Lecture Notes in Computer Scien… 826

Nick Bassiliades Guido Governatori
Adrian Paschke (Eds.)

Rule-Based Reasoning, Programming, and Applications

5th International Symposium, RuleML 2011 – Europe
Barcelona, Spain, July 19-21, 2011
Proceedings

Volume Editors

Nick Bassiliades
Aristotle University of Thessaloniki, Department of Informatics
54124 Thessaloniki, Greece
E-mail: nbassili@csd.auth.gr

Guido Governatori
NICTA, Queensland Research Laboratory
PO Box 6020, St. Lucia, QLD 4067, Australia
E-mail: guido.governatori@nicta.com.au

Adrian Paschke
Freie Universität Berlin, Computer Science Department, Corporate Semantic Web
Königin-Luise-Str. 24/26, 14195 Berlin, Germany
E-mail: paschke@inf.fu-berlin.de

ISSN 0302-9743 e-ISSN 1611-3349
ISBN 978-3-642-22545-1 e-ISBN 978-3-642-22546-8
DOI 10.1007/978-3-642-22546-8
Springer Heidelberg Dordrecht London New York

Library of Congress Control Number: 2011931539

CR Subject Classification (1998): D.2, I.2, C.2.4, H.4, C.2, I.2.11

LNCS Sublibrary: SL 2 – Programming and Software Engineering

Typesetting: Camera-ready by author, data conversion by Scientific Publishing Services, Chennai, India

Printed on acid-free paper

Springer is part of Springer Science+Business Media (www.springer.com)

Preface

The 5th International Symposium on Rules: Research Based and Industry Focused (RuleML-2011@IJCAI), collocated in Barcelona, Spain, with the 22nd International Joint Conference on Artificial Intelligence, was the premier place to meet and to exchange ideas from all fields of rule technology. The aim of RuleML-2011 was to build a bridge between academia and industry in the field of rules and semantic technology, and so to stimulate the cooperation and interoperability between business and research, by bringing together rule system providers, participants in rule standardization efforts, open source communities, practitioners, and researchers. This annual symposium is the flagship event of the Rule Markup and Modeling Initiative (RuleML).

The RuleML Initiative (www.ruleml.org) is a non-profit umbrella organization of several technical groups organized by representatives from academia, industry and government working on rule technology and its applications. Its aim is to promote the study, research and application of rules in heterogeneous distributed environments such as the Web. RuleML maintains effective links with other major international societies and acts as intermediary between various 'specialized' rule vendors, applications, industrial and academic research groups, as well as standardization efforts from, for example, W3C, OMG, and OASIS.

The International Symposium on Rules, RuleML, has evolved from an annual series of international workshops since 2002, international conferences in 2005 and 2006, and international symposia since 2007. In 2011 two instalments of the RuleML Symposium took place. The first one was held in conjunction with IJCAI 2011 (International Joint Conference on Artificial Intelligence) in Barcelona in July, and the second was collocated with the Business Rule Forum in November in Fort Lauderdale, Florida, USA. For RuleML-2011@IJCAI, a selection of the best papers was presented during a joint session with IJCAI, called "Large Track of Best Papers from Sister Conferences." The authors of these papers also submitted a revised version of their papers for inclusion in the IJCAI proceedings.

The technical program showed a carefully selected presentation of current rule research and development in 18 full papers, 8 short papers, 3 invited track papers, and 2 keynote talks (abstracts included) detailed in this book. Accepted papers covered several aspects of rules, such as rule-based distributed/multi-agent systems, rules, agents and norms, rule-based event processing and reaction rules, fuzzy rules and uncertainty, rules and the Semantic Web, rule learning and extraction, rules and reasoning, and finally, rule-based applications. The papers were selected from 58 submissions received from 22 countries. Four of the submissions were selected from some worthy papers on topics related to RuleML originally submitted at IJCAI that marginally missed the acceptance cut-off. In order to increase the quality of the papers, this year a two-round reviewing scheme was adopted to assess the revised papers from IJCAI and revised papers originally submitted to RuleML but not immediately accepted in the first reviewing round.

Due to the above efforts, RuleML-2011, like its predecessors, offered a high-quality technical and applications program, which was the result of the joint effort of the members of the RuleML-2011 Program Committee.

As the future of rule technology lies in the hands of today's students and young researchers, this year RuleML-2011 initiated a doctoral consortium to attract and promote PhD research in this field. The doctoral symposium offers students a close contact with leading experts in the field, as well as the opportunity to present and discuss their ideas in a dynamic and friendly setting. The accepted thesis descriptions span the full range of RuleML topics and were presented to an interested audience and subject to discussion with a panel of senior researchers.

A special thanks is due to the excellent Program Committee for their hard work in reviewing the submitted papers. Their criticism and very useful comments and suggestions were instrumental in achieving a high-quality publication. We also thank the symposium authors for submitting good papers, responding to the reviewers' comments, and abiding by our production schedule. We further wish to thank the keynote speakers for contributing their interesting talks. We are very grateful to the organizers of the 22nd International Joint Conference on Artificial Intelligence for enabling this fruitful collocation with RuleML-2011. Especially, we thank Toby Walsh for his support.

The RuleML-2011 Symposium was financially supported by industrial companies, research institutes and universities and was technically supported by several professional societies. We wish to thank our sponsors, whose financial support helped us to offer this event, and whose technical support allowed us to attract many high-quality submissions.

May 2011

Nick Bassiliades
Guido Governatori
Adrian Paschke

Conference Organization

General Chairs

Jürgen Dix	TU Clausthal, Germany
Georg Gottlob	University of Oxford, UK

Program Chair

Nick Bassiliades	Aristotle University of Thessaloniki, Greece
Guido Governatori	NICTA, Australia
Adrian Paschke	Free University Berlin, Germany

Organization Chairs

Gines Moreno	Universidad de Castilla La Mancha, Spain
Luis Polo	CITIC, Spain

Steering Chairs

John Hall	Model Systems, UK
Christian de Sainte Marie	IBM ILOG, France

Doctoral Consortium Chairs

Carlos Damasio	Universidade Nova de Lisboa, Portugal
Alun Preece	Cardiff University, UK
Umberto Straccia	ISTI – C.N.R., Italy

Publicity Chair

Patrick Hung	University of Ontario Institute of Technology, Canada

Metadata Chairs and Social Media Chairs

Jie Bao	Rensselaer Polytechnic Institute, USA
Richard Cyganiak	DERI Galway, Ireland
Lina Wolf	HPI Potsdam, Germany

Rule Responder Symposium Planner Chair

Zhili Zhao	Free University Berlin, Germany

Sponsorship Chair

Robert Golan	DBMind, USA

Web Chairs

Gökhan Coskun	Free University Berlin, Germany
Ho-Pun (Brian) Lam	NICTA and University of Queensland, Australia

Track Chairs

Automated Reasoning

Grigoris Antoniou	Information Systems Laboratory, FORTH, Greece
Peter Baumgartner	NICTA, Australia

Logic Programming and Non-monotonic Reasoning

Giovambattista Ianni	Università della Calabria, Italy
Kewen Wang	Griffith University, Australia

Rules, Agents and Norms

Antonino Rotolo	CIRSFID, University of Bologna, Italy
Leon van der Torre	University of Luxembourg, Luxembourg

Rule-Based Distributed/Multi-Agent Systems

Costin Badica	University of Craiova, Romania
Lars Braubach	University of Hamburg, Germany

Rule-Based Policies, Reputation and Trust

Piero Bonatti	University of Naples "Federico II", Italy
Daniel Olmedilla	Universidad Autonoma de Madrid, Spain

Rule-Based Event Processing and Reaction Rules

Alexander Artikis	NCRS "Demokritos", Greece
Nenad Stojanovic	FZI, Germany

Fuzzy Rules and Uncertainty

Davide Sottara	University of Bologna, Italy
Giorgos Stamou	National Technical University of Athens, Greece

Rule Transformation and Extraction

Mark Linehan — IBM T.J. Watson Research Center, USA
Erik Putrycz — Apption Software, Canada

Vocabularies, Ontologies, and Business Rules

Ebrahim Bagheri — Athabasca University, Canada
Dragan Gasevic — Athabasca University, Canada

Program Committee

Hassan Ait-Kaci
Patrick Albert
Darko Anicic
Colin Atkinson
Matteo Baldoni
Moritz Y. Becker
Mikael Berndtsson
Pedro Bizarro
Guido Boella
Luiz Olavo Bonino Da Silva Santos
Christoph Bussler
Federico Chesani
Horatiu Cirstea
Matteo Cristani
Célia Da Costa Pereira
Claudia D'Amato
Christian De Sainte Marie
Jens Dietrich
Weichang Du
Schahram Dustdar
Jenny Eriksson LundstrÃűm
Vadim Ermolayev
Opher Etzion
François Fages
Luis Ferreira Pires
Michael Fink
Paul Fodor
Nicoletta Fornara
Enrico Francesconi
Fred Freitas
Aldo Gangemi
Adrian Giurca
Giancarlo Guizzardi
Ioannis Hatzilygeroudis
Stijn Heymans
Rinke Hoekstra
Christopher Hogger
Yuh-Jong Hu
Joris Hulstijn
Minsu Jang
Mustafa Jarrar
Krzysztof Janowicz
Jérôme Lang
Paul Krause
Domenico Lembo
Wolfgang Laun
Francesca Alessandra Lisi
Emiliano Lorini
Jorge Lobo
Michael Maher
Thomas Lukasiewicz
Angelo Montanari
Jing Mei
Chieko Nakabasami
Leora Morgenstern
Georgios Paliouras
Grzegorz J. Nalepa
Jeffrey Parsons
José Ignacio Panach
Fabio Porto
Axel Polleres
Michael Rosemann
Dave Reynolds
Pierangela Samarati
Antonino Rotolo
Marco Seiriö
Giovanni Sartor
Yi-Dong Shen

Guy Sharon
Giorgos Stoilos
Kostas Stathis
Ljiljana Stojanovic
Terrance Swift
Umberto Straccia
Jan Vanthienen
Carlos Viegas Damásio
Wamberto Vasconcelos
George Vouros
Renata Wassermann
Ching-Long Yeh

External Reviewers

Stefano Bragaglia
Minh Dao-Tran
Maxim Davidovsky
Liang Du
Xuan Li
Alessandra Martello
Thierry Martinez
Ella Rabinovich
Insu Song

RuleML 2011 Sponsors

Model Systems OASIS LegalXML

RuleML 2011 Partners

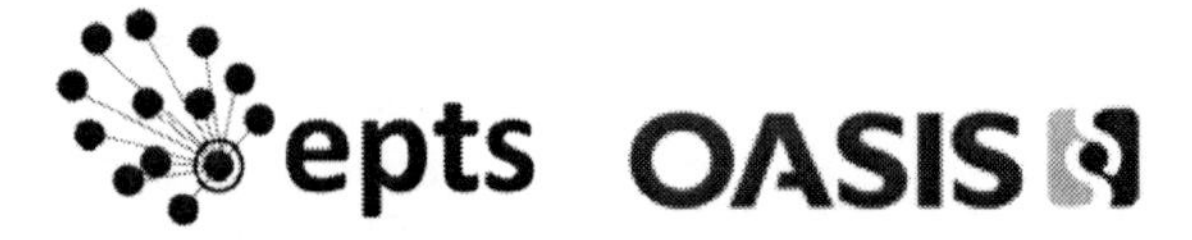

Table of Contents

Keynote Speakers (Abstracts)

Rule-Based Distributed/Multi-Agent Systems

Rules, Agents and Norms

Rule-Based Event Processing and Reaction Rules

Fuzzy Rules and Uncertainty

Rules and the Semantic Web

Rule Learning and Extraction

Rules and Reasoning

Rule-Based Applications

Rule-Based Activity Recognition in Ambient Intelligence

Grigoris Antoniou

Institute of Computer Science, FORTH-ICS, and
Department of Computer Science, University of Crete, Crete, Greece
antoniou@ics.forth.gr

Abstract

Activity recognition is an important, multi-faceted problem with a broad application scope. In this talk we will present a rule-based activity recognition system with the option of using confidence values in our rules and facts. Each activity definition rule has some primary and some optional events and the absence of any of the optional events, only decreases the confidence value of the recognized complex event. We recognize all possible complex events (activities) based on predefined rules, which express temporal and spatial combinations of atomic and complex events. Then we detect all conflicted events (recognized events that overlap but use common resources). The optimal solution is found with an optimization function that takes into account complex event's confidence, temporal duration and number of used atomic events. Adjusting this function, results in higher or lower abstraction levels in our results (more generic events with bigger duration / more specific events with lower duration).

As application domain we use ambient assisted living (e.g. for elderly persons). The approach has been implemented, and tested in a real ambient intelligence environment hosted by the FORTH Institute of Computer Science.

N. Bassiliades et al. (Eds.): RuleML 2011 - Europe, LNCS 6826, p. 1, 2011.

An Overview of the Ciao System

Manuel V. Hermenegildo[1,2], F. Bueno[2], M. Carro[1,2], P. López-García[1,4], R. Haemmerlé[2], E. Mera[3], J.F. Morales[1], and G. Puebla[2]

[1] Madrid Institute of Advanced Studies,
in SW Development Technology (IMDEA Software Institute)
{manuel.hermenegildo,manuel.carro,pedro.lopez,jose.morales}@imdea.org
[2] Universidad Politécnica de Madrid (UPM)
{bueno,mcarro,german,herme}@fi.upm.es
[3] Universidad Complutense de Madrid (UCM)
edison@fdi.ucm.es
[4] Scientific Research Council (CSIC)

Abstract

Ciao is a logic-based, multi-paradigm programming system. One of its most distinguishing features is that it supports a large number of semantic and syntactic language features which can be selectively activated or deactivated for each program module. As a result, a module can be written in, for example, ISO-Prolog plus constraints and higher order, while another can be a pure logic module with a different control rule such as iterative deepening and/or tabling, and perhaps using constructive negation. A powerful and modular extension mechanism allows user-level design and implementation of such features and sub-languages.

Another distinguishing feature of Ciao is its powerful assertion language, which allows expressing many kinds of program properties (ranging from, e.g., moded types to resource consumption), as well as tests and documentation. The compiler is capable of statically finding violations of these properties or verifying that programs comply with them, and issuing certificates of this compliance. The compiler also performs many types of optimizations, including automatic parallelization. It offers very competitive performance, while retaining the flexibility and interactive development of a dynamic language.

We will present a hands-on overview of the system, through small examples which emphasize the novel aspects and the motivations which lie behind Ciao's design and implementation.

Reference

1. Hermenegildo, M.V., Bueno, F., Carro, M., López, P., Mera, E., Morales, J.F., Puebla, G.: An Overview of Ciao and its Design Philosophy. Theory and Practice of Logic Programming (2011), http://arxiv.org/abs/1102.5497

N. Bassiliades et al. (Eds.): RuleML 2011 - Europe, LNCS 6826, p. 2, 2011.

Rule-Based Distributed and Agent Systems

Costin Bădică[1], Lars Braubach[2], and Adrian Paschke[3]

[1] Software Engineering Department,
Faculty of Automatics, Computers and Electronics, University of Craiova
costin.badica@software.ucv.ro
[2] Distributed Systems and Information Systems,
Computer Science Department, University of Hamburg
braubach@informatik.uni-hamburg.de
[3] Corporate Semantic Web,
Computer Science Department, FU Berlin
paschke@inf.fu-berlin.de

Abstract. The paper contains an overview of the roles played by rules and rule-based systems in distributed and multi-agent systems. These roles include an overview of traditional and newly emerging application areas as well as internal agent architectures and frameworks implementing these architectures.

1 Introduction

This paper strives to shed light on the connections of rule based systems and multi-agent systems. In order to give an overview about the different areas rules play an important role in, it is coarsely distinguished between application areas of agents with rules and multi-agent system construction aspects. Interesting application areas of rules and agents that will be discussed include rather traditional fields like parallel and distributed rule-based systems, service oriented architecture, grid and peer-to-peer computing as well as upcoming new trends such as cloud computing, rule based wireless networks and complex event processing scenarios. From a construction perspective it will be shown which role rules play in the context of individual agent architectures and also with respect to multi-agents systems as a whole. The former will delve into various rule inspired agent architectures, distinguishing between reactive, deliberative and hybrid approaches while the latter will primarily deal with rules as part of communication, negotiations and also teamwork approaches.

The rest of the paper is structured as follows. In the next Section 2.1 application areas of rules and agents are presented. Thereafter, in Section 3 the construction-related issues of rules in agents and multi-agent systems are discussed. A conclusion is given in Section 4.

2 Rule-Based Distributed Systems

The early relative success of rule-based expert systems employing more efficient rule-based inference engines, pushed forward the application of rule technologies

N. Bassiliades et al. (Eds.): RuleML 2011 - Europe, LNCS 6826, pp. 3–28, 2011.

to distributed computing and multi-agent systems. This research direction followed the generalization of rule inference to parallel, as well as to distributed computational models. At least two trends can be observed here: (i) improvement of inference algorithms for rule systems using parallel and distributed systems' technology; (ii) exploiting the more declarative nature of rule-based languages as compared to the procedural languages, for the development of more complex systems composed of autonomous components known as *software agents.*

2.1 Parallel Rule-Based Systems

Parallel Forward Chaining Production Systems. Advances of computational models for rule-based production systems, mainly related to the development of the RETE algorithm [39] and its extensions for efficient matching of rule patterns and working memory elements [2], but also addressing concurrent processing and activation of rules in production systems, opened a vivid research path, starting in the second half of the '80s and lasting also during the '90s. The main outcome of these researches was the development of powerful implementation technologies for rule-based systems. Note that most of these works use the terms *production* and *production system* as synonymous to rule and rule-based system, so these terms will be interchangeably used in this paper.

Authors of [46] proposed a new parallel architecture for exploiting fine-grained parallelism of forward chaining inference algorithms for rule-based production systems on multiprocessor systems. The main outcome of this work was the significant improvement of the execution speed of a rule-based production system expressed as number of rule firings/second, as well as working memory element changes/second. Their approach targeted all the phases of the forward chaining inference cycle: matching, conflict resolution and right hand side rule evaluation.

Authors of [53], [54] propose an in-depth analysis of concurrent computational approaches for improving the performance of single and multiple rule systems. The authors start with some considerations regarding the performance of rule-based systems. The book covers: (i) *parallel production systems* including algorithms for parallel rule firings, (ii) *distributed production systems* under distributed control, and *multiagent production systems* as well as their related control issues.

Authors of [5] proposed a parallel and distributed version of the RETE algorithm that uses the master-slave paradigm. The pattern matching system is decomposed into master and slave modules, working in parallel. Each component holds a copy of the RETE network. Rules are activated in parallel by master components. When a rule is activated, it sends all the activating facts to an available slave component that performs the activation and returns the results. Therefore rules can be activated in parallel, while computation of the activations is distributed among the slave components.

Note that parallel firing of multiple rules for improving the execution performance of forward chaining production systems can compromise the consistency or the working memory by possible interference of rules' actions and conditions. Solutions to this problem are outlined in [53] and later in [75].

Authors of [3] introduced an architecture that allows parallel production firing by allowing the concurrent execution of the activities of matching, selecting and acting of productions. The architecture is proved correct with respect to the principle of serialization that relaxes the commutativity principle that was proposed by [53].

Parallel Backward Chaining Rule-Based Systems. Efficient processing in rule-based systems was also addressed for top down inference engines. An early work is [48] that introduced Backpac, a backward-chained inferencing system designed to run on parallel processor machines. More significant achievements in this area are however related to the development of parallelized versions of the well-known logic programming language Prolog that traditionally uses backward chaining as implementation technology. See [47] for an overview of techniques for parallelizing Prolog programs.

Parallel Deductive Databases. Rules played an important role in the development of new databases models, including deductive and active databases [93]. Deductive databases are a suitable model for building large knowledge bases by exploiting both database and knowledge technologies. For example, chapter 6 of [93] contains an overview of parallel processing of rules in production systems, deductive and active databases, while chapter 7 introduces the authors' parallel object-oriented knowledge-based system called $PRACTIC^{KB}$.

Techniques for data and rule partitioning for parallelizing deductive databases are also reported in [94] and [98]. More important, these results were later on exploited for implementing large scale rule reasoning on computer clusters (see Subsection 2.3).

Distributed Jess. Our literature review also revealed efforts for distributing classical state-of-the-art rule based systems shells, including Jess[1] [43].

In paper [27] the authors introduce a model for distributing rule-based inference systems called Web of Inference Systems (WoIS). Each member of WoIS is composed of an inference system (IS) and a rule base, while all ISs operate on a single Shared Working Memory (SWM). WoIS is controlled by a dedicated component called manager (M). Each IS holds a copy of a part of the SWM in its local working memory, while all ISs run independently in parallel. This model was utilized to implement a distributed version of Jess called DJess. Synchronization between interfering rules is achieved by means of shadow facts and ghost facts. A *shadow fact* is a Jess fact linked to a Java bean object. Each shared fact is implemented as a shadow fact, and thus an associated Java bean object is created. All the proxies corresponding to the same shared fact are linked together by means of a Java remote object called *ghost fact*. Access of the ISs to the ghost facts are synchronized by acquiring locks during the transition from the conflict resolution stage to the act stage of an inference cycle.

A different approach for distributing Jess called Octopus was reported in the paper [76]. With the Octopus approach several independent Jess engines

---

[1] `http://www.jessrules.com/`

are interconnected in a star topology as clients of a central server. The server allows them to asynchronously exchange messages using Jess functions for socket communications. The Octopus approach was experimented on a computer cluster running Condor workload management system [90].

2.2 Rule-Based Systems as Agent Reasoning Models

Early works proposed the use of rule-based systems as the basic reasoning model of agents that are part of a multi-agent system. Using this approach, each agent of the system incorporates a rule engine and therefore, its behavior is reduced to performing rule based inference. Agent coordination can be achieved either via a shared working memory or by asynchronous message passing.

Multi-Agent Production Systems. In paper [37] it is described a multi-agent system called MAGSY where each agent is a rule-based system. Agents are able to communicate asynchronously, as well as they are able to provide services to other agents. MAGSY is in fact a general-purpose multi-agent framework. It has been applied in practice for distributing solving of transportation and logistics problems. Each MAGSY agent is a triple comprising facts, rules, and services. The agent can receive messages from other agents that trigger the update of their facts. An agent can also invoke services provided by other agents. As a side-effect, service execution can change the agent's sets of facts and rules. Each MAGSY agent performs rule-based inference using a forward-chaining rule-interpreter based on the well-known RETE algorithm [39].

Author of [53] and [54] consider multi-agent production systems, that are conceptually different from parallel and distributed production systems. While parallel production systems emphasize parallel rule matching and firing and distributed production systems emphasize dynamic distribution of productions among the agents of an organization with the goal of execution performance improvement (the response time), multi-agent production systems concern the integration of multiple independent production systems acting on a shared working memory that is useful for their coordination.

Multi-Agent Jess. Integration of Jess engine into JADE agents [9] is discussed in [29]. This paper is in fact a tutorial showing how a JADE agent can incorporate a Jess engine with the following functionalities: (i) allowing Jess to capture messages received by the agent as Jess facts; (ii) allowing the agent to send messages to other agents directly from Jess; (iii) implementing the agent behavior as Jess inference. Using this approach it is possible to implement rule-based agents in Jess that interact by exchanging FIPA ACL messages using the JADE middleware (see also rule interaction agents, an example of reactive agent architectures discussed in subsection 3.1).

2.3 Rule-Based Grid/Cloud/High-Performance Computing Systems

A recent research trend can be observed in investigating synergies between high-performance computing and rule-based systems and reasoning. On one hand, the higher expressivity of rule-based languages determines an increase of the computational complexity of the inference algorithms, thus limiting the potential of rule-based systems in applications that require large scale reasoning, as it is for example the Semantic Web [10]. On the other hand, the higher expressivity of rule-based languages can help to improve resource and job management in high-performance computing systems, and thus have the potential for improving the overall performance of these systems. Both trends are briefly reviewed in this section of the paper.

Scalable Rule Reasoning. Availability of high-performance computing opened new possibilities for scalable rule reasoning in distributed systems. High-performance computing systems include supercomputers, computer clusters, as well as Grid and more recently Cloud computing infrastructures.

Paper [88] is probably the first reporting the exploitation of the results earlier obtained in parallelizing of deductive databases [94,98] as well as the availability of clusters for parallel computing to investigate the improvement of the reasoning performance for the Semantic Web. The authors of [88] proposed a data partitioning scheme, a parallel algorithm, as well as several optimizations for scalable parallel inference with materialized OWL knowledge bases. The implementation of the algorithm was based on the Jena[2] open source rule-based reasoner and it was experimented on a 16 node computer cluster.

Paper [70] describes MARVIN – a parallel and distributed platform for processing large amounts of RDF data, on a network of loosely coupled peers using a new strategy called divide-conquer-swap. The idea of this approach is to continuously partition the set of RDF triples, compute the closure of each partition in parallel and then swap partitions by exchanges between peers. This technique is shown to eventually reach completeness of reasoning and an efficient strategy called SpeedDate for exchanging data between peers is proposed.

Map-Reduce is a technique for programming large data processing tasks on large computer clusters [33]. Hadoop[3] is an Apache project that "develops open-source software for reliable, scalable, distributed computing" and that also provides a Map-Reduce programming framework. [92] shows how to apply MapReduce on Hadoop for large-scale RDFS reasoning. This work is closely related to: (i) the Large Knowledge Collider (LarKC) project[4] [49] for reasoning with billions of facts and rules that are distributed across different locations, as well as to (ii) WebPIE[5] [91] – a parallel reasoner based on Map-Reduce which aims at reasoning on the scale of the Web.

Rule-based Workflow and Resource Management for Grid and Cloud Computing. Grid and Cloud are modern forms of distributed computing that put a high emphasis on virtualization and software services technologies. Grid is a "coordinated resource sharing and problem solving in dynamic, multi-institutional

[2] `http://jena.sourceforge.net/`

[3] `http://hadoop.apache.org/`

[4] `http://www.larkc.eu/`

[5] `http://www.few.vu.nl/~jui200/webpie.html`

virtual organizations" [40]. Cloud allows provisioning and utilization of computing power with minimal management effort and minimal knowledge of the infrastructure supporting it. This section briefly presents the role that rules and rule reasoning can play to improve resource and workflow management in the Grid. Most of these results apply also to Cloud computing environments.

Paper [85] introduces a new mechanism for on-demand synthesis of available activities in the Grid by applying ontology rules. Rule-based synthesis combines multiple primitive activities to form new compound activities.

Paper [50] introduces WS-CAM – a rule-based application for collaborative awareness management in grid environments. The idea of this work is to represent complex requirements imposed on Grid environments, either behavioral or functional, as business rules implemented using Drools[6].

Paper [66] presents the Active Grid Information Server providing versatile resource management in grid environments, including resource discovery and selection. The server is using an Event-Condition-Action rule-based system that supports dynamically adjustable schedulers.

A recent trend is the representation of grid scheduling algorithms using rule-based formalisms ([71]). Paper [44] proposes a new rule-based languages called SiLK (Simple Language for worKflows) that provides a rule-chaining representation of scientific workflows. SiLK rule-based workflows can be executed and monitored using OSyRIS (Orchestration System using a Rule based Inference Solution) inference engine, as well as with its distributed version D-OSyRIS. The implementation of OSyRIS is based on Drools. SiLK allowed the rule-based representation of several well-known grid scheduling heuristics.

Flexibility of grid resource management can be enhanced by endowing the Grid with semantic descriptions of resources covering the various software and hardware characteristics, as well as their utilization policies. Grid schedulers can thus benefit of these representations by enhancing monitoring and discovery systems with semantic matchmaking capabilities. Performance of resource discovery can be further improved by exploitation of rule-based systems. For an overview of ontology-based semantic approaches for grid resource management the reader is invited to consult reference [4].

Finally, rule-based approaches were shown to be useful for implementing flexible control strategies and decisions that allow the Grid to achieve Quality of Service commitments required by various applications using a Service Level Agreement (SLA) management system. For example, the authors of the paper [72] propose predictive decision rules for adaptive SLA management on the Grid. In [74] a declarative Rule Based Service Level Agreement (RBSLA) framework is described.

2.4 Rule-Based P2P Systems

Peer-to-peer (P2P) is a model of distributed systems in which distributed, equally weighted and directly connected peers collaborate by providing resources and

[6] `http://www.jboss.org/drools`

services to each other. P2P systems have important applications in distributed processing, distributed content management, and ubiquitous computing. The combination of the decentralization of P2P approach with the declarativeness and flexibility of rules enables the development of new types of intelligent distributed systems. Applications are presented in the domains of heterogenous schema mapping and ubiquitous computing.

Heterogenous Schema Mapping. Paper [34] introduces a method for using inference engines to express and process semantics of digital library resources in heterogenous environments. The approach is applied to define metadata mappings between heterogenous schemas in P2P-based digital libraries. The mappings are defined by extracting facts from the XML metadata of resources and then by applying rule-based inference to automatically derive relations between local schemas and other retrieved schemas.

Paper [63] introduces LogicPeer, a P2P extension of Prolog. LogicPeer is a straightforward extension of Prolog with operators that enable goal evaluation over peers in a P2P system. LogicPeer defines two network models: (i) *opaque peer network model* in which each peer does not know the identifiers of its neighbors and a certain query propagation protocol is assumed, and (ii) *transparent peer network model* in which is possible for each peer to obtain the identifiers of its neighbors and thus it allows implementation of customized query propagation protocols. Paper [22] discusses an application of LogicPeer for specifying schema mappings and agents' actions in XML-based data integration tasks.

Ubiquitous Computing. Paper [45] presents the use of Mandarax[7] and Sens-ation sensor platform for creating the new SensBution infrastructure for ubiquitous computing. SensBution abstracts the access to sensor data using rule-base inference, while the underlying P2P network propagates queries between peers. Each peer incorporates a rule base and uses it and rule inference to answer the queries received from the other peer via JXTA[8] network programming environment.

Papers [12] and [11] propose a distributed reasoning solution that could be used in ambient environments modeled as P2P networks of agent. Each agent has a partial view of the environment and it holds a locally consistent theory. Local theories are connected via bridging rules, which may result in inconsistency of the global knowledge base. Dealing with the inconsistency is achieved by representing bridging rules with defeasible logics.

Paper [14] introduces the concept of Intelligent Domotic Environment (IDE) that is capable of providing Ambient Intelligence (AmI) to home environments through rule-based reasoning. Firstly, IDE proposes a formalization of the home environment as DogOnt ontology [13]. Secondly, IDE proposes a new middleware called Domotic OSGi Gateway (DOG) based on OSGi[9] that supports interoperability of hardware and software components of the home automation system. Thirdly, IDE properties are defined from the perspectives of what information

[7] `http://mandarax.sourceforge.net/`

[8] `http://jxta.kenai.com/`

[9] `http://www.osgi.org`

is necessary (state and structural), as well as of the type of inference required (direct, recursive and multi-stage) for their derivation.

2.5 Rule-Based Event Processing Agent Systems

(Complex) Event processing (CEP) is a set of techniques and technologies that helps to understand and control event-driven systems. CEP has emerged as a substantial new field of software engineering and computer science over the last ten years from various research fields addressing event processing. In general, CEP aims at achieving actionable, situational knowledge from distributed systems in real-time or quasi-real-time. CEP tools detect complex event patterns (a.k.a. complex event types) and situations (complex events + conditional contexts), i.e. detecting transitions in the universe of interest that requires action either "reactive" or "proactive" in realtime. It is now one of the fastest growing segments in enterprize middleware software. The decoupled event processing model in distributed event processing systems and in particular intelligent complex event processing systems which exploit rules for processing event messages and making decisions on detected relevant situations can be implemented as event processing networks (EPNs) with distributed event processing agents (EPAs). The Event Processing Technical Society (EPTS) defines an Event processing agent (EPA) (event processing component, event mediator) as a software module that processes events.

Various agent-oriented event processing systems have been developed such as Starview[10], Amit [1], AgentLogic RulePoint [11], Spade [65] and Prova [12].

Amit. The core the Amit (Active Middleware Technology) framework is the IBM Situation Manager Rule Language (SMRL) [1] which is a markup language for describing situations, which are semantic concepts in the customers' domain of discourse and syntactically equivalent to (complex) event patterns. Events in SMRL have a flat structure, and have a unique name and attributes that can be standard or user defined. The conceptual model defines an event type generalization hierarchy. Amit rule engines are deployed as event processing agents in the active middleware.

RulePoint. RulePoint is a server based Event Processing platform based on a reactive agent model. It supports detecting events and is able to responde in reactive manner using event action rule definitions. The agents act as (distributed) realtime alerting systems.

Prova. see 3.2

System-S Spade. System-S Stream Processing Application Declarative Engine (SPADE) [65]. System S is a large-scale, distributed data stream processing middleware developed at the IBM T. J. Watson Research Center. Its runtime can execute a large number of long-running jobs (queries) that take the form of Data-Flow Graphs. A data-flow graph consists of a set of Processing Elements (PEs)

---

[10] `http://www.starviewtechnology.com`

[11] `http://www.agentlogic.com/`

[12] `http://prova.ws/`

connected by streams, where each stream carries a series of Stream Data Objects (SDOs). The PEs implement data stream analytics and are basic execution units that are distributed over the compute event processing agent nodes. The PEs communicate with each other via their input and output ports, connected by streams.

Starview Remote Agents. Starview Remote Agents are based on built-in CEP engines for real-time event processing. The agents can collaborate and cooperate across multiple streams of data by exchanging event messages. The agent follow the "actors" approach where event-processing agents listen for incoming events, and can take action according to predetermined rules.

3 Roles of Rules in Multi-Agent Systems

In this section different roles of rules in agent systems will be presented. This will be done on the micro as well as on the macro layer. The first refers to the meaning of roles for internal agent behavior control, whereas the latter considers rules with multiple agents especially in the context of rule-based interactions.

3.1 Rules on the Micro Layer

The role of rules within agents depends crucially on the *internal agent architecture* employed. According to Wooldridge and Jennings [96, p. 23-24] an agent architecture is defined as follows: "[...] It specifies how [...] the agent can be decomposed into the construction of a set of component modules and how these modules should be made to interact. The total set of modules and their interactions has to provide an answer to the question of how the sensor data and the current internal state of the agent determine the actions [...] and future internal state of the agent. [...]". The definition highlights the architecture's responsibility of deducing agent actions and future state on basis of environmental percepts and its current knowledge. One main difficulty of agent architectures is that reactive and deliberative behavior have to be balanced so that an agent is capable of

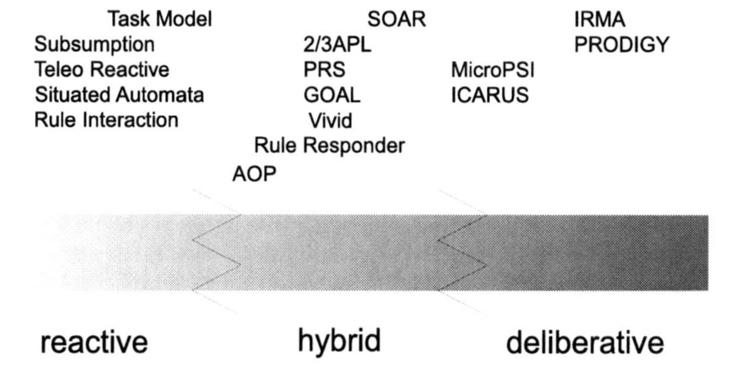

Fig. 1. Agent architecture classification (based on [96])

realtime responses to environmental changes as well as planned actions leading to achievement of its goals. Reactive capabilities require fast decisions whereas deliberative behavior typically needs time to be thoroughly prepared taking into account possible alternatives and occurring difficulties. The question of how reactive and deliberative behavior should be intertwined is further complicated by the fact that an agent is a resource bounded entity meaning that it has to intentionally devote capabilities to the reactive or deliberative decision making processes. Hence, these limitations led to the development of architectures that disregard one in favor of the other.

These considerations also led to a classification scheme of agent architectures according to the nature of their decision making processes [96]. The class of *reactive agent architectures* emphasizes fast decision making based on sensory input, whereas *deliberative architectures* put the focus on planned actions. *Hybrid architectures* are those that try to combine reactive and deliberative aspects. Figure 1 shows these categorization classes alongside with several agent architectures. The classification scheme is considered here as a spectrum with reactive and deliberative architectures as boundaries and hybrid in the middle. At the left hand side of this spectrum so called purely reactive architectures are located, which represent the event action architectures without a model of the world. On the right hand side the spectrum is bordered by purely deliberative approaches that act purely based on cognitive action often based on planning. The spectrum helps understanding the applicability of different architectures. The idea is not considering one architecture as generally superior to another but understanding the application requirements and matching them to the architecture, i.e. if fast responses are indispensable for an application to function an agent architecture should be located in the reactive or hybrid zone. It has further to be noted that the boundaries between the three categories are rather fuzzy and not all architectures can be clearly assigned to one of the categories. In the following rules are discussed with respect to their role in each of the aforementioned internal agent architecture categories.

Reactive Agent Architectures. In a purely reactive rule based agent architecture an agent possesses only reaction rules allowing it to deduce actions from incoming messages or environmental percepts. In the simplest form it can be imagined that the agent behavior completely consists of if-then-else statements containing guards and actions. Its processing would be triggered whenever it receives new input from other agents or the environment. As for nearly all kinds of non-trivial scenarios internal state of an agent is required - otherwise it will repeat wrong behavior over and over again because it cannot remember older outcomes - practical architectures have included mechanisms for autonomous behavior control based on internal state. Though, in contrast to deliberative architectures internal agent state might be kept simple and may not represent a thorough model of the environment. The inclusion of state led to many architectures existing on the boundary between the reactive and hybrid zone and the differences between those and some weakly hybrid architectures are small.

Examples of rather reactive agent architectures include Brook's subsumption architecture [21], task model based architectures [19], as well as several rule based agent architectures (cf. Fig. 1). The subsumption architecture is the prototypical representative for reactive agent architecture and Brooks always insisted on avoiding an internal representation of the world. Despite this fact, even in the subsumption architecture an internal state is preserved in the state machines so that variable values can be saved. Another rather simple but intuitive architecture is the task model, which assumes an agent can be supplied with different behavior snippets called tasks. It has gained some practical attention due to its simplicity and popular agent frameworks such as JADE [8] offering this kind of agent programming abstractions. Both do not rely on rules and thus will not be covered here in more details.

With respect to approaches having relationships to rules teleo-reactive systems [69], situated automata [56] and the rule interaction agent architecture [56] and the rule interaction agent architecture [30] will be discussed.

Teleo-Reactive Agents. Nilsson has conceived a reactive agent architecture and programming language with reactive characteristics called teleo-reactive [69]. In order to achieve instantaneous reactions to environmental changes circuit semantics is introduced, i.e. agent actions are not assumed to be executed atomically but need constant conditional support. The architecture assumes that a teleo-reactive agent is constructed from teleo-reactive behaviors, which consist of a set of conditionally guarded atomic actions or subbehaviors. In case the behavior is active all branches of actions are evaluated in parallel. The first branch with a fulfilled condition is then executed until the condition becomes invalid. As subbehaviors can be used as actions, hierarchical execution structures named teleo-reactive trees can emerge at runtime. The architecture shares interesting similarities with production rule systems with some important differences. The guarded actions of a teleo-reactive program could be interpreted as a set of production rules that are evaluated in order to determine the current execution path. The first difference is that production rule systems are typically flat in the sense that all rules are on the same level. In contrast, teleo-reactive programs are hierarchical having earlier layers fulfilling conditions for the execution of deeper layers. Furthermore, production rule systems assume atomic action execution, whereas teleo-reactive actions are executed continuously as long as its guarding condition holds. Agent platforms supporting teleo-reactive agents are AgentMT(TR) [58] and AgentFactory[13] [31].

Situated Automata. The situated automaton architecture [56] considers an agent as a finite-state machine whose inputs are fed by environmental sensors and whose outputs are directly connected to its actuators. Considering the agent as finite-state machine expressed as a fixed sequential circuit allows for a efficient execution and thus facilitates reactive responses in dynamic environments. The behavior of a an agent is described using goal reduction rules, which help in mapping higher-level goals into more concrete goals. A compiler is then used to

[13] `http://www.agentfactory.com/index.php/Main_Page`

transform the goal rules and top-level goal specification into a simple circuit that is able to map input vectors to output vectors according to the goal rules. This means that symbol manipulation for solving a goal is used only at compile time while at runtime the agent simply behaves according to the generated circuit semantics. To the knowledge of the authors there are no cuurent platforms using the situated automata agent architecture.

Rule Interaction Agents. The rule interaction architecture is based on the idea of combining FIPA speech act communication semantics[41,42] with rule oriented behavior descriptions. In general, the agent architecture consists of a rule engine that contains domain behavior rules as well as specific predefined interaction transformation rules. Whenever an agent receives a message with FIPA-SL content it will automatically execute rules that perform a knowledge representation conversion from FIPA-SL to CLIPS assuming specific semantics of SL speech acts, i.e. in case of an 'inform' the receiver will store the new information in its knowledge base, whereas a 'request' performative act directly leads to action execution. For outgoing message the architecture provides a conversion in the opposite direction. The architecture has been realized based for the JESS and Jamocha Rete rule engines [30].

Deliberative Agent Architectures. A deliberative agent architecture in its purist sense only consists of a thinking process driving the decisions of the agent. The underlying assumption of deliberative agents is the physical symbol system hypothesis of Newell and Simon [86, p. 35] that states: "A physical symbol system has the necessary and sufficient means for general intelligent action." This strong claim assumes that human thinking is effectively based on symbol manipulation so that machines applying symbol manipulation can act intelligently. Hence, in contrast to a reactive agents the internal representation of the world combined with its processing capabilities enables deliberative agents anticipating incidents and adapt itself accordingly [36]. Typically, an deliberative agent is equipped with achievement goals that describe desired world states and applies problem solving methods to find a sequence of actions that form a path from its current state to the desired state. Deliberative architectures in many cases use planning, search or rule techniques or a combination of those in order to realize this kind of problem solving. The advanced cognitive capabilities of deliberative agents are often also reflected in additional architecture skills like learning or knowledge deduction.

IRMA (Intelligent Resource-bounded Machine Architecture) [18], MicroPSI [6] PRODIGY [28] and ICARUS [59] represent internal agent architectures with a focus on deliberative processing tasks. IRMA is an architecture, developed by Pollack and Bratman, that tried to directly adopt Bratman's BDI (belief-desire-intention) model of practical reasoning for agent decision making. It uses the aforementioned attitudes belief, desires and intentions and mainly relies on planning techniques to refine partial plans and deduce agent actions. MicroPSI is based on Dörner's PSI (personality-systems-interactions) theory and includes aspects like perception, thinking, emotions, motivation and memory. MicroPSI realizes the PSI theory by relying on a neural network inspired approach.

In contrast to these architectures Prodigy and ICARUS, which have been implemented as agent systems, employ some rule based ideas and will be presented in more detail in the following.

PRODIGY. The PRODIGY architecture [28] is based on a general problem solver and planner that searches for operator sequences bringing about a set of achievement goals as described in an initial state definition. The search process is guided by control rules that can be domain dependent or independent. Furthermore, PRODIGY enables different kinds of learning mechanisms for control rules. Problem solving in PRODIGY is a two-staged process operating on a tree of nodes, each node representing a world state and the goal set that is to pursue. In the decision phase four kinds of decisions can be controlled via rules: 1) determination of the node to expand, 2) selection of the goal to satisfy, 3) selection of an operator to try, and 4) binding of parameter values of the operator. Thereafter, in the expansion phase the operator is applied and a new node is created for the derived state. In case the operator cannot be executed due to unsatisfied preconditions, a new subgoals for establishing the preconditions are created and also a new node for processing them is created. Control rules in PRODIGY have a specific form. They consist of a left-hand side condition for testing applicability and a right-hand side with an action that can be 'select', 'reject' or 'prefer'. In the first step selection rules are fired to determine the valid set of candidates (node, goal, operator or bindings). If no selection rules trigger all candidates are included. In the next step rejection rules are executed in order to exclude unwanted candidates. Finally, in the last step preference rules are used to order the remaining elements and find the most promising candidates. In case backtracking has to be employed the next most preferred candidate is selected.

ICARUS. ICARUS [59] has been conceived as cognitive architecture mainly for controlling agents in complex physical environments. The ICARUS architecture mainly consists of three components: a perceptual, a planning and an execution system. They are meant to operate concurrently and interact using a specific memory system. This memory system is based on a categorization of concepts in tree form. Whenever new percepts are detected by the perceptual module, these experiences are classified in memory using similarity functions of categories. The organization of the memory in form of a lattice and its operation has similarities with a Rete network used for production system matching [38]. At the heart of the architecture the planner module uses means-end analysis to generate plans. It tries to achieve a goal by comparing the goal state with the initial state and then breaking down the problem into subproblems, which are recursively solved by the planner. The planner uses the memory to retrieve suitable operators called skills based on the problems pre- and postconditions or the reduction of differences between the states it can bring about. In case the planner encounters problems it may backtrack resulting in a heuristic depth-first search. The categorized memory allows the planner learn from previous experiences by fetching entire plans that can be used as starting point for the problem at hand and may be subject to further adaptations or refinements. The architecture has been extended with the possibility of specifying a degree of persistency in performing its activities allowing to adjust its degree of reactivity.

3.2 Hybrid Agent Architectures

Hybrid agent architectures aim at providing a balanced mixture of reactive and deliberative behavior specification means and execution. Due to resource boundedness agent architectures have to solve the question of how much effort to spend for each type of behavior and how often to rethink courses of actions they have committed to. Several experiments have shown the degree of commitment should be dependent on the degree of dynamics exposed by the environment the agent is situated in [78,57]. This has led to the development of architectures with different commitment strategies ranging from bold agents strongly committed to their intentions to cautious agents reconsidering frequently. In contrast to deliberative agent architecture which are often based on planning approaches hybrid architectures rather employ reactive planning or purely rule-based behavior control. Reactive planning, originally stemming from PRS, describes an iterative but very fast planning approach that is based on the idea of planning step by step at runtime taking into account immediate feedback of the environment, i.e. an agent only decides upon the next plan or action and during execution expands subgoals to further plans at runtime. This scheme of acting has been adopted also by many other architectures such as 2/3APL and GOAL, described hereafter.

AOP Agents. The AOP (Agent Oriented Programming) architecture [84] envisions a mentalistic agent description based on the notions beliefs, capabilities and commitments. The fundamental idea is that an agent commits to execute an action for another agent or itself at the current or a future point in time. Actions are described as capabilities with a guard determining the applicability in regard to the agent's context. The means for engaging in commitments is based on commitment rules that may include a message as well as a mental condition. In case a commitment rule fires, a new commitment is added and kept until it got executed or belief changes render the capability's condition invalid. If the latter situation occurs the commitment is removed and a notification to the agent the commitment belong to should be prepared. Rule evaluation is done in each agent deliberation cycle. Frameworks using AOP inspired architectures are AgentFactory [31] and AgentBuilder[14] [81].

PRS Agents. The PRS (procedural reasoning system) architecture [80] builds on the BDI (belief-desire-intention) model of agency [17], which explains human behavior on basis folk-psychological notions, i.e. the BDI model explains rational behavior in the way humans think that they think. Foundation of the BDI model is the process of practical reasoning, which is composed of two subsequent subprocess: goal deliberation and means-end reasoning [95]. The first refers to the responsibility of deciding what goals to pursue, which might be difficult when goals are conflicting. The latter is concerned with determining on

[14] `http://www.agentbuilder.com/`

the means how to achieve a previously selected goal. The PRS architecture only considers means-end resoning by casting BDI to beliefs, goals and plans. Goals appear in form of events that trigger a plan selection and execution process (means-end reasoning). Similar to processing event-condition-action rules the PRS interpreter first selects a subset of applicable plans according to the event type and then selects among those using the first plan with fulfilled preconditions. In case of plan errors the means-end reasoning process can be initiated again and other plans may used out until the goal is achieved or the last plan has been chosen. The traditional PRS architecture has also been described as programming language called AgentSpeak(L) [79]. Architectural extensions of PRS have addressed the inclusion of declarative goal semantics by including different goal types like achievement and maintenance [20] as well as conceptual support for the goal deliberation phase [77,67]. Both forms of extensions emphasize the role of rules in the PRS architectures as goal states have to be observed and trigger actions. The PRS architecture has been used in many agent frameworks including JIAC[15], JACK[16], Jason[17] and Jadex[18][15,16].

2/3APL Agents. 3APL (an abstract agent programming language) [52] and 2APL (a practical agent programming language) [32] are similar approaches for programming agents using mentalistic notions and rules. As 2APL is the successor of 3APL only the former will be described in the following. A 2APL agent is described by the typical BDI attitudes beliefs, goals, and plans and additionally by three types of rules: planning goal rules, procedure call rules and plan repair rules. Beliefs are specified as Prolog facts or belief inference rules that generate additional knowledge based on the agent's beliefs. Goals are represented as formulas describing world states the agent wants to attain. Planning goal rules serve the generation of plans for goals. The condition part of a planning goal rules consist the goal to be present as well as a specific belief state to be valid. The action part contains a plan description composed of an action recipe, which can consist of concrete as well as abstract actions. Procedure call rules are similar to goal planning rules with the difference that as part of the condition instead of goal, message events, environmental events or abstract actions can be used. The usage of both kinds of rules allows for a context based interpretation of goals and runtime expansion of plans. In addition, the third kind of rules called plan repair rule enables reacting on plan failures. Such failures occur when an action of a plan leads to an exception. The condition part of a plan repair rule consists of a belief state check and an action description denoting the beginning of the plan to repair, i.e. the first actions of that plan. The action part contains a replacement plan description that can be used as alternative for the original actions. The 2/3APL architectures have also been implemented in corresponding agent platforms.[19]

[15] http://www.jiac.de/
[16] http://www.aosgrp.com.au/
[17] http://jason.sourceforge.net/Jason/Jason.html
[18] http://jadex-agents.informatik.uni-hamburg.de/
[19] http://apapl.sourceforge.net/, http://www.cs.uu.nl/3apl/

GOAL Agents. A GOAL agent [51] is a BDI style of agent that makes use of the following types of mentalistic notions. It uses knowledge and beliefs as data structures for storing information. In this respect knowledge represents static facts that will not change during runtime and beliefs contains more volatile data that depends on the perceptual input and received messages. Both kinds of structures may also contain knowledge refinement rules for generating additional deduced facts. The motivations of an agent are synthesized as achievement goals using formulas for describing the desired world states. The program logic is defined by action rules referring to actions that are specified similar to STRIPS actions and make use of pre- and postconditions. An action rule is similar to a production rule consisting of a condition and action part. The condition part is a mental state guard that can e.g. check for goal existence or belief states and the action part contains an action that will be executed when the corresponding rule fires. If more than one action rule is activated a GOAL agent arbitrary selects among them yielding non-deterministic agent behavior. The GOAL architecture is implemented in the GOAL agent system.[20]

SOAR Agents. The SOAR (originally for state, operator and result) agent architecture [60,61] has been developed as a candidate for a UTC (unified theories of cognition) [68] helpful for explaining the full gamut of human behavior including e.g. problem solving, learning, and language. SOAR tries to achieve this following the 'parsimony principle', which states that the architecture complexity should be low and it should rely on as few architecture mechanisms as possible. The SOAR architecture is based on the idea of problem solving through operator search and application. In contrast to other architectures SOAR completely relies on production rules for realizing its goal directed behavior. These rules belong to different conceptual groups and their matching and firing is controlled in a sophisticated way by the agent's deliberation cycle. This cycle first transfer sensory input to the SOAR working memory. Thereafter, in the proposal phase, the interpreter fires all activated inference, proposal and comparison rules. Inference rules are used to generate new knowledge from the existing knowledge. Proposal rules serve for operator generation adding them also to the working memory and finally comparison rules are used to establish preferences among the proposed operator instances. In the following decision phase, SOAR has to select exactly one operator. In case the choice is easy and exactly one operator was proposed or one operator is preferred against all others the interpreter directly enters the next application phase. But it may also happen that no operator was selected, several operators are equally well suited or insufficient information is available for operator execution. As the interpreter performs only knowledge decisions it will solve the problem by automatic subgoaling. This means that a subcontext will be established in which SOAR tries to bear new knowledge to resolve the impasse. In the application phase the operator will be executed by firing rules that have been activated by the new operator. In the last phase domain dependent output functions will be called using specific working memory elements

[20] `http://mmi.tudelft.nl/trac/goal`

as parameters. An implementation of SOAR is developed by an active research community[21].

Vivid Agents. Vivid agents [83] is an approach that combines reactive and proactive behavior using rules and planning. The underlying Vivid agent architecture is named CAP (concurrent action and planning) and consists of two independent modules. The reactive module relies on two kinds of rules: reaction and action rules. Reaction rules are similar to event-condition-action rules and are triggered by incoming messages and new environmental percepts. In case the optional condition part is fulfilled the rule is activated and can be fired. In contrast to reaction rules, action rules do not have a triggering event and operate on the agents knowledge only. In Vivid agents three types of (reaction and action) rules are distinguished based on the kind of effects involved: epistemic, physical and communicative. Epistemic rules only have internal effects on the agent's knowledge, whereas physical actions refer to actions performed in the environment and communicative actions deal with sending a message to another agent. The planning module of CAP is responsible for proactive agent behavior. It uses a STRIPS [82] inspired approach that is able to generate a plan for achieving a goal. The planner uses the available action rules as operators and thus produces a plan in form of a sequence of action rules that have to be executed in order to reach the desired world state. After plan generation has been finished the produced plan is executed interleaved with reactive rules. A current implementation of the architecture is not available.

Rule Responder. Rule Responder [73] is a Semantic Web infrastructure for distributed rule-based event processing multi-agent eco-systems. The Rule Responder middleware is based on modern enterprise service technologies and Semantic Web technologies for implementing intelligent rule-based agent services that access data and ontologies, receive and detect events (e.g., for complex event processing in event processing agent networks), and make rule-based inferences and (semi-)autonomous pro-active decisions for reactions based on these representations. The core of a Rule Responder agent (cf. Figure 2) are reasoning engines such as the Prova rule engine [22,23] which implements the decision and behavioral reaction logic of the agents' roles. The Prova rule engine supports different rule types:

- Derivation rules to describe the agent's decision logic
- Integrity rules to describe constraints and potential conflicts
- Normative rules to represent the agent's permissions, prohibitions and obligation policies
- Defeasible rules to priorities rules for, e.g. handling conflicts between agent's goals and modularization of the agent's KB to support multiple roles of an agent

[21] `http://sitemaker.umich.edu/soar/home`

[22] `http://prova.ws`

[23] And other rule engines, such as OO jDREW, DR-Device (initially in Emerald), Euler, or Drools as long as they support Reaction RuleML as general interchange format for agent communication.

- Reaction rules to define reaction logic which are triggered on the basis of detected (complex) events
- Messaging reaction rules to define the agents conversation-based workflow reactions and behavioral logics based on complex event processing

An agent can employ vocabularies defined as Semantic Web ontologies (e.g., based on RDFS or OWL) or Java class hierarchies to give its rules a domain-specific meaning. The vocabularies can be used within the conversation with other agents to enable a semantic and pragmatic interpretation of the messages, e.g. FIPA ACL pragmatic primitives as semantic ontology concepts in messaging reaction rules.

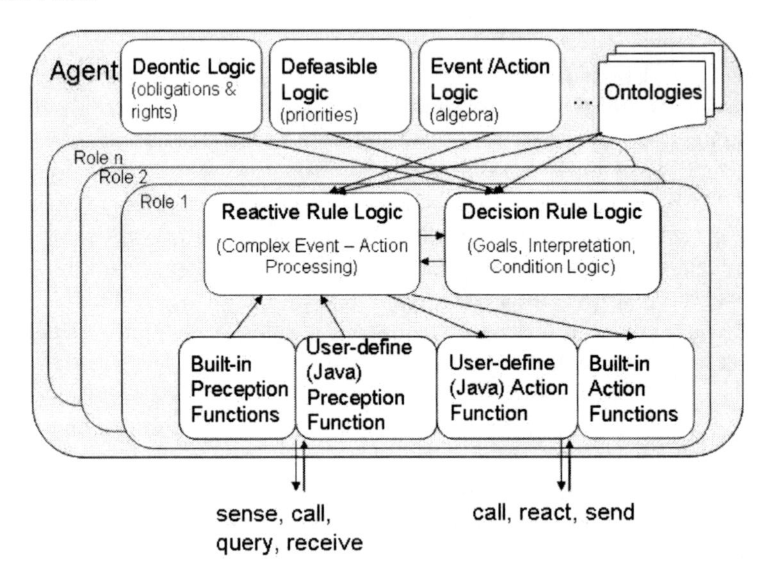

Fig. 2. Rule Responder

For the deployment of agents on the Web and for the communication in agent networks, Rule Responder uses an enterprise service bus (ESB) middleware, which supports a multitude of synchronous and asynchronous transport protocols (>40) such as MS, SMTP, JDBC, TCP, HTTP, XMPP, etc. to transport rulebases, queries and answers between the agents. The de facto standard Reaction RuleML [24] is used as a platform-independent rule interchange format for agent conversation using Reaction RuleML messages. Reaction RuleML incorporates various kinds of production, action, reaction, and knowledge representation temporal/event/action logic rules as well as (complex) event/action messages into the native RuleML standard syntax.

Emerald. Emerald[25] like Rule Responder employs reasoning engines as reasoning services that are implemented as reasoner agents, which intercommunicate

[24] http://reaction.ruleml.org

[25] http://lpis.csd.auth.gr/systems/emerald/rel.html

via FIPA ACL-based communication protocols. EMERALD is built on-top of the JADE multi-agent system. The emerald framework can be used as one platform specific agent framework in the general Rule Responder Semantic Web middleware.

3.3 Rules on the Marco Layer

Rule-Based Negotiation. According to [64], *negotiation* is the process by which a group of agents communicate to try to come to a mutually acceptable agreement on some matter. It is one of the important methods for establishing agent cooperation. Understood in this way, negotiation consists of two parts: (i) *negotiation protocol* that represents the conventions under which negotiation operates as a set of public rules of the agents' interaction process. Agents must comply to the protocol of the negotiation in order to be able to communicate; (ii) *negotiation strategy* that represents the specification of the sequence of actions that an agent plans to make during negotiation and that are supposed to lead to a desired outcome.

Negotiation Protocols. Rules can be used to define a reusable formalization of the semantics of the interaction between several negotiation participants. The participants are required to obey the rules specific to a given negotiation protocol – for example a certain type of auction. One of the first approaches was proposed by paper [62] that introduces AB3D[26] – a rule-based scripting language for expressing auction mechanisms. AB3D allows initialization of auction parameters, definition of rules for triggering auction events, declaration of user variables and definition of rules for controlling bid admissibility.

[7] introduces a conceptual framework for the development of agent-based automated negotiations focused on auctions that consists of: (1) negotiation infrastructure, (2) generic negotiation protocol, and (3) taxonomy of declarative rules, is presented. The *negotiation infrastructure* defines roles of negotiation participants and of a host. Participants exchange proposals within a "negotiation locale" managed by the host. The *generic negotiation protocol* defines three phases of a negotiation: admission, exchange of proposals and formation of an agreement, in terms of how, when and what types of messages should be exchanged between the host and negotiation participants. *Negotiation rules* are used for enforcing the negotiation protocol. Rules are organized into a taxonomy: rules for participants admission to negotiations, rules for checking validity of proposals, rules for protocol enforcement, rules for updating the negotiation status and informing participants, rules for agreement formation and rules for controlling the negotiation termination. [25] presents an implementation of the conceptual negotiation framework introduced in [7] in an agent-based e-commerce system. Furthermore, paper [26] presents a representation of negotiation rules using R2ML[27] markup language for English auctions.

[26] `http://ai.eecs.umich.edu/AB3D/`

[27] `https://oxygen.informatik.tu-cottbus.de/rewerse-i1/?q=R2ML`

[89] proposes a formalization of negotiations that goes beyond the framework of [7]. Its authors suggest usage of an ontology-based approach to expressing negotiation protocols. Specifically, whenever an agent is admitted to negotiation it is to obtain a specification of the negotiation rules in terms of a shared ontology. This approach has been exemplified with a sample scenario by investigating how the ontology can be used to tune the negotiation strategy of participating agents.

Negotiation Strategies. In [87] an implementation of a system of Jade agents that negotiate using strategies expressed in defeasible logic was described. The implementation is demonstrated with a bargaining scenario involving one buyer and one seller agent. The buyer strategy was defined by a defeasible logic program.

Rule-Based Verification of Agent Systems and Workflows. Rules represented in temporal logics can be used to express patterns of properties verification of concurrent and distributed systems [35], including agent systems and workflows. The pattern approach was taken further in [55] to define a set of verification patterns for checking business process models translated into labeled transition systems, using model checking tools. The pattern approach can considerably simplify the verification process by enabling the reuse of software engineering expertise. This technique was applied for checking an agent-based English auction service [23], as well as different types of middle-agents including frontagents, matchmakers, and brokers [24].

4 Conclusion

In this paper we have surveyed several major approaches using rules in (multi) agent systems and distributed agent architectures which run rule engines at their core. The approaches differ, e.g., in their supported rule types, state representation, rule evaluation mechanism, conflict resolution and truth maintenance mechanisms. Depending on their expressiveness and semantics the used rule engines might be capable of implementing agents in the strong sense of cognitive architectures for intelligent agents with goal/task-based, utility-based and learning-based functionalities, or in the weak sense of agent services with simple reflexive functionalities for, e.g., deductive query-answering or simple reactive capabilities. Following the general consensus defined by the strong notion of agency in [97], the use of declarative rules for representing the agents' decision and behavioral reaction logics makes them capable of reactive, proactive, and communicative behavior and supports (semi-)autonomous (intelligent) decisions. Additionally, mentalistic notions can be used in the rule language for describing the agent behavior in an abstract and intuitive way, e.g. in the interactions between agents to communicate the pragmatics of the interchanged information.

References

1. Adi, A., Etzion, O.: Amit - the situation manager. VLDB J. 13(2), 177–203 (2004)
2. Amaral, J.N., Ghosh, J.: Speeding Up Production Systems: From Concurrent Matching to Parallel Rule Firing, ch. 7, pp. 139–160. Elsevier, Amsterdam (1994)
3. Amaral, J.N., Ghosh, J.: A concurrent architecture for serializable production systems. IEEE Transactions on Parallel and Distributed Systems 7(12), 1265–1280 (1996)
4. Amarnath, B.R., Somasundaram, T.S., Ellappan, M., Buyya, R.: Ontology-based grid resource management. Software Practice and Experience 39(17), 1419–1438 (2009)
5. Aref, M.M., Tayyib, M.A.: Lana-match algorithm: A parallel version of the rete-match algorithm. Parallel Computing 24(5-6), 763–775 (1998)
6. Bach, J., Bauer, C., Vuine, R.: Micropsi: Contributions to a broad architecture of cognition. In: Freksa, C., Kohlhase, M., Schill, K. (eds.) KI 2006. LNCS (LNAI), vol. 4314, pp. 7–18. Springer, Heidelberg (2007)
7. Bartolini, C., Preist, C., Jennings, N.: A software framework for automated negotiation. In: Choren, R., Garcia, A., Lucena, C., Romanovsky, A. (eds.) SELMAS 2004. LNCS, vol. 3390, pp. 213–235. Springer, Heidelberg (2005)
8. Bellifemine, F., Caire, G., Greenwood, D.: Developing Multi-Agent systems with JADE. John Wiley & Sons, Chichester (2007)
9. Bellifemine, F.L., Caire, G., Greenwood, D.: Developing Multi-Agent Systems with JADE. John Wiley & Sons Ltd, Chichester (2007)
10. Berners-Lee, T., Hendler, J., Lassila, O.: The semantic web. Scientific American (5) (May 2001)
11. Bikakis, A., Antoniou, G.: Distributed defeasible contextual reasoning in ambient computing. In: Aarts, E., Crowley, J.L., de Ruyter, B., Gerhäuser, H., Pflaum, A., Schmidt, J., Wichert, R. (eds.) AmI 2008. LNCS, vol. 5355, pp. 308–325. Springer, Heidelberg (2008)
12. Bikakis, A., Antoniou, G.: Distributed reasoning with conflicts in an ambient peer-to-peer setting. In: Mühlhauser, M., Ferscha, A., Aitenbichler, E. (eds.) Constructing Ambient Intelligence. CCIS, vol. 11, pp. 24–33. Springer, Heidelberg (2008)
13. Bonino, D., Corno, F.: DogOnt - ontology modeling for intelligent domotic environments. In: Sheth, A.P., Staab, S., Dean, M., Paolucci, M., Maynard, D., Finin, T., Thirunarayan, K. (eds.) ISWC 2008. LNCS, vol. 5318, pp. 790–803. Springer, Heidelberg (2008)
14. Bonino, D., Corno, F.: Rule-based intelligence for domotic environments. Automation in Construction 19(2), 183–196 (2010)
15. Bordini, R., Dastani, M., Dix, J., El Fallah Seghrouchni, A.: Multi-Agent Programming: Languages, Platforms and Applications. Springer, Heidelberg (2005)
16. Bordini, R., Dastani, M., Dix, J., el Fallah-Seghrouchni, A. (eds.): Multi-Agent Programming: Languages, Tools and Applications. Springer, Berlin (2009)
17. Bratman, M.: Intention, Plans, and Practical Reason. Harvard University Press, Cambridge (1987)
18. Bratman, M., Israel, D., Pollack, M.: Plans and Resource-Bounded Practical Reasoning. Computational Intelligence 4(4), 349–355 (1988)
19. Braubach, L.: Architekturen und Methoden zur Entwicklung verteilter agentenorientierter Softwaresysteme. PhD thesis, Universität Hamburg (2007)

20. Braubach, L., Pokahr, A., Moldt, D., Lamersdorf, W.: Goal Representation for BDI Agent Systems. In: Bordini, R., Dastani, M., Dix, J., El Fallah-Seghrouchni, A. (eds.) PROMAS 2004. LNCS (LNAI), vol. 3346, pp. 44–65. Springer, Heidelberg (2005)
21. Brooks, R.A.: How to build complete creatures rather than isolated cognitive simulators. Architectures for Intelligence, 225–239 (1989)
22. Brzykcy, G., Bartoszek, J., Pankowski, T.: Schema mappings and agents' actions in p2p data integration system. Journal of Universal Computer Science 14(7), 1048–1060 (2008)
23. Bădică, A., Bădică, C.: Specification and verification of an agent-based auction service. In: Information System Development. Towards a Service Provision Society (ISD 2008), pp. 239–248. Springer, Heidelberg (2009)
24. Bădică, A., Bădică, C.: Fsp and fltl framework for specification and verification of middle-agents. Applied Mathematics and Computer Science 21(1), 9–25 (2011)
25. Bădică, C., Ganzha, M., Paprzycki, M.: Implementing rule-based automated price negotiation in an agent system. Journal of Universal Computer Science 13(2), 244–266 (2007)
26. Bădică, C., Giurca, A., Wagner, G.: Using rules and R2ML for modeling negotiation mechanisms in E-commerce agent systems. In: Draheim, D., Weber, G. (eds.) TEAA 2006. LNCS, vol. 4473, pp. 84–99. Springer, Heidelberg (2007)
27. Cabitza, F., Dal Seno, B.: Djess - a knowledge-sharing middleware to deploy distributed inference systems. In: Ardil, C. (ed.) The Second World Enformatika Conference, WEC 2005, Enformatika, Çanakkale, Turkey, pp. 66–69 (2005)
28. Carbonell, J.G., Etzioni, O., Gil, Y., Joseph, R., Knoblock, C.A., Minton, S., Veloso, M.M.: Prodigy: An integrated architecture for planning and learning. SIGART Bulletin 2(4), 51–55 (1991)
29. Cardoso, H.L.: Integrating jade and jess (2007)
30. Christoph, U., Krempels, K.-H., Wilden, A.: Jamochaagent - a rule-based programmable agent. In: Filipe, J., Fred, A.L.N., Sharp, B. (eds.) ICAART 2009 - Proceedings of the International Conference on Agents and Artificial Intelligence, pp. 447–454 (2009)
31. Collier, R.W.: Agent Factory: A Framework for the Engineering of Agent-Oriented Applications. PhD thesis, University College Dublin (2001)
32. Dastani, M.: 2apl: a practical agent programming language. International Journal of Autonomous Agents and Multi-Agent Systems (JAAMAS), Special Issue on Computational Logic-based Agents 16(3), 214–248
33. Dean, J., Ghemawat, S.: Mapreduce: Simplified data processing on large clusters. Communications of the ACM 51(1), 107–113 (2008)
34. Ding, H.: Integrating semantic metadata in p2p-based digital libraries. Library Management 26(4/5), 218–229 (2005)
35. Dwyer, M.B., Avrunin, G.S., Corbett, J.C.: Patterns in property specifications for finite-state verification. In: Proc. 21st International Conference on Software Engineering (ICSE 1999), pp. 411–420. IEEE Computer Society Press, Los Alamitos (1999)
36. Ferber, J.: Multi-Agents Systems - An Introduction to Distributed Artificial Intelligence. Addison-Wesley, Reading (1999)
37. Fischer, K., Windisch, H.-M.: Magsy: Ein regelbasiertes multiagentensystem. KI Zeitschrift 6(1), 22–26 (1992)
38. Forgy, C.: Rete: A fast algorithm for the many patterns/many objects match problem. Artificial Intelligence 19(1), 17–37 (1982)

39. Forgy, C.L.: Rete: A fast algorithm for the many pattern/many object pattern match problem. Artificial Intelligence 19(1), 17–37 (1982)
40. Foster, I.T., Kesselman, C., Tuecke, S.: The anatomy of the grid: Enabling scalable virtual organizations. IJHPCA 15(3), 200–222 (2001)
41. Foundation for Intelligent Physical Agents (FIPA). FIPA ACL Message Structure Specification (December 2002), document no. FIPA00061
42. Foundation for Intelligent Physical Agents (FIPA). FIPA SL Content Language Specification (December 2002), document no. FIPA00008
43. Friedman-Hill, E.: Jess in Action: Java Rule-based Systems. Manning Publications Co. (2003)
44. Frîncu, M.E., Petcu, D.: Osyris: a nature inspired workflow engine for service oriented environments. Scalable Computing: Practice and Experience 11(1), 81–97 (2010)
45. Gross, T., Paul-Stueve, T., Palakarska, T.: Sensbution: A rule-based peer-to-peer approach for sensor-based infrastructures. In: Proceedings of the 33rd EUROMICRO Conference on Software Engineering and Advanced Applications, pp. 333–340. IEEE Computer Society, Washington, DC, USA (2007)
46. Gupta, A., Forgy, C.L., Newell, A.: High-speed implementations of rule-based systems. ACM Transactions on Computer Systems 7(2), 119–146 (1989)
47. Gupta, G., Pontelli, E., Ali, K.A.M., Carlsson, M., Hermenegildo, M.V.: Parallel execution of prolog programs: a survey. ACM Transactions on Programming Languages and Systems 23(4), 472–602 (2001)
48. Hall, L.O.: Backpac: A parallel goal-driven reasoning system. Information Sciences 62(1-2), 169–182 (1992)
49. Harmelen, F.: Large scale reasoning on the semantic web: What to do when success is becoming a problem. In: Liu, J., Wu, J., Yao, Y., Nishida, T. (eds.) AMT 2009. LNCS, vol. 5820, p. 3. Springer, Heidelberg (2009)
50. Herrero, P., Bosque, J.L., Salvadores, M., Perez, M.S.: A rule based resources management for collaborative grid environments. International Journal of Internet Protocol Technology 3, 35–45 (2008)
51. Hindriks, K.: Programming Rational Agents in GOAL. In: El Fallah Seghrouchni, A., Dix, J., Dastani, M., Bordini, R. (eds.) Multi-Agent Programming: Languages, Platforms and Applications, pp. 119–157. Springer, Heidelberg (2009)
52. Hindriks, K., de Boer, F., van der Hoek, W., Meyer, J.-J.: Agent Programming in 3APL. Autonomous Agents and Multi-Agent Systems 2(4), 357–401 (1999)
53. Ishida, T.: Parallel, Distributed and Multiagent Production Systems. LNCS, vol. 878. Springer, Heidelberg (1994)
54. Ishida, T.: Parallel, distributed and multi-agent production systems - a research foundation for distributed artificial intelligence. In: Lesser, V.R., Gasser, L. (eds.) Proceedings of the First International Conference on Multiagent Systems, ICMAS, pp. 416–422. The MIT Press, Cambridge (1995)
55. Janssen, W., Mateescu, R., Mauw, S., Fennema, P., van der Stappen, P.: Model checking for managers. In: Dams, D.R., Gerth, R., Leue, S., Massink, M. (eds.) SPIN 1999. LNCS, vol. 1680, pp. 92–107. Springer, Heidelberg (1999)
56. Kaelbling, L.P.: A situated-automata approach to the design of embedded agents. SIGART Bulletin 2, 85–88 (1991)
57. Kinny, D., Georgeff, M.: Commitment and effectiveness of situated agents. In: Proceedings of the 12th International Joint Conference on Artificial Intelligence (IJCAI 1991), pp. 82–88 (February 1991)
58. Knottenbelt, J.: Contract Related Agents. PhD thesis, Imperial College, London (2006)

59. Langley, P., McKusick, K.B., Allen, J.A., Iba, W., Thompson, K.: A design for the icarus architecture. SIGART Bulletin 2(4), 104–109 (1991)
60. Lehman, J.F., Laird, J., Rosenbloom, P.: A gentle introduction to Soar, an architecture for human cognition. In: Sternberg, S., Scarborough, D. (eds.) Invitation to Cognitive Science, vol. 4, pp. 212–249. MIT Press, Cambridge (1996)
61. Lehman, J.F., Laird, J., Rosenbloom, P.: A gentle introduction to Soar, an architecture for human cognition. Technical report, University of Michigan (2006)
62. Lochner, K.M., Wellman, M.P.: Rule-based specification of auction mechanisms. In: 3rd International Joint Conference on Autonomous Agents and Multiagent Systems (AAMAS 2004), pp. 818–825. IEEE Computer Society, Los Alamitos (2004)
63. Loke, S.W.: Declarative programming of integrated peer-to-peer and web based systems: the case of prolog. Journal of Systems and Software 79(4), 523–536 (2006)
64. Lomuscio, A.R., Wooldridge, M., Jennings, N.R.: A classification scheme for negotiation in electronic commerce. Group Decision and Negotiation 12(1), 31–56 (2003)
65. Gedik, B., Kumar, V., Losa, G., Soulé, R., Wu, K.-L., Hirzel, M., Andrade, H.
66. Mohammad Khanli, L., Analoui, M.: Active grid information server for grid computing. The Journal of Supercomputing 50(1), 19–35 (2009)
67. Morreale, V., Bonura, S., Francaviglia, G., Centineo, F., Cossentino, M., Gaglio, S.: Reasoning about goals in BDI agents: the PRACTIONIST framework. In: De Paoli, F., Di Stefano, A., Omicini, A., Santoro, C. (eds.) Proceedings of Joint Workshop "From Objects to Agents" (2006)
68. Newell, A.: Unified Theories of Cognition. Harvard University Press, Cambridge (1990)
69. Nilsson, N.J.: Teleo-reactive programs for agent control. Journal Artificial Intelligence Research 1, 139–158 (1994)
70. Oren, E., Kotoulas, S., Anadiotis, G., Siebes, R., ten Teije, A., van Harmelen, F.: Marvin: Distributed reasoning over large-scale semantic web data. Journal of Web Semantics 7(4), 305–316 (2009)
71. Oskooei, A.R., Mirza-Aghatabar, M., Khorsandi, S.: Introduction of novel rule based algorithms for scheduling in grid computing systems. In: Second Asia International Conference on Modelling and Simulation (AMS 2008), pp. 138–143. IEEE Computer Society, Los Alamitos (2008)
72. Padgett, J., Djemame, K., Dew, P.: Predictive adaptation for service level agreements on the grid. International Journal of Simulation: Systems, Science & Technology 7(2), 29–42 (2006)
73. Paschke, A., Boley, H., Kozlenkov, A., Craig, B.: Rule responder: Ruleml-based agents for distributed collaboration on the pragmatic web. In: Proceedings of the 2nd International Conference on Pragmatic Web, ICPW 2007, pp. 17–28. ACM, New York (2007)
74. Paschke, A., Bichler, M.: Knowledge representation concepts for automated sla management. Decision Support Systems 46(1), 187–205 (2008)
75. Perraju, T.S., Prasad, B.E.: Interference analysis in multiple rule firing systems. Knowledge-Based Systems 13(4), 171–176 (2000)
76. Petcu, D., Petcu, M.: Distributed jess on a condor pool. In: Proceedings of the 9th WSEAS International Conference on Computers, Stevens Point, Wisconsin, USA, pp. 1–5. World Scientific and Engineering Academy and Society, WSEAS (2005)
77. Pokahr, A., Braubach, L., Lamersdorf, W.: A goal deliberation strategy for BDI agent systems. In: Eymann, T., Klügl, F., Lamersdorf, W., Klusch, M., Huhns, M.N. (eds.) MATES 2005. LNCS (LNAI), vol. 3550, pp. 82–93. Springer, Heidelberg (2005)

78. Pollack, M.E., Joslin, D., Nunes, A., Ur, S., Ephrati, E.: Experimental investigation of an agent commitment strategy. Technical Report 94–31, Department of Computer Science, University of Pittsburgh (1994)
79. Rao, A.: AgentSpeak(L): BDI Agents Speak Out in a Logical Computable Language. In: Van de Velde, W., Perram, J. (eds.) MAAMAW 1996. LNCS, vol. 1038, pp. 42–55. Springer, Heidelberg (1996)
80. Rao, A., Georgeff, M.: BDI Agents: from theory to practice. In: Lesser, V. (ed.) Proceedings of the 1st International Conference on Multi-Agent Systems (ICMAS 1995), pp. 312–319. MIT Press, Cambridge (1995)
81. Reticular Systems. AgentBuilder User's Guide, version 1.3 edn (2000), `http://www.agentbuilder.com/`
82. Russell, S., Norvig, P.: Artifical Intelligence: A Modern Approach. Prentice-Hall, Englewood Cliffs (2003)
83. Schroeder, M., Wagner, G.: Vivid agents: Theory, architecture, and applications. Applied Artificial Intelligence 14(7), 645–675 (2000)
84. Shoham, Y.: Agent-oriented programming. Artificial Intelligence 60(1), 51–92 (1993)
85. Siddiqui, M., Villazon, A., Fahringer, T.: Semantic-based on-demand synthesis of grid activities for automatic workflow generation. In: Proceedings of the Third IEEE International Conference on e-Science and Grid Computing, E-SCIENCE 2007, pp. 43–50. IEEE Computer Society, Washington, DC, USA (2007)
86. Simon, H.A.: Cognitive science: the newest science of the artificial. Cognitive Science 4, 33–46 (1980)
87. Skylogiannis, T., Antoniou, G., Bassiliades, N., Governatori, G., Bikakis, A.: Dr-negotiate – a system for automated agent negotiation with defeasible logic-based strategies. Data & Knowledge Engineering 63(2), 362–380 (2007)
88. Soma, R., Prasanna, V.K.: Parallel inferencing for owl knowledge bases. In: 37th International Conference on Parallel Processing, ICPP 2008, pp. 75–82. IEEE Computer Society, Los Alamitos (2008)
89. Tamma, V., Phelps, S., Dickinson, I., Wooldridge, M.: Ontologies for supporting negotiation in e-commerce. Engineering Applications of Artificial Intelligence 18(2), 223–236 (2005)
90. Thain, D., Tannenbaum, T., Livny, M.: Distributed computing in practice: the condor experience. Concurrency and Computation: Practice and Experience 17(2-4), 323–356 (2005)
91. Urbani, J., Kotoulas, S., Maassen, J., van Harmelen, F., Bal, H.E.: Owl reasoning with webpie: Calculating the closure of 100 billion triples. In: Aroyo, L., Antoniou, G., Hyvönen, E., ten Teije, A., Stuckenschmidt, H., Cabral, L., Tudorache, T. (eds.) ESWC 2010. LNCS, vol. 6088, pp. 213–227. Springer, Heidelberg (2010)
92. Urbani, J., Kotoulas, S., Oren, E., Harmelen, F.: Scalable distributed reasoning using mapReduce. In: Bernstein, A., Karger, D.R., Heath, T., Feigenbaum, L., Maynard, D., Motta, E., Thirunarayan, K. (eds.) ISWC 2009. LNCS, vol. 5823, pp. 634–649. Springer, Heidelberg (2009)
93. Vlahavas, I., Bassiliades, N.: Parallel, object-oriented, and active knowledge base systems. Kluwer Academic Publishers, Norwell (1998)
94. Wolfson, O., Ozeri, A.: Parallel and distributed processing of rules by data-reduction. IEEE Transactions on Knowledge and Data Engineering 5(3), 523–530 (1993)
95. Wooldridge, M.: Reasoning about Rational Agents. MIT Press, Cambridge (2000)

96. Wooldridge, M., Jennings, N.: Agent theories, architectures, and languages: A survey. In: Wooldridge, M., Jennings, N. (eds.) ECAI 1994 and ATAL 1994. LNCS, vol. 890, pp. 1–39. Springer, Heidelberg (1995)
97. Wooldrige, M.: An Introduction to MultiAgent Systems. John Wiley & Sons, Chichester (2002)
98. Zhang, W., Wang, K., Chau, S.-C.: Data partition and parallel evaluation of datalog programs. IEEE Transactions on Knowledge and Data Engineering 7(1), 163–176 (1995)

Extending a Multi-agent Reasoning Interoperability Framework with Services for the Semantic Web Logic and Proof Layers

Kalliopi Kravari[1], Konstantinos Papatheodorou[2], Grigoris Antoniou[2], and Nick Bassiliades[1]

[1] Dept. of Informatics, Aristotle University of Thessaloniki, GR-54124 Thessaloniki, Greece
{kkravari,nbassili}@csd.auth.gr
[2] Institute of Computer Science, FORTH, Greece
Department of Computer Science, University of Crete, Greece
{cpapath,antoniou}@ics.forth.gr

Abstract. The ultimate vision of the Semantic Web (SW) is to offer an interoperable and information-rich web environment that will allow users to safely delegate complex actions to intelligent agents. Much work has been done for agents' interoperability; a plethora of proposals and standards for ontology-based metadata and rule-based reasoning are already widely used. Nevertheless, the SW proof layer has been neglected so far, although it is vital for SW agents and human users to understand how a result came about, in order to increase the trust in the interchanged information. This paper focuses on the implementation of third party SW reasoning and proofing services wrapped as agents in a multi-agent framework. This way, agents can exchange and justify their arguments without the need to conform to a common rule paradigm. Via external reasoning and proofing services, the receiving agent can grasp the semantics of the received rule set and check the validity of the inferred results.

Keywords: semantic web, logic layer, proof layer, rules, defeasible reasoning, DR-Prolog, intelligent multi-agent systems, EMERALD.

1 Introduction

The *Semantic Web* (*SW*) [6] is a rapidly evolving extension of the current Web that derives from Sir Tim Berners-Lee's vision of a universal medium for data, information and knowledge exchange, where the semantics of information and services is well-defined, making it possible for people and machines to precisely understand Web content. So far, the fundamental SW technologies (content representation, ontologies) have been established and researchers are currently focusing their efforts on logic and proofs.

Intelligent agents (*IA*s) are software programs intended to perform tasks more efficiently and with less human intervention. They are considered the most prominent means towards realizing the SW vision [1]. The gradual integration of *multi-agent*

N. Bassiliades et al. (Eds.): RuleML 2011 - Europe, LNCS 6826, pp. 29–43, 2011.

systems (*MAS*) with SW technologies will affect the use of the Web in the imminent future; its next generation will consist of groups of intercommunicating agents traversing it and performing complex actions on behalf of their users. Thus, IAs are considered to be greatly favored by the interoperability that SW technologies aim to achieve.

IAs will often interact with other agents, belonging to service providers, e-shops, Web enterprises or even other users. However, it is unrealistic to expect that all intercommunicating agents will share a common rule or logic representation formalism; neither can W3C impose specific logic formalisms in a dynamic environment like the Web. Nevertheless, agents should somehow share an understanding of each other's position justification arguments, i.e. logical conclusions based on corresponding rule sets and facts. This heterogeneity in representation and reasoning technologies comprises a critical drawback in agent interoperation.

A solution to this compatibility issue could emerge via equipping each agent with its own inference engine or reasoning mechanism, which would assist in "grasping" other agents' logics. Nevertheless, every rule engine possesses its own formalism and, consequently, agents would require a common interchange language. Since generating a translation schema from one (rule) language into the other (e.g. *RIF – Rule Interchange Format* [16]) is not always plausible, this approach does not resolve the agent intercommunication issue, but only moves the setback one step further, from argument interchange to rule translation / transformation.

An alternative, more pragmatic, approach was presented in [2, 4], where reasoning services (called Reasoners) are wrapped in IAs, embedded in a common framework for interoperating SW agents, called *EMERALD*. This approach avoids the drawbacks outlined above and allows each agent to effectively exchange its arguments with any other agent, without the need for all involved agents to conform to the same kind of rule paradigm or logic. This way, agents remain lightweight and flexible, while the tasks of inferring knowledge from agent rule bases and verifying the results is conveyed to the reasoning services.

Moreover, trust is a vital feature for Semantic Web. If users (humans and agents) are to use and integrate system answers, they must trust them. Thus, systems should be able to explain their actions, sources, and beliefs. Proofing services are extremely important for this purpose as they let users to trust the inference services' results. Traditional trust models (EMERALD supports some of them) are able to guarantee the agents trustworthiness, including the Reasoners' trustworthiness. However, they cannot guarantee the correctness of the inference service itself, meaning that the results exchanged between agents should be explainable to each other. This includes the ability to provide the proof for a certain claim, as a result of an inference procedure, as well as the ability to validate this proof. Therefore, automating proof generation, exchange and validation are important for every inference task in the Semantic Web.

As the available inference engines list is constantly expanding, the aim of this paper is to extend EMERALD by adding both new defeasible reasoning and proofing services. The rest of the paper is organized as follows. In Section 2, we present EMERALD, a multi-agent knowledge-based framework. Section 3 presents a more thorough description of the reasoning services provided by EMERALD. Section 4 features a new reasoning service supporting DR-Prolog is presented. Section 5 reports on proofs and their validation, namely two new services. Section 6 discusses related work, and finally Section 7 concludes with final remarks and directions for future work.

2 EMERALD: A Multi-agent Knowledge-Based Framework

EMERALD [2] is a multi-agent knowledge-based framework (Fig. 1), which offers flexibility, reusability and interoperability of behavior between agents, based on Semantic Web and FIPA language standards [8]. The main advantage of this approach is that it provides a safe, generic, and reusable framework for modeling and monitoring agent communication and agreements.

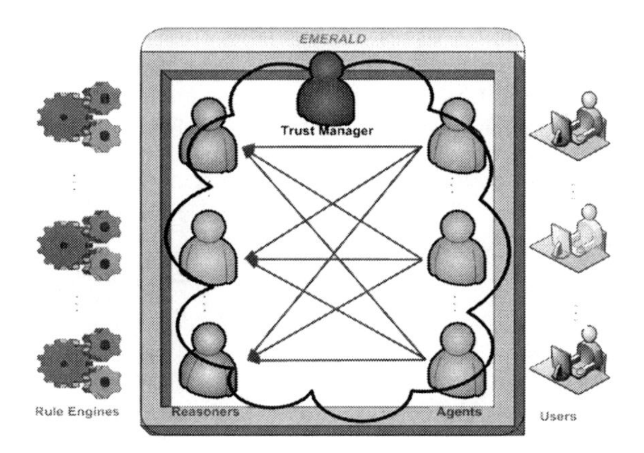

Fig. 1. EMERALD Generic Overview

In order to model and monitor the parties involved in a transaction, a generic, reusable agent prototype for *knowledge-customizable agents* (*KC-Agents*), consisted of an agent model (*KC Model*), a yellow pages service (*Advanced Yellow Pages Service*) and several external Java methods (*Basic Java Library – BJL*), is deployed (Fig. 2).

Agents that comply with this prototype are equipped with a Jess rule engine [4] and a knowledge base (KB) that contains environment knowledge (in the form of facts), behavior patterns and strategies (in the form of Jess production rules). A short description is presented below for better comprehension.

The generic rule format is: *result* $\leftarrow$ *rule* (*preconditions*). The agent's internal knowledge is a set F of facts that consists of subset F_u of user-defined facts and subset F_e of environment-asserted facts: $F_u \equiv \{f_{u1}, f_{u2}, \ldots, f_{uk}\}$, $F_e \equiv \{f_{e1}, f_{e2}, \ldots, f_{em}\}$, $F \equiv F_u \cup F_e$. Agent behavior is a set P of potential actions, expressed as Jess production rules. P consists of rules that derive new facts by inserting them into the KB (subset A) and rules that lead to the execution of a special action (subset S). Special actions can either refer to agent communication (subset C) or Java calls (subset J):

$$P \equiv A \cup S,\ S \equiv C \cup J$$

$$A \equiv \{a | f_e \leftarrow a(f_{u1}, f_{u2}, \ldots, f_{un}) \wedge \{f_{u1}, f_{u2}, \ldots, f_{un}\} \subseteq F_u \wedge f_e \in F_e\}$$

$$C \equiv \{c | ACLMessage \leftarrow c(f_1, f_2, \ldots, f_p) \wedge \{f_1, f_2, \ldots, f_p\} \subseteq F\}$$

$$J \equiv \{j | JavaMethod \leftarrow j(f_1, f_2, \ldots, f_q) \wedge \{f_1, f_2, \ldots, f_q\} \subseteq F\}$$

where *ACLMessage* is a template for defining ACL messages in Jess, while *JavaMethod* refers to user-defined Java methods. A generic specification for the communication rule syntax is:

```
(defrule Communication_Rule
;;; rule preconditions
=>
(ACLMessage (communicative-act ?c) (sender ?s) (receiver ?r) (content ?n)))
```

where *communicative-act*, *sender*, *receiver* and *content* are four template parameters of *ACLMessage*, according to *FIPA* [8] *Fipa2000* description.

The use of the *KC-Agents* prototype offers certain advantages, like interoperability of behavior between agents, as opposed to having behavior hard-wired into the agent's code.

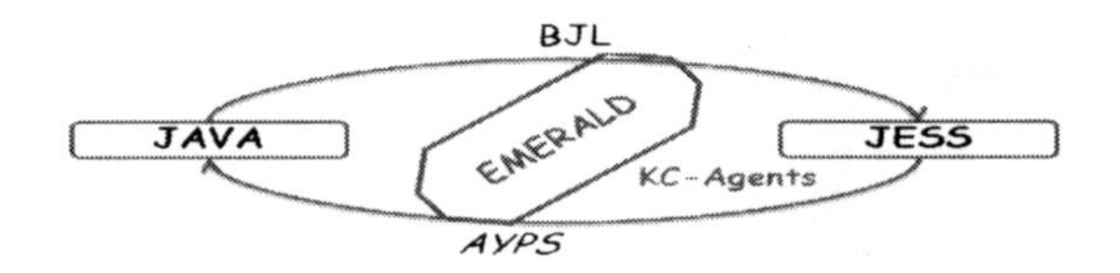

Fig. 2. The KC-Agents Prototype

Finally, as agents do not necessarily share a common rule or logic formalism, it is vital for them to find a way to exchange their position arguments seamlessly. Thus, EMERALD proposes the use of *Reasoners* [4], which are actually agents that offer reasoning services to the rest of the agent community. It is important to mention that although they are embedded in the framework, they can be added in any other multi-agent system.

3 Reasoners

EMERALD's approach for reasoning tasks does not rely on translation between rule formalisms, but on exchanging the results of the reasoning process of the rule base over the input data. The receiving agent uses an external reasoning service to grasp the semantics of the rulebase, i.e. the set of conclusions of the rule base (Fig. 3). The procedure is straightforward: each Reasoner stands by for new requests and as soon as it receives a valid request, it launches the associated reasoning engine and returns the results.

EMERALD implements a number of Reasoners that offer reasoning services in two major reasoning formalisms: deductive and defeasible reasoning. *Deductive reasoning* is based on classical logic arguments, where conclusions are proved to be valid, when the premises of the argument (i.e. rule conditions) are true. *Defeasible reasoning* [17], on the other hand, constitutes a non-monotonic rule-based approach for efficient reasoning with incomplete and inconsistent information. When compared to more mainstream non-monotonic reasoning approaches, the main advantages of defeasible reasoning are enhanced representational capabilities and low computational complexity [18]. Table 1 displays the main features of the four initial reasoning engines.

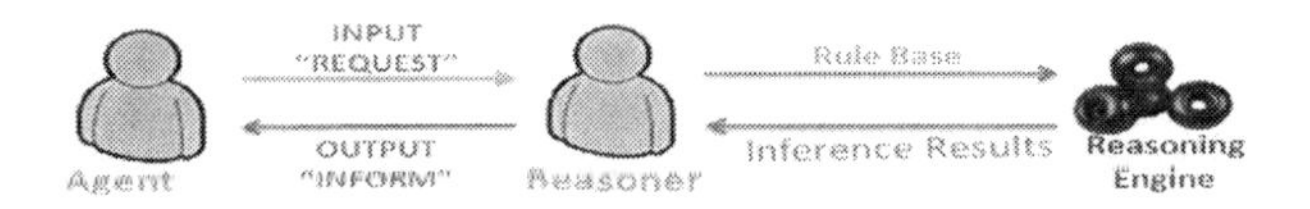

Fig. 3. Input – Output of a Reasoner Agent

The two deductive reasoners, based on the logic programming paradigm, that provides EMERALD are the *R-Reasoner* and the *Prova-Reasoner*. More specifically, the *R-Reasoner* is based on *R-DEVICE* [19], a deductive object-oriented knowledge base system for querying and reasoning about RDF metadata. The system is based on an OO RDF data model, which is different from the established triple-based model, in the sense that resources are mapped to objects and properties are encapsulated inside resource objects, as traditional OO attributes. R-DEVICE features a powerful deductive rule language which is able to express arbitrary queries both on the RDF schema and data, including generalized path expressions, stratified negation, aggregate, grouping, and sorting, functions, mainly due to the second-order syntax of the rule language, i.e. variables ranging over class and slot names, which is efficiently translated into sets of first-order logic rules using metadata. R-DEVICE rules define views which are materialized and incrementally maintained, using forward chaining, fixpoint semantics. R-DEVICE rule language has a RuleML compatible syntax, extending the Datalog with negation-as-failure path of RuleML, having also OO features.

Table 1. Reasoning engine features

	Type of logic	**Implementation**
R-DEVICE	deductive	RDF/CLIPS/RuleML
Prova	deductive	Prolog/Java
DR-DEVICE	defeasible	RDF/CLIPS/RuleML
SPINdle	defeasible	XML/Java
	Order of Logic	**Reasoning**
R-DEVICE	2nd order (restricted)	forward chaining
Prova	1st order	backward chaining
DR-DEVICE	1nd order	forward chaining
SPINdle	zero – order	forward chaining

On the other hand, the *Prova-Reasoner* is based on *Prova* (from Prolog+Java) [20], a rule engine for rule-based Java scripting, integrating Java with derivation rules (for reasoning over ontologies) and reaction rules (for specifying reactive behaviors of distributed agents). Prova supports rule interchange and rule-based decision logic, distributed inference services and combines ontologies and inference with dynamic object-oriented programming. Actually, it is a rule-based system for Java and agent scripting and information integration extending the Mandarax engine with a proper language syntax and enhanced semantics. It combines natural syntax and typing of Java with Prolog-style rules and database wrappers. Java calls may include both constructor and method calls as well as access to public variables in classes. Distributed and agent programming transported via JMS or JADE protocols is based on reaction rules specified in a natural syntax.

Furthermore, the two defeasible reasoners are the *DR-Reasoner* and the *SPINdle-Reasoner*. The *DR-Reasoner* is based on DR-DEVICE [5]. *DR-DEVICE* accepts as input the address of a defeasible logic rule base, written in an OO RuleML-like syntax. The rule base contains only rules; the facts for the rule program are contained in RDF documents, whose addresses are declared in the rule base. Finally, conclusions are exported as an RDF document. DR-DEVICE is based on the OO RDF model of R-DEVICE. Furthermore, defeasible rules are implemented through compilation into the generic rule language of R-DEVICE. DR-DEVICE supports multiple rule types of defeasible logic, both classical (strong) negation and negation-as-failure, and conflicting literals, i.e. derived objects that exclude each other.

The *SPINdle-Reasoner* is based on *SPINdle* [21], an open-source, Java-based defeasible logic reasoner that supports reasoning on both standard and modal defeasible logic; including fact, strict and defeasible rules, defeaters and superiority relation among rules. It accepts defeasible logic theories, represented via a text-based pre-defined syntax or via a custom XML vocabulary, processes them and exports the results via XML. SPINdle only considers rules that are essentially propositional. Rules containing free variables are interpreted as the set of their ground instances.

Finally it is important to mention that Reasoners commit to SW and FIPA standards, such as the RuleML language [6] for representing and exchanging agent policies and e-contract clauses, since it has become a de facto standard and the RDF model [14] for data representation both for the private data included in agents' internal knowledge and the reasoning results generated during the process. For some of them RuleML support is inherent in the original rule engine (such as R-DEVICE and DR-DEVICE), whereas in SPINDLE and Prova, the wrapper agent provides this interface.

4 DR-Prolog Reasoner

At this paper, a new defeasible Reasoner supporting DR-Prolog [22] was implemented. DR-Prolog uses rules, facts and ontologies, and supports all major Semantic Web standards, such as RDF, RDFS, OWL and RuleML. Moreover, it deals with both monotonic and nonmonotonic rules, open and closed world assumption and reasoning with inconsistencies.

Although this Reasoner deals with DR-Prolog, it is important to maintain the EMRALD's general approach. Thus, the Dr-Prolog Reasoner follows the Reasoners' general functionality; it stands by for new requests and as soon as it receives a valid request, it launches the associated reasoning engine and returns the results. However, it has to add some new steps in the procedure in order to be able to process the receiving queries and to send back the appropriate answer in RDF format (Fig. 4).

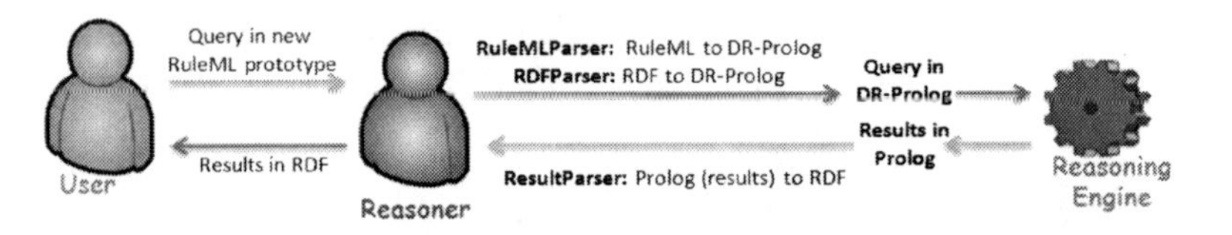

Fig. 4. DR-Prolog Reasoner Functionality

First of all, the DR-Prolog Reasoner receives a new query in RuleML, however the query has to comply with a specific RuleML prototype; an extended RuleML syntax used by DR-Prolog. In order to extract the DR-Prolog rules, that are comprised in the RuleML query, a new parser was implemented called RuleMLParser. RuleMLParser receives the RuleML file containing the query, extracts the DR-Prolog rules and stores them in a new file (*.P) in DR-Prolog format. More specifically, at first the parser sections the RuleML file indicating the rules. Then, each rule is divided and processed. Each processed part of the RuleML rule generates a specific part of the DR-Prolog rule. Eventually, the generated DR-Prolog parts are combined forming the final rules in DR-Prolog format (Fig, 5). In addition, this parser extracts the queries that are included in the RuleML query, indicating whether it is an "answer" or a "proof" query. For instance a query in DR-Prolog format is deployed in Fig. 5.

```
<Implies ruletype="defeasiblerule">
   <oid>r1</oid>
   <head>
      <Atom neg="no">
         <Rel>acceptable</Rel>
         <Slot type="var">X</Slot>
         <Slot type="var">Y</Slot>
         <Slot type="var">Z</Slot>
         <Slot type="var">W</Slot>
      </Atom>
</head>
   <body>
      <part type="atom">
         <Rel>name</Rel>
         <Slot type="var">X</Slot>
         <Slot type="var">X</Slot>
      </part>
         <part type="atom">
         <Rel>price</Rel>
         <Slot type="var">X</Slot>
         <Slot type="var">Y</Slot>
      </part>
         <part type="atom">
         <Rel>size</Rel>
         <Slot type="var">X</Slot>
         <Slot type="var">Z</Slot>
      </part>
         <part type="atom">
         <Rel>size</Rel>
         <Slot type="var">X</Slot>
         <Slot type="var">Z</Slot>
      </part>
         <part type="atom">
          <Rel>gardenSize</Rel>
          <Slot type="var">X</Slot>
          <Slot type="var">W</Slot>
      </part>
       </body>
</Implies>
                                   RuleML
```

```
defeasible(r1,acceptable(X,Y,Z,W),[name(X,X),price(X,Y),size(X,Z),gardenSize(X,W)]).
                                                                        DR-Prolog
```

```
defeasibly(acceptable(X,Y,Z,W))
%(apartment, price, size, gardenSize)
                                         Query in DR-Prolog
```

Fig. 5. RuleMLParser: RuleML to DR-Prolog

However, turning the initial RuleML query into DR-Prolog is not enough. The rule base has to be translated, too. Typically, the rule base is in RDF format, which must be transformed into Prolog facts. For this purpose, another parser was implemented, called RDFParser. This parser uses the SW Knowledge Middleware [23], a set of tools for the parsing, storage, manipulation and querying of Semantic Web (RDF) Knowledge bases, to extract the RDF triples and turn them to Prolog facts (Fig. 7).

```
nonDeterministicGoal(X, defeasibly(acceptable(X,Y,Z,W)), ListModel)
                                                                  Query
```

```
                  Results = [a3,350,65,0,a5,350,55,15]
                                                   Results list in Prolog
```

```
<?xml version="1.0" encoding="UTF-8"?>
<!DOCTYPE rdf:RDF [<!ENTITY rdf 'http://www.w3.org/1999/02/22-rdf-syntax-
ns#'>
<!ENTITY rdfs 'http://www.w3.org/2000/01/rdf-schema#'>
<!ENTITY xsd 'http://www.w3.org/2001/XMLSchema#'>
<!ENTITY dr-device 'file:/c:/jade/EMERALD/conclusions/projectvo58.rdf#'>
]>
<rdf:RDF
      xmlns:dr-
device="file:/c:/jade/EMERALD/conclusions/projectvo58.rdf#"
      xmlns:rdf="http://www.w3.org/1999/02/22-rdf-syntax-ns#"
      xmlns:rdfs="http://www.w3.org/2000/01/rdf-schema#">
      <rdfs:Class rdf:about="acceptable">
            <rdfs:label>acceptable</rdfs:label>
      </rdfs:Class>
      <rdf:Property rdf:about="#X">
            <rdfs:domain rdf:resource="#acceptable"/>
      </rdf:Property>
      <rdf:Property rdf:about="#Y">
            <rdfs:domain rdf:resource="#acceptable"/>
      </rdf:Property>
      <rdf:Property rdf:about="#Z">
            <rdfs:domain rdf:resource="#acceptable"/>
      </rdf:Property>
      <rdf:Property rdf:about="#W">
            <rdfs:domain rdf:resource="#acceptable"/>
      </rdf:Property>
      <dr-device:acceptable rdf:about="#acceptable0">
            <dr-device:X>a3</dr-device:X>
            <dr-device:Y>350</dr-device:Y>
            <dr-device:Z>65</dr-device:Z>
            <dr-device:W>0</dr-device:W>
      </dr-device:acceptable>
      <dr-device:acceptable rdf:about="#acceptable1">
            <dr-device:X>a5</dr-device:X>
            <dr-device:Y>350</dr-device:Y>
            <dr-device:Z>55</dr-device:Z>
            <dr-device:W>15</dr-device:W>
      </dr-device:acceptable>
                                                   Final Results in RDF
</rdf:RDF>
```

Fig. 6. ResultParser: Prolog to RDF

Thus, a new query in DR-Prolog with the associated rule base in Prolog facts is available. The DR-Prolog Reasoner is ready to invoke the engine. As soon as, the inference results (in prolog) are available the Reasoner has to turn them into RDF format and forward them back to the requesting agent. For this purpose, a third parser called ResultParser was implemented. This parser receives the initial query (in DR-Prolog) and the results (a prolog list) and returns the query results in RDF (Fig. 6). It is important to mention that the returned RDF results contain only the results that are required by the initial query and not the complete information that is available at the results' base.

```
<tour:Hotel rdf:ID="CretaMareRoyal">
    <tour:resortID>1</tour:resortID>
    <tour:hotelName>Creta Mare
Royal</tour:hotelName>
    <tour:hotelStars>6</tour:hotelStars>

<tour:hotelCategory>Business</tour:hotelCa
tegory>
    <tour:parking>true</tour:parking>
```

RDF

```
fact(type(CretaMareRoyal,Hotel)).
fact(resortID(CretaMareRoyal,1)).
fact(hotelName(CretaMareRoyal,Creta Mare
Royal)).
fact(hotelStars(CretaMareRoyal,6)).
fact(hotelCategory(CretaMareRoyal,Business
)).
fact(parking(CretaMareRoyal,true)).
fact(swimmingPool(CretaMareRoyal,true)).
fact(breakfast(CretaMareRoyal,true)).
```

DR-Prolog facts

Fig. 7. RDFParser: RDF rule base to DR-Prolog facts

5 Defeasible Proofing Services

In the Semantic Web, the Proof layer is assumed to answer agents about the question of why they should believe the results. At present, there is no technology recommended by W3C to this layer. However, it is a vital issue and thus researchers are now focusing their attention on this direction.

5.1 The Dr-Prolog Reasoner Equipped with a Defeasible Proof Service

The DR-Prolog Reasoner that was presented in the previous section was selected to be updated with a new proofing service. Thus, the Reasoner will be able not only to provide the appropriate results for a receiving query but also to explain them, increasing the trust of the users.

In this context, (defeasible) proof explanation functionality was added to DR-Prolog Reasoner. At first, the Reasoner was equipped with a system, presented in [25], that produces automatically proof explanations using a popular logic programming system (XSB), by interpreting the output from the proof's trace and converting it into a meaningful representation. More specific, this proof explanation system supports explanations in defeasible logic for both positive and negative answers in user queries. Additionally, it uses a pruning algorithm that reads the XSB trace and removes the redundant information in order to formulate a sensible proof.

Although proof explanations are extremely useful there is one more important aspect to deal with. The provided explanations have to be checked. Hence, the DR-Prolog Reasoner was also equipped with a newly developed defeasible proof validator's functionality, presented in the next section. More specific, the proof explanations are fed into the proof validator that verifies the validity of the conclusions. Hence, the Reasoner is now capable of not only processing queries in DR-Prolog but also providing proof explanations (for the inference results) and validity checks (for the proof explanations).

However, the proof explanations and their validity check (though the proof validator) are available only on demand; meaning that the Reasoner can also be used as usual sending back just the results; but whenever it is requested to provide explanations, the service uses its proof generation engine and sends back both the results and their explanation, along with their validity reassurance. More about the project teams that worked in both DR-Prolog Reasoner and Proof Validator can be found at [26].

5.2 The Defeasible Proof Validator

In this context a new defeasible proof checker (Proof Validator) was implemented. It follows the Reasoners' functionality, meaning that it receives requests and returns back a reply; however, it can also be embedded in any other system. Its competence is to decide whether the provided proof, given a theory (in XML), is valid or not. In the case the proof is not valid, an appropriate error message is returned, depending on the nature of the problem.

At first, the proof validator receives the validation request, then parses the received proof and constructs a prolog query based on the claimed proof. The received theory is also constructed and loaded on the prolog engine in support to the proof validator. The XML-formatted proof, contains a lot of redundant or unnecessary information that is omitted from the validation query. Elements declaring provability of a predicate along with the predicate and often the rule name are of major concern, while elements describing the body of a rule or superiority claims are ignored as mentioned. Notice that, due to the lack of an XML schema or a DTD describing the proof constructs the parser does not yet provide any XML validation. It is important to mention that this proof validator uses also DR-Prolog. More details about its structures, rules and facts are described below.

Four assumptions were made during the validator implementation:

1. It is assumed that the theory is the same as the one given to the proof generator. Moreover, any given theory is accepted as valid without any checks.
2. No checks are performed recursively. Thus, any information is required in depth more than one a priori.
3. Any knowledge given in the theory is considered to be definitely provable. For instance all facts are added as definite knowledge regardless of the presence of a statement in the proof supporting it.
4. The minimal information that will contribute to the proof checking process is required.

5.2.1 Data Structures

The proof validator distinguishes between two groups of collections, theory structures and proof deduction structures. The theory structures are four knowledge bases holding the strict rules, defeasible rules, facts and rules hierarchy. These help as retrieve any information used by the proof.

```
:- dynamic strictkb/1.        :- dynamic defeasiblekb/1.
:- dynamic factkb/1.          :- dynamic supkb/1.
```

The proof deduction structures are knowledge bases holding any deduced information already stated by the proof and confirmed by the validator.

```
:- dynamic definitelykb/1.
:- dynamic defeasiblykb/1.
:- dynamic minusdefinitelykb/1.
:- dynamic minusdefeasiblykb/1.
```

For example a rule that adds knowledge to the `defintlykb` is the following:

```
definitelyCheck(X, printOn) :-
  factkb(F), memberchk(X,F), addDefinitely(X).
```

5.2.2 Facts

All facts given in the theory are also added in the definite knowledge base. This means that any stated fact is by default considered by the proof validator, e.g. the following two statements are all accepted, provided that `f` is a fact in the theory:

```
fact(f).    definitely(f).
```

5.2.3 Rules

Generally the rules are not stated explicitly in the contents of the proof validation result, since they are a priori accepted and considered valid (fist assumption in section 5.2). More specifically in the proof, the rules are not stated explicitly (see proof example 5.2.2.), a mere reference of the rule name is used: for example `defeasibly(e,r2)` in the proof means that `e` is derived using rule `r2` which can be found in the rule base of the original theory.

5.2.4 Deductions

A conclusion in D (defeasible) is a tagged literal and may have one of the following forms [27]:

- $+\Delta q$, meaning that q is definitely provable in D.
- $+\partial q$, meaning that q is defeasibly provable in D.
- $-\Delta q$, meaning that q has proved to be not definitely provable in D.
- $-\partial q$, meaning that q has proved to be not defeasibly provable in D.

In order to prove $+\Delta q$, a proof for q consisting of facts and strict rules needs to be established. Whenever a literal is definitely provable, it is also defeasibly provable. In that case, the defeasible proof coincides with the definite proof for q. Otherwise, in order to prove $+\partial q$ in D, an applicable strict or defeasible rule supporting q must exist. In addition, it should also be ensured that the specified proof is not overridden by contradicting evidence. Therefore, it has to be guaranteed that the negation of q is not definitely provable in D. Successively, every rule that is not known to be inapplicable and has head ~q has to be considered. For each such rule s, it is required that there is a counterattacking rule t with head q that is applicable at this point and s is inferior to t.

In order to prove $-\Delta q$ in D, q must not be a fact and every strict rule supporting q must be known to be inapplicable. If it is proved that $-\Delta q$, then it is also proved that $-\partial q$. Otherwise, in order to prove that $-\partial q$, it must firstly be ensured that $-\Delta q$. Additionally, one of the following conditions must hold: (i) None of the rules with head q can be applied, (ii) It is proved that $-\Delta$~q, and (iii) There is an applicable rule r with head ~q, such that no possibly applicable rule s with head q is superior to r.

The proof validator, presented here, uses two separate predicates for strict deductions, namely $+\Delta$ (`definitely`) and $-\Delta$ (`not definitely`) and two for defeasible deductions; predicates `defeasibly` for $+\partial$ and `not defeasibly` for $-\partial$. In general, for positive deductions (+Δ and +∂), when the conclusion is proven by a rule, the name of the rule is required by the proof validator. Otherwise, i.e. when the conclusion is a fact, or when it is already given or deducted at a previous step, it is not required. This approach is followed for the sake of efficiency. On the other hand, for negative deductions, giving the name of the rule would be redundant. That is because, even if a negative result is concluded by one rule, the validator still has to retrieve all existing relevant rules regardless of whether the proof states them or not. For example, the rules that check if a stated literal, claimed to be either a fact or an already proven literal, is definitely provable or not, are the following:

```
definitelyCheck(X,printOn) :-
  factkb(F), memberchk(X,F), addDefinitely(X).
definitelyCheck(X,printOff) :-
  factkb(F), memberchk(X,F).
definitelyCheck(X,_) :-
  definitelykb(K), memberchk(X,K).
definitelyCheck(X,Print) :-
  logError(Print,[X,' is neither a fact nor has yet been proven.']).
```

The second argument is used to state if errors are to be printed or not and it can take two values: `printOn` and `printOff`. The first two rules check if `X` is a fact (i.e. it is a member of the fact knowledge base). The third rule checks if `X` is already a member of the definite knowledge base (it has already been proven that `X` is definitely provable). Should these three rules fail, it means that `X` is neither a fact nor a literal that has been proven definitely, so the fourth rule prints an error message.

5.2.5 Examples

Below the evaluation steps for a complex team defeat example are explained.

```
r1: a => e.   r2: b => e.    r3: c => ~e.   r4: d => ~e.
r1 > r3.      r2 > r4.       a. b. c. d.
```

A valid and correct proof is the following:

```
defeasibly(a), defeasibly(b), defeasibly(c), defeasi-
bly(d), defeasibly(e, r2).
```

The first four statements are deduced in an obvious way, since `a`, `b`, `c`, `d` are facts. The last, i.e. `defeasibly(e,r2)`, has to make some proof checks such as:

1. Is there any rule "r2" in the theory, with head equal to e? →Yes.
2. Is there any attacking rule? →Yes, r3, r4
   - 2.1 Is r2 of higher priority than r3? →No.
     - 2.1.1 Are the conditions of r3 (i.e. c) defeasibly provable? →Yes.
     - 2.1.2 Is there any attacking rule of r3 (different from r2), which defeats r3? →Yes, r1, because its conditions are met and r1 > r3.
   - 2.2 Is r2 of higher priority than r4? →Yes.

6 Related Work

A similar architecture for intelligent agents is presented in [12], where various reasoning engines are employed as plug-in components, while agents intercommunicate via FIPA-based communication protocols. The framework is build on top of the OPAL agent platform [13] and, similarly to EMERALD, features distinct types of reasoning services that are implemented as reasoner agents. The featured reasoning engines are *3APL* [14], *JPRS* (*Java Procedural Reasoning System*) and *ROK* (*Rule-driven Object-oriented Knowledge-based System*) [15]. 3APL agents incorporate BDI logic elements and first-order logic features, providing constructs for implementing agent beliefs, declarative goals, basic capabilities and reasoning rules, through which an agent's goals can be updated or revised. JPRS agents perform goal-driven procedural reasoning and each JPRS agent is composed of a world model (agent beliefs), a plan library (plans that the agent can use to achieve its goals), a plan executor (reasoning module) and a set of goals. Finally, ROK agents are composed of a working memory, a rule-base (consisting of first-order, forward-chaining production rules) and a conflict set. Thus, following a similar approach to EMERALD, the framework integrates the three reasoning engines into OPAL in the form of OPAL micro-agents. The primary difference between the two frameworks lies in the variety of reasoning services offered by EMERALD. While the three reasoners featured in [12] are all based on declarative rule languages, EMERALD proposes a variety of reasoning services, including deductive, defeasible and modal defeasible reasoning, thus, comprising a more integrated solution. Finally, and most importantly, the approach of [12] is not based on Semantic Web standards, like EMERALD, for rule and data interchange.

The *Rule Responder* [24] project builds a service-oriented methodology and a rule-based middleware for interchanging rules in virtual organizations, as well as negotiating about their meaning. Rule Responder demonstrates the interoperation of various distributed platform-specific rule execution environments, based on Reaction RuleML as a platform-independent rule interchange format. We have a similar view of reasoning service for intelligent agents and usage of RuleML. Also, both approaches allow utilizing a variety of rule engines. However, contrary to Rule Responder, our framework (EMERALD) is based on FIPA specifications, achieving a fully FIPA-compliant model and proposes two reputation mechanisms to deal with trust issues. Finally, and most importantly, our framework does not rely on a single rule interchange language, but allows each agent to follow its own rule formalism, but still be able to exchange its rule base with other agents, which will use trusted third-party reasoning services to infer knowledge based on the received ruleset.

7 Conclusions and Future Work

The paper argued that agent technology will play a vital role in the realization of the Semantic Web vision and presented a variety of reasoning services called Reasoners, wrapped in an agent interface, embedded in a common framework for interoperating SW IAs, called *EMERALD*, a JADE multi-agent framework designed specifically for the Semantic Web. This methodology allows each agent to effectively exchange its argument base with any other agent, without the need for all involved agents to conform to the same kind of rule paradigm or logic. Instead, via EMERALD, IAs can utilize third-party reasoning services, that will infer knowledge from agent rule bases and verify the results.

The framework offers a variety of popular inference services that conform to various types of logics. The paper presents how new types of logic were embedded in new Reasoners, as well as it argues about the importance of the SW proof layer and presents how proofing services were designed and embedded also in the system.

As for future directions, it would be interesting to integrate an even broader variety of distinct reasoning and proof validation engines, thus, forming a flexible, generic environment for interoperating agents in the SW. Finally, our intention is to develop methodologies to integrate the generated proofs with the trust mechanism of EMERALD, in order to interconnect the Proof and Trust layers of the SW.

References

1. Hendler, J.: Agents and the Semantic Web. IEEE Intelligent Systems 16(2), 30–37 (2001)
2. Kravari, K., Kontopoulos, E., Bassiliades, N.: EMERALD: A Multi-Agent System for Knowledge-based Reasoning Interoperability in the Semantic Web. In: Konstantopoulos, S., Perantonis, S., Karkaletsis, V., Spyropoulos, C.D., Vouros, G. (eds.) SETN 2010. LNCS, vol. 6040, pp. 173–182. Springer, Heidelberg (2010)
3. JESS, the Rule Engine for the Java Platform, `http://www.jessrules.com/`
4. Kravari, K., Kontopoulos, E., Bassiliades, N.: Trusted Reasoning Services for Semantic Web Agents. Informatica: Int. J. of Computing and Informatics 34(4), 429–440 (2010)
5. Bassiliades, N., Antoniou, G., Vlahavas, I.: A Defeasible Logic Reasoner for the Semantic Web. IJSWIS 2(1), 1–41 (2006)
6. Boley, H., Tabet, S.: RuleML: The RuleML Standardization Initiative (2000), `http://www.ruleml.org/`
7. Berners-Lee, T., Hendler, J., Lassila, O.: The Semantic Web. Scientific American Magazine 284(5), 34–43 (2001) (revised 2008)
8. FIPA Specifications, `http://www.fipa.org/specifications/`
9. Resource Description Framework (RDF) Model and Syntax Specification, `http://www.w3.org/TR/PR-rdf-syntax/`
10. Mule ESB, `http://www.mulesoft.org`
11. Ball, M., Boley, H., Hirtle, D., Mei, J., Spencer, B.: The OO jDREW reference implementation of ruleML. In: Adi, A., Stoutenburg, S., Tabet, S. (eds.) RuleML 2005. LNCS, vol. 3791, pp. 218–223. Springer, Heidelberg (2005)
12. Wang, M., Purvis, M., Nowostawski, M.: An Internal Agent Architecture Incorporating Standard Reasoning Components and Standards-based Agent Communication. In: IEEE/WIC/ACM International Conference on Intelligent Agent Technology (IAT 2005), pp. 58–64. IEEE Computer Society, Washington, DC (2005)
13. Purvis, M., Cranefield, S., Nowostawski, M., Carter, D.: Opal: A Multi-Level Infrastructure for Agent-Oriented Software Development. In: Information Science Discussion Paper Series, number 2002/01. University of Otago, Dunedin, New Zealand (2002) ISSN 1172-602
14. Dastani, M., van Riemsdijk, M.B., Meyer, J.-J.C.: Programming multi-agent systems in 3APL. In: Bordini, R.H., Dastani, M., Dix, J., El Fallah Seghrouchni, A. (eds.) Multi-Agent Programming: Languages, Platforms and Applications. Springer, Berlin (2005)
15. Nowostawski, M.: Kea Enterprise Agents Documentation (2001)

16. Boley, H., Kifer, M.: A Guide to the Basic Logic Dialect for Rule Interchange on the Web. IEEE Transactions on Knowledge and Data Engineering, 1593–1608 (2010)
17. Nute, D.: Defeasible Reasoning. In: 20th Int. C. on Systems Science, pp. 470–477. IEEE, Los Alamitos (1987)
18. Maher, M.J.: Propositional defeasible logic has linear complexity. Theory and Practice of Logic Programming 1(6), 691–711 (2001)
19. Bassiliades, N., Vlahavas, I.: R-DEVICE: An Object-Oriented Knowledge Base System for RDF Metadata. Int. Journal on Semantic Web and Information Systems 2(2), 24–90 (2006)
20. Kozlenkov, A., Penaloza, R., Nigam, V., Royer, L., Dawelbait, G., Schröder, M.: Prova: Rule-based Java Scripting for Distributed Web Applications: A Case Study in Bioinformatics. In: Grust, T., Höpfner, H., Illarramendi, A., Jablonski, S., Fischer, F., Müller, S., Patranjan, P.-L., Sattler, K.-U., Spiliopoulou, M., Wijsen, J. (eds.) EDBT 2006. LNCS, vol. 4254, pp. 899–908. Springer, Heidelberg (2006)
21. Lam, H., Governatori, G.: The Making of SPINdle. In: Governatori, G., Hall, J., Paschke, A. (eds.) RuleML 2009. LNCS, vol. 5858, pp. 315–322. Springer, Heidelberg (2009)
22. Antoniou, G., Bikakis, A.: DR-Prolog: A System for Defeasible Reasoning with Rules and Ontologies on the SW. IEEE Transactions on Knowledge and Data Engineering 19, 2 (2007)
23. Semantic Web Knowledge Middleware, `http://139.91.183.30:9090/SWKM/`
24. Paschke, A., Boley, H., Kozlenkov, A., Craig, B.: Rule responder: RuleML-based Agents for Distributed Collaboration on the Pragmatic Web. In: 2nd International Conference on Pragmatic Web, vol. 280, pp. 17–28. ACM, New York (2007)
25. Antoniou, G., Bikakis, A., Dimaresis, N., Governatori, G.: Proof Explanation for a Non-monotonic Semantic Web Rules Language. Data and Knowledge Engineering 64(3), 662–687 (2008)
26. CS-566 Project 2010, `http://www.csd.uoc.gr/~hy566/project2010.html`
27. Antoniou, G., Billington, D., Governatori, G., Maher, M.J.: Representation results for defeasible logic. ACM Trans. Comput. Logic 2(2), 255–287 (2001)

Cross-Community Interoperation between the EMERALD and Rule Responder Multi-Agent Systems

Kalliopi Kravari[1], Taylor Osmun[2], Harold Boley[2], and Nick Bassiliades[1]

[1] Dept. of Informatics, Aristotle University of Thessaloniki, GR-54124 Thessaloniki, Greece
{kkravari,nbassili}@csd.auth.gr
[2] Inst. for Information Technology, NRC Canada, Fredericton, NB, E3B 9W4, Canada
{taylor.osmun,harold.boley}@nrc.gc.ca

Abstract. The vision of the Semantic Web allows users to delegate complex actions to intelligent agents, which will act on behalf of their users in a variety of real-life applications. This paper focuses on two Semantic Web enabled multi-agent systems, EMERALD and Rule Responder, which can be employed to assist communities of users based on Semantic Web and multi-agent standards such as RDF, OWL, RuleML, and FIPA. The present work demonstrates how these multi-agent systems can interoperate to automate collaboration across communities using a declarative, knowledge-based approach. In addition, a multi-step interaction scenario among agents is presented, demonstrating the usefulness of interoperating between the above systems, exemplifying a general approach to cross-community collaboration.

Keywords: RuleML, Semantic Web, Web Rules, intelligent multi-agent systems, gateway, EMERALD, Rule Responder, SymposiumPlanner.

1 Introduction

The *Semantic Web* (*SW*) [8] is an evolving extension of the current Web, where the semantics of information and services are well-defined, making it possible for people and machines to understand, and act upon, Web content with high precision. The evolution of the SW technologies offer interoperability and, thus, enables Intelligent Agents. Agents are considered the most promising means towards realizing the SW vision [1]. Via the use of agents, programs are extended to perform tasks more efficiently and with less human intervention. The gradual integration of *multi-agent systems* (*MAS*) with SW will affect the use of the Web in the future; the next generation of Web tools will comprise groups of intercommunicating SW agents traversing the Web and performing complex actions on behalf of their users in real-life applications.

At present, a number of multi-agent systems are available; however they are typically isolated, as their organizational philosophies and architectures are typically different, and their agents usually do not share the same logic or rule representation formalism. In this work, two such multi-agent systems, EMERALD [2] and Rule Responder [3], have been analyzed and made interoperable, by extending EMERALD with an appropriate Rule Responder bridge, which can be used in a variety of

N. Bassiliades et al. (Eds.): RuleML 2011 - Europe, LNCS 6826, pp. 44–51, 2011.

interoperation scenarios. Each agent, regardless the MAS it belongs to, has its own policy, a set of private rules representing its requirements, obligations and restrictions, and its idiosyncratic knowledge about the world, which makes interoperation a difficult task.

The aim of this paper is to demonstrate how these multi-agent systems can interoperate to automate collaboration across communities using a declarative, knowledge-based approach, exemplifying the usefulness of a general approach to cross-community collaboration. In this framework, a multi-step interaction scenario among agents is also presented where users are considering sponsoring a symposium modeled by two communities.

In the rest of the paper, we present EMERALD, a multi-agent knowledge-based framework, in Section 2, while Section 3 presents Rule Responder, an open source framework for creating virtual organizations as multi-agent systems. In Section 4, the EMERALD–Rule Responder interoperation gateway is presented, whereas Section 5 illustrates the usefulness of the approach via a multi-step interaction scenario. Section 6 discusses related work, and finally Section 7 concludes with final remarks and directions for future work.

2 EMERALD: A Multi-Agent Knowledge-Based Framework

EMERALD [2] is a multi-agent knowledge-based framework, which offers flexibility, reusability and interoperability of behavior between agents, based on SW and FIPA language standards. The main advantage of this approach is that it provides a safe, generic, and reusable framework for modeling and monitoring agent communication and agreements. EMERALD supported, so far, the implementation of various applications, like brokering, bargaining and agent negotiations.

In order to model and monitor the parties involved in a transaction, a generic, reusable agent prototype for *knowledge-customizable agents* (*KC-Agents*), consisted of an agent model (*KC Model*), a yellow pages service (*Advanced Yellow Pages Service*) and several external Java methods (*Basic Java Library*), is deployed. Agents that comply with this prototype are equipped a knowledge base (KB) that contains environment knowledge, behavior patterns and. The use of the *KC-Agents* prototype offers certain advantages, like interoperability of behavior between agents, as opposed to having behavior hard-wired into the agent's code.

Additionally, as trust has been recognized as a key issue in SW MAS, EMERALD adopts among others two reputation mechanisms, a decentralized and a centralized one [2]. Finally, as agents do not necessarily share a common rule or logic formalism, it is vital for them to find a way to exchange their position arguments seamlessly. Thus, EMERALD proposes the use of *Reasoners* [4], which are actually agents that offer reasoning services to the rest of the agent community. This approach does not rely on translation between rule formalisms, but on exchanging the results of the reasoning process of the rule base over the input data. The receiving agent uses an external reasoning service to grasp the semantics of the rulebase, i.e. the set of conclusions of the rule base. The procedure is straightforward: each Reasoner stands by for new requests and as soon as it receives a valid request, it launches the associated reasoning engine and returns the results.

EMERALD currently implements a number of Reasoners that offer reasoning services in two major reasoning formalisms: deductive and defeasible reasoning. The two deductive reasoners, based on the logic programming paradigm are the *R-Reasoner* (based on *R-DEVICE*) and the *Prova-Reasoner* (based on *Prova*). Furthermore, the two defeasible reasoners are the *DR-Reasoner* (based on DR-DEVICE) and the *SPINdle-Reasoner* (based on *SPINdle*).

Following the above specifications we commit to SW and FIPA standards, namely, we use the RuleML language [6] for representing and exchanging agent policies and e-contract clauses, since it has become a de facto standard. In addition, we use the RDF model for data representation both for the private data included in agents' internal knowledge and the reasoning results generated during the process.

3 Rule Responder

Rule Responder [3] is an open source framework for creating virtual organizations as multi-agent systems that support collaborative teams on the Semantic Web. It comes with a number of official instantiations implementing virtual organizations such as SymposiumPlanner for supporting the chairs of the RuleML Symposia. Rule Responder provides the infrastructure for rule-based collaboration between the distributed members of such a virtual organization. Human members are assisted by semi-autonomous rule-based agents, which use Semantic Web rules that describe aspects of their owners' derivation and reaction logic.

Each Rule Responder instantiation employs four classes of agents, an Organizational Agent (OA), Personal Agents (PAs), External Agents (EAs) and Computational Agents (CAs). The OA represents goals and strategies shared by its virtual organization as a whole, using a global rule base that describes its policies, regulations, opportunities, etc. Each PA assists a single person of the organization, (semi-autonomously) acting on his/her behalf by using a local knowledge base of derivation rules defined by the person. Each EA uses a Web (HTTP) interface, accepting queries from users and passing them to the OA. Each CA can be seen as an (often low level) agent that performs an automated (computing) task.

CAs are comparable to PAs. Their output is meant to assist the OA in answering the query from the EA. They are designed to perform very specific tasks that may involve invoking services independently from the rest of the virtual organization. The OA employs an OWL ontology as a "responsibility assignment matrix" to find a PA that can handle an incoming query. The OA uses reaction rules to send the query to this PA, receive its answer(s), do validation(s), and send answer(s) back to the EA.

Rule Responder uses an Enterprise Service Bus (ESB) called Mule [9] to transfer data. Mule transfers this data via "data endpoints". In the case of Rule Responder, each agent (EAs/OA/PAs) has their own endpoint for which data will travel upon. Additionally, Rule Responder only uses HTTP as a transfer protocol but others can certainly be implemented. Moreover, the supported reasoning engines, with their languages, in Rule Responder are Prova, OO jDREW with POSL and Euler with N3. The present work uses the OO jDREW [10], a deductive reasoning engine for the RuleML web rule language, written in Java. It is an Object Oriented extension to jDREW, which implements Object Oriented extensions to RuleML including Order Sorted Types, Slots and Object Identifiers.

4 EMERALD–Rule Responder Interoperation Gateway

In order to develop an interface between EMERALD and Rule Responder (RR) so that they can interoperate, the two systems were compared regarding among others their agent-connection topologies, their interchange principles, their used subsets of RuleML language and the role of the Prova language (Table 1). Based on this analysis, two uni-directional RuleML gateways between EMERALD and Rule Responder were designed and implemented. Fig. 1, displays the gateways' architecture.

Table 1. Comparison between EMERALD and Rule Responder

	Rule Responder	*EMERALD*
Agent technology	Java servlets / Mule	Java (JADE) agents
Interchange principles	Mule middleware	JADE (ACL)
RuleML	Reaction RuleML	(D)R-DEVICE RuleML
Agent knowledge	Internal rule base Internal & External data-knowledge base	External rule base External data-knowledge base
Reasoning	Multiple reasoning engines and instances of reasoning engines	Multiple reasoning engines (independent external services)
Directory service	NO	AYPS

The EMERALD Rule Responder (EMERALD–RR) Gateway was implemented as a new proxy agent in EMERALD, communicating directly with RR OA. The RRP Agent is an EMERALD agent, acting as a Rule Responder gateway. This RRP agent is flexible and reusable and, thus, not hardwired, meaning that it can receive any (RuleML) query, connect to Rule Responder, forward the query by invoking the proper Rule Responder agent and finally receive the result. Thus, RRP was developed as a Java (EMERALD) agent class that integrates API methods for interacting both with EMERALD agents and Rule Responder's PAs.

On the other hand, the Rule Responder EMERALD (RR–EMERALD) Gateway was implemented as a new CA that handles an appropriate communication channel. CAs in Rule Responder are implemented as Java servlets, which serve as wrappers for

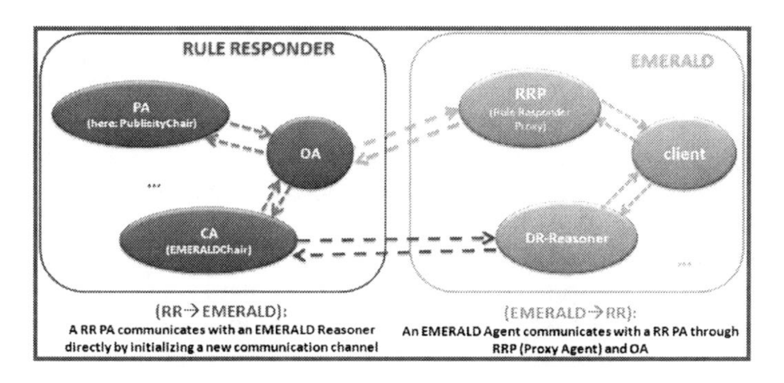

Fig. 1. The EMERALD–Rule Responder gateway architecture

the corresponding reasoning engines. This CA (the gateway) is called EMERALD Chair and has been developed as a Java servlet class that integrates API methods for interacting with EMERALD as well as core RR methods for exchanging messages with the Organizational Agent (OA).

The key feature at EMERALD and Rule Responder collaboration is the interchange of information. RuleML was selected as the data interchange language standard since it is supported by both systems and it has become a de facto standard.

5 A Multi–Step Interaction Scenario

A scenario where an external-to-SymposiumPlanner partner (an EMERALD agent in particular) would like to sponsor the RuleML-20XY Symposium was selected. SymposiumPlanner [5] is a series of use cases based on the RuleML Symposium series (e.g. http://2010.ruleml.org) created with Rule Responder (RR). Using Friend of a Friend (FOAF) profiles, each chair position (e.g. general chair) has a Personal Agent (PA). Each PA has a knowledge base containing the responsibilities of the position in order to answer queries relevant to the chair's role.

In this scenario, the partner has to decide whether or not to sponsor RuleML-20XY Symposium. The decision on the sponsoring level will be based on its personal preferences, related to the benefits of each level. More specifically, the agent has a maximum amount of money to spend but it does not want just to get whatever is available for this amount ("What I get for this amount of money?"). The partner wants to get specific benefits ("If I want these benefits, what amount of money do I have to spend?"), thus it has to get all the sponsoring levels and theirs benefits which can be obtained from the corresponding chair, namely the Publicity Chair.

Thus, the EMERALD agent has to communicate with the PublicityChair in the SymposiumPlanner application. First of all, it sends its query (requesting the sponsoring levels and their benefits) to the RRP agent, the Rule Responder Proxy agent (an EMERALD agent too), in order to forward it to the PA. RRP agent forwards the query and waits for the reply. As soon as, it receives the response, the RRP agent returns it back to the partner. The decision making of the partner is based on rules, and more specifically on defeasible logic rules. Thus, the partner transforms the received RuleML message to RDF, in order to be used as a fact base for the rule base, which is formed in a defeasible RuleML dialect. The rule base contains partner's personal preferences: the partner has a $5000 budget and wants the cheapest sponsoring level providing at least a free registration and a demo for the company's products. Hence, the partner sends the rule base and a link to the data that will be used (RDF file) to the defeasible logic reasoner (DR-Reasoner), hosted by EMERALD, in order to find out the best sponsoring level.

Then, DR-Reasoner calls the associated reasoning engine (DR-DEVICE) in order to perform inference and provide results. As soon as the inference results are available, DR-Reasoner forwards them to the partner. In this case the decision was the Gold sponsoring level, among the five available levels presented in Table 2.

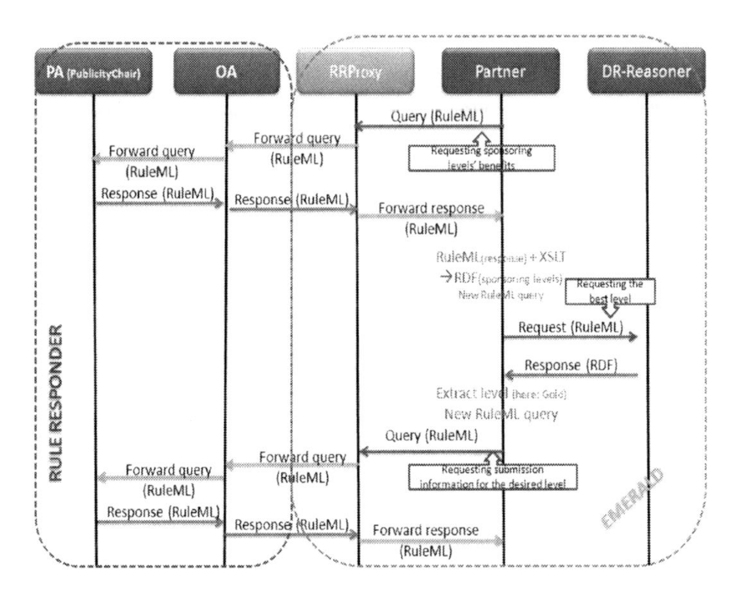

Fig. 2. The scenario overview

Afterwards, the partner receives back DR-Reasoner's response and sends a new query to the PublicityChair (through the RRP agent) requesting the appropriate submission information for that level; e.g. to contact appropriate chair by e-mail/phone or to wait for his/her call. In this case responsible for the sponsorship is the Publicity Chair and the potential partner has to wait for a call. Thus, the partner is able to submit a sponsoring request and wait for the Publicity Chair's phone call or to continue this conversation in order to get any additional information.

Table 2. The Sponsoring Levels

<table>
<tr><td>Bronze
($500)</td><td>Logo on website
Acknowledgement in proceedings</td><td>Silver
($1,000)</td><td>Bronze level benefits +
Sponsor student participants</td></tr>
<tr><td>Gold
($3,000)</td><td>Silver level benefits +
Logo in proceedings
Show demo
1 free registration</td><td rowspan="2">Platinum
($5,000)</td><td rowspan="2">Gold level benefits +
Name included in all advance publicity.
Distribution of material to all participants.
1 additional free registration</td></tr>
<tr><td>Emerald ($ 7,500)</td><td>Platinum level benefits +
1 additional free registration</td></tr>
</table>

Information (and source code) about both the EMERALD – Rule Responder interoperation project and the above scenario is available at the project's site [7].

6 Related Work

The architecture proposed in [14] is similar to ours in terms of system interoperability. However, [14] investigates only FIPA-compliant systems. Another work dealing with agent interoperability was presented in [15]. This work presents an implemented agent that allows interoperability across MAS. The authors describe the issues and design challenges regarding the design and implementation of an interoperator. They define a multiagent system interoperator as an entity that provides agents of one MAS architecture access to the desired capabilities and services offered by another MAS architecture. Our proposal on the other hand deals with heterogeneous systems, FIPA and non-FIPA –compliant, providing the guiding lines for general interoperability architecture by using a variety of SW standards based on system gateways.

A similar to EMERALD architecture for intelligent agents is presented in [11], where various reasoning engines are employed as plug-in components, while agents intercommunicate via FIPA-based communication protocols. The framework is build on top of the OPAL agent platform [12] and, similarly to EMERALD, features distinct types of reasoning services that are implemented as reasoner agents. Following a similar approach to EMERALD, the framework integrates the three reasoning engines into OPAL in the form of OPAL micro-agents. The primary difference between the two frameworks lies in the variety of reasoning services offered by EMERALD. While the three reasoners featured in [11] are all based on declarative rule languages, EMERALD proposes a variety of reasoning services, including deductive, defeasible and modal defeasible reasoning, thus, comprising a more integrated solution. Finally, and most importantly, the approach of [11] is not based on SW standards, like EMERALD and Rule responder, for rule and data interchange.

Speaking for interchange, there are many efforts aiming to rule interchange and building a general rule markup and modeling standard for the (Semantic) Web. Several general standardization efforts including RuleML [6], W3C RIF [13], OMG PRR are already proposed. However, no methodological and architectural design and comprehensive implementation exists which makes this idea of a practical distributed rule layer in the Semantic Web a reality, as the one proposed in this work.

7 Conclusions and Future Work

This paper presents the interoperation between EMERALD and Rule Responder, two SW enabled multi-agent systems. EMERALD is a fully FIPA-compliant MAS, developed on top of JADE, which uses trusted, independently-developed reasoning services. Rule Responder is an open source framework for creating virtual organizations as multi-agent systems that support collaborative teams on the Semantic Web. These two systems were compared and analyzed. Based on this comparison, bidirectional Rule Responder and EMERALD gateways were implemented in order to provide automated collaboration across these communities using a declarative, knowledge-based approach. Finally, the paper presents a use case scenario that illustrates the usability of the framework and the integration of the technologies involved in the EMERALD–Rule Responder Gateway.

In future, we plan to develop a benchmark suite for bidirectional RuleML-based gateways such as between Rule Responder and EMERALD. We also plan to adapt the RuleML gateways to other interoperation needs, such as interchange of proofs between agents or sharing of agent directories. Moreover, we envision formalizing further multi-step interaction scenarios among EMERALD and Rule Responder agents.

Finally, we would like to explore further cross-community agent interoperation needs and provide generalized gateway principles and architectures based on SW standards.

References

1. Hendler, J.: Agents and the Semantic Web. IEEE Intelligent Systems 16(2), 30–37 (2001)
2. Kravari, K., Kontopoulos, E., Bassiliades, N.: EMERALD: A Multi-Agent System for Knowledge-based Reasoning Interoperability in the Semantic Web. In: Konstantopoulos, S., Perantonis, S., Karkaletsis, V., Spyropoulos, C.D., Vouros, G. (eds.) SETN 2010. LNCS, vol. 6040, pp. 173–182. Springer, Heidelberg (2010)
3. Paschke, A., Boley, H., Kozlenkov A., Craig B.: Rule Responder: RuleML-Based Agents for Distributed Collaboration on the Pragmatic Web. In: 2nd ACM Pragmatic Web Conference (ICPW 2007), pp. 17–28 (2007)
4. Kravari, K., Kontopoulos, E., Bassiliades, N.: Trusted Reasoning Services for Semantic Web Agents. Informatica: Int. J. of Computing and Informatics 34(4), 429–440 (2010)
5. Symposium Planner, `http://ruleml.org/SymposiumPlanner/`
6. Boley, H., Paschke, A., Shafiq, O.: The Overarching Specification of Web Rules. In: Dean, M., Hall, J., Rotolo, A., Tabet, S. (eds.) RuleML 2010. LNCS, vol. 6403, pp. 162–178. Springer, Heidelberg (2010)
7. EMERALD – Rule Responder Interoperation Project, `http://tinyurl.com/EMERALDRR`
8. Berners-Lee, T., Hendler, J., Lassila, O.: The Semantic Web. Scientific American Magazine 284(5), 34–43 (2001) (revised 2008)
9. Mule ESB, `http://www.mulesoft.org`
10. Ball, M., Boley, H., Hirtle, D., Mei, J., Spencer, B.: The OO jDREW reference implementation of ruleML. In: Adi, A., Stoutenburg, S., Tabet, S. (eds.) RuleML 2005. LNCS, vol. 3791, pp. 218–223. Springer, Heidelberg (2005)
11. Wang, M., Purvis, M., Nowostawski, M.: An Internal Agent Architecture Incorporating Standard Reasoning Components and Standards-based Agent Communication. In: Proc. IAT 2005, Washington, DC, pp. 58–64 (2005)
12. Purvis, M., Cranefield, S., Nowostawski, M., Carter, D.: Opal: A Multi-Level Infrastructure for Agent-Oriented Software Development. In: Information Science Discussion Paper Series, number 2002/01. University of Otago, New Zealand (2002) ISSN 1172-602
13. Boley, H., Kifer, M.: A Guide to the Basic Logic Dialect for Rule Interchange on the Web. IEEE Transactions on Knowledge and Data Engineering, 1593–1608 (2010)
14. Georgousopoulos, C., Rana, O., Karageorgos, A.: Supporting FIPA Interoperability for Legacy Multi-agent Systems. LNS, vol. 2935, pp. 361–379 (2003)
15. Giampapa, J., Paolucci M., Sycara K.: Agent interoperation across multiagent system boundaries. In: 4th Int. Conf. on Autonomous Agents, pp. 179–186 (2000)

Rules, Agents and Norms: Guidelines for Rule-Based Normative Multi-Agent Systems

Antonino Rotolo[1] and Leendert van der Torre[2]

[1] CIRSFID, University of Bologna,
Bologna, Italy
antonino.rotolo@unibo.it
[2] Computer Science and Communication, University of Luxembourg, Luxembourg
leon.vandertorre@uni.lu

Abstract. In this survey paper we focus on some requirements for developing normative multi-agent systems (NMAS). In particular, we discuss Boella *et al.*'s guidelines proposed for NMAS. Finally, we deal with two more specific questions concerning the role of norms in rule-based NMAS: the concepts of compliance and norm change.

1 Introduction

Normative systems are "systems in the behavior of which norms play a role and which need normative concepts in order to be described or specified" [37, preface]. There has been in the last years an increasing interest in normative systems in the computer science community, due, among the other reasons, to the AgentLink RoadMap [35]'s observation that norms must be introduced in agent technology in the medium term for infrastructure for open communities, reasoning in open environments and trust and reputation. Indeed, NMAS revolve around the idea that, while the main objective of MAS is to design systems of autonomous agents, it is likewise important that agent systems may exhibit global desirable properties. One possible strategy to achieve this goal is that, like in human societies, such desirable properties be ensured if the interaction of artificial agents, too, adopts institutional models whose goal is to regiment agents' behavior through normative systems in supporting coordination, cooperation and decision-making. The deontic-logic and artificial-intelligence-and-law communities, for instance, agree about the rule structure and properties of norms [21]. Hence NMAS, too, has strong and obvious connections with the development of rule-based systems and technologies.

However, despite the widely-acknowledged role that normative concepts can play in MAS, there is no consensus yet in regard to some fundamental research questions, such as the kind of norms to be used, or the way to use them. During the past two decades normative systems have been studied in deontic logic in computer science (ΔEON), and NMAS are the research field where the traditional normative systems and ΔEON meet agent research. Part of this research

N. Bassiliades et al. (Eds.): RuleML 2011 - Europe, LNCS 6826, pp. 52–66, 2011.

community has later converged into a series of NorMAS workshps, during which two consensus definitions of NMAS have been proposed. Here, we will re-discuss and revise some of [8,12,6,7]'s guidelines proposed for NMAS that were motivated by these two consensus definitions (Section 2). The remainder of the paper (Sections 3.1 and 3.2) will highlight, with some more details, research questions concerning two crucial aspects of the role of norms in rule-based NMAS: the concepts of compliance and norm change.

2 NMAS Requirements

The concepts of "norm" and "normative system" have been investigated in many distinct disciplines, such as philosophy, sociology, law, and ethics. Before we consider some general guidelines and requirements for NMAS, it is useful for the remaining discussion to bear in mind some basic achievements of theoretical investigations on the nature of norms and normative systems:

Rule structure of norms. It is widely acknowledged that norms have usually a conditional structure that captures the applicability conditions of the norm and its effects when it is triggered[1]. This very general view highlights an immediate link between the concepts of norm and rule.

Types of norms. There are many types of norms. The common sense meaning of norm refers to having a regulatory and mainly prescriptive character. But norms express not only regulations about how to act. For example, von Wright [43] classified norms into the following main types (among others):

1. determinative rules, which define concepts or constitute activities that cannot exist without such rules. These rules are also called in the literature 'constitutive rules';
2. technical rules, which state that something has to be done in order for something else to be attained;
3. prescriptions, which regulate actions by making them obligatory, permitted, or prohibited. These norms, to be complete, should indicate
   - who (norm-subjects)
   - does what (the action-theme)
   - in what circumstances (conditions of application), and
   - the nature of their guidance (the mood).

Basic features of normative systems. Herbert Hart, among other philosophers, clarified for the law under what conditions normative systems exist [30]. However, Hart's remarks can be somehow generalized and can help us identify some very basic features of almost any other normative domain:

[1] Indeed, norms can be also unconditioned, that is their effects may not depend upon any antecedent condition. Consider, for example, the norm "everyone has the right to express his or her opinion". Unconditioned norms can formally be reconstructed in terms conditionals with no antecedent conditions.

norm recognition and hierarchies: it is possible to state or identify criteria for normative systems to establish whether norms belong to them; also, normative systems can assign to their norms a different ranking status and organize them in hierarchies;

norm application: it is possible to state or identify criteria for normative systems to correctly apply their norms to concrete cases;

norm change: it is possible to state or identify criteria for changing normative systems.

Following [8,12,6,7], we can formulate two definitions of NMAS, which we discuss in the remainder of this section.

2.1 The Norm-Change Definition

The first definition runs as follows:

Definition 1 (The Norm-change definition [8]). *"A normative multiagent system is a multiagent system together with normative systems in which agents on the one hand can decide whether to follow the explicitly represented norms, and on the other the normative systems specify how and in which extent the agents can modify the norms."*

In [6,7] three guidelines for NMAS were derived from Definition 1.

Guideline 1. *Motivate which definition of NMAS is used and so explain whether, either*

1. *norms must be explicitly represented in the system (the 'strong' interpretation), or*
2. *norms must be explicitly represented in the system specification (the 'weak' interpretation), or*
3. *none of the above interpretations should be adopted.*

It was argued in [6,7] that the strong interpretation must be preferred whenever we want to prevent a too generic notion of norm. In fact, we should avoid trivializing this notion, which is a risk when we see any specification requirement as a norm that the system has to comply with. Rather, the weak interpretation is sometimes more suitable to address the following problems:

Problem 1 (Norm compliance). How to check whether a system complies with relevant norms applicable to it?

Problem 2 (Norm implementation). How can we design a system such that it complies with a given set of norms?

Problems 1 and 2 amount to studying the concept of compliance at runtime and at design time, so they can be meaningful also when we adopt for NMAS the strong reading. Notice that both problems require in general to articulate the conditions under which the relevant norms are part of the normative system at hand and can correctly be triggered and applied: these issues correspond, as we said, to the first two basic features of any normative domain.

Finally, notice that any attempt to address Definition 1 and Guideline 1 also requires to preliminarily clarify what types of norm we need to embed within NMAS. This clarification is very relevant, since different types of norms sometimes correspond to different formal (and logical) models and so distinct options may differently affect the choice between the strong and weak interpretations for the explicit representation of norms within NMAS. We have already mentioned von Wright's norm classification. In [21] an extensive analysis of requirements for representing norms has been proposed for the law. Consider the following aspects, which contribute to classify norms and which can be extended to other normative domains besides the law[2]:

Temporal properties [28]. Norms can be qualified by temporal properties, such as:

1. the time when the norm is in force;
2. the time when the norm can produce effects;
3. the time when the normative effects hold.

Normative effects. There are many normative effects that follow from applying norms, such as obligations, permissions, prohibitions and also more articulated effects such as those introduced for the law, for example, by Hohfeld (see [41]). Below is a rather comprehensive list of normative effects [39]:

Evaluative, which indicate that something is good or bad, is a value to be optimised or an evil to be minimised. For example, "Human dignity is valuable", "Participation ought to be promoted";

Qualificatory, which ascribe a normative quality to a person or an object. For example, "x is a citizen";

Definitional, which specify the meaning of a term. For example, "Tolling agreement means any agreement to put a specified amount of raw material per period through a particular processing facility";

Deontic, which, typically, impose the obligation or confer the permission to do a certain action. For example, "x has the obligation to do A";

Potestative, which attribute powers. For example, "A worker has the power to terminate his work contract";

Evidentiary, which establish the conclusion to be drawn from certain evidence. For example, "It is presumed that dismissal was discriminatory";

Existential, which indicate the beginning or the termination of the existence of a normative entity. For example, "The company ceases to exist";

Norm-concerning effects, which state the modifications of norms; for the law: abrogation, repeal, substitution, and so on.

---

[2] Gordon *et al.* also study whether existing rule interchange languages for the legal domain are expressive enough to fully model all the features listed below (and those recalled *infa*, Section 2.2): RuleML, SBVR, SWRL, RIF, and LKIF.

Definition 1 raises other two fundamental research questions, which concern, respectively, whether agents in NMAS can violate norms and how and why norms can be changed in NMAS.

Hence, the second guideline follows from the fact that agents, insofar as are supposed to be autonomous, can decide whether to follow the norms. Indeed, it would be misleading for the specification of a NMAS to disregard "the distinction between normative behavior (as it *should be*) and actual behavior (as it *is*)" [37, preface]. Avoiding to make this distinction is misleading for three reasons: if any "illegal behavior is just ruled out by specification"

- we are unable to "specify what should happen if such illegal but possible behaviors occurs!" [37, preface];
- we fail to adopt a meaningful concept of norm, since philosophers and deontic logicians mostly agree that genuine norms (and their effects) can be violated (as an extreme example, it does not make any sense to say that $A \wedge \neg A$ is forbidden);
- agents cannot violate norms and so we do not model one important aspect of agents' autonomy in normative agent architectures and decision making [16].

Accordingly, a theoretically sound definition of NMAS would assume that agents can violate norms, so if a norm is a kind of constraint, the question immediately is raised what is special about them. While hard constraints are restricted to preventative control systems in which violations are impossible, soft constraints are used in detective control systems where violations can be detected. This justifies the following guideline:

Guideline 2. *Make explicit why your norms are a kind of (soft) constraints that deserve special analysis.*

A typical illustration of how normative soft constraints work is the situation in which one can enter a train without a ticket, but she may be checked and sanctioned. Instead, a supposed illustration of a hard-constraint implementation of a norm is the situation in which one cannot enter a metro station without a ticket [6,7]. However, a closer inspection of the metro example shows that, strictly speaking, this does not correspond to a genuine case where violations are made impossible, but only where they are normally and in most cases prevented to occur: indeed, one could, for instance, break the metro barriers and travel without any ticket. When violations are impossible in any conceivable way, the concept of norm does not make much sense.

On the other hand, if the norms are represented as soft constraints, then how to analyze that detective control is the result of actions of agents and therefore subject to errors and influenceable by actions of other agents? For example, it may be the case that violations are not often enough detected, there are conflicting obligations in the normative system, that agents are able to block the sanction, update the normative system, etc.

More on compliance and norm violation in Section 3.1.

The third guideline follows from the fact that norms can be changed by the agents or by the system. Suppose, for example, that a NMAS must be checked against some legal system. As is well-known, one of the peculiar features of the law is that it necessarily takes the form of a dynamic normative system [33]. Hence, the life-cycle of agents must be described with respect to a changing set of norms. Similar considerations can be applied to many other normative domains, as we argued that it is possible to state or identify criteria for changing many types of normative system:

Guideline 3 (Norm change). *Explain why and how norms can be changed at runtime.*

In general, in NMAS a norm can be made by an agent, as legislators do in a legal system, or there can be an algorithm that observes agent behavior, and suggests a norm when it observes a pattern. The agents can vote on the acceptance of the norm. Likewise, if the system observes that a norm is often violated, then apparently the norm does not work as desired, and it undermines the trust of the agents in the normative system, so the system can suggest that the agents can vote whether to retract or change the norm.

More on norm change in Section 3.2.

2.2 The Mechanism Design Definition

The second definition of NMAS runs as follows:

Definition 2 (The mechanism design definition [12]). *"A normative multiagent system is a multiagent system organized by means of mechanisms to represent, communicate, distribute, detect, create, modify, and enforce norms, and mechanisms to deliberate about norms and detect norm violation and fulfilment."*

Norms are rules used to guide, control, or regulate desired system behavior. A normative multiagent system is a self-organizing system, and norms can be violated. Boella *et al.* [6,7] derive two guidelines from this definition, which focus on the role of norms, either as a mechanism or as part of a larger institution or organization.

Guideline 4. *Discuss the use and role of norms always as a mechanism in a game-theoretic setting.*

Guideline 5. *Clarify the role of norms in your system as part of an organization or institution.*

Both these guidelines lead to handle more specific research problems:

Problem 3 (Norms and games). Games can explain that norms should satisfy various properties and also the role of various kinds of norms in a system. For example, Bulygin [14] explains why permissive norms are needed in normative systems using his "Rex, Minister and Subject" game. Boella and van der Torre introduce a game theoretic approach to normative systems [11] to study violation games, institutionalized games, negotiation games, norm creation games, and control games. Norms should satisfy various properties to be effective as a mechanism to obtain desirable behavior. For example, the system should not sanction without reason, and sanctions should not be too low or too high.

Problem 4 (Norms and their functions). As we mentioned in the previous section, norms may have a number of different effects, and so they do not only impose duties and establish sanctions for their violation. Hence, in a game-theoretic perspective they do not only have a preventive character, but, for instance, also provide incentives. However, moral incentives are very different from financial or legal incentives. For example, the number of violations may *increase* when financial sanctions are imposed, because the moral incentive to comply with the norm is destroyed [34,19, p. 18–20]. Moreover, norms and trust have been discussed to analyze backward induction [31].

Problem 5 (Norms and organizational design). Norms are addressed to roles played by agents [10] and used to model organizations as first class citizens in multiagent systems. In particular, constitutive norms are used to assign powers to agents playing roles inside the organization. Such powers allow to give commands to other agents, make formal communications and to restructure the organization itself, for example, by managing the assignment of agents to roles. Moreover, normative systems allow to model also the structure of an organization and not only the interdependencies among the agents of an organization. Legal institutions are defined by Ruiter [40] as "systems of [regulative and constitutive] rules that provide frameworks for social action within larger rule-governed settings". They are "relatively independent institutional legal orders within the comprehensive legal orders".

Hence, Definition 2, Guideline 4 and 5 and the related research problems require, too, additional clarification on the types of norm we need to model for NMAS. Also in this second perspective, many of Gordon *et al.*'s requirements [21] for specifically representing norms in the law are directly applicable for the roles, organizations and institutions. Important requirements for legal rule languages from the field of AI & Law include the following:

Isomorphism [5]. To ease validation and maintenance, there should be a one-to-one correspondence between the rules in the formal model and the units of natural language text which express the rules in the original normative sources, such as sections of legislation. This entails, for example, that a general rule and separately stated exceptions, in different sections of a statute, should not be converged into a single rule in the formal model.

Rule semantics. Any language for modeling norms should be based on a precise and rigorous semantics, which allows for correctly computing the effects that should follow from a set of norms.

Defeasibility [20,38,41]. When the antecedent of a norm is satisfied by the facts of a case, the conclusion of the rule presumably holds, but is not necessarily true. The defeasibility of norms breaks down in the law into the following issues:

Conflicts [38]. Rules can conflict, namely, they may lead to incompatible legal effects. Conceptually, conflicts can be of different types, according to whether two conflicting rules

- are such that one is an exception of the other (i.e., one is more specific than the other);
- have a different ranking status;
- have been enacted at different times;

Accordingly, rule conflicts can be resolved using principles about rule priorities, such as:

- *lex specialis*, which gives priority to the more specific rules (the exceptions);
- *lex superior*, which gives priority to the rule from the higher authority (see 'Authority' above);
- *lex posterior*, which gives priority to the rule enacted later (see 'Temporal parameters' above).

Exclusionary norms [38,41,20]. Some norms provide one way to explicitly undercut other rules, namely, to make them inapplicable.

Contributory reasons or factors [41]. It is not always possible to formulate precise rules, even defeasible ones, for aggregating the factors relevant for resolving a normative issue. For example: "The educational value of a work needs to be taken into consideration when evaluating whether the work is covered by the copyright doctrine of fair use."

Norm validity [28]. Norms can be invalid or become invalid. Deleting invalid norms is not an option when it is necessary to reason retroactively with norms which were valid at various times over a course of events. For instance, in the law:

1. The *annulment* of a norm is usually seen as a kind of repeal which invalidates the norm and removes it from the legal system as if it had never been enacted. The effect of an annulment applies *ex tunc*: annulreled norms are prevented from producing any legal effects, also for past events.
2. An *abrogation* on the other hand operates *ex nunc*: The norm continues to apply for events which occurred before the rule was abrogated.

Legal procedures. Norms not only regulate the procedures for resolving normative conflicts (see above), but also for arguing or reasoning about whether or not some action or state complies with other, substantive norms [22]. In particular, norms are required for procedures which

1. regulate methods for detecting violations of the law;
2. determine the normative effects triggered by norm violations, such as reparative obligations, namely, which are meant to repair or compensate violations.

Persistence of normative effects [29]. Some normative effects persist over time unless some other and subsequent event terminate them. For example: "If one causes damage, one has to provide compensation". Other effects hold on the condition and only while the antecedent conditions of the rules hold. For example: "If one is in a public office, one is forbidden to smoke".

Values [4]. Usually, norms promote some underlying values or goals. Modeling norms sometimes needs to support the representation of these *values* and *value preferences*, which can play also the role of meta-criteria for solving norm conflicts. (Given two conflicting norms r_1 and r_2, value v_1, promoted by r_1, is preferred to value v_2, promoted by r_2, and so r_1 overrides r_2.)

Some of these requirements, as they are formulated above (they are indeed recalled from [21]), are peculiar of the legal domain only or, at least, of any "codified" system of norms (consider, e.g., the "Isomorphism" requirement). However, almost all can be easily adjusted to fit many other normative domains. Besides some very general requirements, such as "Defeasibility" and "Rule semantics"—which correspond to aspects widely acknowledged for most normative domains—also the other requirements are important for NMAS. Consider, for instance, the problem of the temporal persistence of norm effects, the fact that norms can be valid only under some conditions, or the role of exclusionary reasons.

3 Specific Developments

In the previous sections we mentioned two important issues for the development of NMAS: the role of norms as soft constraints and the compliance problem, and the problem of norm change. In what follows we offer an outline of some research questions related to them.

3.1 How Do Agents Comply with Norms?

There are in general two fundamental strategies to characterize norm enforcement and the concept of compliance in NMAS [32,18,42,9,26]:

- Norms are hard constraints and agent's compliance is achieved by design. This option is usually implemented by adopting the so-called norm regimentation strategy, which can amount to simply designing the system in such a way as illegal states are ruled out and made impossible in it, or by imposing that the occurrence of any illegal states is in theory possible but it leads to the system global failure;
- Norms are soft constraints and so do not limit in advance agents' behavior. Compliance is then ensured by system mechanisms stating that violations should result in sanctions or other normative effects which are supposed to recover from violations.

Of course, there are pros and cons for both options. We have situations which must be avoided and made impossible. Think about a serious failure affecting the system's overall functionality. Hard constraints can be used to this end, but the question is whether this solution can be implemented by invoking, and take advantage of the NMAS paradigm. As we previously argued, a genuine concept of normativity makes sense when norms are in principle violable. Hence, in a game-theoretic approach such as the one proposed in Definition 2, if agents are supposed to coordinate their behavior and NMAS are basically self-organizing systems (but the overall functionality of the system is not directly in jeopardy), then norms (as soft constraints) can play a decisive role to guide and control the desired system behavior.

Some research issues are worthy to be mentioned in regard to what we have already outlined in Section 2. In particular, one of the crucial points is that we need sometimes a rich and expressive language for modeling normative systems, otherwise we cannot truly capture the concept of compliance. However, when such expressive frameworks are required, achieving compliance by design can be very hard:

Problem 6 (Compliance by recovering from violations). Norms often specify obligatory actions to be taken in case of their violations, actions which can vary from penalties to the termination of an interaction itself. Obligations in force after some other obligations have been violated correspond to various types of contrary-to-duty obligations [15]. Among them, we have the reparative obligations, which are meant to 'repair' or 'compensate' violations of primary obligations [22]. These constructions identify situations that are not ideal but still acceptable. The ability to deal with violations is an essential requirement for NMAS where norms are soft constraints, since some failures can occur, but they do not necessarily mean that the whole process has to fail. However, these constructions can give rise to very complex rule dependencies, because we can have that the violation of a single rule can activate other (reparative) rules, which, in case of their violation, refer to other rules, and so forth [24].

Problem 7 (Rich ontologies of norms). NMAS may be regulated by different types of obligations (see Section 2). For instance, when norm effects are temporally qualified, we may have obligations requiring (1) to be always fulfilled during a certain temporal interval or the execution of a certain agent's sub-plan, (2) that a certain condition must occur at least once before a certain temporal deadline or before the execution of a certain action and the obligations persist (or do not) persist after this deadline or action if they are not complied with, (3) that something is done instantaneously [23]. These types of obligation make things more complex when we deal with the compliance of a NMAS with respect to chains of reparative obligations (Problem 6). For example, if the primary obligation is persistent and states to pay before action A, and the secondary (reparative) obligation is to pay a fine in the action B successive to A, we are compliant not only when we pay before A, but also when we do not meet this deadline, pay later and pay the fine at B. If the secondary obligation rather requires to be always fulfilled for all actions successive to A, compliance conditions will change. In addition, other types of obligation can be considered: for instance, we may have provisions stating that some A is obligatory and which are fulfilled even if A was obtained before the provision was in force, whereas other provisions state that A is obligatory but they are complied with only when A holds after they are in force.

Problems 6 and 7 may significantly affect the feasibility of achieving compliance by design:

Problem 8 (Compliance by design: complexity). An approach for achieving compliance with a *preventative* focus can raise complexity problems. This may happen when a rich ontology of obligations is used to regulate agents' plans. Consider, for example, the case where the design and/or execution of agents' actions or plans is described as complex structures such as directed graphs [26,27]. For instance, when plans require the execution of parallel actions which are regulated by obligations such as those mentioned in Problem 7, there are cases where we have to handle the combinatorial explosion of the number of possible execution paths to be verified for compliance.

Similar computational problems (but for different reasons) can be encountered when we try to achieve compliance by design in BDI-like systems, where compliance is obtained at the deliberative stage by imposing that obligations will always prevail over conflicting intentions [13,25]. However, when the system allows us to derive agents' intentions from beliefs (for example, if an agents believes that Amsterdam is in Europe and intends to travel to Amsterdam, if the agent is assumed to be rational we may have reasons to derive the intention to travel to Europe), then achieving compliance by design is an NP-complete problem [25].

3.2 How Do Norms Change?

Obligations can change while the normative system remains the same. For example, due to change in the world or in the agents' knowledge and beliefs, new obligations can be detached from the norms, or an agent can delegate one of its obligations to another agent. This change of obligations and permissions over time is a relatively clear and well studied subject, investigated mostly in the 70s and 80s. Moreover, a code of regulations is itself not static either, but changes over time. For example, a legislative body may want to introduce new norms or to eliminate some existing ones. To study how norm change is different from how obligation change, and how these two are related, several workshops on norm change have been organized (Luxembourg 2007, Amsterdam 2010, Ghent 2011), addressing topics such as:

- Norm revision and contraction, e.g. change of legal code
- Norm evolution, e.g. change of social norms
- Merging normative systems, e.g. the merge of companies

Note that we presuppose a distinction between norms and obligations, which is too often ignored. Norms, imperatives, promises, legal statutes, and moral standards are usually not viewed as being true or false. E.g.: "John, leave the room!" and "Mary, you may enter now" do not describe, but demand or allow a behaviour on the part of John and Mary. Lacking truth values, norms cannot be premise or conclusion in an inference, be termed consistent or contradictory, or be compounded by truth-functional operators. The usual way out is to say that

"John is obliged to leave the room" describes the obligation which follows from the prescriptive "John, leave the room!" [36] raises the question: How can deontic logic be reconstructed in accord with the philosophical position that norms are neither true nor false? The derived problem is: how to How to formalize the relation between norm change and obligation change?

Norm revision. Little work exists on the logic of the revision of a set of norms. To the best of our knowledge, Alchourrón and Makinson were the first to study the changes of a legal code [2,3]. The addition of a new norm n causes an enlargement of the code, consisting of the new norm plus all the regulations that can be derived from n. Alchourrón and Makinson distinguish two other types of change. When the new norm is incoherent with the existing ones, we have an *amendment* of the code: in order to coherently add the new regulation, we need to reject those norms that conflict with n. Finally, *derogation* is the elimination of a norm n together with whatever part of G implies n. In [2] a "hierarchy of regulations" is assumed. Few years earlier, Alchourrón and Bulygin [1] already considered the *Normenordnung* and the consequences of gaps in this ordering. For example, in jurisprudence the existence of precedents is an established method to determine the ordering among norms.

Some of the AGM axioms seem to be rational requirements in a legal context, whereas they have been criticized when imposed on belief change operators. An example is the *success* postulate, requiring that a new input must always be accepted in the belief set. It is reasonable to impose such a requirement when we wish to enforce a new norm or obligation. However, it gives rise to irrational behaviors when imposed to a belief set, as observed for instance in [17]. Below are some relevant research questions:

- Does AGM offer a satisfactory framework for norm revision? Role of minimal change in norm change, revision of conditional norms.
- What triggers the change of a norm? AGM says a new or removed norm
- Do general patterns in the revision of norms exist? If so, how to formalize them?
- Derogation is contraction? How about annulment?

Evolution of norms. How to formalize the evolution of (social) norms? Consider, e.g.,

- E.g., norm about phone calls during meetings;
- No persons who change the norm like in legal code;
- Change of social norm triggered by norm violations;
- Social delegation cycle: relates agent desires and social goals.

Merging sets of norms. We now want to turn to another type of change, that is the aggregation of regulations. This problem has been only recently addressed in the literature and therefore the findings are still very partial.

The first noticeable thing is the lack of general agreement about where the norms that are to be aggregated come from. Some works focus on the merging of conflicting norms that belong to the same normative system, while other works assume that the regulations to be fused belong to different systems. The first situation seems to be more a matter of coherence of the whole system rather than a genuine problem of fusion of norms. However, such approaches have the merit to reveal the tight connections between fusion of norms, non-monotonic logics and defeasible deontic reasoning.

We have seen that the initial motivation for the study of belief revision was the ambition to model the revision of a set of regulations. On the contrary, the generalization of belief revision to *belief merging* is exclusively dictated by the goal to tackle the problem — arising in computer science — of combining information from different sources. The pieces of information are represented in a formal language and the aim is to merge them in an (ideally) unique knowledge base. Can the belief merging framework deal with the problem of merging sets of norms?

4 Summary

In this paper we discussed five guidelines for the development of NMAS proposed in [6,7] and compared them with some of the requirements for legal knowledge representation outlined in [21].

We assumed that norms are used to coordinate, organize, guide, regulate or control interaction among distributed autonomous systems. The so-called 'norm-change' definition supports the derivation of those guidelines that require to motivate which definition of normative multiagent system is used, to make explicit why norms are a kind of soft constraints deserving special analysis, and to explain why and how norms can be changed at runtime. The so-called 'mechanism design' definition entails the guidelines recommending to discuss the use and role of norms as a mechanism in a game-theoretic setting and to clarify the role of norms in the multiagent system. [21]'s formal requirements offer a complementary analysis to [6,7]'s account, as they provide a fine-grained account of the notions of norm and normative system.

Finally, we considered in some detail several research issues concerning two important aspects of NMAS design and implementation: norm compliance and norm change.

References

1. Alchourrón, C.E., Bulygin, E.: The expressive conception of norms. In: Hilpinen, R. (ed.) New Studies in Deontic Logic, pp. 95–125. D. Reidel Publishing Company, Dordrecht (1981)
2. Alchourrón, C.E., Makinson, D.C.: Hierarchies of regulations and their logic. In: Hilpinen, R. (ed.) New Studies in Deontic Logic, pp. 125–148. D. Reidel Publishing Company, Dordrecht (1981)

3. Alchourrón, C.E., Makinson, D.C.: The logic of theory change: Contraction functions and their associated revision functions. Theoria 48, 14–37 (1982)
4. Bench-Capon, T.: The missing link revisited: The role of teleology in representing legal argument. Artificial Intelligence and Law 10(2-3), 79–94 (2002)
5. Bench-Capon, T., Coenen, F.: Isomorphism and legal knowledge based systems. Artificial Intelligence and Law 1(1), 65–86 (1992)
6. Boella, G., Pigozzi, G., van der Torre, L.: Five guidelines for normative multiagent systems. In: JURIX, pp. 21–30 (2009)
7. Boella, G., Pigozzi, G., van der Torre, L.: Normative systems in computer science - ten guidelines for normative multiagent systems. In: Boella, G., Noriega, P., Pigozzi, G., Verhagen, H. (eds.) Normative Multi-Agent Systems, Dagstuhl, Germany. Dagstuhl Seminar Proceedings, vol. 09121, Schloss Dagstuhl - Leibniz-Zentrum fuer Informatik, Germany (2009)
8. Boella, G., Torre, L.V.D.: Introduction to normative multiagent systems. Computational and Mathematical Organization Theory 12, 71–79 (2006)
9. Boella, G., van der Torre, L.: Fulfilling or violating obligations in multiagent systems. In: Procs. IAT 2004 (2004)
10. Boella, G., van der Torre, L.: The ontological properties of social roles in multi-agent systems: Definitional dependence, powers and roles playing roles. Artificial Intelligence and Law Journal, AILaw (2007)
11. Boella, G., van der Torre, L., Verhagen, H.: Normative multi-agent systems. In: Internationales Begegnungs und Porschungszentrum fur Informatik, IBFI (2007)
12. Boella, G., van der Torre, L., Verhagen, H.: Introduction to the special issue on normative multiagent systems. Autonomous Agents and Multi-Agent Systems 17(1), 1–10 (2008)
13. Broersen, J., Dastani, M., Hulstijn, J., van der Torre, L.: Goal generation in the BOID architecture. Cognitive Science Quarterly 2(3-4), 428–447 (2002)
14. Bulygin, E.: Permissive norms and normative systems. In: Martino, A., Natali, F.S. (eds.) Automated Analysis of Legal Texts, pp. 211–218. Publishing Company, Amsterdam (1986)
15. Carmo, J., Jones, A.: Deontic logic and contrary to duties. In: Gabbay, D., Guenther, F. (eds.) Handbook of Philosophical Logic, 2nd edn. Kluwer, Dordrecht (2002)
16. Conte, R., Castelfranchi, C., Dignum, F.: Autonomous norm-acceptance. In: Papadimitriou, C., Singh, M.P., Müller, J.P. (eds.) ATAL 1998. LNCS (LNAI), vol. 1555, pp. 99–112. Springer, Heidelberg (1999)
17. Gabbay, D.M., Pigozzi, G., Woods, J.: Controlled revision - an algorithmic approach for belief revision. J. Log. Comput. 13(1), 3–22 (2003)
18. Garca-Camino, A., Rodrguez-Aguilar, J., Sierra, C., Vasconcelos, W.: Constraint rule-based programming of norms for electronic institutions. Autonomous Agents and Multi-Agent Systems 18, 186–217 (2009), doi:10.1007/s10458-008-9059-4
19. Gneezy, U., Rustichini, A.: A fine is a price. The Journal of Legal Studies 29(1), 1–18 (2000)
20. Gordon, T.F.: The Pleadings Game; An Artificial Intelligence Model of Procedural Justice. Springer, New York (1995)
21. Gordon, T.F., Governatori, G., Rotolo, A.: Rules and norms: Requirements for rule interchange languages in the legal domain. In: Governatori, G., Hall, J., Paschke, A. (eds.) RuleML 2009. LNCS, vol. 5858, pp. 282–296. Springer, Heidelberg (2009)
22. Governatori, G.: Representing business contracts in RuleML. International Journal of Cooperative Information Systems 14(2-3), 181–216 (2005)

23. Governatori, G., Hulstijn, J., Riveret, R., Rotolo, A.: Characterising deadlines in temporal modal defeasible logic. In: Orgun, M.A., Thornton, J. (eds.) AI 2007. LNCS (LNAI), vol. 4830, pp. 486–496. Springer, Heidelberg (2007)
24. Governatori, G., Rotolo, A.: An algorithm for business process compliance. In: JURIX, pp. 186–191 (2008)
25. Governatori, G., Rotolo, A.: Bio logical agents: Norms, beliefs, intentions in defeasible logic. Autonomous Agents and Multi-Agent Systems 17(1), 36–69 (2008)
26. Governatori, G., Rotolo, A.: How do agents comply with norms? In: Web Intelligence/IAT Workshops, pp. 488–491 (2009)
27. Governatori, G., Rotolo, A.: A conceptually rich model of business process compliance. In: 7th Asia-Pacific Conference on Conceptual Modelling (APCCM 2010), vol. 110, pp. 3–12. ACS (2010)
28. Governatori, G., Rotolo, A.: Changing legal systems: Legal abrogations and annulments in defeasible logic. The Logic Journal of IGPL (forthcoming)
29. Governatori, G., Rotolo, A., Sartor, G.: Temporalised normative positions in defeasible logic. In: 10th International Conference on Artificial Intelligence and Law (ICAIL 2005), pp. 25–34. ACM Press, New York (2005)
30. Hart, H.: The concept of law. Clarendon, Oxford (1994)
31. Hollis, M.: Trust within reason. Cambridge University Press, Cambridge (1998)
32. Jones, A.J.I., Sergot, M.: On the characterization of law and computer systems: the normative systems perspective, pp. 275–307. John Wiley and Sons Ltd., Chichester (1993)
33. Kelsen, H.: General theory of norms. Clarendon, Oxford (1991)
34. Levitt, S.D., Dubner, S.J.: Freakonomics: A Rogue Economist Explores the Hidden Side of Everything. William Morrow, New York (May 2005)
35. Luck, M., McBurney, P., Preist, C.: Agent Technology: Enabling Next Generation Computing. AgentLink (2003), electronically `http://www.agentlink.org/roadmap/`
36. Makinson, D.C.: On a fundamental problem of deontic logic. In: Prakken, H., McNamara, P. (eds.) Norms, Logics and Information Systems. New Studies in Deontic Logic and Computer Science, pp. 29–54. IOS Press, Amsterdam (1998)
37. Meyer, J.-J., Wieringa, R.: Deontic Logic in Computer Science: Normative System Specification. John Wiley & Sons, Chichester (1993)
38. Prakken, H., Sartor, G.: A dialectical model of assessing conflicting argument in legal reasoning. Artificial Intelligence and Law 4(3-4), 331–368 (1996)
39. Rubino, R., Rotolo, A., Sartor, G.: An OWL ontology of fundamental legal concepts. In: Proceedings of JURIX 2006, pp. 101–110 (2006)
40. Ruiter, D.: A basic classification of legal institutions. Ratio Juris 10(4), 357–371 (1997)
41. Sartor, G.: Legal Reasoning: A Cognitive Approach to the Law. Springer, Dordrecht (2005)
42. Tinnemeier, N., Dastani, M., Meyer, J.-J.: Roles and norms for programming agent organizations. In: Proceedings of The 8th International Conference on Autonomous Agents and Multiagent Systems, AAMAS 2009, Richland, SC, vol. 1, pp. 121–128. International Foundation for Autonomous Agents and Multiagent Systems (2009)
43. von Wright, G.H.: Norm and Action. Routledge, London (1963)

Rule-Based Agents, Compliance, and Intention Reconsideration in Defeasible Logic

Antonino Rotolo

CIRSFID, University of Bologna, Italy
antonino.rotolo@unibo.it

Abstract. This paper shows how belief revision techniques can be used in Defeasible Logic to change rule-based theories characterizing the deliberation process of cognitive agents. We discuss intention reconsideration as a strategy to make agents compliant with the norms regulating their behavior.

1 Introduction and Background

Many works in MAS on cognitive agents combined two different perspectives [7, 10–13, 40]: (a) a classical (BDI-like) cognitive model of agents that specifies their mental attitudes; (b) a model of agents' behaviour based on normative concepts. This combination leads to an account of agents' deliberation and behaviour in terms of the interplay between mental attitudes and normative (external) factors such as obligations.

A crucial aspect in this trend is that reasoning about agents is embedded in rule-based non-monotonic systems, as one the most interesting problems concerns the cases where the agent's intentions are in conflict with obligations. Indeed, it is important that agent systems may exhibit desirable properties and obligations are precisely meant to ensure them. However, if intentions prevail over obligations, this poses the question of agents' norm compliance.There are in general two strategies to get compliance in MAS:

- Norm compliance (i.e., the fact that intentions are not incompatible with obligations) is achieved by design, namely, by stating that rules supporting the derivation of obligations always prevail over rules supporting conflicting intentions [7, 20].
- Norms should not limit in advance agents' behaviour, but would instead provide soft constraints which can be violated [4]. Getting compliance is then ensured by stating that violations should result in sanctions or other normative effects [21].

There are of course pros and cons in both approaches. But, independently of this, a research issue is still overlooked in the literature: what's the relation between norm compliance and intention reconsideration? Indeed, agents cannot simply maintain intentions, once adopted, without ever stopping to reconsider. It is necessary from time to time for them to check whether the intention has been achieved or whether it is no longer achievable. Most of the existing models of intentional systems view the reconsideration of intention as either a costly computational process or mainly dependent on the dynamics of beliefs [6, 8, 9, 30–33, 35–37, 39, 41]. However, agents' deliberation can be itself a computationally costly process and may require an appropriate intention reconsideration policy which helps the agent to deliberate only when necessary.

N. Bassiliades et al. (Eds.): RuleML 2011 - Europe, LNCS 6826, pp. 67–82, 2011.

In this picture, it is still overlooked the problem of changing intentions not because of the change of beliefs, but because the normative constraints require so.

In this paper, we will thus address this research issue: how to characterize intention reconsideration with the specific purpose of making agents compliant with obligations? More precisely, we will explore how different types of intention reconsiderations can be modeled by applying techniques from revision theory to an extension of Defeasible Logic (DL) which embeds modalities for obligations and intentions [20, 23] and also—this is another novelty—makes use of path labels to keep track of the reasoning chains leading to "illegal" intentions.

The layout of the paper is as follows. Section 2 presents the extension of DL with path labels to reason about intentions and obligations; the purpose is to develop a formalism able to handle intention reconsideration when intentions conflict with obligations. Section 3 recalls a classification between different types of intentions and then shows how different techniques from revision theory can used in the proposed logical framework.

2 The Logical Framework

In line with [20, 23] we develop a constructive account of the modalities **O** and **I** corresponding to obligations and intentions: rules for these concepts are thus meant to devise suitable logical conditions for introducing modalities. For example, rules such as $a_1,\ldots,a_n \Rightarrow_{\mathbf{O}} b$ and $d_1,\ldots,d_n \Rightarrow_{\mathbf{I}} e$ if applicable, will allow for deriving $\mathbf{O}b$ and $\mathbf{I}e$, meaning the former that b is obligatory, the latter that e is an intention of an agent.

In our language, for $X \in \{\mathbf{O},\mathbf{I}\}$, *strict rules* have the form $\phi_1,\ldots,\phi_n \rightarrow_X \psi$. *Defeasible rules* have the form $\phi_1,\ldots,\phi_n \Rightarrow_X \psi$. A rule of the form $\phi_1,\ldots,\phi_n \rightsquigarrow_X \psi$ is a *defeater*. Strict rules support indisputable conclusions whenever their antecedents, too, are indisputable; defeasible rules can be defeated by contrary evidence; defeaters cannot lead to any conclusion but are used to defeat some defeasible rules by producing evidence to the contrary.

Definition 1 (Language). *Let* PROP *be a set of propositional atoms,* $\mathrm{MOD} = \{\mathbf{O},\mathbf{I}\}$, *and* Lbl *be a set of labels. The sets defined below are the smallest ones closed under the given construction conditions:*

Literals

$$\mathrm{Lit} = \mathrm{PROP} \cup \{\neg p | p \in \mathrm{PROP}\}$$

If q is a literal, $\sim q$ denotes the complementary literal (if q is a positive literal p then $\sim q$ is $\neg p$; and if q is $\neg p$, then $\sim q$ is p);

Modal literals

$$\mathrm{ModLit} = \{X\,l, \neg X\,l | X \in \{\mathbf{O},\mathbf{I}\}, l \in \mathrm{Lit}\}$$

Rules $\mathrm{Rul} = \mathrm{Rul}^X_{\mathrm{s}} \cup \mathrm{Rul}^X_{\mathrm{d}} \cup \mathrm{Rul}^X_{\mathrm{dft}}$, *where* $X \in \{\mathbf{I},\mathbf{O}\}$, *such that*

$$\mathrm{Rul}^X_{\mathrm{s}} = \{r : \phi_1,\ldots,\phi_n \rightarrow_X \psi | r \in \mathrm{Lbl}, A(r) \subseteq \mathrm{Lit} \cup \mathrm{ModLit}, \psi \in \mathrm{Lit}\}$$
$$\mathrm{Rul}^X_{\mathrm{d}} = \{r : \phi_1,\ldots,\phi_n \Rightarrow_X \psi | r \in \mathrm{Lbl}, A(r) \subseteq \mathrm{Lit} \cup \mathrm{ModLit}, \psi \in \mathrm{Lit}\}$$
$$\mathrm{Rul}^X_{\mathrm{dft}} = \{r : \phi_1,\ldots,\phi_n \rightsquigarrow_X \psi | r \in \mathrm{Lbl}, A(r) \subseteq \mathrm{Lit} \cup \mathrm{ModLit}, \psi \in \mathrm{Lit}\}$$

We use some obvious abbreviations, such as superscripts for the rule mode ($\mathbf{I}, \mathbf{O}$)*, subscripts for the type of rule, and* $\text{Rul}[\phi]$ *for rules whose consequent is* ϕ*, for example:*

$$\text{Rul}^{\mathbf{I}} = \{r : \phi_1, \ldots, \phi_n \hookrightarrow_{\mathbf{I}} \psi | \hookrightarrow \in \{\rightarrow, \Rightarrow, \rightsquigarrow\}\}$$
$$\text{Rul}^{X}_{\text{sd}} = \{r : \phi_1, \ldots, \phi_n \hookrightarrow_{X} \psi | X \in \text{MOD}, \hookrightarrow \in \{\rightarrow, \Rightarrow\}\}$$
$$\text{Rul}_{\text{s}}[\psi] = \{\phi_1, \ldots, \phi_n \rightarrow_{X} \psi | \forall X \in \text{MOD}\}$$

We use $A(r)$ *to denote the set* $\{\phi_1, \ldots, \phi_n\}$ *of* antecedents *of the rule* r*, and* $C(r)$ *to denote the* consequent ψ *of the rule* r*.*

An agent theory is the knowledge base which is used to reason about the agent's intentions and their interplay with a set of normative rules regulating the agent's deliberation.

Definition 2 (Agent Theory). *An agent theory* D *is a structure* $(F, R^{\mathbf{O}}, R^{\mathbf{I}}, \succ)$ *where*

- $F \subseteq \text{Lit} \cup \text{ModLit}$ *is a finite set of facts;*
- $R^{\mathbf{O}} \subseteq \text{Rul}^{\mathbf{O}}$ *is a finite set of obligation rules;*
- $R^{\mathbf{I}} \subseteq \text{Rul}^{\mathbf{I}}$ *is a finite set of intention rules;*
- $\succ$ *is an acyclic (superiority) relation over* $(R^{\mathbf{I}} \times R^{\mathbf{I}}) \cup (R^{\mathbf{O}} \times R^{\mathbf{O}})$.

Definition 3. *A* path *based on an agent theory* D *is a structure*

$$[\alpha_{1_1}, \ldots, \alpha_{n_1}]_1 [\alpha_{1_2}, \ldots, \alpha_{n_2}]_2 \ldots [\omega]_j$$

where α_{l_w}, $1 \leq w \leq j-1$ *and* $1_w \leq l_w \leq n_w$*, is either a literal, modal literal, or a rule, such that* $j \geq 0$*. If* $j \geq 1$*, then*

- *either*
  - $\omega = -r$ *where* $r \in R^{\mathbf{O}} \cup R^{\mathbf{I}}$*; or*
  - $\omega \in R^{\mathbf{O}}_{\text{sd}} \cup R^{\mathbf{I}}_{\text{sd}}$ *such that, if* $j = 1$ *then* $A(\omega) = \emptyset$*; or*
  - *if* $\omega \in R^{\mathbf{O}}_{\text{sd}} \cup R^{\mathbf{I}}_{\text{sd}}$ *and* $j > 1$*, then* $\forall b \in A(\omega)\ \exists \alpha_{k_{j-1}}$ *such that either*
    * *if* $b \in \text{Lit}$*, then* $\alpha_{k_{j-1}} = b \in F$*, or*
    * *if* $b = Xl \in \text{ModLit}$*, then either* $\alpha_{k_{j-1}} = b \in F$ *or* $l = C(\alpha_{k_{j-1}}) : \alpha_{k_{j-1}} \in R^{X}_{\text{sd}}$*;*
- $\forall \alpha_{x_t}$, $1 < t \leq j-1$, $\alpha_{x_t} \in R^{\mathbf{O}}_{\text{sd}} \cup R^{\mathbf{I}}_{\text{sd}}$ *such that* $\forall b \in A(\alpha_{x_t})\ \exists \alpha_{y_{t-1}}$ *such that either*
  - *if* $b \in \text{Lit}$*, then* $\alpha_{y_{t-1}} = b \in F$*, or*
  - *if* $b = Xl \in \text{ModLit}$*, then either* $\alpha_{y_{t-1}} = b \in F$ *or* $l = C(\alpha_{y_{t-1}}) : \alpha_{y_{t-1}} \in R^{X}_{\text{sd}}$.

An empty path *is a path where* $j = 0$*. A* broken path *is a path where* $\omega = -r$*. A rule* r *occurs in a path iff* $r = \alpha_{l_w}$*, or* $r = \omega$*.*

Example 1. A path recalls the notion of argument for a literal l of [18]:

$$\begin{array}{c} \mathbf{O}c \\ \widehat{\mathbf{O}a\ \mathbf{I}b} \\ |\quad\ | \\ \mathbf{I}f\ \ \mathbf{I}g \\ |\quad\ | \\ \mathbf{O}e\ \ d \end{array}$$

$r : \mathbf{O}e \Rightarrow_{\mathbf{I}} f$
$s : \mathbf{I}f \Rightarrow_{\mathbf{O}} a$
$t : d \Rightarrow_{\mathbf{I}} g$
$u : \mathbf{I}g \Rightarrow_{\mathbf{I}} b$
$w : \mathbf{O}a, \mathbf{I}b \Rightarrow_{\mathbf{O}} c$
$z : \Rightarrow_{\mathbf{O}} e$
$d \in F$

The tree on the left side is the argument for the modal literal $\mathbf{O}c$ we can build using the rules r, s, t, u, w, z and the fact d, which are shown on the right side. From this structure we can obtain, e.g., the path $[z,d]_1[r,t]_2[s,u]_3[w]_4$.

Proofs are sequences of literals and modal literals together with the so-called proof tags $+\Delta$, $-\Delta$, $+\partial$ and $-\partial$. These tags can be labeled by modalities and paths: the modality indicates the mode of the conclusion (if it is an intention or an obligation), the path keeps track of the facts and rules used to obtain it. Hence, if $X \in \{\mathbf{O},\mathbf{I}\}$, given an agent theory D, $+\Delta^X \mathscr{L} q$ means that literal q is provable as modalized with X (e.g., $\mathbf{O}q$, if $X = \mathbf{O}$) in D using the facts and strict rules in the path $\mathscr{L}$, $-\Delta^X \mathscr{L} q$ means that it has been proved in D that q is not definitely provable in D, $+\partial^X \mathscr{L} q$ means that q is defeasibly provable as modalized with X in D using the facts and rules in $\mathscr{L}$, and $-\partial^X \mathscr{L} q$ means that it has been proved in D that q is not defeasibly provable in D. We will clarify later the structure of paths in the case of the negative proof tags.

Definition 4. *Given an agent theory D, a proof in D is a linear derivation, i.e, a sequence of labelled formulas of the type $+\Delta^X \mathscr{L} q$, $-\Delta^X \mathscr{L} q$, $+\partial^X \mathscr{L} q$ and $-\partial^X \mathscr{L} q$, where the proof conditions defined in the rest of this section hold.*

Definition 5. *Let D be an agent theory. Let $\# \in \{\Delta,\partial\}$ and $X \in \{\mathbf{O},\mathbf{I}\}$, $\mathscr{L}$ be any path based on D, and $P = (P(1),\ldots,P(n))$ be a proof in D. A literal q is* $\#\mathscr{L}$-provable *in P if there is a line $P(m)$, $1 \leq m \leq n$, of P such that either*

1. *q is a modal literal Xp and $P(m) = +\#^X \mathscr{L} p$ or*
2. *q is a modal literal $\neg Xp$ and $P(m) = -\#^X \mathscr{L} p$.*

A literal q is $\#\mathscr{L}$-rejected *in P if there is a line $P(m)$ of P such that*

1. *q is a modal literal Xp and $P(m) = -\#^X \mathscr{L} p$, or*
2. *q is a modal literal $\neg Xp$ and $P(m) = +\#^X \mathscr{L} p$.*

The definition of Δ^X describes just forward (monotonic) chaining of strict rules: given $1 \leq j \leq n$

If $P(n+1) = +\Delta^X \mathscr{L}[\alpha_1,\ldots,\alpha_n][r]q$ then
  (1) $\exists x \in R_s^X[q]$:
    (1.1) $x = r$ and
    (1.2) $\forall a \in A(r)$ either
      (1.2.1) $a \in F$, or
      (1.2.2) a is $\Delta\mathscr{L}[\alpha_j]$-provable.

If $P(n+1) = -\Delta^X \mathscr{L}[\alpha_1,\ldots,\alpha_n][r]q$ then
  (1) $\forall x \in R_s^X[q]$ either
    (1.1) $x \neq r$ or
    (1.2) $\exists a \in A(r)$:
      (1.2.1) $a \notin F$, and
      (1.2.2) a is $\Delta\mathscr{L}[\alpha_j]$-rejected.

The path supporting q is built step by step by including the rules and facts used to obtain it. In the case of negative proof tags, any path involved is in fact empty, since there is no reasoning chain supporting q. See also Proposition 1 below.

Example 2. Suppose I am obliged to go to Italy (because, for example, I have to renew my passport, which is going to expire) and I have the intention to eat good tortellini. In this case, if I have this intention, then by necessity I also have the intention to go to Bologna (no way to eat good tortellini elsewhere!). As a conclusion, if I have this last intention, by necessity I will also have the intention to go to Italy, thus complying with the obligation:

$$\begin{aligned}
F &= \{\mathbf{O}\mathit{GoToItaly}, \mathbf{I}\mathit{GoodTortellini}\}\\
R &= \{r_1 : \mathbf{I}\mathit{GoodTortellini} \rightarrow_{\mathbf{I}} \mathit{GoToBologna},\\
&\quad r_2 : \mathbf{I}\mathit{GoToBologna} \rightarrow_{\mathbf{I}} \mathit{GoToItaly}\}\\
\succ &= \emptyset
\end{aligned}$$

Let us work on the proof conditions to illustrate them. The obligation $\mathbf{O}\mathit{GoToItaly}$ does not trigger any rule. The fact $\mathbf{I}\mathit{GoodTortellini}$ triggers r_1 (condition (1.1)): hence we obtain $+\Delta^{\mathbf{I}}[\mathbf{I}\mathit{GoodTortellini}][r_1]\mathit{GoToBologna}$. Now, using proof condition (1.2), we trigger r_2 to get $+\Delta^{\mathbf{I}}[\mathbf{I}\mathit{GoodTortellini}][r_1][r_2]\mathit{GoToItaly}$. This last conclusion shows that the agent's deliberation is intuitively compliant.

Consider now proof conditions for ∂^X: given $1 \leq j \leq n$,

If $P(n+1) = +\partial^X \mathscr{L}[\alpha_1,\ldots,\alpha_n][r]q$ then
(1) $+\Delta^X \mathscr{L}[\alpha_1,\ldots,\alpha_n][r]q$ or
(2) (2.1) $-\Delta^X \mathscr{X} \sim q \in P[1..n]$ and
(2.2) $\exists x \in R^X_{\mathrm{sd}}[q]$:
(2.2.1) $x = r$ and
(2.2.2) $\forall a \in A(r)$
(2.2.2.1) $a \in F$, or
(2.2.2.2) a is $\partial \mathscr{L}[\alpha_j]$-provable, and
(2.3) $\forall s \in R^X[\sim q]$ either $\exists a \in A(s)$:
a is $\partial \mathscr{Y}$-rejected, or
(2.3.1) $\exists t \in R^X[q]$: $\forall a \in A(r)$
a is $\partial \mathscr{Z}$-provable and $t \succ s$.

If $P(n+1) = -\partial^X \mathscr{L}[\alpha_1,\ldots,\alpha_n][r]q$ then
(1) $-\Delta^X \mathscr{L}[\alpha_1,\ldots,\alpha_n][r]q$ and
(2) (2.1) $+\Delta^X \mathscr{X} \sim q \in P[1..n]$ or
(2.2) $\forall x \in R^X_{\mathrm{sd}}[q]$ either
(2.2.1) $x \neq r$, or
(2.2.2) $\exists a \in A(r)$:
(2.2.2.1) $a \notin F$, and
(2.2.2.2) a is $\partial \mathscr{L}[\alpha_j]$-rejected, or
(2.3) $\exists s \in R^X[\sim q]$: $\forall a \in A(s)$
a is $\partial \mathscr{Y}[s]$-provable, and
(2.3.1) $\forall t \in R^X[q]$, $\exists a \in A(r)$:
a is $\partial \mathscr{Z}$-rejected or $t \not\succ s$,
where $[r] = [-r]$ if $\forall a \in A(r)$
$a \in F$, or
a is $\partial \mathscr{L}[\alpha_j]$-provable.

To show that a literal q is defeasibly provable with the mode X we have two choices: (a) We show that q is already definitely provable; or (b) We need to argue using the defeasible part of an agent theory D. For this second case, some (sub)conditions must be satisfied: First, we need to consider possible reasoning chains in support of $\sim q$ with the mode X, and show that $\sim q$ is not definitely provable with that mode (2.1 above). Second, we require that there must be a strict or defeasible rule with mode X for q which can be applied (2.2 above). Third, we must consider the set of all rules which are not known to be inapplicable and which permit to get $\sim q$ with the mode X (2.3 above). Essentially, each such a rule s attacks the conclusion q. For q to be provable, s must be counterattacked by a rule t for q with the following properties: t must be applicable and must prevail over s. Thus each attack on the conclusion q must be counterattacked by a stronger rule. In other words, r and the rules t form a team (for q) that defeats the rules s. The mechanism for handling paths is basically the one for definite conclusions. The only difference is that here we can have broken paths when a rule is made applicable but is defeated by a stronger rule: in this case, the path keeps track of the defeated rule r, which is marked as $-r$.

Proposition 1. *(a) For $-\Delta$: if condition (1) holds, then $\mathscr{L}[\alpha_1,\dots\alpha_n][r]$ is an empty path.*
(b) For $-\partial$: if condition (2.2) holds, then $\mathscr{L}[\alpha_1,\dots\alpha_n][r]$ is an empty path;
(c) For $-\partial$: if condition (2.3) holds and $\mathscr{L}[\alpha_1,\dots\alpha_n][r]$ is broken, then rule r is applicable.

Proof (Sketch). Consider the case (a): if condition (1) holds, this means that there is no path and proof supporting q, and so $\mathscr{L}[\alpha_1,\dots\alpha_n][r]$ must be empty. The same argument applies to the case (b). Consider case (c): here, by construction there is a path and a proof supporting the antecedents of r, even though any r is defeated. Hence r is applicable.

Example 3. Let us expand the theory in Example 2:

$$
\begin{aligned}
F &= \{\mathbf{O}\mathit{GoToItaly}, \mathbf{I}\mathit{GoodTortellini}, \mathit{Hungry}\}\\
R &= \{r_1 : \mathbf{I}\mathit{GoodTortellini} \rightarrow_{\mathbf{I}} \mathit{GoToBologna},\\
&\quad r_2 : \mathbf{I}\mathit{GoToBologna} \rightarrow_{\mathbf{I}} \mathit{GoToItaly},\\
&\quad r_3 : \leadsto_{\mathbf{O}} \neg \mathit{EatModerately},\\
&\quad r_4 : \mathbf{I}\mathit{GoodTortellini} \Rightarrow_{\mathbf{O}} \mathit{EatModerately},\\
&\quad r_5 : \mathit{Hungry} \Rightarrow_{\mathbf{I}} \neg \mathit{EatModerately},\\
&\quad r_6 : \Rightarrow_{\mathbf{I}} \neg \mathit{EatModerately},\\
&\quad r_7 : \mathbf{I}\neg \mathit{EatModerately}, \mathbf{I}\mathit{GoodTortellini} \Rightarrow_{\mathbf{O}} \mathit{Abstinence}\}
\end{aligned}
$$

$$\succ = \{r_4 \succ r_3\}$$

Since the defeasible part of the theory cannot affect the derivation obtained using the monotonic part (which is the same of Example 2), the following conclusions still hold:

$$+\Delta^{\mathbf{I}}[\mathbf{I}\mathit{GoodTortellini}][r_1]\mathit{GoToBologna} \qquad +\Delta^{\mathbf{I}}[\mathbf{I}\mathit{GoodTortellini}][r_1][r_2]\mathit{GoToItaly}$$

Let us briefly comment the new rules: r_3 works as a permission, since it is supposed to block the opposite conclusion (that *EatModerately* is obligatory) [22]; r_4 states that eating moderately is obligatory whenever the agent intends to eat good tortellini; r_5 says that, when hungry, the agents intends not to eat moderately; r_6 assumes that the agent is greedy, as she normally intends not eat moderately in general; r_7 states that, when the agent intends not to eat moderately and to eat good tortellini, then she obliged to have abstinence afterwards. What are our conclusions? The fact **I***GoodTortellini* triggers r_4, which conflicts with r_3; if r_3 could prevail, we would have $-\partial^{\mathbf{O}}[-r_3]EatModerately$, but this is not the case since r_4 is stronger than r_3, thus leading to

$$+\partial^{\mathbf{O}}[\mathbf{I}GoodTortellini][r_4]EatModerately \tag{1}$$

The fact *Hungry* makes r_5 applicable, and so

$$+\partial^{\mathbf{I}}[Hungry][r_5]\neg EatModerately \tag{2}$$

The rule r_6 is always applicable, thus supporting

$$+\partial^{\mathbf{I}}[r_6]\neg EatModerately \tag{3}$$

Finally, since **I***GoodTortellini* is a fact and we have both (2) and (3), we will obtain

$$+\partial^{\mathbf{O}}[Hungry][r_5,\mathbf{I}GoodTortellini][r_7]Abstinence$$
$$+\partial^{\mathbf{O}}[r_6,\mathbf{I}GoodTortellini]Abstinence$$

Definition 6. *Given an agent theory D, $D \vdash \pm\#^X l$ (i.e., $\pm\#^X l$ is a conclusion of D), where $\# \in \{\Delta,\partial\}$ and $X \in \{c,\mathbf{O},\mathbf{I}\}$, iff there is a proof $P = (P(1),\dots,P(n))$ in D such that $P(n) = \pm\#^X l$.*

Proposition 2. *Let D be an agent theory where the transitive closure of $\succ$ is acyclic. For every $\# \in \{\Delta,\partial\}$, $X \in \{\mathbf{O},\mathbf{I}\}$ and every pair of paths $\mathscr{L}$ and $\mathscr{M}$ (where, possibly, $\mathscr{L} = \mathscr{M}$):*

- *It is not possible that both $D \vdash +\#^X \mathscr{L} p$ and $D \vdash -\#^X \mathscr{M} p$;*
- *if $D \vdash +\partial^X \mathscr{L} p$ and $D \vdash +\partial^X \mathscr{M} {\sim}p$, then $D \vdash +\Delta^X \mathscr{L} p$ and $D \vdash +\Delta^X \mathscr{M} {\sim}p$.*

Proof. The proof is a trivial variation of the ones for Theorems 1 and 2 in [24]. Proposition 2 shows the soundness of the logic: it is not possible to derive a tagged conclusion and its opposite, and that we cannot defeasibly prove both p and its complementary unless the definite part of the theory proves them; this means that inconsistency can be derived only if the theory we started with is inconsistent, and even in this case the logic does not collapse to the trivial extensions (i.e., everything is provable).

Definition 7. *Given a theory D, the* universe *of D (U^D) is the set of all the atoms occurring in D; the* extension *of D (E^D), is defined as follows:*

$$E^D = (\Delta^+(D),\Delta^-(D),\partial^+(D),\partial^-(D))$$

where for $X \in \{\mathbf{I},\mathbf{O}\}$

$$\Delta^+(D) = \{Xl|D \vdash +\Delta^X \mathscr{L}l\} \qquad \Delta^-(D) = \{Xl|D \vdash -\Delta^X \mathscr{L}l\}$$
$$\partial^+(D) = \{Xl|D \vdash +\partial^X \mathscr{L}l\} \qquad \partial^-(D) = \{Xl|D \vdash -\partial^X \mathscr{L}l\}.$$

3 Compliance and Revising Intentions

3.1 Conceptual Background

Suppose the agent's intentions conflict with some obligations. If we assume that obligations are unchangeable, the possibility to avoid violations relies on the possibility to handle rules for intentions.

As we argued elsewhere [20, 23], we can conceptually distinguish between different types of intentions: unchangeable intentions, strong intentions and weak intentions. The first type corresponds in our logic to intentional facts of an agent theory (elements of F), the second type to definite conclusions ($+\Delta^{\mathbf{I}}$), the third to defeasible conclusions ($+\partial^{\mathbf{I}}$). Unchangeable intentions cannot be reconsidered in any case (see [23] for a discussion on this issue). To give up a strong intention we have necessarily to change (revise) the theory (i.e., we have to modify the strict rules), while we can abandon a weak intention if we have an exception to it without having to change the theory. To illustrate this point let us consider the following rules:

$$r_1 : a \rightarrow_{\mathbf{I}} b \qquad\qquad r_2 : c \rightarrow_{\mathbf{I}} \neg b \tag{4}$$

Suppose the same connections are expressed as defeasible rules:

$$r_1' : a \Rightarrow_{\mathbf{I}} b \qquad\qquad r_2' : c \Rightarrow_{\mathbf{I}} \neg b \qquad\qquad r_2' \succ r_1' \tag{5}$$

In both cases we obtain $\mathbf{I}b$ given a as a fact. However if both a and c are given then from (4) we get an inconsistency, since definite conclusions cannot be blocked and we have to revise the theory. If we use belief revision to change the theory then we have to remove r_1 from the theory. A consequence of this operation is that we are no longer able to derive $\mathbf{I}b$ from a. An alternative would be to use base revision instead of belief revision. If this strategy is taken then r_1 is changed into

$$r_1'' : a, \neg c \rightarrow_{\mathbf{I}} b \tag{6}$$

Again, it is not possible to obtain $\mathbf{I}b$ from a. To derive it we have to supplement the theory with the information whether c or $\neg c$ is definitely the case, increasing then the cognitive burden on the agent.

If the same information were encoded as weak intentions, as in (5), then we would not suffer from the above drawback, since (5) prevents the conclusion of an inconsistency (in case we do not specify that r_2' is stronger than r_1', we are not able to conclude $\mathbf{I}b$ nor $\mathbf{I}\neg b$). Indeed, the defeasibility of weak intentions makes it possible to block the application of the intention to the particular case without reconsidering it. This is in agreement with [6]. This way the amount of deliberation required for intention reconsideration can be minimized to some extent.

Unfortunately, if the first and compelling purpose is to make agents compliant, not in all cases the defeasibility of intentions is *the* solution. Indeed, if a theory containing (5) allows for deriving $\mathbf{O}b$, there is no way to recover, unless we change the theory.

3.2 A Simple Model

Let us first formally characterize the notion of compliance to a norm:

Definition 8 (Rule Fulfilment and Violation). *An agent theory* $D = (F, R^{\mathbf{O}}, R^{\mathbf{I}}, \succ)$ fulfil *a rule* $r \in R^{\mathbf{O}}_{\mathrm{sd}}$ *iff, if* $D \vdash +\partial^{\mathbf{O}}\mathscr{L}C(r)$*, then, either*

- *if* $C(r)$ *is a positive literal* l *(*r *is a conditional obligation), then there is an* $\mathscr{Y}$ *such that* $D \vdash +\partial^{\mathbf{I}}\mathscr{Y}l$*, or*
- *if* $C(r)$ *is a negative literal* $\neg l$ *(*r *is a conditional prohibition) for any* $\mathscr{L}$*,* $D \vdash -\partial^{\mathbf{I}}\mathscr{L}l$*.*

D violates *the rule* r *whenever* D *does not fulfil* r*.* D *is compliant iff* D *does not violate any rule in it.*

As we briefly discussed in Section 3.1, an option to recover from violations and reinstate compliance is to revise intentions by using AGM techniques. This idea looks natural (see e.g. [8, 30]). However, it is far from obvious how to do it in DL. Fortunately, AGM fundamental operations have been defined for propositional DL in [2].

The first step is thus to extend [2]'s notions of expansion and contraction to cover DL with modalities, which is trivial. Consider an agent theory D and suppose we want to expand the extension of D with $c = \mathbf{I}p_1, \ldots, \mathbf{I}p_n$:

$$D^+_c = \begin{cases} D & \text{if } \exists i \in \{1, \ldots n\}\colon \mathbf{I}{\sim}p_i \in \partial^+(D) \\ D & \text{if } \exists i, j \in \{1, \ldots n\}\colon {\sim}p_i = p_j \\ (F, R^{\mathbf{O}}, R^{\mathbf{I}'}, \succ') & \text{otherwise} \end{cases}$$

$$\begin{aligned} &\text{where} \\ &R^{\mathbf{I}'} = R^{\mathbf{I}} \cup \{w_1 :\Rightarrow_{\mathbf{I}} p_1, \ldots, w_n :\Rightarrow_{\mathbf{I}} p_n\} \\ &\succ' = (\succ \cup \{w_i \succ r \mid 1 \le i \le n, r \in R^{\mathbf{I}}[{\sim}p]\}) - \\ &\qquad \{r \succ w_i \mid 1 \le i \le n, r \in R^{\mathbf{I}}[{\sim}p]\}. \end{aligned} \tag{7}$$

Thus, we add rules that prove $p_1, \ldots p_n$ as intentions; these rules are always applicable and are strictly stronger than any possibly contradicting rules. This solution looks useful to deal with many cases of violation.

Example 4. Consider the following theory D.

$$\begin{aligned} &F = \{a\} \\ &R = \{r_1 : a \rightarrow_{\mathbf{I}} b, r_2 : \mathbf{I}b \Rightarrow_{\mathbf{O}} c, r_3 : a \leadsto_{\mathbf{I}} \neg c, r_4 : \mathbf{I}b \Rightarrow_{\mathbf{I}} c\} \\ &\succ = \emptyset \end{aligned}$$

Here we obtain, among other conclusions, $+\partial^{\mathbf{O}}[a][r_1][r_2]c$. To be compliant, we should be able to derive that c is intended, but this is not possible. We have here that $-\partial^{\mathbf{I}}[a][r_1][-r_4]c$. What we can do is to expand D with $\mathbf{I}c$ by simply adding an intention rule w for c and applying (7). Since this operation satisfies AGM postulates for expansion [2], $\mathbf{I}c$ is successfully added to the positive extension of D. Hence, we obtain $+\partial^{\mathbf{I}}[w]c$ and make D compliant.

Let us define the procedure explained in Example 4.

Definition 9 (Positive Revision). *Let $D = (F, R^{\mathbf{O}}, R^{\mathbf{I}}, \succ)$ be an agent theory. If D* violates *the rules $r_1, \ldots, r_n \in R^{\mathbf{O}}$, then D_c^+ where $c = \mathbf{I}p_1, \ldots, \mathbf{I}p_n$ such that $C(r_1) = p_1, \ldots, C(r_n) = p_n$.*

Let us adjust [2]'s definition of contraction. Here, too, we trivially extends [2]'s approach. If we want to contract $c = \mathbf{I}p_1, \ldots, \mathbf{I}p_n$ in D, then:

$$D_c^- = \begin{cases} D & \text{if } \mathbf{I}p_1, \ldots, \mathbf{I}p_n \notin \partial^+(D) \\ (F, R^{\mathbf{O}} R^{\mathbf{I}'}, \succ') & \text{otherwise} \end{cases}$$

$$\begin{aligned} &\text{where} \\ &R^{\mathbf{I}'} = R^{\mathbf{I}} \cup \{s : \mathbf{I}p_1, \ldots, \mathbf{I}p_{i-1}, \mathbf{I}p_{i+1}, \ldots, \mathbf{I}p_n \rightsquigarrow_{\mathbf{I}} \sim p_i | \\ &\qquad 1 \leq i \leq n\} \\ &\succ' = \succ - \{r \succ s \mid r \in R^{\mathbf{I}'} - R^{\mathbf{I}}\}. \end{aligned} \tag{8}$$

(8) blocks the proof of $\mathbf{I}p_1, \ldots, \mathbf{I}p_n$. It is ensured that at least one of the $\mathbf{I}p_i$s will not be derived. The new rules in $R^{\mathbf{I}'}$ are such that, if all but one $\mathbf{I}p_i$ have been obtained, a defeater with head $\sim p_j$ is triggered. The defeaters are not weaker than any other rules, so the defeater cannot be "counterattacked" by another rule, and p_j will not be proven as an intention.

Example 5. Consider the following theory D.

$$\begin{aligned} &F = \{a, \mathbf{I}d\} \\ &R = \{r_1 : a \rightarrow_{\mathbf{I}} b, r_2 : \mathbf{I}b \Rightarrow_{\mathbf{O}} c, r_3 : \mathbf{I}d \Rightarrow_{\mathbf{I}} \neg c\} \\ &\succ = \emptyset \end{aligned}$$

We obtain, among other conclusions, $+\partial^{\mathbf{O}}[a][r_1][r_2]c$. To be compliant, we should derive that $\mathbf{I}c$, but we obtain the opposite through r_3. More precisely, we get $+\partial^{\mathbf{I}}[\mathbf{I}d][r_3]\neg c$. What we can do is to contract $\mathbf{I}\neg c$ by simply adding a defeater $s : \rightsquigarrow_{\mathbf{I}} c$ and thus applying (8). Since this operation satisfies AGM postulates for contraction [2], $\mathbf{I}\neg c$ is successfully removed from the positive extension of D and added to the negative extension.

Definition 10 (Negative Revision). *Let $D = (F, R^{\mathbf{O}}, R^{\mathbf{I}}, \succ)$ be an agent theory. If D* violates *the rules $r_1, \ldots, r_n \in R^{\mathbf{O}}$, then D_c^- where $c = \mathbf{I}p_1, \ldots, \mathbf{I}p_n$ such that $C(r_1) = \neg p_1, \ldots, C(r_n) = \neg p_n$.*

Definitions 9 and 10 guarantee to recover from violations, are very simple, and directly exploit techniques and results from [2]. Also, they do not make any essential use of paths, which sometimes may look cumbersome. However, they have two serious drawbacks: (a) They work only on the defeasible part of agent theories, and so cannot be used to recover from violations when these are caused by strong intentions (see the discussion in Section 3.1); (b) They apply only to the last rule of the reasoning chains supporting "illegal" intentions.

To overcome the above difficulties, DL with paths is useful.

3.3 Refinements: Using Paths

The advantage of using paths is that we can easily identify (i) which rules have been violated, and (ii) which rules for intentions have determined the violation of an obligation.

Let us see when Definitions 9 and 10 clearly fail while DL with paths succeeds.

Example 6 (Strong Intentions). Consider this theory:

$$F = \{a, \mathbf{I}b\}$$
$$R = \{r_1 : a \rightarrow_{\mathbf{I}} \neg c, r_2 : \mathbf{I}b \Rightarrow_{\mathbf{O}} c, r_3 : \mathbf{I}b \rightarrow_{\mathbf{I}} d,$$
$$r_4 : \mathbf{I}d, a \rightarrow_{\mathbf{I}} \neg c\}$$
$$\succ = \emptyset$$

We have two reasons for the violation of r_2 (indeed, we obtain $+\partial^{\mathbf{O}}[\mathbf{I}b][r_2]c$). In fact, we can derive $+\Delta^{\mathbf{I}}[a][r_1]\neg c$ and $+\Delta^{\mathbf{I}}[\mathbf{I}b][r_3, a][r_4]\neg c$. Since strict rules cannot be defeated, the only solution is rule removal. Hence, we have to operate over r_1 but we are free to remove either r_3 or r_4. For example, if we prefer not to remove r_4, we will successfully get compliance by removing r_1 and only r_3.

Definition 11 (Rule Removal). *Let $D = (F, R^{\mathbf{O}}, R^{\mathbf{I}}, \succ)$ be an agent theory. For each $r \in R^{\mathbf{O}}_{\mathrm{sd}}$ such that the paths $\mathscr{L}_1, \ldots \mathscr{L}_n$ are the ones based on D such that $D \vdash +\Delta^{\mathbf{I}}\mathscr{L}_1 p, \ldots,$ $D \vdash +\Delta^{\mathbf{I}}\mathscr{L}_n p$ and $D \vdash +\partial^{\mathbf{O}}\mathscr{Y}C(r)$, where $C(r) = \neg p$, the theory D_{-X} is such that*

- *$X = \{w_1, \ldots, w_m\}$ is the smallest set of rules in $R^{\mathbf{I}}$ such that, for each $k \in \{1, \ldots, n\}$, there is at least a $w_j \in X$ that occurs in $\mathscr{L}_k$,*
- *$R^{\mathbf{I}}_{-X} = R^{\mathbf{I}} - X$, and*
- *$F_{-X} = F$, $R^{\mathbf{O}}_{-X} = R^{\mathbf{O}}$, and $\succ_{-X} = \succ$.*

Let us work on weak intentions only. The following definition proposes intention retraction for DL with paths by exploiting the contraction of intentions as framed in (8).

Definition 12 (Contraction with Paths). *Let $D = (F, R^{\mathbf{O}}, R^{\mathbf{I}}, \succ)$ be an agent theory. For each $r \in R^{\mathbf{O}}_{\mathrm{sd}}$ such that the paths $\mathscr{L}_1, \ldots \mathscr{L}_n$ are the ones based on D such that $D \vdash +\partial^{\mathbf{I}}\mathscr{L}_1 p, \ldots, D \vdash +\partial^{\mathbf{I}}\mathscr{L}_n p$ and $D \vdash +\partial^{\mathbf{O}}\mathscr{Y}C(r)$, where $C(r) = \neg p$, the theory $D_{\flat p} = (F, R^{\mathbf{O}}, R^{\mathbf{I}'}, \succ')$ is such that*

(i) $R^{\mathbf{I}'} = R^{\mathbf{I}} \cup \{s : \leadsto_{\mathbf{I}} \sim q\} \cup \{t : \leadsto_{\mathbf{I}} \sim x\}$,
(ii) $\succ' = \succ - [\{r_k \succ s \mid r_k \in R^{\mathbf{I}}[\sim C(s)], r_k$ occurs in $\mathscr{L}_k\ \forall k \in \{1, \ldots, n\}\} \cup \{w \succ t \mid$ for each path $\mathscr{M}[-w]$ based on D such that $C(w) = x$, either $x = p$ or w occurs in $\mathscr{L}_k\ \forall k \in \{1, \ldots, n\}\}]$.

Example 7 (Paths). Consider the following agent theory:

$$F = \{a, \mathbf{I}b\}$$
$$R = \{r_1 : a \Rightarrow_{\mathbf{I}} \neg c, r_2 : \mathbf{I}b \Rightarrow_{\mathbf{O}} c, r_3 : \mathbf{I}b \Rightarrow_{\mathbf{I}} d, r_4 : \mathbf{I}d, a \Rightarrow_{\mathbf{I}} \neg c$$
$$r_5 : g \Rightarrow_{\mathbf{I}} \neg c\}$$
$$\succ = \emptyset$$

Like in Example 6, we obtain $+\partial^{\mathbf{O}}[\mathbf{I}b][r_2]c$. We also derive $+\partial^{\mathbf{I}}[a][r_1]\neg c$ and $+\partial^{\mathbf{I}}[\mathbf{I}b][r_3,a][r_4]\neg c$, which violate rule r_2. Definition 12 allow us to add, for example, a defeater for c which is stronger than r_1 and another defeater for $\neg d$ which is stronger than r_3. Hence, as we have already seen in Example 6, Definition 12 does not only provide tools to affect the rules r_1 and r_4 that directly prove illegal intentions, but also rules preceding them in the involved path (e.g., r_3).

Finally, notice that we can use paths also with positive revisions (expansion), but only when the literal we want to add is in fact the one which directly would support compliance:

Example 8. Suppose we have the following:

$$
\begin{aligned}
F &= \{a\} \\
R &= \{r_1 : a \Rightarrow_{\mathbf{I}} \neg c, r_2 : a \Rightarrow_{\mathbf{O}} d, r_3 : \mathbf{I}\neg c \Rightarrow_{\mathbf{I}} b, r_4 : \mathbf{O}d, \mathbf{I}b \Rightarrow_{\mathbf{I}} d, \\
&\qquad r_5 : \Rightarrow_{\mathbf{I}} \neg b\} \\
\succ &= \{r_5 \succ r_3\}
\end{aligned}
$$

Here the reasoning chain supporting $\mathbf{I}d$ is broken at r_3. Hence the only path available to work with is $[a][r_1][-r_3]$, which is not explicitly linked with the potential derivation of $\mathbf{I}d$. The idea could work if r_5 would attack r_4. In this case, we would have a path like $[a][a,r_1][r_2,r_3][-r_4]$: since the head of r_4 is d, we could add a new rule which defeats r_5. However, this is nothing but an application of Definition 9.

The following proposition shows that the proposed operations for reconsidering intentions are successful:

Proposition 3 (Success). *Let $D = (F, R^{\mathbf{O}}, R^{\mathbf{I}}, \succ)$ be an agent theory. If, for each $r \in R^{\mathbf{O}}_{\mathrm{sd}}$ we have $D \vdash +\partial^{\mathbf{O}}\mathscr{Y}C(r)$, where $C(r) = \neg p$, and for the paths $\mathscr{L}_1, \dots \mathscr{L}_n$ based on D*

(a) $D \vdash +\Delta^{\mathbf{I}}\mathscr{L}_1 p, \dots, D \vdash +\Delta^{\mathbf{I}}\mathscr{L}_n p$, then $\mathbf{I}p \notin \Delta^+(D_{-X})$;
(b) $D \vdash +\partial^{\mathbf{I}}\mathscr{L}_1 p, \dots, D \vdash +\partial^{\mathbf{I}}\mathscr{L}_n p$, then $\mathbf{I}p \notin \partial^+(D_{\flat p})$ unless $\mathbf{I}p \in \Delta^+(D)$.

Proof (Sketch). Case (a): By construction, Definition 11 guarantees that at least one strict intention rule is removed in every path based on D supporting $\mathbf{I}p$.

Case (b): An inspection of the proof conditions for ∂ shows that Definition 12 successfully blocks the derivation of $\mathbf{I}p$, unless it is derived using only strict rules. Notice that condition (ii) in Definition 12 ensures that, in case the attacks made by the defeaters s activate other (previously defeated) rules supporting $\mathbf{I}p$, these last potential derivations are made unsuccessful.

4 Related Work

This paper investigates how to model the norm compliance of rule-based agents by providing different theory-revision strategies for reconsidering agents' intentions. To the best of our knowledge, this is the first work which jointly address these two specific research issues.

The literature on norm compliance in MAS is large (see, e.g., [1, 3, 5, 14–16, 26, 27, 29]). Independently of the specific techniques proposed, all these works adopt one or both of the two fundamental strategies to characterize norm enforcement [4, 17, 21, 28, 38]: (a) norms are hard constraints and agent's compliance is achieved by design; (b) norms are soft constraints and so do not limit in advance agents' behavior. As far as cognitive (BDI-like) agents are concerned, the problem amounts to model the relation between intentions and obligations. In this regard, the main approach proposed in the literature adopts the first of the two above mentioned strategies [7, 20]: compliance is then obtained at the deliberative stage by introducing the notion of social agent, i.e., by imposing that obligations always prevail over conflicting intentions. No role for intention reconsideration is acknowledged in this context.

Intention reconsideration, too, is a topic widely investigated in the MAS literature, which is classically related with the problem of persistence of intentions [6, 9, 39]. Indeed, following [6] it is often assumed that intentions obey the law of inertia and resist retraction or revision, since the deliberation of resource-bounded agents would be too expensive if all intentions were susceptible of being changed without any constraints. A typical condition under which intentions can be reconsidered is when new relevant, and significant information comes in. In Section 1 we mentioned a list of works in this field and provided some general comments. Let us focus on some of them, which are closer to our approach and discuss how to apply theory revision techniques. Such techniques are discussed in this context by, e.g., [8, 30]: their approaches, though inspired by different ideas and purposes, consider AGM operations but not in the context of rule-based non-monotonic frameworks. A very sophisticated work is [39], where beliefs are modeled as sets of Linear Temporal Logic formulas and intentions are derived from the agents current active plans. A dynamic update operator is introduced and the revision of intentions is determined by the dynamics of agents' beliefs. No reference however is made here in regard to the role of other factors, such as obligations.

5 Summary and Future Work

In this paper we presented an extension of DL with path labels to reason about intentions and obligations The formalism was able to handle intention reconsideration when the agent's intentions conflict with obligations. In particular, we showed that the reconsideration of different types of intentions can be modeled using various techniques from revision theory.

This is a preliminary step towards modeling intention reconsideration in DL. A number of open issues should be addressed.

- According to [25] if I violate a norm r but I comply with an obligation which is meant to compensate the violation of r, I am still compliant. In [10] we introduced the operator $\otimes$ to handle compensations in a version of DL with modalities but without paths. What happens if we combine $\otimes$ with DL with paths?
- In [20] we showed that the extensions of agent theories, in some modal versions of DL, can be computed in linear time. We will have to check whether this is preserved in the new logic.

- We have to investigate the properties of the new operations over agent theories. In particular, we have to better study how to minimize changes.
- Another possibility is not to revise the set of rules for intention, but to change rule priorities [19]. Also this question is left to a future research.

Acknowledgments. This paper benefited from conversations with Guido Governatori and Leon van der Torre. A different version of it was published in the IJCAI 2011 proceedings [34].

References

1. Alberti, M., Gavanelli, M., Lamma, E., Chesani, F., Mello, P., Torroni, P.: Compliance verification of agent interaction: a logic-based software tool. Applied Artificial Intelligence 20(2-4), 133–157 (2006)
2. Billington, D., Antoniou, G., Governatori, G., Maher, M.J.: Revising nonmonotonic theories: The case of defeasible logic. In: Burgard, W., Christaller, T., Cremers, A.B. (eds.) KI 1999. LNCS (LNAI), vol. 1701, pp. 101–112. Springer, Heidelberg (1999)
3. Boella, G., Broersen, J., van der Torre, L.: Reasoning about constitutive norms, counts-as conditionals, institutions, deadlines and violations. In: Bui, T.D., Ho, T.V., Ha, Q.T. (eds.) PRIMA 2008. LNCS (LNAI), vol. 5357, pp. 86–97. Springer, Heidelberg (2008)
4. Boella, G., van der Torre, L.: Fulfilling or violating obligations in multiagent systems. In: Proc. IAT 2004 (2004)
5. Bou, E., López-Sánchez, M., Rodríguez-Aguilar, J.A.: Adaptation of autonomic electronic institutions through norms and institutional agents. In: O'Hare, G.M.P., Ricci, A., O'Grady, M.J., Dikenelli, O. (eds.) ESAW 2006. LNCS (LNAI), vol. 4457, pp. 300–319. Springer, Heidelberg (2007)
6. Bratman, M.E.: Intentions, Plans and Practical Reason. Harvard University Press, Cambridge (1987)
7. Broersen, J., Dastani, M., Hulstijn, J., van der Torre, L.: Goal generation in the BOID architecture. Cognitive Science Quarterly 2(3-4), 428–447 (2002)
8. Cawsey, A., Galliers, J., Logan, B., Reece, S., Sparck Jones, K.: Revising beliefs and intentions: A unified framework for agent interaction. In: Proc. 9th Biennial Conference of the Society for the Study of Artificial Intelligence and Simulation of Behaviour. IOS Press, Amsterdam (1993)
9. Cohen, P.R., Levesque, H.J.: Intention is choice with commitment. Artificial Intelligence 42(1), 213–261 (1990)
10. Dastani, M., Governatori, G., Rotolo, A., van der Torre, L.: Programming cognitive agents in defeasible logic. In: Sutcliffe, G., Voronkov, A. (eds.) LPAR 2005. LNCS (LNAI), vol. 3835, pp. 621–636. Springer, Heidelberg (2005)
11. Dastani, M., Governatori, G., Rotolo, A., van der Torre, L.: Preferences of agents in defeasible logic. In: Zhang, S., Jarvis, R. (eds.) AI 2005. LNCS (LNAI), vol. 3809, pp. 695–704. Springer, Heidelberg (2005)
12. Dignum, F.: Autonomous agents with norms. Artificial Intelligence and Law 7(1), 69–79 (1999)
13. Dignum, F., Morley, D., Sonenberg, L., Cavedon, L.: Towards socially sophisticated BDI agents. In: ICMAS 2000, pp. 111–118 (2000)
14. Esteva, M., Rosell, B., Rodríguez-Aguilar, J.A., Arcos, J.L.: Ameli: An agent-based middleware for electronic institutions. In: Proc. AAMAS 2004. ACM, New York (2004)

15. Flores, R.A., Chaib-draa, B.: Modelling flexible social commitments and their enforcement. In: Gleizes, M.-P., Omicini, A., Zambonelli, F. (eds.) ESAW 2004. LNCS (LNAI), vol. 3451, pp. 139–151. Springer, Heidelberg (2005)
16. Gaertner, D., Garcia-Camino, A., Noriega, P., Rodriguez-Aguilar, J.-A., Vasconcelos, W.: Distributed norm management in regulated multiagent systems. In: Proc. AAMAS 2007. ACM, New York (2007)
17. Garca-Camino, A., Rodrguez-Aguilar, J., Sierra, C., Vasconcelos, W.: Constraint rule-based programming of norms for electronic institutions. Autonomous Agents and Multi-Agent Systems 18, 186–217 (2009), doi:10.1007/s10458-008-9059-4
18. Governatori, G., Maher, M.J., Billington, D., Antoniou, G.: Argumentation semantics for defeasible logics. Journal of Logic and Computation 14, 675–702 (2004)
19. Governatori, G., Olivieri, F., Scannapieco, S., Cristani, M.: Superiority based revision of defeasible theories. In: Dean, M., Hall, J., Rotolo, A., Tabet, S. (eds.) RuleML 2010. LNCS, vol. 6403, pp. 104–118. Springer, Heidelberg (2010)
20. Governatori, G., Rotolo, A.: Bio logical agents: Norms, beliefs, intentions in defeasible logic. Autonomous Agents and Multi-Agent Systems 17(1), 36–69 (2008)
21. Governatori, G., Rotolo, A.: How do agents comply with norm? In: Web Intelligence/IAT Workshops, pp. 488–491 (2009)
22. Governatori, G., Rotolo, A., Sartor, G.: Temporalised normative positions in defeasible logic. In: Proc. ICAIL 2005, pp. 25–34. ACM, New York (2005)
23. Governatori, G., Padmanabhan, V., Rotolo, A., Sattar, A.: A defeasible logic for modelling policy-based intentions and motivational attitudes. Logic Journal of the IGPL 17(3), 227–265 (2009)
24. Governatori, G., Rotolo, A.: A computational framework for institutional agency. Artif. Intell. Law 16(1), 25–52 (2008)
25. Governatori, G., Rotolo, A.: A conceptually rich model of business process compliance. In: APCCM, pp. 3–12 (2010)
26. Grossi, D., Aldewereld, H., Dignum, F.: Ubi lex, ibi poena: Designing norm enforcement in e-institutions. In: Noriega, P., Vázquez-Salceda, J., Boella, G., Boissier, O., Dignum, V., Fornara, N., Matson, E. (eds.) COIN 2006. LNCS (LNAI), vol. 4386, pp. 101–114. Springer, Heidelberg (2007)
27. Fred Hübner, J., Boissier, O., Bordini, R.H.: From organisation specification to normative programming in multi-agent organisations. In: Dix, J., Leite, J., Governatori, G., Jamroga, W. (eds.) CLIMA XI. LNCS, vol. 6245, pp. 117–134. Springer, Heidelberg (2010)
28. Jones, A.J.I., Sergot, M.: On the characterization of law and computer systems: the normative systems perspective, pp. 275–307. John Wiley and Sons Ltd., Chichester (1993)
29. López y López, F., Luck, M., d'Inverno, M.: Constraining autonomy through norms. In: Proc. AAMAS 2002. ACM, New York (2002)
30. Lorini, E.: Variations on intentional themes: From the generation of an intention to the execution of an intentional action. PhD thesis, University of Siena (2007)
31. Lorini, E., Herzig, A.: A logic of intention and attempt. Synthese 163(1), 45–77 (2008)
32. Meyer, J.-J.C., van der Hoek, W., van Linder, B.: A logical approach to the dynamics of commitments. Artif. Intell. 113, 1–40 (1999)
33. Rao, A.S., Georgeff, M.P.: Modelling rational agents within a BDI-architecture. In: Proc. KR 1991. Morgan Kaufmann, San Francisco (1991)
34. Rotolo, A.: Norm compliance of rule-based cognitive agents. In: Proc. IJCAI 2011. AAAI Press, Menlo Park (2011)
35. Shoham, Y.: Agent-oriented programming. Artif. Intell. 60, 51–92 (1993)
36. Singh, M.P.: On the commitments and precommitments of limited agents. In: Proc. IJCAI 1991 Workshop on Theoretical and Practical Design of Rational Agents (1991)

37. Singh, M.P., Asher, N.M.: A logic of intentions and beliefs. Journal of Philosophical Logic
38. Tinnemeier, N., Dastani, M., Meyer, J.-J.: Roles and norms for programming agent organizations. In: Proc. AAMAS 2009, pp. 121–128. IFAAMS, Richland (2009)
39. van der Hoek, W., Jamroga, W., Wooldridge, M.: Intention is choice with commitment. Artificial Intelligence 42(1), 213–261 (1990)
40. van der Torre, L., Boella, G., Verhagen, H. (eds.) Normative Multi-agent Systems, Special Issue of JAAMAS, vol. 17(1) (2008)
41. Wooldridge, M.: Reasoning about rational agents. MIT Press, Cambridge (2000)

A Dynamic Metalogic Argumentation Framework Implementation

Jenny S.Z. Eriksson Lundström[1], Giacomo Aceto[2,⋆], and Andreas Hamfelt[3]

[1] Dept of Informatics and Media, Uppsala University, Sweden
[2] Faculty of Engineering, University of Bologna, Italy
{jenny.eriksson,andreas.hamfelt}@im.uu.se, giacomo.aceto@gmail.com

Abstract. One of the main challenges that faces the AI-community is to express close approximations of human reasoning as computational formalizations of argument. In this paper we present a full implementation and accompanying software for defeasible adversarial argumentation. The work is based on the metalogic framework of defeasible adversarial argumentation games of [9]. The software we developed consists of: a meta-interpreter, a declarative implementation of the argumentation game model and a graphical interface developed in Java that shows the results of the game execution and the construction of the argumentation derivation tree[1].

1 Introduction

A core endeavor of formal argumentation is to contribute to formal philosophy a characterization of argumentation, capturing aspects of its phenomena in a way precise enough for scientific evaluation and prediction. However, to also present this characterization in the form of a specification executable by computer systems is essential for enabling the evolution of software directed towards the addressed domain; here computational aid for the advancement and scrutinizing of argumentation. It turn, such implementations provide a contribution to formal philosophy as they may enhance the acceptance and spread of the means of formal description of the identified phenomena. As an example, research in general defeasible argumentation has presented some large scale implementations adapted for eg. robotics [5] and the semantic web [2]. Both making significant contributions to the field of defeasible reasoning and formal argument.

For formal models of disputes, there exist comprehensive approaches to defeasible logic and argumentation in the field of AI and law cf. e.g. [24][7].

As an early example [11] presents a normative formalization and fully implemented computational model, using conditional entailment while identifying issues in the argumentation. For rule-based logic frameworks, a full implementation of defeasible logic in Prolog was presented in [20]. However, surveying the

⋆ This paper was written when this author was a visiting student at the Department of Informatics and Media, Uppsala University, Sweden.

[1] The source code of the software and accompanying documentation are available on the web site [splogad.altervista.org].

N. Bassiliades et al. (Eds.): RuleML 2011 - Europe, LNCS 6826, pp. 83–98, 2011.

Table 1. Won and lost dialogues. Source: [10], [9]

	won	lost
pro	$\vdash \kappa$	$\vdash \neg\kappa$
	$\mid\!\sim \kappa \wedge$ opp-rep exhausted	$\not\mid\!\sim \kappa \wedge$ prop-rep exhausted
	some valid move leads to lost for the opponent (at turntaking)	all valid moves lead to won for the opponent (at turntaking)
opp	$\vdash \neg\kappa$	$\vdash \kappa$
	$\mid\!\sim \neg\kappa \wedge$ prop-rep exhausted	$\mid\!\sim \kappa \wedge$ opp-rep exhausted
	some valid move leads to lost for the proponent (at turntaking)	all valid moves lead to won for the proponent (at turntaking)

legal argumentation literature, after [11], the contributions are mostly theoretical studies of extensions to the framework of [8]. Thus, making it less straightforward to incorporate these contributions in the evolution of software in the legal domain.

In this paper we present a full implementation and accompanying software for defeasible adversarial argumentation. Our findings are illustrated by an application of defeasible logic by means of an argumentation framework for legal debate, based on [9]. The argumentation framework is based on a metalogic formalization of adversarial dispute of two debating parties. The argumentation draws on game trees for unraveling the debate.

The paper is outlined as follows: In Section 2 the metalogic argumentation framework of [9] is discussed. In Section 3 we present our defeasible meta-interpreter. In Section 4 the time and space complexity of our approach is analyzed. In Section 5, we present the graphical interface of the system. In Section 6, we touch upon related work, and in Section 7, we conclude.

2 Metalogic and Argumentation

Human argumentation can be seen as dynamic and non-monotonic in its nature. To us this suggests that argumentation and the validity of arguments need to be scrutinized in a dynamical and flexible setting where the interaction is influenced by the parties previous arguments. In addition, while disputing, each party choose to put forward their arguments from separate and private repositories that, until presented by the party itself, remains hidden from the adversary. The metalogic framework for adversarial argumentation analysis is a dynamical, flexible and exhaustive approach to the logical analysis and formalization of argumentation and dispute cf. e.g. [14][9]. It presents a customizable framework and computational system utilizing AI methods for the formal modeling and analysis of argumentation. In its current form, we have in mind situations in which the case circumstances, the applicable background knowledge as well as the parties pleas and argumentation strategies are available, eg. in legal audits concerning the correctness of a litigation, as an alternative approach to dynamic priorities of rules; or if the complete knowledge is yet to be presented, for intermediate analysis of the current standing of a dispute, eg. for assessing the strategic burden of proof discussed in [23]. The model and system is inspired by and adheres to the four layers of legal argumentation proposed by [22]. A distinguishing feature of the framework is the close approximation of the dynamic progression taking place in an adversarial dispute. Hence, focus is placed on the formalization of the interaction between the logical layer of defeasible argumentation and the dynamic progression in the argumentation. Thus, in the model we find a dynamical, exhaustive procedural layer of dialectical disputation, in which the control of the game reasoning mechanism that captures the nondeterministic nature of the argumentation process as a dialectic process is explicitly exercised via the metalogic formalism. A computational dynamical defeasible logic dialectical layer is devised, in which the logical and dialectical layers are handled by a defeasible logic framework that is inspired by [1,12]. Adhering to our key objectives described above, a key difference of our approach is that the parties in general advance their available knowledge stepwise.

The model provides a closer approximation of key aspects of argumentation, as it accommodates that in most non-trivial disputes, the parties lack insight in the future moves of the other player. Hence, each party has the possibility to withhold arguments in order to strengthen its own position. Stated in metalogic the layers are clearly stratified although joined into seamless interaction. This caters for a dynamical and flexible computation of the game, drawing on the strengths of the AI-techniques of game tree analysis.

2.1 Argumentation Games

Consider an adversarial argumentation game as an interaction between two parties, the Proponent and the Opponent. Debating over a topic, the parties take turn in putting forward a subset of these arguments, i.e. move, with the sole purpose of justifying their claim. From these arguments, logical consequences of the claims and the available common knowledge could be deduced. The challenge of the game is to conduct a winning strategy analogous to the elaboration of a winning strategy in a board game like chess.

The game is governed by a protocol for admissible moves and the conditions for winning/losing the game. For this purpose, the analogy to board games have been used when formalizing the termination criteria, i.e. e.g. the notions won and lost cf Table 1. We note that in many cases the game may be expected to come out as a draw. This is the case in situations where the proponent can defend her claim against attack, but cannot justify it by the logical means available, e.g. available evidence, and presented arguments.

The knowledge of the players is separated into private knowledge and public knowledge. Hence, each party has its own private repository of sentences from which they can put forward during the dispute. We are inspired by the defeasible logic of [1,12] in which sentences take form of implication clauses comprising a body of premises and a head. Ordinary strict clauses use the implication symbol

$\rightarrow$, whereas defeasible clauses use $\Rightarrow$. Arguments are generally single rules and multi-steps moves are allowed without a specific order, that means that if a player has got the following rules: $\Rightarrow p$, $\rightarrow p$ and the opponent has the following ones $\Rightarrow s$, $\Rightarrow t$, then both players can choose which rules to put forward from their private repository. In order to prevent the party from repeating itself, and thus, to prevent the argumentation game from reducing to a blackboard trivialization, when a party makes a move, the rules have to be retracted from the private knowledge base. The arguments put forward are required to be consistent in the sense that a party cannot contradict herself. The outcome of a dispute is not to depend only on the arguments available, but also on the strategy played by the party. Hence, a special clause 'resting' is used to express that the party is refraining from putting forward additional arguments.

The public knowledge forms the common set of arguments in the form of propositional statements in a defeasible logic. A distinction is made between strict rules, expressing indisputable assertions and the defeasible rules representing beliefs that can be overruled by additional information. The model allows for reasoning on the strength of different rules of the same type. The public knowledge and propositions that form the object language clauses are encoded as terms in metalogic.

A certain state in the argumentation game is like a state in the board game. Initially this public knowledge base is like the initial situation of a board game like chess. The computational analysis of the argumentation game then proceeds in analogy to the analysis of game trees for board games having been studied extensively in artificial intelligence, cf. *e.g.*, [18]. During the argumentation, the knowledge base is extended with the arguments put forward by the parties. For a comprehensive presentation of the intuitions constraining the arguments to be presented during the dispute cf. [9].

2.2 A Sample Legal Case in Defeasible Logic

Let us consider a simplified legal dispute concerned with prescriptive rights[2].

A prescriptive right is a legal right principle dating back to Roman law, enabling the obtaining of ownership by sustained use or possession of land or physical objects. However, legal ownership is not granted if the possessor has obtained or received permission or has engaged in a contract with the legal owner. As a main rule, the possession must have lasted without interruption at least for twenty years, possibly through a succession of possessors.

In the common knowledge base we find the following clauses:

$possession \Rightarrow ownership$
$possession \wedge permission \rightarrow \neg ownership$
$permission \rightarrow possession$

The first two clauses formalize the principle of prescriptive right. The third clause expresses that granting of an unrequested permission implies that possession has taken place.

[2] The example was introduced in [14].

We set up a particular argumentation game by specifying repositories of the two parties and a key claim.

Repository of the Proponent: $\Rightarrow possession$

The keyclaim κ of the proponent is *ownership*. The clause $\Rightarrow possession$ denotes that the proponent claims that possession has taken place.

Repository of the Opponent: $\Rightarrow \neg possession$ $\quad \rightarrow permission$

The opponent has the option of claiming that possession has not taken place. On the other hand, she has also at her disposal the second clause enabling her to disclose a permission, meant here as evidence which is not to be disputed.

For this simple example the argumentation game tree unfolds as follows:

The proponent initiates the argumentation by uttering her sole clause. Then the opponent can choose between the two clauses available in her repository. If the opponent utters the first clause the dispute becomes a draw, because the question of possession remains unsettled and hence, ownership is not established. Neither the key claim nor the negation of the key claim is justified. However, the opponent may choose another move, namely putting forward evidence of a permission being granted. In this case the negation of the key claim is justified in the defeasible logic and the game is then won by the opponent, in spite of possession being acknowledged.

The upshot of this argumentation game analysis is that the opponent, by playing her second choice, can win the argumentation despite that the proponent's claim remains undisputed. Hence, we note that the outcome of this particular dispute depends not only on the arguments available, but also on the strategy played by the party.

2.3 Metalogic Program Formalization

In the argumentation game exploration, we determine the state of the game by the current state (S). (S) consists of the common knowledge base and the two repositories. Extending the termination criteria from Table 1 to all argumentation states, an argumentation state is said to be *won* if there exists a move to a subsequent state that is lost for the other party. An argumentation state is *lost* if all admissible moves leading to a subsequent state are won by the other party.

Appealing to negation as failure for the definition of mutually recursive clauses for the non-terminal states of won and lost (using existential and universal quantification alternately), we may obtain the game tree explorer with the Prolog clauses:

$$won(S) \leftarrow move(S, S') \wedge lost(S')$$
$$lost(S) \leftarrow \; not \; defensible(S)$$
$$defensible(S) \leftarrow move(S, S') \wedge \; not \; won(S')$$

where *defensible* is an auxiliary predicate.

We implement *move* as the argumentation state transition from state S to the subsequent state S' by means of a selected proposition according to appropriate contextual and termination criteria for the argumentation.

As the dynamical defeasible logic dialectical layer is clearly separated from the elaboration at the formal metalevel, an easy replacement of the defeasible logic can be achieved. In fact, in [9] both an ambiguity propagating defeasible logic prover and an ambiguity blocking defeasible logic prover, inspired by [12], are realized in metalogic programming. Due to space limitations, the interested reader is conferred to [9] for the full formalization.

The argumentation game tree explorer is to appeal to the defeasible logic prover with a termination criterion to check whether the key claim or its denial hold, *i.e.* whether the keyclaim or its denial has become irrefutably defeasible in the current argumentation state. The game tree explorer is invoked with the initial state comprising the common knowledge resource and the two repositories.

Given the above presented, the advantage of a logic formalization of argumentation becomes visible. The logic formalization provides a symbolic knowledge representation while preserving a comprehensible behavior of the devised knowledge representation systems reasoning. The non-monotonic nature of the defeasible logic layer accommodates the representational issues, and the metalogic program establishes the sound computation and how to interpret the semantics of the computation.

3 Implementation: A Dynamical Meta-Interpreter for DL

We now turn our interest from the metalogic characterization to the implementation issues of a software directed towards the addressed domain; computational aid for the advancement and scrutinizing of legal argumentation.

Using Prolog (Sictus 1.4) we developed an implementation of a non-ground defeasible meta-interpreter. Prolog fits well with our approach as it uses the same data structures to represent programs as well as data. In addition, the non-monotonic nature of the defeasible logic is facilitated by Prolog as it allows for easy knowledge base update and new goal evaluations.

As stated in the previously presented Section 2.1, we emphasize a clear stratified architecture. It caters for the modularity and scalability of our implementation. Given an object language (a defeasible theory expressed as Prolog-clauses), its evaluation is performed by our defeasible meta-interpreter. As described above, the assessment is conducted at a meta-level able to reason on the object-level language. Thus, our first issue is to implement the defeasible logic dialectic layer (extending the expressivity to include defeasible arguments and defeasible derivability), and, second we have to find a representative and computationally efficient way to implement the argumentation game model with its metalogic representation encoding of variables, constants and the other terms of our defeasible logic theory (a type-free language) as terms in our meta-language.

3.1 Implementation: The Dynamical Defeasible Logic Prover

Our point of departure was the Prolog-defeasible logic implementation presented by [20]. A key difference in our approach is that we aim to handle human argumentation in general and legal dispute in particular, and thus need to be able to handle conflicting superiority relations that requires meta-superiority relations to be resolved. Due to the structure of legal rules and exceptions to such, these are quite common in the legal domain cf. the Italian Villa example discussed by [22]. In the example this is illustrated by that if a building needs restructuring then its exterior can be modified. However, there also exists an earlier rule saying that if a building is a protected building because of archeological or historical values, then it cannot be modified. Those rules clearly conflict, and cannot be straightforwardly handled by a single level superiority relation.

Basic features
Strict rules are represented by the " $: -/2''$ operator in Prolog:
`flies(X):- bird(X).`
In order to extend the Prolog engine to handling defeasible reasoning, we defined a new kind of rules (defeasible rules). As common in the literature, the defeasible rules are represented by the " $:= /2''$ operator, as follows:
`flies(X) := bird(X).`

In our defeasible logic prover, besides from negation as failure, classical negation is implemented to cater for the non-monotonic and dynamical behavior of possibly incompatible defeasible arguments. We represent classical negation, i.e. when something is not the case, by the operator $neg/1$. In contrast to negation as failure in use in a traditional Prolog clause, this operator allows us to put the negation at the head of a clause.
`neg flies(X) :- house(X).`
Although the argumentation game assessment is governed by the argumentation game model interpreter, i.e. the dynamical procedural layer of the application, the dynamical defeasible logic prover can evaluate the following basic features of a theory that we put forward:

Derivability[3]**.** Given a rule the system tries to derive it using the rules in the knowledge bases. The derivation can be:

- **Strict:** The system tries to evaluate a goal by only using strict rules.
- **Defeasible:** The system derives a goal using both strict rules and defeasible rules.

Attackability. With attackability the system addresses potential conflicts between defeasible rules in the knowledge base:

- **Rebutting attacks** in which a new conclusion is proposed in opposition to an existing rule, and
- **Undercutting attacks** in which the conclusion is blocked.

We could fit our defeasible logic prover as an integration of [19] and [17] as it is able to execute both ambiguity propagation and ambiguity blocking (cf. [4]). In our system we can perform either ambiguity propagation or ambiguity blocking by changing the criteria for the evaluation. This impacts the assessment

[3] It should be noted that in this evaluation we don't distinguish between derivable rules and supportive rules as in [3]. Our system finds all supportive rules for a given goal automatically, as it investigates both the conclusions and the conclusions of the supportive rules in the body of the clause.

of attackability. If a defeasible rule (that is defeasibly derivable) is attacked by another defeasibly derivable rule we implemented two different behaviors: For ambiguity propagation we say that a rule R is rebutted by a rule R' iff both rules are derivable and there exists a superiority relation in favor of R'; otherwise for ambiguity blocking, we say a rule R is rebutted by a rule R' iff both rules are derivable and there do not exist a superiority relation in favor of R.

This implementation provides a more general definition of ambiguities more suitable for programming logic due to its scalability and as it better represents the state of each nested derivability predicates invocation.

Decision Criteria

In order to properly address the complexities of human argumentation in general and legal dispute in particular, one important class of rules that is needed to solve potential conflicts of arguments is *decision criteria.* Hence, the defeasible logic prover is augmented by features such as defeasible incompatibility rules, defeasible superiority relations, multiple superiority relations evaluation, and a loop detector equipped to handle inconsistent superiority relations.

- **Incompatibility:** An incompatible rule can be considered as a *special* undercutting criterion. We say that two rules R and R' are incompatible if R and R' are defeasible rules, which both are derivable, and there exists a rule $incompatible(R, R)$. In other words, it means that the system cannot reach a conclusion since *R'* conflicts with *R*.

  An alternative approach is to define priorities between rules.
- **Superiority relations:** we say that a rule *R* is *superior* to another rule, say, *R'* if there exists a strict superiority rule arguing that:
  1. there exists a strict superiority rule arguing that and its body is derivable.
  2. there exists a superiority rule in favor of *R* and there are no derivable superiority rules in favor of *R'*;
  3. there is a superiority rule *sup_rule1* in favor of *R* and there is a superiority rule *sup_rule2* in favor of *R'*, but those rules are included in a third superiority relation that argues that *sup_rule1* is superior to *sup_rule2.*

  The superiority relation is expressed by a *sup*/2 predicate stating that in case of conflict, the former argument is superior to the latter.

  For the special case of superiority we find specificity cf. [25][6] as an additional criterion for choosing between two conflicting rules.
- **Specificity:** In our implementation the *Specificity* predicate belongs to superiority relation one. If the above criteria fail, we check if the condition of *R* is more specific than the condition of *R'*, i.e. if the body of *R'* is derivable using the body of *R* and the contrary does not hold.

Rejecting criterion: when we add information to our knowledge base (in the form of rules), we introduce a consistency check. If the newly introduced rule is the negation of a rule that already belongs to our common knowledge base then the rule is to be rejected. This criterion is valid for the introduction of both new *strict* as well as new *defeasible* rules.

The criteria presented above emphasize the flexibility of the implementation as its complex behavior is the result of mutual and multiple invocation of the various predicates. In addition, inspired by [20] the defeasible logic prover provides additional tools able to investigate the reasons of a given derivation failure/success.

3.2 Implementation: The Dynamical Game Model Interpreter

Our second objective was to find a representative and computationally efficient way to implement the dynamic exhaustive metalayer. For this purpose, a non-ground representation, a Vanilla-like meta-interpreter, was chosen as the point of departure[4].

The Vanilla-interpreter is well equipped to handle propositional defeasible logic as quantifier problems are not to arise. In addition, it requires less resources to hold the terms of the object language, and it is straightforward to implement, as the object-language variables are encoded as meta-language variables, instead of constants as in a ground representation. The idea is to represent the whole object-language in the meta-level in order to manipulate and execute the object-level predicates without translation. Thus, the otherwise needed, rather complicated definitions for the built-in logical predicate about unification, renaming, et c are superfluous.

We present an implementation of the dynamical exhaustive procedural layer of dialectical disputation in which the control of the game reasoning mechanism captures the nondeterministic nature of an adversarial argumentation dispute as discussed in Section 2. It should be noted that for the evaluation we can assume different protocols for the argumentation game analysis. The implemented protocol is based on [9](Chapter 10) regarding the definition of the two fundamental predicates *won* and *lost*. In the following we present the argumentation game implementation for the 'won_proponent' characterization, cf. Figure 1.

We implement the argumentation game as an AND/OR-graph. Hence, the tree structure is built starting from the root. Recursively it traverses down to the leaf nodes acquiring the generated data.

In an ambiguity propagating setting, given the characterization presented in the table, we will see some complexity issues arising due to a possible double deliberation for the *lost* predicate. Indeed we need to implement two different alternatives of the *lost* predicate. For this purpose, in the implementation both of the two following different approaches are considered:

1. We allow for an asymmetrical interpretation of the *lost* predicate and accept the increased complexity resulting from a double evaluation.
2. We only use the interpretation of an explicit negation of the keyclaim and switch to a skeptical semantics in order to avoid that both the keyclaim and its negation could be true.

As the game involves two players, we distinguish among each player's private repository of information and a public knowledge called CKB. Indeed, when one

[4] Differences between ground and non-ground meta-interpreter are discussed by [15], who elaborates on the advantages and disadvantages of each approach respectively.

```
won(pro,CKB, ProKB, OppKB,Tree,NewTree):-
  keyclaim(Keyclaim),
  assertall(CKB),
  strict_der(KB, Keyclaim),
  nl,write('Proponent won...strict!'),nl,
  append(Tree,[[ 'Proponent won',♯, []]],NewTree),
  unassertall(CKB),!.

won(pro,CKB, ProKB, OppKB, Tree, NewTree):-
  isEmpty(OppKB),
  keyclaim(Keyclaim),
  assertall(CKB),
  def_der(KB, Keyclaim),
  append(Tree,[['Proponent won',♯, []]],NewTree),
  unassertall(CKB),!,
  nl,write('The keyclaim is defeasible
  and the opponent repository is exhausted!').

  won(pro,CKB,_,_,_,_) :-
  unassertall(CKB),fail.
  won(pro,CKB,ProKB,OppKB,Tree,NewTree):-
   orand,
   countPlayer(ProKB,ProItem),
   findall([X,'♯',NewTreeLost],
  (
   member(X,ProKB),
  move(X,CKB),
  append(CKB,[X],NewCKB),
  delete(X, ProKB, NewProKB),
  nl,write('Calling 'lost(opp)' and adding: '),
  write(X),
  lost(opp,NewCKB,NewProKB,OppKB,Tree,
  NewTreeLost),
  List),
  )
  append(Tree,List,NewTree),nl,
  countPlayer(List,N),
  N == ProItem.

won(pro,CKB,ProKB,OppKB,Tree,NewTree):-
  \+ orand,
  countPlayer(ProKB,ProItem),
  findall([X,'♯',NewTreeLost],
  (
  member(X,ProKB),
  move(X,CKB),
  append(CKB,[X],NewCKB),
  delete(X, ProKB, NewProKB),
  nl,write('Calling "lost(opp)" and adding: '),
  write(X),
  lost(opp,NewCKB,NewProKB,OppKB,Tree,
  NewTreeLost),
  List),
  )
  append(Tree,List,NewTree),
  countPlayer(List,N),
  List ≡ [].
```

Fig. 1. Implementation for the 'won_proponent' characterization

of the players puts forward a new rule, the system will have to remember which of the players moved and in which node the player made its move, thus, each branch represents a unique evolution of the keyclaim evaluation.

Each node represents a new state characterized by a new rule being put forward by one of the parties, we have a node for each move, and for each branch that rule is put forward in different levels. As, our meta-interpreter is based on a non-monotonic logic, it means that by evaluating the derivability of the keyclaim in different nodes, the evaluation of the keyclaim could change. Hence, in each node of the particular argumentation game tree we should evaluate the keyclaim asserting a related set of rules that are valid for that particular node. The root is the keyclaim, and its children are all the possible moves that the adversary can put forward. It ensures the exhaustiveness of our approach cf. Section 2. If there exists (OR) at least one branch in which the proponent wins in the subsequent step for each (AND) of her/his moves, the debate is won by the proponent, and vice versa. Actually, the game trees that we have to explore are two, the first one tries to derive a victory for the proponent, the second tree tries to establish a victory of the opponent.

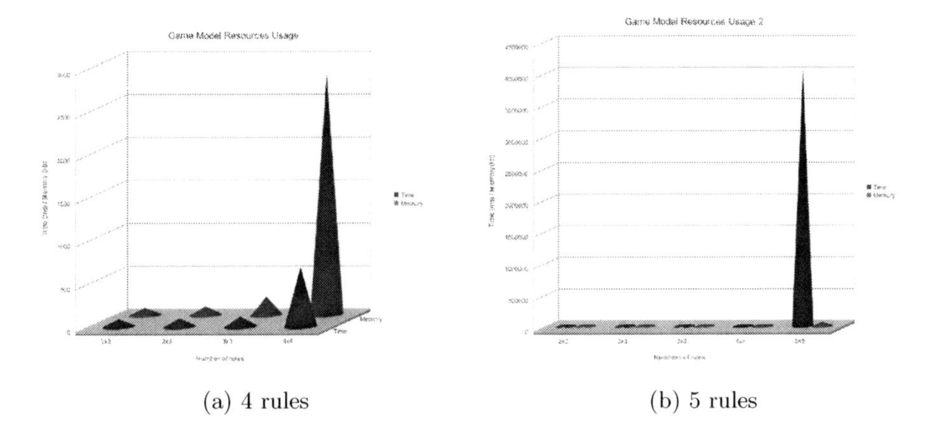

(a) 4 rules

(b) 5 rules

Fig. 2. Resources Usage

4 Complexity

In this section we discuss some performance tests of our system and we propose some coding improvements in order to enable a better performance. Our assessment provides information about the time (measured in ms) to finish an argumentation game and the total amount of memory used during the task execution. We tested the application adding some theories with a growing number of rules, on a Centrino 2 T2300@1.66Ghz, 1Gb Ram, kernel Linux 2.6.32.22-generic. Initially, we were not able to get a result (except for trivial examples) due to the stack limitation blocking our application. The system slowed down and arrived at a deadlock. On the Linux OS, this problem was easily solved as we are able to switch the stack limitation to unlimited performance.

In a simple challenge between two parties whose private KB contains not more than 5 rules for each one, the system spent 1h11min. to reach a conclusion, and it required more than 70mb. In Figure 2 we show the complexity results.

In the lefthand chart of Figure 2 we notice in a four times four rule example that we get excessive usage of memory, although the time for the evaluation is approximately 2.5 seconds. It is not a great result, but considering that the application is not yet optimized it may be acceptable. Unfortunately, the resource usage explodes just by adding one more rule for each party. In the righthand chart of Figure 2 we can see that the time needed for a five times five rule evaluation is 4.079.490 ms (approx. 1h and 8 minutes), and the task requires more than 69MB of memory. This result is cumbersome as a non-trivial theory should contain a large number of possible rules to put forward, cf. e.g. [16,13].

4.1 Complexity Analysis

This problem is due to the fact that the argumentation game tree is built starting from the root recursing to the leaf nodes while requiring the generated data via backwards reasoning. Given the exhaustiveness of this approach, it means that in a particular node, after won/lost predicate invocation, Prolog cannot remove the invoking predicate from the stack as it must remain open and wait until the sub-tree explorations are completed. Since each node represents the addition of a new rule by one of the parties, we have a node for each move, and all branches are permutations of a branch in which all the rules are inserted.

To better understand the causes of this huge increase of time and memory we measure the complexity of the system:

State Space Complexity: Given k and q, where k is number of rules of the proponent and q opponent number of rules, the number of total nodes would be the following succession:$nodenumber = 1 + k + k * q + k * q * (k - 1) + ... + k * q * (k - 1) * (q - 1) * (k - 2) * (q - 2) + ...$that could be expressed with a recursive function. We can round down this number only by using depth and branch factors. In this case we use a depth (d) of k+q (in the worst case) and a branching factor (b) that is the average among k, q which renders the complexity to approximately $O(b^d)$;

Game Tree Size: The game tree size represents the number of conclusions that we can reach, i.e. the number of child nodes of our tree, namely, $k! * q!$;

Game Tree Complexity: The complexity of the game tree represents the minimum number of leaves that we have to explore. It coincides with the total number of leaves, $k! * q!$;

Computational Complexity: The computational complexity depends on the number of input arguments, hence, we can see that the number of items increases factorially. Furthermore, for each node instance we would create a data structure containing three different lists (Common KB and two private KB). It should be noted that in a 5X5 rules dispute we would have 14400 leaf nodes, each containing a different data structure whose size is between 1Kb-3Kb (in our simple examples). It means that just for the children nodes we would need approx. 50MB of memory. It is easy to demonstrate that this problem is an ***ExpTime*** problem. Also in terms of memory we have an exponential complexity for task execution.

4.2 Complexity Reduction

In this section we suggest some possible code optimizations by means of parallelism and recursion optimization. As stated in the previous Section 3.2, our bottleneck is caused by the mutual and multiple recursion. In other words, that in a given node, after won/lost predicate invocation, Prolog cannot remove the invoking predicate from the stack and it must remain open and wait till the end of the generated sub-tree explorations.

Taking a look on the code, we notice that in our implementation, the *find-all* predicate causes two separate problems: First, even in the case that it is invoked by the last rule in the clause, the execution of the *find-all* predicate requires multiple invocation of the same predicate and thus, leaves us with the situation that tail recursion can only be partially implemented. Secondly, the *find-all* predicate cannot be the last rule to be executed, because after an execution of the *find-all* predicate we need to evaluate whether the won/lost predicate is verified for all child nodes of the argumentation game tree. Hence, a possible solution is to re-design our algorithm to prevent that the recursion fills the stack, or at least prevent the excessive usage of the processor during execution. To fix this we can *completely change our recursive approach* and edit our algorithm regarding the forward tree building, the *find-all* parallelism or by delaying the AND/OR check.

Forward Tree Building

Forward-tree building concerns one of the heaviest recursive issues, namely, that before completing its result a parent node has to wait until all the children sub-executions have completed the building of their respective sub-lists. To perform this task the processor slows down due to the extensive memory usage. Thus, it would be a better solution if each parent node sent its "up-list" to its child nodes. This also goes for the case that the tail-recursion cannot completely close the parent predicate. In this way we can save memory as the allocation decreases.

Find-All *Parallelism*

The time needed for a complete execution of a last invocation, of the *find-all* predicate is a thorny problem as multiple recursion is not easily prevented. In our implementation, however, the nested execution of the *find-all* arguments is completely independent. It means that we can execute its argument in parallel by exploiting the Muse framework, provided by SicstusProlog[5], and thereby improve our performance. In the literature, there are some examples that report a speed up to about 3.8. In our example argumentation game of 5X5 rules, it means that we could reduce the time from 1h8min. to 17min. It is a promising result, but we still have to remember that in our case the time increases exponentially and the 5X5 rule example is just an elementary example. Nevertheless, by a combination of all the changes we may achieve an even better result.

Delaying the AND/OR Check

Finally, we said that the *find-all* predicate cannot be the last rule as we need to check whether at least for one branch (OR) the proponent wins and for all branches (AND) whether the opponent loses. In the implementation all the child nodes, before completion, create tracks of their list.The list is forwarded in a data structure, and thus, we are able to build the argumentation tree in a bottom-up fashion.

Furthermore, there are more solutions such as a *complete rewriting of the code* in a strongly typed language. In particular we suggest Erlang, which has been invented in order to improve recursion performance and thanks to this provides efficient implementations of concurrent programming.

5 Ubongo

The graphical interface Ubongo consists of the following components: *The Application Engine*: The core of the application that has the job to manage the

[5] This framework asserts a new predicate "muse_flag(num_workers,_, <number_of_workers>)" while leaving the Prolog syntax unchanged.

other components; *The Prolog Parser*: An extended Prolog parser that accepts also defeasible rules and initialization rules in order to configure the challenge; *The TreeViewer*: A simple viewer that draws the derivation tree; *The Defeasible Meta-Interpreter.*

Ubongo has been developed using Java(TM) SE Runtime Environment (*build* $1.6.0_{2}0 - b02$),, eclipse Galileo and javacc 5.0. The application is the graphical interface front-end that provides some examples by default. It takes the theory from the text viewer and sends it to the parser that is responsible for evaluating the syntax. It is a Prolog parser built over YProlog. The parser has been modified to also be able to handle evaluation of defeaters, defeasible rules and initialization rules, which are used to instigate the initialization of a game. The following rules are available:

- rule(key, <keyclaim>) : the rule that we have to use in order to put forward the keyclaim;
- rule(pro, <rule>) : <rule> is a rule that belongs to the private knowledge base of the Proponent;
- rule(opp, <rule>) : <rule> is a rule that belongs to the private knowledge base of the Opponent;
- rule(ambiguity_blocking, <on/off>) : enables or disables the ambiguity propagation;
- rule(defeasible_priority, <on/off>) : enables or disables defeasible priority;
- rule(orandTree, <on/off>) : enables or disables the AND/OR tree derivation;
- rule(metaSupRel, <on/off>) : enables or disables the meta superiority relation level, it controls possible paradoxes that are put forward in the common knowledge base CKB;
- rule(mess, <rule>) : is a rule that we can use to add a message rule as for example write('<text-to-write>');

It should be noted that in this way Ubongo facilitates writing a theory and its subsequent execution. The application uses an instance of pParser to check whether the theory is correctly written. When a correct theory is introduced, and the execution button is clicked (after the parser evaluation) Ubongo tries to access a script and execute Maggie from java. Maggie loads the theory and provides the assessment. This task is performed by opening a command editor (shell in Linux) whose stack size is increased to unlimited value. The external usage of Maggie allow us to simply add a folder in the root directory of Ubongo, providing us with a completely modular scenario. This facilitates the easy replacement of the meta-interpreter version, i.e. by just changing the folder, you are able to choose between the latest beta-release, Maggie 0.7 or a customized version of the system. Actually, there is no direct invocation from java to Prolog, since our aim is to leave this application non Sicstus-dependent, so by changing the path of the Prolog engine a new script for Prolog invocation will be built and executed. The result is presented as a tree built by gTreeViewer.

6 Related Work

The first defeasible meta interpreter was presented in [20] and based on the formalism (LDR1 in [19]) in which competition was among Prolog rules. This implementation provided both ambiguity blocking and ambiguity propagation and a first attempt to define superiority relations. Nevertheless, this metainterpreter was not able to solve most of the common problems in literature because some limitations such as only one level of superiority relations and non-defeasible incompatibility relations. The implementations accounted for in domains such as robotics [5] and the semantic web [2] are all inspired by the defeasible meta interpreter by [20] and draws on Nutes' defeasible logic. They implemented a formalism able to cope with problems such as team defeat, prove disjunction and failure by loop. A main difference to our approach is that the authors focus on drawing conclusions from a given theory, while in our case the resulting mechanism addresses sequences of defeasible (meta) theories, and uses meta-reasoning (meta-rules or high level rules) to assess the acceptability and priorities of rules for the theories at lower levels. Our goal was to provide a full Nute metainterpreter evolution for such adversarial argumentation games, in order to solve problems such as the Roman Villa example described by [21] which we find arises in human language domains in general and the legal field in particular.

7 Conclusion and Future Work

We have presented a full implementation and accompanying software for defeasible adversarial argumentation as an approach to expressing close approximations of human reasoning as computational formalizations of argument. Hence, we dealt with knowledge representations, non-monotonic logics and a game-model that make possible building a human reasoning simulator able to contend a legal debate between two parties. We proposed a meta-interpreter that provides some features proposed in the literature over the years eg. defeasible superiority relations. In addition, we propose some approaches in order to reduce the argumentation game-model complexity. We noticed that the performance of our dynamical meta interpreter is quite satisfactory as it is able to solve most of the problems presented in the literature. We go forth with a deep theoretical analysis to shed light on the intrinsical complexity of the system.

References

1. Antoniou, G., Billington, D., Governatori, G., Maher, M.J.: A flexible framework for defeasible logics. In: 17th American National Conference on Artificial Intelligence, AAAI 2000 (2000)
2. Antoniou, G., Billington, D., Governatori, G., Maher, M.J., Rock, A.: A family of defeasible reasoning logics and its implementation. In: Proc. of the 14th European Conference on Artificial Intelligence, pp. 459–463. IOS Press, Amsterdam (2000)
3. Antoniou, G., Bikakis, A.: Dr-prolog: A system for defeasible reasoning with rules and ontologies on the semantic web. IEEE Trans. on Knowl. and Data Eng. 19, 233–245 (2007)
4. Billington, D.: The proof algorithms of plausible logic form a hierarchy. In: Zhang, S., Jarvis, R.A. (eds.) AI 2005. LNCS (LNAI), vol. 3809, pp. 796–799. Springer, Heidelberg (2005)
5. Billington, D., Estivill-Castro, V., Hexel, R., Rock, A.: Using temporal consistency to improve robot localisation. In: Lakemeyer, G., Sklar, E., Sorrenti, D.G., Takahashi, T. (eds.) RoboCup 2006: Robot Soccer World Cup X. LNCS (LNAI), vol. 4434, pp. 232–244. Springer, Heidelberg (2007)

6. Brewka, G.: A reconstruction of rescher's theory of formal disputation based on default logic. In: Proceedings of the 11th European Conference on Artificial Intelligence, pp. 336–370 (1994)
7. Chesñevar, C.I., Maguitman, A.G., Loui, R.P.: Logical models of argument. ACM Computing Surveys, 32(4) (2000)
8. Dung, P.M.: On the acceptability of arguments and its fundamental role in nonmonotonic reasoning and logic programming and n-person game. Artificial Intelligence 77, 321–357 (1995)
9. Eriksson Lundström, J.: On the Formal Modeling of Games of Language and Adversarial Argumentation - A Logic-Based Artificial Intelligence Approach (2009)
10. Eriksson Lundström, J., Hamfelt, A., Fischer Nilsson, J.: A common framework for board games and argumentation games. In: EJC 2008. IOS Press, Amsterdam (2008)
11. Gordon, T.: The Pleadings Game: An artificial intelligence model of procedural justice. Journal of Artificial Intelligence and Law, 2(4) (1993)
12. Governatori, G., Antoniou, G., Billington, D., Maher, M.J.: Argumentation semantics for defeasible logics. Journal of Logic and Computation 14(5) (2004)
13. Grosof, B.N.: Representing e-commerce rules via situated courteous logic programs in ruleml. Electronic Commerce Research and Applications 3(1), 2–20 (2004)
14. Hamfelt, A., Eriksson Lundström, J., Nilsson, J.F.: A metalogic formalization of legal argumentation as game trees with defeasible reasoning. In: ICAIL 2005, Int. Conference on AI and Law, Bologna, Italy, pp. 250–251 (2005)
15. Hill, P.M., Lloyd, J.W.: Analysis of Meta-Programs. In: Abramson, H., Rogers, M.H. (eds.) Meta-Programming in Logic Programming. MIT Press, Cambridge (1989)
16. Maher, M.J., Rock, A., Antoniou, G., Billington, D., Miller, T.: Efficient defeasible reasoning systems. International Journal on Artificial Intelligence Tools 10(4), 483–501 (2001)
17. Nute, D., Maier, F.: Ambiguity propagating defeasible logic and the well-founded semantics. In: Fisher, M., van der Hoek, W., Konev, B., Lisitsa, A. (eds.) JELIA 2006. LNCS (LNAI), vol. 4160, pp. 306–318. Springer, Heidelberg (2006)
18. Nilsson, N.J.: Artificial Intelligence: A New Synthesis. Morgan Kaufmann, California (1998)
19. Nute, D.: Defeasible logic. In: Handbook of Logic in Artificial Intelligence and Logic Programming, vol. 3, pp. 353–395. Oxford University Press, Oxford (1994)
20. Nute, D., Covington, M.A., Vellino, A.: Prolog Programming in Depth. Scott Foresman and Co., Chicago (1998)
21. Prakken, H., Sartor, G.: Presumptions and burdens of proof. In: Jurix 2006, pp. 21–30. IOS Press, Amsterdam (1996)
22. Prakken, H., Sartor, G.: Modelling reasoning with precedents in a formal dialogue game. AI and Law 2(4), 231–287 (1998)
23. Prakken, H., Sartor, G.: Formalising arguments about the burden of persuation. In: ICAIL 2007, pp. 97–106. ACM Press, New York (2007)
24. Prakken, H., Vreeswijk, G.: Logical systems for defeasible argumentation. In: Gabbay, D.M. (ed.) Handbook of Philosophical Logic, pp. 219–318 (2002)
25. Reiter, R.: A logic for default reasoning. AI 13(1), 81–132 (1980)

Integrating Written Policies in Business Rule Management Systems*

Adeline Nazarenko, Abdoulaye Guissé, François Lévy,
Nouha Omrane, and Sylvie Szulman

LIPN, Université Paris 13 & CNRS (UMR 7030), France

Abstract. Knowledge acquisition is a key issue in the business rule methodology. As Natural Language (NL) policies and regulations are often important or even contractual sources of knowledge, we propose a framework for acquisition and maintenance of business rules based on NL texts. It enables business experts to author the specification of rule applications without the help of knowledge engineers. This framework has been created as part of the ONTORULE project, which is defining an integrated platform for acquisition, maintenance and execution of business-oriented knowledge bases combining ontologies and rules.

Our framework relies on a data structure, called "index", encompassing and connecting the source text, the ontology and a textual representation of rules. Textual rules are as close to the Structured English representation of SBVR as possible for business users in charge of rule elicitation. The index relies on W3C technologies, which makes the tools interoperable and enable semantic search. We show that such an index structure supports the parallel maintenance of policy documents and knowledge bases (acquisition, consistency check and update).

Two detailed examples with preliminary results are provided, one from air travel and the other from the automotive industry.

1 Introduction

Even if rule-based applications rely on powerful rule engines, several challenges must still be met to ensure their development. From this perspective, the ONTORULE project has set three main objectives: 1) provide methodology and software tools that use open standards, especially SBVR, PRR, RIF and OWL; 2) enable specification of these applications at the business modeling level rather than in terms of information systems data models, as typically happens in current practice, and in the form of "business rules models" composed a business vocabulary and of business rules based on that vocabulary; 3) support business users in owning and driving the specifications, by defining and owning the ontologies and rules on which the specifications are based.

* This work was realised as part of the FP7 231875 ONTORULE project (http://ontorule-project.eu). We thank to our partners for the fruitful discussions, especially to John Hall (Model Systems) for introducing us to the SBVR world and to Audi for the collaboration on their use case. We are also grateful to American Airline who is the owner of one of our working corpora.

N. Bassiliades et al. (Eds.): RuleML 2011 - Europe, LNCS 6826, pp. 99–113, 2011.

In this perspective, acquisition remains a knowledge engineering bottleneck. This paper describes a text-based approach for acquisition of business rule models (BR models) to be exploited by BRMS. It combines automated natural language processing (NLP) and tactical human intervention to develop models that: 1) are compliant with the policies given in the documents, 2) take the form of ontologies and rule models that serve as the basis for specification of information systems, and 3) are expressed using business vocabulary, *i.e.* in the terms that business expert use so that they are able to author, validate and maintain them without having to rely on IT people.

Our approach is part of the platform developed in ONTORULE which is designed for the acquisition, authoring, maintenance and execution of BR models. The methodology focuses on the first part of the acquisition process, namely the knowledge elicitation, that must be driven and controlled by business people. The resulting model might be semi-formal but it is intended to be a comprehensive and explicit specification that can be passed on to knowledge engineers for further formalization and transformation into an executable model.

Another originality of this text-based approach is in the assumption that BR models are designed from documents but cannot be directly extracted from them. We argue that NLP can help, not by translating policy documents into business rules automatically, but by supporting the modelling activity and indexing the source documents with respect to the resulting knowledge base. The result is a "documented business rule model", which index structure is a critical resource for acquiring the BR models, for consistency maintenance, for the traceability of decisions and to bring models up to date when regulations change.

Within ONTORULE, our acquisition and index-based approach has been tested on two use cases for which two real BR models and rule applications had to be defined, exploiting available sources of information. The *AAdvantage use case* aims at developing a classification application that determines the benefits that an airline customer retention program member has earned over a given period. In the *Audi use case*, a rule application is being defined to certify the conformance of Audi procedures with vehicle safety international regulations.

Section 2 presents the state of the art. Section 3 describes the index structure that underlies our approach. The following section shows how the acquisition methodology and tools enable a business expert to build a BR model and to index the source documents with respect to it. The knowledge bases and index structures built for the use cases are presented in Section 5. The last section illustrates how such an index structure can be exploited for the joint management of BR models and policy documents.

2 Related Works

2.1 Business Modelling

Some attempts have been made to exploit NLP tools in order to parse written policies and transform them into formal statements.

A first approach takes as input the statements written by business experts during the modelling process. It is embodied for instance in Oracle Policy Modeling[1] suite, which may feed eligibility applications with the executable business rules resulting from the parsing of the rules written in NL. However the input is controlled rather than natural language: one simple sentence per line and with explicit 'and', 'or', 'if ... then' relations. The IBM SPARCLE policy workbench [4] also offers entering of policies in NL and generation of a machine readable version of the policy. It had encouraging results for usability but the input must be written according to strict templates allowing its automatic translation. Similarly, semantic wikis are now proposed for collaborative ontology management in controlled languages, such as Attempto Controlled English, and as knowledge engineering environments [8,3]. In all these cases, however, acquisition does not start from existing plain NL documents as regulations or policies often are.

A second approach takes as input texts which have not been written on purpose for rule modelling, such as [6] which aims at checking conformance of organisational procedures to regulations. It consists of parsing the source regulation and representing it as a set of Abstract Syntax Trees that a knowledge engineer then edits and transforms into logical CTL formulae[2]. ASTs thus provide an intermediary structure between text and rules, but the operations transforming ASTs into formulas are not described.

No approach handles the complete automated translation of NL texts into exploitable models. Such a process actually involves complex transformations that business rules practitioners are accustomed to make but which depend on the target application and use case as well as on the rule executable language and technology. Business rules are not fully explicit in documents and human interpretation is involved in their modelling, even when relying on regulations.

The importance of human conceptualisation has been long recognised in the domain of ontology acquisition. Although attempts have been made for automatically "learning" ontologies from texts [5], most approaches integrate human control in the conceptualisation process, either by incorporating human validation in an iterative classification process [7] or by revising an automatically built ontology [12]. The terminological approach, as it is for instance embodied in TERMINAE [2], relies on NLP tools for extracting textual clues but also on the strong belief that those textual elements and conceptual ones differ in nature and that the latter ones cannot be automatically derived from the former ones.

Beyond acquisition, the Object Management Group has developed the standard Semantics of Business Vocabulary and Business Rules (SBVR)[3] for documenting the semantics of business vocabularies, fact types, and rules. SBVR supports the role of human expertise in business model acquisition and management and encourages making models understandable by business people. It defines business models as a combination of a conceptual vocabulary used by the target business community, the structural rules that defines the structure of

[1] www.oracle.com/technology/products/applications/policy-automation/index.html
[2] CTL is a temporal logic frequently used in model checking.
[3] http://www.omg.org/spec/SBVR/1.0/

an organisation and the operative rules that control its operation. By making business experts authoring ontologies and rules, we adopt a similar approach.

2.2 Semantic Annotation

As knowledge cannot be extracted from written policies but nevertheless need to be acquired from and maintained together with those policies, we propose an approach based on semantic annotation. This is a way to ease the "transitions on the knowledge formalization continuum" as proposed by [3].

Several projects have proposed to articulate texts with a semantic model in order to be able to query both the text and its semantic model, the two approaches being complementary. Our approach differs from previous works which either annotate controlled language [8] or consider a single type of link (*e.g.* to individuals [9,1]). We exploit a richer annotation of NL texts where any ontological element (concepts, roles, their instances) or rule can be linked to a textual element. However, as previous works on semantic annotation, our framework relies on W3C technologies and standards.

In the following, we propose a new way to work with written policies, which is based on semantic annotation. We show that articulating a policy document with a rich semantic model gives a "documented business rule model" and enables powerful search functionalities, which meets the needs for the documentation and maintenance of BR models. [11] builds a similar index linking documentation, business rules and code, for the need of expert validation and rule maintenance, although the reverse engineering workflow is opposite of ours (from code to rules, then to documents) and the nature of documents is quite different (the technical data descriptions are plain lists of property-value pairs).

3 A Core Index Structure

For integrating policy documents into BRMS, we propose to design "documented business rule models". This approach relies on an index structure[4] that encompasses and links the source documents and the BR model, be it under construction or ready for execution. Since the BR model is not equivalent to the source text, it is actually important that the written policy remains accessible during the whole lifetime of the rule application. This is achieved through the semantic annotation of the source documents with respect to a semantic model, the BR model which itself combines ontology and rules. As will be shown in Sections 4 and 6, the index structure is built during the acquisition phase which progressively relies on it and it is exploited for controlling the resulting BR model, for its maintenance and for traceability.

The index defines a common structure that integrates and links together the source documents on the one hand, and the ontology and the rules that form

[4] We use "index" in the generic sense of a system designed to make finding information easier and by analogy with the "back-of-the-book index" which is a semantic structure (keyword list or thesaurus) built upon a document and linked to it.

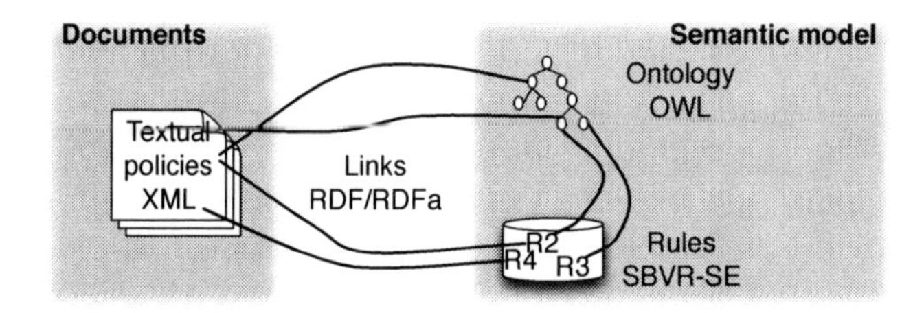

Fig. 1. Index structure representing a documented business rule model

the semantic model, on the other hand (Fig. 1). Such an index builds a semantic space in which one can navigate from any piece of text to the related rules and vice-versa, from the rules to the ontology and from the ontology to the text or rules. The semantic structure associated to the text allows for search and reasoning that cannot be done on the source document.

Document model. The document model defines which textual elements or document units can be annotated. So far, we have adopted a simple document model allowing any character sequence as document unit. In the future however, the document model should be an XML structure, thus allowing constraints on the linguistic types of the document units (*e.g.* word, sentences) and reference to the structure of the document. The semantic annotations embedded in the document are represented in RDFa (RDF in attributes) and can be visualized by HTML navigators (Fig. 5).

Semantic model. The semantic model represents the BR model which is progressively enriched during acquisition. It combines an ontology and rules. The ontology is conventionally represented in OWL-DL but a specific rule format has been defined for rules in the perspective of BR model acquisition.

The rule base is a list of candidate rules (CR) statements expressing any type of static constraint or operative rule relevant for the specification of the target application as in SBVR. We call them "candidate" as they are not yet totally formalized and will require further interpretation to be transformed into executable rules. It is also possible that only part of the candidate rules can be integrated in the formal model at the end but our acquisition methodology makes explicit which parts of the business expert specification are left over. The underlying idea is that CRs are progressively revised by business experts during the elicitation and authoring process until they can be turned into RIF formulae by a knowledge engineer. A CR statement can be 1) in plain natural language, 2) in annotated or semi-controlled language if some words belong to the conceptual vocabulary, or 3) in controlled language, if it is a well-formed SBVR Structured English (SBVR-SE) statement[5] combining keywords and conceptual elements.

Each candidate rule is represented in RDF by a rule ID and is associated with various properties, one of which being its NL statement (`ruleText`).

[5] SBVR-SE is the controlled language associated to SBVR and used in ONTORULE but our approach makes no specific assumption on the type of controlled language.

4 Acquiring a Business Rule Model

Acquisition is an important part of ONTORULE's methodology. The BR model is composed of an ontology that sets the business vocabulary in use in a given business community and a set of business rules expressed as most as possible in these terms. The acquisition process encompasses two main phases (Fig. 2). The ontology, which models the underlying business domain and which is supposed to be relatively stable, is designed first and the rules, which are more frequently updated, are then built on that ontological knowledge.

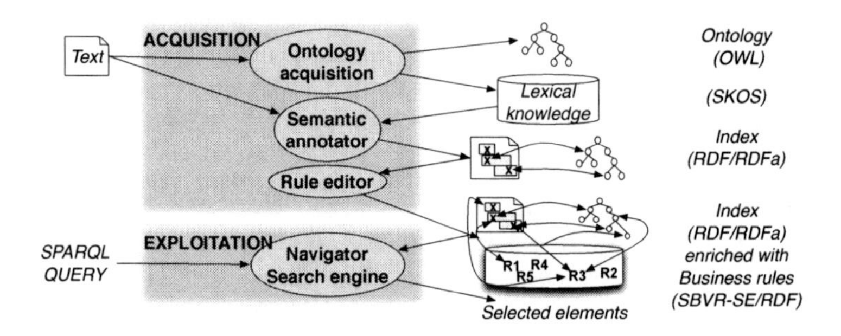

Fig. 2. Overall of the acquisition process

Part of ONTORULE's rationale is that the ontology with its structural constraints and the operative rules are owned by different business user roles, even if for a BR model of limited scope, both roles may be played by the same business expert. ONTORULE's goal is to enable them to design, author and maintain ontologies and rules without having to rely on specialists of information technologies, and relying on professional knowledge engineers only for formalization. We show, in the following, how tools support this acquisition process.

4.1 Acquisition of a Domain Ontology

Even when one relies on textual documentation, designing ontologies is a conceptualisation process that requires some human interpretation. This process cannot be fully automated but acquisition tools can ease and guide it.

ONTORULE's methodology for ontology acquisition relies on TERMINAE [2], a method and tool for building domain ontologies from texts. An ontology is designed in three stages:

- Automatic extraction of the textual units – terms and named entities – and relations that seem semantically relevant in the domain to be modelled, starting from the source text and using NLP tools.
- Normalizing that initial terminological description in a termino-conceptual network: terms which are variants of each other are clustered into a single

termino-concept; ambiguous terms are decomposed into several; irrelevant terms are eliminated and termino-conceptual relations are added[6].
– Formalization into a conceptual or ontological structure.

For instance, in the AAdvantage use case, at the terminological level, the business expert has selected the term *airline participant* in the initial term list and clustered the variant forms (*Airline participant*, *participant*) under the same canonical form (*participant*). As the term is relevant for the domain, a termino-concept ***Participant*** has been created but, since it is ambiguous[7], it is linked to a second distinct termino-concept, ***Member***, also termed *participant* in some contexts. Two concepts, **Participant** and **Member**, were also created to model those termino-concepts at the conceptual or ontological level. Similarly, verbs such as *belongs to* are turned into termino-conceptual relations and formalized into conceptual roles (**belongs_to** with **Member** and **Program** as domain and range).

The whole acquisition process is interactive. At each level, the business expert has to select the relevant items and to organise them, a complex and tedious task that is supported by TERMINAE interfaces. Figure 3 shows the interface presented at the termino-conceptual level: a hierarchical view of the termino-concepts is presented on the left and the right part details the features of the selected termino-concept (*Sapphire* in the present case) to help the business expert's analysis. The new version of TERMINAE tool can be plugged into the Neon Toolkit[8] which ontology editor is exploited to work at the conceptual level.

The originality of this approach lies in the links that relate one level to another. An OWL concept or class at the conceptual level is linked, through an unambiguous termino-concept, to several terms at the terminological level and usually some of their occurrences in the source text. This ensures the traceability of the resulting ontology and produces the intermediate lexical knowledge required to annotate documents with respect to that ontology.

4.2 Semantic Annotation

In the business rule perspective, ontologies are used for modelling and must be incorporated as soon as possible in rule design. One way to achieve this is to annotate the policy document with respect to the ontology, which emphasizes the terms and phrases referring to ontological entities in the source policy.

Achieving such a semantic annotation requires a relevant lexicalised ontology as produced by TERMINAE, where concepts, individuals and roles are related to termino-conceptual and terminological elements. In practice, the termino-conceptual and terminological levels of TERMINAE form a thesaurus which can be exported in a SKOS[9] format and used for the annotation of texts.

---

[6] TERMINAE also allows to give explicit termino-conceptual elements NL definitions and differential properties but, in pratice, this is seldom done in a systematic way.

[7] *Participant* alternatively refers to the companies that participate or collaborate in the program and the customers who are members of it and benefit from it.

[8] http://neon-toolkit.org

[9] http://www.w3.org/2004/02/skos/

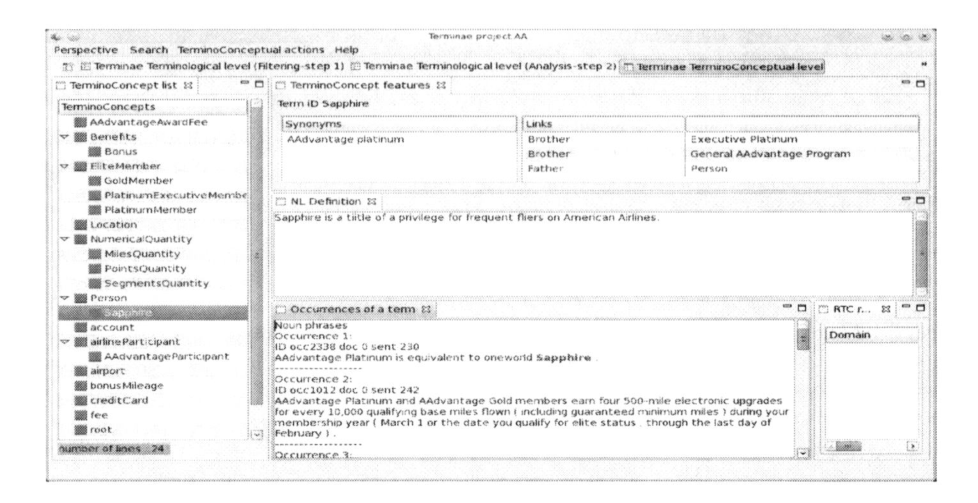

Fig. 3. Termino-concept *Sapphire*

For instance, in the Audi use case, the business expert has created the termino-concepts ***Adjusting device*** and ***Low-temperature chamber*** and associated each one with a set of synonymous terms (resp. *adjusting device/belt adjustment device* and *low-temperature chamber/refrigerated cabinet*) represented as preferred and alternate labels in the SKOS exported file. Annotating the source policy with the concept **AdjustingDevice** or the role **tested_by** consists in tagging the label occurrences with the corresponding concept or role, NLP tools allowing to take into account the surface variations that labels undergo in texts (*e.g. adjusting device(s), device for belt adjustement*).

Semantically annotating the source document is a first step in the creation of the index structure described above. It links ontological and document units.

4.3 Acquisition of Business Rules

Designing rules requires a detailed analysis and reformulation of the source text. SemEx, the tool designed for rule elicitation and exploration in ONTORULE, supports that rule editing process and enables the business expert to progressively reformulate the source text as a set of candidate rules that form a detailed business rule specification. Any candidate rule is a SBVR-SE-like statement expressing a constraint or operative rule relevant for the target application but still has to be formalized according to the specific rule engine features.

Our rule design methodology relies on the following SemEx functionalities:

- The navigation perspective (Fig. 5) presents the current index structure with the loaded ontology on the left and the annotated policy on the right, so that the business expert can easily explore the source document. Rule acquisition actually strongly relies on the conceptual vocabulary formalized in ontology.
- A list of generic linguistic markers (*e.g.* modals, *if-then*) are automatically emphasized to help the expert locating rule fragments in large documents.

- R13 The test shall be carried out at a temperature between 15 and 30 C.
  - R14 The micro_slip_test shall be carried out at a temperature between 15 and 30 C.
    - R15 The temperature of the micro_slip_test must be between 15 and 30 C.
      - R17 The temperature of the micro_slip_test must be lesser than 30 C.
      - R16 The temperature of the micro_slip_test must be greater than 15

Fig. 4. Example of rule derivation

- To edit a rule, the business expert selects a relevant fragment of text, opens a rule editor perspective (Fig. 6) and progressively reformulates the initial fragment into a self-contained, unambiguous and simplified CR statement which words belong either to a set of predefined keywords (orange words in the examples in Fig. 4) or to the conceptual vocabulary defined by the ontology (green, red and blue resp. for concepts, individuals and roles). The coloured annotation inspired from SBVR-SE gives an immediate feedback to the user. The remaining black text requires further revision.
- The business expert can save as many versions of a rule as necessary. Each version is an additional CR that is linked to the previous version by a `previousForm` link (*e.g.* R14 in the rule hierarchy of Figure 4).
- The business expert can also decompose a CR into several ones, which are linked to their parent rule by a `subRule` link (*e.g.* R16 and R17).

The typical transformations made on CRs consist in normalizing the vocabulary to conform to the ontology, simplifying the syntax (*e.g.* the transformation from R14 to R15), making explicit some contextual information (*e.g.* in the context of R13, *test* must be understood as *micro slip test*).

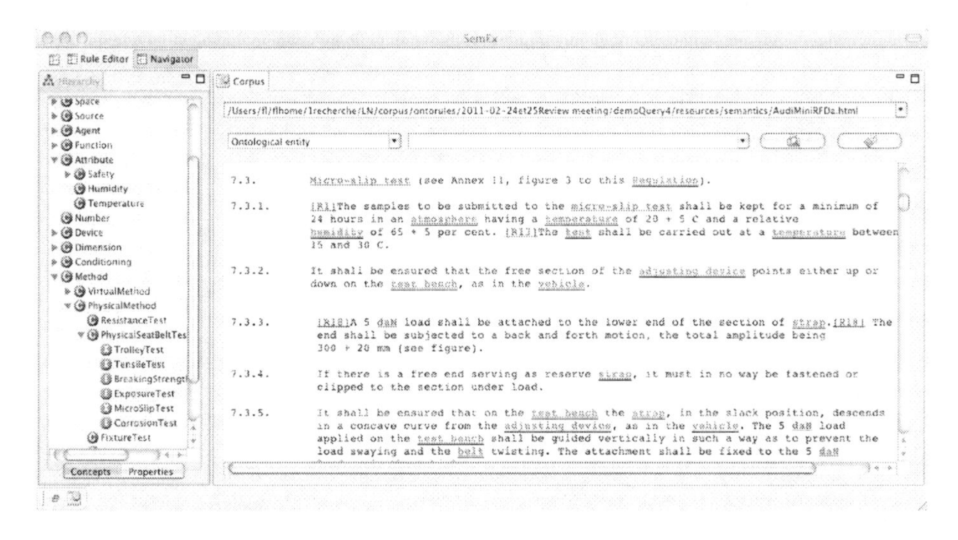

Fig. 5. SemEx - Navigation perspective. The class hierarchy of the ontology is presented on the left. The right window shows the source document annotated wrt. the ontology.

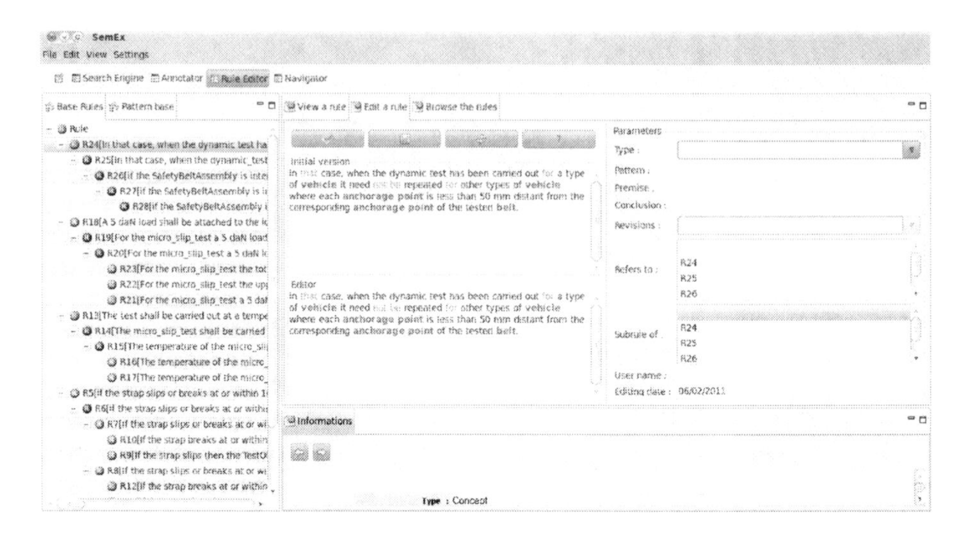

Fig. 6. SemEx - Rule Editor. The rule base is presented on the left as a derivation hierarchy. The old and new versions of the edited rule appear in the middle zone. The right form allows the business expert to describe the properties of the new rule.

The editing process enriches the index, as all the rules derived from the source text are linked to the sentence(s) from which they are originated (text to rule links) and because the CR content is itself annotated with respect to the ontology (rule to ontology links).

5 Results

Our acquisition methodology has been tested on the two use cases presented above. The BR models are built from the various sources: for AAdvantage use case, documentation downloaded from the American Airlines (AA) web site, in particular the Terms and Conditions (5,744 words), which describes different membership statuses and the associated benefits; for Audi use case, the Chapter 7 of the regulation n°16 of the UNO agreement "concerning the adoption of uniform technical prescriptions for wheeled vehicles" (3,704 words).

These source texts are typical of those rather short documents that are nevertheless difficult to master simply by reading and require careful analysis. TERMINAE has been used to build the AAdvantage and Audi ontologies from those texts. The resulting ontologies have been exploited for modelling candidate rules. The final rule bases and underlying ontologies form the BR models to be used by the BRMS developed within ONTORULE.

Ontologies. In the AAdvantage use case, an existing ontology of the legal domain, Lkif[10], has been exploited to model the upper level concepts organizing the

[10] http://www.estrellaproject.org/lkif-core/

domain specific concepts. In the current state, the AA ontology is composed of 210 concepts, among which 32 have been imported from Lkif. The Audi ontology is smaller but should be progressively extended as new regulations are considered. The detailed figures of these ontologies are presented in Table 1.

Rules. In the AAdvantage use case, 101 independent candidate rules have been created but they have not been edited and transformed yet. In the Audi use case, the complete rule editing methodology has been applied on a first regulation: 83 candidate rules have been created, half of them being revision or decomposition of other rules. Results are presented in Table 1.

Table 1. Semantic models built for the two use-cases. Ontologies are described in terms of concepts (OWL classes), individuals (class instances) and roles (properties). Various types of rules are distinguished depending on how they have been created (directly from the text or by revision/decomposition of another rule).

Ontology	Use case	Concepts	Individuals	Roles	
	AAdvantage	210	25	74	
	Audi	77	31	19	
Business rules	Use case	Initial rules	Revised rules	Decomposed rules	Total
	AAdvantage	101	0	0	101
	Audi	40	27	16	83

Index. The resulting indexes are dense structures where ontologies and rules are strongly related to each other and to the source text (Table 2). The coverage of the source text by the ontology and the rules (O2T or R2T coverage[11]) gives an idea of the density of the index. For instance, in the Audi use case, 1/3 of words are covered (or annotated) by the ontology and 1 sentence of the text out of 3 is linked to a rule. It is also interesting to compare the coverage of the ontology on the text taken as a whole and on the part that support the rules (O2T *vs.* O2R coverage). Both ontologies better fit the text of the rules than the rest of the text, which shows that the ontologies have been designed for rule modelling.

Beyond their density, it is difficult to evaluate the quality of the resulting indexes which cannot be assessed independently of their use in rule applications.

[11] *O2T coverage* = AnnTextOcc/TextOcc where *AnnTextOcc* is the number of word occurrences in the text which are annotated wrt. the ontology and *TextOcc* is the total number of word occurrences. Only the occurrences of open class words (OCW, that is nouns, verbs and adjectives) are considered.
R2T coverage = RuleSentences/TextSentences where *RuleSentences* is the number of sentences of the text that are linked to a rule and *TextSentences* is the total number of sentences in the text.
O2R coverage = AnnRuleOcc/RuleOcc where *AnnRuleOcc* is the number of OCW occurrences which are annotated wrt. the ontology and *RuleOcc* is the total number of OCW occurrences, both in the part of the text that supports the rules.

Table 2. Density of the index for the two use-cases

Use Case	Ontology to text coverage (O2T coverage)	Ontology to rules coverage (O2R coverage)	Rule to Text coverage (R2T coverage)
AAdvantage	46.4 %	54.8 %	41 %
Audi	33.8%	40 %	33.8 %

6 Exploiting and Exploring the Resulting Index

The resulting ontologies, rules bases and annotation links build a rich index structure which is time-consuming to build for business experts but crucial for the elicitation and management of BR models. This section illustrates how the indexes built for the AAdvantage and Audi use cases can be searched and exploited and how they support the overall business rule methodology of ONTORULE (acquisition, consistency checking and maintenance).

6.1 Semantic Search

The semantic search engine integrated in SemEx is a key component for exploiting the index. It allows navigation within and across models.

The three resources that compose the index (document, ontology and rules) can be explored independently of each other:

- Traditional text search allows for locating the various occurrences of a word and navigating from one to another; additional browsing functionalities exploit the text structure (*e.g.* sections) if it is encoded in XML.
- Navigating in the ontological structure can be used to explore the hierarchy of concepts, to identify the instances subsumed by a given concept, to ckeck the properties associated with any concept or instance.
- Browsing the rule base is useful to understand how a given rule has been revised and decomposed or to visualize the list of candidate rules resulting from the editing process.

The annotation links also allow for navigating from one resource to another. One can go from the document to the semantic model and vice-versa but also navigate between the ontology and rule base that compose the semantic model. One can visualize the concepts or rules associated with a given text fragment and, conversely, the document units associated to any concept or rule.

Beyond the browsing functionalities accessible from the navigation interface, SemEx also offers a semantic search interface. It allows the business expert to run queries for a deeper and personalised exploration of the index semantic space (Fig. 7). Since the user is not expected to design complex SPARQL queries, a user-friendly interface will be designed for a set of predefined useful queries.

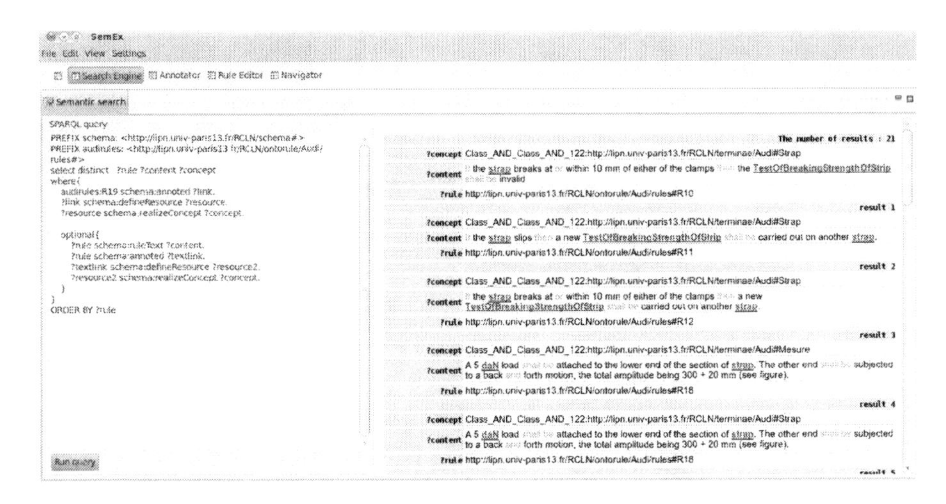

Fig. 7. SemEx - Search engine perspective. Running the SPARQL query presented on the left returns the candidate rules that share a common concept with the rule R19.

6.2 Acquisition

The index structure supports the acquisition process itself. Actually the index is built in parallel with the BR model:

- The first annotation links are built by TERMINAE as a help for the ontology conceptualisation work: browsing the sentences referring to a given concept helps to capture its precise semantics, for instance.
- An extensive annotation of the source text is performed once the ontology is stabilized or after any ontology revision. This is a way to normalize the text vocabulary and to emphasize the conceptual elements in the document. It is a first step towards reformulating the rules.
- When rules are extracted from the source policy, additional rule annotations are associated to the corresponding text fragments. These text-to-rule links help to identify holes in the coverage of the rule base under construction.
- Finally the rule statements are annotated wrt. the ontology in the same way the source document is. This helps reformulating and comparing the rules.

6.3 Support for Consistency Checking

Checking the consistency of BR models is a critical issue for any rule application. Combined with the consistency checking module developed in ONTORULE framework, the index can support the diagnosis and resolution of some inconsistencies.

The inconsistent rules detected by the consistency checker can be traced back to the textual fragments from which they have been derived. This helps to understand whether the inconsistency comes from the source text which must be revised or is due to an error of interpretation in the rule editing process.

It is also interesting to analyze the rule base *a priori*, *i.e.* before rule execution, at the candidate rule level. Knowing what types of inconsistency problems often occur [10], generic SPARQL queries can be predefined to bring potential problems to light, and added as navigation features for use by non technical users. For instance, since inconsistency is frequently due to the incompleteness of the rule base (some cases are covered by no rule), it is useful to cluster all the rules whose premise contain a given concept or any of its subconcept, and analyze them together to check for missing cases.

6.4 Maintenance

As regulations are often updated, BR models must be carefully maintained to remain up to date. The rules are changing faster but the ontology may also evolve. Since the indexing links ensure the traceability of the BR model to the text and vice-versa, one can identify the semantic elements impacted by a change in the source documentation, and which parts of the regulation must be revised when the BR model is updated. A future functionality should enable the marking of units as potentially obsolete or as new candidates and allow for a global analysis of the revised BR model prior to its update.

7 Conclusion

This paper presents a text-based approach for rule acquisition, which is part of ONTORULE's methodology. It is designed for business experts that have to elicit, author and maintain the BR models of rule-applications. We propose a method and tools enabling them to build domain ontologies and business rules which are anchored in the source policies, serve as specification for the targeted application and enable the parallel maintenance of BR models and policies.

Our framework exploits semantic annotation as well as OMG and W3C standards and technologies. It relies on an index structure that encompasses and inter-links the knowledge sources of rule-based applications: source NL policies, ontology and rules. An interactive method has been proposed for the design of such documented BR models: the associated tools, TERMINAE and SemEx guide the modelling of ontology and rules. The resulting indexed resources form a semantic space, in which one can navigate from one textual element to the ontology or a rule, from the ontology to the associated pieces of text and rules and from a rule to its source text or ontological elements. The documented model can also be explored by a semantic search engine: the tracing, updating and analysis functionalities are useful for maintaining the BR models of rule applications.

The proposed approach has been tested and illustrated on two real use cases. Even if they will be extended in the next future, these experiments show the validity of our approach. Acquisition remains a time-consuming activity but NLP, knowledge engineering and semantic web techniques provide guidance so that business experts can author and maintain comprehensive and understandable business rule models that serve as semi-formal specification for rule applications.

References

1. Amardeilh, F., Laublet, P., Minel, J.L.: Document annotation and ontology population from linguistic extractions. In: Proc. of the 3rd Int Conf. on Knowledge Capture, pp. 161–168. ACM, New York (2005)
2. Aussenac-Gilles, N., Després, S., Szulman, S.: The terminae method and platform for ontology engineering from texts. In: Buitelaar, P., Cimiano, P. (eds.) Bridging the Gap between Text and Knowledge: Selected Contributions to Ontology learning from Text, pp. 199–223. IOS Press, Amsterdam (2008)
3. Baumeister, J., Reutelshoefer, J., Puppe, F.: Knowwe: A semantic wiki for knowledge engineering. Applied Intelligence (in press, 2011)
4. Brodie, C., Karat, C.M., Karat, J.: An empirical study of natural language parsing of privacy policy rules using the sparcle policy workbench. In: SOUPS 2006 (2006)
5. Cimiano, P.: Ontology Learning and Population from Text: Algorithms, Evaluation And Applications. Springer, New York (2006)
6. Dinesh, N., Joshi, A., Lee, I., Sokolsky, O.: Reasoning about conditions and exceptions to laws in regulatory conformance checking. In: van der Meyden, R., van der Torre, L. (eds.) DEON 2008. LNCS (LNAI), vol. 5076, pp. 110–124. Springer, Heidelberg (2008)
7. Faure, D., Nédellec, C.: Knowledge acquisition of predicate argument structures from technical texts using machine learning: the system asium. In: Stude, R., Fensel, D. (eds.) Proc. of the 11th Int. Conf. on Knowledge Engineering and Knowledge Management, pp. 329–334. Springer, Heidelberg (1999)
8. Nalepa, G.J.: Collective knowledge engineering with semantic wikis. Journal of Universal Computer Science 16(7), 1006–1023 (2010)
9. Popov, B., Kiryakov, A., Ognyanoff, D., Manov, D., Kirilov, A.: Kim – a semantic platform for information extraction and retrieval. Nat. Lang. Eng. 10(3-4), 375–392 (2004)
10. Pührer, J., El Ghali, A., Chniti, A., Korf, R., Schwichtenberg, A., Lévy, F., Heymans, S., Xiao, G., Eiter, T.: D2.3 consistency maintenance. Intermediate report, ONTORULE IST-2009-231875 Project (December 2010), `http://ontorule-project.eu/deliverables`
11. Putrycz, E., Kark, A.W.: Connecting legacy code, business rules and documentation. In: Bassiliades, N., Governatori, G., Paschke, A. (eds.) RuleML 2008. LNCS, vol. 5321, pp. 17–30. Springer, Heidelberg (2008)
12. Wang, Y., Volker, J., Haase, P.: Towards semi-automatic ontology building supported by large-scale knowledge acquisition. In: AAAI Fall Symp. On Semantic Web for Collaborative Knowledge Acquisition, vol. FS-06-06, pp. 70–77. AAAI Press, Arlington (2006)

On Complex Event Processing for Real-Time Situational Awareness

Nenad Stojanovic[1] and Alexander Artikis[2]

[1] FZI Karlsruhe, 76131 Karlsruhe, Germany
Nenad.Stojanovic@fzi.de
[2] NCSR Demokritos, Athens 15310, Greece
a.artikis@iit.demokritos.gr

Abstract. In this paper we give an overview of the existing research results and open research challenges in applying complex event processing for real-time situational awareness. We consider two different viewpoints: better detection of emerging complex situations and prediction of future situations. In order to illustrate these viewpoints we consider two application areas: activity recognition from the video content and social media observation, respectively.

Keywords: Situation awareness, Social media observation, Activity recognition.

1 Introduction

Real-time data processing has become very important for many applications, such as item-tracking in RFID-supported logistics, social-media channels observation, activity recognition from video content, computer network monitoring, patient monitoring and trader behavior evaluation in financial markets. In all of these applications the amount of data being generated requires on–the-fly processing and immediate reaction in order to be managed in an efficient way. Indeed, such real-time orientation enables the detection of problems (e.g. a damaged item in a delivery, or bad image of a company in recently posted tweets) as soon as they happen, so that a corresponding reaction can be successfully performed.

In the nutshell of this mechanism is the ability to recognize in real-time[1] (or even ahead of time) some interesting situations, what is called "real-time situational awareness". Note that this goes beyond the traditional (static) situational awareness that is focused on the understanding a situation (if possible in real-time). Real-time situational awareness introduces the notion of real-time emergency: the main goal is to recognize a situation of interest as soon as possible in order to be able to react to it properly.

Such a process introduces several challenges for the processing of data:

1. it should be very efficient in order to deal with a huge amount of events,
2. it should be intelligent in order to enable an early recognition of interesting situations,

[1] We consider „business real-time" as the criteria for declaring something to be processed in real-time.

N. Bassiliades et al. (Eds.): RuleML 2011 - Europe, LNCS 6826, pp. 114–121, 2011.

3. it should be very flexible in order to deal with various and dynamically changing patterns (situations) of interests (that should be recognized in real-time), and
4. it should be tolerant to various types of noise.

Due to its real-time processing orientation, complex event processing (CEP) is a technology that aims to resolve these challenges. Indeed, CEP is in the nutshell about efficient management of the pattern detection process in the huge and dynamic data streams and as such it is very suitable for detecting/recognizing complex real-time situations. However, CEP can be also viewed as a technology for detecting trends in the flow of data that leads to predicting some future situations. In this paper we give an overview of the application of complex event processing for the real-time situational awareness from these two different viewpoints:

- better detection of emerging complex situations (complex real-time-situation awareness) and
- prediction of future situations (future-situation awareness).

In order to illustrate these viewpoints we consider two application areas: a) activity recognition from the video content, and b) social media observation, respectively.

Indeed, in the area of activity recognition one has to deal with several of the problems faced by traditional event processing systems such as the real-time recognition of long-term activities given large amounts of detected short-term activities the continuous, automated refinement of long-term activity representation for increased recognition accuracy, as well as the accurate recognition in the presence of noise.

Social media observation is dealing with detecting interesting information in the streams of data coming from various social media channels. These channels have become very important sources for monitoring public opinion in order to, e.g. (re)define marketing strategies. Recently the term real-time marketing intelligence has been coined for describing the need for reacting immediately on the threats/opportunities for having more and more satisfied customers.

Moreover, this paper discusses about the application of two machine learning approaches in CEP:

- using unsupervised learning for predicting novel situations and
- using supervised learning for automatically refining complex event representations and handling noise.

2 Activity Recognition

2.1 Motivation

One of the objectives of computer vision research is to recognize in an automated way what happens in scenes depicted by video sequences. An automatic video interpretation system takes video sequences as input and produces as output the interpretation of these sequences. Such a system is typically composed of two main components. The first component produces a symbolic representation of the mobile objects detected on raw video sequences, as well as of the 'short-term activities' of the mobile objects – simple events, in the terminology of event processing – such as when a person is walking, running, stays inactive, moves abruptly, and so on. The second component recognizes various types of 'long-term activity' – complex events – such as when a person leaves an object unattended, two people are fighting, etc. A long-term activity is defined as a set of temporal, spatial and/or logical constraints on a set of short-term activities.

Automatic video interpretation systems have to deal with several of the problems faced by traditional event processing systems:

- They have to recognise in real-time long-term activities given thousands of short-term activities per second.
- They are required to recognize long-term activities that are possibly about to take place, such as when a person is about to leave an object unattended.
- They need machine learning techniques to automatically and continuously refine what constitutes a long-term activity. Such a refinement increases recognition accuracy.
- They have to deal with uncertainty, as the detection of short-term activities from video content is often noisy.

In following we discuss how some of the above issues are being addressed in the field of activity recognition, as we believe that several of the methods of this field are directly applicable to complex event processing.

2.2 A Representative Approach

Several approaches have been proposed in the literature for long-term activity recognition – [3, 5, 7, 7, 8] are but a few recent examples. To address the issue of uncertainty mentioned above, various probabilistic reasoning frameworks have been adopted. One such framework, that is increasingly gaining attention, is Markov Logic Networks (MLN) [4]. MLN combine first-order logic and probabilistic graphical models. The use of first-order logic allows for the representation of long-term activities including complex temporal constraints – this is opposed to sequential graphical models that allow for restricted temporal representation. The main concept behind MLN is that the probability of a world increases as the number of formulas it violates decreases. Therefore, a world violating formulas becomes less probable, but not impossible as in first-order logic. Syntactically, each formula F_i in Markov logic is represented in first-order logic and it is associated with a weight w_i. The higher the value of the weight, the stronger the constraint represented by F_i. Semantically, a set of Markov logic formulas (F_i, w_i) represents a probability distribution over possible worlds.

MLN have been recently used for long-term activity recognition – consider, for example, [3, 8]. (A detailed account of the use of MLN for activity recognition and complex event processing in general may be found in [1].) The MLN inference algorithms take into consideration the weights attached to the short-term activities detected by the underlying computer vision component. As mentioned above, it is often the case that short-term activity detection is noisy and, therefore, this feature of MLN is very helpful for long-term activity recognition. Furthermore, using MLN one may attach weights to the first-order logic rules expressing a long-term activity. Strong weights are given to rules that are almost always true, while weak weights are given to rules that describe exceptions.

An important feature of MLN is that they are supported by a variety of machine learning algorithms. More precisely, it is possible to estimate the weights of the first-order rules expressing a long-term activity and/or the rules themselves, given a set of training data, that is, short-term activities annotated with long-term activities. Weight learning in MLN is performed by optimising a likelihood function, which is a statistical measure of how well the probabilistic model (MLN) fits the training data. Weights can be learned by either generative or discriminative estimation. Generative learning attempts to optimise the joint distribution of all variables in the model. In contrast, discriminative learning attempts to optimise the conditional distribution of a set of outputs, given a set of inputs.

In addition to weight learning, the structure of a MLN, that is, the rules expressing long-term activities, can be learned from training data. A variety of structure learning methods have been proposed for MLN. These methods build upon the techniques of Inductive Logic Programming (ILP) [6]. In brief, the MLN structure learning methods can be classified into top-down and bottom-up methods [4]. Top-down structure learning starts from an empty or existing MLN and iteratively constructs clauses by adding or revising a single predicate at a time, using typical ILP operations and a search procedure. However, as the structure of a MLN may involve complex long-term activities, the space of potential top-down refinements may become intractable. For this reason, bottom-up structure learning can be used instead, starting from training data and searching for more general hypotheses. This approach usually leads to a more specialised model, following a search through a manageable set of generalisations.

Long-term activity recognition in MLN involves querying a ground Markov network about long-term activities. A ground Markov network is produced by grounding all first-order logic rules expressing long-term activities using a finite set of constants concerning the application under consideration. Complete grounding of MLN, even for simple long-term activity knowledge bases, results in complex and large networks, compromising inference efficiency. For this reason, we may employ 'lazy inference methods', or 'lifted inference methods' which can answer queries without grounding the entire network [4].

2.3 Research Challenges

Markov Logic Networks (MLN) combine the strengths of logical and probabilistic inference. Consequently, they address, to a certain extent, the following issues that often arise in activity recognition and complex event processing in general: incomplete simple event (short-term activity) streams, erroneous simple event detection, and inconsistent annotation of simple events and complex events (long-term activities). MLN also offer a very expressive framework, as the full power of first-order logic is available.

Being based on logic, MLN benefit from a formal and declarative semantics, a variety of inference mechanisms, and methods for learning a knowledge base of complex events from data. Compared to procedural methods, logic-based ones facilitate efficient development and management of complex event representations, which are clearly separated from the generic inference mechanism. Moreover, compared to methods exhibiting informal semantics, logic-based approaches support validation and traceability of results.

Although MLN are increasingly being used for activity recognition and, in general, complex event processing, there are several issues that need to be resolved still, such as the incorporation and use of numerical temporal constraints in MLN inference, and the simultaneous learning of numerical parameters — for example, weights and numerical temporal constraints — and the logical structure of the knowledge base expressing complex events.

3 Future-Situation Awareness in Social Media

3.1 Motivation

The power of data processing has migrated in recent years from explaining the past using very efficient (web) search mechanisms (answering on the question "What happened?") into understanding the present through different social media-based filtering mechanisms (answering on the question "What is happing now?"). Indeed, in last two years there is a huge proliferation of systems for the real-time analyses of the streams from news portals, discussion forums, Twitter, etc. leading to different types of services for filtering interesting information, e.g. automatic notification in the case that interesting information has appeared. This feature enables developing of very efficient reactive systems that will react as soon as a problem/opportunity appears. It boosts the competitiveness through the real-time awareness that increases the speed of reaction. In this case the data is used for an efficient detection of some already known and already-happened situations. However, an extreme dynamicity and complexity of the modern business implies the need for creating awareness of that what can happen in order to be able not only to react on problems, but to avoid that they will happen at all (the task of the so-called proactive systems).

On the other hand, there are new, community-driven, sources of information and influences that can be considered and exploited for estimating what can happen, like the wisdom of crowds, the power of an individual blogger to impact a company's image, the fact that consumers now buy as communities, and the potential radical restructuring of classic functions like product design because consumers are designing their own products. In that case the data should be used for an efficient prediction that some situations might happen, including the detection of prior unknown situations (answering on the question "*What will happen?*"). This data-driven proactivity opens possibilities to provide new solutions for new situations and from the business point of view it will boost *competitiveness trough innovativeness*. Many added value services based on this proactivity can be envisioned, starting from calculating specific, context-based predictions that can point to new business threats or opportunities, till providing efficient actions based on predictions. Just as short example imagine a SME that can produce small series of specialized chips and can discover (using specific predictions calculated from data streams) that in a segment of the market there would be, in a shorter period of time, either problems in the supply or new demand for specific types of chips (small series).

Obviously, this posts new requirements for processing streams of data[2] in the future, which the following two are the most important of: a) generating streams of interesting information out of streams of data (interestingness is defined through the statistics-based notion of unusuality) and b) generating different trend-based analytics (incl. relevant predictions) out of streams of interesting information. We argue that these two processing steps define a basic pipeline for the so-called *proactive processing of streams* that will enable the creation of many business models around various derivatives of streams of data.

3.2 State of the Art/Current Situation

The need for predicting some parameters of the business is well recognized and mainly supported by predictive analytics, which encompasses a variety of techniques from statistics, data mining and game theory that analyze current and historical facts to make predictions about future events. However, predictive analytics is usually used for defining some operative data (like what revenue can be expected and from what channels - direct sales, partners, etc.) and it is based on developing very formal mathematical models (e.g. a customer profile can include more than 200 descriptive variables, such as income, age group, gender, occupation, and education level). As such it doesn't exploit the potential of data streams for listening to the rumors and finding weak signals in the marketplace that can be used for the competitive advantage.

On the other hand, many portals have been developed in last two years around available real-time data streams (like twitter) with the goal of using them for building different (real-time) opinion maps, usually as a part of analyzing effects of some marketing activities. We have analyzed more than 230 solutions (mainly from USA and Germany) in the area of social media monitoring. Social media monitoring tools are used to observe user-generated-content in order to gain marketing relevant insight. Radia6 (acquired by Salesforce recently), Sysomos, Lithum, Attensity360 are the most popular solutions in this area. Almost more than the half of them analyzes content only from blogs, Twitter and Facebook. The remaining systems are built either for Twitter or Facebook. Usage of other available sources, like crawling discussion forums and web pages is missing in these systems. None of the systems consider mining techniques in order to gain intelligent insights. Prediction based on collected data is also not in the focus of these systems. There is no existing solution which deals with an advanced analysis of the data (like providing unusual information) or working towards predicting some trends for the future. To the best of our knowledge there is only one approach which deals scientifically with the predictions based on the data from social media [10]. This approach uses the chatter from Twitter.com to forecast box-office revenues for movies and outperform other prediction methods. However, this approach, like above mentioned predictive analytics, deals with predicting some operative data and the goal approach aims to discover/predict completely new/unexpected business threats and opportunities, that couldn't be detected otherwise.

---

[2] Note that we consider as streams of data all data which is coming with a time stamp from a data source, independently of the frequency of changes. For example, publishing changes/updates in a web page represents such a stream of data. Other examples are updates from discussion forums, twitter and facebook (wall). Note that we are talking mainly about community-driven data.

3.3 Research Challenges and Beyond State of the Art

New research work should be mainly focused on developing efficient and scalable solutions for finding unusuality (changes) in the data flow: the value of data streams is determined not only by the data itself (i.e. data value) but rather by the context the data values have appeared in. For example, if there are two complaints coming from the gold-customer about X in a short period of time, one will react on that differently depending on that if that customer complains very rarely or quite often including multiple complaints. This will enable finding interesting information in data streams (see previous section). This will require methods for the detection of unusual situations in textual data streams.

Discovering unusual situations have been studied widely through many different fields of science and economy. In [11] the authors isolate outliers to assure high quality of stored data. In [12] and [13] a feature-based clustering algorithm is presented. They mark that previous approaches considers outliers as binary properties and introduced LOF (local outlier actor) to measure the degree of an outlier.

From the data mining point of view, very important is the work of [14], who provides a framework for effective examining of multidimensional data streams with the use of "velocity density estimation". It allows both a fast computation and to derive a visual perspective of the changes. The idea behind it is to estimate the changing rate of the data based on some user-defined temporal window.

As a short conclusion, most approaches in this field are using unsupervised learning techniques to detect unusualness. The large number of such approaches is due to the possibility for fast computation. However, they are only adjusted to some specific domains. In unpredictable situations it is not desirable to readjust the underlying parameter. Further, none of the presented approaches, aside Data Stream Mining solutions, has real-time capabilities.

4 Conclusions

Although CEP is in the nutshell about efficient management of the pattern detection process in the huge and dynamic data streams, it can be also viewed as a technology for detecting trends in the flow of data that leads to predicting some future situations. In this paper we give an overview of the application of complex event processing for the real-time situational awareness from these two different viewpoints: better detection of emerging complex situations (complex real-time-situation awareness) and prediction of future situations (future-situation awareness). In order to illustrate these viewpoints we consider two application areas: a) activity recognition from the video content, and b) social media observation, respectively. We presented the most important research challenges for these areas and gave guidelines for the further research in these directions.

Acknowledgments

Alexander Artikis is supported by the EU-funded PRONTO project (FP7-ICT 231738). Nenad Stojanovic is partially financed by EU in the following FP7 projects: ALERT (ICT-258098) and PLAY (ICT-258659).

References

1. Thirunarayan, K., Henson, C., Sheth, A.: Situation Awareness via Abductive Reasoning for Semantic Sensor Data: A Preliminary Report. In: Proc. 2009 Int. Symposium on Collaborative Technologies and Systems (CTS 2009), Baltimore, MD (May 18-22, 2009)
2. Artikis, A., Porter, F., Skarlatidis, A., Paliouras, G.: Logic-based representation, reasoning and machine learning for event recognition. In: International Conference on Distributed Event-Based Systems (DEBS), pp. 282–293. ACM, New York (2010)
3. Biswas, R., Thrun, S., Fujimura, K.: Recognizing activities with multiple cues. In: Elgammal, A., Rosenhahn, B., Klette, R. (eds.) Human Motion 2007. LNCS, vol. 4814, pp. 255–270. Springer, Heidelberg (2007)
4. Domingos, P., Lowd, D.: Markov Logic: An Interface Layer for Artificial Intelligence. Morgan & Claypool Publishers (2009)
5. Hakeem, A., Shah, M.: Learning, detection and representation of multi-agent events in videos. Artificial Intelligence 171(8-9), 586–605 (2007)
6. Muggleton, S.: Inductive logic programming. New Generation Computing 8(4), 295–318 (1991)
7. Shet, V., Neumann, J., Ramesh, V., Davis, L.: Bilattice-based logical reasoning for human detection. In: Proceedings of International Conference on Computer Vision and Pattern Recognition (CVPR), pp. 1–8. IEEE, Los Alamitos (2007)
8. Thonnat, M.: Semantic activity recognition. In: Proceedings of European Conference on Artificial Intelligence (ECAI), pp. 3–7 (2008)
9. Tran, S.D., Davis, L.S.: Event modeling and recognition using markov logic networks. In: Proceedings of Computer Vision Conference, pp. 610–623 (2008)
10. Asur, S., Huberman, B.A.: Predicting the Future with Social Media, wi-iat. In: 2010 IEEE/WIC/ACM International Conference on Web Intelligence and Intelligent Agent Technology, vol. 1, pp. 492–499 (2010)
11. Last, M., Kandel, A.: Automated Detection of Outliers in Real-World Data. In: Proc. of the Second International Conference on Intelligent Technologies, pp. S292–S301 (2001)
12. Minh, L.M., Nguyen, Q., Omiecinski, E.: A Fast Feature-Based Method to Detect Unusual Patterns in Multidimensional Datasets. Springer, Heidelberg (2009)
13. Breunig, M.M., Kriegel, H.-P., Ng, R.T., Sander, J.L.: identifying density-based local outliers. SIGMOD Rec. 29(2), S93–S104 (2000)
14. Aggarwal, C.: A Framework for Diagnosing Changes in Evolving Data Streams. In: ACM SIGMOD Conference, S575–S586 (2003)

Retractable Complex Event Processing and Stream Reasoning

Darko Anicic[1], Sebastian Rudolph[2], Paul Fodor[3], and Nenad Stojanovic[1]

[1] FZI Research Center for Information Technology, Germany
[2] AIFB, Karlsruhe Institute of Technology, Germany
[3] State University of New York at Stony Brook, USA

Abstract. Complex Event Processing (CEP) deals with processing of continuously arriving events with the goal of identifying meaningful *patterns* (complex events). In existing stream database approaches, CEP is manly concerned by temporal relations between events. This paper advocates for a *knowledge-rich* CEP with Stream Reasoning capabilities. Secondly, we address the problem of *revision* in event processing. Events are often assumed to be immutable and therefore always correct. Revision in event processing deals with the circumstance that certain events may be revoked. This necessitates to reconsider complex events which might have been computed based on the original, flawy history as soon as part of that history is corrected.

In this paper, we present a novel approach for *knowledge-based CEP* and *Stream Reasoning*, including revisions of events too. We present a *rule-based language* for pattern matching over event streams with a precise syntax and the declarative semantics. We devise an execution model for the proposed formalism, and provide a prototype implementation. Extensive experiments have been conducted to demonstrate the efficiency and effectiveness of our approach.

1 Introduction

While existing semantic technologies and reasoning engines are constantly being improved in dealing with *time invariant* domain knowledge, they lack in support for processing *real-time* streaming data. Real-time data on Web is valuable only if it is captured, processed, and delivered instantly. Examples include traffic monitoring, real-time financial services, web click analysis and advertisement, various social web and real-time collaboration tools, and so forth.

Complex Event Processing (CEP) is a set of techniques and tools that help us in understanding and controlling real-time and event-driven systems [11]. As such, it is a technology that can help in processing real-time data on the Web too. CEP deals with processing continuously arriving events with the goal of identifying meaningful event patterns (complex events). An *event* represents something that occurs, happens, or changes the current state of affairs. For example, an event may represent a stock price change, a complied transaction, a new piece of information, knowledge made available by a Web service, and so forth. In all these situations, to structure the course of affairs and describe more complex *dynamic* situations, we compose simple (atomic) events into *complex* events. Today's CEP systems [1,13,4], however, focus on high throughput

N. Bassiliades et al. (Eds.): RuleML 2011 - Europe, LNCS 6826, pp. 122–137, 2011.

and timeliness as two important characteristics, while they do not meet the *complexity* requirements of event-driven applications. Pattern matching over streams poses two new challenges directly impacting the complexity of CEP systems:

Knowledge-based CEP & Stream Reasoning. According to [11], the *time critical* actions are supposed to be taken upon complex events. The question is, however, whether event patterns detectable by today's CEP systems are expressive enough to capture complex (business) events in all their aspects. How likely is that *critical* decisions are taken merely on event patterns of type, e.g., "event a is followed by event b in last 10 seconds"? For some applications such patterns are expressive enough; however, for *knowledge-rich* applications, they are certainly not. In such applications real-time actions are triggered not only by events, but also upon additional *knowledge*. This knowledge captures the *domain* of interest, or *context* related to business critical actions and decisions. Its purpose is to be evaluated during detection of complex events in order to *enrich* events with background information (context); or to detect more complex *situations*. The task of reasoning over streaming data (events) and the background knowledge constitutes a new challenge known as *Stream Reasoning* [15].

The Linked Open Data (LOD) initiative[1] has made available on the Web hundreds of datasets and ontologies. Examples also include the New York Times dataset[2], financial ontologies[3], encyclopedic data (e.g., DBpedia), Linked-GeoData[4], and so forth. This knowledge is commonly represented as *structured* data (e.g., using RDFS). Structured data enable machines to *reason* over explicit knowledge in order to infer new (implicit) information. However, current CEP systems [1,13,4] cannot utilize the structured knowledge, and they cannot do stream reasoning.

To achieve the aforementioned goal, various approaches have been proposed [6,5,10]. They are capable to process either additional background or structured knowledge (though varying in Complex Event Processing capabilities they provide). In this paper, we propose an approach that is capable to do both, Complex Event Processing and Stream Reasoning. Moreover, the goal of this paper is to provide an additional feature (in comparison to [6,5,10]), namely, *event revision*.

Non-blocking event revision. CEP systems such as [1,13,4] detect complex events based on reported atomic events. Once a complex event has been detected, typically there is no chance to *revise* this event later. Events are assumed to be immutable and therefore always correct. In practice, there is a number of reasons requiring *revisions* in event stream processing. For example, an event was reported by mistake, but did not happen in reality (and the mistake was realized later); an event happened, but it was not reported (due to failure of either a sensor, or failure of the event transmission system); or an event was triggered and later revoked due to the transaction failure. Also very often streaming data sources contend with noise (e.g., financial data feeds, Web streaming data, updates etc.) resulting in erroneous inputs and, therefore, erroneous complex event results. As recognised in [14], event stream sources may issue "revision tuples"

[1] such as e.g., `http://linkeddata.org/`

[2] Linked Open Data from the New York Times `http://data.nytimes.com/`

[3] Financial ontology: `http://www.fadyart.com/`

[4] LinkedGeoData: `http://linkedgeodata.org`

(revision events) that amend previously issued events. A CEP system should therefore be capable to take these revisions into account and produce correct revision outputs. There exist approaches for dealing with revision in event processing [9,12]). However, these approaches (as rooted in stream databases) cannot do Stream Reasoning.

The goal of this work is to provide a fundamental framework for processing event streams, exceeding the capabilities of today's CEP systems. We propose a formalism featuring an expressive *declarative* and *rule-based* semantics. As such, the formalism enables effective Complex Event Processing and Stream Reasoning. Apart from this, our approach naturally captures *revision* of acquired knowledge[5]. Extensive experiments have been conducted to demonstrate the practical efficiency and effectiveness of our approach.

2 Formal Model for Knowledge-Based Event Processing with Revision

We have defined a basic language for CEP in [3]. In this section, we extend the language to handle *retractions*. In order to keep the presentation of the overall formalism self-contained, we will also recall basics of the language from [3].

2.1 Event Processing Language Syntax

In this section, we present the formal syntax of our language for event processing, while in the remaining sections of the paper, we will gradually introduce other aspects of the language (i.e., the declarative and operational semantics as well as the performance of a prototypical implementation based on the language).

The syntax of our language allows for the description of *time* and *events*. We represent time instants as well as durations as nonnegative rational numbers $q \in \mathbb{Q}^+$. Events can be atomic or complex. An *atomic event* refers to an instantaneous occurrence of interest. Atomic events are described by ground atoms (i.e., predicates followed by arguments which are terms not containing variables). Intuitively, the arguments of a ground atom describing an atomic event denote information items (i.e., event data) that provide additional information about that event.

Atomic events can be composed to form *complex events* via *event patterns*. We use event patterns to describe how events can (or have to) be temporally situated relative to other events or absolute time points. The language P of event patterns is formally defined by

$$P ::= \texttt{pr}(t_1, \ldots, t_n) \mid P \text{ WHERE } t \mid q \mid (P).q \mid P \text{ BIN } P \mid \text{NOT}(P).[P, P]$$

Thereby, $\texttt{pr}$ a predicate name with arity n, t_i denote terms, t is a term of type Boolean, q is a nonnegative rational number, and BIN is one of the binary operators SEQ, AND, PAR, OR, EQUALS, MEETS, DURING, STARTS, or FINISHES. As a side condition, in every expression p WHERE t, all variables occurring in t must also occur in the pattern p. Finally, an *event rule* is defined as a formula of the following form:

[5] We focus on revision of *events*. Revision of background knowledge is out of scope.

$$\texttt{pr}(t_1, \ldots, t_n) \leftarrow p$$

where p is an event pattern containing every variable occurring in $\texttt{pr}(t_1, \ldots, t_n)$ at least once outside any function application.

Figure 1 demonstrates the various ways of constructing complex event descriptions from simpler ones in our language for event processing. Moreover, the figure informally introduces the semantics of the language, which will be formally defined in Section 2.3.

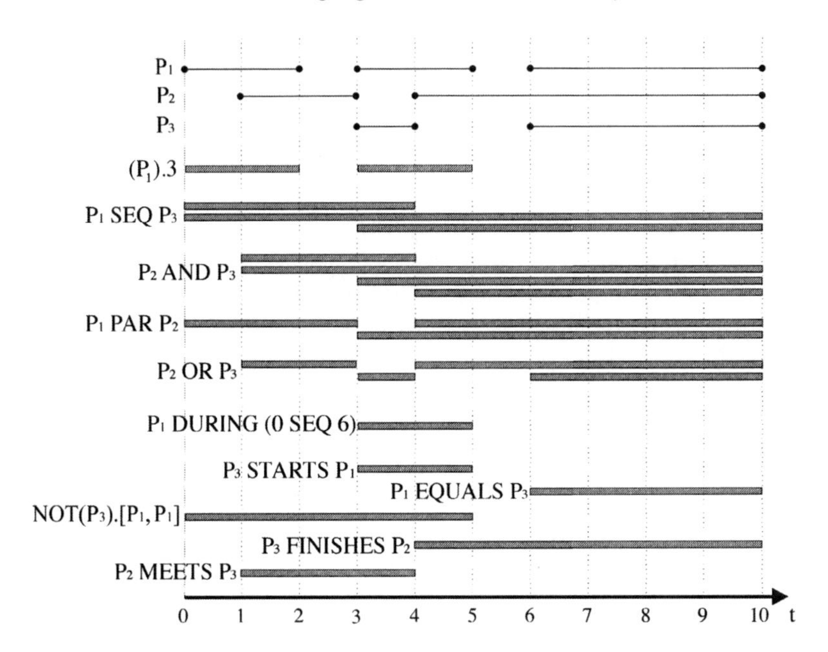

Fig. 1. Language for Event Processing - Composition Operators

It is worth noting that the language captures the set of all possible 13 relations on two temporal intervals as defined in [2] and can therefore be used for extensive temporal reasoning.

2.2 Examples

Let us briefly review the modeling capabilities of the presented pattern language.

General examples. One might be interested in defining an event matching stock market working days:

$$\texttt{workingDay()} \leftarrow \text{NOT}(\texttt{marketCloses()})[\texttt{marketOpens()}, \texttt{marketCloses()}].$$

Moreover, we might be interested in detecting the event of two bankruptcies happening on the same market working day:

$$\texttt{dieTogether}(X, Y) \leftarrow (\texttt{bankrupt}(X)\,\text{SEQ}\,\texttt{bankrupt}(Y))\ \text{DURING}\ \texttt{workingDay()}.$$

This event rule also shows how event information (about involved institutions, provenance, etc.) can be "passed" on to the defined complex events by using variables. Furthermore, variables may be employed to conditionally group events into complex ones if they refer to the same entity:

$\texttt{indirectlyAcquires}(X, Y) \leftarrow \texttt{buys}(Z, Y)$ AND $\texttt{buys}(X, Z)$

Knowledge-based patterns. Let us consider an example demonstrating *knowledge-based* pattern detection. Suppose that we want to detect the stock price increase in a supply chain system of companies. The following pattern monitors two stock price increases in two companies (occurred within certain time window), and checks whether the companies are parts of the supply chain system.

$\texttt{trendIncrease}() \leftarrow \big(\texttt{stockIcr}(CompanyA)$ SEQ $\texttt{stockIcr}(CompanyB)\big).10$
AND $\texttt{inSupChain}(CompanyA, CompanyB)$.

The supply chain system is represented as a set of explicit links between companies, e.g., with $\texttt{linked}(A, B)$ we represent two interconnected businesses involved in the ultimate provision of a product. We assume that such explicit relationships are continuously being updated via *information events* as, for instance, our data mining tool processes different information sources, delivering events of the form:

$\texttt{linked}(CompanyA, CompanyB)$
...
$\texttt{linked}(CompanyY, CompanyZ)$

The above set of linked relations can be represented, with no restriction, as a set of RDF triples too. Our prototype implementation (see Section 4) uses Semantic Web Library[6] to represent an RDFS ontology as a set of Prolog rules and facts.

The following transitive closure pattern can then be used to span over semantic relationships between companies scenario where direct supply relationships are represented explicitly, and hence discover implicit relationships, i.e., whether two stock price increases also covered the whole supply chain system.

$\texttt{inSupChain}(X, Y) \leftarrow \texttt{linked}(X, Y)$.
$\texttt{inSupChain}(X, Z) \leftarrow \texttt{linked}(X, Y)$ AND $\texttt{inSupChain}(Y, Z)$.

To generalize, for a given set of events that satisfy certain *temporal* relationships, our approach may be used to additionally check whether these events satisfy certain *semantic* relationships with respect to domain knowledge that itself may be dynamically collected. Semantic relationships between occurring events is an important dimension, neglected in today's CEP systems. It helps discovering the *context* in which events occurred by combining *knowledge management* techniques (e.g., *deductive reasoning*) with event stream processing.

Event revision. To illustrate how *event revision* can be useful in practise, let us consider the following example. An automated stock brokerage system sells stocks to its clients. The system emits an event described by availableStock to a client every time

[6] SWI-Prolog: http://www.swi-prolog.org/pldoc/package/semweb.html

when the respective stocks become available. The event contains information about the company's stock ID, the current price Pri, and the available amount of stocks Amt. A client (identified by CID) may now signal the request to buy the offered stocks by sending an event `trChecked` back to the system, stating the wanted amount Amt_1 of stocks. Event `availableStock` followed by event `trChecked` will trigger a complex event `buyStocks` according to the following rule:

$$\texttt{buyStocks}(CID, ID, Pri, Amt_1) \leftarrow \texttt{availableStock}(ID, Pri, Amt) \\ \quad \text{SEQ } \texttt{trChecked}(CID, ID, Pri, Amt_1) \text{ WHERE } Amt_1 \leq Amt.$$

Upon detection, event `buyStocks` will trigger two transactions: the first transaction transfers money from the client's account to the broker's account, the second transaction maintains the balance of available stocks, by subtracting Amt_1 from Amt. The maintenance is necessary as available stocks are also offered to other interested clients. Since the stock trading is carried out in real-time, it is important that execution in the stock brokerage system is automated and that the transaction of one client does not block executions of other clients (as long as $Amt > 0$). Now, suppose that event `balanceChange` is triggered whenever the balance of available stocks changes from Amt_2 to Amt_3 by customer identified as CID (i.e., whenever the second transaction completes). For example, these events may be used for transaction execution monitoring, statistical analysis, etc. Let us furthermore assume that the following pattern is used to detect stock trades of suspiciously large volume, which may hint at a potential fraud.

$$\texttt{bigTrade}(CID, ID, Amt_1) \leftarrow \texttt{buyStocks}(CID, ID, Pri, Amt_1) \\ \quad \text{SEQ } \texttt{balanceChange}(CID, Amt_2, Amt_3) \text{ WHERE } (Amt_2 - Amt_3) > 10000.$$

Many transactions concurrently change the balance, and after each change, event `balanceChange` is triggered. Now let us suppose that an event `bigTrade` has been detected, and a fraud investigation was initiated. Just a second afterwards, the money transfer transaction fails (due to insufficient account balance of a customer). In this situation, the amount of available stocks will be restored by executing a compensation transaction. Moreover, the corresponding `balanceChange` event needs to be retracted. Finally, the `bigTrade` complex event needs to be revoked too, leading to the cancelation of the fraud investigation.

The automated stock brokerage system operates with flexible policies, allowing customers to cancel their transaction within certain time. If after detection of event `bigTrade`, a customer cancels her transaction (by *retracting* event `trChecked`) the atomic event `buyStocks` will be revoked too, which in turn will necessitate the retraction of event `bigTrade`.

2.3 Declarative Semantics

We define the declarative formal semantics of our language for event processing in a model-theoretic way.

Note that we assume a fixed interpretation of the occurring function symbols, i.e., for every function symbol f of arity n, we presume a predefined function $f^* : Con^n \to Con$. That is, in our setting, functions are treated as built-in utilities.

As usual, a *variable assignment* is a mapping $\mu : Var \rightarrow Con$ assigning a value to every variable. We let μ^* denote the extension of μ to terms defined in the usual way:

$$\mu^* : \begin{cases} v \mapsto \mu(v) & \text{if } v \in Var, \\ c \mapsto c & \text{if } c \in Con, \\ f(t_1, \ldots, t_n) \mapsto f^*(\mu^*(t_1), \ldots, \mu^*(t_n)) & \text{otherwise.} \end{cases}$$

In addition to the set of rules $\mathcal{R}$, we define an *event stream* $\mathcal{S} = (\mathbb{E}, \mathsf{ev}, \mathsf{occ}, \mathsf{rev})$. Thereby, $\mathbb{E}$ is a set of events, $\mathsf{ev} : \mathbb{E} \rightarrow Ground$ a function assigning a ground atom (specifying the event type and possibly additional information) to every event and $\mathsf{occ}, \mathsf{rev} : \mathbb{E} \nrightarrow \mathbb{Q}^+$ partial functions assigning to events time points at which they occur or are revoked, respectively. As a side condition, we presume that for all $e \in \mathbb{E}$ with $\mathsf{rev}(e)$ defined, $\mathsf{occ}(e)$ is defined as well and $\mathsf{occ}(e) < \mathsf{rev}(e)$, i.e., an event can only be revoked after it has occurred. Moreover, we require the event stream to be free of accumulation points, i.e., for every $q \in \mathbb{Q}^+$, the set $\{q' \in \mathbb{Q}^+ \mid q' < q \text{ and } q' = \mathsf{occ}(e) \text{ for some } e \in \mathbb{E}\}$ is finite.

Given an event stream $\mathcal{S} = (\mathbb{E}, \mathsf{ev}, \mathsf{occ}, \mathsf{rev})$ and a time "viewpoint" $v \in \mathbb{Q}^+$, we now define the auxiliary function $\epsilon_v : Ground \rightarrow 2^{\mathbb{Q}^+}$ from ground atoms into sets of nonnegative rational numbers by

$$\epsilon_v(at) := \mathsf{occ}\big(\mathsf{ev}^{-1}(at) \cap \big(\mathsf{occ}^{-1}([0, v]) \setminus \mathsf{rev}^{-1}([0, v])\big)\big)$$

It thereby indicates at what time instants what event types occur according to all the (occurrence and revocation) information obtained up to the time viewpoint v.

Now, we define an interpretation $\mathcal{I} : Ground \rightarrow 2^{\mathbb{Q}^+ \times \mathbb{Q}^+}$ as a mapping from the ground atoms to sets of pairs of nonnegative rationals, such that $q_1 \leq q_2$ for every $\langle q_1, q_2 \rangle \in \mathcal{I}(g)$ for all $g \in Ground$.

Given an event stream $\mathcal{S}$ and a viewpoint $v \in \mathbb{Q}^+$, we call an interpretation $\mathcal{I}$ *model* for a rule set $\mathcal{R}$ – written as $\mathcal{I} \models^v_{\mathcal{S}} \mathcal{R}$ – if the following conditions are satisfied:

C1 $\langle q, q \rangle \in \mathcal{I}(g)$ for every $g \in Ground$ and $q \in \epsilon_v(g)$.
C2 for every rule $atom \leftarrow pattern$ and every variable assignment μ we have $\mathcal{I}_\mu(atom) \subseteq \mathcal{I}_\mu(pattern)$ where $\mathcal{I}_\mu$ is inductively defined as displayed in Figure 2.

Given an interpretation $\mathcal{I}$ and some $q \in \mathbb{Q}^+$, we let $\mathcal{I}|_q$ denote the interpretation defined via $\mathcal{I}|_q(g) = \mathcal{I}(g) \cap \{\langle q_1, q_2 \rangle \mid q_2 - q_1 \leq q\}$.

Given two interpretations $\mathcal{I}$ and $\mathcal{J}$, we say that $\mathcal{I}$ is *preferred* to $\mathcal{J}$ if there exists a $q \in \mathbb{Q}^+$ with $\mathcal{I}|_q \subset \mathcal{J}|_q$.

A model $\mathcal{I}$ is called *minimal* if there is no other model preferred to $\mathcal{I}$. It is easy to show that for every event stream $\mathcal{S}$, viewpoint $v \in \mathbb{Q}^+$, and rule base $\mathcal{R}$ there is a unique minimal model $\mathcal{I}^{\mathcal{S},v,\mathcal{R}}$.

Finally, given an atom a and two rational numbers q_1, q_2, we say that the event $a^{[q_1,q_2]}$ is a *consequence* of the event stream ϵ and the rule base $\mathcal{R}$ at the viewpoint v (written $\mathcal{S}, v, \mathcal{R} \models a^{[q_1,q_2]}$), if $\langle q_1, q_2 \rangle \in \mathcal{I}_\mu^{\mathcal{S},v,\mathcal{R}}(a)$ for some variable assignment μ.

Clearly, the problem of deciding $\mathcal{S}, v, \mathcal{R} \models a^{[q_1,q_2]}$ is time polynomial with respect to the combined size of $\mathcal{R}$ and $\mathcal{S}$, given bounded arity of the used predicates and polynomial computation time for the built-in functions. This result is a straightforward consequence from the fact that there only polynomially many $a^{[q_1,q_2]}$ to be considered

pattern	$\mathcal{I}_\mu$(pattern)
$\mathtt{pr}(t_1,\ldots,t_n)$	$\mathcal{I}(\mathtt{pr}(\mu^*(t_1),\ldots,\mu^*(t_n)))$
p WHERE t	$\mathcal{I}_\mu(p)$ if $\mu^*(t) = \mathit{true}$ $\emptyset$ otherwise.
q	$\{\langle q,q\rangle\}$ for all $q \in \mathbb{Q}^+$
$(p).q$	$\mathcal{I}_\mu(p) \cap \{\langle q_1,q_2\rangle \mid q_2 - q_1 = q\}$
p_1 SEQ p_2	$\{\langle q_1,q_4\rangle \mid \langle q_1,q_2\rangle \in \mathcal{I}_\mu(p_1)$ and $\langle q_3,q_4\rangle \in \mathcal{I}_\mu(p_2)$ for some $q_2,q_3 \in \mathbb{Q}^+$ with $q_2 < q_3\}$
p_1 AND p_2	$\{\langle \min(q_1,q_3),\max(q_2,q_4)\rangle \mid \langle q_1,q_2\rangle \in \mathcal{I}_\mu(p_1)$ and $\langle q_3,q_4\rangle \in \mathcal{I}_\mu(p_2)$ for some $q_2,q_3 \in \mathbb{Q}^+\}$
p_1 PAR p_2	$\{\langle \min(q_1,q_3),\max(q_2,q_4)\rangle \mid \langle q_1,q_2\rangle \in \mathcal{I}_\mu(p_1)$ and $\langle q_3,q_4\rangle \in \mathcal{I}_\mu(p_2)$ for some $q_2,q_3 \in \mathbb{Q}^+$ with $\max(q_1,q_3) < \min(q_2,q_4)\}$
p_1 OR p_2	$\mathcal{I}_\mu(p_1) \cup \mathcal{I}_\mu(p_2)$
p_1 EQUALS p_2	$\mathcal{I}_\mu(p_1) \cap \mathcal{I}_\mu(p_2)$
p_1 MEETS p_2	$\{\langle q_1,q_3\rangle \mid \langle q_1,q_2\rangle \in \mathcal{I}_\mu(p_1)$ and $\langle q_2,q_3\rangle \in \mathcal{I}_\mu(p_2)$ for some $q_2 \in \mathbb{Q}^+\}$
p_1 DURING p_2	$\{\langle q_3,q_4\rangle \mid \langle q_1,q_2\rangle \in \mathcal{I}_\mu(p_1)$ and $\langle q_3,q_4\rangle \in \mathcal{I}_\mu(p_2)$ for some $q_2,q_3 \in \mathbb{Q}^+$ with $q_3 < q_1 < q_2 < q_4\}$
p_1 STARTS p_2	$\{\langle q_1,q_3\rangle \mid \langle q_1,q_2\rangle \in \mathcal{I}_\mu(p_1)$ and $\langle q_1,q_3\rangle \in \mathcal{I}_\mu(p_2)$ for some $q_2 \in \mathbb{Q}^+$ with $q_2 < q_3\}$
p_1 FINISHES p_2	$\{\langle q_1,q_3\rangle \mid \langle q_2,q_3\rangle \in \mathcal{I}_\mu(p_1)$ and $\langle q_1,q_3\rangle \in \mathcal{I}_\mu(p_2)$ for some $q_2 \in \mathbb{Q}^+$ with $q_1 < q_2\}$
NOT$(p_1).[p_2,p_3]$	$\mathcal{I}_\mu(p_2$ SEQ $p_3) \setminus \mathcal{I}_\mu(p_2$ SEQ p_1 SEQ $p_3)$

Fig. 2. Definition of extensional interpretation of event patterns. We use $p_{(x)}$ for patterns, $q_{(x)}$ for rational numbers, $t_{(x)}$ for terms, and pr for predicates .

and their validity can be computed in a bottom-up way with increasing interval length. The computational overhead introduced by event revision is not measurable in terms of worst-case complexity which is PTime with and without the revision component.

In the sequel, we will see how this declarative, time-dependent semantics is realized incrementally, as v proceeds, i.e., the "computed semantics" at some time viewpoint v is revised to obtain the semantics at some latter stage, instead of computing everything from scratch.

3 A Rule-Based Execution Model

This section starts with a brief explanation on how complex events can be computed with *event-driven backward chaining* (EDBC) rules [3]. This is our basic mechanism for derivation of complex events in a data-driven fashion (with logic rules). Later on, we extend the mechanism to handle event revision too.

Sequence with event revision. Let us consider a sequence of events represented as a rule: e $\leftarrow$ a SEQ b SEQ c. Event e is detected when event a[7] is followed by b and in turn followed by event c. We can always represent the above pattern as $e \leftarrow ((a$ SEQ $b)$ SEQ $c)$.

We refer to this way of "coupling events" as *binarization* of events. Effectively, in binarization we introduce *two-input* intermediate events (goals). For example this allows us to rewrite the above sequence as $ie_1 \leftarrow a$ SEQ b, and $e \leftarrow ie_1$ SEQ c. Every monitored event (either atomic or complex), including intermediate events, will be assigned with one or more *logic rules*, fired whenever that event occurs.

In the following, we give more details about assigning rules to each monitored event. Algorithm 1 accepts as input a rule referring to a binary sequence $e_i \leftarrow a$ SEQ b, and produces executable rules for the sequence pattern. A detected sequence can also be *retracted* by the given transformation. If this occurs, the retraction is further propagated amongst other patterns (built upon that sequence).

[7] More precisely, by "event a" is meant an *instance* of the event of type a.

Algorithm 1. Sequence

Output: event-driven backward chaining rules for SEQ operator including revision.
Each event binary goal $\mathtt{ie_1} \leftarrow \mathtt{a}$ SEQ $\mathtt{b}$ is converted into: {

```
         a(ID, [T1, T2]) :- for_each(a, 1, ID, [T1, T2]).
      a(1, ID, [T1, T2]) :- assert(goal(b(_, [_, _]), a(ID, [T1, T2]), ie1(_, [_, _]))).
     rev_a(ID, [T3, T4]) :- for_each(rev_a, 1, ID, [T3, T4]).
  rev_a(1, ID, [T3, T4]) :- goal(b(_, [_, _]), a(ID, [T1, T2]),
                            ie1(_, [_, _])), retract(goal(b(_, [_, _]), a(ID, [T1, T2]))).
  rev_a(2, ID, [T3, T4]) :- (ie_1(ID, [T1, T2]),
                            retract(ie_1(ID, [T1, T2])), rev_ie1(ID, [T1, T2])); true.
         b(ID, [T3, T4]) :- for_each(b, 1, ID, [T3, T4]).
      b(1, ID, [T3, T4]) :- goal(b(_, [_, _]), a(ID, [T1, T2]),
                            ie1(_, [_, _])), T2 < T3, ie1(ID, [T1, T4]).
     rev_b(ID, [T5, T6]) :- for_each(rev_a, 1, ID, [T5, T6]).
  rev_b(1, ID, [T5, T6]) :- (ie1(ID, [T1, T4]),
                            retract(ie1(ID, [T1, T4])), rev_ie1(ID, [T1, T4])); true.
      ie_1(ID, [T1, T4]) :- for_each(ie_1, 1, ID, [T1, T4]).
   ie_1(1, ID, [T1, T4]) :- assert(ie_1(ID, [T1, T4])).}
}
```

The binarization step must precede the rule transformation. We first consider rules that handle sequence without event revision. These rules in Algorithm 1 do not have prefix *rev_event_name* (e.g., $rev\_a(1, ID, [T_3, T_4])$), and belong to one of two different classes of rules[8]. We refer to the first class as to *goal inserting rules*. The second class corresponds to *checking rules*. For example, the second rule in Algorithm 1 (i.e., with $\mathtt{a}(1, ID, [T_1, T_2])$ in the rule head) belongs to the first class of rules, as it inserts $goal(b(\_,\_), a(T_1, T_2), ie_1(\_,\_))$. This rule will fire when an event of type a occurs, and the meaning of the inserted goal is as follows: "an event a has occurred at $[T_1, T_2]$,[9] and we are waiting for event b to happen in order to detect event $\mathtt{ie_1}$." Obviously, the goal does not carry information about times for b and $\mathtt{ie_1}$, as we don't know when they will occur. In general, the *second* event in a goal always denotes the event that has just occurred. The role of the *first* argument is to specify what we are waiting for, to detect an event that is on the *third* position.

The rule with $\mathtt{b}(1, ID, [T_3, T_4])$ in the rule head (see Algorithm 1) belongs to the second class (i.e., *checking rule*). This rule checks whether certain prerequisite goals already have been asserted, in which case it triggers the more complex event. In this example, the rule will fire whenever event b occurs. The rule checks whether $goal(\mathtt{b}(\_, [\_, \_]), \mathtt{a}(ID, [T_1, T_2]), \mathtt{ie_1}(\_, [\_, \_]))$ already exists (i.e., a has previously happened), in which case the rule triggers $\mathtt{ie_1}$, by calling $\mathtt{ie_1}(ID, [T_1, T_4])$. After detection of event $\mathtt{ie_1}$, $goal(\mathtt{b}(\_, [\_, \_]), \mathtt{a}(ID, [T_1, T_2]), \mathtt{ie_1}(\_, [\_, \_]))$ could be removed from

[8] There exist the third class of rules too (with `for_each` predicate). However these auxiliary rules, implementing a sort of "for each" loop, and ensuring that whenever an event of certain type happens, all rules with that event in the head fire.

[9] Apart from the timestamp, an event may carry other data parameters. They are omitted here for the sake of readability.

the database to free up memory (as it is "consumed"). However this is not the case, as the goal still may be useful if the revision of event a takes place (see below the case when event rev_a happens).

The time occurrence of $\mathtt{ie}_1$ (i.e., $[T_1, T_4]$) is defined based on the occurrence of constituting events (i.e., $\mathtt{a}(ID, [T_1, T_2])$, and $\mathtt{b}(ID, [T_3, T_4])$, see Section 2.3). By calling $\mathtt{ie}_1(ID, [T_1, T_4])$, this event will be inserted as a fact (see Algorithm 1). If later on, the revision process takes place, this fact will serve as a proof that event $\mathtt{ie}_1$ occurred and hence may be retracted. If event $\mathtt{ie}_1$ is further used in composition of other complex events, there will exist another rule with $\mathtt{ie}_1$ in the rule head (apart from the current rules). The purpose of those rules would be to propagate the occurrence of event $\mathtt{ie}_1$ upward (since it is an intermediate event).

Let us now explain how Algorithm 1 handles *event revision* in a sequence of two events. If once detected, event $\mathtt{ie}_1$ may be retracted by an occurrence of either event rev_a or rev_b. That is why there are two sets of *revision* rules: rev_a and rev_b, see Algorithm 1. Additionally, events rev_a and rev_b may retract other detected events, if they were used in their detections and their IDs match. The identification (ID) is used to make a distinction between possible retractions of instances of the same event types.

If an event rev_a happens, rules $\mathtt{rev\_a}(1, ID, [T_3, T_4])$ and $\mathtt{rev\_a}(2, ID, [T_3, T_4])$ aim to nullify a prior occurrence of an event a. In particular, if an event a has happened, a goal $goal(\mathtt{b}(\_, [\_, \_]), \mathtt{a}(ID, [T_1, T_2]), \mathtt{ie}_1(\_, [\_, \_]))$ will be inserted into the database. Therefore the subsequent occurrence of rev_a needs to delete that goal. The rule $\mathtt{rev\_a}(1, ID, [T_3, T_4])$ does that. If the following sequence of events occurs: $\mathtt{a}, \mathtt{rev\_a}, \mathtt{b}$, then event $\mathtt{ie}_1$ will not be detected (as rev_a has nullified the occurrence of a). If event rev_a happens after event b, event $\mathtt{ie}_1$ will need to be retracted (as it has already been detected). The rule with $\mathtt{rev\_a}(2, ID, [T_3, T_4])$ in the head is used in the latter scenario.

In the previously described algorithm, we assumed that all events in a binarized pattern have the same ID (i.e., $\mathtt{ie}_1(ID) \leftarrow \mathtt{a}(ID)$ BIN $\mathtt{b}(ID)$). It is worth noting that some intermediate or complex events may be composed of events with different IDs. In such cases, an additional ID may be added, e.g., $\mathtt{ie}_1(ID_1, ID_2)$. ID_1 will then denote an ID of the left-hand-side event ($\mathtt{a}(ID_1)$), and ID_2 will denote an ID of the right-hand-side event ($\mathtt{b}(ID_2)$). Checking these IDs when certain events are retracted allows to employ event revision using the presented algorithms with no further restriction.

Rules produced by the transformation in Algorithm 1 are executable rules (Prolog rules). With no restriction these rules may be accompanied by other Prolog rules, used for example to express the background or domain *knowledge* (see Example "Knowledge-based patterns" from Section 2.2). To also enable use of existing online knowledge bases expressed as RDFS ontologies (e.g., from LOD initiative and other sources, see Section 1), we use existing tools for conversion of RDFS to Prolog, such as SWI-Prolog Semantic Web Library. This conversion is done at design-time, and has no impact at run-time characteristics of our framework.

Rule transformations for other language constructs – defined in Section 2 – are omitted for space reasons.

4 Experimental Results

As a proof of concept, we have provided a prototype implementation of the presented framework for knowledge-based CEP with event revision capabilities. The implementation is part of our open-source engine for event processing called ETALIS[10]. Since our approach is based on deductive rules, it was convenient to provide the implementation in Prolog.[11] The prototype automatically compiles the user-defined complex patterns, written in the presented language (see Section 2) into Prolog rules. Also, our engine can automatically load an accompanied RDFS ontology (as a domain background knowledge base) into Prolog. YAP Prolog version 5.1.3[12] is then used to execute the compiled rules. All tests were carried out on a workstation with Intel Core Quad CPU Q9400 2,66GHz, 8GB of RAM, running Windows Vista x64. To run tests on streaming data, we have implemented an event stream generator that creates time series data with probabilistic events. We present a test with real data set too.

Knowledge-based CEP test. As a concrete example, we show the evaluation of the *trendIncrease* complex pattern from Section 2.2. We varied the pool of companies in the transitive closure, ranging from 100 to 100,000 *linked* companies. Figure 3(a) shows the throughput in thousands of events/second, obtained after detection of *stockIcr* events. To prove the supply-chain connectivity between two companies, the system needs to evaluate transitive closure rules, i.e., it needs to perform Stream Reasoning (see *inSupChain* rules from Section 2.2). It can be seen that the computation of the recursive relation *inSupChain* has a relatively small effect, $\sim$10%, on the overall complex processing execution time (even when the system needs to traverse 100,000 *links* in between two *stockIcr* events). Our system detects more 20000 complex events per second, where for each complex event, the system additionally needed to process background knowledge consisting of 100000 facts (or RDF triples).

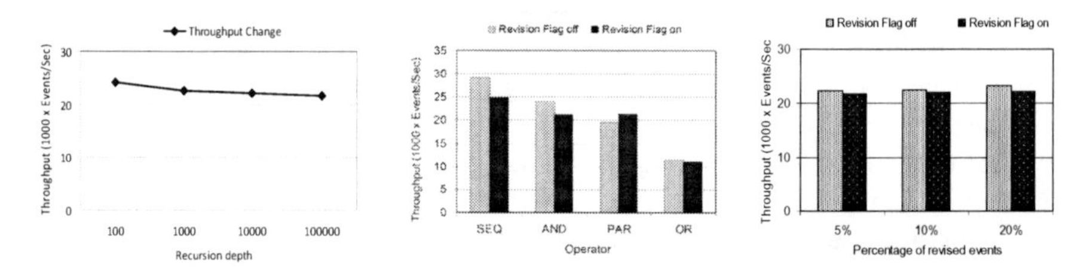

Fig. 3. (a) CEP with Stream Reasoning (b) Throughput comparison (c) Negation and revision

Event revision CEP experiments. Figure 3(b) shows experimental results we obtained for an event pattern represented by rule (1). In particular, Figure 3(b) shows the throughput comparison with and without handling event revision. We did the measurement for a pattern that exhibits different event operators (i.e., BIN instantiated by SEQ, AND, OR) of two events and the join operation on their ID attribute. The y-axis shows the

[10] ETALIS: `http://code.google.com/p/etalis/`

[11] With similar effort, our revision model could be implemented in other rule languages too.

[12] YAP Prolog: `http://www.dcc.fc.up.pt/~vsc/Yap/`

event throughput achieved by our prototype when events are, and are not, retractable. The x-axis shows different event operators in rule (1). The performance loss when revision is handled is moderate, and it happens mainly due to the fact that more events (goals) are kept in memory; hence more data needs to be indexed and processed.

$$\mathtt{e}(ID) \leftarrow \mathtt{a}(ID)\ \textsc{bin}\ \mathtt{b}(ID). \quad (1)$$

We also present an in-comparison throughput for negation. The tested pattern with negation is depicted by rule (2). The pattern detects an event a followed by an event b, with no occurrence of an event c in between (provided that all event instances must have the same ID). Figure 3(c) shows evaluation results for this pattern. We compare two throughputs, one obtained by processing streams without retracted events; and another with retracted events. The percentage of negated events (i.e., those of type c) in both streams varies from 5% to 20%. Additionally, streams with retracted events contain negated events with the same percentage (i.e., from 5% to 20%). The achieved results are similar to those from other operators.

$$\mathtt{e}(ID) \leftarrow \textsc{not}(\mathtt{c}(ID)).[\mathtt{a}(ID)\ \textsc{seq}\ \mathtt{b}(ID)]. \quad (2)$$

We have also tested the *latency* caused by retraction of a hierarchy of complex events (i.e., not only complex events detected directly from an input stream). Complex events in this tests are chained events, as represented by rule (3). That is, when event $\mathtt{e_1}$ occurs, it will trigger other n events in a chain. Also if event $\mathtt{e_1}$ is retracted, all n chained events will be retracted. We have created event chains of different sizes, ranging from 1000 events to 50000 events. Once the chains are created, we retract the first event in the chain and measure the time required to retract all other triggered events. Figure 4 shows the experiment results. Retraction of 1000 event is done in 31 ms and all up to 10000 events the delay seems fairly negligible (less than a second). However to retract 20000 and specially for 50000 events, the time increases exponentially (i.e., approx. 3 s and 16 s). Note that this test is rather hard as we assumed that all 50000 events have the same ID, so no goal could have been removed while computing and retracting all of them. Obviously, this fact has its consequences on the performance.

$$\begin{aligned} &\mathtt{e_2}(ID) \leftarrow \mathtt{e_1}(ID).\\ &\mathtt{e_3}(ID) \leftarrow \mathtt{e_2}(ID).\\ &\ldots\\ &\mathtt{e_{n+1}}(ID) \leftarrow \mathtt{e_n}(ID). \end{aligned} \quad (3)$$

All presented tests so far were carried out with probabilistic synthetic data streams. We could not find available real data sets with revision tuples (as they are usually kept proprietarily). Still to present a more realistic scenario, we took a stream of IBM stocks from 1962 year up to now, provided by Yahoo Finance[13]. We artificially inserted 5% of revision tuples to this stream. Format of events provided by Yahoo Finance is $\mathtt{stock}(ID, Date, Opn, High, Low, Cls, Vol, Adj)$ where ID is a company ID; $Date$ is a current date; $Opn, High, Low, Cls$ denote the opening, the highest, the lowest, and closing price, respectively; Adj is the closing price adjusted for dividends and splits.

[13] Yahoo Finance: `http://finance.yahoo.com/`

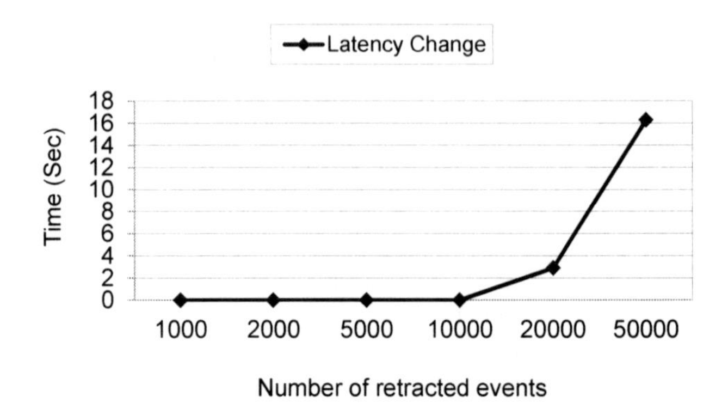

Fig. 4. Event latency

The event pattern is represented by rule (4). We monitored the price increase of two successive stock updates w.r.t *Adj* data. Additionally a filter for the price increase was specified by X, where X varied between 0% and 10%. Figure 5(b) compare results obtained for the original stream and the one modified with revision tuples.

$$\begin{aligned}
&\texttt{stockIncr}(ID, Adj_1, Adj_2) \leftarrow \\
&\quad \texttt{stock}(ID, Date_1, Opn_1, High_1, Low_1, Cls_1, Vol_1, Adj_1) \\
&\quad \text{SEQ} \\
&\quad \texttt{stock}(ID, Date_2, Opn_2, High_2, Low_2, Cls_2, Vol_2, Adj_2) \\
&\quad \text{WHERE } (Adj_1 * X < Adj_2).
\end{aligned} \tag{4}$$

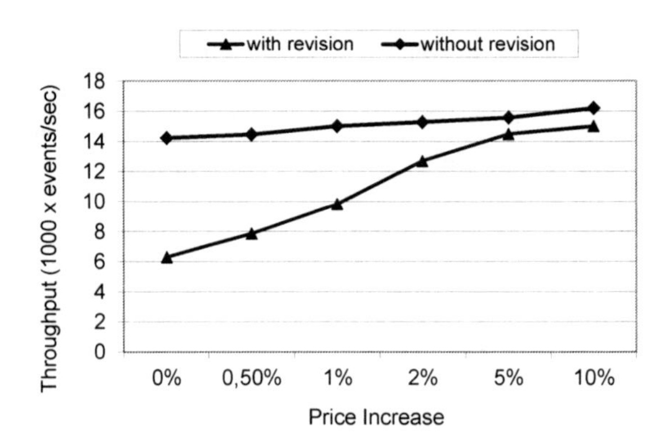

Fig. 5. Stock price change on a real data set

First, we see that the throughput without revision is lower than the one obtained from a similar test (see Figure 3(b)). Our closer investigation has shown that this difference was not caused by the use of real data set. Instead it has to do with more efficient indexing in the former test (Figure 3(b)). Note that in the real stream, all events are of the same type (i.e., *stock*) whereas in the synthetic data set we have two types (i.e.,

a and b). Our engine is more effective when events are discriminated upon their types (rather than on data attributes, e.g., an ID). Second, we can observe that the throughput without revision slightly increases as the filter condition gets tighter. This result is understandable, since in this case, less complex events, are computed and the throughput (based on the input stream) raises up.

At the end, it is worth mentioning that costs of compilation of an event program (written in the formalism, proposed in Section 2) into Prolog rules are minor. Typically, a program is compiled in few micro seconds, and the compilation is done only once at the design-time. Hence, the compilation does not cause a significant overhead.

5 Related Work

Work related to ours goes in two directions. The first direction reviews existing approaches from Data Stream Management Systems (DSMS) that also handle event revision (retraction). The other discusses Knowledge-based CEP & Stream Reasoning. We are not aware of any approach covering both aspects.

DSMS approaches. The Borealis CEP engine [9] features a mechanism for revision processing. The mechanism handles erroneous input events by generating corrections of previously output query results on data streams.

This work has been extended in [12] by proposing a revision model based on "replay" of event history. The technique assumes that a stream engine maintains an archive of recent data seen on each of its input streams. These archives are revised when revision tuples occur, and reprocessing (replaying) the sequence of input tuples than generates any of the query results invalidated by the revision.

While this technique is general and works well for all classes of patterns supported by Borealis system [9], it requires the event history to be kept (persisted). The history is kept as long as revision needs to be guaranteed. In our approach we also need to keep extra data in order to enable revision. However we saw (in Section 3) that we do not need to keep the *whole* event history (i.e., during the period of time in which revision is guaranteed). We keep only intermediate results (goals) relevant w.r.t detected complex events. Moreover we do not need to *replay* the whole history when computing revisions. The intermediate results (goals) represent partial results, hence they enable us to obtain revisions without re-computing them from scratch.

In [7] revision is considered as a problem caused by out of order events, i.e., it is possible to revise the occurrence time as well as the time when an event is reported to the system. We consider a general case where not only times can be revised, but the whole event can be retracted. Moreover, the consequences of that retraction are amended not only on detected patterns but also on complex patterns that are built out of them (i.e., hierarchies of complex events). The work in [7] is based on *buffering* and synchronization points. An input stream may be *blocked* in between synchronization points until events are reordered. On the other hand, we propose an approach that never blocks the input events. Further on, we never buffer the input stream and reorder it.

Knowledge-based CEP & Stream Reasoning. Continuous SPARQL (C-SPARQL) [5] is a language for continuous query processing over streams of RDF data. It extends the SPARQL language by adding support for window and aggregation operations. The work in [8] introduces Streaming SPARQL. The approach is built on temporal relational algebra, and the authors provide an algorithm to transform SPARQL queries to that algebra. As in [5], the approach is lacking event processing capabilities, i.e., detecting RDF triple sequences occurring in a specific time relatedness.

Finally, in [10] an approach for integrating sensor streams with LOD background knowledge has been presented. As a part of this work, a continuous query language, CQELS, has been proposed. The language supports sliding windows, aggregations, and other operators supported by SPARQL language (which are now adapted to stream processing).

Our work is similar to this and other, previously mentioned, approaches. We, however, follow completely a deductive rule-based paradigm, providing an effective solution for CEP and Stream Reasoning. Additionally our approach handles revision in event processing too.

6 Conclusions and Future Work

Complex Event Processing (CEP) deals with processing of continuously arriving events with the goal of identifying meaningful patterns, (complex events). In existing CEP approaches complex events consist merely of more simple (temporally situated) events. We proposed a *knowledge-based* event processing, advocating a richer formalism for CEP, capable not only to match patterns based on *temporal* relations among events but also to evaluate *contextual knowledge* and prove their *semantic* relations. Moreover, we proposed a framework which enables *revision* in pattern matching. We have demonstrated that our deductive rule-based approach for CEP represents a natural way to realize knowledge-based CEP with Stream Reasoning, and express routines required for event revisions.

Acknowledgments

This work was partially supported by the European Commission funded project PLAY (FP7-20495) and by the ExpresST project funded by the German Research Foundation (DFG). We thank Jia Ding and Ahmed Khalil Hafsi for their help in implementation and testing ETALIS.

References

1. Agrawal, J., Diao, Y., Gyllstrom, D., Immerman, N.: Efficient pattern matching over event streams. In: SIGMOD, pp. 147–160 (2008)
2. Allen, J.F.: Maintaining knowledge about temporal intervals. Communications of the ACM 26, 832–843 (1983)
3. Anicic, D., Fodor, P., Rudolph, S., Stühmer, R., Stojanovic, N., Studer, R.: A rule-based language for complex event processing and reasoning. In: Hitzler, P., Lukasiewicz, T. (eds.) RR 2010. LNCS, vol. 6333, pp. 42–57. Springer, Heidelberg (2010)

4. Arasu, A., Babu, S., Widom, J.: The cql continuous query language: semantic foundations and query execution. VLDB Journal 15, 121–142 (2006)
5. Barbieri, D.F., Braga, D., Ceri, S., Grossniklaus, M.: An execution environment for c-sparql queries. In: EDBT, pp. 441–452 (2010)
6. Barbieri, D.F., Braga, D., Ceri, S., Valle, E.D., Grossniklaus, M.: Incremental reasoning on streams and rich background knowledge. In: Aroyo, L., Antoniou, G., Hyvönen, E., ten Teije, A., Stuckenschmidt, H., Cabral, L., Tudorache, T. (eds.) ESWC 2010. LNCS, vol. 6088, pp. 1–15. Springer, Heidelberg (2010)
7. Barga, R.S., Goldstein, J., Ali, M.H., Hong, M.: Consistent streaming through time: A vision for event stream processing. In: Proceedings of the 3rd Biennial Conference on Innovative Data Systems Research (CIDR 2007), pp. 363–374 (2007)
8. Bolles, A., Grawunder, M., Jacobi, J.: Streaming SPARQL - extending SPARQL to process data streams. In: Bechhofer, S., Hauswirth, M., Hoffmann, J., Koubarakis, M. (eds.) ESWC 2008. LNCS, vol. 5021, pp. 448–462. Springer, Heidelberg (2008)
9. Carney, D., et al.: Monitoring streams: a new class of data management applications. In: VLDB 2002, pp. 215–226 (2002)
10. Le-Phuoc, D., Parreira, J.X., Hausenblas, M., Hauswirth, M.: Unifying stream data and linked open data. DERI Technical Report (August 15, 2010)
11. Luckham, D.: The Power of Events: An Introduction to Complex Event Processing in Distributed Enterprise Systems. Addison-Wesley, Reading (2002)
12. Maskey, A.S., Cherniack, M.: Replay-based approaches to revision processing in stream query engines. In: SSPS, pp. 3–12 (2008)
13. Mei, Y., Madden, S.: Zstream: a cost-based query processor for adaptively detecting composite events. In: SIGMOD, pp. 193–206 (2009)
14. Ryvkina, E., Maskey, A.S., Cherniack, M., Zdonik, S.: Revision processing in a stream processing engine: A high-level design. In: ICDE 2006, USA, pp. 141–143 (2006)
15. Valle, E.D., Ceri, S., van Harmelen, F., Fensel, D.: It's a streaming world! reasoning upon rapidly changing information. IEEE Intelligent Systems 24, 83–89 (2009)

A Declarative Framework for Matching Iterative and Aggregative Patterns against Event Streams

Darko Anicic[1], Sebastian Rudolph[2], Paul Fodor[3], and Nenad Stojanovic[1]

[1] FZI Research Center for Information Technology, Germany
[2] AIFB, Karlsruhe Institute of Technology, Germany
[3] State University of New York at Stony Brook, USA

Abstract. Complex Event Processing as well as pattern matching against streams have become important in many areas including financial services, mobile devices, sensor-based applications, click stream analysis, real-time processing in Web 2.0 and 3.0 applications and so forth. However, there is a number of issues to be considered in order to enable effective pattern matching in modern applications. A language for describing patterns needs to feature a well-defined semantics, it needs be rich enough to express important classes of complex patterns such as iterative and aggregative patterns, and the language execution model needs to be efficient since event processing is a real-time processing. In this paper, we present an event processing framework which includes an expressive language featuring a precise semantics and a corresponding execution model, expressive enough to represent iterative and aggregative patterns. Our approach is based on a logic, hence we analyse deductive capabilities of such an event processing framework. Finally, we provide an open source implementation and present experimental results of our running system.

1 Introduction

Pattern matching against event streams is a paradigm of processing continuously arriving events with the goal of identifying meaningful *patterns* (complex events). For instance, occurrence of multiple events form a complex event pattern by matching certain *temporal*, *relational* or *causal* conditions. Complex Event Processing (CEP) has recently aroused significant interest due to its wide applicability in areas such as financial services (e.g., dynamic tracking of stock fluctuations, surveillance for frauds and money laundering etc.), sensor-based applications (e.g., RFID monitoring), network traffic monitoring, Web click analysis etc.

While the pattern matching over continuously arriving events has been well studied [1,10,5,6,9], so far the focus was mostly on the high-performance and the pattern language expressivity. A common approach for stream query processing has been to use select-join-aggregation queries [5,6,9]. While such queries can specify a wide range of patterns, they are unable to express *Kleene* closure. Kleene closure can be used to extract from the input stream a finite yet

N. Bassiliades et al. (Eds.): RuleML 2011 - Europe, LNCS 6826, pp. 138–153, 2011.

unbounded number of events with a particular property. Recent study [1] has presented that non-deterministic finite automate (NFA) are suitable for pattern matching, including also the matching on unbounded events streams.

In this work, we propose a *logic rule-based* approach that supports the class of patterns expressible with select-join-aggregation queries, as well as with Kleene closure and transitive closure. In our formalism these patterns are realized as *iterative* rules.

We advocate here a *logic rule-based* approach because a rule-based formalism is expressive enough and convenient to represent diverse complex event patterns. Rules can easily express complex relationships between events by matching certain temporal, relational or causal conditions. Detected patterns may further be used to build more complex patterns (i.e., the head of one rule may be used in the body of other rule, thereby creating more and more complex events). Also declarative rules are free of side-effects. Moreover, with our rule-based formalism it is possible to realize not only a set of event patterns, but rather the whole *event-driven* application (realized in a single, uniform formalism). Ultimately, a logic-based event model enables *reasoning* over events, their relationships, entire state, and possible contextual *knowledge*. This knowledge captures the *domain* of interest, or *context* related to business critical actions and decisions (that are triggered in real-time by complex events). Its purpose is to be evaluated during detection of complex events in order to *enrich* recorded events with background information; to detect more complex *situations*; to propose certain intelligent *recommendations* in real-time; or to accomplish complex event *classification*, *clustering*, and *filtering*.

Our approach is based on an efficient, *event-driven*, model for detecting event patterns. The model has inference capabilities and yet good run-time characteristics (comparable or better than approaches with no reasoning capabilities). It provides a flexible transformation of complex patterns into *intermediate patterns* (i.e., *goals*) updated in the dynamic memory. The status of achieved goals at the current state shows the progress toward matching of one or more event patterns. Goals are automatically asserted as relevant events occur. They can persist over a period of time "waiting" in order to support detection of a more complex goal or complete pattern. Important characteristics of these goals are that they are asserted only if they are used later on (to support a more complex goal or an event pattern), goals are all unique, and goals persist as long as they remain relevant (after the relevant period they are deleted). Goals are asserted by declarative rules, which are executed in the backward chaining mode. We have implemented the proposed language in a Prolog-based prototype called ETALIS, and evaluated the implementation in Section 4.

2 A Language for Complex Event Processing

We have defined a basic language for CEP in [4]. In this and the following sections, we extend the language to handle *iterative* and *aggregative* event patterns. In order to keep the presentation of the overall formalism self-contained, in this section we also recall basics of the language from [4].

The syntax and semantics of the ETALIS formalism features (i) static rules accounting for static background information about the considered domain and (ii) event rules that are used to capture the dynamic information by defining patterns of complex events. Both parts may be intertwined through the use of common variables. Based on a combined (static and dynamic) specification, we will define the notion of entailment of complex events by a given event stream.

We start by defining the notational primitives of the ETALIS formalism. An ETALIS rule base is based on:

- a set $\mathbf{V}$ of *variables* (denoted by capitals X, Y, ...)
- a set $\mathbf{C}$ of *constant symbols* including *true* and *false*
- for $n \in \mathbb{N}$, sets $\mathbf{F}_n$ of *function symbols* of arity n
- for $n \in \mathbb{N}$, sets $\mathbf{P}^{\mathrm{s}}_n$ of *static predicates* of arity n
- for $n \in \mathbb{N}$, sets $\mathbf{P}^{\mathrm{e}}_n$ of *event predicates* of arity n, disjoint from $\mathbf{P}^{\mathrm{s}}_n$

Based on those, we define *terms* by:

$$t ::= v \mid c \mid \mathtt{p}^{\mathrm{s}}_n(t_1,\ldots,t_n) \mid \mathtt{f}_n(t_1,\ldots,t_n)$$

We define the set of *(static or event) atoms* as the set of all expressions $\mathtt{p}_n(t_1,\ldots,t_n)$ where $\mathtt{p}$ is a (static or event) predicate and $t_1,\ldots t_n$ are terms.

An ETALIS *rule base* $\mathcal{R}$ is composed of a static $\mathcal{R}^{\mathrm{s}}$ and an event part $\mathcal{R}^{\mathrm{e}}$. Thereby, $\mathcal{R}^{\mathrm{s}}$ is a set of Horn clauses using the static predicates $\mathbf{P}^{\mathrm{s}}_n$. Formally, a *static rule* is defined as $a : -a_1,\ldots,a_n$ with $a, a_1,\ldots,a_n$ static atoms. Thereby, every term that a contains must be a variable. Moreover, all variables occurring in any of the atoms have to occur at least once in the rule body outside any function application.

The event part $\mathcal{R}^{\mathrm{e}}$ allows for the definition of patterns based on *time* and *events*. Time instants and durations are represented as nonnegative rational numbers $q \in \mathbb{Q}^+$. Events can be atomic or complex. An *atomic event* refers to an instantaneous occurrence of interest. Atomic events are expressed as ground event atoms (i.e., event predicates the arguments of which do not contain any variables). Intuitively, the arguments of a ground atom representing an atomic event denote information items (i.e. event data) that provide additional information about that event.

Atomic events are combined to *complex events* by *event patterns* describing temporal arrangements of events and absolute time points. The language P of event patterns is defined by

$$\begin{aligned} P ::= \mathtt{p}^{\mathrm{e}}(t_1,\ldots,t_n) &\mid P \text{ WHERE } t \mid q \mid (P).q \\ &\mid P \text{ BIN } P \mid \text{NOT}(P).[P,P] \end{aligned}$$

Thereby, $\mathtt{p}^{\mathrm{e}}$ is an n-ary event predicate, t_i denote terms, t is a term of type boolean, q is a nonnegative rational number, and BIN is one of the binary operators SEQ, AND, PAR, OR, EQUALS, MEETS, DURING, STARTS, or FINISHES[1]. As a

[1] Hence, the defined pattern language captures all possible 13 relations on two temporal intervals as defined in [2].

side condition, in every expression p WHERE t, all variables occurring in t must also occur in the pattern p.

Finally, an *event rule* is defined as a formula of the shape

$$\mathrm{p}^{\mathrm{e}}(t_1, \ldots, t_n) \leftarrow p$$

where p is an event pattern containing all variables occurring in $\mathrm{p}^{\mathrm{e}}(t_1, \ldots, t_n)$.

We define the declarative formal *semantics* of our formalism in a model-theoretic way. Note that we assume a fixed interpretation of the occurring function symbols, i.e. for every function symbol f of arity n, we presume a predefined function $f^* : Con^n \to Con$. That is, in our setting, functions are treated as built-in utilities.

As usual, a *variable assignment* is a mapping $\mu : Var \to Con$ assigning a value to every variable. We let μ^* denote the canonical extension of μ to terms:

$$\mu^* : \begin{cases} v \mapsto \mu(v) & \text{if } v \in Var, \\ c \mapsto c & \text{if } c \in Con, \\ f(t_1, \ldots, t_n) \mapsto f^*(\mu^*(t_1), \ldots, \mu^*(t_n)) & \text{for } f \in \mathbf{F}_n, \\ \mathrm{p}(t_1, \ldots, t_n) \mapsto \begin{cases} \mathit{true} & \text{if } \mathcal{R}^{\mathrm{s}} \models p(\mu^*(t_1), \ldots, \mu^*(t_n)), \\ \mathit{false} & \text{otherwise.} \end{cases} \end{cases}$$

Thereby, $\mathcal{R}^{\mathrm{s}} \models p(\mu^*(t_1), \ldots, \mu^*(t_n))$ is defined by the standard least Herbrand model semantics.

In addition to $\mathcal{R}$, we fix an *event stream*, which is a mapping $\epsilon : Ground^{\mathrm{e}} \to 2^{\mathbb{Q}^+}$ from event ground predicates into sets of nonnegative rational numbers. It indicates what elementary events occur at which time instants.

Moreover, we define an interpretation $\mathcal{I} : Ground^{\mathrm{e}} \to 2^{\mathbb{Q}^+ \times \mathbb{Q}^+}$ as a mapping from the event ground atoms to sets of pairs of nonnegative rationals, such that $q_1 \leq q_2$ for every $\langle q_1, q_2 \rangle \in \mathcal{I}(g)$ for all $g \in Ground^{\mathrm{e}}$. Given an event stream ϵ, an interpretation $\mathcal{I}$ is called a *model* for a rule set $\mathcal{R}$ – written as $\mathcal{I} \models_\epsilon \mathcal{R}$ – if the following conditions are satisfied:

C1 $\langle q, q \rangle \in \mathcal{I}(g)$ for every $q \in \mathbb{Q}^+$ and $g \in Ground$ with $q \in \epsilon(g)$
C2 for every rule *atom* $\leftarrow$ *pattern* and every variable assignment μ we have $\mathcal{I}_\mu(atom) \subseteq \mathcal{I}_\mu(pattern)$ where $\mathcal{I}_\mu$ is inductively defined as displayed in Fig. 1.

For an interpretation $\mathcal{I}$ and some $q \in \mathbb{Q}^+$, we let $\mathcal{I}|_q$ denote the interpretation defined by $\mathcal{I}|_q(g) = \mathcal{I}(g) \cap \{\langle q1, q2 \rangle \mid q2 - q1 \leq q\}$. Given interpretations $\mathcal{I}$ and $\mathcal{J}$, we say that $\mathcal{I}$ is *preferred* to $\mathcal{J}$ if $\mathcal{I}|_q \subset \mathcal{J}|_q$ for some $q \in \mathbb{Q}^+$. A model $\mathcal{I}$ is called *minimal* if there is no other model preferred to $\mathcal{I}$. Obviously, for every event stream ϵ and rule base $\mathcal{R}$ there is a unique minimal model $\mathcal{I}^{\epsilon,\mathcal{R}}$.

Finally, given an atom a and two rational numbers q_1, q_2, we say that the event $a^{[q_1,q_2]}$ is a *consequence* of the event stream ϵ and the rule base $\mathcal{R}$ (written $\epsilon, \mathcal{R} \models a^{[q_1,q_2]}$), if $\langle q_1, q_2 \rangle \in \mathcal{I}_\mu^{\epsilon,\mathcal{R}}(a)$ for some variable assignment μ.

It can be easily verified that the behavior of the event stream ϵ beyond the time point q_2 is irrelevant for determining whether $\epsilon, \mathcal{R} \models a^{[q_1,q_2]}$ is the case[2]. This

[2] More formally, for any two event streams ϵ_1 and ϵ_2 with $\epsilon_1(g) \cap \{\langle q, q' \rangle \mid q' \leq q_2\} = \epsilon_2(g) \cap \{\langle q, q' \rangle \mid q' \leq q_2\}$ we have that $\epsilon_1, \mathcal{R} \models a^{[q_1,q_2]}$ exactly if $\epsilon_2, \mathcal{R} \models a^{[q_1,q_2]}$.

pattern	$\mathcal{I}_\mu$(pattern)
$\mathtt{pr}(t_1,\ldots,t_n)$	$\mathcal{I}(\mathtt{pr}(\mu^*(t_1),\ldots,\mu^*(t_n)))$
p WHERE t	$\mathcal{I}_\mu(p)$ if $\mu^*(t) = true$ $\emptyset$ otherwise.
q	$\{\langle q,q\rangle\}$ for all $q \in \mathbb{Q}^+$
$(p).q$	$\mathcal{I}_\mu(p) \cap \{\langle q_1,q_2\rangle \mid q_2 - q_1 = q\}$
p_1 SEQ p_2	$\{\langle q_1,q_4\rangle \mid \langle q_1,q_2\rangle \in \mathcal{I}_\mu(p_1)$ and $\langle q_3,q_4\rangle \in \mathcal{I}_\mu(p_2)$ and $q_2 < q_3\}$
p_1 AND p_2	$\{\langle \mathsf{min}(q_1,q_3),\mathsf{max}(q_2,q_4)\rangle \mid \langle q_1,q_2\rangle \in \mathcal{I}_\mu(p_1)$ and $\langle q_3,q_4\rangle \in \mathcal{I}_\mu(p_2)\}$
p_1 PAR p_2	$\{\langle \mathsf{min}(q_1,q_3),\mathsf{max}(q_2,q_4)\rangle \mid \langle q_1,q_2\rangle \in \mathcal{I}_\mu(p_1)$ and $\langle q_3,q_4\rangle \in \mathcal{I}_\mu(p_2)$ and $\mathsf{max}(q_1,q_3) < \mathsf{min}(q_2,q_4)\}$
p_1 OR p_2	$\mathcal{I}_\mu(p_1) \cup \mathcal{I}_\mu(p_2)$
p_1 EQUALS p_2	$\mathcal{I}_\mu(p_1) \cap \mathcal{I}_\mu(p_2)$
p_1 MEETS p_2	$\{\langle q_1,q_3\rangle \mid \langle q_1,q_2\rangle \in \mathcal{I}_\mu(p_1)$ and $\langle q_2,q_3\rangle \in \mathcal{I}_\mu(p_2)\}$
p_1 DURING p_2	$\{\langle q_3,q_4\rangle \mid \langle q_1,q_2\rangle \in \mathcal{I}_\mu(p_1)$ and $\langle q_3,q_4\rangle \in \mathcal{I}_\mu(p_2)$ and $q_3 < q_1 < q_2 < q_4\}$
p_1 STARTS p_2	$\{\langle q_1,q_3\rangle \mid \langle q_1,q_2\rangle \in \mathcal{I}_\mu(p_1)$ and $\langle q_1,q_3\rangle \in \mathcal{I}_\mu(p_2)$ and $q_2 < q_3\}$
p_1 FINISHES p_2	$\{\langle q_1,q_3\rangle \mid \langle q_2,q_3\rangle \in \mathcal{I}_\mu(p_1)$ and $\langle q_1,q_3\rangle \in \mathcal{I}_\mu(p_2)$ and $q_1 < q_2\}$
NOT$(p_1).[p_2,p_3]$	$\mathcal{I}_\mu(p_2$ SEQ $p_3) \setminus \mathcal{I}_\mu(p_2$ SEQ p_1 SEQ $p_3)$

Fig. 1. Definition of extensional interpretation of event patterns. We use $p_{(x)}$ for patterns, $q_{(x)}$ for rational numbers, $t_{(x)}$ for terms and **pr** for event predicates.

justifies to take the perspective of ϵ being only partially known (and continuously unveiled along a time line) while the task is to detect event-consequences as soon as possible.

The theoretical properties of the presented formalism heavily depend on the conditions put on the formalism's signature. On the negative side, without further restrictions, the formalism turns out to be ExpTime-complete as a straightforward consequence from according results in [7]. On the other side, the formalism turns not only decidable but even tractable if both $\mathbf{C}$ and the arity of functions and predicates is bounded:

Theorem 1. *Given natural numbers k, m, the problem of detecting complex events in an event stream ϵ with an ETALIS rule base $\mathcal{R}$ which satisfies $|\mathbf{C}| \leq k$ and $\mathbf{F}_n = \mathbf{P}^{\mathrm{s}}_n = \mathbf{F}^{\mathrm{e}}_n = \emptyset$ for all $n \geq m$ is* PTIME*-complete w.r.t. $|\mathcal{R}| + |\epsilon|$.*

Proof. PTIME-hardness directly follows from the fact that the formalism subsumes function-free Horn logic which is known to be hard for PTIME, see e.g. [7].

For containment in PTIME, recall that in our formalism, function symbols have a fixed interpretation. Hence, given an ETALIS rule base $\mathcal{R}$ with finite $\mathbf{C}$, we can transform it into an equivalent function-free rule base $\mathcal{R}'$: we eliminate every n-ary function symbol $\mathtt{f}$ by introducing an auxiliary $n+1$-ary predicate $\mathtt{p_f}$ and "materializing" the function by adding ground atoms $\mathtt{p_f}(c_1,\ldots,c_n,\mathtt{f}^*(c_1,\ldots,c_n))$. This can be done in time polynomial time, given the above mentioned arity bound. Naturally, also the size of $\mathcal{R}'$ is polynomial compared to the size of $\mathcal{R}$.

Next, observe that under the above circumstances, the least Herbrand model of $\mathcal{R}^{s\prime}$ (which is then arity-bounded and function-free) can be computed in polynomial time (as there are only polynomially many ground atoms). Finally, note that the number of time points occurring in an event stream ϵ is linearly bounded by $|\epsilon|$, whence there are only polynomially many relevant "interval-endowed ground predicates" $a^{[q_1,q_2]}$ possibly entailed by ϵ and $\mathcal{R}^{e\prime}$. Finally these entailments can be checked in polynomial time in a forward-chaining manner against the respective (polynomial) grounding of $\mathcal{R}^{e\prime}$. This concludes the proof.

Example. The following pattern rules (1) demonstrates the usage of the ETALIS formalism by defining a common financial pattern called the "tick-shape" pattern. Let's consider a simple day trader pattern that looks for a peak followed by a continuous fall in price of stocks, followed by a rise in price. We are interested in a raise only if (and as soon as) it grows higher than the beginning price. The "tick-shape" pattern is monitored for each company symbol over online stock events, see rules (1).

$$\begin{aligned}
\mathtt{down}(I,P1,P2) &\leftarrow \textsc{not}(\mathtt{stock}(I,P)).[\mathtt{stock}(I,P1),\\
&\quad\ \mathtt{stock}(I,P2)]\ \textsc{where}\ P1 < P2.\\
\mathtt{down}(I,P1,P3) &\leftarrow \textsc{not}(\mathtt{stock}(I,P)).[\mathtt{down}(I,P1,P2),\\
&\quad\ \mathtt{stock}(I,P3)]\ \textsc{where}\ P2 > P3.\\
\mathtt{up}(I,P1) &\leftarrow \mathtt{stock}(I,P1).\\
\mathtt{up}(I,P2) &\leftarrow \textsc{not}(\mathtt{stock}(I,P)).[\mathtt{up}(I,P1),\mathtt{stock}(I,P2)]\\
&\quad\ \textsc{where}\ P1 < P2.\\
\mathtt{tickShape}(I) &\leftarrow \mathtt{down}(I,P1,P2)\ \textsc{meets}\\
&\quad\ \textsc{not}(\mathtt{stock}(I,P)).[\mathtt{up}(I,P3),\mathtt{stock}(I,P4)]\\
&\quad\ \textsc{where}\ P3 < P1\ \wedge\ P4 > P1.
\end{aligned} \tag{1}$$

In this example, we first start detecting a short increase (in order to detect the peak) and subsequent fall in price using $\mathtt{down}(I, P1, P2)$ iterative rules. Thereby, I takes the identifier of the monitored company, $P1$ the price at the peak directly preceding the decrease and $P2$ the price at the end of the interval. The usage of the NOT pattern ensures that no `stock` events in between are left out and hence, the decrease in price is monotone. Similarly we can detect a rise in price, defined by $\mathtt{up}(I, P1)$ (where $P1$ assumes the price at the end of the interval). Finally, $\mathtt{tickShape}(I)$ will be triggered when a `down` event meets an `up` event which ends at a prize value below the preceding peak, and the next incoming stock event for I reports a prize above that peak value.

2.1 Iterations and Aggregate Functions

In this section, we show how unbound iterations of events, possibly in combination with aggregate functions can be expressed within our defined formalism.

Many of the formalisms concerned with Complex Event Processing feature operators indicating that an event may be iterated arbitrarily often. Mostly, the notation of these operators is borrowed from regular expressions in automata theory: the *Kleene star* $(\cdot^*)$ matches zero or more occurrences whereas the *Kleene plus* $(\cdot^+)$ indicates one or more occurrences.

For example, the pattern expression a SEQ b^+ SEQ c would match any of the event sequences abc, $abbc$, $abbbc$ etc. It is easy to see that – given our semantics – this pattern expression is equivalent to the pattern a SEQ b SEQ c (as essentially, it allows for "skipping" occurring events)[3]. Likewise, all patterns in which this kind of Kleene iteration occurs can be transformed into non-iterative ones.

However, frequently iterative patterns are used in combination with *aggregate functions*, i.e. a value is accumulated over a sequence of events. Mostly, CEP formalisms define new language primitives to accommodate this feature. However, within the ETALIS formalism, this situation can be handled via recursive event rules.

As an example, assume an event should be triggered by a sequence of repeated selling events if the total income generated by them is above 100000$. For this, we have to sum over the single incomes indicated by the atomic selling events. This can be realized by the below set of rules.

$$\begin{aligned} \texttt{income}(Price) &\leftarrow \texttt{sell}(Item, Price). \\ \texttt{income}(P1 + P2) &\leftarrow \texttt{income}(P1) \text{ SEQ } \texttt{sell}(Item, P2). \\ \texttt{bigincome} &\leftarrow \texttt{income}(Price) \text{ WHERE } Price > 100000. \end{aligned} \tag{2}$$

In the same vein, every aggregative pattern can be expressed by sets of recursive rules, where we introduce auxiliary events that carry the intermediate results of the aggregation as arguments.

As a further remark, note that for a given natural number n, the n-fold sequential execution of an event a (a pattern usually written as a^n) can be recognized by $\texttt{iteration}(a, n)$ defined as follows:

$$\begin{aligned} \texttt{iteration}(a, 1) &\leftarrow a. \\ \texttt{iteration}(a, k+1) &\leftarrow a \text{ SEQ } \texttt{iteration}(a, k). \end{aligned} \tag{3}$$

This allows us to express patterns where events are repeated many times in a compact way.

A common scenario in event processing is to detect patterns on moving *length-based windows*. Such a pattern is detected when certain events are repeated as many times as the window length is. A sliding window moves on each new event to detect a new complex event (defined by the length of a window). Rules (4) implement such a pattern in ETALIS for the length equal to n (n is typically predefined). For instance, for n=5, e will be triggered every time when the system encounters five occurrences of a.

$$\begin{aligned} \texttt{iteration}(a, 1) &\leftarrow a. \\ \texttt{iteration}(a, k+1) &\leftarrow \text{NOT}(a).[a, \texttt{iteration}(a, k)]. \\ \texttt{e} &\leftarrow \texttt{iteration}(a, n). \end{aligned} \tag{4}$$

3 Execution Model

Complex event patterns that a user can create with the language proposed in Section 2 are not convenient to be used for *event-driven* computation. These are

[3] Note that due to the chosen semantics, this encoding would also match sequences like *acbbc* or *abbacbc*. However, if wanted, these can be excluded by using the slightly more complex pattern (a SEQ b SEQ c) EQUALS NOT(a OR c).[a, c].

rather Prolog-style rules suitable for *backward chaining* evaluation. Such rules are understood as goals which, at certain time, either can or cannot be proved by an inference engine. The difficulty is that such an inference process cannot be done in an *event-driven* fashion.

Our execution model is based on a *goal-directed event-driven* rules. The approach is established on decomposition of complex event patterns into *two-input intermediate events* (i.e., *goals*). The status of achieved goals at the current state shows the progress toward completeness of an event pattern. Goals are automatically asserted by rules as relevant events occur. They can persist over a period of time "waiting" in order to support detection of a more complex goal or pattern. In the remaining part of this subsection we explain the *transformation* of user-defined patterns into goal-directed event-driven rules (i.e., executable rules capable to detect events as soon as they really occur).

Algorithm 1. Sequence

Input: event binary goal $\mathtt{e} \leftarrow \mathtt{a}$ SEQ $\mathtt{b}$ WHERE $\mathtt{t}$.
Output: event-driven backward chaining rules for SEQ operator and a static rule $\mathtt{t}$.
Each event binary goal $\mathtt{ie} \leftarrow \mathtt{a}$ SEQ $\mathtt{b}$ is converted into: {

$\mathtt{a}(T_1, T_2) :- \mathtt{for\_each}(\mathtt{a}, 1, [T_1, T_2]).$
$\mathtt{a}(1, T_1, T_2) :- \mathtt{assert}(\mathtt{goal}(\mathtt{b}(\_, \_), \mathtt{a}(T_1, T_2), \mathtt{ie}(\_, \_))).$
$\mathtt{b}(T_3, T_4) :- \mathtt{for\_each}(\mathtt{b}, 1, [T_3, T_4]).$
$\mathtt{b}(1, T_3, T_4) :- \mathtt{goal}(\mathtt{b}(T_3, T_4), \mathtt{a}(T_1, T_2), \mathtt{ie}), T_2 < T_3,$
$\quad \mathtt{retract}(\mathtt{goal}(\mathtt{b}(T_3, T_4), \mathtt{a}(T_1, T_2), \mathtt{ie}(\_, \_))), \mathtt{ie}(T_1, T_4).$

}
$\mathtt{ie}(T_1, T_4) :- \mathtt{t}, \mathtt{e}(T_1, T_4).$

Let us first consider a sequence of events $e \leftarrow p_1$ SEQ p_2 SEQ p_3... SEQ p_n where e is detected when an event p_1 is followed by p_2,.., followed by p_n. We can always represent the above pattern as $e \leftarrow (((p_1$ SEQ $p_2)$ SEQ $p_3)$... SEQ $p_n)$. We refer to this coupling of events as *binarization* of events. Effectively, in binarization we introduce intermediate events (goals), e.g., $ie_1 \leftarrow p_1$ SEQ p_2, $ie_2 \leftarrow ie_1$ SEQ p_3, etc. Every monitored event (either atomic or complex), including intermediate events, will be assigned with one or more *logic rules* which are fired whenever that event occurs. Using the binarization, it is more convenient to construct *event-driven* rules. First, it is easy to implement an event operator when events are considered on a "two by two" basis. Second, the binarization increases the *sharing* among events and intermediate events (when detecting complex patterns). Third, the binarization eases the management of rules. For example, each new use of an event (in a pattern) amounts to appending only one rule to the existing rule set.

Algorithm 1 accepts as input a binary sequence $\mathtt{e} \leftarrow \mathtt{a}$ SEQ $\mathtt{b}$ WHERE $\mathtt{t}$, and produces event-driven backward chaining rules (i.e., executable rules). Additionally a user needs to define a static rule for a predicate $\mathtt{t}$ and add it into a rule base. As discussed, $\mathtt{t}$ is application specific, and can be used for event enrichment, filtering, querying historical data, as well as for reasoning about the context.

Event-driven backward chaining rules produced by Algorithm 1 belong to two different classes of rules. We refer to the first class as to rules used to *generate goals*. The second class corresponds to *checking rules*.

When an a event occurs at some (T_1, T_2) it will trigger the first rule, which in turn will trigger each $\mathtt{a}(n, T_1, T_2)$[4]. In this case $n = 1$, since the a event is used only once in the pattern. In general there can be more than one rule of this type, e.g., $\mathtt{a}(1, T_1, T_2)...\mathtt{a}(3, T_1, T_2)$, if the a event appears three times in user's complex event patterns.

$\mathtt{a}(1, [T_1, T_2])$ is a rule that generates $goal(\mathtt{b}([\_, \_]), \mathtt{a}([T_1, T_2]), \mathtt{ie}([\_, \_]))$. Its interpretation is that "an event a has occurred at $[T_1, T_2]$[5], and we are waiting for b to happen in order to detect ie". Obviously, the goal does not carry information about times for b and ie, as we don't know when they will occur. In general, the *second* event in a goal always denotes an event that has just occurred. The role of the *first* event is to specify what we are waiting for to detect an event that is on the *third* position. $\mathtt{b}(1, [T_3, T_4])$ belongs to the *checking rules*. They check whether certain goals already exist in the database, in which case they trigger more complex events. For example, rule $\mathtt{b}(1, [T_3, T_4])$ will fire whenever b occurs. The rule checks whether $goal(\mathtt{b}([T_3, T_4]), \mathtt{a}([T_1, T_2]), \mathtt{ie}([\_, \_]))$ already exists (i.e., an a has previously happened), in which case it triggers ie (by calling $\mathtt{ie}([T_1, T_4])$. The time occurrence of ie (i.e. $[T_1, T_4]$) is defined based on the occurrence of constituting events (i.e. $\mathtt{a}[T_1, T_2]$, and $\mathtt{b}[T_3, T_4]$).

The $\mathtt{ie}([T_1, T_4])$ event will trigger the last rule. If the static predicate, t, evaluates to true, then the rule will call the e event. Calling $\mathtt{e}[T_1, T_4]$, this event is effectively propagated either upward (if it is an intermediate event) or triggered as a complex event.

More detailed description of event-driven computation in ETALIS (including other operators from the language too) can be found in [3]. Other issues regarding the execution model, such as the various consumption policies and memory management were also studied in [8].

3.1 Kleene Plus Closure

The main principle behind the execution model of Kleene closure is similar as for the sequence operator. To explain how this closure can be computed in ETALIS let us go back to example rules (2), Section 2.1. Algorithm 1 can be used to transform these rules into event-driven backward chaining rules, which can be directly executed by ETALIS prototype.

Essentially these rules handle an unbounded stream of *sell* (*Item*, *Price*) events, compute the sum of their prices and detect *bigincome* if the sum is greater than 100000 \$. The first rule sets a condition which defines when the pattern detection should start[6]. In our example it is just an occurrence of *start*

---

[4] By using a predicate, for_each. Implementation details for this predicate can be found in [3].

[5] Apart from the time stamp, an event may carry other data parameters that are omitted here in order to make the presentation more readable.

[6] It also sets the starting *Price* value to 0.

event (e.g. it can be at the beginning of a day, a month or just an event occurrence denoting that something significant to our business happened). An occurrence of $start([T_1, T_2])$ event[7] will unconditionally cause an occurrence of *income* event with $Price = 0$, and the same timestamp $[T_1, T_2]$. As *income* is used to build a sequence of events in the second rule, $goal(sell\ (Item, P2,\ [\_, \_]),$ $income(P1,\ [T_1, T_2]),\ income(P1 + P2,\ [\_, \_]))$ will be inserted. The goal states that an instance of *income* event occurred at $[T_1, T_2]$, and the CEP engine waits for *sell* to happen to detect another *income* (iteratively). If *sell* occurs at some $[T_3, T_4]$, $T_2 < T_3$, a corresponding checking rule will check whether $goal(sell$ $(Item, P2, [\_, \_]),\ income(P1, [T_1, T_2]),\ income(P1 + P2, [\_, \_]))$ is already in the database, in which case it will trigger $income(P1 + P2, [T_1, T_4])$ (adding price $P2$ to the current aggregated value, $P1$). Events of type *income* are intermediate events in our overall complex pattern. The third rule monitors these events in order to detect *bigincome*. The rule sets a condition which defines when the pattern detection should stop (taking into account that we deal with an unbounded stream of events).

3.2 Implementation of Iterative Rules and Common Aggregate Functions

The aggregate functions are computed incrementally, by starting with an initial value for the increment, and iterating the aggregate function over events. However, window size and the sliding window require us to use efficient data structures and algorithms in Logic Programming (e.g., in Prolog) to obtain fast implementations.

For any aggregate function we implement the following two rules.

$$\begin{aligned}
&\texttt{iteration}(StartCntr = 0, StartVal) \leftarrow \texttt{start_event}(StartVal).\\
&\texttt{iteration}(OldCntr + 1, NewVal) \leftarrow\\
&\qquad \texttt{iteration}(OldCntr, OldVal)\ \textsc{seq}\ \texttt{a}(AggArg)\\
&\qquad \textsc{where}\ \{\texttt{assert}(AggArg),\\
&\qquad\qquad \texttt{window}(WndwSize, OldCntr, OldVal, AggArg, NewVal)\}.
\end{aligned} \tag{5}$$

The first rule starts the iteration process (when `start_event`) occurs with its initial value and possible condition on that value (see the first rule). The second rule defines the iteration itself, i.e., whenever an event participating in the iteration occurs (event `a`), it will trigger the rule and generate a new `iteration` event.

In each iteration it is possible to calculate certain operations (an aggregate function). To achieve this, the iterative rule contains the static part (the WHERE clause) for two reasons: to save data from the seen events as history relevant w.r.t the aggregation function (see `assert`($AggArg$)), and to compute the sliding window incrementally (i.e., to delete events that expired from the sliding window and calculate the aggregate function on the rest, see the `window` expression).

[7] As *start* is an atomic event, $T_1 = T_2$.

The functionality of `assert` predicate is simply to add data on which aggregation is applied (i.e., an aggregation argument $AggArg$) to database. Sliding `window` functionality is also simple, and it is realized by rule (6).

$$\begin{aligned}
&\texttt{window}(WndwSize, OldCntr, OldVal, AggArg, NewVal) :- \\
&\quad OldCntr + 1 >= WindowSize -> \\
&\quad \texttt{retract}(LastItem), \\
&\quad \texttt{spec_aggregate}(OldValue, AggArg, NewValue); \\
&\quad \texttt{spec_aggregate}(OldValue, AggArg, NewValue).
\end{aligned} \tag{6}$$

We check whether the current counter value (i.e., the incremented old counter, $OldCntr + 1$) exceeds the window size (line 2) in which case we retract the last item from the window (line 3) and compute a specific aggregate function (line 4). Recall that new data element (AggArg) was previously added by the iteration rule (`assert`($AggArg$)). If the counter does not exceed the window's value, we simply compute a specific aggregate function (line 5).

Based on these iterative pattern and sliding window rules we can implement other various aggregation functions. The iterative rules (7) (SUM aggregate function) implement the sum of certain values from selected events (see *SUM aggregate function*).

As we already explained, the iteration begins when `start_event` occurs and sets the $StartVal$. The iteration is further continued whenever event `a` occurs. Note that events `start_event` and `a` can be of the same type. We can additionally have WHERE clause to set filter conditions for both $StartVal$ and $AggArg$. We omit filters here to keep the pattern rules simple, however it is clear that neither every `start_event` must start the iteration nor that every `a` must be accepted in an ongoing iteration. The `assert` predicate adds new data ($AggArg$) to the current sum, and the window rule deducts the expired (last) value from the window in order to produce $NewSum$.

Note that the same rules can be used to compute the moving average (AVG) (hence we omit to repeat them to save space). As we have the current sum and the counter value, we can simply add $AvgVal = NewSum/(OldCntr+1)$ in the WHERE clause of the second rule.

$$\begin{aligned}
&\texttt{sum}(StartCntr = 0, StartVal) \leftarrow \texttt{start_event}(StartVal). \\
&\texttt{sum}(OldCntr + 1, NewSum) \leftarrow \\
&\quad \texttt{sum}(OldCntr + 1, OldSum) \text{ SEQ } \texttt{a}(AggArg) \\
&\quad \text{WHERE } \{\texttt{assert}(AggArg), \\
&\qquad \texttt{window}(WndwSize, OldCntr, \\
&\qquad OldSum + AggArg, AggArg, NewSum)\}. \\
\\
&\texttt{window}(WndwSize, OldCntr, CurrSum, NewSum) :- \\
&\quad OldCntr + 1 >= WindowSize- > \\
&\quad \texttt{retract}(LastItem), \\
&\quad NewSum = CurrSum - LastItem; \\
&\quad NewSum = CurrSum - LastItem.
\end{aligned} \tag{7}$$

In general, the iterative rules give us possibility to realize essentially any aggregate functions on event streams, no matter whether events are *atomic* or *complex* (note that there is no assumption whether event a is atomic or complex). We can also have *multiple* aggregations, computed on a single iterative pattern (when they are supposed to be calculated on the same event stream). For instance, the same iterative rules can be used to compute the average and the standard deviation. This feature can potentially save computation resources and increase the overall performance. Finally, it is worth noting that we are not constrained to compute the Kleene plus closure only on *sequences* of events (as it is common in other approaches [1,10]). With no restriction, instead of SEQ we can also put (in line 3) other event operators such as AND or PAR . The following iterative pattern computes the *maximum* over a sliding window of events.

$$
\begin{aligned}
&\texttt{max}(StartCntr = 0, StartVal) \leftarrow \texttt{start\_event}(StartVal).\\
&\texttt{max}(OldCntr + 1, NewMax) \leftarrow\\
&\qquad \texttt{max}(OldCntr + 1, OldMax)\ \textsc{seq}\ \texttt{a}(AggArg)\\
&\qquad\ \textsc{where}\ \{\texttt{assert}(AggArg),\\
&\qquad\qquad\qquad \texttt{window}(WndwSize, OldCntr, NewMax)\}.
\end{aligned}
\tag{8}
$$

$$
\begin{aligned}
&\texttt{window}(WndwSize, OldCntr, NewMax) : -\\
&\qquad OldCntr + 1 >= WindowSize- >\\
&\qquad \texttt{retract}(LastItem),, get(NewMax);\\
&\qquad get(NewMax).
\end{aligned}
$$

The rules are very similar to rules for other aggregation functions (e.g., see rules (8)). However there is one difference in implementation of the window rule. The history of events necessary for computing aggregations on sliding windows can be kept in the memory using different data structures. Essentially we need a *queue* where the latest event (or its aggregation value) is inserted into the queue and the oldest event from the window is removed. For example, we implemented efficiently the sum and the average using two data structures: *stacks* and *difference lists*. Stacks can be easy implemented in Prolog using *assert* and *retract* commands, and difference list are convenient as the cost for deleting the oldest element that expired from the window is O(1).

Queues with difference lists are however not good enough for computing aggregations such as the *maximum* and the *minimum*. For these functions, searching the maximum (or the minimum) in a sliding window when the current maximum (minimum) is deleted requires a price of O(Window) (to find the new maximum or the minimum). Still to provide an efficient implementation we use balanced binary search trees. We know what is the event that will be deleted from the history queue. We keep a red-black (RB) balanced tree to be indexed on the aggregate argument, so that we can do cleanup of overdue events efficiently. In each node, we keep a counter with how many times that an event with the aforementioned key came. At each time the maximum (minimum) is the rightmost (leftmost) leaf. Additionally we can also keep the timestamp of events. This allows us also to prune events (data) based on the *time* w.r.t the sliding window.

With the balanced tree this search is reduced to O(logN). For instance, for a window of 1000 events, the price of 1000 operations is reduced to at most 10 at each step ($2^{10} = 1024$).

Pruning events based on their timestamps is the basis for *time-based* sliding windows. So far we have discussed *count-based* sliding windows (i.e., the pruning is based on the number of events in the window). For event patterns with time-based sliding windows, we do not need the window rule (e.g., rule (6)). Instead, we use only iterative patterns with a garbage collector (set to prune events out of the specified sliding window). Events are stored internally in order as they come (we index them on the timestamp information $[T_2, T_1]$). This eases the process of pruning expired events, using either of our two memory management techniques.

$$
\begin{aligned}
&\texttt{iteration}(StartCntr = 0, StartVal) \leftarrow \texttt{start\_event}(StartVal).\\
&\texttt{iteration}(NewCntr) \leftarrow\\
&\qquad \texttt{iteration}(OldCntr) \text{ SEQ } \texttt{a}(AggArg)\\
&\qquad \text{WHERE } \{NewCntr = \texttt{getCount}([T_2, T_1]), \texttt{window}(3min)\}.
\end{aligned} \tag{9}
$$

The *count* aggregation is typically used on time-based sliding windows, see the pattern (9). Whenever a relevant event occurs (e.g., event a), its timestamp will be asserted by the *getCount* predicate and the current counter number will be returned. Additionally we set a garbage collector to incrementally remove outdated timestamps, so that *getCount* always returns the correct result. In the same vein, we have realized other aggregate functions with the time-based sliding windows (i.e., SUM, AVG, MAX, MIN).

4 Performance Evaluation

We have implemented the proposed framework for iterative and aggregative patterns. In this section we present experimental results we have obtained with our open-source implementation, called ETALIS[8]. Experimental results compare our logic programming-based implementation with Esper 3.3.0[9]. Esper is a state-of-the-art engine primarily relying on NFA. We choose Esper as it is available as open source, and also it is a commercially proven system.

We have evaluated the *sum* aggregation function, defined by iterative pattern (7) (we omit rewriting the pattern here to save space). The moving sum is computed over the stream of complex events. Complex events are defined as a *conjunction* of two events, joined on their ID (see pattern rule (10)). The sum is aggregated on the attribute X of complex events $\texttt{a}(ID, X, Y)$. Figure 2(a) shows the performance results. In particular, the figure shows how the throughput depends on different sizes of the sliding window. Our system ETALIS was run in two modes: using the window implementation based on the stack and

[8] ETALIS, can be found on: `http://code.google.com/p/etalis/`

[9] Esper: `http://esper.codehaus.org`

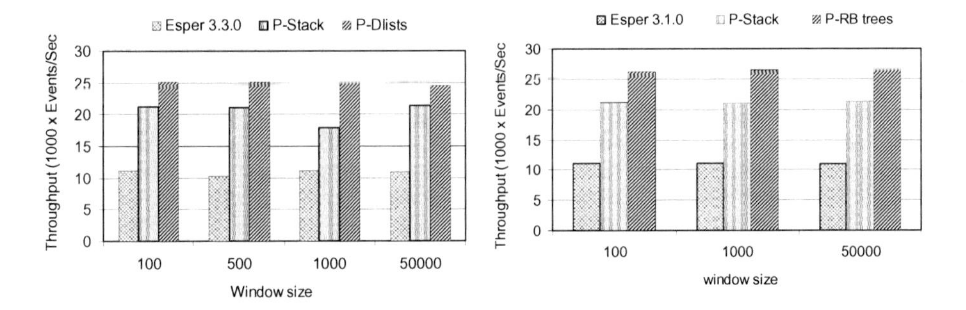

Fig. 2. (a) SUM-AND: throughput vs. window size (b) AVG-SEQ: throughput vs. window size

difference lists, denoted as P-Stack and P-Dlists, respectively. In both modes our implementation has outperformed Esper 3.3.0 (see Figure 2(a)).

$$\mathtt{a}(ID, X, Y) \leftarrow \mathtt{b}(ID, X) \text{ AND } \mathtt{c}(ID, Y). \tag{10}$$

In the next test we computed the moving *average* (avg) over the stream of complex events. Complex events were defined by rule (10) where operator AND was replaces with the *sequence* SEQ . Again ETALIS was run with windows implemented with the stack and different lists. Results are presented in Figure 2(b), showing again the dominance of our system.

Example application: supply chain. CEP can be combined with evaluation of the *background knowledge* to detect (near) real-time situations of interest. To demonstrate this functionality, let us consider the following example. Suppose we monitor a shipment delivery process in a supply chain system. The following rules represent a complex pattern (`delivery` event), triggered by every `shipment` event. This iterative pattern may be used to *aggregate* certain values carried by `shipment` events.

$$\begin{aligned} \mathtt{delivery}(start, start) &\leftarrow \mathtt{shipment}(start). \\ \mathtt{delivery}(From, To) &\leftarrow \mathtt{delivery}(From, PrevTo) \\ &\qquad \text{SEQ } \mathtt{shipment}(To) \\ &\qquad \text{WHERE } \mathtt{inSupChain}(From, To). \end{aligned} \tag{11}$$

Additionally there is a constraint that every shipment on its way needs to pass a number of sites, defined with a *delivery path.* Valid paths are represented as sets of explicit links between sites, e.g., with $\mathtt{linked}(site_3, site_4)$ we represent two connected sites. If for that shipment there exists also another connection $\mathtt{linked}(site_4, site_5)$, the system can *infer* that the path $site_3, site_4, site_5$ is a valid path (performing the *reasoning* over the following transitive closure and available background knowledge).

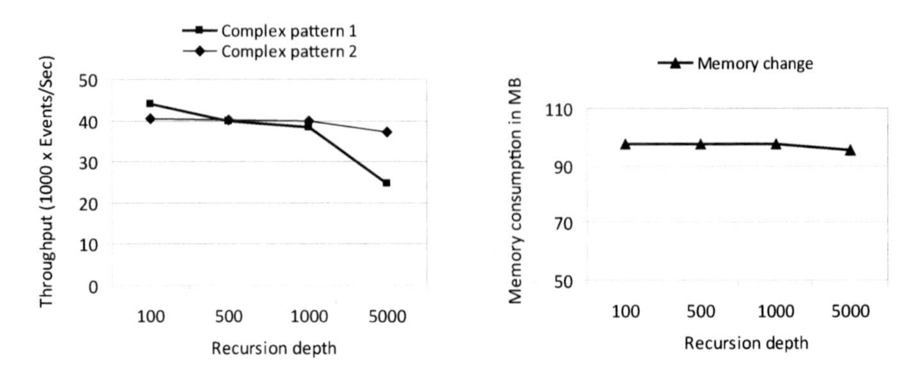

Fig. 3. (a) Throughput comparison (b) Memory consumption

$\texttt{inSupChain}(X, Y) :- \texttt{linked}(X, Y).$
$\texttt{inSupChain}(X, Z) :- \texttt{linked}(X, Y)$ AND $\texttt{inSupChain}(Y, Z).$

We have evaluated the iterative `delivery` pattern for different sizes of supply chain paths (between 100 and 5000 links), see Figure 3 (a). In "Complex pattern 1" we enforce that for each new `shipment` event, the valid path must be proved from its beginning (see $\texttt{inSupChain}(From, To)$ in rule (11)). For longer paths (e.g., 5000 links) this is a significant overhead, and we see that the throughput declines. But if we relax the check so that for every new event the path must be checked with respect only to the last `delivery` event, i.e., we replace $\texttt{inSupChain}(From, To)$ with $\texttt{inSupChain}(PrevTo, To)$ in rule (11)) we obtain the throughput which is almost constant (see "Complex pattern 2" in Figure 3 (a)). Figure 3 (b) shows the total memory consumption for the presented test. There is no difference in memory consumption for complex patterns 1 and 2, hence we present only one curve.

5 Conclusions

We have presented an extended formalism for logic-based event processing. The formalism is rather general, however in this paper we put emphasis on handling iterative and aggregative patterns matched against unbounded event streams. The paper presents syntax and declarative semantics of ETALIS Language for Events, demonstrates its use for more knowledge-oriented and intelligent event processing, provides an execution model, and finally shows performance evaluation of our prototype implementation.

Acknowledgments

This work was partially supported by the European Commission funded project PLAY (FP7-20495) and by the ExpresST project funded by the German Research Foundation (DFG). We thank Jia Ding and Ahmed Khalil Hafsi for their help in implementation and testing ETALIS.

References

1. Agrawal, J., Diao, Y., Gyllstrom, D., Immerman, N.: Efficient pattern matching over event streams. In: SIGMOD, pp. 147–160 (2008)
2. Allen, J.F.: Maintaining knowledge about temporal intervals. Communications of the ACM 26, 832–843 (1983)
3. Anicic, D., Fodor, P., Rudolph, S., Sthmer, R., Stojanovic, N., Studer, R.: Reasoning in Event-based Distributed Systems. In: Etalis: Rule-Based Reasoning in Event Processing. Series in Studies in Computational Intelligence, Sven Helmer, Alex Poulovassilis and Fatos Xhafa (2010)
4. Anicic, D., Fodor, P., Rudolph, S., Stühmer, R., Stojanovic, N., Studer, R.: A rule-based language for complex event processing and reasoning. In: Hitzler, P., Lukasiewicz, T. (eds.) RR 2010. LNCS, vol. 6333, pp. 42–57. Springer, Heidelberg (2010)
5. Arasu, A., Babu, S., Widom, J.: The cql continuous query language: semantic foundations and query execution. VLDB Journal 15, 121–142 (2006)
6. Chandrasekaran, S., Cooper, O., Deshpande, A., Franklin, M.J., Hellerstein, J.M., Hong, W., Krishnamurthy, S., Madden, S., Raman, V., Reiss, F., Shah, M.A.: Telegraphcq: Continuous dataflow processing for an uncertain world. In: Proceedings of the 1st Biennial Conference on Innovative Data Systems Research, CIDR 2003 (2003)
7. Dantsin, E., Eiter, T., Gottlob, G., Voronkov, A.: Complexity and expressive power of logic programming. ACM Computing Surveys 33, 374–425 (2001)
8. Fodor, P., Anicic, D., Rudolph, S.: Results on out-of-order event processing. In: Rocha, R., Launchbury, J. (eds.) PADL 2011. LNCS, vol. 6539, pp. 220–234. Springer, Heidelberg (2011)
9. Krämer, J., Seeger, B.: Semantics and implementation of continuous sliding window queries over data streams. ACM Transactions on Database Systems 34 (2009)
10. Mei, Y., Madden, S.: Zstream: a cost-based query processor for adaptively detecting composite events. In: SIGMOD, pp. 193–206 (2009)

Entity-Based State Management for Complex Event Processing Applications

Hannes Obweger[1], Josef Schiefer[1], Martin Suntinger[1], and Robert Thullner[2]

[1] UC4 Senactive Software GmbH, Vienna, Austria
[2] Secure Business Austria, Vienna, Austria
hannes.obweger@uc4.com

Abstract. Complex Event Processing (CEP) using Event-Condition-Action (ECA) rules has proved particularly suitable for detecting noteworthy business situations of a defined length and structure. By contrast, challenges arise when the state of a complex, durable entity – e.g., a counter, a server, or a task queue – shall be derived from continuous streams of low-level updates. In this paper, we present a novel approach to state management for CEP applications. We propose business entity providers, which encapsulate arbitrary state-calculation logic and manage state in the form of typed, application-wide data structures. Using a plug-in-based component model, business entity providers can be integrated into an application based on the specific requirements of a business scenario. We present an ECA rule model that allows accessing business entities well-integrated with event-pattern detection and demonstrate our approach in a real-world scenario from the workload automation domain.

Keywords: Complex Event Processing, ECA rules, state management.

1 Introduction

Complex Event Processing (CEP) [12] has emerged a new paradigm for monitoring business environments and automated, reactive decision making. CEP systems define monitoring logic on an event-based abstraction of the underlying business environment, where relevant state changes or actions are transformed into events of respective event types. On the resulting, continuous stream of events, specialized pattern-detection algorithms can be applied to detect noteworthy event patterns in near real time. Event-Condition-Action (ECA) rules, defined in a tailored Event Processing Language (EPL), have proved suitable for describing event-processing logic in a way that is understandable to business users. In an ECA rule, a (possibly complex) event is associated with sets of Boolean conditions and actions. When the triggering pattern is detected in a stream of events and all conditions are fulfilled, the actions are executed.

ECA-based CEP works particularly well for detecting noteworthy business situations of a defined temporal extent and structure, where the focus lies on relationships between the involved events. In the logistics domain, for instance, an ECA rule could be used to detect all transports of a specific carrier that are delayed by x hours or longer, and trigger a notification event in response.

N. Bassiliades et al. (Eds.): RuleML 2011 - Europe, LNCS 6826, pp. 154–169, 2011.

By contrast, ECA-based CEP faces significant challenges when the overall state of a complex, durable business entity – e.g., a counter, a server, or a task queue – shall be derived from a incremental, low-level updates of that state, and each update is represented by a (possibly complex) event. The state of such entities may, however, be of paramount importance for the monitoring of a system, both during event processing and for the ex-post analysis of historic event data. Consider an example from the workload automation domain: Provided events of type "Task enqueued" and "Task started" as emitted by the source system, a system administrator might wish to be notified whenever the average sojourn time of a task queue exceeds a specified threshold, or investigate the development of a queue's load over the past weeks.

We identified the following challenges for state-of-the-art, ECA-based CEP:

- **Durable entity state.** Many CEP engines use sliding time windows to detect event patterns of a defined length and to limit the number of events which must be kept in memory. While this strategy is suitable for event-pattern detection, it generally contradicts with the idea of durable business entities. By contrast, entity data require a separate, non-volatile data-management layer that can be updated based on incoming events and takes into account the specific characteristics of the managed entities. Entity data, their development over time and possible relationships to event data may eventually provide valuable insights to the behavior of a system and should be available for ex-post analysis.
- **Complex state-calculation logic.** Calculating the overall state of an entity from low-level updates may be of considerable complexity; consider, for instance, the above calculation of average sojourn time from a series of "add" and "remove" operations. Implementing such logic directly within ECA rules easily bloats an application and makes it difficult to read and maintain. Calculation of entity state should instead be encapsulated and decoupled from end-user-defined business logic.
- **Active entity monitoring.** In many CEP frameworks, durable data can only be accessed at the occurrence of an event, in the "condition" or "action" part of a rule. As a consequence, to continuously check entities for exceptional states, high-level monitoring logic must be based on the same event patterns that are used for updating these entities. To avoid a tight coupling between these aspects, a framework should instead enable rules to actively react to entity-level state changes, generally independent from the events and rules that originally caused these state changes.
- **Context-aware data access.** Concepts such as *contexts* [2] and *correlation sets* [18] have been developed to partition the overall set of events based on user-defined relations between events. For the sake of consistency across event-pattern detection and state management, access to entity data should be integrated with contexts and related concepts, if such are available.
- **Ease of use.** Usability from an end-user perspective is seen as a key issue in the future development of CEP (cf. [6, 8]). As a general concern, the definition of application-specific state-management logic, the monitoring of business entities as well as their integration with event-pattern detection should therefore be oriented towards business users and require as little technical expertise as possible.

In this paper, we present a novel approach to state management for Complex Event Processing applications. We introduce *business entity providers*, which encapsulate custom state-calculation logic and manage virtual entities as system-wide, typed data structures. The presented architecture allows business entity providers to be implemented as plug-in-like components that can be incorporated depending on the specific requirements of a given business scenario. Within this architecture, plugged-in business entity providers expose easy-to-use interfaces for updating and querying entities to end-user-defined event-processing logic. We eventually present a business-user-oriented, ECA-based rule model that has been extended towards business entity providers and allows accessing entities fully integrated with event-pattern detection.

Fig. 1 shows the presented approach from a high-level perspective. On the "updating" side of a business entity provider, ECA rules are applied on the incoming stream of business incidents for filtering, transformation and aggregation purposes, as well as to detect events that signify updates to the state of an entity. In the action part of such rule, the concerned business-entity instance is identified from the detected event pattern and the respective update operation is invoked on the business entity provider. To support a decoupling between updating and monitoring business entities, the proposed architecture provides for updating rules to be defined generally independent from possible monitoring logic; by contrast, these rules are specified with the general goal of keeping the various business entities of an application "up to date".

On the "monitoring" side, ECA rules may then use the query interface of a business entity provider to monitor business entity states for exceptional values, e.g., to test the load of a task queue against a specified threshold. The proposed architecture supports two access modes: On the one hand, ECA rules may run a query *on demand*, e.g., at the occurrence of an event. On the other hand, ECA rules may evaluate a condition *continuously* and immediately react to exceptional states independent from the events that originally caused that update. Depending on the used data-management approach, a business entity provider may eventually provide historic entity data to tailored data mining and visualization tools for the ex-post analysis of a system.

Facilitating the integration of custom state calculation and management logic, the presented solution enables companies to exploit the benefits of CEP also in entity-centric business scenarios, which are difficult, if not impossible, to approach with

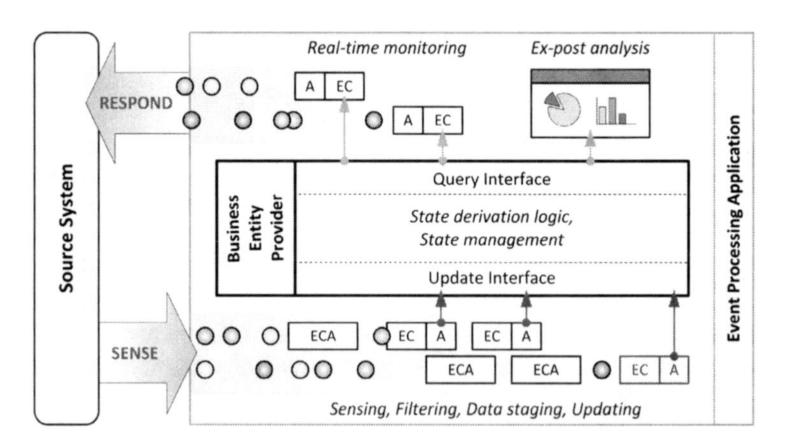

Fig. 1. A High-Level View on Business Entity Providers

purely event-based strategies. Exposing their functionality through easy-to-use interfaces, business entity providers simplify end-user-defined event-processing logic, which may now focus on event-pattern detection rather than low-level calculations. The proposed architecture furthermore supports a clear *separation of concerns* between state updating and state monitoring: Updating rules can be defined with the general goal of keeping business entities up-to-date, independently from possible monitoring logic. Conversely, monitoring rules can focus on high-level decision making and may be added and removed without having to touch the low-level infrastructure of an application. In many cases, the resulting decoupling complies with the organizational framework conditions of an enterprise: While high-level business logic would typically be administrated by business users and change frequently, low-level integration logic would typically be administrated by technical personnel and be more stable over time. The presented architecture eventually outperforms problem-specific, ad-hoc solutions by providing full integration with the framework's rule model independent from plugged-in business-entity provider implementations.

The remainder of this paper is structured as follows: In Section 2, we discuss related work. Section 3 presents the meta model for business entity providers, along with reference implementations for commonly needed kinds of entities. An extended, ECA-based rule model for updating and monitoring entities is presented in Section 4. Section 5 discusses the implementation architecture of our approach. In Section 6, we demonstrate our solution by a concrete example from the workload automation domain. Section 7 concludes this paper and gives an outlook to future work.

2 Related Work

Since introduced to a wider community by Luckham [12], Complex Event Processing has inspired numerous projects of academic (e.g., [1, 2, 3, 4, 21]) as well as commercial nature (cf. [9]). Although listed as one of seven key building blocks for CEP applications by Etzion and Niblett [8], the issue of *state management* – i.e., the handling of durable data and their integration into event-based, real-time decision making – has received little attention in research on stream and ECA-based CEP. In the following, we discuss existing CEP solutions and their approaches to state management, if such are available. Our survey is roughly structured by the basic ideas and paradigms underlying these solutions; detailed discussions on the different perspectives on CEP, their strengths and weaknesses can be found in the literature [15].

In inference-based approaches, reasoning about (complex) events is naturally integrated with reasoning about durable data, with both kinds of data being managed as *facts* in working memory. Logic-based approaches based on Event Calculus [10] and its variants (e.g., [14]) use *fluents* to model entity state; in principle, a fluent represents "anything whose value is subject to change over time" [22]. In the following, we focus on approaches that perform event-pattern detection directly on volatile (streams of) events and do not per se set up on an underlying knowledge base.

Many approaches to stream and ECA-based event processing are entirely event-based and do not provide access to non-event data (e.g., [12, 21]). If supported at all, monitoring the state of an entity based on low-level updates requires a system to collect all events for that entity and re-calculate its state whenever new updates occur. Such approach primarily suffers from time-window issues, but also leads to complex rules and a tight coupling between state calculation and monitoring.

In stream-oriented event processing, *query tables* [23] and related concepts have been introduced to make durable data joinable with event data and updatable within event-stream queries. While query tables provide means for persistent data management, the calculation of entity state must still be defined as part of a rule, using the framework's EPL. *FlexStreams* [25] allow incorporating procedural, potentially stateful logic as part of a query. Kozlenkov et al. [10] present a context-aware approach to state management that builds upon a separation between stream processing and (inference-based) state management. In both cases, state management is well encapsulated and allows users to define event-processing logic in a decoupled manner. Yet, to our best knowledge, both approaches dictate a certain style of programming (procedural vs. inference-based); as a consequence, their usefulness could vary depending on the given application scenario and the data to be managed.

Several ECA-based event processing frameworks allow accessing persistent data sources – e.g., Web data such as XML or RDF [5], or databases – in the "condition" and "action" part of a rule. When using passive data storages such as files or non-active databases, entity state must be calculated directly within rules and explicitly be retrieved in order to be monitored. Active object databases [16] allow encapsulating durable data along with functions for updating these data, and furthermore provide means for active entity monitoring. Rules in active databases are, however, internally-oriented (i.e., limited to events that occur within the underlying database) and typically defined with a global scope (cf. [15]).

Our survey shows that several approaches to stream and ECA-based CEP provide access to durable data; however, many of these approaches require state-calculation logic to be written directly within rules. Only few approaches have been proposed where state management is well encapsulated. In ECA-based event processing, we are not aware of any approach that combines support for encapsulated state-calculation logic, entity-aware data management, and full CEP capabilities. Neither in stream nor in ECA-based CEP, we are aware of any approach that allows incorporating arbitrary state-management logic in a way that it is seamlessly integrated with the framework's EPL and can easily be adapted to the specific requirements of a use case.

This paper presents a novel approach to state management for the generic event-processing framework *Sense-and-Respond Infrastructure* (SARI) [20]. Our solution is based on the idea of *business entities* [7, 13], which we understand as typed, identifiable, system-wide data structures. Being identifiable via (possibly composite) keys and accessible through easy-to-use interfaces, business entities are, in some respects, comparable to *objects* in (active) object databases. By contrast, our framework provides an additional layer of abstraction that allows incorporating arbitrary state-calculation logic and data-management strategies. In addition, a type model is provided that enables end users to easily configure plugged-in business entity providers based on the specific requirements of an application scenario.

3 Business Entity Provider Model

The presented framework is designed as a generic state-management layer that can be equipped with plug-in-like *business entity providers* depending on the requirements of a given use case. Each business entity provider encapsulates state-management logic for a certain "kind" of entity; a business entity provider could, for instance, be provided for *queues* as discussed in Section 1. Apart from a basic structure prescribed by the framework, this state-management logic can be defined freely by the implementer of a business entity provider – e.g., using OOP and in-memory data management, SQL statements, or any other suitable approach – and optimized with respect to the managed data. In the following, we present a meta model for business entity providers and discuss exemplary realizations for commonly needed kinds of entities.

3.1 Meta Model

Fig. 2 sketches the meta model for business entity providers, defining the basic structure a business entity provider must adhere to in order to be used in the proposed framework. The meta model is roughly separated into a non-empty collection of *business entity types*, a collection of *business entities* conforming to these types, as well as collections of *update* and *query interfaces* for accessing business entities.

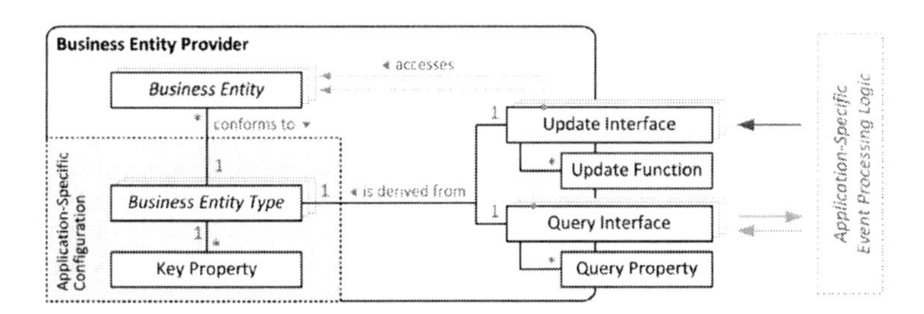

Fig. 2. Business Entity Provider Meta-Model

Business entity types. While the basic semantics of a business entity provider are given through its implementation, the proposed framework allows tailoring a provider to the specific application in which it is used, through a non-empty collection of *business entity types*. Each type thereby specifies the exact structure of a class of business entities to be managed: For example, given a business entity provider for queues, a business entity type could describe a class "Task queue" of queues, with respective characteristics. Albeit business entity types are generally provider-specific – see Section 3.2 for concrete examples – the proposed architecture requires all business entity types to define a (possibly composite) key, through a non-empty collection of typed *key properties* K. At run time, a tuple of key-property values can then be used to identify a specific instance of that type, e.g., when updating or querying its state.

Business entities. During run time, business entity providers manage state as collections of *business entities*. Each business entity conforms to exactly one business entity type $T = (K, \ldots)$ and is uniquely identified by a tuple of *key-property values* V_K for all key properties in K. By definition, the key of a business entity is immutable.

Update and query interfaces. Business entity providers eventually provide access to managed data through easy-to-use interfaces for updating and querying business entities. These interfaces are exposed per business entity type; therefore, in order to access an interface, a caller must first specify the concerned business entity type.

The update interface for a business entity type $T = (K, \ldots)$ is defined by a non-empty collection of *update functions* for creating, modifying and destroying T-typed entities. By definition, an update function takes as input a non-empty collection of *key property values* V_K (indentifying the entity to which the update shall apply) and a collection of *function parameters* V_f, further specifying the demanded update. The query interface provides access to the managed T-entities through a non-empty collection of typed *query properties*. Provided the unique key of an entity, these properties may be used to define conditions on the current state of that entity; for instance, a rule could test if the query property "Size" of a queue is greater than 100. Query properties are typically provided for all (type-specific and type-independent) properties of entities. In addition, properties may be available for aggregates over multiple updates and meta information such as the last update time stamp.

3.2 Exemplary Business Entity Providers

Based on the above meta model, the proposed framework enables application developers to integrate arbitrary business-entity provider implementations according to the specific problems that need to be solved. In the following, we illustrate the presented model by the example of three commonly needed kinds of entities: *Base entities, scores* and *sets*. Business entity providers for these entities have been implemented as part of our prototype (see Section 5 for further details) and showed to be useful in many practical application scenarios. In their type model, all of the following examples provide a Boolean *history* flag, indicating whether the provider shall maintain the complete history of an entity, as well as a Boolean *persistence* flag, indicating whether entity states shall be kept persistent in a database or managed in memory only.

Base entities. Base entities associate a tuple of key properties with a collection of *entity properties*, which can be updated and queried via the provider's interfaces. Base entities are typically used as virtual representations of complex real-world entities such as customers or products: Whenever an event indicates an update to a real-world entity, this update is "mirrored" to the respective base-entity instance. Monitoring rules are typically used to detect exceptional events based on the current state of a related entity; for instance, a rule could trigger an alert if a delay is signified for an order of a customer with the property "Rating" set to "Premium".

Scores. Scores associate a tuple of key properties with a single, numeric *score value*. Through the provider's update interface, this value can be set, increased and decreased by a user-defined delta. Query properties are available for the current score value and a collection of "moving" aggregates, such as the moving average and median; the number of values to be considered for these aggregates is defined as part of a score type. Albeit simple, scores form the basis for concepts such as counters and Key Performance

Indicators and are part of almost any practical SARI installation. Monitoring rules are typically used to detect scores that are above/below a certain threshold.

Sets. Sets are an extension to above-described *base entities* that allow modeling collection data such as FIFO queues, priority queues, or stacks. Besides grouping a number of *entity properties*, sets act as a container for multi-variate *set elements*, which by themselves are defined by a *set element identifier* and a collection of *set element properties*. Through the update interface, set elements can be inserted and removed. Via the query interface, the current set elements, their sojourn time, and metrics such as the overall number of elements fulfilling a certain condition can be retrieved.

4 Rule Model

In the proposed architecture, ECA rules are applied for both updating business entities based on low-level events and monitoring these entities for exceptional states. In the following, we present the rule model of *Sense-and-Respond Infrastructure* (SARI), along with diverse extensions for its integration with business entity providers.

4.1 Base Rule Model

SARI features a two-layered rule model, which conceptually, as well as technically, is separated into *event correlation* and *pattern detection*. Event correlation denotes the grouping of events that are generally related to each other, e.g., with respect to a common real-world process from which they arise. From the resulting event situations, pattern detection picks those that are *noteworthy* in a certain sense and triggers reaction logic in response. The described separation between event correlation and pattern detection enables users to define these aspects in decoupled, simplified (sub-) models and facilitates reuse of correlation information, e.g., across rule definitions, during event processing, as well as for the ex-post analysis of a system (cf. [18]).

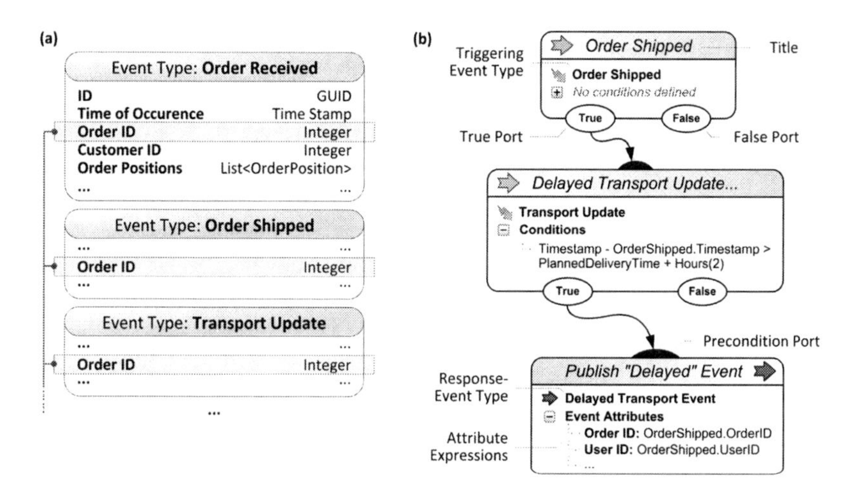

Fig. 3. Exemplary SARI Rule

A complete SARI rule eventually associates with each other a user-defined *correlation set*, describing a basic relation between events of different event types, and a user-defined *decision graph*, describing those aspects of an event situation that make it noteworthy in the given context plus reaction logic. Fig. 3[1] sketches a simple rule "Delayed transport" from the logistics domain; for detailed discussions on correlation sets and decision graphs, the interested reader may refer to Schiefer et al. [18, 19].

Correlation set. The rule's correlation set "Transport process" (Fig. 3a) describes a relation between events of type "Order received", "Order shipped", and "Transport update", which are to be correlated by their "Order ID". When an event is correlated based on this definition, it is assigned to the respective *correlation session* – e.g., all events of a certain transport #42 – or, if no session exists, establishes a new one.

Decision graph. Setting up on the so-defined correlation set, the rule's decision graph (Fig. 3b) picks from all transports those that are delayed by two hours or longer and generates a "Delayed transport" event in response. Decision graphs orchestrate understandable pieces of event-processing logic – so-called *rule components* – in a directed, acyclic graph. During event-pattern detection, predecessors in the decision graph are then considered as preconditions in the evaluation process; to activate a component c, an event situation must conform to (at least) one valid path through the decision graph. Depending on the evaluation result of c, further parts are activated, and so forth. Multiple preconditions may be combined using AND, OR, or XOR.

In the base decision-graph model, two kinds of rule components are available: *Event conditions* specify a "triggering" event type T as well as a Boolean expression x_b on the underlying event situation; when all preconditions are fulfilled and a T-event occurs, x_b is evaluated and the correct output port is activated. *Response event actions* specify an abstract response-event template, which consists of an event type U and expression for all event attributes in U. Whenever all preconditions are fulfilled, a response event is instantiated and published to the event-processing network.

4.2 Correlation Model Extensions

In practical scenarios, semantic relations may exist not only between events, but also between events and entities, and different kinds of entities. As a first extension to SARI's rule model, we therefore present a generalization of the original correlation model [18], enabling users to define relationships on event types as well as business entity types; while the former are correlated based on event attributes, the latter are correlated based on key properties. Within a SARI rule, the so-defined relationship then identifies the business entities that are generally concerned with the occurrence of an event or the status change of a business entity: For state-management rule components as discussed in the following sections, those entities that are related to the active correlation session serve as the basic target for update and query operations. An exemplary correlation set from the logistics domain is shown in Fig. 4 below.

[1] SARI's rule modeling facilities enable users to model correlation sets as well as decision graphs in an entirely visual, business-user-oriented fashion; while XML-based representations are used internally, these are not currently optimized for readability. Fig. 3 and all following example figures are therefore based on the standard renderings of SARI's graphical rule editors.

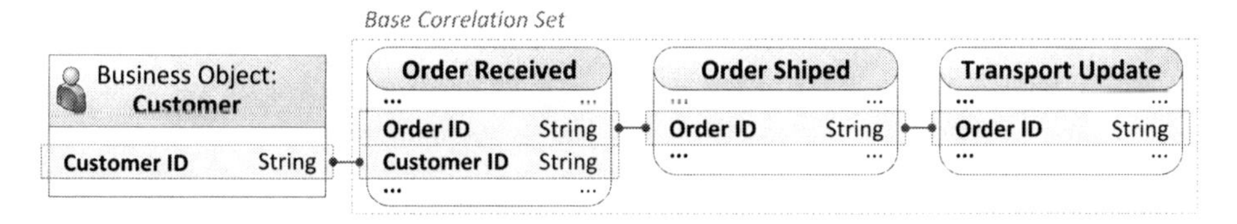

Fig. 4. An exemplary extended correlation set on the event of an order process and a base entity of type "Customer". As shown here, the granularity of correlation sessions is not necessarily equal to the granularity of business entities: While correlation sessions exist per process ID, entities exist per customer ID; thus, a single entity may be associated with several correlation sessions. Conversely, in other scenarios, a single correlation session could equally be associated with several entities.

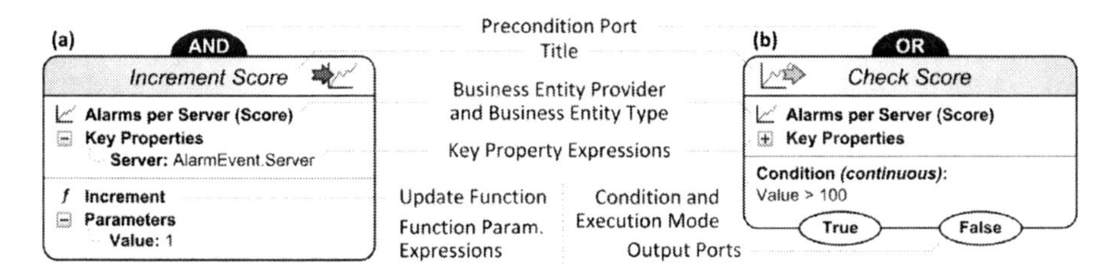

Fig. 5. Exemplary Business Entity Action (a) and Business Entity Condition (b)

4.3 Business Entity Actions

On the updating side of a business entity provider, ECA rules are applied to detect the (possibly complex) events that indicate updates to an entity and trigger the respective update operation at the provider. To support the described behavior in SARI's rule model, we extend the base decision-graph model as discussed in Section 4.1 by so-called *business entity actions*, rule components that, whenever activated, directly and synchronously call a user-defined update function on a business entity provider.

Fig. 5a. shows an exemplary action for incrementing the value of a score "Alarms per Server". A business entity action $a = (p, T, X_K, f, X_f)$ is defined by:

- a business entity provider p
- a business entity type $T = (K, \ldots)$ for p
- an optional collection of *key-property expressions* X_K for selected key properties in K. Evaluated on the active correlation session prior to the actual updating process, the resulting values allow further restricting the set of concerned business entities.
- an update function f for T
- a collection of *function parameter expressions* X_f for each function parameter of f

Whenever a so-defined rule component is activated, the component's key-property expressions in X_K are evaluated on the active correlation session, resulting in a collection of concrete values for selected key properties. In a second step, the specified update is applied for all instances of T that are

a. correlated to the activate correlation session, and
b. conform to the calculated key-property values, if available.

4.4 Business Entity Conditions

In the proposed framework, so-called monitoring rules are applied for the real-time detection of noteworthy entity states. From practical use cases, we identified two access modes required for ECA-based monitoring: In *on demand* access mode, the state of an entity shall be checked at a certain point in time – e.g., on the occurrence of an event – while subsequent developments of that entity are not taken into account. In *continuous* access mode, the state of an entity shall be checked continuously, enabling rules to react on noteworthy states independent from the exact point in time in which they occur. To support business-entity monitoring in SARI's rule model, we extend the base decision-graph model by so-called *business entity conditions*. Business entity conditions allow evaluating a Boolean expression on one or more business entities and activate downstream rule logic according to the result of such evaluation.

Fig. 5b. shows an exemplary condition for scores of type "Alarms per server", testing the current value of a score against a specified threshold. A business entity condition $c = (p, T, X_K, x_b, q, c)$ is defined by:

- a business entity provider p, a business entity type $T = (K, ...)$ for p and an optional collection of key-property expressions X_K
- a Boolean *condition* x_b on business entities of type T. x_b is to be defined based on the set of query properties for T and may furthermore consider events of the active correlation session; for instance, a condition could test a score value against an event-attribute value of a preceding event. The syntax of x_b is oriented towards SARI's business-user-oriented event-access language [17], which aims to support an integrated approach to event-pattern detection and state management.
- a binary connective $c \in \{\text{AND, OR, XOR}\}$, indicating whether *all*, *at least one* or *exactly one* business entity must conform to x_b
- an *execution mode* $m \in \{\text{on demand, continuous}\}$

Whenever a so-defined business entity condition is evaluated, x_b is calculated for all T-instances that are correlated to the activate correlation session and conform to the calculated key-property values, if such are available. Depending on the results of these calculations and the chosen connective c, the component's output port for "true" or "false" is activated. In case of *on demand* execution, the described evaluation process is executed *on activate*, i.e., every time the preconditions of the condition are fulfilled. In case of *continuous* execution, the evaluation process is triggered whenever a correlated, T-typed business entity is updated at the business entity provider. As a consequence, the component allows reacting to state changes actively and fully decoupled from low-level updating logic.

5 Implementation

In the course of our research, we implemented the presented approach as an experimental extension to SARI. Reference business-entity providers are available for base entities, scores and sets (see Section 3.2). In the following, we give an overview to SARI's basic rule evaluation approach and discuss the architecture of our solution.

5.1 Rule Evaluation in SARI

SARI's rule model is generally based on a separation between *event correlation* – i.e., the grouping of events that are generally related to each other – and *pattern detection*, which picks from the resulting event situations those that are noteworthy in a certain sense. At run time, SARI uses a rule's correlation set to correlate events before starting the actual decision-graph evaluation. For each of the resulting correlation sessions, SARI maintains a separate decision-graph state, which, among others, includes the set of activated output ports. An incoming event e is then said to *activate* the decision graph for the correlation session $S \ni e$ to which it belongs, and is processed with the associated decision-graph state. In its pattern-detection engine, SARI forwards e to all active rule components (in bottom-up direction), which process e based on the encapsulated rule logic and activate their output ports accordingly.

5.2 State-Management Architecture

In the extended SARI architecture, business entity providers must be provided in the form of .NET assemblies and referenced in a configuration file. Given the unique ID of a business entity type, a business entity provider must provide XML-formatted descriptions of the respective update and query interfaces; during the design time of a SARI application, these descriptions are used for the type-safe definition of ECA rules. While data management is generally implementation-specific, business entity providers are provided access to an application's default *event-data repository*.

Fig 6a sketches the run-time architecture of a SARI application. Plugged-in business entity providers are managed in a central *provider management service*, which performs common tasks such as inter-service communication and the evaluation of complex conditions based on a provider's query properties. In an application's event-processing network, so-called *rule services* evaluate sets of rules on incoming event streams. If a *business entity action* or an *on-demand business-entity condition* is activated within such rule, the rule service calls the provider management and passes all data necessary for performing the update or query. On the update interface of a business entity provider, function calls are received generally independent from triggering events and their exact time of creation. Thus, if a strict ordering of events is required, this must be ensured explicitly through a preceding *resequencer service*.

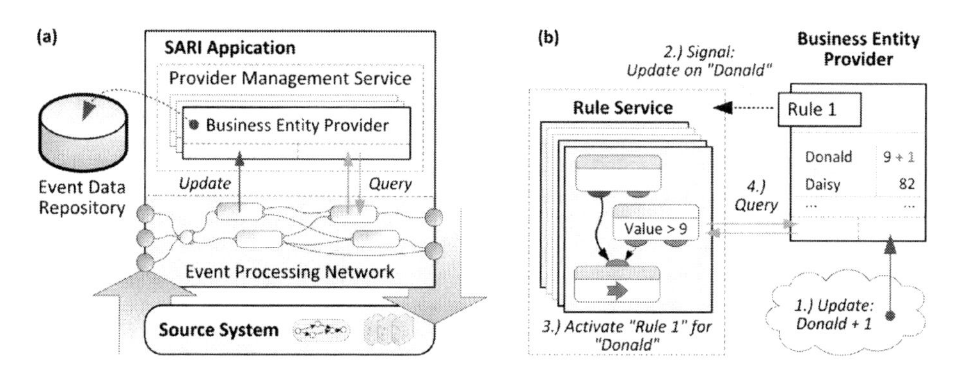

Fig. 6. Business Entity Providers in SARI (a), Continuous Monitoring Implementation (b)

Fig. 6b sketches the approach to *continuous* entity monitoring. On start up, all rules containing a continuous business-entity condition are registered as listeners at the concerned business entity providers. At run time, whenever an update to a business entity is performed, a special notification – a so-called *signal* – is published to all registered rule services. Here, SARI's basic correlation mechanism is used to retrieve the decision-graph states for all related correlation sessions. For each session, the incoming signal is then tested against the condition's key-property expressions; if the condition is concerned with the update, the provider management is called as with on-demand evaluations. Note that signals – just like any "common" event – are processed asynchronously by default; thus, a (potentially noteworthy) state at time stamp t_1 may be re-set before the actual evaluation is triggered at time stamp t_2. While such issues showed to be of little relevance in many practical use cases, we implemented an alternative, synchronous execution mode to the expense of overall event-processing performance; further improvements to this mode are subject to future work.

6 Example

In the following, we demonstrate our framework in a real-world example from the workload automation domain. One of the major challenges observed in corporations with distributed, inhomogeneous IT landscapes is to manage the proper execution of IT processes and ensure the performance of potentially thousands of servers across disconnected data centers. Traditional workload automation has been developed to overcome these difficulties, but is driven by scheduled batch execution, and lacks capabilities for flexible, event-driven execution. We applied SARI on top of an automation engine to fill this gap and add an additional layer of flexibility and control.

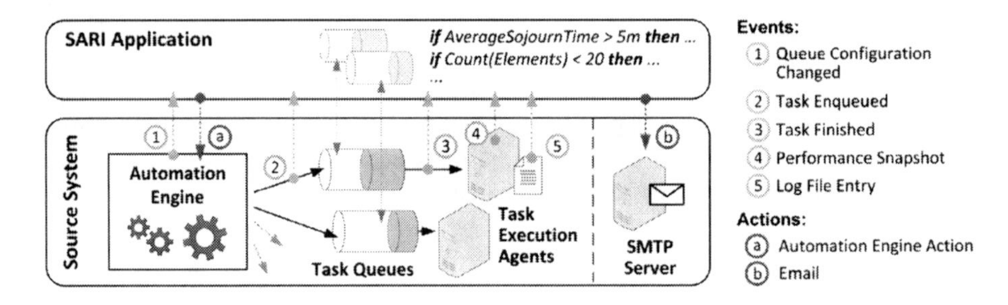

Fig. 7. Example Overview

Fig 7. sketches the presented scenario. In the source system, an automation platform distributes tasks on a network of (virtual or physical) *task execution agents*. To control the load on such agents, the platform uses extended *task queues* as an intermediate layer between its engine and the executing agents: Besides providing priority-aware queuing functionality, such a queue allows configuring a certain number of *execution slots*; all tasks that lie within these slots are then executed in parallel on the associated agent. During run time, the number of slots can be adapted dynamically, e.g., based on a schedule or on demand by a user. SARI continuously senses the given

IT landscape at several integration points: Events of type "Task enqueued", "Task finished" and "Queue configuration changed" are retrieved directly from the platform. On agent hosts, "Performance snapshot" events are published at regular intervals. "Log file" events are generated whenever message are written to the log. Conversely, SARI may trigger actions directly on the platform and send email notifications.

The described scenario illustrates many of the challenges ECA-based CEP is faced with in entity-centric environments: Serving as a key indicator to the health of a system, the overall state of task queues needs to be calculated from incremental, low-level updates and made accessible to ECA-based decision making. Counteractions will typically be required whenever a task queue reaches an exceptional state, e.g., whenever its load exceeds a certain threshold; to support this behavior decoupled from low-level updating logic, means for *active entity monitoring* must be provided. Eventually, the application's business logic is likely to change over time and should be understandable and editable to business users with restricted technical skills.

In the example's SARI application, a set type "Task Queue" is used to track the overall state of underlying, real-world task queues and make it accessible to ECA-based monitoring logic. It is defined by a single key property "Host ID" (identifying a queue by the host to which it belongs), a set of entity properties including an Integer-typed property "Execution Slots", as well as a collection of set-element properties including a task's ID, type and priority. Fig. 8a shows an exemplary rule for updating the resulting business entities: In response to incoming "Task enqueued" events, the "insert" operation is called for the correlated task queue. Further updating rules are applied to remove tasks and to update the number of slots. Fig 8b shows a simple monitoring rule for detecting overload situations: Executed in *continuous* access mode, a condition triggers an "Email" event whenever a queue's load exceeds the number of execution slots by a factor greater than four. Fig 8c demonstrates *on demand* access to task queues: Here, the number of high-priority file transfers is retrieved and tested against a threshold whenever an event of type "Recurring file-write error" occurs; in response, the automation engine could be instructed to throttle the number of file transfers or to provision an additional agent. Recurring file-write errors are detected through a preceding ECA rule from accumulations of "Log file" events.

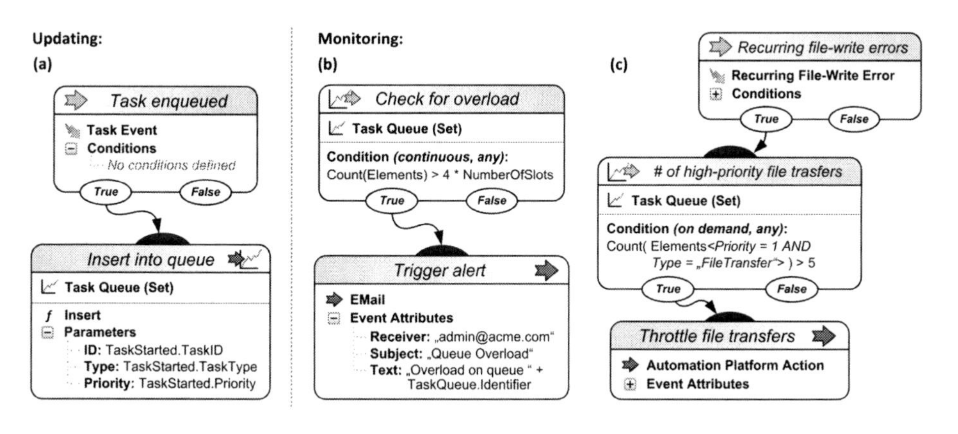

Fig. 8. Example Rules

7 Conclusion and Future Work

In this paper, we presented a novel approach to state management for Complex Event Processing. It is based on the idea of *business entities*, which we understand as identifiable, typed data structures that are accessible across an application. The proposed framework allows integrating arbitrary *business entity providers* as plug-in-like components, depending on the specific requirements of a business scenario. The model is fully integrated with SARI's ECA-based rule model, which enables users to define event patterns fully integrated with updating and monitoring business entities.

Existing challenges with state-of-the-art, ECA-based CEP as discussed in Section 1 of this paper are addressed as follows:

- **Durable entity state, complex state-calculation.** Within SARI applications, business entity providers fully encapsulate the calculation of complex entity states from low-level updates, as well as the management of resulting data over time. Access to business entities is provided through easy-to-use *update* and *query interfaces*.
- **Active entity monitoring.** In the proposed framework, business entities can be monitored based on two "access modes – *on-demand* vs. *continuous access*. In the latter case, a rule evaluates its conditions whenever an update to a business entity is signified, independent from the events that originally caused that update.
- **Context-aware data access.** The concept of business entities is fully integrated with SARI's *correlation model*, which enables users to define semantic relations between events and the business entities to which they belong. In an ECA rule, updates and queries are implicitly directed towards those business entities of a user-defined type that are associated with the triggering event or business entity.
- **Ease of use.** The presented approach explicitly focuses on usability from a business-user perspective. For the simple definition of state-management logic, a type model for business entities is presented that enables end users to configure prepared state-management logic according to the specific requirements of their application. Access to so-defined business entities is well integrated with SARI's visual rule model and can be defined using predefined, easy-to-use *rule components*.

The presented work is part of a long-term research effort towards user-oriented rule management for CEP. Apart from improvements in the evaluation of business entities at run time, future work will especially focus on the entity-driven analysis of historical event data; while a line-chart based visualization for scores has been implemented and incorporated into SARI's event-analysis framework [24], tailored visualization methods for business objects and sets are still to be designed.

References

1. Abadi, D.J., Carney, D., Cetintemel, U., Cherniack, M., Convey, C., Lee, S., Stonebraker, M., Tatbul, N., Zdonik, S.: Aurora: A new model and architecture for data stream management. VLDB J. 12(2), 120–139 (2003)
2. Adi, A., Etzion, O.: AMiT – The situation manager. VLDB J. 13(2), 177–203 (2004)
3. Brenna, L., Demers, A., Hong, M., Ossher, J., Panda, B., Riedewald, M., Thatte, M., White, W.: Cayuga: A high-performance event processing engine. In: Proc. 2007 ACM SIGMOD Int. Conf. on Management of Data, pp. 1100–1102 (2007)

4. Bry, F., Eckert, M.: Rule-based composite event queries: The language XChange^{EQ} and its semantics. In: Marchiori, M., Pan, J.Z., Marie, C.d.S. (eds.) RR 2007. LNCS, vol. 4524, pp. 16–30. Springer, Heidelberg (2007)
5. Bry, F., Eckert, M., Pătrânjan, P.-L.: Reactivity on the Web: Paradigms and applications of the language XChange. J. of Web Engineering 5(1), 3–24 (2006)
6. Chandy, K.M., Schulte, W.R.: Event Processing: Designing IT Systems for Agile Companies. McGraw Hill, New York (2009)
7. Cohn, D., Hull, R.: Business artifacts: A data-centric approach to modeling business operations and processes. IEEE Data Engineering Bulletin 32(3), 3–9 (2009)
8. Etzion, O., Niblett, P.: Event Processing in Action. Manning (2010)
9. Gualtieri, M., Rymer, J.R.: The Forrester Wave: Complex Event Processing (CEP) Platforms, Q3 2009. Forrester Research, Cambridge, MA, USA (2009)
10. Kowalski, R.A., Sergot, M.J.: A Logic-Based Calculus of Events. New Generation Computing 4, 67–95 (1986)
11. Kozlenkov, A., Jeffery, D., Paschke, A.: State management and concurrency in event processing. In: Proc. 3rd ACM Int. Conf. on Distributed Event-Based Systems, DEBS 2009 (2009)
12. Luckham, D.: The Power of Events: An Introduction to Complex Event Processing in Distributed Enterprise Systems. Additions-Wesley, Reading (2001)
13. Nandi, P., König, D., Moser, S., Hull, R., Klicnik, V., Clausen, J., Kloppmann, M., Vergo, J.: Data4BPM, Part 1: Introducing Business Entities and the Business Entity Definition Language (BEDL). IBM Corp., Riverton (2010)
14. Paschke, A.: ECA-RuleML/ECA-LP: A homogenous Event-Condition-Action logic programming language. In: Proc. Int. Conf. on Rules and Rule Markup Languages for the Semantic Web, RuleML 2006 (2006)
15. Paschke, A., Kozlenkov, A.: Rule-based event processing and reaction rules. In: Governatori, G., Hall, J., Paschke, A. (eds.) RuleML 2009. LNCS, vol. 5858, pp. 53–66. Springer, Heidelberg (2009)
16. Paton, N.W., Díaz, O.: Active database systems. ACM Comput. Surv. 31(1), 63–103 (1999)
17. Rozsnyai, S., Obweger, H., Schiefer, J.: Event Access expressions: A business user language for analyzing event streams. In: Proc. 25th Int. Conf. on Advanced Information Networking and Applications (AINA 2011), pp. 191–199 (2011)
18. Schiefer, J., Obweger, H., Suntinger, M.: Correlating business events for event-triggered rules. In: Governatori, G., Hall, J., Paschke, A. (eds.) RuleML 2009. LNCS, vol. 5858, pp. 67–81. Springer, Heidelberg (2009)
19. Schiefer, J., Rozsnyai, S., Rauscher, C., Saurer, G.: Event-driven rules for sensing and responding to business situations. In: Proc. 2007 Int. Conf. on Distributed Event-Based Systems (DEBS 2007), pp. 198–205 (2007)
20. Schiefer, J., Seufert, A.: Management and controlling of time-sensitive business processes with Sense & Respond. In: Proceedings of the Int. Conf. on Computational Intelligence for Modelling, Control and Automation (CICMA 2005), pp. 77–82 (2005)
21. Seiriö, M., Berndtsson, M.: Design and implementation of an ECA rule markup language. In: Adi, A., Stoutenburg, S., Tabet, S. (eds.) RuleML 2005. LNCS, vol. 3791, pp. 98–112. Springer, Heidelberg (2005)
22. Shanahan, M.: The Event Calculus explained. In: Wooldridge, M.J., Veloso, M. (eds.) Artificial Intelligence Today. LNCS (LNAI), vol. 1600, pp. 409–430. Springer, Heidelberg (1999)
23. StreamBase Systems, Inc., StreamBase 7.0.3 (2011)
24. Suntinger, M., Obweger, H., Schiefer, J., Gröller, M.E.: The Event Tunnel: Exploring event-driven business processes. IEEE Comput. Graph. Appl. 28(5), 46–55 (2008)
25. Sybase, Inc., Beyond relational operators: Programming with FlexStreams in the Sybase Aleri Streaming Platform. Technical Note (2010)

Declarative Traces into Fuzzy Computed Answers*

Pedro-Jose Morcillo, Ginés Moreno, Jaime Penabad, and Carlos Vázquez

University of Castilla-La Mancha,
Faculty of Computer Science Engineering,
2071, Albacete, Spain
{pmorcillo,cvazquez}@dsi.uclm.es
{Gines.Moreno,Jaime.Penabad}@uclm.es

Abstract. Fuzzy logic programming is a growing declarative paradigm aiming to integrate fuzzy logic into logic programming. In this setting, the so-called *Multi-Adjoint Logic Programming* approach, MALP in brief, represents an extremely flexible fuzzy language for which we are developing the FLOPER tool (*Fuzzy LOgic Programming Environment for Research*). Currently, the platform is useful for compiling (to standard Prolog code), executing and debugging fuzzy programs in a safe way and it is ready for being extended in the near future with powerful transformation and optimization techniques designed in our research group in the recent past. In this paper, we focus in a nice property of the system regarding its ability for easily collecting declarative traces at execution time, without modifying the underlying procedural principle. The clever point is the use of lattices modeling truth degrees (beyond $\{true, false\}$) enriched with constructs for directly *visualizing* on fuzzy computed answers not only the sequence of program rules exploited when reaching solutions, but also the set of evaluated fuzzy connectives together with the sequence of primitive (arithmetic) operators they call, thus giving a detailed description of their computational complexities.

Keywords: Fuzzy Logic Programming, Declarative Traces, Lattices.

1 Introduction

Logic Programming (LP) [16] has been widely used as a formal method for problem solving and knowledge representation in the past. Nevertheless, traditional LP languages do not incorporate techniques or constructs to treat explicitly with uncertainty and approximated reasoning. To fulfill this gap, *Fuzzy Logic Programming* has emerged as an interesting and still growing research area trying to consolidate the efforts for introducing fuzzy logic into logic programming.

During the last decades, several fuzzy logic programming systems have been developed, such as [3,4,6,15,13,30], the QLP scheme of [27] and the many-valued

* This work was supported by the EU (FEDER), and the Spanish Science and Innovation Ministry (MICINN) under grants TIN 2007-65749 and TIN2011-25846, as well as by the Castilla-La Mancha Administration under grant PII1I09-0117-4481.

N. Bassiliades et al. (Eds.): RuleML 2011 - Europe, LNCS 6826, pp. 170–185, 2011.

logic programming language of [28,29], where the classical inference mechanism of SLD–Resolution has been replaced by a fuzzy variant which is able to handle partial truth and to reason with uncertainty.

This is also the case of *multi-adjoint logic programming* approach MALP [19,17,18], a powerful and promising approach in the area. In this framework, a program can be seen as a set of rules each one annotated by a truth degree and a goal is a query to the system plus a substitution (initially the empty substitution, denoted by *id*). *Admissible steps* (a generalization of the classical *modus ponens* inference rule) are systematically applied on goals in a similar way to classical resolution steps in pure logic programming, thus returning a state composed by a computed substitution together with an expression where all atoms have been exploited. Next, during the so called interpretive phase (see [10,21,24]), this expression is interpreted under a given lattice, hence returning a pair $\langle$*truth degree*; *substitution*$\rangle$ which is the fuzzy counterpart of the classical notion of computed answer used in pure logic programming.

The main goal of the present paper is to present the benefits of introducing different notions of multi-adjoint lattices for managing truth degrees even in a single FLOPER's work-session without changing a given MALP program and goal. In particular, we are especially interested now in showing the collateral effect of these actions regarding debugging capabilities (i.e., the generation of declarative traces inside fuzzy computed answers).

The structure of the paper is as follows. In Section 2, we summarize the main features of multi-adjoint logic programming, both language syntax and procedural semantics. Section 3 presents a discussion on multi-adjoint lattices and their nice representation by using standard Prolog code, in order to facilitate its further assimilation inside the FLOPER tool. As described in Section 4, we propose too a sophisticated kind of lattices capable for taking into account details on declarative traces, such as the sequence of computations (regarding program rules, fuzzy connectives and primitive operators) needed for evaluating a given goal. Finally, in Section 5 we give our conclusions and some lines of future work.

2 Multi-Adjoint Logic Programming

This section summarizes the main features of multi-adjoint logic programming (see [19,17,18] for a complete formulation of this framework). In what follows, we will use the abbreviation MALP for referencing programs belonging to this setting.

2.1 MALP Syntax

We work with a first order language, $\mathcal{L}$, containing variables, constants, function symbols, predicate symbols, and several (arbitrary) connectives to increase language expressiveness: implication connectives ($\leftarrow_1, \leftarrow_2, \ldots$); conjunctive operators (denoted by $\&_1, \&_2, \ldots$), disjunctive operators ($\vee_1, \vee_2, \ldots$), and hybrid operators (usually denoted by $@_1, @_2, \ldots$), all of them are grouped under the name of "aggregators".

Aggregation operators are useful to describe/specify user preferences. An aggregation operator, when interpreted as a truth function, may be an arithmetic mean, a weighted sum or in general any monotone application whose arguments are values of a complete bounded lattice L. For example, if an aggregator @ is interpreted as $[\![@]\!](x, y, z) = (3x + 2y + z)/6$, we are giving the highest preference to the first argument, then to the second, being the third argument the least significant.

Although these connectives are binary operators, we usually generalize them as functions with an arbitrary number of arguments. So, we often write $@(x_1, \ldots, x_n)$ instead of $@(x_1, \ldots, @(x_{n-1}, x_n), \ldots)$. By definition, the truth function for an n-ary aggregation operator $[\![@]\!] : L^n \to L$ is required to be monotonous and fulfills $[\![@]\!](\top, \ldots, \top) = \top$, $[\![@]\!](\bot, \ldots, \bot) = \bot$.

Additionally, our language $\mathcal{L}$ contains the values of a multi-adjoint lattice $\langle L, \preceq, \leftarrow_1, \&_1, \ldots, \leftarrow_n, \&_n \rangle$, equipped with a collection of *adjoint pairs* $\langle \leftarrow_i, \&_i \rangle$, where each $\&_i$ is a conjunctor which is intended to the evaluation of *modus ponens* [19]. More exactly, in this setting the following items must be satisfied:

- $\langle L, \preceq \rangle$ is a bounded lattice, i.e. it has bottom and top elements, denoted by $\bot$ and $\top$, respectively.
- Each operation $\&_i$ is increasing in both arguments.
- Each operation $\leftarrow_i$ is increasing in the first argument and decreasing in the second.
- If $\langle \&_i, \leftarrow_i \rangle$ is an *adjoint pair* in $\langle L, \preceq \rangle$ then, for any $x, y, z \in L$, we have that: $x \preceq (y \leftarrow_i z)$ if and only if $(x \&_i z) \preceq y$.

This last condition, called *adjoint property*, could be considered the most important feature of the framework (in contrast with many other approaches) which justifies most of its properties regarding crucial results for soundness, completeness, applicability, etc.

In general, L may be the carrier of any complete bounded lattice where a L-expression is a well-formed expression composed by values and connectives of L, as well as variable symbols and *primitive operators* (i.e., arithmetic symbols such as $*, +, min$, etc...).

In what follows, we assume that the truth function of any connective @ in L is given by its corresponding *connective definition*, that is, an equation of the form $@(x_1, \ldots, x_n) \triangleq E$, where E is a L-expression not containing variable symbols apart from $x_1, \ldots, x_n$. For instance, in what follows we will be mainly concerned with the following classical set of adjoint pairs (conjunctors and implications) in $\langle [0, 1], \leq \rangle$, where labels L, G and P mean respectively *Łukasiewicz logic*, *Gödel intuitionistic logic* and *product logic* (which different capabilities for modeling *pessimist*, *optimist* and *realistic scenarios*, respectively):

$$\&_{\mathtt{P}}(x, y) \triangleq x * y \qquad \leftarrow_{\mathtt{P}} (x, y) \triangleq \min(1, x/y) \qquad \textit{Product}$$

$$\&_{\mathtt{G}}(x, y) \triangleq \min(x, y) \qquad \leftarrow_{\mathtt{G}} (x, y) \triangleq \begin{cases} 1 & \text{if } y \leq x \\ x & \text{otherwise} \end{cases} \qquad \textit{Gödel}$$

$$\&_{\mathtt{L}}(x, y) \triangleq \max(0, x + y - 1) \qquad \leftarrow_{\mathtt{L}} (x, y) \triangleq \min\{x - y + 1, 1\} \qquad \textit{Łukasiewicz}$$

A *rule* is a formula $H \leftarrow_i \mathcal{B}$, where H is an atomic formula (usually called the *head*) and $\mathcal{B}$ (which is called the *body*) is a formula built from atomic formulas $B_1, \ldots, B_n$ — $n \geq 0$ —, truth values of L, conjunctions, disjunctions and aggregations. A *goal* is a body submitted as a query to the system. Roughly speaking, a multi-adjoint logic program is a set of pairs $\langle \mathcal{R}; \alpha \rangle$ (we often write "$\mathcal{R}$ *with* α"), where $\mathcal{R}$ is a rule and α is a *truth degree* (a value of L) expressing the confidence of a programmer in the truth of rule $\mathcal{R}$. By abuse of language, we sometimes refer a tuple $\langle \mathcal{R}; \alpha \rangle$ as a "rule".

2.2 MALP Procedural Semantics

The procedural semantics of the multi–adjoint logic language $\mathcal{L}$ can be thought of as an operational phase (based on admissible steps) followed by an interpretive one. In the following, $\mathcal{C}[A]$ denotes a formula where A is a sub-expression which occurs in the –possibly empty– context $\mathcal{C}[]$. Moreover, $\mathcal{C}[A/A']$ means the replacement of A by A' in context $\mathcal{C}[]$, whereas $\mathcal{V}ar(s)$ refers to the set of distinct variables occurring in the syntactic object s, and $\theta[\mathcal{V}ar(s)]$ denotes the substitution obtained from θ by restricting its domain to $\mathcal{V}ar(s)$.

Definition 1 (Admissible Step). *Let $\mathcal{Q}$ be a goal and let σ be a substitution. The pair $\langle \mathcal{Q}; \sigma \rangle$ is a* state *and we denote by $\mathcal{E}$ the set of states. Given a program $\mathcal{P}$, an* admissible computation *is formalized as a state transition system, whose transition relation $\rightarrow_{AS} \subseteq (\mathcal{E} \times \mathcal{E})$ is the smallest relation satisfying the following* admissible rules *(where we always consider that A is the selected atom in $\mathcal{Q}$ and $mgu(E)$ denotes the* most general unifier *of an equation set E [14]):*

1) $\langle \mathcal{Q}[A]; \sigma \rangle \quad \rightarrow_{AS} \quad \langle (\mathcal{Q}[A/v \&_i \mathcal{B}])\theta; \sigma\theta \rangle$,
if $\theta = mgu(\{A' = A\})$, $\langle A' \leftarrow_i \mathcal{B}; v \rangle$ in $\mathcal{P}$ and $\mathcal{B}$ is not empty.

2)[1] $\langle \mathcal{Q}[A]; \sigma \rangle \quad \rightarrow_{AS} \quad \langle (\mathcal{Q}[A/v])\theta; \sigma\theta \rangle$,
if $\theta = mgu(\{A' = A\})$ and $\langle A' \leftarrow_i; v \rangle$ in $\mathcal{P}$.

3) $\langle \mathcal{Q}[A]; \sigma \rangle \rightarrow_{AS} \langle (\mathcal{Q}[A/\bot]); \sigma \rangle$,
if there is no rule in $\mathcal{P}$ whose head unifies with A.

Note that 3th case is introduced to cope with (possible) unsuccessful admissible derivations (this kind of step is useful when evaluating, for instance, an expression like "$\vee(p, 0.8)$", which returns a value different from 0 even when there is no program rule defining p). As usual, rules are taken renamed apart. We shall use the symbols $\rightarrow_{AS1}$, $\rightarrow_{AS2}$ and $\rightarrow_{AS3}$ to distinguish between computation steps performed by applying one of the specific admissible rules. Also, the application of a rule on a step will be annotated as a superscript of the $\rightarrow_{AS}$ symbol.

[1] Note that this case could be subsumed by the first one, after expressing each fact $\langle A' \leftarrow_i; v \rangle$ as a program rule of the form $\langle A' \leftarrow_i \top; v \rangle$.

Multi-adjoint logic program $\mathcal{P}$:

$$\begin{array}{lllllll}
\mathcal{R}_1: & p(X) & \leftarrow_{\mathtt{P}} & \&_{\mathtt{G}}(q(X), @_{\mathtt{aver}}(r(X), s(X))) & \mathit{with} & 0.9 \\
\mathcal{R}_2: & q(a) & \leftarrow & & \mathit{with} & 0.8 \\
\mathcal{R}_3: & r(X) & \leftarrow & & \mathit{with} & 0.7 \\
\mathcal{R}_4: & s(X) & \leftarrow & & \mathit{with} & 0.5
\end{array}$$

Admissible derivation:

$$\begin{array}{ll}
\langle \underline{p(X)};\ id\rangle & \rightarrow_{AS1}{}^{\mathcal{R}_1} \\
\langle \&_{\mathtt{P}}(0.9, \&_{\mathtt{G}}(\underline{q(X_1)}, @_{\mathtt{aver}}(r(X1), s(X1)))); \{X/X_1\}\rangle & \rightarrow_{AS2}{}^{\mathcal{R}_2} \\
\langle \&_{\mathtt{P}}(0.9, \&_{\mathtt{G}}(0.8, @_{\mathtt{aver}}(\underline{r(a)}, s(a)))); \{X/a, X_1/a\}\rangle & \rightarrow_{AS2}{}^{\mathcal{R}_3} \\
\langle \&_{\mathtt{P}}(0.9, \&_{\mathtt{G}}(0.8, @_{\mathtt{aver}}(0.7, \underline{s(a)}))); \{X/a, X_1/a, X_2/a\}\rangle & \rightarrow_{AS2}{}^{\mathcal{R}_4} \\
\langle \&_{\mathtt{P}}(0.9, \&_{\mathtt{G}}(0.8, @_{\mathtt{aver}}(0.7, 0.5))); \{X/a, X_1/a, X_2/a, X_3/a\}\rangle &
\end{array}$$

Interpretive derivation:

$$\begin{array}{ll}
\langle \&_{\mathtt{P}}(0.9, \&_{\mathtt{G}}(0.8, \underline{@_{\mathtt{aver}}(0.7, 0.5)})); \{X/a\}\rangle & \rightarrow_{IS} \\
\langle \&_{\mathtt{P}}(0.9, \underline{\&_{\mathtt{G}}(0.8, 0.6)}); \{X/a\}\rangle & \rightarrow_{IS} \\
\langle \underline{\&_{\mathtt{P}}(0.9, 0.6)}; \{X/a\}\rangle & \rightarrow_{IS} \\
\langle 0.54; \{X/a\}\rangle. &
\end{array}$$

Fig. 1. MALP program $\mathcal{P}$ with admissible/interpretive derivations for goal $p(X)$

Definition 2. *Let $\mathcal{P}$ be a program, $\mathcal{Q}$ a goal and "id" the empty substitution. An* admissible derivation *is a sequence $\langle \mathcal{Q}; id\rangle \rightarrow_{AS} \dots \rightarrow_{AS} \langle \mathcal{Q}'; \theta\rangle$. When $\mathcal{Q}'$ is a formula not containing atoms (i.e., a L-expression), the pair $\langle \mathcal{Q}'; \sigma\rangle$, where $\sigma = \theta[\mathcal{V}ar(\mathcal{Q})]$, is called an* admissible computed answer *(a.c.a.) for that derivation.*

Example 1. Let $\mathcal{P}$ be the multi-adjoint fuzzy logic program described in Figure 1 where the equation defining the average aggregator $@_{\mathtt{aver}}$ must obviously has the form: $@_{\mathtt{aver}}(x_1, x_2) \triangleq (x_1 + x_2)/2$. Now, we can generate the admissible derivation shown in Figure 1 (we underline the selected atom in each step). So, the admissible computed answer (a.c.a.) in this case is composed by the pair: $\langle \&_{\mathtt{P}}(0.9, \&_{\mathtt{G}}(0.8, @_{\mathtt{aver}}(0.7, 0.5))); \theta\rangle$, where θ only refers to bindings related with variables in the goal, i.e., $\theta = \{X/a, X_1/a, X_2/a, X_3/a\}[\mathcal{V}ar(p(X))] = \{X/a\}$.

If we exploit all atoms of a given goal, by applying admissible steps as much as needed during the operational phase, then it becomes a formula with no atoms (a L-expression) which can be then directly interpreted w.r.t. lattice L by applying the following definition we initially presented in [10]:

Definition 3 (Interpretive Step). *Let $\mathcal{P}$ be a program, $\mathcal{Q}$ a goal and σ a substitution. Assume that $[\![@]\!]$ is the truth function of connective @ in the lattice $\langle L, \preceq \rangle$ associated to $\mathcal{P}$, such that, for values $r_1, \ldots, r_n, r_{n+1} \in L$, we have that $[\![@]\!](r_1, \ldots, r_n) = r_{n+1}$. Then, we formalize the notion of* interpretive computation *as a state transition system, whose transition relation $\rightarrow_{IS} \subseteq (\mathcal{E} \times \mathcal{E})$ is defined as the least one satisfying:*

$$\langle \mathcal{Q}[@(r_1, \ldots, r_n)]; \sigma \rangle \quad \rightarrow_{IS} \quad \langle \mathcal{Q}[@(r_1, \ldots, r_n)/r_{n+1}]; \sigma \rangle$$

Definition 4. *Let $\mathcal{P}$ be a program and $\langle \mathcal{Q}; \sigma \rangle$ an a.c.a., that is, $\mathcal{Q}$ is a goal not containing atoms (i.e., a L-expression). An* interpretive derivation *is a sequence $\langle \mathcal{Q}; \sigma \rangle \rightarrow_{IS} \ldots \rightarrow_{IS} \langle \mathcal{Q}'; \sigma \rangle$. When $\mathcal{Q}' = r \in L$, being $\langle L, \preceq \rangle$ the lattice associated to $\mathcal{P}$, the state $\langle r; \sigma \rangle$ is called a* fuzzy computed answer *(f.c.a.) for that derivation.*

Example 2. If we complete the previous derivation of Example 1 by applying 3 interpretive steps in order to obtain the final f.c.a. $\langle 0.54; \{X/a\} \rangle$, we generate the interpretive derivation shown in Figure 1.

3 Truth-Degrees and Multi-Adjoint Lattices in Practice

In [23] we describe a very easy way to model truth-degree lattices for being included into the FLOPER tool. All relevant components of each lattice are encapsulated inside a Prolog file which must necessarily contain the definitions of a minimal set of predicates defining the set of valid elements (including special mentions to the "`top`" and "`bottom`" ones), the full or partial ordering established among them, as well as the repertoire of fuzzy connectives which can be used for their subsequent manipulation. In order to simplify our explanation, assume that file "bool.pl" refers to the simplest notion of (a binary) adjoint lattice, thus implementing the following set of predicates:

- `member/1` which is satisfied when being called with a parameter representing a valid truth degree. In the case of finite lattices, it is also recommend to implement `members/1` which returns in one go a list containing the whole set of truth degrees. For instance, in the Boolean case, both predicates can be simply modeled by the Prolog facts: `member(0).`, `member(1).` and `members([0,1]).`
- `bot/1` and `top/1` obviously answer with the top and bottom element of the lattice, respectively. Both are implemented into "bool.pl" as `bot(0).` and `top(1).`
- `leq/2` models the ordering relation among all the possible pairs of truth degrees, and obviously it is only satisfied when it is invoked with two elements verifying that the first parameter is equal or smaller than the second one. So, in our example it suffices with including into "bool.pl" the facts: `leq(0,X).` and `leq(X,1).`

– Finally, if we have some fuzzy connectives of the form $\&_{label_1}$ (conjunction), $\vee_{label_2}$ (disjunction) or $@_{label_3}$ (aggregation) with arities n_1, n_2 and n_3 respectively, we must provide clauses defining the *connective predicates* "`and_`$label_1$`/(`n_1`+1)`", "`or_`$label_2$`/(`n_2`+1)`" and "`agr_`$label_3$`/(`n_3`+1)`", where the extra argument of each predicate is intended to contain the result achieved after the evaluation of the proper connective. For instance, in the Boolean case, the following two facts model in a very easy way the behaviour of the classical conjunction operation: `and_bool(0,_,0). and_bool(1,X,X).`

The reader can easily check that the use of lattice "bool.pl" when working with MALP programs whose rules have the form:

$$\text{“}A \quad \leftarrow_{bool} \quad \&_{bool}(B_1, \ldots, B_n) \quad with \quad 1\text{”}$$

.... being A and B_i typical atoms[2], successfully mimics the behaviour of classical Prolog programs where clauses accomplish with the shape "$A \quad :- \quad B_1, \ldots, B_n$". As a novelty in the fuzzy setting, when evaluating goals according to the procedural semantics described in Section 2, each output will contain the corresponding Prolog's substitution (i.e., the *crisp* notion of computed answer obtained by means of classical SLD-resolution) together with the maximum truth degree 1.

On the other hand and following the Prolog style regulated by the previous guidelines, in file "num.lat" we have included the clauses shown in Figure 2. Here, we have modeled the more flexible lattice (that we will mainly use in our examples, beyond the boolean case) which enables the possibility of working with truth degrees in the infinite space (note that this condition disables the implementation of the consulting predicate "`members/1`") of the real numbers between 0 and 1, allowing too the possibility of using conjunction and disjunction operators recasted from the three typical fuzzy logics proposals described before (i.e., the *Łukasiewicz*, *Gödel* and *product* logics), as well as a useful description for the hybrid aggregator *average*.

Note also that we have included definitions for auxiliary predicates, whose names always begin with the prefix "`pri_`". All of them are intended to describe primitive/arithmetic operators (in our case $+$, $-$, $*$, $/$, min and max) in a Prolog style, for being appropriately called from the bodies of clauses defining predicates with higher levels of expressivity (this is the case for instance, of the three kinds of fuzzy connectives we are considering: conjuntions, disjunctions and agreggations).

Since till now we have considered two classical, fully ordered lattices (with a finite and infinite number of elements, collected in files "bool.pl" and "num.pl", respectively), we wish now to introduce a different case coping with a very simple lattice where not always any pair of truth degrees are comparable. So, consider the following partially ordered multi-adjoint lattice in the diagram below for which the conjunction and implication connectives based on the *Gödel* intuitionistic logic described in Section 2 conform an adjoint pair.... but with the

[2] Here we also assume that several versions of the classical conjunction operation have been implemented with different arities.

```
member(X) :- number(X),0=<X,X=<1. % no members/1 (infinite lattice)

bot(0).                 top(1).                 leq(X,Y) :- X=<Y.

and_luka(X,Y,Z) :- pri_add(X,Y,U1),pri_sub(U1,1,U2),pri_max(0,U2,Z).
and_godel(X,Y,Z):- pri_min(X,Y,Z).
and_prod(X,Y,Z) :- pri_prod(X,Y,Z).

or_luka(X,Y,Z)  :- pri_add(X,Y,U1),pri_min(U1,1,Z).
or_godel(X,Y,Z) :- pri_max(X,Y,Z).
or_prod(X,Y,Z)  :- pri_prod(X,Y,U1),pri_add(X,Y,U2),pri_sub(U2,U1,Z).

agr_aver(X,Y,Z) :- pri_add(X,Y,U),pri_div(U,2,Z).
agr_aver2(X,Y,Z):- or_godel(X,Y,Z1),or_luka(X,Y,Z2),agr_aver(Z1,Z2,Z).

pri_add(X,Y,Z)  :- Z is X+Y.     pri_min(X,Y,Z) :- (X=<Y,Z=X;X>Y,Z=Y).
pri_sub(X,Y,Z)  :- Z is X-Y.     pri_max(X,Y,Z) :- (X=<Y,Z=Y;X>Y,Z=X).
pri_prod(X,Y,Z) :- Z is X * Y.   pri_div(X,Y,Z) :- Z is X/Y.
```

Fig. 2. Multi-adjoint lattice modeling truth degrees in the real interval [0,1] ("num.pl")

particularity now that, in the general case, the *Gödel*'s conjunction must be expressed as $\&_{\mathtt{G}}(x, y) \triangleq inf(x, y)$, where it is important to note that we must replace the use of "*min*" by "*inf*" in the connective definition.

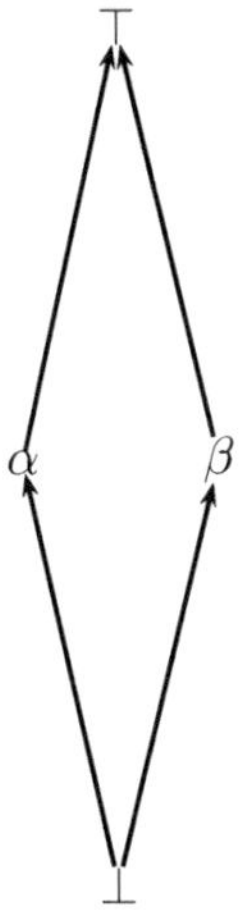

$\top$, α, β, $\bot$

```
member(bottom).   member(alpha).
member(beta).     member(top).

members([bottom,alpha,beta,top]).

leq(bottom,X). leq(alpha,alpha). leq(alpha,top).
leq(beta,beta). leq(beta,top). leq(X,top).

and_godel(X,Y,Z) :- pri_inf(X,Y,Z).

pri_inf(bottom,X,bottom):-!.
pri_inf(alpha,X,alpha):-leq(alpha,X),!.
pri_inf(beta,X,beta):-leq(beta,X),!.
pri_inf(top,X,X):-!.
pri_inf(X,Y,bottom).
```

To this end, observe in the Prolog code accompanying the figure above that we have introduced five clauses defining the new primitive operator "`pri_inf/3`" which is intended to return the *infimum* of two elements. Related with this fact, we must point out the following aspects:

- Note that since truth degrees α and β (or their corresponding representations as Prolog terms "`alpha`" and "`beta`" used for instance in the definition(s) of "`members(s)/1`") are incomparable then, any call to goals of the form "`?- leq(alpha,beta).`" or "`?- leq(beta,alpha).`" will always fail.

- Fortunately, a goal of the form "`?- pri_inf(alpha,beta,X).`", or alternatively "`?- pri_inf(beta,alpha,X).`", instead of failing, successfully produces the desired result "`X=bottom`".

- Note anyway that the implementation of the "`pri_inf/1`" predicate is mandatory for coding the general definition of "`and_godel/3`".

4 Declarative Traces into f.c.a.'s Using FLOPER

As detailed in [1,20,23,24,25], our parser has been implemented by using the classical DCG's (*Definite Clause Grammars*) resource of the Prolog language, since it is a convenient notation for expressing grammar rules. Once the application is loaded inside a Prolog interpreter (in our case, Sicstus Prolog v.3.12.5), it shows a menu which includes options for loading, parsing, listing and saving fuzzy programs, as well as for executing fuzzy goals.

All these actions are based in the translation of the fuzzy code into standard Prolog code. The key point is to extend each atom with an extra argument, called *truth variable* of the form "$\_TV_i$", which is intended to contain the truth degree obtained after the subsequent evaluation of the atom. For instance, the first clause in our target program is translated into:

```
p(X,_TV0)  :-  q(X,_TV1),
               r(X,_TV2),
               s(X,_TV3),
               agr_aver(_TV2,_TV3,_TV4),
               and_godel(_TV1,_TV4,_TV5),
               and_prod(0.9,_TV5,_TV0).
```

Moreover, the second clause in our target program in Figure 1, becomes the pure Prolog fact "`q(a,0.8)`" while a fuzzy goal like "`p(X)` ", is translated into the pure Prolog goal: "`p(X, Truth_degree)`" (note that the last truth degree variable is not anonymous now) for which the Prolog interpreter returns the desired fuzzy computed answer [$\texttt{Truth\_degree} = 0.54, \texttt{X} = \texttt{a}$]. The previous set of options suffices for running fuzzy programs (the "`run`" choice also uses the clauses contained in "num.pl", which represent the default lattice): all internal computations (including compiling and executing) are pure Prolog derivations whereas inputs (fuzzy programs and goals) and outputs (fuzzy computed answers) have always a fuzzy taste, thus producing the illusion on the final user of being working with a purely fuzzy logic programming tool.

On the other hand, in [23] we explain that FLOPER has been recently equipped with new options, called "`lat`" and "`show`", for allowing the possibility of respectively changing and displaying the multi-adjoint lattice associated to a given program. Assume that "new_num.pl" contains the same Prolog code than "num.pl" with the exception of the definition regarding the average aggregator). Now, instead of computing the average of two truth degrees, let us consider a new version which computes the average between the results achieved after applying to both elements the disjunctions operators described by Gödel and Łukasiewicz, that is: $@_{\mathtt{aver}}(x_1, x_2) \triangleq (\vee_{\mathtt{G}}(x_1, x_2) + \vee_{\mathtt{L}}(x_1, x_2)) * 0.5$. The corresponding Prolog clause modeling such definition into the "new_num.pl" file could be:

```
agr_aver(X,Y,Z)  :-   or_godel(X,Y,Z1),
                      or_luka(X,Y,Z2),
                      pri_add(Z1,Z2,Z3),
                      pri_prod(Z3,0.5,Z).
```

and now, by selecting again the "`run`" option (without changing the program and goal), the system would display the new solution: [`Truth_degree` = 0.72, `X` = `a`].

Let us consider now the so called *domain of weight values* $\mathcal{W}$ used in the QLP (*Qualified Logic Programming*[3]) framework of [27], whose elements are intended to represent proof costs, measured as the weighted depth of proof trees (although close to MALP, the QLP scheme allows a lesser repertoire of connectives in the body of program rules). In essence, $\mathcal{W}$ can be seen as lattice $\langle \mathbb{R} \cup \infty, \geq \rangle$, where $\geq$ is the reverse of the usual numerical ordering (with $\infty \geq d$ for any $d \in \mathbb{R}$) and thus, the bottom elements is ∞ and the top element is 0 (and not vice versa).

By using again the "`lat`" option of FLOPER, we can associate this lattice $\mathcal{W}$ to the program seen before after changing the "weights" of each program rule to 1 (the underlying idea is that "the use of each program rule in a derivation implies the application of one admissible step"). Moreover, since in this lattice the arithmetic operation "+" plays the role of a conjunction (*t-norm*) connective, we assume the definitions of the set of connectives appearing in the program *mapped* to "+" (i.e. $\&_{\mathtt{P}}(x, y) \triangleq x + y$, $\&_{\mathtt{G}}(x, y) \triangleq x + y$ and $@_{\mathtt{aver}}(x, y) \triangleq x + y$). Now, for goal "$p(X)$" we could generate an admissible derivation similar to the one seen in Figure 1, but ending now with $\langle \&_{\mathtt{P}}(1, \&_{\mathtt{G}}(1, @_{\mathtt{aver}}(1, 1))); \{X/a\}\rangle$ And since: $\&_{\mathtt{P}}(1, \&_{\mathtt{G}}(1, @_{\mathtt{aver}}(1, 1))) = +(1, +(1, +(1, 1))) = 4$, the final fuzzy computed answer or f.c.a. $\langle 4; \{X/a\}\rangle$ indicates that goal "$p(X)$" holds when X is a, as proved after applying 4 admissible steps, as wanted.

Moreover, we can also conceive a more powerful lattice expressed as the *cartesian product* of the one seen in Figure 2 (real numbers in the interval $[0, 1]$) and $\mathcal{W}$. Now, each element has two components, coping with truth degrees and cost measures. In order to be loaded into FLOPER, we must define in Prolog the new lattice, whose elements could be expressed, for instance, as data terms of the form "`info(Fuzzy_Truth_Degree,Cost_Number_Steps)`". Moreover, the clauses defining some predicates required for managing them are:

[3] Although close to MALP, the QLP scheme allows a lesser repertoire of connectives into the body of program rules.

```
member(info(X,Y)) :- number(X), 0=<X, X=<1, number(Y), Y=<0.
leq(info(X1,Y1),info(X2,Y2)) :- X1=<X2, Y1>=Y2.        top(info(1,0)).
and_godel(info(X1,Y1),info(X2,Y2),info(X3,Y3)) :-  pri_min(X1,X2,X3),
                                                   pri_add(Y1,Y2,Y3).
```

Finally, if the weights assigned to the rules of our running example be "`info(0.9,1)`" for $\mathcal{R}_1$, "`info(0.8,1)`" for $\mathcal{R}_2$, "`info(0.7,1)`" for $\mathcal{R}_3$ and "`info(0.5,1)`" for $\mathcal{R}_4$, then, for goal "$p(X)$" we would obtain the desired fuzzy computed answer $\langle \texttt{info}(0.54, 4); \{X/a\}\rangle$ with the obvious meaning that we need 4 admissible steps to prove that the query is true at a 56 % degree when X is a".

One step beyond, in what follows we are going to design a much more complex lattice to cope with declarative traces. Its elements must have two components, taking into account truth degrees and "labels" collecting information about the program rules, fuzzy connectives and primitive operators used when executing programs. In order to be loaded into FLOPER, we need to define again the new lattice as a Prolog program, whose elements will be expressed now as data terms of the form "`info(Fuzzy_Truth_Degree, Label)`" as shown in Figure 3 (note that the complex version of the *average connective* is called here `agr_aver2` and invokes the simple version `agr_aver`).

Here, we see that when implementing for instance the conjunction operator of the Product Logic, in the second component of our extended notion of "truth degree", we have *appended* the labels of its arguments with the label `'&PROD.'` (see clauses defining `and_prod, pri_app` and `append`). Of course, in the fuzzy program to be run, we must also take into account the use of labels associated to the program rules. For instance, in set of rules of our example (where we use the complex version of average, i.e., `@aver2` in the first rule) must have the form:

```
p(X) <prod &godel(q(X),@aver2(r(X),s(X))) with info(0.9,'RULE1.').
q(a) with   info(0.8,'RULE2.').
r(X) with   info(0.7,'RULE3.').
s(X) with   info(0.5,'RULE4.').
```

Now, the reader can easily tests that, after executing goal `p(X)`, we obtain the desired fuzzy computed answers which includes the desired declarative trace regarding program-rules/connective-calls/primitive-operators evaluated till finding the final solution:

```
>> run.

[Truth_degree=info(0.72,  RULE1.RULE2.RULE3.RULE4.
                          @AVER2.|GODEL.#MAX.|LUKA.
                          #ADD.#MIN.@AVER.#ADD.#DIV.
                          &GODEL.#MIN.&PROD.#PROD.),      X=a]
```

In this fuzzy computed answer we obtain both the truth value (0.72) and substitution ($X = a$) associated to our goal, but also the sequence of program rules exploited when applying admissible steps as well as the proper fuzzy connectives evaluated during the interpretive phase, also detailing the set of primitive operators (of the form #*label*) they call.

```
member(info(X,_)):-number(X),0=<X,X=<1.                bot(info(0,_)).

top(info(1,_)).                   leq(info(X1,_),info(X2,_)):- X1 =< X2.

and_prod(info(X1,X2),info(Y1,Y2),info(Z1,Z2)) :-
                    pri_prod(X1,Y1,Z1,DatPROD),pri_app(X2,Y2,Dat1),
                    pri_app(Dat1,'&PROD.',Dat2),pri_app(Dat2,DatPROD,Z2).
or_godel(info(X1,X2),info(Y1,Y2),info(Z1,Z2)):-
                    pri_max(X1,Y1,Z1,DatMAX),pri_app(X2,Y2,Dat1),
                    pri_app(Dat1,'|GODEL.',Dat2),pri_app(Dat2,DatMAX,Z2).
or_luka(info(X1,X2),info(Y1,Y2),info(Z1,Z2)):-
                    pri_add(X1,Y1,U1,DatADD),pri_min(U1,1,Z1,DatMIN),
                    pri_app(X2,Y2,Dat1),pri_app(Dat1,'|LUKA.',Dat2),
                    pri_app(Dat2,DatADD,Dat3),pri_app(Dat3,DatMIN,Z2).
agr_aver(info(X1,X2),info(Y1,Y2),info(Z1,Z2)):-
                    pri_add(X1,Y1,Aux,DatADD),pri_div(Aux,2,Z1,DatDIV),
                    pri_app(X2,Y2,Dat1),pri_app(Dat1,'@AVER.',Dat2),
                    pri_app(Dat2,DatADD,Dat3),pri_app(Dat3,DatDIV,Z2).
agr_aver2(info(X1,X2),info(Y1,Y2),info(Z1,Z2)):-
                    or_godel(info(X1,''),info(Y1,''),Za),
                    or_luka(info(X1,''),info(Y1,''),Zb),
                    agr_aver(Za,Zb,info(Z1,Dat3)),pri_app(X2,Y2,Dat1),
                    pri_app(Dat1,'@AVER2.',Dat2),pri_app(Dat2,Dat3,Z2).

pri_add(X,Y,Z,'#ADD.') :- Z is X+Y.   pri_sub(X,Y,Z,'#SUB.'):- Z is X-Y.
pri_prod(X,Y,Z,'#PROD.'):-Z is X * Y. pri_div(X,Y,Z,'#DIV.'):- Z is X/Y.
pri_min(X,Y,Z,'#MIN.') :- (X=<Y,Z=X;X>Y,Z=Y).
pri_max(X,Y,Z,'#MAX.') :- (X=<Y,Z=Y;X>Y,Z=X).
pri_app(X,Y,Z) :-     name(X,L1),name(Y,L2),append(L1,L2,L3),name(Z,L3).
append([],X,X).                    append([X|Xs],Y,[X|Zs]):-append(Xs,Y,Zs).
```

Fig. 3. Multi-adjoint lattice modeling truth degrees with labels

Strongly related with this, in [21] we proposed a variant of the original notion of interpretive step (see Definition 3) which was able to distinguish calls to fuzzy connectives (conjunctions, disjunctions and aggregations) and computations devoted to the evaluation of primitive operators, thus providing cost measures about the complexity of connectives. Such new notion, called *small interpretive step*, has been recently implemented into FLOPER, as described in [24], in order to generate "evaluation trees" like the one shown in Figure 4. However, compared with our present approach where we don't need any additional modification of the underlying execution machinery, the implementation of [24] required strong changes in the core of the systems, including a new representation of the fuzzy code much more involved than the one based in the compilation to Prolog code described at the beginning of this section.

The research line on cost measures mentioned above was motivated after evidencing in our fuzzy fold/unfold framework described in [26,5,9] that it is possible to improve the "shape" of a set of program rules but with the "risk" of

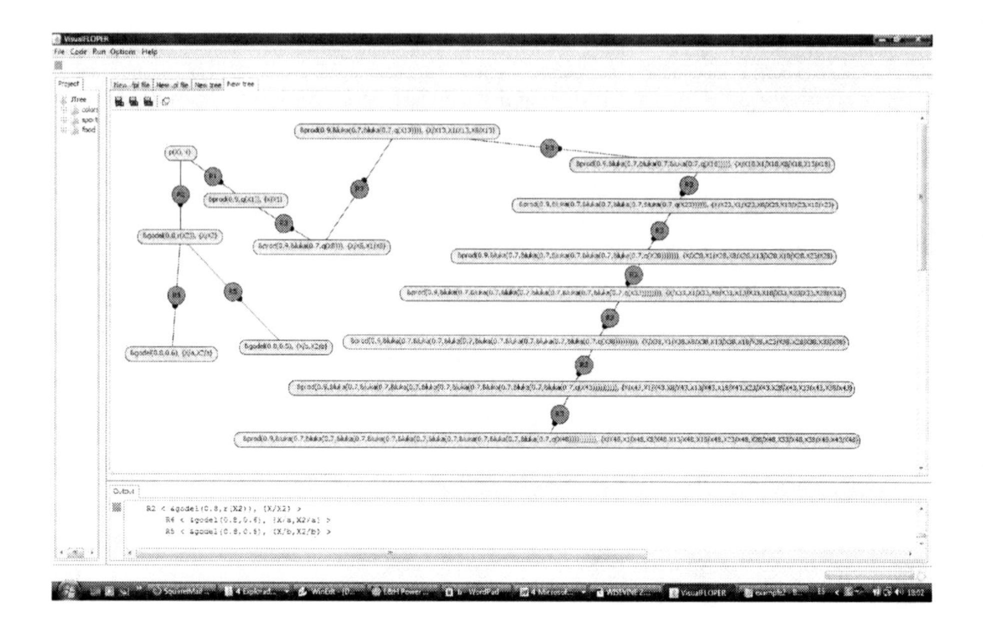

Fig. 4. Building a graphical interface for FLOPER

automatically generating a set of artificial connectives (see the definition of the *aggregation transformation* described in [5]) which necessarily invoke other connectives, thus producing nested definitions of aggregators. For this reason, it is very important to "calibrate" the complexities of these new connectives (i.e., to visualize the number of direct/indirect calls they perform to other connectives and/or primitive operators) in order to detect if the whole transformation process really returns improved sets of program rules and connective definitions. In this sense, the present work can be seen as a first stage to achieve this goal.

5 Conclusions and Future Work

The experience acquired in our research group regarding the design of techniques and methods based on fuzzy logic in close relationship with the so-called multi-adjoint logic programming approach ([10,26,5,9,11,12,7,8,21,22]), has motivated our interest for putting in practice all our developments around the design of the FLOPER environment [20,24,23]. Our philosophy is to friendly connect this fuzzy framework with Prolog programmers: our system, apart for being implemented in Prolog, also translates the fuzzy code to classical clauses (in two different representations) and, what is more, in this paper we have also shown that a wide range of lattices modeling powerful and flexible notions of truth degrees also admit a nice rule-based characterizations into Prolog. The main purpose of this work has been the illustration of an interesting kind of lattices where truth-degrees are accompanied with labels, having the ability of augmenting fuzzy computed answers with declarative traces (i.e., by listing the sequence of program rules, connective calls and primitive operators used for finding solutions) without requiring additional cost.

Apart for our ongoing efforts devoted to providing FLOPER with a graphical interface as illustrated in Figure 4[4], nowadays we are especially interested in extending the tool with testing techniques for automatically checking that lattices modeled according the Prolog-based method established in this paper, verify the requirements of our fuzzy setting (with special mention to the *adjoint property*).

In a more practical way, we are currently working in our ongoing application available from `http://dectau.uclm.es/fuzzyXPath/`, where we propose a flexible extension of the popular XPath language for querying XML documents. The material presented in [2] represents the first real-world application developed with the fuzzy logic language MALP (using too our FLOPER tool), by showing its capabilities for easily modeling scenarios where concepts somehow based on fuzzy logic play a crucial role.

For the future, we plan to implement all the manipulation tasks developed in our group on fold/unfold transformations [5,9], partial evaluation [12] and thresholded tabulation [8].

References

1. Abietar, J.M., Morcillo, P.J., Moreno, G.: Designing a software tool for fuzzy logic programming. In: Simos, T.E., Maroulis, G. (eds.) Proc. of the International Conference of Computational Methods in Sciences and Engineering, ICCMSE 2007. Computation in Modern Science and Engineering, vol. 2, pp. 1117–1120. American Institute of Physics (distributed by Springer) (2007)
2. Almendros-Jiménez, J.M., Luna, A., Moreno, G.: A Flexible XPath-based Query Language Implemented with Fuzzy Logic Programming. In: Bassiliades, N., Governatori, G., Pasckhe, A. (eds.) RuleML 2011. LNCS, vol. 6826, p. 8. Springer, Heidelberg (2011)
3. Baldwin, J.F., Martin, T.P., Pilsworth, B.W.: Fril- Fuzzy and Evidential Reasoning in Artificial Intelligence. John Wiley & Sons, Inc., Chichester (1995)
4. Guadarrama, S., Muñoz, S., Vaucheret, C.: Fuzzy Prolog: A new approach using soft constraints propagation. Fuzzy Sets and Systems 144(1), 127–150 (2004)
5. Guerrero, J.A., Moreno, G.: Optimizing fuzzy logic programs by unfolding, aggregation and folding. Electronic Notes in Theoretical Computer Science 219, 19–34 (2008)
6. Ishizuka, M., Kanai, N.: Prolog-ELF Incorporating Fuzzy Logic. In: Joshi, A.K. (ed.) Proceedings of the 9th Int. Joint Conference on Artificial Intelligence, IJCAI 1985, pp. 701–703. Morgan Kaufmann, San Francisco (1985)
7. Julián, P., Medina, J., Moreno, G., Ojeda, M.: Thresholded tabulation in a fuzzy logic setting. Electronic Notes in Theoretical Computer Science 248, 115–130 (2009)
8. Julián, P., Medina, J., Moreno, G., Ojeda, M.: Efficient thresholded tabulation for fuzzy query answering. Studies in Fuzziness and Soft Computing (Foundations of Reasoning under Uncertainty) 249, 125–141 (2010)

[4] Here we show an unfolding tree evidencing an infinite branch where states are colored in yellow and program rules exploited in admissible steps are enclosed in circles.

9. Julián, P., Moreno, G., Penabad, J.: On Fuzzy Unfolding. A Multi-adjoint Approach. Fuzzy Sets and Systems 154, 16–33 (2005)
10. Julián, P., Moreno, G., Penabad, J.: Operational/Interpretive Unfolding of Multi-adjoint Logic Programs. Journal of Universal Computer Science 12(11), 1679–1699 (2006)
11. Julián, P., Moreno, G., Penabad, J.: Measuring the interpretive cost in fuzzy logic computations. In: Masulli, F., Mitra, S., Pasi, G. (eds.) WILF 2007. LNCS (LNAI), vol. 4578, pp. 28–36. Springer, Heidelberg (2007)
12. Julián, P., Moreno, G., Penabad, J.: An Improved Reductant Calculus using Fuzzy Partial Evaluation Techniques. Fuzzy Sets and Systems 160, 162–181 (2009), doi:10.1016/j.fss.2008.05.006
13. Kifer, M., Subrahmanian, V.S.: Theory of generalized annotated logic programming and its applications. Journal of Logic Programming 12, 335–367 (1992)
14. Lassez, J.L., Maher, M.J., Marriott, K.: Unification Revisited. In: Minker, J. (ed.) Foundations of Deductive Databases and Logic Programming, pp. 587–625. Morgan Kaufmann, Los Altos (1988)
15. Li, D., Liu, D.: A fuzzy Prolog database system. John Wiley & Sons, Inc., Chichester (1990)
16. Lloyd, J.W.: Foundations of Logic Programming, 2nd edn. Springer, Berlin (1987)
17. Medina, J., Ojeda-Aciego, M., Vojtáš, P.: Multi-adjoint logic programming with continuous semantics. In: Eiter, T., Faber, W., Truszczyński, M. (eds.) LPNMR 2001. LNCS (LNAI), vol. 2173, pp. 351–364. Springer, Heidelberg (2001)
18. Medina, J., Ojeda-Aciego, M., Vojtáš, P.: A procedural semantics for multi-adjoint logic programming. In: Brazdil, P.B., Jorge, A.M. (eds.) EPIA 2001. LNCS (LNAI), vol. 2258, pp. 290–297. Springer, Heidelberg (2001)
19. Medina, J., Ojeda-Aciego, M., Vojtáš, P.: Similarity-based Unification: a multi-adjoint approach. Fuzzy Sets and Systems 146, 43–62 (2004)
20. Morcillo, P.J., Moreno, G.: Programming with fuzzy logic rules by using the FLOPER tool. In: Bassiliades, N., Governatori, G., Paschke, A. (eds.) RuleML 2008. LNCS, vol. 5321, pp. 119–126. Springer, Heidelberg (2008)
21. Morcillo, P.J., Moreno, G.: Modeling interpretive steps in fuzzy logic computations. In: Di Gesù, V., Pal, S.K., Petrosino, A. (eds.) WILF 2009. LNCS, vol. 5571, pp. 44–51. Springer, Heidelberg (2009)
22. Morcillo, P.J., Moreno, G.: On cost estimations for executing fuzzy logic programs. In: Arabnia, H.R., de la Fuente, D., Olivas, J.A. (eds.) Proceedings of the 11th International Conference on Artificial Intelligence, ICAI 2009, Las Vegas, Nevada, USA, July 13-16, pp. 217–223. CSREA Press (2009)
23. Morcillo, P.J., Moreno, G., Penabad, J., Vázquez, C.: A Practical Management of Fuzzy Truth Degrees using FLOPER. In: Dean, M., Hall, J., Rotolo, A., Tabet, S. (eds.) RuleML 2010. LNCS, vol. 6403, pp. 20–34. Springer, Heidelberg (2010)
24. Morcillo, P.J., Moreno, G., Penabad, J., Vázquez, C.: Modeling interpretive steps into the FLOPER environment. In: Arabnia, H.R., et al. (eds.) Proceedings of the 12th International Conference on Artificial Intelligence, ICAI 2010, Las Vegas, Nevada, USA, July 12-15, pp. 16–22. CSREA Press (2010)
25. Morcillo, P.J., Moreno, G., Penabad, J., Vázquez, C.: Fuzzy Computed Answers Collecting Proof Information. In: Cabestany, J., Rojas, I., Joya, G. (eds.) IWANN 2011, Part II. LNCS, vol. 6692, pp. 445–452. Springer, Heidelberg (2011)
26. Moreno, G.: Building a Fuzzy Transformation System. In: Wiedermann, J., Tel, G., Pokorný, J., Bieliková, M., Štuller, J. (eds.) SOFSEM 2006. LNCS, vol. 3831, pp. 409–418. Springer, Heidelberg (2006)

27. Rodríguez-Artalejo, M., Romero-Díaz, C.: Quantitative logic programming revisited. In: Garrigue, J., Hermenegildo, M. (eds.) FLOPS 2008. LNCS, vol. 4989, pp. 272–288. Springer, Heidelberg (2008)
28. Straccia, U.: Query answering in normal logic programs under uncertainty. In: Godo, L. (ed.) ECSQARU 2005. LNCS (LNAI), vol. 3571, pp. 687–700. Springer, Heidelberg (2005)
29. Straccia, U.: Managing uncertainty and vagueness in description logics, logic programs and description logic programs. In: Baroglio, C., Bonatti, P.A., Małuszyński, J., Marchiori, M., Polleres, A., Schaffert, S. (eds.) Reasoning Web. LNCS, vol. 5224, pp. 54–103. Springer, Heidelberg (2008)
30. Vojtáš, P.: Fuzzy Logic Programming. Fuzzy Sets and Systems 124(1), 361–370 (2001)

A Flexible XPath-Based Query Language Implemented with Fuzzy Logic Programming*

Jesús M. Almendros-Jiménez[1], Alejandro Luna[2], and Ginés Moreno[2]

[1] Dep. of Languages and Computation, University of Almería, Spain
jalmen@ual.es
[2] Dep. of Computing Systems, University of Castilla-La Mancha, Spain
{Gines.Moreno,Alejandro.Luna}@uclm.es

Abstract. In this paper we present an extension of the XPath query language for the handling of flexible queries. In order to provide ranked answers, our approach proposes fuzzy variants of *and*, *or* and *avg* operators for XPath conditions, as well as two structural constraints, called *down* and *deep*, for which a certain degree of relevance is associated. Our proposal has been implemented with a fuzzy logic language to take profit of the clear sinergies between both target and source fuzzy languages.

1 Introduction

The *XPath* language [3] has been proposed as a standard for XML querying and it is based on the description of the path in the XML tree to be retrieved. XPath allows to specify the name of nodes (i.e., tags) and attributes to be present in the XML tree together with boolean conditions about the content of nodes and attributes. XPath querying mechanism is based on a boolean logic: the nodes retrieved from an XPath expression are those matching the path of the XML tree. Therefore, the user should know the *XML schema* in order to specify queries. However, even when the XML schema exists, it can not be available for users. Moreover, XML documents with the same XML schema can be very different in structure. Let us suppose the case of XML documents containing the curriculum vitae of a certain group of persons. Although they can share the same schema, each one can decide to include studies, jobs, training, etc. organized in several ways: by year, by relevance, and with different nesting degree.

Therefore, in the context of semi-structured databases, the need for *flexible query languages* arises, in which the user can formulate queries without taking into account a rigid schema database. In addition, they should be equipped with a mechanism for obtaining a certain *ranked list* of answers. The ranking of answers can provide *satisfaction degree* depending on several factors. In a structural XPath-based query, the main criteria to provide a certain degree of

* This work has been partially supported by the EU, under FEDER, and the Spanish Science and Innovation Ministry (MICINN) under grants TIN 2008-06622-C03-03, TIN 2007-65749 and TIN2011-25846, as well as by the Castilla-La Mancha Administration under grant PII1I09-0117-4481.

N. Bassiliades et al. (Eds.): RuleML 2011 - Europe, LNCS 6826, pp. 186–193, 2011.

satisfaction depends on the *hierarchical deepness* and *document order*. Therefore the query language should provide mechanisms for giving *priority* to answers when they occur in different parts of the document.

In this paper we present an extension of the XPath query language for the handling of flexible queries. Our approach proposes two structural constraints called *down* and *deep* for which a certain degree of relevance can be associated. In such a way that *down* provides a ranked set of answers depending on the path is found from "top to down" in the XML document, and *deep* provides a set of answers depending on the path is found from "left to right" in the XML document. Both structural constraints can be combined. In addition, we provide fuzzy operators *and*, *or* and *avg* for XPath conditions. In this way, users can express the priority they give to answers. Such fuzzy operators can be combined to provide ranked answers. Our approach has been implemented by means of multi-adjoint logic programming and the FLOPER tool.

The need for providing flexibility to XPath has recently motivated the investigation of extensions of the XPath language. The most relevant ones are [4,5] in which authors introduce in XPath flexible matching by means of fuzzy constraints called *close* and *similar* for node content, together with *below* and *near* for path structure. In addition, they have studied *deep-similar* notion for tree matching. In order to provide ranked answers they adopt a *Fuzzy set theory*-based approach in which each answer has an associated numeric value (the membership degree). The numeric value represents the *Retrieval Status Value (RSV)* of the associated item. In the work of [7], they propose a satisfaction degree for XPath expressions based on associating a degree of importance to XPath nodes, and they study how to compute the best k answers. In both cases, authors allow the user to specify in the query the degree in which the answers will be penalized. On the other hand, in [6], they have studied how to relax XPath queries by means of rewriting in order to improve information retrieval in the presence of heterogeneous data resources.

Our work is similar to the proposed by [4,5]. The *below* operator of [4,5] is equivalent to our proposed *down*: both extract elements that are direct descendants of the current node, and the penalization is proportional to the distance. The *near* operator of [4,5], which is defined as a generalization of *below*, ranks answers depending of the distance to the required node, in any XPath axis. Our proposed *deep* ranks answers depending of the distance to the current node, but the nodes considered can be direct and non direct descendants. Therefore our proposed *deep* combined with *down* is a particular case of *near*. However, our aim is to extend the number of constraints and fuzzy operators of our approach thanks to the expressivity power of our framework based on fuzzy logic programming. The so-called *multi-adjoint logic programming* approach, MALP in brief [9], is an extension of logic programming for covering with fuzzy logic. Such framework provides theoretical basis for defining flexibility to XPath in many directions. In addition, the framework provides mechanism for customizing ranked answers as assigning priority of elements with independence when they occur.

With respect to *similar* and *close* operators proposed in [4,5], our framework lacks on similarity relations, rather than it focus on structural (i.e. path-based) flexibility. With regard to tree matching, the operator *deep-similar* defined in [4,5] can be simulated by means of *deep* and *down* operators. We believe that we could also work in the future in adapting our framework for working with degree of importance to XPath nodes in the line of [7], and relaxing XPath expressions by rewriting in the line [6]. In both cases, our framework could provide ranked answers w.r.t. the degree of importance, and degree of matching. Our proposal makes use of the multi-adjoint logic programming framework for defining new fuzzy operators for XPath: *and*, *or* and *avg*. Such operators are used in XPath conditions on nodes and attribute values. They provide fuzzy combinations for ranking answers.

Finally, let us remark that our work is an extension of previous works about the implementation of XPath by means of logic programming [2], which has been extended to XQuery in [1]. The proposed extension follows the same encoding proposed in [1] in which a predicate called *xpath* is defined by means of Prolog rules, which basically traverse the Prolog representation of the XML tree by means of a Prolog list. In order to implement the flexible extension of XPath by means of the «*Fuzzy LOgic Programming Environment for Research*» FLOPER (which is devoted to the management of MALP programs [10,11]), we proceed similarly to the Prolog implementation of XPath, but proposing a new (fuzzy) predicate called *fuzzyXPath* implemented in MALP. The new query language returns a set of ranked answers each one with an associated RSV. Such RSV is computed by easily using MALP rules (thus exploiting the correspondences between the languages *for-being* and *to-be* implemented), where the notion of *RSV* is modeled inside a multi-adjoint lattice, and usual fuzzy connectives of the MALP language act as ideal resources to represent new flexible XPath operators.

The structure of the paper is as follows. Whereas in Section 2 we present our fuzzy extension of XPath, Section 3 is devoted to describe the main elements of the implementation of XPath in MALP and FLOPER. Finally, Section 4 concludes by also planning future work.

2 Flexible XPath

Our flexible XPath is defined by means of the following rules:

```
   xpath := [deepdown]path
    path := literal | text() | node | @att |
            node/path | node//path
    node := QName | QName[cond]
    cond := path op path
deepdown := DEEP=degree,DOWN=degree
      op := > | = | < | and | or | avg
```

```
<bib>
  <book year="2001" price="45.95">
    <title>Don Quijote de la Mancha</title>
    <author>Miguel de Cervantes Saavedra</author>
    <publications> <book year="1997" price="35.99">
                   <title>La Galatea</title>
                   <author>Miguel de Cervantes Saavedra</author>
                   <publications>
                          <book year="1994" price="25.99">
                          <title>Los trabajos de Persiles y Segismunda</title>
                          <author>Miguel de Cervantes Saavedra</author></book>
                   </publications></book>
    </publications></book>
  <book year="1999" price="25.65">
    <title>La Celestina</title>
    <author>Fernando de Rojas</author></book>
  <book year="2005" price="29.95">
    <title>Hamlet</title>
    <author>William Shakespeare</author>
    <publications>
      <book year="2000" price="22.5">
        <title>Romeo y Julieta</title>
        <author>William Shakespeare</author></book>
    </publications></book>
  <book year="2007" price="22.95">
    <title>Las ferias de Madrid</title>
    <author>Felix Lope de Vega y Carpio</author>
    <publications>
      <book year="1996" price="27.5">
        <title>El remedio en la desdicha</title>
        <author>Felix Lope de Vega y Carpio</author> </book>
      <book year="1998" price="12.5">
        <title>La Dragontea</title>
        <author>Felix Lope de Vega y Carpio</author></book>
    </publications></book>
</bib>
```

Fig. 1. Input XML document in our examples

Basically, our proposal extends XPath as follows:

- A given XPath expression can be adorned with «[DEEP $= r_1$, DOWN $= r_2$]» which means that the *deepness* of elements is penalized by r_1 and that the *order* of elements is penalized by r_2, and such penalization is proportional to the distance. In particular, «[DEEP = 1, DOWN $= r_2$]» can be used for penalizing only w.r.t. document order. *DEEP* works for //, and *DOWN* works for / and //.
- Moreover, the classical *and* and *or* connectives admit here a fuzzy behavior based on fuzzy logic, i.e., assuming two given *RSV*'s r_1 and r_2, operator *and* is defined as $r_3 = r_1 * r_2$ and operator *or* returns $r_3 = r_1 + r_2 - (r_1 * r_2)$. In addition, the *avg* operator is defined as $r_3 = (r_1 + r_2)/2$.

In general, an extended XPath expression defines, w.r.t. a XML document, a sequence of subtrees of the XML document where each subtree has an associated RSV. XPath conditions, which are defined as fuzzy operators applied to XPath expressions, compute a new RSV from the RSVs of the involved XPath expressions, which at the same time, provides a RSV to the node. In order to illustrate

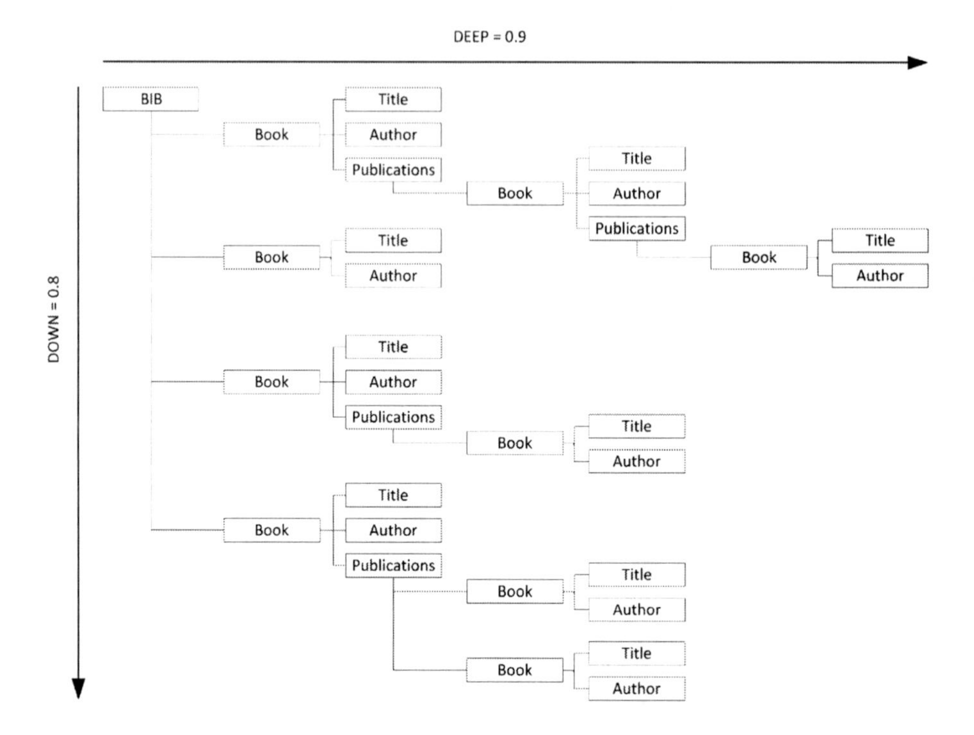

Fig. 2. XML skeleton represented as a tree

these explanations, let us see some examples of our proposed fuzzy version of XPath according to the XML document shown in Figure 1, whose *skeleton* is depicted in Figure 2.

Document	**RSV computation**
<result>	
<title **rsv**="0.81">Don Quijote de la Mancha</title>	$0.81 = 0.9^2$
<title **rsv**="0.6561">La Galatea</title>	$0.6561 = 0.9^4$
<title **rsv**="0.531441">Los trabajos de Persiles y ...</title>	$0.531441 = 0.9^6$
<title **rsv**="0.648">La Celestina</title>	$0.648 = 0.9^2 * 0.8$
<title **rsv**="0.5184">Hamlet</title>	$0.5184 = 0.9^2 * 0.8^2$
<title **rsv**="0.419904">Romeo y Julieta</title>	$0.419904 = 0.9^4 * 0.8^2$
<title **rsv**="0.41472">Las ferias de Madrid</title>	$0.41472 = 0.9^2 * 0.8^3$
<title **rsv**="0.3359232">El remedio en la desdicha</title>	$0.3359232 = 0.9^4 * 0.8^3$
<title **rsv**="0.26873856">La Dragontea</title>	$0.26873856 = 0.9^4 * 0.8^4$
</result>	

Fig. 3. Output of a query using *DEEP/DOWN*

Example 1. Suppose the XPath query: « [DEEP=0.9,DOWN=0.8]//title », that requests *title*'s penalizing the occurrences from the document root by a proportion of 0.9 and 0.8 by nesting and ordering, respectively, and for which we obtain the file listed in Figure 3. In such document we have included as attribute of each subtree, its corresponding RSV. The highest RSVs correspond the main *book*'s of the document, and the lowest RSVs represent the *book*'s occurring in nested positions (those annotated as related *publication*'s).

Document	RSV computation
<result>	
<book **rsv**="0.5" ...> <title>Don Quijote ...</title> ...</book>	$0.5 = (0 + 1)/2$
<book **rsv**="1.0"...><title>La Celestina</title> ...</book>	$1 = (1 + 1)/2$
<book **rsv**="1.0" ...><title>Hamlet</title> ...</book>	$1 = (1 + 1)/2$
<book **rsv**="0.5" ...><title>Las ferias de Madrid</title> ...</book>	$0.5 = (1 + 0)/2$
</result>	

Fig. 4. Output of a query using *AVG*

Document	RSV computation
<result>	
<title **rsv**="0.3645">La Galatea</title>	$0.3645 = 0.9^3 * 1/2$
<title **rsv**="0.295245">Los trabajos de Persiles y... </title>	$0.295245 = 0.9^5 * 1/2$
<title **rsv**="0.72">La Celestina</title>	$0.72 = 0.9 * 0.8 * 1$
<title **rsv**="0.288">Hamlet</title>	$0.288 = 0.9 * 0.8^2 * 1/2$
<title **rsv**="0.2304">Las ferias de Madrid</title>	$0.2304 = 0.9 * 0.8^3 * 1/2$
<title **rsv**="0.2985984">El remedio en la desdicha</title>	$0.2985984 = 0.9^3 * 0.8^4 * 1$
<title **rsv**="0.11943936">La Dragontea</title>	$0.11943936 = 0.9^3 * 0.8^5 * 1/2$
</result>	

Fig. 5. Output of a query using all operators

Example 2. Figure 4 shows the answer associated to the XPath expression: « /bib/book[@price<30 avg @year<2006] ». Here we show that books satisfying a *price* under 30 and a *year* before 2006 have the highest RSV.

Example 3. Finally, combining all operators «[DEEP=0.9,DOWN=0.8] //book [(@price>25 and @price<30) avg (@year<2000 or @year>2006)]/title», the RSV values are more scattered, as shown in Figure 5.

3 Some Implementation Hints Using MALP

In this section we assume familiarity with logic programming and its most popular language Prolog [8], for which MALP [9] (*Multi-Adjoint Logic Programming*[1]) allows a wide repertoire of *fuzzy connectives* connecting atoms in the bodies of clauses.

Although the core of our application is written with (fuzzy) MALP rules, our implementation is based on the following items:

(1) We have reused/adapted several modules of our previous Prolog-based implementation of (crisp) XPath described in [1,2].
(2) We have used the SWI-Prolog library for loading XML files, in order to represent a XML document by means of a Prolog term[2].
(3) The parser of XPath has been extended to recognize the new keywords *deep, down, avg*, etc... with their proper arguments.

---

[1] See also [10,11] and visit `http://dectau.uclm.es/floper` for downloading our prototype system FLOPER.

[2] The notion of *term* (i.e., data structure) is just the same in MALP and Prolog.

```
[element(bib,[],
   [element(book,[year=2001,price=45.95],
           [element(title,[],[Don Quijote de la Mancha]),
           element(author,[],[Miguel de Cervantes Saavedra]),
           element(publications,[],
                       [element(book,[year=1997,price=35.99],
                               [element(title,[],[La Galatea]),
                               element(author,[],[Miguel de Cervantes Saavedra]),
                            element(publications,[],...])...]),])])
```

Fig. 6. A data-term representing a XML document

(4) Each tag is represented as a data-term of the form: `element(Tag, Attributes, Subelements)`, where `Tag` is the name of the XML tag, `Attributes` is a Prolog list containing the attributes, and `Subelements` is a Prolog list containing the subelements (i.e. subtrees) of the tag. For instance, the document of Figure 1 is represented in SWI-Prolog like in Figure 6. Loading of documents is achieved by the predicate `load_xml(+File,-Term)` and writing by the predicate `write_xml(+File,+Term)`.

(5) A predicate called `fuzzyXPath` where `fuzzyXPath(+ListXPath,+Tree,+Deep,+Down)` receives four arguments: (1) `ListXPath` is the Prolog representation of an XPath expression; (2) `Tree` is the term representing an input XML document and (3) `Deep/Down` which have the obvious meaning.

(6) The evaluation of the query generates a *truth value* which has the form of a tree, called *tv tree*. For instance, the query shown in Example 1, generated the one illustrated in Figure 7. The main power of a fuzzy logic programming language like MALP w.r.t. Prolog, is that instead of answering questions with a simple *true/false* way, solutions are reported in a much more tinged, documented form. Basically, the `fuzzyXPath` predicate traverses the Prolog tree representing a XML document annotating into the *tv tree* the corresponding *deep/down* values according to the movements performed in the horizontal and vertical axis, respectively. In addition, the *tv tree* is annotated with the values of *and*, *or* and *avg* operators in each node.

(7) Finally, the *tv tree* is used for computing the output of the query, by multiplying the recorded values. A predicate called `tv_to_elem` has been implemented to output the answer in a pretty way.

```
tv(0.9,[[],
   tv(0.9,[element(title,[],[Don Quijote de la Mancha]),[],
   tv(1,[[],[],
   tv(1,[[],
      tv(0.9,[[],
         tv(0.9,[element(title,[],[La Galatea]),[],
         tv(1,[[],[],
         tv(1,[[],
            tv(0.9,[[],
               tv(0.9,[element(title,[],[Los trabajos de Persiles..]),...]),
   tv(0.8,[[],
     tv(0.9,[element(title,[],[La Celestina]),[],[]]),...
```

Fig. 7. Example of a *MALP* output

More details about our implementation of the flexible version of XPath reported in this paper, are available on: `http://dectau.uclm.es/fuzzyXPath/`

4 Conclusions and Future Work

In this paper we have enriched XPath with new constructs (both structural -*deep* and *down*- and constraints -*avg* and fuzzy versions of classical *or/and* operators-) in order to flexibly query XML documents. This paper represents the first real-world application developed with the fuzzy logic language MALP, by showing its capabilities for easily modeling scenarios where concepts somehow based on fuzzy logic play a crucial role. We think that this research line promises fruitful developments in the near future by reinforcing the power of fuzzy XPath commands, extensions to cope with XQuery and the semantic web, etc.

References

1. Almendros-Jiménez, J.M.: An Encoding of XQuery in Prolog. In: Bellahsène, Z., Hunt, E., Rys, M., Unland, R. (eds.) XSym 2009. LNCS, vol. 5679, pp. 145–155. Springer, Heidelberg (2009)
2. Almendros-Jiménez, J.M., Becerra-Terón, A., Enciso-Baños, F.J.: Querying XML documents in logic programming. TPLP 8(3), 323–361 (2008)
3. Berglund, A., Boag, S., Chamberlin, D., Fernandez, M.F., Kay, M., Robie, J., Siméon, J.: XML path language (XPath) 2.0. W3C (2007)
4. Campi, A., Damiani, E., Guinea, S., Marrara, S., Pasi, G., Spoletini, P.: A fuzzy extension of the XPath query language. Journal of Intelligent Information Systems 33(3), 285–305 (2009)
5. Damiani, E., Marrara, S., Pasi, G.: FuzzyXPath: Using fuzzy logic an IR features to approximately query XML documents. In: Melin, P., Castillo, O., Aguilar, L.T., Kacprzyk, J., Pedrycz, W. (eds.) IFSA 2007. LNCS (LNAI), vol. 4529, pp. 199–208. Springer, Heidelberg (2007)
6. Fazzinga, B., Flesca, S., Furfaro, F.: On the expressiveness of generalization rules for XPath query relaxation. In: Proceedings of the Fourteenth International Database Engineering & Applications Symposium, pp. 157–168. ACM, New York (2010)
7. Fazzinga, B., Flesca, S., Pugliese, A.: Top-k Answers to Fuzzy XPath Queries. In: Bhowmick, S.S., Küng, J., Wagner, R. (eds.) DEXA 2009. LNCS, vol. 5690, pp. 822–829. Springer, Heidelberg (2009)
8. Lloyd, J.W.: Foundations of Logic Programming, 2nd edn. Springer, Berlin (1987)
9. Medina, J., Ojeda-Aciego, M., Vojtáš, P.: Similarity-based Unification: a multi-adjoint approach. Fuzzy Sets and Systems 146, 43–62 (2004)
10. Morcillo, P.J., Moreno, G.: Programming with Fuzzy Logic Rules by using the FLOPER Tool. In: Bassiliades, N., Governatori, G., Paschke, A. (eds.) RuleML 2008. LNCS, vol. 5321, pp. 119–126. Springer, Heidelberg (2008)
11. Morcillo, P.J., Moreno, G., Penabad, J., Vázquez, C.: A Practical Management of Fuzzy Truth Degrees using FLOPER. In: Dean, M., Hall, J., Rotolo, A., Tabet, S. (eds.) RuleML 2010. LNCS, vol. 6403, pp. 20–34. Springer, Heidelberg (2010)

A RIF-Style Semantics for RuleML-Integrated Positional-Slotted, Object-Applicative Rules

Harold Boley

Institute for Information Technology,
National Research Council of Canada,
Fredericton, NB, E3B 9W4, Canada

Abstract. In F-logic and RIF, objects (frames) are defined entirely separately from function and predicate applications. In POSL and RuleML, these fundamental notions are integrated by permitting applications with optional object identifiers and, orthogonally, arguments that are positional or slotted. The resulting positional-slotted, object-applicative (psoa) terms are given a novel formalization, reducing the number of RIF terms by generalizing its positional and slotted (named-argument) terms as well as its frame terms and class memberships. Like multi-slot frames accommodate for (Web-)distributed slotted descriptions of the same object identifier (IRI), multi-tuple psoa terms (e.g., shelves) do for positional descriptions. The syntax and semantics of these integrated terms and rules over them are defined as PSOA RuleML in the style of RIF-BLD. The semantics provides a novel first-order model-theoretic foundation, blending frame slotribution, as in F-logic and RIF (as well as shelf tupribution) with integrated psoa terms, as in POSL and RuleML.

1 Introduction

Logic-based (e.g., FOL, Horn, LP) as well as object-oriented (and frame-based) paradigms (e.g., CLOS, RDF, N3) have been employed for knowledge representation and problem solving in AI, the (Semantic) Web, and IT at large. In search for a unified paradigm for AI/(Sem)Web languages, there have been various approaches to combining these paradigms in Description Logics (DLs), Object-Oriented Databases (OODBs) / Deductive Object-Oriented Databases (DOODs), and object-oriented logic languages such as LIFE [AK93] and F-logic [KLW95]. The W3C Rule Interchange Format (RIF) [BK10a] adopted a semantics based on F-logic with a serialization syntax based on RuleML [BPS10].

While F-logic and RIF have accommodated the standard first-order model-theoretic semantics [CL73] for the incorporation of objects (frames), these are added separately from function and predicate applications to arguments. The resulting complexity of the object-extended semantics can be reduced by integrating objects with applications. In this paper we present an integration based on the positional-slotted, object-applicative rules of POSL and RuleML [Bol10]. F-logic's model-theoretic semantics in the style of RIF is also the starting point of our integrated semantics. Our integration permits applications with optional

N. Bassiliades et al. (Eds.): RuleML 2011 - Europe, LNCS 6826, pp. 194–211, 2011.

object identifiers and, orthogonally, arguments that are positional or slotted. Structured by these independent dimensions of defining features, language constructs can then be freely combined.

The integration is based on **p**ositional-**s**lotted, **o**bject-**a**pplicative (***psoa***) terms and rules over them. A psoa term applies a function or predicate symbol, possibly instantiated by an object, to zero or more positional or slotted (named) arguments. In the interpretation of a psoa term as an atomic formula, the predicate symbol is both the class (type) of the object and the relation between the arguments, which describe the object. Each argument of a psoa term can be a psoa term that applies a function symbol.

The intuition behind the fundamental distinctions in the taxonomy of psoa terms is as follows. Psoa terms that apply a predicate symbol (as a relation) to *positional arguments* can be employed to make factual assertions. An example, in simplified RIF (presentation) syntax,[1] is the term `married(Joe Sue)` for the binary predicate `married` applied to `Joe` and `Sue`, where the positional (left-to-right) order can be used to identify the husband, as the first argument, and wife, as the second argument.

Psoa terms that apply a predicate symbol (as a class) to *slotted arguments* correspond to typed attribute-value descriptions. An example is the psoa term `family(husb->Joe wife->Sue)` or `family(wife->Sue husb->Joe)` for the `family`-typed attribute-value pairs (slots) {<`husb,Joe`>, <`wife,Sue`>}. Such a description can be easily extended with further slots, e.g. by adding one or more children, as in `family(husb->Joe wife->Sue child->Pete)`.[2] Usually, slotted terms describe an object symbol, i.e. an object identifier (OID), maintaining object identity even when slots of their descriptions are added or deleted. This leads to (typed) frames in the sense of F-logic. For example, using RIF's membership syntax `#`, the OID `inst1`, as a member of the class `family`, can be described by `inst1#family(husb->Joe wife->Sue)`, by `inst1#family(husb->Joe wife->Sue child->Pete)`, etc. Psoa terms can also specialize to class membership terms, e.g. `inst1#family()`, abridged `inst1#family`, represents `inst1` $\in$ `family`.

While positional and slotted, object-oriented and applicative terms have mostly been treated separately, psoa terms integrate them, allowing for all intermediate forms. Like OID-describing slotted terms constitute a (multi-slot) 'frame', positional terms that describe an object constitute a (single-tuple) 'shelf', similar to a (one-dimensional) array describing its name. Thus, in the `family` example, the `husb` and `wife` slots can be positionalized as in the earlier `married` example: `inst1#family(Joe Sue)` describes `inst1` with the argument tuple `[Joe Sue]`. *Combined positional-slotted* psoa terms are allowed, as in XML elements (tuple$\rightsquigarrow$subelements, slots$\rightsquigarrow$attributes), optionally describing an object,

---

[1] In this introduction, we omit RIF's namespace prefixes for simplicity.

[2] As in RDF and RIF, attributes are multi-valued by default, allowing, e.g., `family(... child->Pete child->Jane)`. Duplications of entire slots are also syntactically permitted, e.g., `family(... child->Pete child->Pete)`, but will be semantically treated as duplicate-free, e.g., `family(... child->Pete)`.

as always required by RDF descriptions (object⇝subject, slots⇝properties).[3] For example, `inst1#family(Joe Sue child->Pete)` describes `inst1` with two positional and one slotted argument.

On the other hand, the positional `married` example could be made slotted, leading to `married(husb->Joe wife->Sue)`, and even be used to describe a (marriage) object: positionally, as in `inst2#married(Joe Sue)`, or slotted, as in `inst2#married(husb->Joe wife->Sue)`.

Summarizing, an object's description or an application's arguments can consist of slots as well as a tuple of values. This includes object-describing atomic formulas playing the role of frames, shelves, or the combination of both.

A frame without an explicit class is semantically treated as typing its object with the root class $\top$ (syntactically, `Top`). For example, the (untyped) frame `inst3[color->red shape->diamond]` in square-bracketed F-logic/RIF syntax is equivalent to our parenthesized `inst3#Top(color->red shape->diamond)`.[4]

An atomic formula without an OID is treated as having an implicit OID. An OID-less application is *objectified* by a syntactic transformation as follows: *The OID of a ground fact is a new constant generated by the 'new local constant' (a stand-alone `_`); the OID of a non-ground fact or of an atomic formula in a rule conclusion, `f(...)`, is a new, existentially scoped variable `?i`, leading to `Exists ?i (?i#f(...))`; the OID of any other atomic formula is a new variable generated by the 'anonymous variable' (a stand-alone `?`).* Objectification allows compatible semantics for an atom constructed as a RIF-like slotted (named-argument) term and a corresponding frame, solving an issue with RIF's named-argument terms.[5]

For example, the slotted-fact assertion `family(husb->Joe wife->Sue)` is syntactically objectified to the assertion `_#family(husb->Joe wife->Sue)`, and – if `_1` is the first new constant from `_1`, `_2`, ... – to `_1#family(husb->Joe wife->Sue)`. This typed frame, then, is semantically *slotributed* to `_1#family(husb->Joe)` and `_1#family(wife->Sue)`. The query `family(husb->Joe)` is syntactically objectified to the query `?#family(husb->Joe)`, i.e. – if `?1` is the first new variable in `?1`, `?2`, ... – to `?1#family(husb->Joe)`. Posed against the fact, it succeeds with the first slot, unifying `?1` with `_1`. Slotribution ('slot distribution') avoids POSL's 'rest-slot' variables [Bol10]: a frame's OID 'distributes' over the slots of a description.

Rules can be defined on top of psoa terms in a natural manner. A rule derives (a conjunction of possibly existentially scoped) conclusion psoa atoms from (a formula of) premise psoa atoms. Let us consider an introductory example with a rule deriving `family` frames; this will be modified in Example 4 of Section 4.

Example 1 (Rule-defined anonymous family frame). A `Group` is used to collect a rule and two facts. The `Forall` quantifier declares the original universal argument variables as well as the generated universal OID variables `?2`, `?3`, `?4`. The

[3] See earlier XML/RDF unification: http://www.dfki.uni-kl.de/~boley/xmlrdf.html.

[4] `Top` will allow us to always use parenthesized typed frames, and to reserve square brackets for enclosing positional tuples.

[5] See Dave Reynolds' point: http://lists.w3.org/Archives/Public/public-rif-wg/2008Jul/0000.html.

:- infix separates the conclusion from the premises of a rule, which derives an anonymous/existential `family` frame from a `married` relation `And` from a `kid` relation of the `husb` `Or` `wife` (the left-hand side is objectified on the right).

```
Group (
 Forall ?Hu ?Wi ?Ch (

  family(husb->?Hu wife->?Wi child->?Ch) :-
   And(married(?Hu ?Wi)
       Or(kid(?Hu ?Ch) kid(?Wi ?Ch))) )
 married(Joe Sue)
 kid(Sue Pete)
     )
```

```
Group (
 Forall ?Hu ?Wi ?Ch ?2 ?3 ?4 (
  Exists ?1 (
   ?1#family(husb->?Hu wife->?Wi child->?Ch)) :-
    And(?2#married(?Hu ?Wi)
        Or(?3#kid(?Hu ?Ch) ?4#kid(?Wi ?Ch))) )
 _1#married(Joe Sue)
 _2#kid(Sue Pete)
     )
```

Semantically, this example is modeled by predicate extensions corresponding to the following set of ground facts (the subdomain of individuals $\boldsymbol{D}_{\text{ind}}$ will be defined in Section 3.1):

{*o#family(husb->Joe wife->Sue child->Pete)* } ∪
{*_1#married(Joe Sue)*, *_2#kid(Sue Pete)*}, where $o \in \boldsymbol{D}_{\text{ind}}$.

A language incorporating this integration, PSOA RuleML, is defined here. The rest of the paper is organized as follows. Section 2 gives the human-readable presentation syntax of PSOA RuleML. Section 3 gives its model-theoretic semantics. Section 4 concludes the paper and discusses future work.

2 The Presentation Syntax

The presentation syntax of PSOA RuleML is built on the one of RIF-BLD and described in "mathematical English". An EBNF syntax is then given, although it cannot fully capture the presentation syntax, as the latter is not context-free.

2.1 Alphabet of PSOA RuleML

Definition 1 (Alphabet). *The **alphabet** of the presentation language of PSOA RuleML consists of the following disjoint sets:*

- *A countably infinite set of **constant symbols** `Const` (including the root class `Top` ∈ `Const` and the positive-integer-enumerated local constants `_1`, `_2`, ... ∈ `Const` as well as individual, function, and predicate symbols).*
- *A countably infinite set of **variable symbols** `Var` (including the positive-integer-enumerated variables `?1`, `?2`, ... ∈ `Var`).*
- *The connective symbols `And`, `Or`, and `:-`.*
- *The quantifiers `Exists` and `Forall`.*
- *The symbols `=`, `#`, `##`, `->`, `External`, `Import`, `Prefix`, and `Base`.*
- *The symbols `Group` and `Document`.*
- *The auxiliary symbols `(`, `)`, `<`, `>`, `^^`, and `_`.*

Constants have the form `"literal"^^symspace`, where `literal` is a sequence of Unicode characters and `symspace` is an identifier for a symbol space. An example is `"_123"^^rif:local`. Constants can use shortcuts as defined in [PBK10], *including the underscore notation* `_literal` *(e.g.,* `_123`*) for the above form with* `symspace` *specialized to* `rif:local`*.* `Top` *is a new shortcut for the root class constant* `"Top"^^psoa:global` *in PSOA RuleML's global symbol space.*

Anonymous variables are written as a stand-alone question mark symbol (`?`*); named variables, as Unicode strings preceded with the question mark symbol.*

The symbols `=` *and* `##` *are used in formulas that define equality and subclass relationships. The symbols* `#` *and* `->` *are used in positional-slotted, object-applicative formulas for class memberships and slots, respectively. The symbol* `External` *indicates that an atomic formula or a function term is defined externally (e.g., a built-in) and the symbols* `Prefix` *and* `Base` *enable abridged representations of IRIs (Internationalized Resource Identifiers).* □

The language of PSOA RuleML is the set of formulas built using the above alphabet according to the construction methods given below.

2.2 Terms

The main parts of rules are called *terms*. PSOA RuleML defines several kinds of terms: *constants* and *variables*, *psoa* terms, *equality*, *subclass*, and *external* terms. Thus "*term*" will be used to refer to any one of these constructs.

Below, the phrase *base term* means a simple term, an anonymous psoa term (i.e., an anonymous frame term, single-tuple psoa term, or multi-tuple psoa term), or a term of the form `External(t)`, where `t` is an anonymous psoa term. An anonymous term can be *deobjectified* (by omitting the main `?#`) if its re-objectification (cf. Section 1) results in the original term (i.e., re-introduces `?#`).

Definition 2 (Term). *PSOA RuleML defines several different types of logic terms. Here we describe the syntax of the most important ones.*

1. *Constants and variables. If* `t` $\in$ `Const` *or* `t` $\in$ `Var` *then* `t` *is a* **simple term***.*
2. *Equality terms.* `t = s` *is an* **equality term** *if* `t` *and* `s` *are base terms.*
3. *Subclass terms.* `t##s` *is a* **subclass term** *if* `t` *and* `s` *are base terms.*
4. *Positional-slotted, object-applicative terms.* $o\#f([t_{1,1} \ldots t_{1,n_1}] \ldots [t_{m,1} \ldots t_{m,n_m}]\ p_1\text{->}v_1 \ldots p_k\text{->}v_k)$ *is a* **positional-slotted, object-applicative (psoa) term** *if* $f \in$ `Const` *and* $o, t_{1,1}, \ldots, t_{1,n_1}, \ldots, t_{m,1}, \ldots, t_{m,n_m}, p_1, \ldots, p_k, v_1, \ldots, v_k$*,* $m \geq 0$*,* $k \geq 0$*, are base terms.*
   Psoa terms can be specialized in the following way.[6]
   - *For* `m = 0` *they become* **(typed or untyped) frame terms** $o\#f(p_1\text{->}v_1 \ldots p_k\text{->}v_k)$*. We consider two overlapping subcases.*
     - *For* `k = 0` *they become* **class membership terms** `o#f()`*, abridged to* `o#f`*, corresponding to those in F-logic and RIF.*

---

[6] Distinctions similar to those for `m = 1`, and further ones, could be made for `m > 1`, i.e. ***multi-tuple psoa terms***, but for space reasons we leave most of them implicit in the general psoa term definition here. We do note that for `m > 1` and `k = 0` multi-tuple psoa terms specialize to ***multi-tuple shelf terms***. Also, for `o` being the anonymous variable `?`, these terms become ***anonymous multi-tuple psoa terms***.

- *For* $k \geq 0$ *they can be further specialized in two ways, which can be orthogonally combined.*
  - ∗ *For* `o` *being the anonymous variable* `?`*, they become* ***anonymous frame terms (slotted terms)*** `?#f(p1->v1 ... pk->vk)`*, deobjectified* `f(p1->v1 ... pk->vk)`*, corresponding to* terms with named arguments *in RIF.*
  - ∗ *For* `f` *being the root class* `Top`*, they become* ***untyped frame terms*** `o#Top(p1->v1 ... pk->vk)` *corresponding to* frames *in the abridged form* `o[p1->v1 ... pk->vk]` *of F-logic and RIF, where square brackets are used instead of round parentheses.*

– *For* `m = 1` *they become* ***single-tuple psoa terms*** `o#f([t1,1 ... t1,n1] p1->v1 ... pk->vk)`*, abridged to* `o#f(t1,1 ... t1,n1 p1->v1 ... pk->vk)`*. These can be further specialized in two ways, which can be orthogonally combined:*[7]

- *For* `o` *being the anonymous variable* `?`*, they become* ***anonymous single-tuple psoa terms*** `?#f(t1,1 ... t1,n1 p1->v1 ... pk->vk)`*, deobjectified* `f(t1,1 ... t1,n1 p1->v1 ... pk->vk)`*.*
  These can be further specialized:
  - ∗ *For* `k = 0`*, they become* ***positional terms*** `?#f(t1,1 ... t1,n1)`*, deobjectified* `f(t1,1 ... t1,n1)`*, corresponding to the usual terms and atomic formulas of classical first-order logic.*
- *For* `f` *being the root class* `Top`*, they become* ***untyped single-tuple psoa terms*** `o#Top(t1,1 ... t1,n1 p1->v1 ... pk->vk)`*.*
  These can be further specialized:
  - ∗ *For* `k = 0`*, they become* ***untyped single-tuple shelf terms*** `o#Top(t1,1 ... t1,n1)` *describing the object* `o` *with the positional arguments* `t1,1, ..., t1,n1`*.*

5. *Externally defined terms. If* `t` *is an anonymous psoa term then* `External(t)` *is an* ***externally defined term****.*
   External terms represent built-in function or predicate invocations as well as "procedurally attached" function or predicate invocations. Procedural attachments are often provided by rule-based systems, and external terms constitute a way of supporting them in PSOA RuleML. □

The notion of psoa term is generalized here from allowing a single tuple, as in [Bol10], to allowing a bag (multi-set) of tuples. Together with 'tupribution' (cf. definition 5, item 3), this accommodates for distributed positional descriptions of the same OID. For multiple tuples (m>1) each tuple is enclosed by square brackets, which can be omitted for a single tuple (m=1). The special case $n_1 = \ldots = n_m$ is useful to describe the distributed object with 'homogeneous' equal-length tuples of a relation: the OID names the extension of the relation's tuples.

Observe that the argument names of psoa terms, $p_1, \ldots, p_n$, are base terms, hence can be constants or variables. Since psoa terms include anonymous frames

[7] The combination of `o = ?` and `f = Top` leads to ***anonymous, untyped psoa terms***, describing anonymous variables without a class/type, which could be further specialized for `m = 0` and for `k = 0`.

(slotted terms), this generalizes RIF, where the corresponding named-argument terms can only use argument names from a separate set `ArgNames`, to reduce the complexity of unification [BK10a]. PSOA RuleML could emulate such a special treatment of slotted terms based on reserving an `ArgNames`-style subset of `Const` for argument names. On the other hand, as shown in Section 1, since PSOA RuleML's slotted terms via objectification are conceived as frames, they can be queried by slotribution rather than unification.

2.3 Formulas

An ***atomic formula*** is any psoa term of the form `f(...)` or `o#f(...)`, with `f` being a predicate symbol and `o` a simple term (constant or variable), or any equality or subclass term, or any externally defined term of the form `External(`φ`)`, where φ is an atomic formula. Simple terms are *not* formulas. More general formulas are built from atomic formulas via logical connectives.

Definition 3 (Formula).
*A **formula** can have one of the following forms:*

1. *Atomic: An atomic formula is also a formula.*
2. *Condition formula: A **condition formula** is either an atomic formula or a formula that has one of the following forms:*
   - *Conjunction: If φ_1, ..., φ_n, $n \geq 0$, are condition formulas then so is `And(`φ_1 ... φ_n`)`, called a **conjunctive** formula. As a special case, `And()` is allowed and is treated as a tautology, i.e., a formula that is always true.*
   - *Disjunction: If φ_1, ..., φ_n, $n \geq 0$, are condition formulas then so is `Or(`φ_1 ... φ_n`)`, called a **disjunctive** formula. As a special case, `Or()` is considered as a contradiction, i.e., a formula that is always false.*
   - *Existentials: If φ is a condition formula and ?V_1, ..., ?V_n, n>0, are distinct variables then `Exists` ?V_1 ... ?V_n(φ) is an **existential** formula.*
3. *Rule implication: φ `:-` ψ is a formula, called **rule implication**, if:*
   - *φ is a head formula or a conjunction of head formulas, where a head formula is an atomic formula or an existentially scoped atomic formula,*
   - *ψ is a condition formula, and*
   - *none of the atomic formulas in φ is an externally defined term (i.e., a term of the form `External(...)`).*

   Note that external terms can occur in the arguments of atomic formulas in the rule conclusion, but they cannot occur as atomic formulas.
4. *Universal rule: If φ is a rule implication and ?V_1, ..., ?V_n, n>0, are distinct variables then `Forall` ?V_1 ... ?V_n(φ) is a universal rule formula. It is required that all the free variables in φ occur among the variables ?V_1 ... ?V_n in the quantification part. Generally, an occurrence of a variable ?v is free in φ if it is not inside a subformula of φ of the form `Exists` ?v (ψ) and ψ is a formula. Universal rules are also referred to as* PSOA RuleML rules.
5. *Universal fact: If φ is an atomic formula and ?V_1, ..., ?V_n, n>0, are distinct variables then `Forall` ?V_1 ... ?V_n(φ) is a universal fact formula, provided that all the free variables in φ occur among the variables ?V_1 ... ?V_n. Universal facts are treated as rules without premises.*

6. *Group: If φ_1, ..., φ_n are PSOA RuleML rules, universal facts, variable-free rule implications, variable-free atomic formulas, or group formulas then* `Group(`φ_1 ... φ_n`)` *is a group formula.*
   Group formulas are used to represent sets of rules and facts. Note that some of the φ_i's can be group formulas themselves, i.e. groups can be nested.
7. *Document: An expression of the form* `Document(`*directive*$_1$ ... *directive*$_n$ Γ`)` *is a PSOA RuleML document formula, if*
   - *Γ is an optional group formula; it is called the group formula associated with the document.*
   - *directive$_1$, ..., directive$_n$ is an optional sequence of directives. A directive can be a base directive, a prefix directive or an import directive. For details see [BK10a].* □

2.4 Well-Formed Formulas

Not all formulas or documents are well-formed in PSOA RuleML. The well-formedness restriction is similar to standard first-order logic: it is required that no constant appear in more than one context. Informally, unique context means that no constant symbol can occur within the same document as an individual or a (plain or external) function or predicate symbol in different places. The detailed definitions are as in RIF-BLD, found in [BK10b], Section 2.5.

2.5 EBNF Grammar for the Presentation Syntax of PSOA RuleML

Until now, we have been using mathematical English to specify the syntax of PSOA RuleML. Since tool developers might prefer a more succinct overview of the syntax using familiar grammar notation, our PSOA RuleML specification also supplies an EBNF definition. For instance, a condition formula in mathematical English becomes a `FORMULA` nonterminal in EBNF.

The EBNF grammar for the PSOA RuleML presentation syntax is as follows:

Rule Language:

```
Document ::= 'Document' '(' Base? Prefix* Import* Group? ')'
Base     ::= 'Base' '(' ANGLEBRACKIRI ')'
Prefix   ::= 'Prefix' '(' Name ANGLEBRACKIRI ')'
Import   ::= 'Import' '(' ANGLEBRACKIRI PROFILE? ')'
Group    ::= 'Group' '(' (RULE | Group)* ')'
RULE     ::= ('Forall' Var+ '(' CLAUSE ')') | CLAUSE
CLAUSE   ::= Implies | ATOMIC
Implies  ::= (HEAD | 'And' '(' HEAD* ')') ':-' FORMULA
HEAD     ::= ATOMIC | 'Exists' Var+ '(' ATOMIC ')'
PROFILE  ::= ANGLEBRACKIRI
```

Condition Language:

```
FORMULA  ::= 'And' '(' FORMULA* ')' |
             'Or' '(' FORMULA* ')' |
             'Exists' Var+ '(' FORMULA ')' |
```

```
               ATOMIC |
               'External' '(' Atom ')'
ATOMIC    ::= Atom | Equal | Subclass
Atom      ::= PSOA
Equal     ::= TERM '=' TERM
Subclass ::= TERM '##' TERM
PSOA      ::= TERM '#' TERM '(' TUPLE* (TERM '->' TERM)* ')'
TUPLE     ::= '[' TERM* ']'
TERM      ::= Const | Var | Expr | 'External' '(' Expr ')'
Expr      ::= PSOA
Const     ::= '"' UNICODESTRING '"^^' SYMSPACE | CONSTSHORT
Var       ::= '?' UNICODESTRING?
SYMSPACE ::= ANGLEBRACKIRI | CURIE
```

The following subsections explain and illustrate the two parts of the syntax; first the foundational language of positive conditions, then the language of rules.

EBNF for the Condition Language. The Condition Language represents formulas that can be used as queries or in the premises of PSOA RuleML rules.

The production for the non-terminal `FORMULA` represents *PSOA RuleML condition formulas* (cf. definition 3, item 2). The connectives `And` and `Or` define conjunctions and disjunctions of conditions, respectively. `Exists` introduces existentially quantified variables. Here `Var+` stands for the list of variables that are free in `FORMULA`. A PSOA RuleML `FORMULA` can also be an `ATOMIC` term, i.e., an `Atom`, `Equal`, or `Subclass`. A `TERM` can be a constant, variable, `Expr`, or `External Expr`.

Example 2 (PSOA RuleML conditions). This example shows conditions that are composed of psoa terms (`"Opticks"` is a shortcut for `"Opticks"^^xs:string`).

```
Prefix(bks  <http://eg.com/books#>)
Prefix(auth <http://eg.com/authors#>)
Prefix(cts  <http://eg.com/cities#>)
Prefix(cpt  <http://eg.com/concepts#>)
```

Formula that uses an anonymous psoa (positional term):
```
?#cpt:book(auth:Newton "Opticks")
```
Deobjectified version:
```
cpt:book(auth:Newton "Opticks")
```

Formula that uses an anonymous psoa (slotted term):
```
?#cpt:book(cpt:author->auth:Newton cpt:title->"Opticks")
```
Deobjectified version:
```
cpt:book(cpt:author->auth:Newton cpt:title->"Opticks")
```

Formula that uses a named psoa (typed frame):
```
bks:opt1#cpt:book(cpt:author->auth:Newton cpt:title->"Opticks")
```

Formula that uses a named psoa (untyped frame):
```
bks:opt1#Top(cpt:author->auth:Newton cpt:title->"Opticks")
```

Deobjectified version of a formula that uses an anonymous psoa (multi-tuple term):
```
cpt:book([auth:Newton "Opticks"] [cts:London "1704"^^xs:integer])
```

Deobjectified version of a formula that uses an anonymous psoa (positional-slotted term):
```
cpt:book(auth:Newton "Opticks" cpt:place->cts:London cpt:year->"1704"^^xs:integer)
```

EBNF for the Rule Language. The EBNF for PSOA RuleML rules and documents is given in Section 2.5. A PSOA RuleML `Document` consists of an optional `Base` directive, followed by any number of `Prefix`es and then any number of `Import`s. These may be followed by an optional `Group`. `Base` and `Prefix` are employed by the shortcut mechanisms for `IRI`s. An `Import` directive indicates the location of a document to be imported and an optional profile. A PSOA RuleML `Group` is a collection of any number of `RULE` elements along with any number of nested `Group`s.

Rules are generated using `CLAUSE` elements via two `RULE` alternatives:

- In the first, a `CLAUSE` is in the scope of the `Forall` quantifier. In that case, all variables mentioned in `CLAUSE` are required to also appear among the variables in the `Var+` sequence.
- In the second alternative, `CLAUSE` appears on its own. In that case, `CLAUSE` cannot have variables.

`Var`, `ATOMIC`, and `FORMULA` were defined as part of the syntax for positive conditions in Section 2.5. In the `CLAUSE` production, `ATOMIC` is what is usually called a *fact*. An `Implies` *rule* can have a `HEAD` element or a conjunction of `HEAD` elements as its conclusion; a `HEAD` is an `ATOMIC` element or an `Exists` of an `ATOMIC` element. The `Implies` has a `FORMULA` as its premise. Note that, by Definition 3, externally defined atoms (i.e., formulas of the form `External(Atom)`) are not allowed in the conclusion part of a rule (`ATOMIC` does not expand to `External`).

Example 3 (PSOA RuleML business rule). This example adapts a business rule from a POSL logistics use case [Bol10]. The ternary `reciship` conclusion represents `reci`procal `ship`pings, at a total cost (as the single positional argument), between a `source` and a `dest`ination (as two slotted arguments). The first two premises apply a 4-ary `shipment` relation that uses an anonymous cargo and named cost variables as two positional arguments, as well as `reciship`'s slotted arguments (in both 'directions'). The third premise is an `External`-wrapped `numeric-add` built-in [PBK10] applied on the right-hand side of an equality to sum up the `shipment` costs for the total cost. With the two facts, `?cost` = `?57.0`.

```
Prefix(cpt  <http://eg.com/concepts#>)
Prefix(mus  <http://eg.com/museums#>)
Prefix(func <http://www.w3.org/2007/rif-builtin-function#>)
Prefix(xs   <http://www.w3.org/2001/XMLSchema#>)
Group (
  Forall ?cost ?cost1 ?cost2 ?A ?B (
    cpt:reciship(?cost cpt:source->?A cpt:dest->?B) :-
      And(cpt:shipment(? ?cost1 cpt:source->?A cpt:dest->?B)
          cpt:shipment(? ?cost2 cpt:source->?B cpt:dest->?A)
          ?cost = External(func:numeric-add(?cost1 ?cost2)) )
                                                          )
  shipment("PC"^^xs:string "47.5"^^xs:float cpt:source->mus:BostonMoS cpt:dest->mus:LondonSciM)
  shipment("PDA"^^xs:string "9.5"^^xs:float cpt:source->mus:LondonSciM cpt:dest->mus:BostonMoS)
     )
```

The rule can be objectified as follows (`External`s are not being transformed):

```
Forall ?cost ?cost1 ?cost2 ?A ?B ?2 ?3 (
  Exists ?1 (?1#cpt:reciship(?cost cpt:source->?A cpt:dest->?B)) :-
    And(?2#cpt:shipment(? ?cost1 cpt:source->?A cpt:dest->?B)
```

```
        ?3#cpt:shipment(? ?cost2 cpt:source->?B cpt:dest->?A)
        ?cost = External(func:numeric-add(?cost1 ?cost2)) )
                                              )
```

Further, it can be tupributed and slotributed thus (actually done by the semantics):

```
Forall ?cost ?cost1 ?cost2 ?A ?B ?2 ?3 (
  Exists ?1 (And(?1#cpt:reciship(?cost)
                 ?1#cpt:reciship(cpt:source->?A)
                 ?1#cpt:reciship(cpt:dest->?B))) :-
    And(?2#cpt:shipment(? ?cost1)
        ?2#cpt:shipment(cpt:source->?A)
        ?2#cpt:shipment(cpt:dest->?B)
        ?3#cpt:shipment(? ?cost2)
        ?3#cpt:shipment(cpt:source->?B)
        ?3#cpt:shipment(cpt:dest->?A)
        ?cost = External(func:numeric-add(?cost1 ?cost2)) )
                                              )
```

3 Semantics

The formalization of the PSOA RuleML semantics in this section is in the style of RIF-BLD [BK10a], which in some respects is more general than what would be actually required. The reason for this generality is the need to ensure that the semantics stay comparable, and that a future RIF logic dialect could be specified to cater for PSOA (e.g., via an updated RIF-FLD [BK10c]).

For the interpretation of (multiple) PSOA RuleML documents, we refer to the RIF-BLD article [BK10a]. We mention that a *local* constant, marked by an underscore prefix (e.g., `_uvw`), is encapsulated within documents, i.e. it can be interpreted differently in different documents. Based on that, in a given document, the *new local constant* generator, written as a stand-alone `_`, denotes the first new local constant $\_i$, $i \geq 1$, from the sequence `_1`, `_2`, ... that does not already occur in that document (cf. *anonymous ID symbols* in [YK03]). For each document we will assume OID-less psoa terms to be objectified by the transformation of Section 1, whose head existentials make PSOA RuleML non-Horn.

To save space, in describing the semantics we omit lists and datatypes, and simplify the semantics of external functions and predicates, all found in the RIF-BLD specification [BK10b].

3.1 Semantic Structures

The semantics of PSOA RuleML is an extension of the standard semantics for Horn clauses. This semantics is specified using *general models* while the semantics for Horn clauses is usually given via *Herbrand models* [Llo87]. Without head existentials, the two semantics become equivalent. We will use $\boldsymbol{TV}$ to denote $\{\mathbf{t},\mathbf{f}\}$–the set of truth values used in the semantics. $\boldsymbol{TV}$ is used in RIF because it is intended to address (through RIF-FLD [BK10c]) a range of logic languages, including those that are based on multi-valued logics. Since PSOA RuleML is based on the classical two-valued logic, its set $\boldsymbol{TV}$ is particularly simple.

Truth valuation of PSOA RuleML formulas will be defined as a mapping $TVal_{\mathcal{I}}$ in two steps: 1. A mapping $\boldsymbol{I}$ generically bundles the various mappings from the semantic structure, $\mathcal{I}$; $\boldsymbol{I}$ maps a formula to an element of the domain $\boldsymbol{D}$. 2. A mapping $\boldsymbol{I}_{\text{truth}}$ takes such a domain element to $\boldsymbol{TV}$. This indirectness allows HiLog-like generality, as detailed at the beginning of Section 3.2.

The key concept in a model-theoretic semantics for a logic language is the notion of *semantic structures* [End01], which is defined next.

Definition 4 (Semantic structure). *A* ***semantic structure****, $\mathcal{I}$, is a tuple of the form* $<\boldsymbol{TV}, \boldsymbol{DTS}, \boldsymbol{D}, \boldsymbol{D}_{ind}, \boldsymbol{D}_{func}, \boldsymbol{I}_C, \boldsymbol{I}_V, \boldsymbol{I}_{psoa}, \boldsymbol{I}_{sub}, \boldsymbol{I}_{=}, \boldsymbol{I}_{external}, \boldsymbol{I}_{truth}>$*. Here* $\boldsymbol{D}$ *is a non-empty set of elements called the* ***domain*** *of* $\mathcal{I}$*, and* $\boldsymbol{D}_{ind}$*,* $\boldsymbol{D}_{func}$ *are nonempty subsets of* $\boldsymbol{D}$*. The domain must contain at least the root class:* $\top \in \boldsymbol{D}$*.* $\boldsymbol{D}_{ind}$ *is used to interpret the elements of* `Const` *that play the role of individuals.* $\boldsymbol{D}_{func}$ *is used to interpret the constants that play the role of function symbols. As before,* `Const` *denotes the set of all constant symbols and* `Var` *the set of all variable symbols.* $\boldsymbol{DTS}$ *denotes a set of identifiers for primitive datatypes.*

The remaining components of $\mathcal{I}$ *are total mappings defined as follows:*

1. $\boldsymbol{I}_C$ *maps* `Const` *to* $\boldsymbol{D}$*. This mapping interprets constant symbols. In addition:*
   - *If a constant,* $\mathtt{c} \in$ `Const`*, is an individual then it is required that* $\boldsymbol{I}_C(\mathtt{c}) \in \boldsymbol{D}_{ind}$*.*
   - *If* $\mathtt{c} \in$ `Const` *is a function symbol then it is required that* $\boldsymbol{I}_C(\mathtt{c}) \in \boldsymbol{D}_{func}$*.*
   - *It is required that* $\boldsymbol{I}_C(\mathtt{Top}) = \top$*.*
2. $\boldsymbol{I}_V$ *maps* `Var` *to* $\boldsymbol{D}_{ind}$*. This mapping interprets variable symbols.*
3. $\boldsymbol{I}_{psoa}$ *maps* $\boldsymbol{D}$ *to total functions that have the general form* $\boldsymbol{D}_{ind} \times \mathtt{SetOfFiniteBags}(\boldsymbol{D^*}_{ind}) \times \mathtt{SetOfFiniteBags}(\boldsymbol{D}_{ind} \times \boldsymbol{D}_{ind}) \rightarrow \boldsymbol{D}$*. This mapping interprets psoa terms, uniformly combining positional, slotted, and frame terms, as well as class memberships. An argument* $\mathtt{d} \in \boldsymbol{D}$ *of* $\boldsymbol{I}_{psoa}$ *uniformly represents the function or predicate symbol of positional terms and slotted terms, and the object class of frame terms, as well as the class of memberships. An element* $\mathtt{o} \in \boldsymbol{D}_{ind}$ *represents an object of class* `d`*, which is described with two bags.*
   - *A finite bag of finite tuples* $\{<t_{1,1}, ..., t_{1,n_1}>, \ldots, <t_{m,1}, ..., t_{m,n_m}>\} \in \mathtt{SetOfFiniteBags}(\boldsymbol{D^*}_{ind})$*, possibly empty, represents positional information. Here* $\boldsymbol{D^*}_{ind}$ *is the set of all finite tuples over the domain* $\boldsymbol{D}_{ind}$*. Bags rather than sets of tuples are used since the order of the tuples in a psoa term is immaterial and tuples may repeat, e.g.,* `o#d([a b c][a b c])`*. Such repetitions arise through variable instantiations as explained below for slots.*
   - *A finite bag of attribute-value pairs* $\{<\mathtt{a1,v1}>, ..., <\mathtt{ak,vk}>\} \in \mathtt{SetOfFiniteBags}(\boldsymbol{D}_{ind} \times \boldsymbol{D}_{ind})$*, possibly empty, represents slotted information. Bags are again used since the order of the attribute-value pairs in a psoa term is immaterial and pairs may repeat, e.g.,* `o#d(a->b a->b)`*. Such repetitions arise naturally when variables are instantiated with constants. For instance,* `o#d(?A->?B ?C->?D)` *becomes* `o#d(a->b a->b)` *if variables* `?A` *and* `?C` *are instantiated with the symbol* `a` *and* `?B`*,* `?D` *with* `b`*. (We shall see later that* `o#d(a->b a->b)` *is actually equivalent to* `o#d(a->b)`*.)*

In addition:

- *If* $\mathtt{d} \in \boldsymbol{D}_{func}$ *then* $\boldsymbol{I}_{psoa}(\mathtt{d})$ *must be a* ($\boldsymbol{D}_{ind}$*-valued) function* $\boldsymbol{D}_{ind} \times$ $\mathtt{SetOfFiniteBags}(\boldsymbol{D}^*_{ind}) \times \mathtt{SetOfFiniteBags}(\boldsymbol{D}_{ind} \times \boldsymbol{D}_{ind}) \to \boldsymbol{D}_{ind}$.
- *This implies that when a function symbol is applied to arguments that are individual objects then the result is also an individual object.*

We will see shortly how $\boldsymbol{I}_{psoa}$ *is used to determine the truth valuation of psoa terms.*

4. $\boldsymbol{I}_{sub}$ *gives meaning to the subclass relationship. It is a total mapping of the form* $\boldsymbol{D}_{func} \times \boldsymbol{D}_{func} \to \boldsymbol{D}$.
An additional restriction in Section 3.2 ensures that the operator `##` *is transitive, i.e., that* `c1 ## c2` *and* `c2 ## c3` *imply* `c1 ## c3`.
5. $\boldsymbol{I}_{=}$ *is a mapping of the form* $\boldsymbol{D}_{ind} \times \boldsymbol{D}_{ind} \to \boldsymbol{D}$. *It gives meaning to the equality operator.*
6. $\boldsymbol{I}_{external}$ *is a mapping that is used to give meaning to* `External` *terms. It maps symbols in* `Const` *designated as external to fixed functions of appropriate arity. Typically, external terms are invocations of built-in functions or predicates, and their fixed interpretations are determined by the specification of those built-ins.*
7. $\boldsymbol{I}_{truth}$ *is a mapping of the form* $\boldsymbol{D} \to \boldsymbol{TV}$. *It is used to define truth valuation for formulas.*

We also define the following generic mapping from terms to $\boldsymbol{D}$, *which we denote by* $\boldsymbol{I}$.

- $\boldsymbol{I}(k) = \boldsymbol{I}_C(k)$, *if* k *is a symbol in* `Const`
- $\boldsymbol{I}(?v) = \boldsymbol{I}_V(?v)$, *if* $?v$ *is a variable in* `Var`
- $\boldsymbol{I}(o\#f([t_{1,1} \ldots t_{1,n_1}] \ldots [t_{m,1} \ldots t_{m,n_m}]\ a_1\text{->}v_1 \ldots a_k\text{->}v_k)) =$
$\boldsymbol{I}_{psoa}(\boldsymbol{I}(f))(\boldsymbol{I}(o),$
$\{<\boldsymbol{I}(t_{1,1}), \ldots, \boldsymbol{I}(t_{1,n_1})>, \ldots, <\boldsymbol{I}(t_{m,1}), \ldots, \boldsymbol{I}(t_{m,n_m})>\},$
$\{<\boldsymbol{I}(a_1),\boldsymbol{I}(v_1)>, \ldots, <\boldsymbol{I}(a_k),\boldsymbol{I}(v_k)>\})$
Here {...} *again denote* bags *of tuples and attribute-value pairs. Section 3.2 will show that duplicate elements in such a bag do not affect the value of* $\boldsymbol{I}_{psoa}(\boldsymbol{I}(f))$. *For instance,* $\boldsymbol{I}(o\#f(a\text{->}b\ a\text{->}b)) = \boldsymbol{I}(o\#f(a\text{->}b))$.
- $\boldsymbol{I}(c1\#\#c2) = \boldsymbol{I}_{sub}(\boldsymbol{I}(c1), \boldsymbol{I}(c2))$
- $\boldsymbol{I}(x\texttt{=}y) = \boldsymbol{I}_{=}(\boldsymbol{I}(x), \boldsymbol{I}(y))$
- $\boldsymbol{I}(External(p(s_1 \ldots s_n))) = \boldsymbol{I}_{external}(p)(\boldsymbol{I}(s_1), \ldots, \boldsymbol{I}(s_n))$.

In addition, PSOA RuleML imposes certain restrictions on datatypes so that they would be interpreted as intended (for instance, that the constants in the symbol space `xs:integer` *are interpreted by integers). Details are found in [BK10b].* □

3.2 Formula Interpretation

This section establishes how semantic structures determine the truth value of PSOA RuleML formulas other than document formulas. Truth valuation of document formulas is as defined in RIF-BLD [BK10a]. Here we define a mapping, $TVal_{\mathcal{I}}$, from the set of all non-document formulas to $\boldsymbol{TV}$.

Observe that in case of an atomic formula ϕ, $TVal_{\mathcal{I}}(\phi)$ is defined essentially as $\boldsymbol{I}_{\text{truth}}(\boldsymbol{I}(\phi))$. Recall that $\boldsymbol{I}(\phi)$ is just an element of the domain $\boldsymbol{D}$ and $\boldsymbol{I}_{\text{truth}}$ maps $\boldsymbol{D}$ to truth values in $\boldsymbol{TV}$. This might surprise those used to textbook-style definitions, since normally the mapping $\boldsymbol{I}$ is defined only for terms that occur as arguments to predicates, not for atomic formulas. Similarly, truth valuations are usually defined via mappings from instantiated formulas to $\boldsymbol{TV}$, not from the interpretation domain $\boldsymbol{D}$ to $\boldsymbol{TV}$. This HiLog-style definition [CKW93] is inherited from RIF-FLD [BK10c] and is equivalent to a standard one for first-order languages such as RIF-BLD and PSOA RuleML. In RIF-FLD, this style of definition is a provision for enabling future RIF dialects that support higher-order features, such as those of HiLog, Relfun, and FLORA-2 [YKZ03].

Definition 5 (Truth valuation). ***Truth valuation*** *for well-formed formulas in PSOA RuleML is determined using the following function, denoted* $TVal_{\mathcal{I}}$*:*

1. *Equality:* $TVal_{\mathcal{I}}(\mathtt{x = y}) = \boldsymbol{I}_{truth}(\boldsymbol{I}(\mathtt{x = y}))$.
   - *To ensure that equality has precisely the expected properties, it is required that:*

     $\boldsymbol{I}_{truth}(\boldsymbol{I}(\mathtt{x = y})) = \boldsymbol{t}$ *if* $\boldsymbol{I}(x) = \boldsymbol{I}(y)$ *and that* $\boldsymbol{I}_{truth}(\boldsymbol{I}(\mathtt{x = y})) = \boldsymbol{f}$ *otherwise.*
   - *This can also be expressed as* $TVal_{\mathcal{I}}(\mathtt{x = y}) = \boldsymbol{t}$ *if and only if* $\boldsymbol{I}(x) = \boldsymbol{I}(y)$.
2. *Subclass:* $TVal_{\mathcal{I}}(\mathtt{sc\#\#cl}) = \boldsymbol{I}_{truth}(\boldsymbol{I}(\mathtt{sc\#\#cl}))$.
   In particular, for the root class, `Top`*, and all* $\mathtt{sc} \in \boldsymbol{D}$, $TVal_{\mathcal{I}}(\mathtt{sc\#\#Top}) = \boldsymbol{t}$.
   To ensure that `##` *is transitive, i.e.,* `c1 ## c2` *and* `c2 ## c3` *imply* `c1 ## c3`*, the following is required:*
   - *For all* `c1`, `c2`, $\mathtt{c3} \in \boldsymbol{D}$, *if* $TVal_{\mathcal{I}}(\mathtt{c1\#\#c2}) = TVal_{\mathcal{I}}(\mathtt{c2\#\#c3}) = \boldsymbol{t}$ *then* $TVal_{\mathcal{I}}(\mathtt{c1\#\#c3}) = \boldsymbol{t}$.
3. *Psoa formula:*

   $TVal_{\mathcal{I}}(\mathtt{o\#f([t_{1,1} \ldots t_{1,n_1}] \ldots [t_{m,1} \ldots t_{m,n_m}]\ a_1\text{->}v_1 \ldots a_k\text{->}v_k)}) =$
   $\boldsymbol{I}_{truth}(\boldsymbol{I}(\mathtt{o\#f([t_{1,1} \ldots t_{1,n_1}] \ldots [t_{m,1} \ldots t_{m,n_m}]\ a_1\text{->}v_1 \ldots a_k\text{->}v_k)}))$.
   *Since the formula consists of an object-typing membership, a bag of tuples representing a conjunction of all the object-centered tuples (*tupribution*), and a bag of slots representing a conjunction of all the object-centered slots (*slotribution*), the following restriction is used, where* $\mathtt{m} \geq 0$ *and* $\mathtt{k} \geq 0$*:*

   - $TVal_{\mathcal{I}}(\mathtt{o\#f([t_{1,1} \ldots t_{1,n_1}] \ldots [t_{m,1} \ldots t_{m,n_m}]\ a_1\text{->}v_1 \ldots a_k\text{->}v_k)}) = \boldsymbol{t}$
     if and only if
     $TVal_{\mathcal{I}}(\mathtt{o\#f}) =$
     $TVal_{\mathcal{I}}(\mathtt{o\#Top([t_{1,1} \ldots t_{1,n_1}])}) = \ldots = TVal_{\mathcal{I}}(\mathtt{o\#Top([t_{m,1} \ldots t_{m,n_m}])}) =$
     $TVal_{\mathcal{I}}(\mathtt{o\#Top(a_1\text{->}v_1)}) = \ldots = TVal_{\mathcal{I}}(\mathtt{o\#Top(a_k\text{->}v_k)}) =$
     $\boldsymbol{t}$.
     Observe that on the right-hand side of the "if and only if" there are $1+\mathtt{m}+\mathtt{k}$ *subformulas splitting the left-hand side into an object membership,* `m` *object-centered positional formulas, each associating the object with a tuple, and* `k` *object-centered slotted formulas, i.e. 'triples', each*

associating the object with an attribute-value pair. All parts on both sides of the "if and only if" are centered on the object `o`*, which connects the subformulas on the right-hand side (the first subformula providing the* `o`*-member class* `f`*, the remaining* `m+k` *ones using the root class* `Top`*).*

For the root class, `Top`*, and all* $o \in \mathbf{D}$, $TVal_{\mathcal{I}}(\texttt{o \# Top}) = \mathbf{t}$.
To ensure that all members of a subclass are also members of its superclasses, i.e., `o # f` *and* `f ## g` *imply* `o # g`*, the following restriction is imposed:*

- *For all* `o`, `f`, `g` $\in \mathbf{D}$, *if* $TVal_{\mathcal{I}}(\texttt{o \# f}) = TVal_{\mathcal{I}}(\texttt{f \#\# g}) = \mathbf{t}$ *then* $TVal_{\mathcal{I}}(\texttt{o \# g}) = \mathbf{t}$.

4. *Externally defined atomic formula:* $TVal_{\mathcal{I}}(\texttt{External(t)}) = \mathbf{I}_{truth}(\mathbf{I}_{external}(\texttt{t}))$.
5. *Conjunction:* $TVal_{\mathcal{I}}(\texttt{And}(c_1 \; ... \; c_n)) = \mathbf{t}$ *if and only if* $TVal_{\mathcal{I}}(c_1) = ... = TVal_{\mathcal{I}}(c_n) = \mathbf{t}$. *Otherwise,* $TVal_{\mathcal{I}}(\texttt{And}(c_1 \; ... \; c_n)) = \mathbf{f}$. *The empty conjunction is treated as a tautology:* $TVal_{\mathcal{I}}(\texttt{And()}) = \mathbf{t}$.
6. *Disjunction:* $TVal_{\mathcal{I}}(\texttt{Or}(c_1 \; ... \; c_n)) = \mathbf{f}$ *if and only if* $TVal_{\mathcal{I}}(c_1) = ... = TVal_{\mathcal{I}}(c_n) = \mathbf{f}$. *Otherwise,* $TVal_{\mathcal{I}}(\texttt{Or}(c_1 \; ... \; c_n)) = \mathbf{t}$. *The empty disjunction is treated as a contradiction:* $TVal_{\mathcal{I}}(\texttt{Or()}) = \mathbf{f}$.
7. *Quantification:*

   - $TVal_{\mathcal{I}}(\texttt{Exists} \; ?v_1 \; ... \; ?v_n \; (\varphi)) = \mathbf{t}$ *if and only if for some* $\mathcal{I}^*$*, described below,* $TVal_{\mathcal{I}^*}(\varphi) = \mathbf{t}$.
   - $TVal_{\mathcal{I}}(\texttt{Forall} \; ?v_1 \; ... \; ?v_n \; (\varphi)) = \mathbf{t}$ *if and only if for every* $\mathcal{I}^*$*, described below,* $TVal_{\mathcal{I}^*}(\varphi) = \mathbf{t}$.

   Here $\mathcal{I}^*$ *is a semantic structure of the form* $<\mathbf{TV}, \mathbf{DTS}, \mathbf{D}, \mathbf{D}_{ind}, \mathbf{D}_{func}, \mathbf{I}_C, \mathbf{I}^*_V, \mathbf{I}_{psoa}, \mathbf{I}_{sub}, \mathbf{I}_{=}, \mathbf{I}_{external}, \mathbf{I}_{truth}>$*, which is exactly like* $\mathcal{I}$*, except that the mapping* $\mathbf{I}^*_V$*, is used instead of* $\mathbf{I}_V$. $\mathbf{I}^*_V$ *is defined to coincide with* $\mathbf{I}_V$ *on all variables except, possibly, on* $?v_1, ..., ?v_n$.
8. *Rule implication:*

   - $TVal_{\mathcal{I}}(conclusion \;\text{:-}\; condition) = \mathbf{t}$*, if either* $TVal_{\mathcal{I}}(conclusion) = \mathbf{t}$ *or* $TVal_{\mathcal{I}}(condition) = \mathbf{f}$.
   - $TVal_{\mathcal{I}}(conclusion \;\text{:-}\; condition) = \mathbf{f}$ *otherwise.*
9. *Groups of rules:*

   If Γ *is a group formula of the form* $\texttt{Group}(\varphi_1 \; ... \; \varphi_n)$ *then*

   - $TVal_{\mathcal{I}}(\Gamma) = \mathbf{t}$ *if and only if* $TVal_{\mathcal{I}}(\varphi_1) = ... = TVal_{\mathcal{I}}(\varphi_n) = \mathbf{t}$.
   - $TVal_{\mathcal{I}}(\Gamma) = \mathbf{f}$ *otherwise.*

   In other words, rule groups are treated as conjunctions. □

The tupribution and slotribution in item 3 render their syntactic counterparts (cf. Example 3) unnecessary.

4 Conclusions

As a W3C Recommendation, RIF-BLD has provided a reference semantics for extensions, e.g. with negations, and for continued efforts, as described here. Implementations of RIF-BLD engines are currently being planned or developed, including as extensions to the F-logic engine Flora 2 and the POSL and RuleML engine OO jDREW. Flora 2, OO jDREW, and other engines could be extended for the PSOA RuleML semantics of this paper. A subset of PSOA RuleML with single-tuple psoa terms has already been prototyped in OO jDREW.

The PSOA RuleML syntax of this paper is built on RIF-BLD's presentation syntax, which in OO jDREW will be complemented with a generalized POSL syntax. A psoa term $\texttt{o\#f(}[t_{1,1} \ldots t_{1,n_1}] \ldots [t_{m,1} \ldots t_{m,n_m}]\ p_1\texttt{->}v_1 \ldots p_k\texttt{->}v_k\texttt{)}$ corresponds to $\texttt{f(o\^{}}t_{1,1}, \ldots, t_{1,n_1}; \ldots; t_{m,1}, \ldots, t_{m,n_m}; p_1\texttt{->}v_1; \ldots; p_k\texttt{->}v_k\texttt{)}$ in POSL, where the OID moves into the argument list, separated from the other arguments by a hat infix, and tuple brackets are replaced with comma infixes that have precedence over the tuple- and slot-separating semicolon infixes. The generalization here with respect to the POSL publication [Bol10] is multi-tuple psoa terms.[8] Their PSOA RuleML/XML serialization can build on the XML schemas of Hornlog RuleML (with some FOL RuleML) and RIF-BLD (with some RIF-FLD), adding a <Tuple> element, different from RuleML's <Plex> and RIF's <List>. On the other hand, POSL's *explicit* rest-slot variables are avoided through frame slotribution.

Our semantics gives a first-order model-theoretic foundation for a revised POSL and PSOA RuleML, showing how a RIF-style semantics can be adapted for them. By blending *implicit* rest slots from F-logic and RIF with integrated psoa terms from POSL and RuleML, the advantages of both rule approaches have thus been combined. This is a crucial step in RIF-RuleML convergence, which could lead to a RIF-PSOA dialect corresponding to PSOA RuleML and, ultimately, to a joint RIF-PSOA RuleML.

Future work on psoa terms includes encoding (multi-)slots and slotribution as (multi-)tuples and tupribution; conversely, tuples could be encoded as multi-list values of a `tuple` slot. Web ontologies, especially taxonomies, in OWL 2, RDF Schema, etc. could be reused for PSOA RuleML's OID type systems by alignments rooted in their classes `owl:Thing`, `rdfs:Resource`, etc. and in `Top`. While the base terms used as (function-applying) arguments of a psoa term currently are anonymous psoa terms, uses of *named base terms* could be studied. PSOA RuleML could incorporate more features of POSL such as *signature declarations*. Membership of an object, e.g. `atv1`, in multiple classes, e.g. `car` and `ship`, is written as a conjunction of psoa terms, e.g. `And(atv1#car(borne->land drive->wheel) atv1#ship(borne->water drive->propeller))`; instead using DL-style *class intersection*, e.g. `atv1#Intersect(car ship)(... slot union ...)`, may be feasible.

Further efforts concern Horn rules. Notice Example 1 is not Horn in that there is a head existential after objectification. To address this issue, it can be modified as follows.

---

[8] For `m = 1` they gracefully degenerate to $\texttt{f(o\^{}}t_{1,1}, \ldots, t_{1,n_1}; p_1\texttt{->}v_1; \ldots; p_k\texttt{->}v_k\texttt{)}$.

Example 4 (Rule-extended named family frame). This Horn-rule version of Example 1 retrieves a `family` frame with a named OID variable in the premise and uses its binding to extend that frame in the conclusion (the left-hand side is objectified on the right).

```
Group (
 Forall ?Hu ?Wi ?Ch ?o (
  ?o#family(husb->?Hu wife->?Wi child->?Ch) :-
   And(?o#family(husb->?Hu wife->?Wi)
       Or(kid(?Hu ?Ch) kid(?Wi ?Ch))) )
  inst4#family(husb->Joe wife->Sue)
  kid(Sue Pete)
      )
```

```
Group (
 Forall ?Hu ?Wi ?Ch ?o ?1 ?2 (
  ?o#family(husb->?Hu wife->?Wi child->?Ch) :-
   And(?o#family(husb->?Hu wife->?Wi)
       Or(?1#kid(?Hu ?Ch) ?2#kid(?Wi ?Ch))) )
  inst4#family(husb->Joe wife->Sue)
  _1#kid(Sue Pete)
      )
```

It leads to a simpler semantics corresponding to the following set of ground facts: {*inst4#family(husb->Joe wife->Sue child->Pete), _1#kid(Sue Pete)*}.

Various sublanguages of PSOA RuleML could be defined to reflect Horn rules and other restrictions, both syntactic and semantic. It will be interesting to precisely align these with existing RuleML sublanguages as well as RIF dialects. While the current PSOA RuleML is closest to Hornlog RuleML and RIF-BLD, its integrated psoa terms with implicit rest slots could be 'lifted' to full FOL RuleML and RIF-FLD as well as 'lowered' to Datalog RuleML and RIF-Core, further advancing the unified RIF RuleML effort for Web rule interchange.

Acknowledgements

Many thanks go to Michael Kifer and all colleagues in the RuleML Technical Groups and the W3C RIF Working Group for Web rule collaboration. Also thanks to Tara Athan, Jidi Zhao, and Alexandre Riazanov for helpful discussions on drafts of this paper. Further thanks go to the RuleML-2011@IJCAI reviewers and editors. NSERC is thanked for its support through Discovery Grants.

References

[AK93] Aït-Kaci, H.: An Introduction to LIFE: Programming with Logic, Inheritance, Functions, and Equations. In: Miller, D. (ed.) Proceedings of the 1993 International Symposium on Logic Programming, Vancouver, B.C., Canada, pp. 52–68. MIT Press, Cambridge (October 1993)

[BK10a] Boley, H., Kifer, M.: A Guide to the Basic Logic Dialect for Rule Interchange on the Web. IEEE Transactions on Knowledge and Data Engineering 22(11), 1593–1608 (2010)

[BK10b] Boley, H., Kifer, M.: RIF Basic Logic Dialect, W3C Recommendation (June 2010), http://www.w3.org/TR/rif-bld

[BK10c] Boley, H., Kifer, M.: RIF Framework for Logic Dialects, W3C Recommendation (June 2010), http://www.w3.org/TR/rif-fld

[Bol10] Boley, H.: Integrating Positional and Slotted Knowledge on the Semantic Web. Journal of Emerging Technologies in Web Intelligence 4(2), 343–353 (2010), http://ojs.academypublisher.com/index.php/jetwi/article/view/0204343353

[BPS10] Boley, H., Paschke, A., Shafiq, O.: RuleML 1.0: The Overarching Specification of Web Rules. In: Dean, M., Hall, J., Rotolo, A., Tabet, S. (eds.) RuleML 2010. LNCS, vol. 6403, pp. 162–178. Springer, Heidelberg (2010)

[CKW93] Chen, W., Kifer, M., Warren, D.S.: HiLog: A Foundation for Higher-Order Logic Programming. Journal of Logic Programming 15(3), 187–230 (1993)

[CL73] Chang, C.L., Lee, R.C.T.: Symbolic Logic and Mechanical Theorem Proving. Academic Press, London (1973)

[End01] Enderton, H.B.: A Mathematical Introduction to Logic. Academic Press, London (2001)

[KLW95] Kifer, M., Lausen, G., Wu, J.: Logical Foundations of Object-Oriented and Frame-Based Languages. Journal of ACM 42, 741–843 (1995)

[Llo87] Lloyd, J.W.: Foundations of Logic Programming, 2nd edn. Springer, Heidelberg (1987)

[PBK10] Polleres, A., Boley, H., Kifer, M.: RIF Datatypes and Built-ins 1.0, W3C Recommendation (June 2010), `http://www.w3.org/TR/rif-dtb`

[YK03] Yang, G., Kifer, M.: Reasoning about Anonymous Resources and Meta Statements on the Semantic Web. In: Spaccapietra, S., March, S.T., Aberer, K. (eds.) Journal on Data Semantics I. LNCS, vol. 2800, pp. 69–97. Springer, Heidelberg (2003)

[YKZ03] Yang, G., Kifer, M., Zhao, C.: FLORA-2: A Rule-Based Knowledge Representation and Inference Infrastructure for the Semantic Web. In: Chung, S., Schmidt, D.C. (eds.) CoopIS 2003, DOA 2003, and ODBASE 2003. LNCS, vol. 2888, pp. 671–688. Springer, Heidelberg (2003)

CORОR: A COmposable Rule-Entailment Owl Reasoner for Resource-Constrained Devices

Wei Tai, John Keeney, and Declan O'Sullivan

Knowledge and Data Engineering Group,
School of Computer Science & Statistics, Trinity College Dublin, Ireland
{TaiW,John.Keeney,Declan.OSullivan}@cs.tcd.ie

Abstract. OWL (Web Ontology Language) reasoning has been extensively studied since its standardization by W3C. While the prevailing research in the OWL reasoning community has targeted faster, larger scale and more expressive OWL reasoners, only a small body of research is focused on OWL reasoning for resource-constrained devices such as mobile phones or sensors. However the ever-increasing application of semantic web technologies in pervasive computing, and the desire to push intelligence towards the edge of the network, emphasizes the need for resource-constrained reasoning. This paper presents COROR a COmposable Rule-entailment Owl Reasoner for resource-constrained devices. What distinguishes this work from related work is the use of two novel reasoner *composition* algorithms that dynamically dimension a rule-based reasoner at runtime according to the features of the *particular* semantic application. This reasoner is implemented and evaluated on a resource-constrained sensor platform. Experiments show that the composition algorithms outperform the original non-composable reasoner while retaining the same level of reasoning capability.

Keywords: Composable Reasoner, Resource-Constrained Reasoning, OWL Reasoning, Rule-engine Optimization, OWL.

1 Introduction

Quite a few OWL reasoners, using different reasoning technologies, have been developed to provide OWL reasoning services for different purposes. For example some Description Logic (DL) tableau-based reasoners, e.g. Pellet [12], RacerPro [14] and FaCT++ [13], aim to provide sound and complete OWL reasoning services. Some reasoners, e.g. KAON2 [16] and QuOnto [17], are designed to support efficient query services over large data sets. Reasoners such as CEL [18] are specifically dimensioned to provide an efficient subsumption algorithm for some applications (e.g. medical or bio-informatics). Yet more reasoners such as OWLIM [19] and Oracle 11g [22] provide certain levels of embedded OWL (entailment) reasoning services in (large) data stores.

Much of the existing OWL reasoning research aims to develop faster, larger-scale and more expressive OWL reasoners, while there exists only limited work on OWL reasoners for resource-constrained devices such as embedded devices, mobile phones

N. Bassiliades et al. (Eds.): RuleML 2011 - Europe, LNCS 6826, pp. 212–226, 2011.

or sensor platforms. However, as more intelligent embedded systems become pervasive, and with the proliferation of smarter mobile devices, the need for "on-device" semantic reasoning becomes more pronounced, for example, information filtering in context-aware mobile personal information system [28], localized fault diagnoses in wireless sensor networks [29] and context-addressable messaging services in mobile ad-hoc networks [30].

This paper presents COROR, a COmposable Rule-entailment Owl Reasoner for resource-constrained devices. The key contribution of this work is the use of two composition algorithms, i.e. a selective rule loading algorithm and a two-phase RETE algorithm. Instead of selecting a static reasoner configuration, or selecting a-priori from a set of known reasoners or reasoner configurations, composition algorithms try to dimension the OWL entailment rule set and the reasoning algorithm on-the-fly during execution by considering the particular semantic features of the ontology to be reasoned. Our reasoner COROR is implemented and evaluated on a resource-constrained sensor platform (SunSPOT). Experiments show our composition algorithms result in a large reduction in memory and reasoning time while retaining the same amount of reasoning capabilities, freeing up resources on resource-constrained devices or allowing larger ontologies to be reasoned.

This work is currently based on OWL (rather than OWL2) since a de-facto standard OWL2RL rule-set had yet become available. However, the composition algorithms presented in this work are independent of any particular OWL semantic level and they can be equally applied to OWL2 without any fundamental modifications. This selection of a candidate OWL2RL rule-set is subject of ongoing work.

Section 2 presents background and related work. Section 3 details the two composition algorithms implemented in COROR. Details of the implementation are given in section 4, while experiment design, setup and results are discussed in detail in section 5. Section 6 concludes with a discussion of ongoing and further work.

2 Background and Related Work

Background and related work are briefly discussed in this section, including OWL and its sublanguages, the RETE algorithm [5] and some of its optimizations, and finally other resource-constrained semantic reasoners.

2.1 OWL and OWL Sublanguages

OWL is an ontology modelling language standardized by the W3C, consisting of a set of formally defined OWL constructs each of which is given a logic-based semantic [24]. The formal definition of OWL enables reasoning, e.g. entailment computation, to be performed automatically over OWL ontologies. OWL has three standard sublanguages, i.e. OWL-Full, OWL-DL and OWL-Lite, varying in the set of constructs supported, the semantic expressivity, and the complexity of reasoning tasks. Non-standard OWL sublanguages, such as pD* semantics family [4], DL-Lite family [23] and DLP [51], are also designed for different usages according to the OWL features supported.

In this research we choose the pD* semantics family due to its provision of a definitive entailment rule set and tractable entailment. Some OWL-DL constructs are missing, such as cardinality constructs (cardinality, minCardinality and maxCardinality), some (in)equality constructs (allDifferent and distinctMembers), Boolean combination constructs (unionOf, complementOf and intersectionOf), and oneOf, but still a substantial subset of OWL-DL constructs is kept. Given the resource-constrained context where this work will be applied, any ontology will be generally less complex than OWL-DL. We feel that the pD* family generally have sufficient expressivity and semantics to model our domain to an acceptable degree. COROR is configured to use the pD*sv entailments that extend the pD* semantics with OWL's *iff* semantics for *owl:someValuesFrom*, but at the cost of possibly intractable entailment. Nevertheless, COROR can be configured to use the pD* semantics by simply altering the rule set in use for better computational complexity.

2.2 RETE and RETE Optimizations

The RETE algorithm is a fast pattern matching algorithm for forward-chaining production systems. It forms the basis for most modern production engines, and is the underlying algorithm for COROR. In general RETE builds a discrimination network, termed RETE network, matching and joining facts in the network. A typical RETE network consists of an alpha network and a beta network. The alpha network performs intra-condition matching for individual condition elements in the left hand side (l.h.s.) of each rule. For each rule, successfully matched facts for each condition element, said to partially match the rule, are stored in alpha memory as intermediate results and are propagated into the beta network. In the beta network inter-condition joins are performed by pairwise checking the consistency of variable bindings for intermediate values (i.e. pairwise joins of condition elements). New intermediate results are generated for consistent pairs and they are passed down the beta network for further matching. The final join results that eventually satisfy all condition elements are termed the instantiations of a rule and are added into a conflict set for firing (i.e. fire the r.h.s. action of the corresponding rule). Firing rules may add/remove facts into/from the fact base triggering another RETE cycle as described above.. Multiple RETE cycles are usually required for full entailment of a fact base. The RETE algorithm completes when no more new facts are generated.

Caching intermediate results can substantially speeds up join operations. However an inappropriately ordered sequence of joins can cause very excessive unnecessary memory usage and processing time in the beta network, in particular when two condition elements have no common variables, which leads to a production join. Several heuristics, such as 'most specific condition first', 'pre-evaluation of join connectivity', etc, have been developed to cope with the excessive memory overhead from inappropriate join sequences. Direct application of these can result in optimized RETE networks, however, they have several shortcomings. Firstly direct application of heuristics relies largely on human tuning of the original rule set (e.g. manual order of condition elements in rules) according to heuristics. This is a very onerous task where reasoners are deployed in an environment with diverse or changing rule sets or changing dataset characteristics. For example in sensor networks different sensors may have different rule sets, and rules may change over time. Secondly, direct application of heuristics [2, 3] usually only considers the rule-set therefore they usually cannot produce optimal join structures for different fact bases [1], where diversity in fact bases and their structure is commonplace in sensor networks.

Researchers have proposed some approaches to automatically optimize join sequences while taking account of the fact base. These optimizations are usually hard to implement and in most cases require modification of the RETE algorithm. However they do not require input from humans and can give different optimizations for different fact bases. Ishida in [1] proposes to use a trial execution before the real execution to collect statistics about the fact set. A predefined cost model is used to evaluate a set of candidate RETE structures and the RETE structure with the minimal cost is selected. This approach can find an optimal RETE structure however its obvious drawback is that a trial execution may not always be practical, particularly where memory, processing ability and power are limited.

Other join structures are also studied to reduce the resource required by RETE network. Work in [10] studies the combination of RETE and TREAT [11] such that the size of beta network can change automatically. The Gator network [50] is proposed as a generalized RETE join network. However Gator and TREAT are not considered as at this stage for COROR as it designed as an experimental reasoner for investigating composition algorithms on rule-entailment OWL reasoners, where the adoption of RETE in rule-entailment OWL reasoners is prevalent.

2.3 Mobile Reasoners

Other work has been devoted to porting semantic reasoning capability onto resource-constrained devices. *MiRE4OWL* [25] is a resource-constrained rule-entailment OWL reasoner developed using C++ for PPC. It adopts two mechanisms to reduce the memory usage of the RETE engine. One is to restrict the number of facts of the same type and the other is to use a primary key to detect duplication of facts and to use an update key to specify the operation to take for duplications. These mechanisms are useful for keeping a light-weight and up-to-date fact base with continuously incoming facts. However its RETE implementation is not optimized and therefore it is likely that inefficient production joins may occur if rules are not tuned by rule experts.

μOR [26] is a resolution-based OWL-DL reasoner for ambient intelligent devices (J2ME CDC compliance). A dynamic rule generation mechanism (similar to the one used in [7]) is used to automatically generate specific inference rules for all concepts/properties/individuals. This approach can construct small specific rules leading to a small (or no) beta network, and scales well for large ABoxes. The drawback, however, is obvious: the size of rule set will increase rapidly with the increase on the size of the TBox.

Bossam [21] is a forward-chaining OWL reasoner for the J2ME CDC platform. However rather than on reducing the runtime memory footprint, Bossam concentrates on providing web-friendly and distributed reasoning.

The above reasoners are the most relevant research to COROR, however their target platform is much less constrained than that of COROR, i.e. SunSPOT (CLDC 1.1 conformant). Some other less related work exists. They are mostly mobile DL tableaux reasoners. *Pocket KRHyper* [27] is a mobile DL reasoner based on hyper tableaux algorithm. Work in [8] introduces an ontology-based context fusion framework for context-aware computing using a sequential rule matching algorithm. Work in [9] discusses *mTaleaux*, a tableaux algorithm for resource-constrained devices. However, they are not directly comparable to our work and due to space considerations will not be discussed in detail here.

3 Composition Algorithms

This section briefly presents our composition algorithms, i.e. the selective rule loading algorithm and the two-phase RETE algorithm that are implemented in COROR.

3.1 Selective Rule Loading Algorithm

The selective rule loading algorithm automatically composes a reasoner rule-base depending on the reasoning capabilities required. It dimensions a selected entailment rule set by estimating which entailment rules are required or desired for reasoning specific ontologies and then selectively loading only these rules into the reasoner. Estimation is performed by comparing OWL constructs used in the ontology against OWL constructs in the l.h.s. of each entailment rule. All OWL constructs used by the ontology are inserted into a *construct set*. Each rule is then individually checked for usefulness. A rule is considered as useful if all OWL constructs used in its l.h.s. are included in the construct set, and it is selected as it *could* be fired for reasoning this ontology. OWL constructs used in the right-hand side (r.h.s.) of each selected rule are then inserted into the construct set as its firing could lead to the insertion of these OWL constructs into the ontology. This process iterates over the remaining unselected rules until all useful rules are identified, while the remaining rules are not used, resulting in a resource saving.

Note that not all selected rules will be fired as the existence of a rule's OWL constructs in the target ontology does not necessitate successful instantiation of that rule. However, unselected rules cannot be fired even if they were loaded due to the absence of relevant OWL constructs in the ontology. A prototype desktop-based implementation and an initial evaluation of this algorithm can be found in [6]. Experiment results show a moderate amount of memory usage reduction but scarcely any reduction in reasoning time in this implementation.

3.2 Two-Phase RETE Algorithm

Rather than optimizing based on reasoning capabilities, as per the selective rule loading algorithm, the two-phase RETE algorithm composes the reasoner at the RETE algorithm level. A novel interrupted RETE network construction mechanism is adopted that performs only the first RETE cycle immediately after the construction the alpha network (first phase). This enables some information about the ontology to be collected without requiring a full pre-match or traversal of the fact-base. The construction of the beta network resumes after the first-phase matching and a customized RETE network can be composed for the second-phase, tuned for the particular ontology by taking collected information into account. The first RETE cycle resumes after the construction of entire RETE network and the following cycles are performed as in the normal RETE algorithm. The following subsections discuss each phase in detail.

First Phase. In the first phase a shared alpha network is built and the first RETE cycle starts by matching triples against individual rule condition elements in the alpha network. Matched triples are cached in alpha memory awaiting further propagation into the beta network (which is not yet constructed at this stage). A variety of informative statistics about the ontology, e.g. the size of each alpha memory node, the join selectivity factor, etc., can be collected during or after this phase without introducing extra efforts such as specific traversal of the ontology or pre-matching all rules. In our prototype only the number of matched triples for each condition element is gathered. This helps to order beta network join sequences later. An alpha node sharing mechanism is also used to allow condition elements common across different rules to share the same alpha node, thereby reducing the size of the alpha memory and also fact matching time to 1/n for an alpha node (condition element) shared by n rules.

As multiple RETE cycles may be required for reasoning a fact base, information collected at this stage can only be used to optimize the first RETE cycle. However, we notice that for most ontologies that we experimented on (see section 5), the majority of (alpha network) matches and (beta network) joins occur in the first RETE iteration: 15 of a total of 19 ontologies have an average of 75% joins performed in the first iteration (for the remaining 4 ontologies this is still above 50%). Furthermore an average of 83% inferred facts are generated in this iteration. Hence it is appropriate to optimize the RETE network by applying first-cycle optimization heuristics.

Second Phase. In the second phase a beta network is constructed heuristically and the first RETE cycle resumes propagating partially matched intermediate results down through the beta network as condition elements are pairwise joined. However information collected in the first phase enables the application of heuristics to rely not only on characteristics of rules but also on characteristics of the ontology such that a customized beta network (rather than a generally optimized one) can be composed for the particular ontology. Two join sequence optimization heuristics, i.e. the *most specific condition first* heuristic and the *connectivity* heuristic, are implemented in the beta network construction. Their applications are discussed in detail in the following paragraphs.

The ***most specific condition first*** heuristic orders join sequences according to their specificity to avoid long chain effects [3], i.e. where the absence of successful joins is only detected after a large amount of expensive join operations have been performed, leading to a waste of computational resources, in particularly beta network memory. In a previous study [2] Özacar et al assert that using the number of matched facts of a condition element as a criterion to estimate its specificity can guarantee to find the most specific condition elements. However, this metric can only be calculated after matching, which makes it useless in normal RETE implementations. However we argue that this information can be collected in the first phase of our novel interrupted RETE construction mechanism without introducing extra effort and thereafter it *can* be used here as a straight forward criterion to estimate the specificity: the more facts matched for a condition element's alpha-network node the less specific that condition element is for the particular ontology. A corollary presents where fewer triples match, a condition is more specific. Although the following RETE cycles may affect this specificity ordering (i.e. number of matching facts), it is still sufficient as most joins and intermediate values are generated in the first RETE cycle.

More sophisticated criteria can be introduced for specificity estimation, for example including the cardinality of values to be joined. At this stage we did not implement such heuristics, but the approach taken is equally applicable and, as described later, the approach taken substantially reduces memory and reasoning time.

The ***connectivity*** heuristic ensures that all joining condition elements have variables in common. This prevents product joins and thus can further reduce the amount of intermediate results in the beta network. The connectivity test is performed after the 'most specific condition first' join ordering heuristic: if a condition C_{uncon} is found to be not connectable to all previous conditions C_{pre}, then C_{uncon} is swapped with the first condition after C_{uncon} in the join sequence that *is* connectable to C_{pre}, say C_{con}. As the join sequence has already been ordered by the most specific condition first heuristic, C_{con} is then the one that connects with C_{pre} and with the least specificity of all later connectable conditions. This ensures connectivity in the join sequence and also maintains the specificity ordering of joins where possible.

3.3 Analytical Comparisons between Composition Algorithms

In this section analytical comparisons between the two composition algorithms are presented from three aspects, including reasoning algorithm independence, semantic independence and flexibility in handling changes. Empirical analyses and comparisons can be found in section 5.

As the selective rule loading algorithm constructs a selective ruleset only by analyzing the constructs used in the entailment rules themselves, it is completely independent of reasoning algorithm or ruleset used. This feature enables it to be applied in all forward-chaining rule-entailment reasoners regardless the reasoning algorithms such as RETE or DBMS. Furthermore its application does not need to change the reasoning algorithm and hence it is relative easy to be applied. The two-phase RETE algorithm can only be applied for the RETE algorithm and therefore is not reasoning algorithm independent. In addition its implementation involves changes to the reasoning algorithm i.e. interrupting RETE construction, so is harder to implement compared to the selective rule loading algorithm. Both algorithms are semantic independent. Both the two-phase RETE algorithm and the selective rule loading algorithm are completely independent of the particular ontology or entailment rule set in use.

Addition and deletion are discussed separately with respect to flexibility of handling dynamic changes in the fact-base. Additions can be handled incrementally by the two-phase RETE algorithm due to the intrinsic capability of RETE to handle addition incrementally. Simple deleting facts may lead to logical errors (e.g. deleting facts with different justifications) and therefore may require truth maintenance mechanisms. As truth maintenance is not yet implemented on COROR re-reasoning the entire ontology is required for every deletion. However given that many existing semantic applications only need to reason on static ontology rather than changing KBs, COROR is still sufficient for them. Additions may introduce previously unseen OWL constructs which may cause a problem with the selective rule loading algorithm. In this case re-execution of the selective rule loading algorithm and re-reasoning of the entire ontology are required.

The semantic independence feature of both composition algorithms enables the extension of COROR to support OWL 2 RL without *any* fundamental modification.

Given growing adoption of OWL 2 the extension of COROR to support OWL 2 RL is considered as an important task in future work.

4 Implementation

COROR is implemented on the SunSPOT [48] sensor board emulator with SDK v4.0 (blue). The *μJena* framework [49], a cut down J2ME version of *Jena* [15], is used to read and handle OWL ontologies. It provides a powerful interface for ontology access and modification, e.g. parse ontology definitions, support to assert/retrieve OWL axioms, query resources and so on. Rule handling and reasoning are not supported by *μJena*. Given the close connection between *μJena* and *Jena* we ported the *Jena* RETE engine (and relevant modules) into *μJena* rather than implementing them from scratch. As the SunSPOT is only conformant with CLDC 1.1, a subset of J2ME, substantial modifications were required to port the *Jena* rule engine onto *μJena* and SunSPOT.

The selective rule loading algorithm is implemented as a Java class (*RuleSetComposer*) outside of the RETE engine. To enable faster OWL construct identification, instead of analyzing entailment rules at runtime using *μJena* APIs, we manually analyze them beforehand: OWL constructs from both l.h.s. and r.h.s. are identified and coded as rule-construct mappings in a text file which will be loaded and analyzed by the selective rule loading algorithm. A drawback of this approach is it requires different rule-construct mappings to be created manually for different entailment rule sets. The checking for OWL constructs in any ontology is performed automatically at load-time by enumerating the OWL constructs using the *μJena* ontology manipulation API.

The two-phase RETE algorithm is implemented inside the RETE engine (*RETEEngine* class). One problem encountered in the implementation is *Jena*'s extensive use of Java arrays as variable binding vectors where bound values are stored in the corresponding positions in the array as in the rule. This hampers the sharing of common conditions between rules, thereby requiring extensive code refactoring. Four composition modes, i.e. *NonComposable* mode, *Selective Rule Loading* mode, *Two-Phase RETE* mode, and *Hybrid* mode, are implemented corresponding to the use of no, one or both composition algorithms. In the Hybrid mode both composition algorithms are used and the selective rule loading algorithm first dynamically constructs a selective entailment ruleset for use in the two-phase RETE algorithm.

Entailment is the key reasoning task implemented by COROR. However, some common reasoning tasks can be realized by querying the ontology with all entailments calculated, coined entailment closure (at the moment COROR supports only single-triple-based query). For example, subsumption between two classes C and D can be reduced to querying the entailment closure with the triple *C rdfs:subClassOf D*, instantiation of C as querying with the triple *?x rdf:type C*, where *?x* is a variable and satisfiability of a class C as querying with the triple *C rdfs:subClassOf owl:Nothing*, checking if x is an instance of class C as querying for the triple *x rdf:type C*, and so on. Some other reasoning tasks are not directly supported by this approach. For example, realization of an instance a requires finding the most specialized class that a instantiates, which requires pairwise subsumption checking for all classes retrieved using *a rdf:type ?x*.

A configuration file is used where users can specify the composition mode, the ruleset to be used, and specify the ontology to be reasoned. Rules are encoded in the *Jena* rule format in a separate rule file, giving users flexibility to modify the rule set, in particular providing simple support for application-specific reasoning.

5 Experiments and Discussions

This section presents and discusses two experiments carried out to evaluate COROR from both the performance and the correctness perspectives.

5.1 Design and Execution

Experiments were performed to investigate the performance impacts of composition algorithms on rule-entailment reasoners.

The memory usage and execution time required to fully calculate entailments of a selected set of ontologies on the SunSPOT emulator (v 4.5.0) is compared for different composition algorithms. These metrics were selected since they directly represent changes in reasoning performance. Some other metrics used to evaluation other OWL reasoners were not selected here as they are not quite suitable for COROR. For example, conjunctive query answering time is not yet implemented in the current version of COROR; reasoning speed on ever enlarging KB is also omitted here as COROR performs load-time reasoning for resource-constrained devices and therefore small or medium ontologies with static sizes are the target of this work. The separate evaluation of individual reasoning tasks such as classification are also not performed in this work as entailment is the key reasoning task in COROR and all other tasks are reduced to querying the entailment closure (as discussed in Section 4).

The memory usage and execution time of COROR (configured to use the hybrid mode) were also compared with other OWL reasoners. As *MiRE4OWL* and *μOR* are not accessible, *Bossam* and three other desktop rule-entailment reasoners, i.e. Jena 2.6.3, BaseVISor 1.5.0 [20], and swiftOWLIM v3.0.1, were selected in this comparison due to their similarity with COROR in terms of expressivity and reasoning algorithm. Note that although Bossam supports J2ME CDC we failed to port it onto SunSPOT as java.util.List is widely used in Bossam while not supported by CLDC 1.1. Jena was configured to used RETE engine only and also the pD*sv rule set. Pellet was also included in this comparison giving readers an intuition of the performance of COROR comparing to a full fledged DL tableau reasoner. As it has proved time prohibitive to port these reasoners onto SunSPOT platform this second evaluation step was performed using a J2SE platform on a desktop computer with Dual Core CPU @ 2.4GHz, Java SE 6 Update 14, and maximum heap size as 128MB (the SunSPOT emulator ran on the same desktop machine).

In total 17 ontologies varying in size and expressiveness were used in our experiments, including: teams [31], owls-profile [32], koala[33], university [34], beer [35], mindswapper [36], foaf [37], mad_cows [38], biopax [39], food [40], miniTambis [41], atk-portal [42], wine [43], amino-acid [44], pizza [45], tambis-full [46] and nato [47]. These ontologies are of small or medium size and are from different domains therefore their usage can avoid any unintentional bias where some OWL constructs are over- or under-used by some ontology designers in different application domains.

They are well known and commonly used, and so are relatively free from errors. Due to the low memory and processing power available on SunSPOT only 11 of the 17 ontologies were used in the experiment on the SunSPOT platform while all 17 ontologies were used in the comparison with other reasoners.

5.2 Results and Discussion

The memory usage and reasoning time required by different composition modes on SunSpot COROR implementation are illustrated in figure 1 and 2. Results show that all composition modes use less memory and reasoning time than the NonComposable mode. Note that some tests produced no data e.g. the memory usage required to reason the food ontology in the NonComposable mode, required manual termination before completion due to a long reasoning time (over 30 minutes).

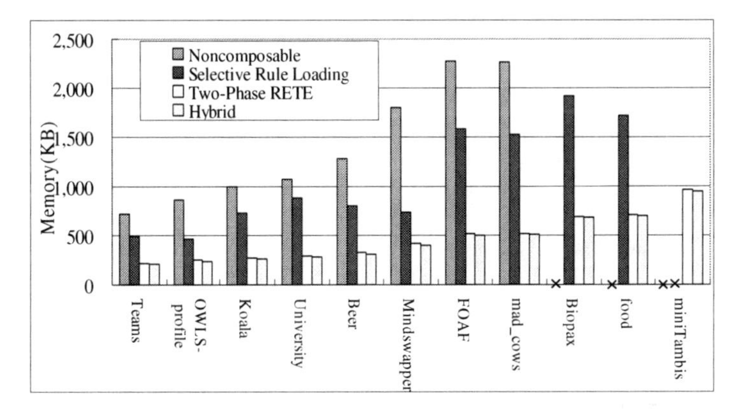

Fig. 1. Memory usage for different composition algorithms (KB)

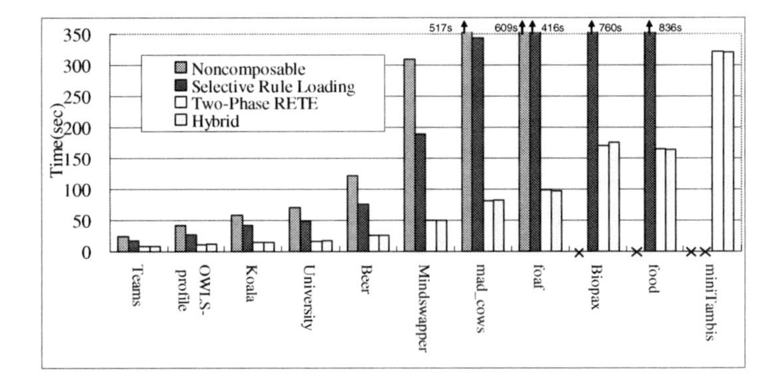

Fig. 2. Reasoning execution time for different composition algorithm (second)

Different composition algorithms vary in their performances. The two-phase RETE algorithm outperforms the selective rule loading algorithm for all tested ontologies. In addition the time/memory reductions in hybrid mode are also limited (comparing to the two-phase RETE mode). We can conclude the reasons for these performance differences by analysing the algorithms, rulesets and ontologies used. The selective rule loading algorithm reduces memory and time by unloading rules. Loaded rules are not optimized. Heuristics used in the two-phase RETE algorithm, however, apply to all rules, even rules that could have been omitted. The two-phase RETE algorithm reorders join sequences of rules according to the number of matched facts of each condition, so any condition element from an unneeded rule with no matching OWL facts is placed at the start of the join sequence. In this way join sequences of unneeded rules can be reordered such that no join operation is needed, as if they are "unloaded". Despite this, some shared alpha network nodes may still be created for the other condition elements of these unneeded rules reducing the size of alpha network, which is not in the selective rule loading algorithm. Hence the two-phase RETE algorithm can have better performance than the selective rule loading algorithm. This also explains the limited benefit in hybrid mode beyond the two-phase mode.

In depth investigations into composition algorithms are performed to identify the sources for the time/memory reductions. Several metrics are selected. As join and match are respectively the two major operations in alpha and beta network, changes on the *number of matches* (*#M*) and the *number of joins* (*#J*) are used to respectively represent changes on the reasoning time in alpha and beta network. Similarly changes on the *number of intermediate results* (*#IR*) generated by matches/joins ($\#IR_M/\#IR_J$) are used to represent changes on memory in the corresponding network. By enumerating the *#M*, *#J* and *#IR* values by rule for each ontology under the selective rule loading mode we find that these metrics all drop to zero for unneeded/unloaded rules leading to the reduction of memory usage and reasoning time. For loaded rules these metrics remains the exact same as for the NonComposable mode. These metrics and a close comparison of the results of all modes show that the optimizations applied do not in any way change the results of the entailment process, so the correctness of the process is not affected.

Insights into the two-phase RETE algorithm show that the alpha node sharing mechanism in alpha network contributes most *memory reduction* in this experiment as the reduced $\#IR_M$ occupies the majority of the total reduced *#IR* (an average of 95% of the intermediate result reductions occur in the alpha network for all tested ontologies). However, it is reductions in both the *#M* and *#J* values (in both the alpha- and beta-networks) that contribute to the decrease in *reasoning time*, but due to the differences in the processing time required for different per match/join operations it is difficult to conclude which contributes more.

Close investigation of the rule set explain the limited memory reduction resulting from the join-reordering in the beta network. The selected pD*sv ruleset is already manually optimized in terms of condition ordering and therefore nearly no automatic optimization is required for this ruleset. This leads to only small reductions in the $\#IR_J$ (and therefore small contribution to the memory reduction). To show that the two-phase RETE algorithm is able to greatly reduce the reasoning time and memory the pD*sv rule set was re-processed to re-order conditions elements for each rule in a sub-optimal manner (as would be typical for user-authored or application specific rules). Tests performed in figure 1 and 2 were re-executed for the rearranged non-optimized rule set and results show that the NonComposable mode required *substantially* more time and memory than it required before. However the two-phase RETE algorithm required the exact same amounts of time and memory as shown in figures 1 and 2, which shows the ability of two-phase RETE algorithm to greatly reduce reasoning time and memory with sub-optimal ordering of rule conditions. These results show that the approach and heuristics selected for COROR are capable of automatically optimizing rules condition ordering to an extent comparable to that of a rule authoring expert.

The comparisons of reasoning time and memory usage between COROR and other state of the art reasoners are given in Figures 3 and 4. The time-based performance COROR is comparable to Jena and BaseVISor. For some small ontologies it runs slightly faster than BaseVISor. Generally Jena requires a longer time to finish its reasoning mainly due to its complicated design to enable flexible ontology manipulation rather than fast reasoning. However, the reasoning execution time of COROR is substantially worse than OWLIM and Bossam.

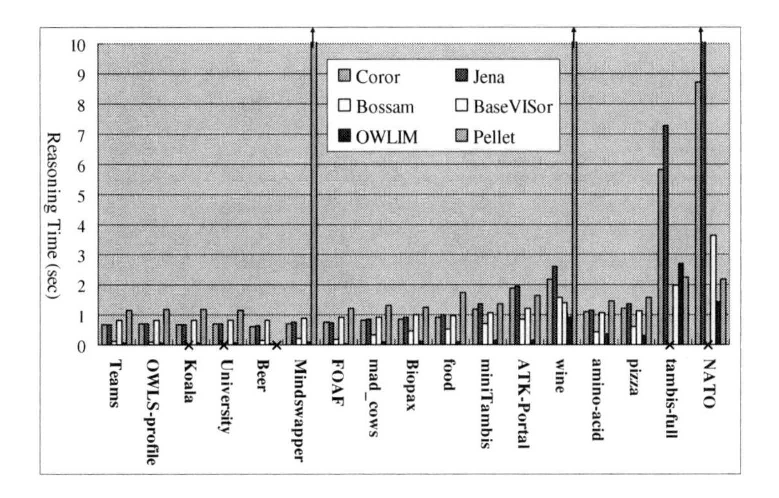

Fig. 3. Comparison of reasoning execution time with other OWL reasoners

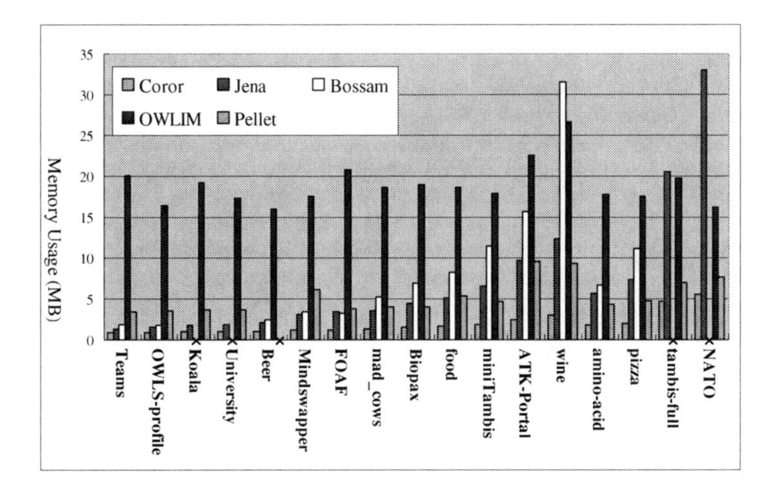

Fig. 4. Comparison of memory usage with other OWL reasoners

On the other hand the memory performance of COROR is much better than the other reasoners. It uses the least memory for all tested ontologies, which indicates much smaller memory footprint can be gained when COROR is applied on resource-constrained devices. Bossam failed for some ontologies so there are no values for them. BaseVISor hides its reasoning process from external inspection so we cannot accurately measure its memory usage and it is omitted from the memory comparison.

The correctness of algorithms (in terms of the pD* semantics) were tested by comparing results of the mode based on the original Jena RETE engine (NonComposable mode) with results from the other composition modes. All the four composition modes generate identical results for all 17 ontologies. Given the tight relationship between the NonComposable mode and Jena RETE engine, we can conclude that our algorithms do not affect correctness.

6 Conclusion and Future Work

We present COROR, a composable reasoner for resource constrained devices. It implements two novel complementary algorithms to compose a custom OWL reasoner at the entailment ruleset level and at the RETE algorithm level. The selective rule loading algorithm establishes a perfect-fit entailment rule subset for the target ontology by selecting only the entailment rules required for that ontology and then loading them into the reasoner. The two-phase RETE algorithm dynamically collects optimization statistics during the reasoning process and uses them to optimize the RETE network building process. This reasoner was implemented on the SunSPOT platform. Experiments show that all combinations of the composition algorithms require less memory and time than the non-optimized version of the reasoner, and require substantially less memory than other off-the-shelf rule-based reasoners.

Further work is actively addressing a number of outstanding topics. First different types of statistics can be collected in the first phase and more sophisticated heuristics can be designed or selected. For example, as mentioned earlier the heuristics we are currently using to evaluate the specificity of a condition is relatively simplistic, despite its good performance. Secondly the capability to process conjunctive queries needs to be included. This allows richer queries, characteristic of sensor applications. Thirdly, indexing and other join methods, e.g. merge-join, can be studied and tested for better efficiency. Finally, consideration of the recently published W3C OWL2 standard, and the selection of a candidate OWL 2 RL rule set is ongoing.

Acknowledgement

This work is supported by the Irish Government in the "Network Embedded Systems" project (NEMBES), part of the Higher Education Authority's Programme for Research in Third Level Institutions (PRTLI) cycle 4, and by Science Foundation Ireland via grant 08/SRC/I1403 - "Federated, Autonomic Management of End-to-End Communications Services" (FAME).

References

1. Ishida, T.: An optimization algorithm for production systems. IEEE Transactions on Knowledge and Data Engineering 6, 549–558 (1994)
2. Ozacar, T., Ozturk, O., Unalir, M.O.: Optimizing a Rete-based Inference Engine using a Hybrid Heuristic and Pyramid based Indexes on Ontological Data. J. of Computers 2, 41 (2007)
3. Scales, D.J.: Efficient Matching Algorithm for the OAR/OPS5 Production System. Technical Report KSL-86-47, Department of Computer Science, Stanford University (1986)
4. ter Horst, H.J.: Completeness, decidability and complexity of entailment for RDF Schema and a semantic extension involving the OWL vocabulary. Web Semantics: Science, Services and Agents on the World Wide Web 3, 79–115 (2005)
5. Forgy, C.: Rete: A Fast Algorithm for the many pattern/many object pattern match problem. Artificial Intelligence 19, 17–37 (1982)
6. Tai, W., Brennan, R., Keeney, J., O'Sullivan, D.: An Automatically Composable OWL Reasoner for Resource Constrained Devices. In: Proc. Intl. Conf. on Semantic Computing (2009)
7. Meditskos, G., Bassiliades, N.: A Rule-Based Object-Oriented OWL Reasoner. IEEE Transactions on Knowledge and Data Engineering 20, 397–410 (2008)
8. Gu, T., Kwok, Z., Koh, K.K., Pung, H.K.: A Mobile Framework Supporting Ontology Processing and Reasoning. In: Proc. Workshop on Requirements and Solutions for Pervasive Software Infrastructures (2007)
9. Steller, L., Krishnaswamy, S.: Pervasive Service Discovery: mTableaux Mobile Reasoning. In: Proc. Intl. Conf. on Semantic Systems (2008)
10. Wright, I., Marshall, J.: The execution kernel of RC++: RETE*, a faster RETE with TREAT as a special case. Int. J. of Intelligent Games and Simulation 2 (2003)
11. Miranker, D.P.: TREAT: A better match algorithm for AI production systems. In: Proc. of AAAI Conf., pp. 42–47 (1987)
12. Pellet reasoner, `http://clarkparsia.com/pellet/`
13. FaCT++, `http://owl.man.ac.uk/factplusplus/`
14. RacerPro, `http://www.racer-systems.com/`
15. Jena, `http://jena.sourceforge.net/`
16. KAON2 reasoner, `http://kaon2.semanticweb.org/`
17. QuOnto, `http://www.dis.uniroma1.it/~quonto/`
18. CEL, `http://lat.inf.tu-dresden.de/systems/cel/`
19. OWLIM, `http://www.ontotext.com/owlim/`
20. BaseVISor, `http://vistology.com/basevisor/basevisor.html`
21. Bossam, `http://bossam.wordpress.com/about-bossam/`
22. Oracle Database Semantic Technologies, `http://www.oracle.com/technetwork/database/options/semantic-tech/index.html`
23. Calvanese, D., De Giacomo, G., Lembo, D., Lenzerini, M., Rosati, R.: Tractable Reasoning and Efficient Query Answering in Description Logics: The DL-Lite Family. Journal of Automated Reasoning 39, 385–429 (2007)
24. Patel-Schneider, P.F., Hayes, P., Horrocks, I.: Web Ontology Language (OWL) Abstract Syntax and Semantics, W3C Recommendation (2004)
25. Kim, T., Park, I., Hyun, S.J., Lee, D.: MiRE4OWL: Mobile Rule Engine for OWL. In: Proc. Intl. Workshop on Middleware Engineering, ME 2010 (2010)

26. Ali, S., Kiefer, S.: μOR - A Micro OWL DL Reasoner for Ambient Intelligent Devices. In: Abdennadher, N., Petcu, D. (eds.) GPC 2009. LNCS, vol. 5529, pp. 305–316. Springer, Heidelberg (2009)
27. Sinner, A., Kleemann, T.: KRHyper - In Your Pocket. In: Nieuwenhuis, R. (ed.) CADE 2005. LNCS (LNAI), vol. 3632, pp. 452–457. Springer, Heidelberg (2005)
28. Kleemann, T., Sinner, A.: User Profiles and Matchmaking on Mobile Phones. In: Umeda, M., Wolf, A., Bartenstein, O., Geske, U., Seipel, D., Takata, O. (eds.) INAP 2005. LNCS (LNAI), vol. 4369, pp. 135–147. Springer, Heidelberg (2006)
29. Brennan, R., Tai, W., O'Sullivan, D., Aslam, M.S., Rea, S., Pesch, D.: Open Framework Middleware for Intelligent WSN Topology Adaption in Smart Buildings. In: Proc. Intl. Conf. on Ultra Modern Telecommunications & Workshops (2009)
30. Koziuk, M., Domaszewicz, J., Schoeneich, R.O., Jablonowski, M., Boetzel, P.: Mobile Context-Addressable Messaging with DL-Lite Domain Model. In: Roggen, D., Lombriser, C., Tröster, G., Kortuem, G., Havinga, P. (eds.) EuroSSC 2008. LNCS, vol. 5279, pp. 168–181. Springer, Heidelberg (2008)
31. Teams, http://owl.man.ac.uk/2005/sssw/teams
32. OWLS-profile, http://www.daml.org/services/owl-s/1.1/Profile.owl
33. Koala, http://protege.stanford.edu/plugins/owl/owl-library/koala.owl
34. University, http://www.mindswap.org/ontologies/debugging/university.owl
35. Beer, http://www.purl.org/net/ontology/beer
36. Mindswapper, http://www.mindswap.org/2004/owl/mindswappers
37. FOAF, http://xmlns.com/foaf/0.1/
38. mad_cows, http://www.cs.man.ac.uk/~horrocks/OWL/Ontologies/mad_cows.owl
39. Biopax, http://www.biopax.org/release/biopax-level1.owl
40. food, http://www.w3.org/2001/sw/WebOnt/guide-src/food
41. miniTambis, http://www.mindswap.org/ontologies/debugging/miniTambis.owl
42. ATK-Portal, http://www.aktors.org/ontology/portal
43. wine, http://www.w3.org/2001/sw/WebOnt/guide-src/wine
44. amino-acid, http://www.co-ode.org/ontologies/amino-acid/2005/10/11/amino-acid.owl
45. pizza, http://www.co-ode.org/ontologies/pizza/pizza_20041007.owl
46. tambis-full, http://www.mindswap.org/ontologies/tambis-full.owl
47. NATO, http://www.mindswap.org/ontologies/IEDMv1.0.owl
48. SUN SPOT, http://www.sunspotworld.com/
49. µJena, http://poseidon.elet.polimi.it/ca/?page_id=59
50. Hanson, E.N., Hasan, M.S.: Gator: An Optimized Discrimination Network for Active Database Rule Condition Testing. Tech. Report, CIS Dept, University of Florida (1993)
51. Grosof, B.N., Horrocks, I., Volz, R., Decker, S.: Description logic programs: combining logic programs with description logic. In: Proc. Intl. Conf. on World Wide Web (2003)

Rule-Based Trust Assessment on the Semantic Web

Ian Jacobi[1], Lalana Kagal[1], and Ankesh Khandelwal[2,*]

[1] MIT CSAIL,
Cambridge, MA 02139
{jacobi,lkagal}@csail.mit.edu
[2] Rensselaer Polytechnic Institute,
Troy, NY 12180
ankesh@cs.rpi.edu

Abstract. The Semantic Web is a decentralized forum on which anyone can publish structured data or extend and reuse existing data. This inherent openness of the Semantic Web raises questions about the trustworthiness of the data. Data is usually deemed trustworthy based on several factors including its source, users' prior knowledge, the reputation of the source, and the previous experience of users. However, as rules are important on the Semantic Web for checking data integrity, representing implicit knowledge, or even defining policies, additional factors need to be considered for data that is inferred. Given an existing trust measure, we identify two trust axes namely data and rules and two trust categories namely content-based and metadata-based that are useful for trust assignments associated with Semantic Web data. We propose a meta-modeling framework that uses trust ontologies to assign trust values to data, sources, rules, etc. on the Web, provenance ontologies to capture data generation, and declarative rules to combine these values to form different trust assessment models. These trust assessment models can be used to transfer trust from known to unknown data. We discuss how AIR, a Web rule language, can be used to implement our framework and declaratively describe assessment models using different kinds of trust and provenance ontologies.

1 Introduction

The rise of the Semantic Web and Linked Data, and the machine-understandable interlinked data they promise, has led to an increased reuse of data. Vocabularies such as RDF Schema (RDFS) [7] and the Web Ontology Language (OWL) [2,25] have been developed to enable consumers of Semantic Web data to exchange data with some knowledge of the meaning of this data, allowing not only for the reuse of data, but the reuse of schemas and terminology as well.

Given the inherent openness of the Semantic Web, where anyone can say anything, the reliability and usefulness of web data depends on evaluating its

* Author names are arranged in alphabetic order.

N. Bassiliades et al. (Eds.): RuleML 2011 - Europe, LNCS 6826, pp. 227–241, 2011.

trustworthiness. Users need to make decisions about their subjective belief of whether the data is true; such decisions may be based on a number of factors, including which sources to rely on, their prior knowledge, the reputation of the source, and their experience [1]. However, trust assessment becomes challenging when the consumers of this data are applications and agents. In order to automate the assignment of "truthfulness" or trustworthiness measures, it must be possible for trust values to be associated with different aspects of the data such as the actual content of the data, the data sources, recency of updates, the schemas being used, and the creator, and for these, trust values be combined together to evaluate trust in the actual data. For example, there might be multiple Friend Of a Friend (FOAF)[1] files for Tim Berners-Lee that describe his social profile in Resource Description Framework (RDF), but the one that is most trusted is the one available at the W3C website. This is because the trustworthiness of the source, W3C, is higher than that of the other sources. Different trust levels may also be assigned to sources relative to their contents. For example, a hospital may be trusted with information about a potential virus outbreak but may not be trusted with respect to its economic predictions. We suggest that the trust associated with any Web data is some combination of these different trust values associated with the content of the data as well as meta-data about the data such as its source, creator, etc.

Rules are often used with Semantic Web data to check its integrity or represent implicit knowledge as well as to define policies and business logic. As the machine-understandability of Semantic Web data encourages the use of this data by software agents, mechanisms for the automated evaluation of inferred data becomes important. The trustworthiness of inferred data may be evaluated from its provenance, metadata describing how data came to be known. This provenance could be as simple as the source of the data or contain the entire deduction trace. These justifications or deduction traces may provide detailed provenance information, including the data sources, facts used, and rules applied, to allow the evaluation of the particular result. Any number of reasons may exist to assign different levels of trust in a rule or rule set (or the derivations produced therefrom), including differing levels of expertise, familiarity with domain knowledge, or even malicious intent. Thus, the ability to assign or determine a level of *trust in a rule* and its conclusions are required for trust on the Semantic Web. In case of inferred data, the trust value is a combination of trust values associated with its data as well as its rules that in turn can be calculated from the trust associated with their content as well as meta-data.

In this paper we focus on developing models that involve non-statistical functions to assess trust in Semantic Web data in terms of the content and meta-data (source, creator, recency, provenance, reputation, etc.) of data and rules. Along with the trust values associated with the data used, we propose that the trust assignments of rules used in data generation is an important factor in the trust evaluation of the generated data. We suggest that there are two main trust categories for Semantic Web data from which different trust assessment models may

[1] http://www.foaf-project.org/

be derived: **content-based trust** and **metadata-based trust**. In content-based trust, we derive our trust values from the contents of the data or rule itself. The metadata-based trust category is more helpful when calculating trust based on circumstantial facts about the data or rule such as reputation assignments, user ratings, and provenance, rather than the content itself. We propose a *meta-modeling framework* that uses trust ontologies to assign metadata-based and content-based trust values to data, sources, rules, etc. on the Web, provenance ontologies to capture justification/deduction traces, and declarative rules to combine these values to form different trust assessment models. We show how this meta-modeling system can be used to define a range of trust assessment strategies in AIR, a Semantic Web rule language.

This paper is structured as follows: we begin by introducing existing work dealing with trust on the Web. In Section 3, we discuss trust problems on the Semantic Web and discuss different possible trust representations and assessment strategies. The next section provides an overview of the AIR language. In Section 5 we describe how AIR can be used for different trust assessment strategies on the Web. Section 6 identifies the contributions of our work and finally, Section 7 provides a summary and directions for future work.

2 Related Work

Well-known trust management systems such as PolicyMaker [19], KeyNote [6], REFEREE [8], and Delegation Logics [17] view trust management as an authorization problem. That is, they define mechanisms for inferring whether a requester (software or human agent) is permitted to perform a certain action or access a certain resource based on a set of constraints defined by the action/data owner. Our goals are different in that we look at the role of trust in rule based reasoning. Our framework is focused on expressing trustworthiness of data on the open Web, evaluating trustworthiness of inferred data and on allowing mechanisms for decisions based off trust and trust computations to be declaratively specified.

[22,11,12,16] discuss how trust values for users and data sources can be computed. Richardson et al. enable users to maintain trust for other users and provide functions to merge these values into trust values for all users by leveraging the path of trust between users [22]. Kuter et al. allow users to maintain trust values or trust estimates for data sources and provide a probabilistic technique to use that information to compute a trust estimate for a data source [16]. Our approach can be thought of as a meta-modeling approach that allows different trust frameworks to be declaratively developed and possibly combined. It provides a rule language, mechanisms for accessing the Web and cryptographic, math, string and other related functions that may be used to specify how trust is assigned and calculated.

The WIQA framework [5] is also related to the trust assessment framework that we've developed using AIR, however, it is much simpler. The WIQA framework allows RDF data to be filtered according to policies expressed as graph patterns (Please refer to Section 3.3 for more information about patterns) and provides an explanation for this filtering by identifying the matched patterns. Our framework supports more than just filtering as graph patterns are part of rule definitions and filtered data take part in some rule based reasoning. Furthermore, data may be filtered not just based on some patterns but also based on trust assigned (or assessed) to data as well as patterns.

SAOR [13] and Straccia et al. [24] incorporate trust in rule based reasoning. They employ different trust representations and use trust differently. While Straccia et al. assume that every triple is annotated with trust (and other annotations such as fuzziness), SAOR doesn't consider trust valuation of triples in isolation. At the rule application time, trust on a triple is evaluated based on what it is being used to prove, and the trust value is binary, i.e. a triple is either considered authoritative for that instance of rule application or is not used for derivation. In contrast every triple is used for derivation in the framework proposed by Straccia et al. and the inferred triples are associated with trust derived from that of triples required for inferring it. AIR reasoner is not trust aware in the sense that SAOR and the framework proposed by Straccia et al. are, but we show that the language features of AIR give a lot of freedom to reason about knowledge base annotated with trust. In the approach proposed, the trust valuations are incorporated in the rule conditions and may be used for different affects. For instance a pattern with trust smaller than 7 may be rejected for one rule, and accepted with lower trust value of 6 for other (because it is rejected for trust value less than 5). Furthermore, we treat rules as part of the knowledge that people may have varying degrees of trust.

3 Semantic Web and Trust

The reliability and usefulness of Web data depends on evaluating its trustworthiness, the subjective measure of the belief which a user has that the data is "true". Our approach supports the vision provided by the Semantic Web layer-cake[2] by building trust out of rules about provenance and proofs/justifications related to data on the Semantic Web. Thus, in order to better understand how trust might be modeled in the Semantic Web, it is important to understand the underlying concepts employed by the Resource Description Framework (RDF), which serves as the foundation for all Semantic Web data.

3.1 Resource Description Framework (RDF)

Resource Description Framework (RDF) is the data modeling framework for the Semantic Web and it uses 3-tuples, or triples, to represent facts. RDF is described in more detail in [3], but we will proceed to give a short outline below.

Each triple in an RDF model consists of a subject, predicate, and object, much like the subject, predicate, and object of a natural language sentence. For example, one possible triple representing the rating of a movie, **:citizenkane**

[2] http://www.w3.org/2004/Talks/0412-RDF-functions/slide4-0.html

:stars "5".[3], consists of a subject **:citizenkane**, a predicate **:stars** and an object **"5"**. Triples may also be thought of as logical predicates taking two arguments, such as $stars(citizenkane, 5)$.

In the RDF data model, each triple may be thought of as a directed edge in a labelled *RDF graph*, where the subject and object are nodes in the graph, and the predicate is a labelled edge. Nodes may be uniquely identified by a Uniform Resource Identifier (URI), and thus, subjects and objects may be specified by a URI. Nodes may also be made anonymous, without such an identifier. Such anonymous nodes are called blank nodes, or bnodes.

Predicates are also identified by a URI. Unlike subjects and objects, however, these URIs do not identify a unique edge, but rather identify the type/meaning of the edge linking the two entities. Objects may also be a *literal*, that is, a string or a simply-typed object (such as an integer or date), but these do not uniquely identify a node.

3.2 Models of Trust for the Semantic Web

When speaking of a trust metric, $\mathcal{T}$ (a quantitative measurement of trust), which is applicable to the RDF data derived from rules, we must ground such trust in the two inputs needed to draw such conclusions: trust in the data from which the conclusion was drawn, $\mathcal{T}(f)$, and trust in the rule which generated the conclusion, $\mathcal{T}(r)$. These two axes of trust are independent of each other, but must be considered together in order to draw a meaningful idea of the trust that may be placed in any conclusions.

If we consider rules to be black boxes, we must necessarily separate trust in rules from trust in data in this way. Any inferences generated by a rule may be generated locally or by a third party in exactly the same way. Because inferences may be generated by an unknown third party, it is difficult to offer strong guarantees about the trust of any inferences made. RDF and rule systems do not innately have any semantics pertaining to trust, and, as trust is subjective in any case, it is difficult to offer any universal guarantees in how input data might be used or how output data might be generated in order to determine the level of trust that might apply to a particular inferred fact. Thus, as in certain modal logics of trust, we must ground the degree of trust in the output data in the degree of trust we have in the particular rule which generated that particular data [18].

Similarly, provenance-based approaches to trust evaluation necessarily consider the "paths" by which data came to be (i.e. from whom data came from, as well as the processes which generated them, which may include rule systems) [9]. Thus, when calculating the trust in a derived fact, we must necessarily consider the trust in the rule which generated the conclusion, $\mathcal{T}(r)$ in any meta-modeling system capable of assessing trust.

[3] Throughout this paper, we use Turtle syntax for RDF (`http://www.w3.org/TeamSubmission/turtle/`), which is a subset of the Notation 3 syntax compatible with the RDF abstract syntax.

Furthermore, as rules may depend on external knowledge to create conclusions, our trust in these conclusions must, necessarily, be no greater than our trust in this input knowledge. This differs from our trust in rules in much the same way that a quantitative process or algorithm may generate precise results without necessarily being accurate (perhaps due to some bias in the input data). Thus, while a trusted rule may generate reliable output data (i.e. it is precise), the output data may only be reliable for other purposes to the extent that the input data is reliable (i.e. its results may not be accurate).

Although both axes should be considered when determining whether or not to trust a conclusion, the trust model used for drawing such conclusions may vary from one "invocation" of a rule to the next. The trust model used for one axis may differ from that used for the other, but both generally must consist of a synthesis of two different categories of trust: **content-based trust**, and **metadata-based trust** [10,5].

In content-based trust, we derive our trust values from the contents of the facts asserted. Thus, any metric $\mathcal{T}$ would be defined in terms of one or more facts, $f \in \mathcal{F}$, the set of all facts known. For example, one trust metric might determine trust in external statements about the actors in certain movies if the source happens to agree with certain statements about the directors of the movies known a priori ($\mathcal{T} \sim |\mathcal{F}_{\text{known}} \cap \mathcal{F}_{\text{source}}|$). Similarly, one might place a higher trust value on statements which use a well-defined and well-used ontology rather than an ill-defined one ($\mathcal{T} \sim \forall_{f \in \mathcal{F}_{\text{source}}} \mathit{predicate}(f)$).

Metadata-based trust is more helpful when calculating trust based on circumstantial facts about the data, rather than facts in the data itself. Each fact $f \in \mathcal{F}$ may be considered to have a vector of corresponding "metadata" facts $M(f)$ which describe additional information regarding the fact, such as authorship, creation times, data sources, and other such derivative data. Metadata-based trust subsumes all data that might describe a given fact, including the provenance of the fact and any user-generated trust values or ratings of the source from which the fact is derived. Any of these metadata-facts may then be used to calculate $\mathcal{T}$.

For example, one may have a higher trust value in statements made by one's friends than those made by arbitrary people ($\mathcal{T} \sim M_{\text{source}}(f)$). Such a trust value depends not on the data being said, but rather on the *source* of the data. Similarly, if, during a science experiment, a bad sensor is identified and replaced, different trust values may be assigned to the data recorded at different times in the experiment ($\mathcal{T} \sim \mathit{time} - M_{\text{time}}(f)$). In this case, the trust value depends on the *time* data was collected, $M_{\text{time}}(f)$, rather than in the data itself (which may have no information indicating its accuracy or lack thereof).

Content-based trust and metadata-based trust may be synthesized in any number of ways to create a trust metric. For example, we may trust statements made about the actors of the movie to a different degree from statements about the creators of the movie. In constrast, metadata-based trust allows us to assign different trust values to statements made by the creators of the movie, Avatar, separate from statements made by the actors of the movie. Thus content-based trust is associated with the statements themselves whereas metadata-based trust may be based on facts related to the statements such as their authors.

As mentioned previously, these two trust categories apply not only to the facts that caused the deduction of new facts, but also to the rules themselves. For example, we may have metadata-based trust in a rule and be able to trust rules that deduce information about a movie's rating that have been written by a movie critic, but not necessarily the same rules written by a director interested in promoting his own movies.

Any language seeking to be used for the purpose of calculating trust in rules or using trust levels to make deductions must be able to model trust metrics not only based on the rules and facts, but it should be able to synthesize trust values based on both metadata about the data, and the data itself. We believe that the AIR rule language is capable of doing so, and we will illustrate this in the following sections.

3.3 Possible Trust Representations in RDF

Given any trust measure, there are numerous ways trust assignments may be made using RDF. One of the simplest ways to declare binary trust is by defining two classes of trust such as *Trusted* and *UnTrusted* and declare URIs, sources, rules, or any resource, to be one or the other. We demonstrate such a model in example (a) in Figure 1, where Isabel trusts two resources, `:RobertEbert` and `:Karl`, but does not trust the resource identified by the URI, <http://example.org/critix.n3>.

The above trust assignment is simple and only allows users to classify resources as trusted or not. In order to have finer grained trust values, it is possible to define a property such as *trustvalue* and use it to assign values (either quantitative or qualitative) to resources. This property can also be used to model fuzzy RDF where triples are annotated with a degree of truth in [0, 1] as defined by Straccia et al. [24]. For example, 'Rome is a big city to degree 0.8' can be represented in Notation 3 (Please refer to Section 4.1 for more information about Notation 3) as **{:Rome :a :BigCity} :trustvalue 0.8**. In example (b) from Figure 1, Isabel defines trust as her confidence in the accuracy of the data/resource and associates trust values with `:RogerEbert`, <http://example.org/critix.n3>, a rule, `:KarlWatchRule`, and a statement about CitizenKane.

Instead of using a quantitative approach as above, an alternate approach would be to create properties for every discrete type of trust possible such as the model for social networks proposed by Golbeck et al. [12]. Golbeck defines individual properties for different trust relationship between users — distrusts absolutely, distrusts highly, distrusts moderately, distrusts slightly, trusts neutrally, trusts slightly, trusts moderately, trusts highly, and trusts absolutely. In example (c) from Figure 1, Isabel highly trusts `:RogerEbert` but trusts `:Karl` moderately.

Additionally, it is possible to trust certain sources or documents with certain information but not all information they contain. For example, a hospital may be trusted with information about a potential virus outbreak but may not be

```
# Example (a)

# Isabel's trust declaration
:RogerEbert a :Trusted .
<http://example.org/critix.n3> rdf:type :Untrusted .
:Karl a :Trusted .

# Example (b)

# Isabel's trust declaration
:RogerEbert :trustvalue 5 .
<http://example.org/critix.n3> :trustvalue 9 .
:KarlWatchRule :trustvalue 7 .
{:CitizenKane :rating :ThumbsUp} :trustvalue 8 .

# Example (c)

# Isabel's trust declaration
:Isabel :trustsHighly :RogerEbert .
:Isabel :trustsModerately :Karl .

# Example (d)

# Isabel's trust declarations
<http://example.org/critix.n3> :istrustedwith :some-t.
:some-t rdf:type :TrustInfo;
    :tval 95;
    :tpattern  { :RogerEbert ?p ?o } .
```

Fig. 1. Trust Representations

trusted with respect to its economic predictions. This could be modeled in Notation 3 (Please refer to Section 4.1 for more information about Notation 3) in several ways, one of which is to use quoted formulae [4]. A property, *istrusted-with* is defined whose object is of type *TrustInfo* and is associated with data sources. The *TrustInfo* class has two properties *tpattern* and *tval*. The *tpattern* is a graph pattern that describes the facts that are trusted from that particular source. The *tval* is similar to the *trustvalue* property and is a trust value associated with all those facts that match the (graph) pattern. The example (d) in Figure 1 shows how these properties are defined and Isabel's trust declaration states that she assigns a quantitative trust value of 95 to all statements made about `:RogerEbert` described in document <http://example.org/critix.n3>.

4 AIR Web Rule Language

AIR is made up of a set of built-in functions and two independent ontologies — the first is for the specification of AIR rules, and the second deals with describing justifications for the inferences made by AIR rules [14]. The built-in functions allow rules to access (Semantic) Web resources, query remote RDF databases, as well as to perform basic math, string and cryptographic operations. We describe the syntax and functionality of the AIR language and the Rule ontology next. The AIR justification ontology is derived from PML [20] and customized for AIR reasoning, and is described in detail at [15]. However, we will use only the PML vocabulary in the paper, as the specifics of AIR reasoning are not important.

```
@prefix s: <http://s.example.org/ontology#> .
@prefix a: <http://a.example.org/instance#> .
@prefix foaf: <http://xmlns.com/foaf/0.1/> .
@prefix rdf: <http://www.w3.org/1999/02/22-rdf-syntax-ns#> .
@prefix : <http://src1.example.org/JohnAnalyst#> .

:Jim rdf:type foaf:Person.
:Matt rdf:type foaf:Person.

a:StarWars s:rec s:Watch.
a:TheRoom s:rec s:DontWatch.
a:TheGraduate s:rec s:Watch.

:RogerEbert :said {a:CitizenKane :rating :ThumbsUp}.
```

Fig. 2. Content of an RDF Data Source

4.1 Syntax

AIR extends Notation 3 (N3) [3], a syntax based on the RDF abstract syntax. N3 makes use of a number of basic concepts from RDF, including the concept of triples. N3 extends RDF's abstract syntax by adding formula quoting, which allows for RDF Graphs to be treated as subjects or objects, and variable quantification. Figure 2 provides some examples of N3 statements. Please refer to `http://www.w3.org/2000/10/swap/Primer` for an overview of N3.

AIR uses N3's formula quoting and variable quantification to describe graph patterns, which are similar to the Basic Graph Pattern (BGP) of SPARQL queries[4], that are to be matched before rules may fire.

4.2 Rule Ontology

The AIR rule vocabulary consists of several key classes and properties. ***Belief-rule*** is a class of resources representing the set of all rules. These rules may then have the properties ***if***, ***then***, and ***else*** associated with them to represent the N3 pattern to be matched, and the actions to take if the pattern matches, or does not match, respectively. ***then*** and ***else*** actions may be described in terms of the facts they assert (using the ***assert*** property) or the rules they cause to match next (using the ***rule*** property).

If the graph pattern or condition matches the current state of the world, defined as the facts known or inferred to be true so far, then all the actions under ***then*** are fired, otherwise all the actions under ***else*** are fired. The condition matches the current state if there is a subgraph of known facts that matches the graph pattern.

Figure 3 demonstrates how the AIR rule vocabulary can be used to define the recommendation rule Isabel uses. The rule suggests that Isabel only watch movies, ***air:assert { :Isabel s:shouldWatch :MOVIE}***, if there is a five-star rating, ***:MOVIE s:starRating 5*** . The same rule is illustrated in a tabular representation in Figure 4. For clarity we use this tabular representation of AIR rules for the remainder of this paper.

[4] `http://www.w3.org/TR/rdf-sparql-query/#BasicGraphPatterns`

```
@forAll :MOVIE.
:IsabelWatchRule a air:Belief-rule;
   air:if { :MOVIE s:starRating 5  };
   air:then [ air:assert { :Isabel s:shouldWatch :MOVIE } ].
```

Fig. 3. Example AIR Syntax

```
:IsabelWatchRule a air:Belief-rule .

@forAll :MOVIE .

IF    # Implicitly trust all 5-star ratings.
      :MOVIE s:starRating 5 .

THEN  assert :Isabel s:shouldWatch :MOVIE .
```

Fig. 4. Example AIR Rule: `IsabelWatchRule` implicitly encodes **content-based trust** into the rule by explicitly trusting all stated 5-star ratings to the full degree without regard to how the ratings were generated or who stated them. Although there is no reliance on trust values of the statement or its pattern itself, it is the same as if complete trust was placed in all such statements.

5 Trust Assessment Framework

Our trust assessment framework is not restricted to any specific trust measure such as reputation, degree of truth, or completeness. As long as the trust assignment can be captured in RDF, it can be used by our framework. However, it is up to the user developing the trust assessment model to ensure that the semantics associated with different trust assignments is maintained when combining different trust values.

In this section we show how our framework can be used to evaluate trust in a movie recommendation scenario. Assume that a movie streaming service, WebCinema, offers several different methods of movie recommendations to its clients. Isabel, a member of WebCinema, uses one of WebCinema's metrics, which recommends movies that have at least one five-star rating. WebCinema permits users to select the critics giving the five-star ratings, so as to ignore reviews from critics users disagree with, and Isabel has chosen to make use of this feature. Some of WebCinema's customers may create their own rules which merge the results of several of WebCinema's built-in rules. Karl uses WebCinema's rating-based rules as part of his decision making process, but does not entirely trust them. Karl may wish to only partially trust WebCinema's ratings-based rules, depending additionally on the trust he places on the facts used by the rules to make recommendations.

For this scenario, we assume that trust declarations are made using the *istrustedwith* property, where we trust a source with respect to certain data, and the *trustvalue* property, where we associate a trust value with a resource, as defined in Section 3.3. The rule in Figure 5, `:IsabelWatchRule`, uses metadata-based trust and assigns trust to sources of data with respect to watch recommendations and creators of data. The rule looks for patterns referring to watch recommendations in sources whom she trusts more than 75 with the specified pattern

```
:IsabelWatchRule a air:Belief-rule .
@forAll :CRITICREVIEWS, :VARIABLE, :MOVIE, :STRUST,
:CREATOR, :CTRUST, :VAL, :TRUST .

IF    :CRITICREVIEWS
          t:istrustedwith [ t:pattern { :VARIABLE s:rec s:Watch . } ;
                    t:value :STRUST ] .
      :STRUST math:notLessThan 75 .
      :CRITICREVIEWS log:includes { :MOVIE s:rec s:Watch . }.
      :CRITICREVIEWS foaf:maker :CREATOR .
      :CREATOR t:trustvalue :CTRUST .
      (:STRUST 100) math:integerQuotient :VAL .
      (:CTRUST :VAL) math:product :TRUST .
      :TRUST math:notLessThan 80 .
THEN  assert :Isabel s:shouldWatch :MOVIE .
```

Fig. 5. Compute trust in data using metadata-based trust: `IsabelWatchRule` uses the trust ontology described in section 3.3 to assign trust to critics with respect to watch recommendations. The source is only searched if the trust in the source is greater than 75. The trust in the new information is calculated from the trust in the source website and creator of the information.

{ :VARIABLE s:rec s:Watch . }. If the source contains this information, the rule calculates trust for this new information based on her trust in the source and the creator of the data and recommends that she watch it if the trust is greater than 80.

As AIR is a general purpose reasoner, AIR rules can be written to consume these trust declarations and combine them in different ways in order to compute trust values for data or inferences of interest. `IsabelWatchRule` as defined in Figure 4 uses metadata-based trust and assigns trust to critics with respect to watch recommendations. `:IsabelWatchRule` recommends that Isabel watch a movie if there is a watch recommendation made by a critic with trust value greater than 7.

As rules themselves could have trust values associated with them, as described in Section 3.3, it is possible to reason about the trustworthiness of *rules* and use them to deduce trust in the inferences made by them. AIR's support for the ***air:justifies*** property allows for the execution of other rules which we may be able to query for trust. The rule `:KarlWatchRule` in Figure 6 encapsulates such a rule (which synthesizes rule-trust with data-trust); it recommends that Karl watch a movie only if both the rule and data used to justify the recommendation are trusted by Karl with an average trust value greater than or equal to 7.

In `:KarlWatchRule`, ***air:justifies*** is used to run the rules at the URL <http://webcinema.example.com/rules> against some trusted data. The result of this reasoning is stored in the output variable `:RULEJUST`, which may be used with other built-in functions, like ***log:includes***, to determine not only which facts are asserted by the rules, but also the justifications for such. These justifications may then be used to determine the rules which caused some conclusion to be found to be true and their trust values.

```
:KarlWatchRule a air:Belief-rule .
@forAll :RULESET, :RULEJUST, :MOVIE, :RULEAPPEVENT,
    :EXTRACTIONEVENT, :SOURCE, :RULE, :RULETRUST, :SOURCETRUST,
    :TRUSTSUM, :TRUSTAVG .
    <http://webcinema.example.com/rules> log:semantics :RULESET .
    ((:RULESET) (:DATA)) air:justifies :RULEJUST .
    :RULEJUST log:includes {
        @forSome :RULEAPPEVENT .
        :Karl s:shouldWatch :MOVIE .
        :RULEAPPEVENT pmlj:outputdata { :Karl s:shouldWatch :MOVIE . } .
        :RULEAPPEVENT pmll:operation :RULE .
IF      :RULEAPPEVENT pmll:antecedent :EXTRACTIONEVENT .
        :EXTRACTIONEVENT pmlp:source :SOURCE .
    } .
    :RULE t:trustvalue :RULETRUST .
    :SOURCE t:trustvalue :SOURCETRUST .
    (:RULETRUST :SOURCETRUST) math:sum :TRUSTSUM .
    (:TRUSTSUM 2) math:quotient :TRUSTAVG .
    :TRUSTAVG math:notLessThan 7 .
THEN assert :Karl s:shouldWatch :MOVIE .
```

Fig. 6. Compute trust in data using metadata-based trust in rules: `KarlWatchRule` uses the trust ontology described in section 3.3 to assign trust to the rules used by WebCinema to generate recommendations. If the average trust in the rule used to generate a watch recommendation and the data used by the rule has a trust value greater than or equal to 7, then the rule recommends that Karl should watch that movie.

We could use a similar rule to more generally judge the output of rules based on where the output came from. While the above rule checks trust values in the rule and source individually, rules could also be written to expressly generate trust based on properties of the rule or data, as well as the trust measurements themselves (for example, we could check the "author" of a rule to implicitly trust all rules authored by WebCinema, giving their results a high trust value.)

Provenance models such as the Open Provenance Model (OPM) [21] or Provenir [23] are also supported by our framework. OPM and Provenir are high-level, general-purpose provenance models that may be encoded in RDF and be queried using the AIR language in a manner similar to that shown above. As long as it is possible to identify the URIs of rules used in a particular fact's derivation, one need only express an appropriate pattern which may be used to find and bind the rule's identifier to search for an appropriate trust value for the rule.

For example, content-based trust models may be used together with languages like OPM and Provenir to identify and determine trust in particular products of generic scientific processes. The faulty scientific sensor example discussed in Section 3.2 may be easily implemented in our framework when the provenance is encoded in OPM as can be observed in the sample rule in Figure 7.

```
:BadSensorRule a air:Belief-rule .
@forAll :DATA, :PROCESS, :TIME, :UNIXTIME .
IF    :DATA a opm:Artifact ;
           opm:wasGeneratedBy :PROCESS ;
           opm:wasGeneratedAt :TIME .
      :PROCESS owl:sameAs :BadSensorProcess .
      :TIME time:inSeconds :UNIXTIME .
THEN  activate-rule :BadSensorTimeRule
---------------------------------------------------
:BadSensorTimeRule a air:Belief-rule .
IF    :UNIXTIME math:greaterThan :BadSensorFixedTime .
THEN  assert :DATA t:trustvalue 7.
ELSE  assert :DATA t:trustvalue 3.
```

Fig. 7. Deriving trust from OPM provenance: `BadSensorRule` uses provenance metadata about some datum encoded in OPM to assign trust to the datum depending on the time the data was generated by the faulty sensor

6 Contributions

As demonstrated above, our framework has several unique features that make it useful for trust assessment and modeling thanks to its foundation in the Semantic Web. First, its use of the RDF data model and ability to uniquely identify and specify rules allows for the augmentation of existing rulesets with trust data. Trust values and metrics may be defined separate from the data for which trust is being assigned. This also allows third-party representations of trust, which may not be possible in all trust model implementations. Furthermore, its rule-based nature allows for more nuanced trust-assessment on the web than a simple binary trust model, although binary trust models are also supported.

Although the examples in this paper make use of specific terms for trust and PML and OPM ontologies for provenance, the general principles employed in the motivating use case implementations can be used with **any other trust and provenance vocabularies** that have an RDF representation. Our framework may serve to construct and evaluate trust metrics in general, regardless of the vocabularies used to encode provenance and trust.

Second, as a generic Semantic Web rule language, AIR is capable of reasoning over several different semantic representations of trust metrics, including straightforward numerical values like that in Figure 7 and trust values assigned on a per-pattern basis, such as in Figure 5. Thus, existing trust metrics may be integrated with framework needing only a suitable mapping into the RDF data model, and users may thus choose a trust model that best captures their requirements.

Finally, our framework identifies two trust categories, namely content-based and metadata-based, for assigning trust and recognizes that trust in rules is as important as trust in data on the Semantic Web as rules are used frequently to make inferences over Web data. So far as we can tell, there exists no literature regarding these categories or axes of trust within the context of rule systems.

7 Summary and Future Work

In this paper, we discussed the importance of trust on the Semantic Web and identified two trust axes namely data and rules and two trust categories namely content-based and metadata-based that are useful for trust declarations associated with Semantic Web data. Furthermore, we outlined a meta-modeling trust framework and demonstrated how an implementation of this framework in the AIR Web rule language could be used to develop different trust assessments models.

Though this work demonstrates the usefulness of AIR, it relies on user-generated rules for handling trust. As part of our future work, we will work on general rules that will handle trust transparently such that users do not need to explicitly know about or handle trust in their systems but will be able to customize these rules to do it for them. We also intend to evaluate the addition of trust as a first-class entity within AIR, potentially adding explicit support for trust in built-in functions. Although the benefits to adding trust as an implicit part of a rules language may be great, it is possible that the flexibility of trust models is preferable to forcing one particular trust model on the language.

Acknowledgements

This paper is based upon work supported by the National Science Foundation under Award No. CNS-0831442 and by the Air Force Office of Scientific Research under Award No. FA9550-09-1-0152.

References

1. Artz, D., Gil, Y.: A Survey of Trust in Computer Science and the Semantic Web. Web Semantics 5, 58–71 (2007)
2. Bechhofer, S., van Harmelen, F., Hendler, J., Horrocks, I., McGuinness, D.L., Patel-Schneider, P.F., Stein, L.A.: OWL Web Ontology Language Reference, W3C Recommendation (February 10, 2004), http://www.w3.org/TR/owl-ref/
3. Berners-Lee, T.: Primer: Getting into RDF and Semantic Web using N3 (2005), http://www.w3.org/2000/10/swap/Primer
4. Berners-Lee, T., Connolly, D., Kagal, L., Scharf, Y., Hendler, J.: N3Logic: A Logical Framework For the World Wide Web. Journal of Theory and Practice of Logic Programming (2007)
5. Bizer, C., Cyganiak, R.: Quality-driven information filtering using the WIQA policy framework. Journal of Web Semantics 7, 1–10 (2009)
6. Blaze, M., Feigenbaum, J., Ioannidis, J., Keromytis, A.: The KeyNote Trust Management System Version. Internet RFC 2704 (September 1999)
7. Brickley, D., Guha, R.: RDF Vocabulary Description Language 1.0: RDF Schema, W3C Recommendation (February 2002), http://www.w3.org/TR/rdf-schema

8. Chu, Y.-H., Feigenbaum, J., LaMacchia, B., Resnick, P., Strauss, M.: REFEREE: Trust management for Web Applications. Computer Networks and ISDN Systems 29(8-13), 953–964 (1997)
9. Dai, C., Lin, D., Hwang, J., Kantarcioglu, M.: An Approach to Evaluate Data Trustworthiness Based on Data Provenance. In: Jonker, W., Petković, M. (eds.) SDM 2008. LNCS, vol. 5159, pp. 82–98. Springer, Heidelberg (2008), doi:10.1007/978-3-540-85259-9_6
10. Gao, Q., Houben, G.-J.: A Framework for Trust Establishment and Assessment on the Web of Data. In: Proceedings of the 19th International Conference on World Wide Web, WWW 2010, pp. 1097–1098. ACM, New York (2010)
11. Gil, Y., Ratnakar, V.: Trusting Information Sources One Citizen at a Time. In: Horrocks, I., Hendler, J. (eds.) ISWC 2002. LNCS, vol. 2342, pp. 162–176. Springer, Heidelberg (2002)
12. Golbeck, J., Parsia, B., Hendler, J.: Trust Networks on the Semantic Web. In: Proceedings of Cooperative Intelligent Agents, pp. 238–249 (2003)
13. Hogan, A., Harth, A., Polleres, A.: SAOR: Authoritative Reasoning for the Web. In: Domingue, J., Anutariya, C. (eds.) ASWC 2008. LNCS, vol. 5367, pp. 76–90. Springer, Heidelberg (2008)
14. Kagal, L., Hanson, C., Weitzner, D.: Using Dependency Tracking to Provide Explanations for Policy Management. In: IEEE Policy 2008 (2008)
15. Kagal, L., Jacobi, I., Khandelwal, A.: Gasping for AIR: Why we need linked rules and justifications on the Semantic Web. Technical Report MIT-CSAIL-TR-2011-023, Massachusetts Institute of Technology (April 2011)
16. Kuter, U., Golbeck, J.: SUNNY: a new algorithm for trust inference in social networks using probabilistic confidence models. In: Proceedings of the 22nd National Conference on Artificial Intelligence, pp. 1377–1382. AAAI Press, Menlo Park (2007)
17. Li, N., Grosof, B.N., Feigenbaum, J.: Delegation Logic: A Logic-based Approach to Distributed Authorization. ACM Transactions on Information Systems Security (TISSEC) 6(1) (February 2003)
18. Liau, C.-J.: Belief, information acquisition, and trust in multi-agent systems–A modal logic formulation. Artificial Intelligence 149, 31–60 (2003)
19. Blaze, M., Feigenbaum, J., Lacy, J.: Decentralized Trust Management. In: Proceedings of IEEE Conference on Privacy and Security (1996)
20. McGuinness, D.L., Ding, L., da Silva, P.P., Chang, C.: PML 2: A Modular Explanation Interlingua. In: AAAI 2007 Workshop on Explanation-aware Computing (2007)
21. Moreau, L., Plale, B., Miles, S., Goble, C., Missier, P., Barga, R., Simmhan, Y., Futrelle, J., Mcgrath, R.E., Myers, J., Paulson, P., Bowers, S., Ludaescher, B., Kwasnikowska, N., Bussche, J.V.D., Ellkvist, T., Freire, J., Groth, P. (eds.): The Open Provenance Model (v1.01) (2008), http://eprints.ecs.soton.ac.uk/16148/1/opm-v1.01.pdf
22. Richardson, M., Agrawal, R., Domingos, P.: Trust Management for the Semantic Web. In: Fensel, D., Sycara, K., Mylopoulos, J. (eds.) ISWC 2003. LNCS, vol. 2870, pp. 351–368. Springer, Heidelberg (2003)
23. Sahoo, S.S., Sheth, A.: Provenir ontology: Towards a Framework for eScience Provenance Management. In: Microsoft eScience Workshop (October 2009)
24. Straccia, U., Lopes, N., Lukacsy, G., Polleres, A.: A General Framework for Representing and Reasoning with Annotated Semantic Web Data. In: AAAI (2010)
25. W3C OWL Working Group. OWL 2 Web Ontology Language, W3C Recommendation (October 27, 2009), http://www.w3.org/TR/owl2-overview/

SOWL: A Framework for Handling Spatio-temporal Information in OWL 2.0

Sotiris Batsakis and Euripides G.M. Petrakis

Department of Electronic and Computer Engineering,
Technical University of Crete (TUC),
Chania, Greece
{batsakis,petrakis}@intelligence.tuc.gr

Abstract. We propose SOWL, an ontology for representing and reasoning over spatio-temporal information in OWL. Building upon well established standards of the semantic web (OWL 2.0, SWRL) SOWL enables representation of static as well as of dynamic information based on the 4D-fluents (or, equivalently, on the N-ary) approach. Both RCC-8 topological and cone-shaped directional relations are integrated in SOWL. Representing both qualitative temporal and spatial information (i.e., information whose temporal or spatial extents are unknown such as "left-of" for spatial and "before" for temporal relations) in addition to quantitative information (i.e., where temporal and spatial information is defined precisely) is a distinctive feature of SOWL. The SOWL reasoner is capable of inferring new relations and checking their consistency, while retaining soundness, completeness, and tractability over the supported sets of relations.

1 Introduction

Ontologies offer the means for representing high level concepts, their properties, and their interrelationships. Dynamic ontologies in addition enable representation of information evolving in time and space. Welty and Fikes [2] showed how quantitative temporal information (i.e., in the form of temporal intervals whose left and right endpoints are well defined) as well as the evolution of concepts in time can be represented effectively in OWL using the so-called "4D-fluents approach".

In our previous work [1], we extended this approach in certain ways: (a) the 4D-fluents mechanism was enchanced with qualitative (in addition to quantitative) temporal expressions allowing for the representation of temporal intervals with unknown endpoints by means of their relation (e.g., "before", "after") to other time intervals, and (b) spatial information was also supported. Accordingly, the spatial representation supports both quantitative and qualitative expressions. However, only basic (non-disjunctive) relations were supported. Neither soundness nor completeness of reasoning were guaranteed.

This work handles all these issues. The expressiveness of the model increases by introducing sets of disjunctive relations by means of SWRL rules and OWL 2.0

N. Bassiliades et al. (Eds.): RuleML 2011 - Europe, LNCS 6826, pp. 242–249, 2011.

constructs. Both, the 4D-fluents and the N-ary relations approach are expanded to accommodate this information. Reasoning implements path consistency [4] and it is sound and complete.

Related work in the field of knowledge representation is discussed in Section 2. This includes issues related to representing and reasoning about information evolving in time and space. The SOWL representation model is presented in Section 3 and the corresponding reasoning mechanism in Section 4, followed by conclusions and issues for future work in Section 5.

2 Background and Related Work

The OWL-Time temporal ontology[1] describes the temporal content of Web pages and the temporal properties of Web services. Apart from language constructs for the representation of time in ontologies, there is still a need for mechanisms for the representation of the evolution of concepts (e.g., events) in time.Representation of time in the Semantic Web can be achieved using *Reification, N-ary relations*[2], *temporal RDF* [3], *named graphs* [10] or *4D-fluents* [2].

Reification is a general purpose technique for representing n-ary relations using a language such as OWL that permits only binary relations. Specifically, an n-ary relation is represented as a new object that has all the arguments of the n-ary relation as objects of properties. Fig. 1(a) illustrates the relation *Works-For(Employee, Company, TimeInterval)* representing the fact that an employee works for a company during a time interval. Reification offers limited OWL reasoning capabilities [2] since the n-ary relation is represented as the object of a property and thus OWL semantics over properties (e.g., inverse properties), are no longer applicable. Following the *N-ary relations* approach, the temporal property is represented by two properties each one related with the new object (Fig.1(b)). This approach requires only one additional object for every temporal interval, it maintains property semantics, but it suffers from data redundancy in the case of inverse and symmetric properties (e.g., the inverse of a relation is added explicitly twice instead of once as in 4D-fluents).

The *4D-fluents* (perdurantist) approach [2] suggests that concepts in time are represented as 4-dimensional objects with the 4th dimension being the time (*timeslices*). Following the approach by Welty and Fikes [2], to add a time dimension to an ontology, classes *TimeSlice* and *TimeInterval* with properties *TimeSliceOf* and *timeInterval* are introduced. Properties having a time dimension are called fluent properties and connect instances of class *TimeSlice* (see Fig.1(c)). The 4D-fluents approach still suffers from proliferation of objects, but it maintains full OWL expressiveness and reasoning support.

Representing spatio-temporal knowledge has also motivated research within the Semantic Web community. Katz et al. [5] propose representing RCC-8 topologic relations as OWL-DL class axioms (instead of object properties as in [1]), but this approach has limited scalability as shown in [11]. In our previous work

[1] http://www.w3.org/TR/owl-time

[2] http://www.w3.org/TR/swbp-n-aryRelations

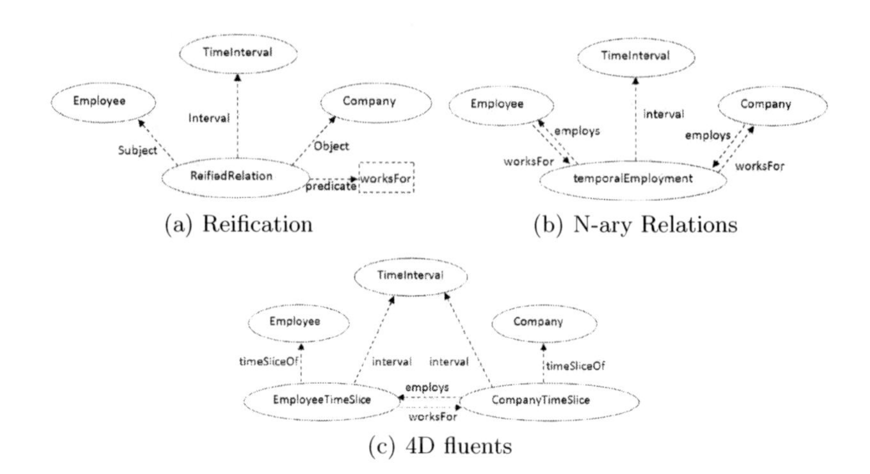

Fig. 1. Example of (a) Reification (b) N-ary Relations and (c) 4D-fluents

[1], we proposed a spatio-temporal representation model supporting both quantitative and qualitative information. The qualitative relations were restricted to basic (non disjunctive) relations.

3 SOWL Ontology

In SOWL, the 4D-fluents (or the N-ary representation), is enhanced with qualitative temporal relations holding between time intervals whose left and right endpoints are not specified. This is implemented by introducing temporal relationships as object relations between time intervals. This can be one of the 13 pairwise disjoint Allen's relations [8]. In addition, SOWL supports several types of qualitative spatial relations. These can be either topologic or directional [4]. Fig. 2(a) illustrates the ontology representation of a static (non moving) object. Since the location of the object is a static property, it is a property of the object and not of a timeslice of the object (or the intermediate object introduced by the N-ary approach). Class *Location* has attribute *name* (of type string). Moreover, a *Location* object can be optionally connected with a *footprint* class with subclasses *Point, Line, Polyline, and MBR*, representing points, line segments, surrounding contours of objects (or regions) as sets of consecutive line segments, and Minimun Bounding Rectangles, respectively. In case of a moving object the location is a property of a timeslice belonging to a specific time interval (Fig. 2(b)) or the intermediate object introduced by the N-ary approach.

In an ontology, each *spatialRelation* connects two locations and has two subproperties, namely, *topologicRelation* and *directionalRelation.* The topologic spatial relations between regions can be extracted from their surrounding *MBRs* by comparing their coordinates or contours using computational geometry. In case of point-based representations, directional relations are computed using their formal definitions [7,13], while, in case of regions, the directional relations are

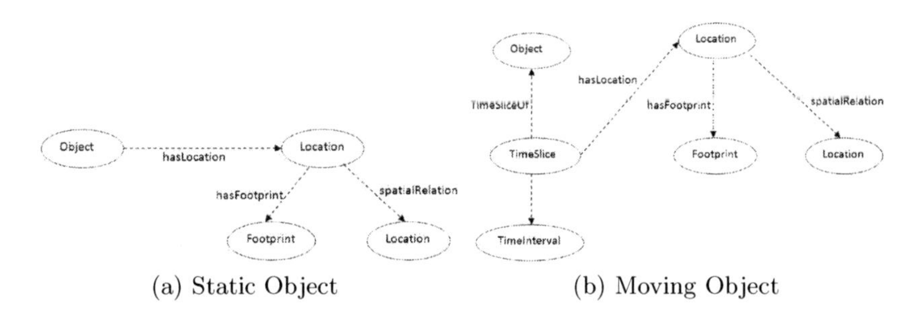

(a) Static Object (b) Moving Object

Fig. 2. Ontology representation of (a) Static and (b) Moving objects

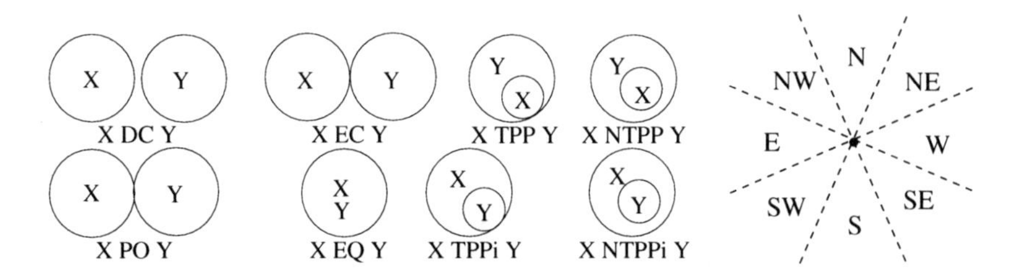

Fig. 3. Topologic relations (left) Directional relations (right)

defined using their centroids. If quantitative information (i.e., location coordinates) is not given, qualitative relations can be asserted into the ontology instead. In this case, the reasoning mechanism will infer additional relations and detect inconsistencies.
The topologic relations holding between two regions *x,y (DC, EC, EQ, NTPP, NTPPi, TPP, TPPi, PO)*, are referred to as RCC-8 relations [6], as shown in Fig. 3 Direction relations holding between two points are defined based on cone-shaped areas [7,13], as shown in Fig. 3. Nine direction relations can be identified, namely, North (N), North East (NE), East (E), South East (SE), South (S), South West (SW), West (W) North West (NW), and the identical point relation (O), following the cone-shaped areas approach of Frank [7]. Directional relations apply to objects represented by points (e.g., by their centroid).

4 Reasoning in SOWL

Reasoning in SOWL is realized by introducing a set of SWRL[3] rules operating on spatial (topologic or directional) relations as well as by a set of temporal Allen rules for asserting inferred temporal relations. Notice that, OWL does not support role intersection and that (in order to retain decidability[4]) transitivity of properties cannot be combined with property disjointess . In SOWL, path

[3] http://www.w3.org/Submission/SWRL
[4] http://www.w3.org/TR/2009/REC-owl2-syntax-20091027

consistency is implemented using SWRL. Reasoners that support DL-safe rules such as Pellet[5] can be used for inference and consistency checking over spatio-temporal relations.

The temporal reasoner implements the compositions of the 13 basic Allen relations defined in [8]. These relations are: *Before, After, Meets, Metby, Overlaps, Overlappedby, During, Contains, Starts, Startedby, Ends, Endedby* and *Equals*. Not all compositions yield a unique relation as a result. For instance, the composition of relations *During* and *Meets* yields the relation *Before* as result, while the composition of relations *Overlaps* and *During* yields the three possible relations *Starts, Overlaps, and During.* Rules corresponding to compositions of relations *R1, R2* yielding a unique relation *R3* can be expressed in SWRL as follows:

$$R1(x, y) \wedge R2(y, z) \rightarrow R3(x, z)$$

An example of temporal inference rule is the following:

$$During(x, y) \wedge Meets(y, z) \rightarrow Before(x, z)$$

Rules yielding a set of possible relations cannot be represented in SWRL since disjuctions of atomic formulas are not permitted as a rule head. Instead, disjunctions of relations are represented using new relations whose compositions have been defined and asserted into the knowledge base. For example, if the relation *DOS* represents the disjunction of relations *During, Overlaps* and *Starts*, then the composition of *Overlaps* and *During* is expressed as:

$$Overlaps(x, y) \wedge During(y, z) \rightarrow DOS(x, z)$$

In addition to the above, inverse axioms (relations *After, Metby, Overlappedby, Startedby, Contains* and *Finishedby* are the inverses of *Before, Meets, Overlaps, Starts, During* and *Finishes*, respectively) and rules defining the relation holding between two intervals with known starting and ending points (e.g., if the end of *interval*1 is smaller than the start of *interval2*, then *interval1* is *before interval2*) are also asserted into the knowledge base.

Notice that, starting and ending points of intervals are represented using concrete datatypes such as *xsd:date* that support ordering relations. Axioms concerning relations that represent disjunctions of basic relations are defined using the corresponding axioms for these basic relations. Specifically, compositions of disjunctions of basic relations are defined as the disjunction of the compositions of these basic relations. Similarly, the inverse of a disjunction of basic relations is the disjunction of the inverses of these basic relations. For example, the inverse of the disjunction of relations *Before* and *Meets* is the disjunction of the inverse relations of *Before* and *Meets* (*After* and *MetBy*, respectively).

By applying compositions of relations, the implied relations may be inconsistent. Consistency checking is achieved using path consistency [4]. Path consistency is implemented by consecutive applications of suitable instances of the following formula:

[5] http://clarkparsia.com/pellet

$$\forall x, y, k \; R_s(x, y) \leftarrow R_i(x, y) \cap (R_j(x, k) \circ R_k(k, y))$$

representing intersection of compositions of relations with existing relations (the symbol $\cap$ denotes intersection and the symbol $\circ$ denotes composition and symbols R_i, R_j, R_k, R_s denote Allen relations). The formula is applied until a fixed point is reached (i.e., application of rules does not yield new inferences) or until the empty set is reached, implying that the ontology is inconsistent.

An additional set of rules defining the result of intersection of relations holding between two intervals are also introduced. These rules have the form:

$$R1(x, y) \wedge R2(x, y) \rightarrow R3(x, y)$$

where $R3$ can be the empty relation. For instance, the intersection of relation *DOS* (that represents the disjunction of *During, Overlaps and Starts*), and the relation *During* yields the relation *During* as result:

$$DOS(x, y) \wedge During(x, y) \rightarrow During(x, y)$$

Intersection of relations *During* and *Starts* yields the empty relation, and an incosistency is detected:

$$Starts(x, y) \wedge During(x, y) \rightarrow \bot$$

The maximal tractable subset of Allen relations containing all basic relations when applying path consistency comprises of 868 relations [12]. Tractable subsets of Allen relations containing 83 or 188 relations [12] can be used for reasoning as well, offering reduced expessivity, but increased efficiency over the maximal subset. Notice that, the proposed temporal reasoning mechanism affects only relations of temporal intervals and can work equally well in conjunction with either the 4D-fluents or the N-ary relations approach.

The SOWL spatial reasoner implements rules for RCC-8 relations and cone-shaped direction relations using SWRL and OWL 2.0 property axioms. All basic relations are pairwise disjoint. Their inverse relations (e.g., *North* is the inverse of *South*) are defined as well. Furthermore, the point identity relation (O) is handled using the OWL *SameAs* keyword applied on points instead of explicity asserting the relation. Path consistency is implemented by introducing rules defining compositions and intersections of supported relations until a fixed point is reached or until an incosistency is detected [9,13].

The directional relations in SOWL (under the assumption that the line separating two 2D cone shaped areas, e.g., *North* from *North-West*, is part of one of these areas, preserving the disjointness of basic relations) are a special case of the revised Star Calculus [13] and therefore are decided by path consistency when applied on basic relations. Furthermore, given a tractable set of relations and by applying compositions, intersections and inverse operations until a set of relations that is closed under these operations is yielded, the resulting set of relations is also tractable [4]. By applying this method (*closure method*) on the basic directional relations, a tractable set of relations containing the basic directional relations and all relations appearing as the result of their composition is yielded. This set of directional relations is used for directional spatial reasoning.

Reasoning on RCC-8 relations also combines OWL property axioms along with a set of composition rules (i.e., rules defining compositions of RCC-8 relations) and intersection rules. Specifically, relations *DC, EC* and *PO* are symmetrical, and relations *NTPPi* and *TPPi* are inverse of *NTPP* and *TPP*, respectively. In SOWL, the spatial reasoner implements the RCC-8 composition rules defined in [9]. Notice that, extracting spatial relations from the raw spatial data depends on the application and is not part of the reasoning mechanism. In contrast to the model presented in [1], the proposed model is extended with additional relations corresponding to disjunctions of basic relations. Notice that using the full set of relations ($2^8 - 1$ relations in case of RCC-8) leads to intractability since this set cannot be decided by path consistency. However, tractable subsets of the full set are known to exist [4,12]. Such subsets are used in this work offering increased expressive power while retaining tractability.

The resulting OWL ontology it is decidable, since it complies with OWL 2 specifications. and does not contain role inclusion axioms with cyclic dependences or restrictions on composite (e.g., transitive) properties. Introducing the set of temporal qualitative rules of Section 4 retains decidability since rules are DL-safe rules[6] and they apply only on named individuals of the ontology Abox using Pellet (which support DL-safe rules). Furthermore, computing the rules has polynomial time complexity since tractable subsets of Allen's temporal and RCC-8 and directional spatial relations are used. The selection of these tractable subsets is a design decision representing a tradeoff between expressiveness and efficiency.

As shown in [4], by restricting the supported relations set to a tractable subset of Allen's interval algebra (and the corresponding RCC-8 and directional spatial relations), path consistency has $O(n^5)$ worst time complexity (with n being the number of intervals) and is sound and complete. Also, any time interval (or location) can be related with every other interval (or location) by at most k relations, where k is the size of the set of supported relations. Therefore, for n intervals or locations, using $O(k^2)$ rules, at most $O(kn^2)$ relations can be asserted into the knowledge base. Note that, extending the model to the full set of relations would result into an intractable reasoning procedure. Applying the *closure method* over Allen, RCC-8, and directional relations, the minimal tractable sets containing the basic relations consist of 29,49, and 33 relations, respectively. For these sets, the required number of OWL axioms and SWRL rules are 983, 1439, and 964, respectively.

5 Conclusions and Future Work

We introduce SOWL, an ontology capable of handling spatio-temporal information in ontologies. The SOWL model extends our previous work [1] to handle

[6] http://www.w3.org/TR/rif-rdf-owl

both quantitative and qualitative spatial and spatio-temporal information using a sound and complete reasoning method based on path consistency. Incorporating additional forms of information (e.g., size and distance information) and addressing performance and scalability issues for large scale applications are important issues for future research.

References

1. Batsakis, S., Petrakis, E.G.M.: SOWL: Spatio-temporal Representation, Reasoning and Querying over the Semantic Web. In: 6th International Conference on Semantic Systems, Graz, Austria, September 1-3, pp. 1–9 (2010)
2. Welty, C., Fikes, R.: A Reusable Ontology for Fluents in OWL. Frontiers in Artificial Intelligence and Applications 150, 226–236 (2006)
3. Gutierrez, C., Hurtado, C., Vaisman, A.: Introducing Time into RDF. IEEE Trans. on Knowledge and Data Engineering 19(2), 207–218 (2007)
4. Renz, J., Nebel, B.: Qualitative Spatial Reasoning using Constraint Calculi. In: Handbook of Spatial Logics, pp. 161–215. Springer, Netherlands (2007)
5. Katz, Y., Grau, B.: Representing Qualitative Spatial Information in OWL-DL. In: Proc. of Int. Workshop: OWL Experiences and Directions, Galway, Ireland (2005)
6. Randell, D., Cui, Z., Cohn, A.: A Spatial Logic Based on Regions and Connection. In: Proc. 3rd Int. Conf. on Knowledge Representation and Reasoning, pp. 165–176. Morgan Kaufmann, San Mateo (1992)
7. Frank, A.: Qualitative Spatial Reasoning: Cardinal Directions as an Example. Int. Journal of Geographic Information Systems 10(3), 269–290 (1996)
8. Allen, J.F.: Maintaining Knowledge About Temporal Intervals. Communications of the ACM 26, 832–843 (1983)
9. Cohn, A., Bennett, B., Goodayand, J., Gotts, N.: Qualitative Spatial Representation and Reasoning with the Region Connection Calculus. GeoInformatica 1(3), 275–316 (1997)
10. Tappolet, J., Bernstein, A.: Applied Temporal RDF: Efficient Temporal Querying of RDF Data with SPARQL. In: Aroyo, L., Traverso, P., Ciravegna, F., Cimiano, P., Heath, T., Hyvönen, E., Mizoguchi, R., Oren, E., Sabou, M., Simperl, E. (eds.) ESWC 2009. LNCS, vol. 5554, pp. 308–322. Springer, Heidelberg (2009)
11. Stocker, M., Sirin, E.: PelletSpatial: A Hybrid RCC-8 and RDF/OWL Reasoning and Query Engine. In: CEUR Workshop Proceedings, OWLED 2009, vol. 529, pp. 2–31 (2009)
12. Renz, J.: Maximal Tractable Fragments of the Region Connection Calculus: A Complete Analysis. In: Int. Joint Conference on Artificial Intelligence, vol. 16, pp. 448–455 (1999)
13. Renz, J., Mitra, D.: Qualitative Direction Calculi with Arbitrary Granularity. In: Zhang, C., Guesgen, H.W., Yeap, W.-K. (eds.) PRICAI 2004. LNCS (LNAI), vol. 3157, pp. 65–74. Springer, Heidelberg (2004)

Conditional Learning of Rules and Plans by Knowledge Exchange in Logical Agents

Stefania Costantini[1], Pierangelo Dell'Acqua[2], and Luís Moniz Pereira[3]

[1] Dip. di Informatica, Università di L'Aquila, Coppito 67010, L'Aquila, Italy
stefania.costantini@univaq.it
[2] Dept. of Science and Technology - ITN, Linköping University, Norrköping, Sweden
pierangelo.dellacqua@liu.se
[3] Dept. de Informática, Centro de Inteligência Artificial (CENTRIA), Universidade Nova de Lisboa, 2829-516 Caparica, Portugal
lmp@di.fct.unl.pt

Abstract. This paper is related to logical agents and in particular discusses issues related to learning sets of rules from other agents. In principle, the approach extends to agent societies a feature which is proper of human societies, i.e., the cultural transmission of abilities. However, the new knowledge cannot be blindly accepted and incorporated, but should instead be evaluated (and thus possibly discarded) according to its usefulness. We propose a technique and its formalization.

1 Introduction

Adaptive autonomous agents are capable of adapting their behavior according to changes in the environment, by means of some kind of approach. As it is widely acknowledged, the effects of learning should include at least one of the following: (i) the range of behaviors is expanded: the agent can do more; (ii) the accuracy on tasks is improved: the agent can do things better; (iii) the speed is improved: the agent can do things faster.

In this paper, we discuss an approach to learning centered on the possibility of acquiring sets of rules from other agents, namely "learning by being told". We assume in fact that, whatever the formalism they are based upon, the agents that we are considering have a rule-based knowledge base. The acquired sets of rules can either define a reaction to a previously unknown event, or they can represent a plan to reach an objective. Indeed, learning from others is a fairly practical and economical way of increasing abilities, widely used by human beings: in fact, avoiding the cost of learning is an important benefit of imitation. An agent that learns and re-elaborates the learned knowledge may become itself an information producer, from which others can learn in turn.

However, agents should not blindly incorporate the new knowledge. Rather, they should be able to evaluate how useful the new knowledge is, and on this basis decide whether to keep or discard it. To this aim, we propose to associate to the acquired knowledge a specific objective and (possibly) a set of conditions, including a time limit. The purpose is that the new rules should help the agent reach that objective and fulfill the conditions within the given time limit. After a while, the agent will evaluate whether (or to what extent) this has been achieved. More sophisticated conditions/constraints that have to be verified can also be specified. If the evaluation is unsatisfactory, the new

N. Bassiliades et al. (Eds.): RuleML 2011 - Europe, LNCS 6826, pp. 250–265, 2011.

knowledge will be discarded or possibly deactivated for future re-trial in a modified context. There is a clear similarity between our approach and reinforcement learning, where here the action that is to be evaluated is the use of the new knowledge.

The approach is developed in the context of a general agent model proposed in [1], that provides high flexibility in how an agent is built and may evolve. In fact, we equip an agent with forms of understanding and awareness that are "situated" at different control layers. Beyond the basic control layer we introduce in fact a meta-control, where non-trivial supervising and tuning tasks can be performed, based on suitable control and meta-control information. It is at the meta-control level that we introduce the check for the evaluation of the acquired knowledge.

The present work was initiated by the experiments with the prototype implementation presented in [2], developed in DALI [3,4]. Later on, we have empowered the implementation with the temporal-logic-like operators that we introduced in [5,6], and we have performed some experiments in Ambient Intelligent applications [7]. In this paper, we present a further evolution of our approach, which as mentioned has been enriched with a meta-evaluation component, and generalized so as to make it usable in many rule-based agent-oriented approaches.

The paper is organized as follows. In Section 2 we further discuss motivations and potential usefulness of the proposed approach, and we outline the features of our proposal that we illustrate in more detail in Section 3. We introduce the semantics in Section 4. In Section 5 we propose a case-study, formalized in the language of our implementation: namely, we define an artificial fish able to learn from its shoal what to do in certain situations. Finally, we discuss related work and conclude in Section 6. In the Appendix we present the DALI language, as in fact our approach has been implemented in DALI and is under some respects inspired to features of the DALI language and architecture.

2 Motivations and Overall Framework

Learning may allow agents to survive and reach their goals in environments where a static knowledge is insufficient. The environmental context can change, cooperative or competitive agents can appear or disappear, ask for information, require resources, propose unknown goals and actions. Then, agents may try to improve their potential by interacting with other entities so as to perform unknown or difficult tasks.

One of the key features of MAS is the ability of "sub-contracting" computations to agents that may possess the ability to perform them. More generally, agents can try to achieve a goal by means of cooperative distributed problem-solving. However, on the one hand not all tasks can be delegated, and on the other agents may need or may want to acquire new abilities to cope with unknown situations. In our view, an improvement in the effectiveness of MAS may consist in introducing a key feature of human societies, i.e., cultural transmission of abilities. Without this possibility, agents are limited under two important respects:

- they are unable to expand the set of perceptions they can recognize, elaborate on and react to;
- they are unable to expand their range of expertise.

In fact, a well-known and particularly difficult problem in AI is the so-called "brittleness" problem: automated systems tend to "break" when confronted with even slight deviations from the situations specifically anticipated by their designers. Indeed, the flexibility and thus the "intelligence" of agents may increase if they become able not only to refine but also to enlarge their own capabilities. The need of acquiring new knowledge can be recognized by an agent at least in relation to the following situations:

1. There is an objective that the agent has been unable to reach: it has been unable to relate a plan (in the KGP perspective [8]) or intention (in a BDI perspective [9]) to that objective (or desire) and it has to acquire new knowledge (beliefs)[1]. As a particular case, there is a situation the agent is unable to cope with; for instance, there is an exogenous event that the agent does not recognize.

   Use case. An agent located in a network router for security management has to recognize and respond to attacks, and perform repairs. It is impossible to delegate this tasks, it is instead possible in some cases to learn suitable behaviors from trusted agents. For instance, the agent may perceive an unknown external event that presumably corresponds to an unknown attack: it can try to learn how to respond. Also, the agent can recognize an attack, and devise a plan for response and repair, but some step of this plan fails: the agent can try to learn alternative ways to reach the objective.
2. There is some kind of computation that the agent is unable to perform.

   Use case. An agent which acts as a mediator in a data integration context is responsible for reformulating, at runtime, queries defined on a (virtual) mediated schema into the local(actual) schemata of the underlying data sources. Most mediator systems use wrappers to handle the task of data access, data retrieval, and data translation: a wrapper module is able to access specific data sources, extract selected data, and translate source data formats into a common data model designed for the integration system. If a new data source is added to the system, a suitable wrapper may be missing. Delegating the wrapping is unpractical and would in most cases unacceptably spoil efficiency. The agent can try to acquire the wrapper from another and thus "learn" how to cope with the new data format.

Assuming that the agent establishes that it cannot resort to cooperation to get its task performed, it can still resort to cooperation in order to try to acquire the necessary piece of knowledge from another agent. The problems involved in this issue are at least the following: how to ask for what the agent needs; how to evaluate the actual usefulness of the new knowledge; and, how this kind of acquisition can be semantically justified in a logical agent.

In this paper, we make the simplifying assumption that there are ways for asking other agents and obtaining the potentially needed new knowledge. In our view it should not in principle be required that the involved agents be based on the same inference mechanism. It is reasonable however to assume that they are somehow "compatible":

[1] By some abuse of notation, we use the words 'knowledge' and 'belief' as synonyms when referring to agents. In fact, we implicitly consider autonomous agents that are in general not able to resort to 'knowledge' as such but only have their possibly subjective 'beliefs'.

in particular, we assume that all the involved agents are rule-based and are able to incorporate prolog-like sets of rules.

In order to show that indeed we do not neglect this issue, we briefly summarize the learning rules process that we have defined and experimented in the prototype implementation of [2]. This solution is based on the introduction of a *mediator agent* that we called $yellow\_rules\_agent$, keeping track of the agents specialization and reliability, and of which pieces of knowledge they are willing to share with others. When an entity needs to learn something, it asks the $yellow\_rules\_agent$ for the names of agents having a certain specialization and being more reliable, that have declared to possess the needed piece of knowledge. In particular, in our implementation the requester provides the $yellow\_rules\_agent$ with a set of keywords that the latter will try to match with the current contents of its directory.

Once obtained this information, the agent may acquire the desired knowledge by some of them. If the agent will finally decide to incorporate the learned rules in its program because they work correctly, it will also send to $yellow\_rules\_agent$ a message indicating satisfaction. This will result in an increment of the reliability of the agent that has provided the rules. A negative experience will imply an unfavorable dispatch. In the present implementation agents return a numeric value indicating the "level of trust". In updating the level of trust, our $yellow\_rules\_agent$ adopts a model that updates trust only when the information is sufficient, i.e., after a certain number of reports which are in accordance, sent by reliable agents (we have treated this topic at some length in [10]).

However, as described in the Appendix the DALI language provides a communication layer where meta-rules can be defined so as to filter incoming and out-coming communications. These meta-rules are defined independently of the main agent program, so that the communication behavior of an agent can be "tuned" in an elaboration-tolerant way. This allows one to equip an agent with specific meta-rules, according to the strategy of trust management and knowledge retrieval that one wants to adopt. Therefore, our implementation is easily customizable to accommodate any strategy.

In summary, when an agent needs some knowledge it will first obtain the names of one or more agents that it is possible to ask for missing rules. Then it will contact (some of) them according to both the society's and the personal reliability evaluation of these agents. Finally, it will get the required item in a standard format (see e.g. the case-study in Section 5) so as to be able to use it. The exchanged piece of knowledge should include all the *relevant rules* in the sense of [11], i.e., all the rules which are required (directly or indirectly) for actually using that knowledge. Also, acquired rules should be submitted to a suitable renaming process so as not to overlap or interfere with the original knowledge base of the receiver agent.

At this stage, the receiver agent has to face two problems:

(a) establish whether the new knowledge is consistent, or at least compatible, with its knowledge base, and also self-consistent given the facts and the knowledge base. This is a topic which has long been studied in belief revision [12], and that we do not discuss here.
(b) establish whether the new knowledge is actually useful to the purposes for which it has been acquired. If so, it can possibly be definitely asserted in the knowledge base. Otherwise, it can possibly be discarded.

Thus, agents should be able to evaluate how useful the new knowledge is. Similarly to reinforcement learning, techniques must be identified so as to make this evaluation feasible with reasonable efficiency. The discussion of heuristics for the evaluation is outside the scope of this paper, where we intend to outline the general setting, that can however accommodate several possibilities in a modular fashion. In fact, as discussed in the next section, the evaluation will be performed by means of a set of meta-rules that can be modularly defined independently of the "main" agent program. However, in general in our framework usefulness will not be evaluated by a simulation (which would be time-costly and would possibly worsen the problem of brittleness), rather it will be evaluated based on practical usage. This makes the topic of trustworthiness particularly relevant, as knowledge obtained by reliable sources is assumed to be maybe "not so good" but however not harmful for the receiving agent. Simple techniques to cope with this problem that we have already to some extent experimented in our prototype implementation are the following.

1. The new knowledge has been acquired in order to cope with an unknown event so as to fulfill some conditions: the agent can confirm/discharge the new knowledge according to the conditions being satisfied or not.
2. The new knowledge has been acquired in order to reach an objective: the agent can confirm/discharge the new knowledge according to its reaching/not reaching the objective. This evaluation can be related to additional parameters, like e.g. time, amount of resources needed, quality of results.
3. The new knowledge has been acquired for performing a computation: results which are not "sufficiently good" (given some sort of evaluation) lead to the elimination of the related piece of knowledge. The agent can possibly acquire the same type of knowledge from several sources, and compare/combine the results.

When some new knowledge is received, it will be used by the agent, one or more times, to the aim for which it has been acquired. After these trials, the receiver agent is able to assess the usefulness of the new knowledge, and decide whether it can be confirmed (i.e., permanently added to the knowledge base) or discarded. Possibly, rather than totally discarded the new knowledge can be de-activated for future possible re-trial or usage in a modified context.

The main point of our approach and the novel aspect proposed in this paper is that a meta-level device will be responsible of checking the usefulness of the new knowledge. Meta-level axioms will state on which basis the knowledge has to be evaluated. In fact, it is widely recognized (see, e.g., [13]) that coping with unexpected situations involves, for an agent, meta-level monitoring, reasoning about, and, when necessary, altering its own behavior. The agent meta-control, based on a meta-history, will then determine assimilation or discarding or deactivation of the new knowledge, by performing the checks for deciding whether to keep it.

Though our experiments have been performed in DALI, we do not intend to commit to a specific agent formalism or language. In fact, the semantic that we propose in Section 4 is general enough to accommodate many agent-oriented rule-based approaches.

3 The Approach

In this Section we illustrate the specific features of the proposed approach. Let A be an agent defined according to some logic-based agent model $\mathcal{M}$. Assume that A has reached some stage of its operation where it recognizes the need of acquiring new knowledge from the outside in order to cope with a situation that cannot be managed by means of the knowledge which is presently available. A learning step is thus in order.

We introduce the possibility for the agent to learn reactive rules and plans. Once acquired, the new knowledge is stored in two forms.

- As plain knowledge added to the set of beliefs, so that the agent is able to use it.
- As meta-information, that allows the agent to "trace" the new knowledge, in the sense of recording what has been acquired, when and with which expectations. The meta-information allows the agent to perform meta-reasoning on these aspects. If the agent should conclude that the new rules must be removed because the expectations have not been met, the meta-information will be used to locate the rules in the beliefs and remove them.

The syntax that we adopt both in this Section and in the case-study of Section 5 is often reminiscent of logic programming: variables in upper case, constants and predicates in lower case, connective $\leftarrow$ (or :- like in many practical systems) between the head (conclusion) of a rule, and its body (conditions). Syntax is also reminiscent of the DALI language, where some new connectives are introduced (e.g., :> is a new connective that defines a reactive rule).

However, this syntax (which is the syntax of our implementation) is in general terms by no means mandatory, as it is basically aimed at illustrating on the one hand the conceptual elements of the approach and on the other hand how it can be put at work. A suitable variant of the syntax can be developed when applying the approach to some other practical setting.

We may assume for instance that the meta-information associated to a set of rules that an agent learns from the outside for coping with a previously unknown event has the following form:

react(R, event(E), rules(R1,. . . ,Rn), cond(pos(P), neg(N)), time(T))

where R is an identifier for this set of rules (a constant); E specifies the event to be coped with; $R1, \ldots, Rn$ are the acquired reactive rules plus their required auxiliary rules; *cond* specifies in the *pos* part the positive condition(s) that have to be fulfilled after reaction ensues, and in the *neg* part the negative conditions; time specifies the time threshold allowed for condition fulfillment. For example:

react(r1,event(rains), rules((head(rains),body(open_umbrella))),
cond(pos(true),neg(wet)), time())

means that $r1$ is a rule acquired for coping with external event of rain, and that the condition to be fulfilled via the reaction is not getting wet. One rule is provided, in particular a reactive rule where the head is the event that has occurred, i.e., *rains* and the body specifies the action to be undertaken then, i.e., *open_umbrella*.

Analogously, we assume that the meta-information associated to a set of rules that an agent learns from the outside and that represent a plan for coping with an objective that previously could not be reached has the following form:

plan(P, obj(O), steps(S1,. . . ,Sn), cond(pos(P), neg(N)), time(T))

where P is an identifier for this plan (a constant); O specifies the objective to be reached via this plan; $S1, \ldots, Sn$ represent the steps of the plan plus the needed auxiliary rules; *cond* specifies in the *pos* part the positive condition(s) that have to be fulfilled while reaching for the objective, and in the *neg* part the negative conditions; time specifies the time threshold allowed for reaching the objective. Example:

plan(toAirport, objective(atAirport), steps(. . .),
cond(pos(moneySpent $\leq$ *200), neg(lostPlane)), time(18:30))*

meaning that plan *toAirport* is aimed at getting at the airport while spending less that an amount 200 and avoiding to lose the plane.

Supervising activities will in general rely upon a *meta-history* generated during the agent's operation, that integrates in time the existing meta-control information. The meta-history should contain at least a list of:

- which goals have been set and at which time;
- which goals resulted in being successful/failed/timed-out and at which time;
- which incoming external events were known to the agent (and thus have been reacted to) and which ones were unknown instead.

The basic supervising activity can be based upon a mechanism similar to that of the *internal events* of the DALI logic programming agent-oriented language [3,4]. I.e., expectations related to each piece of new knowledge are (automatically) checked from time to time, and actions are undertaken on awareness of their violation.

Various properties that should be respected by the agent behavior can be expressed over the meta-history, also in terms of (adapted versions of) temporal statements, such as those introduced in [5,6]. When goal g is set, a record $goal\_set(g) : t_1, t_2$ is added to the meta-history, meaning that the agent has decided at time t_1 to pursue this goal, that should be achieved by time t_2.

Whenever a goal is either reached, or failed or timed-out, a record of the form $successful(g) : t$ or $failed(g) : t$ or $timed\_out(g) : t$ is added to the meta-history, where t is the time where the meta-conclusion about the outcome has been reached. Assume that time-stamps can be omitted if not needed.

Whenever an external event e that reaches the agent is recognized, a record of the form $known(e) : t$ is added to the meta-history, where t is the time when the event occurred. If instead the event is not recognized, a record of the form $unknown(e) : t$ is instead added.

4 Semantics of Learning by Rule Exchange

We adopt here the general agent model of [1], which does not stick to any specific approach for defining logical agents. Rather, the specific agent model $\mathcal{M}$ that one intends to embrace is an "input parameter" of the overall framework. As we will see however, it is defined in terms of components that, together, constitute and agent program, and is thus particularly suitable to represent rule-based agents.

An *agent* in this framework is characterized by an agent program $\mathcal{P}$ (defined in terms of the specific instance agent model $\mathcal{M}$) and a suitable underlying operational mechanism $\mathcal{U}$ that can be understood as an implementation which is able to run the agent program. $\mathcal{P}$ encompasses an explicit control component $\mathcal{C}$, operating on suitable control information $\mathcal{CI}$.

To the aims of the approach that we are introducing in this paper, below we augment the framework of [1] by introducing a meta-control component $\mathcal{MC}$, operating on suitable control information $\mathcal{MCI}$. Correspondingly, the underlying operational mechanism is enriched by a meta-control mechanism $\mathcal{H}$. Formally:

Definition 1. *Let $\mathcal{M}$ be an agent model. An agent program or simply "agent" $\mathcal{P}$ is a tuple $\langle \mathcal{B}, \mathcal{DI}, \mathcal{SC}, \mathcal{BM}, \mathcal{CS}, \mathcal{A}, \mathcal{C}, \mathcal{CI}, \mathcal{MC}, \mathcal{MCI} \rangle$ of software components where: $\mathcal{B}$ is the set of the agent's beliefs; $\mathcal{DI}$ the set of desires and intentions; $\mathcal{SC}$ is the sensing and communication component; $\mathcal{BM}$ is the belief management; $\mathcal{CS}$ a set of constraints; $\mathcal{A}$ is the set of actions that the agent has devised to perform; $\mathcal{C}$ is the object-level control component and $\mathcal{CI}$ the control information; $\mathcal{MC}$ is the meta-control component and $\mathcal{MCI}$ the meta-control information. Each component of the tuple is defined (or omitted) according to $\mathcal{M}$.*

The operational behavior of the agent will result from the control and meta-control components $\mathcal{C}$ and $\mathcal{MC}$ given the control and meta-control information $\mathcal{CI}$ and $\mathcal{MCI}$. In general, this information will be partly specified in advance and partly updated/generated later. The agent actual functioning in the environment where its is situated relies on underlying control and meta-control mechanisms $\mathcal{U}$ and $\mathcal{H}$ that implement the practical counterpart of the agent model.

Definition 2. *Let $\mathcal{M}$ be an agent model and $\mathcal{P}$ an agent program. Let the initial agent $A_0 = \mathcal{P}$ Let $\mathcal{E} = \{E_0, \ldots, E_n\}$ be a sequence of sets of events. The* underlying control mechanism *$\mathcal{U}$ of $\mathcal{M}$ is a transformation function that transforms (E_0, A_0) step by step into a sequence of agents $A_1, \ldots, A_n$. This transformation exploits the events E_i and the components C_i and $\mathcal{CI}_i$ of every agent A_i ($i \geq 0$):*

$$(E_i, A_i) \xrightarrow{\mathcal{U}(C_i, \mathcal{CI}_i)} A_{i+1}$$

The meta-control acts by means of single steps, similarly to the control. Then, given as before an agent program $\mathcal{P}$, and an initial agent $A_0 = \mathcal{P}$:

Definition 3. *Let $\mathcal{E} = \{E_0, \ldots, E_n\}$ be a sequence of sets of events. The* underlying meta-control mechanism *$\mathcal{H}$ of $\mathcal{M}$ is a transformation function that transform (E_0, A_0) into a sequence of agents $A_1, \ldots, A_n$. This transformation exploits the events E_i and the components $\mathcal{MC}_i$ and $\mathcal{MCI}_i$ of every agent A_i ($i \geq 0$):*

$$(E_i, A_i) \xrightarrow{\mathcal{H}(\mathcal{MC}_i, \mathcal{MCI}_i)} A_{i+1}$$

Based on suitable (meta-)control information, the meta-control can be exploited either in a domain-dependent or in a domain-independent fashion for supervising, checking, tuning many aspects.

Definition 4. *Let $\mathcal{M}$ be an agent model and $\mathcal{P}$ an extended agent program. Given a sequence of sets of events $\mathcal{E} = \{E_0, \ldots, E_n\}$, the* operational behavior *of $\mathcal{P}$ is defined as a sequence of transformation steps interleaving control and meta-control.*

We thus assume to perform some steps of meta-control after a number of steps of control. We do not specify here how many these steps are: they may be specified either in advance (built-in in $\mathcal{U}^{\mathcal{M}}$ and $\mathcal{H}^{M}$) or in the control information.

Our approach to rule exchange fits in this semantic framework: in fact, the history and the meta-history will be included into the control and meta-control information $\mathcal{CI}$ and $\mathcal{MCI}$. Among the actions devised by an agent at each step there may be a request for new rules to other agents. An incoming event can be the arrival of such new rules that will be managed, as exemplified in Section 5, by the meta-control $\mathcal{MC}$ and thus made available to the control component $\mathcal{C}$.

For the declarative semantics, we refer to the general setting introduced in [14]. where changes, either external (e.g., agent's reception of exogenous events) or internal (e.g., courses of actions undertaken based on internal conditions) are considered as producing a corresponding change in the agent program, which is a logical theory, and in its semantics (however defined). For such a change to be represented, we understand this change as the application of a program-transformation function. Also belief revision can be seen as a step of program transformation that in this case results in the updated theory.

In order to cope with adding and deleting the new knowledge we rely on the approach of EVOLP [3], that allows (sets of) rules to be conditionally added or deleted from a program. The EVOLP approach can be smoothly merged into our semantics: some of the evolution steps determined by the meta-control will be (a series of) EVOLP steps that imply requiring, adding or dropping some knowledge pieces.

5 Case Study: An Artificial Fish

The case-study that we consider is in the realm of adaptive controllers, where an adaptive controller can change its behavior in response to changes in the dynamics of the process and the disturbances [15]. In particular, we consider hybrid control systems, i.e., systems whose behavior is defined by processes of diverse characteristics. In our setting, such a controller is modeled ad depicted in Fig 1.

Its architecture consists of two loops. The inner loop is an ordinary feedback loop composed of the process and the controller. The behavior of the controller is adjusted by the outer loop which consists of a supervisory controller, that coincides with the meta-control component. In this context, we assume that the rules included in the controller are not completely available from the beginning, but instead are learned when needed and then evaluated by the supervisor.

We consider as a scenario a virtual marine world inhabited by a variety of fish. They autonomously explore their dynamic world in search for food. Hungry predator fish

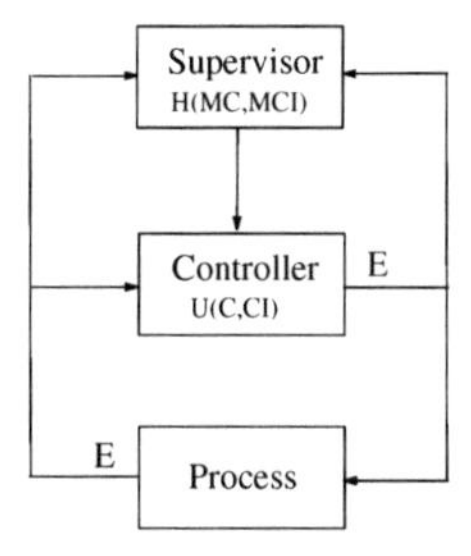

Fig. 1. Supervisory control system architecture

stalk smaller fish who scatter in terror. For simplicity, the behavior of a fish is reduced to eating food and escaping, and is determined by the motivation of it being satiated and safe. In [16], McCarthy considers that "A fish cannot take instruction from a more experienced fish in how to swim better" as an example of a handicap that prevents fish from improving their behavior. Next, we show how our artificial fish can overcome this obstacle by receiving instructions, say from members of its shoal. In the reality, it will most presumably just imitate its mates. In our setting, this behavior is realized by asking for rules that will help it cope with an unknown situation.

Each fish is described by variables with values in the range $[0\ 1]$ with higher values indicating a stronger desire to eat or to avoid predators. In the formalization, we let t denote the clock time of the system.

- *hungry*: it expresses how hungry the fish is and it is approximated by

$$\text{hungry}(t) = \min\{\Delta T \times a, 1\}$$

  where ΔT denotes the time since the last meal and a indicates the appetite of the fish;
- *fear*: it quantifies the fear of the fish by taking into account the distance $d(t)$ of the fish to visible predators

$$\text{fear}(t) = \min\{D/d(t), 1\}$$

  where D indicates how coward the fish is.

The input vector to the controller is

$$\tilde{x}(t) = \begin{bmatrix} hungry(t) \\ fear(t) \end{bmatrix}$$

The fish behavior as well as its internal state (i.e., its beliefs) are modeled by means of an agent program

$$\mathcal{M} = \langle \mathcal{B}, \mathcal{C}, \mathcal{CI}, \mathcal{MC}, \mathcal{MCI} \rangle$$

where $\mathcal{B}$ is the fish's beliefs component (the remaining components are omitted as not necessary for this application). The controller and its supervisor are formalized via $\mathcal{C}$

and $\mathcal{CI}$, and $\mathcal{MC}$ and $\mathcal{MCI}$, respectively. Assume that at some state α the meta-control information component $\mathcal{MCI}_\alpha$ contains the rules

$$\begin{aligned} &\mathit{prop1(E)} \leftarrow \mathit{SOMETIMES\ not\ know(E)} \\ (r1)\ &\mathit{prop1(E)}{:>}\mathit{learn(new\_rule\_for(E))} \\ &\mathit{know(hunger)} \end{aligned}$$

stating that any time there exists an unknown event, then a new rule to cope with that event must be learned. Suppose that at state α the fish knows that it has to search for food when it is hungry. This is formalized in $\mathcal{CI}_\alpha$ with the reactive rule (see Appendix):

$$\mathit{hunger(X)}, X \geq 0.5, \mathit{not\ food} :> \mathit{search(food)}$$

where X is the value of hungriness. Note that the stimuli of the fish (i.e., its input vector $\tilde{x}(t)$) are represented at the controller level via the notion of event. For example, the value v of the stimulus *hungry(t)* of the process is represented as *hunger(v)*.

Suppose that the fish perceives the stimulus of fear. Being this stimulus unknown, $\mathcal{MC}$ requires a new rule to handle the unknown event via the reactive rule (r1).

Assume that at a later state α_2, the meta-control receives in response to its request the rule:

$$\begin{aligned} (r2)\ &\mathit{react(\#2, event(fear), rules(}\ulcorner \mathit{fear(X)}, X \geq 0.5, \mathit{nearby(predator)} :> \mathit{flee}\urcorner), \\ &\mathit{cond(\ pos(true), neg(nearby(predator))), time(10))} \end{aligned}$$

Here, $\ulcorner r \urcorner$ abbreviates the representation of a rule r and $\#2$ is a unique rule identifier. Rule r2 is a meta-rule, and is aimed at producing actual object-level rules to be employed by the fish. In particular, upon reception of r2 rules r4 and r5 are generated in a standard way and added to the fish belief base. r2 looks highly domain-specific, as it is supposed to be provided by some other fish of the shoal. However, its structure is general, and it can be seen as the instance of a meta-meta rule for encoding sets of rules to be shared with other agents. In this setting, we suppose that the supervisor also receives a related *evaluation rule* which is more detailed than r2 and declaratively expresses how to evaluate r2. In principle, different evaluation rules might be associated to the same learned meta-rule.

$$\begin{aligned} (r3)\ &\mathit{eval(\#2, act(pos(nearby(predator)), neg(false)),} \\ &\mathit{obj(\ pos(true), neg(nearby(predator))\ ),} \\ &\mathit{time(20), criticality(high), action(drop\_rule)\ )} \end{aligned}$$

Abstracting away from domain-specific aspects, it can be seen that r3 is an instance of a meta-meta rule and in fact it states (in addition to what already expressed in r2): the activation conditions to start the evaluation (in this case, the simple fact that r2 has been received); the objectives that need to be achieved as well as the time interval to achieve them (in this case they add nothing to r2, but more conditions might be stated), the criticality level of the rule under evaluation; the action to be undertaken if the objectives are not fulfilled within the time constraints. From r3, rules r6-r9 below can be automatically generated.

Then, the extended agent program (representing the overall behavior of the fish) $A_{\alpha 2}$ evolves through a meta-control step as follows:

$$(E_{\alpha_2}, A_{\alpha_2}) \xrightarrow{\mathcal{H}(\mathcal{MC}_{\alpha_2}, \mathcal{MCI}_{\alpha_2})} A_{\alpha_2+1}$$

where

$E_{\alpha_2} = \{r2, r3\}$
$A_{\alpha_2} = \langle \mathcal{B}_{\alpha_2}, \mathcal{C}_{\alpha_2}, \mathcal{CI}_{\alpha_2}, \mathcal{MC}_{\alpha_2}, \mathcal{MCI}_{\alpha_2} \rangle$
$A_{\alpha_2+1} = \langle \mathcal{B}_{\alpha_2+1}, \mathcal{C}_{\alpha_2+1}, \mathcal{CI}_{\alpha_2+1}, \mathcal{MC}_{\alpha_2+1}, \mathcal{MCI}_{\alpha_2+1} \rangle$ (defined below)

The aim of this meta-control step is to incorporate the new learned rules into the extended agent program A_{α_2}. These new rules may be possibly de-activated later if they are considered not useful. When a rule is acquired it is assumed to be *active*. Every learned rule is exploited only if active. Whenever the supervisor takes the decision to drop a rule, it simply drops the assumption of the rule being active. This leaves the way open to a possible later re-activation of the rule.

As mentioned, the rules that are added at the object level so as to make the incoming rules r2 and r3 operative are rules r4-r12 (specified below in the same syntax that we have already employed in Section 3). Rule r4 states that the reactive rule related to r2 (and denoted by its identifier #2) can be applied whenever: (i) it is active and (ii) the corresponding event (left-hand side) has occurred. In this case the reaction (right-hand side) will take place. Rule r5 states that #2 is active. Rule r6 sets the objectives specified in the evaluation rule r3, while r7 asserts the related meta-history item. Rules r8 checks whether the objective has been achieved in time, while r9 asserts the related meta-history item.

Rules r10-r12 can be considered to be specific of this particular agent, and state what to do whenever the evaluation of knowledge acquired from outside is negative. In particular, rule r10 specifies that an objective must never go timed-out (which in this setting subsumes failure) and r11 states what to do if this requirement is violated: drop rule #2. This will consist, as discussed above, in performing an $assert(not\ active(\#2))$ to de-activate the rule.

$(r4)$ *active(#2), fear(X), X* $\geq$ *0.5, nearby(predator) :> flee*
$(r5)$ *active(#2)*

$(r6)$ *obj(#2, cond(pos(true), neg(nearby(predator)))*) $\leftarrow$
nearby(predator), active(#2)
$(r7)$ *obj(#2,X), not obj_set(#2,_), current_time(T) :> assert(obj_set(#2,X):T,T+10)*

$(r8)$ *obj_achieved(#2):T* $\leftarrow$
obj_set(#2,cond(pos(P),neg(N))):T1,T2,
P, not N, current_time(T), T $\leq$ *T2*
$(r9)$ *obj_achieved(#2):T :> assert(obj_achieved(#2):T)*

$(r10)$ *prop3* $\leftarrow$ *NEVER obj_set(#2,_), timed_out(#2)*
$(r11)$ *not prop3 :> drop(#2)*
$(r12)$ *timed_out(#2)* $\leftarrow$
not obj_achieved(#2), obj_set(#2,_):T1,T2
current_time(T), T > T2

The extended agent program A_{α_2+1} is therefore defined as follows (where in EVOLP notation $\circ$ denotes rule assertion):

$$\begin{array}{l} \mathcal{CI}_{\alpha_2+1} = \mathcal{CI}_{\alpha_2} \circ \{r4, r5\} \\ \mathcal{MCI}_{\alpha_2+1} = \mathcal{MCI}_{\alpha_2} \circ \{r5 - r12\} \\ \text{and } \mathcal{MC}_{\alpha_2+1} = \mathcal{MC}_{\alpha_2} \\ \mathcal{B}_{\alpha_2+1} = \mathcal{B}_{\alpha_2} \circ \{\} \\ \mathcal{C}_{\alpha_2+1} = \mathcal{C}_{\alpha_2} \circ \{\} \\ \mathcal{MC}_{\alpha_2+1} = \mathcal{MC}_{\alpha_2} \circ \{\} \end{array}$$

That is, A_{α_2+1} is obtained by updating (wrt. the EVOLP semantics) the components of A_{α_2} with the specified sets of rules.

In this kind of setting, preferences/priorities among events are particularly important (in DALI, such priorities can be provided in the initial control information associated to an agent program). In fact, in our example fear must be given higher priority than hunger. Otherwise, paradoxical behavior may arise: suppose that in a later state α_3, the controller and the supervisor perceive high values for both the fear and the hunger stimuli, and the event that a predator is nearby, that is, $E_{\alpha_3} = \{$*nearby(predator),fear(0.7), hunger(0.6)*$\}$. In such a situation, the controller has two alternative choices: either search for food or flee. Suppose that, without priorities having been stated, it selects the first alternative. Then, it is easy to see that if the time interval of 10 passes by, *time_out(#2)* holds in $\mathcal{MCI}_{\alpha_3+i}$, for some i. Being the objective set for #2, *prop3* holds by rule r10. This will trigger the reactive rule r11 thus resulting in the removal (more precisely, in the de-activation) of rule r4. That is, $\mathcal{CI}_{\alpha_3+i+1}$ would be $\mathcal{CI}_{\alpha_3+i} \circ \{$*assert(not active(#2))*$\}$.

6 Related Work and Concluding Remarks

We have proposed an approach that allows logical agents to adopt a form of learning which consists in improving each agent's skills by acquiring new knowledge from other agents. We believe that this kind of technique can be often useful, and in some application contexts it can even be a key feature.

The problem that we have tackled here is specific to the particular realm of agents, that are able to acquire knowledge from other agents, i.e., from the "society" to which they belong. This is not in contrast with an agent adopting direct ("deep") learning techniques, rather it is complementary. In fact, as deep learning is time-consuming and costly, each agent in a society may apply a combination of deep learning and imitation.

We have illustrated a specific instance of the approach, that we have implemented in DALI, and we have discussed a case-study. The implementation, though prototypical and specific for DALI agents, constitutes a proof-of-concept for the effectiveness of the approach. However, in the overall framework that we have depicted we did not stick to a specific formalism or language for logical agents. In fact, the approach and its semantics are general enough to allow for a wide applicability.

Our approach brings some similarity with the approach of [17,18]. There, a BDI agent not possessing a plan to manage an event, is able to ask agents from a certain set S for such a plan. Symmetrically, an agent can define each of its plans as private, public, or sharable with a set of trusted agents. This copes with the problem of where to find the needed knowledge. Their approaches has been implemented and applied for instance to the scenario of service-oriented computing. Our approach adds the aspect of meta-reasoning for evaluating, activating and de-activating the new knowledge, where this evaluation may in principle affect the level of trust of source agent.

The works in [19,20] are aimed, again in a BDI context, at filtering new percepts according to their expected relevance to the current agent's ongoing desires and intentions. This may also help an agent to understand when to reconsider her deliberations. The latter proposal adopts meta-reasoning techniques for doing so. The principles and methods outlined in these works might be suitably integrated in our approach so as to evaluate how relevant the acquired new knowledge can be to the current context: in our experiments we considered quite rough methods for knowledge evaluation, while the mentioned approaches propose more involved evaluation techniques. As however our approach is modular w.r.t. this aspect, we can in future work implement such techniques in the communication layer of our architecture. In fact, [20] explicitly advocates this kind of meta-reasoning to be performed in a preprocessing module on incoming information. Future work will certainly be concerned with more involved techniques for knowledge retrieval and evaluation. To this aim, we intend to design meta-meta levels for controlling knowledge exchange.

Finally, we intend to fully implement an instance of the proposed framework, accommodating not only DALI agents but also other kinds of agents and architectures.

References

1. Costantini, S., Tocchio, A., Toni, F., Tsintza, P.: A multi-layered general agent model. In: Basili, R., Pazienza, M.T. (eds.) AI*IA 2007. LNCS (LNAI), vol. 4733, pp. 121–132. Springer, Heidelberg (2007)
2. Costantini, S., Tocchio, A.: Learning by knowledge exchange in logical agents. In: Proc. of WOA 2005, From Objects to Agents: Intelligent Systems and Pervasive Computing (2005) ISBN 88-371-1590-3
3. Costantini, S., Tocchio, A.: A logic programming language for multi-agent systems. In: Flesca, S., Greco, S., Leone, N., Ianni, G. (eds.) JELIA 2002. LNCS (LNAI), vol. 2424, p. 1. Springer, Heidelberg (2002)
4. Costantini, S., Tocchio, A.: The DALI logic programming agent-oriented language. In: Alferes, J.J., Leite, J. (eds.) JELIA 2004. LNCS (LNAI), vol. 3229, pp. 685–688. Springer, Heidelberg (2004)
5. Costantini, S., Dell'Acqua, P., Pereira, L.M.: A multi-layer framework for evolving and learning agents. In: Proc. of the AAAI 2008 Workshop on Metareasoning: Thinking about Thinking. Stanford University, AAAI Press (2008)

6. Costantini, S., Dell'Acqua, P., Pereira, L.M., Tsintza, P.: Runtime verification of agent properties. In: Proc. of the Int. Conf. on Applications of Declarative Programming and Knowledge Management, INAP 2009 (2009)
7. Costantini, S., Dell'Acqua, P., Pereira, L.M., Toni, F.: Learning and evolving agents in user monitoring and training. In: Proc. of the AICA Italian Conference, L'Aquila, Italy (2010)
8. Bracciali, A., Demetriou, N., Endriss, U., Kakas, A., Lu, W., Mancarella, P., Sadri, F., Stathis, K., Terreni, G., Toni, F.: The KGP model of agency: Computational model and prototype implementation. In: Priami, C., Quaglia, P. (eds.) GC 2004. LNCS, vol. 3267, pp. 340–367. Springer, Heidelberg (2005)
9. Rao, A.S., Georgeff, M.: Modeling rational agents within a bdi-architecture. In: Proc. of the Second Int. Conf. on Principles of Knowledge Representation and Reasoning (KR 1991), pp. 473–484. Morgan Kaufmann, San Francisco (1991)
10. Costantini, S., Tocchio, A., Verticchio, A.: Communication and trust in the DALI logic programming agent-oriented language. J. of the Italian Association of Artificial Intelligence, Intelligenza Artificiale 2(1) (2005) (in English)
11. Dix, J.: A classification theory of semantics of normal logic programs: I. strong properties. Fundamenta Informaticae 22(3) (1995)
12. Antoniou, G.: Nonmonotonic Reasoning. The MIT Press, Cambridge (1997), with contributions by M.-A. Williams, ISBN 0-262-01157-3
13. Anderson, M.L., Perlis, D.R.: Logic, self-awareness and self-improvement: The metacognitive loop and the problem of brittleness. Journal of Logic and Computation 15(1) (2005)
14. Costantini, S., Tocchio, A.: About declarative semantics of logic-based agent languages. In: Baldoni, M., Endriss, U., Omicini, A., Torroni, P. (eds.) DALT 2005. LNCS (LNAI), vol. 3904, pp. 106–123. Springer, Heidelberg (2006)
15. Åstrom, K.J., Wittenmark, B.: Computer-Controlled Systems. Theory and Design. Prentice Hall Internal Inc., Englewood Cliffs (1990)
16. McCarthy, J.: Making robots conscious of their mental states. Machine Intelligence 15, 3–17 (1995)
17. Ancona, D., Mascardi, V., Hübner, J.F., Bordini, R.H.: Coo-agentspeak: Cooperation in AgentSpeak through plan exchange. In: 3rd International Joint Conference on Autonomous Agents and Multiagent Systems (AAMAS 2004), New York, NY, USA, August 19-23, pp. 696–705. IEEE Computer Society, Los Alamitos (2004)
18. Bozzo, L., Mascardi, V., Ancona, D., Busetta, P.: Coows: Adaptive BDI agents meet service-oriented computing. In: EUMAS 2005 - Proceedings of the Third European Workshop on Multi-Agent Systems, Brussels, Belgium, December 7-8, p. 473. Koninklijke Vlaamse Academie van Belie voor Wetenschappen en Kunsten (2005)
19. Lorini, E., Piunti, M.: Introducing relevance awareness in BDI agents. In: Braubach, L., Briot, J.-P., Thangarajah, J. (eds.) ProMAS 2009. LNCS, vol. 5919, pp. 219–236. Springer, Heidelberg (2010)
20. Koster, A., Koch, F., Dignum, F., Sonenberg, L.: Augmenting bdi with relevance: Supporting agent-based, pervasive applications. In: Proc. of Pervasive Mobile Interaction Device, PERMID 2008 (2008)
21. Costantini, S., D'Alessandro, S., Lanti, D., Tocchio, A.: DALI web site, download of the interpreter (2010), `http://www.di.univaq.it/stefcost/Sito-Web-DALI/WEB-DALI/index.php`, With the contribution of many undergraduate and graduate students of Computer Science, L'Aquila. For beta-test versions of the interpreter (latest advancements) please ask the authors

A The DALI Language and Architecture

DALI [3,4] is an Active Logic Programming language designed for executable specification of logical agents. The DALI interpreter is freely available [21]. A DALI agent is a logic program that contains a particular kind of rules, reactive rules, aimed at interacting with an external environment. The environment is perceived in the form of external events, that can be exogenous events, observations, or messages by other agents. In response, a DALI agent can perform actions, send messages, adopt goals, etc. The reactive and proactive behavior of the DALI agent is triggered by several kinds of events: external events, internal, present and past events.

External events are syntactically indicated by the postfix *E*. When an event arrives to the agent from its "external world", the agent can perceive it and decide to react. The reaction is defined by a reactive rule which has in its head that external event (or, possibly, a conjunction of external events). The special token :>, used instead of :-, indicates that reactive rules performs forward reasoning. The agent remembers to have reacted by converting an external event into a *past event* (postfix *P*).

However, when an agent perceives an event from the "external world", it doesn't necessarily react to it immediately: it has the possibility of reasoning about the event, before (or instead of) triggering a reaction. In this situation, the event is called present event and is indicated by the postfix *N*.

In DALI, actions (indicated with postfix *A*) may have or not preconditions: in the former case, the actions are defined by actions rules, in the latter case they are just action atoms. An action rule is just a plain rule, but in order to emphasize that it is related to an action, we have introduced the new token :<, thus adopting the syntax $action :< preconditions$. Similarly to events, actions are recorded as past actions.

Internal events make a DALI agent agent proactive. An internal event is syntactically indicated by the postfix *I*, and its description is composed of two rules. The first one contains the conditions (knowledge, past events, procedures, etc.) that must be true so that the reaction (in the second rule) may happen. Thus, a DALI agent is able to react to its own conclusions. Internal events are automatically attempted with a default frequency customizable by means of directives in the initialization file.

The DALI communication architecture consists of four layers. The first layer implements the DALI/FIPA communication protocol and a filter on communication, i.e. a set of rules that decide whether or not to receive or send a message. The second layer includes a meta-reasoning user-customizable module that tries to understand message contents, possibly based on ontologies and/or on forms of commonsense reasoning. The third layer consists of the DALI interpreter. The fourth layer implements a filter for the out-coming and incoming messages.The DALI/FIPA protocol consists of the main FIPA primitives, plus few new primitives which are particular to DALI.

A Framework for the Automatic Extraction of Rules from Online Text

Saeed Hassanpour, Martin J. O'Connor, and Amar K. Das

Stanford Center for Biomedical Informatics Research,
Stanford, CA 94305, U.S.A.
{saeedhp,martin.oconnor,amar.das}@stanford.edu

Abstract. The majority of knowledge on the Web is encoded in unstructured text and is not linked to formalized knowledge, such as ontologies and rules. A potential solution to this problem is to acquire this knowledge through natural language processing and text mining methods. Prior work has focused on automatically extracting RDF- or OWL-based ontologies from text; however, the type of knowledge acquired is generally restricted to simple term hierarchies. This paper presents a general-purpose framework for acquiring more complex relationships from text and then encoding this knowledge as rules. Our approach starts with existing domain knowledge in the form of OWL ontologies and Semantic Web Rule Language (SWRL) rules and applies natural language processing and text matching techniques to deduce classes and properties. It then captures deductive knowledge in the form of new rules. We have evaluated our framework by applying it to web-based text on car rental requirements. We show that our approach can automatically and accurately generate rules for requirements of car rental companies not in the knowledge base. Our framework thus rapidly acquires complex knowledge from free text sources. We are expanding it to handle richer domains, such as medical science.

Keywords: Knowledge Acquisition, Rule Extraction, Natural Language Processing, Text Mining, Ontology, SWRL, OWL.

1 Introduction

There is an increasing need for RDF and OWL ontologies to support the Semantic Web and intelligent systems. The linked data community (linkeddata.org), for example, is focused on providing large amounts of information in the form of ontologies. Knowledge acquisition remains a bottleneck; this problem has driven research in the area of acquiring knowledge directly from unstructured sources [1-4]. Researchers have attempted to glean information from publicly available text-based sources using a variety of standard natural language processing (NLP) techniques. One of the earliest goals of these efforts was finding terms in text to acquire vocabularies. Commonly available text processing tools can perform tasks such as word stemming, and tools like WordNet [5] can find synonyms or identify parts of speech. The vocabularies

N. Bassiliades et al. (Eds.): RuleML 2011 - Europe, LNCS 6826, pp. 266–280, 2011.

created by these tools can be used to generate domain ontologies, which can be used to process documents with similar content.

Recent work has attempted to infer logical relationships between terms in a source. These efforts have used more complex NLP techniques to process text. Instead of simply extracting terms, these techniques analyze the grammatical structure of sentences to determine term usage. They then infer possible is-a relationships between terms, which can be used to build classification hierarchies. The hierarchies themselves are useful, and can greatly support intelligent search capabilities. For example, when users search for a particular term, the search mechanism can consider not just direct term matches, but also the hierarchies of both the term and candidate matches. This expansion can produce more intelligent search results.

There has been much less work in extracting more complex relationships from text. In particular, rule-like information is common in many sources, but has not been the focus of prior work. Online documents frequently contain rule-like specifications of regulations or policies or rule-like definition of concepts. Common examples include item return policies, car rental requirements, late fee policies, and shipping rate calculations. For instance, a typical example of eligibility to rent requirements from a car rental company could look as follows:

All Drivers Must: Meet the renting location's minimum age requirements. Have a valid driver's license. Present a major credit card in their name at the time of rental or meet the location's cash qualification requirements.

Clearly, these rule-like requirements cannot be represented as ontology term hierarchies. Instead, a representation encoding the knowledge using a rule-like formalism is required. Automatically acquiring this type of knowledge can be of great benefit in developing rule bases directly from online content.

A number of challenges must be met to address this knowledge acquisition requirement. These challenges include:

(1) The ability to recognizing domain concepts in the text, such as, for example, *drivers*, *locations*, and *minimum age requirements*. To robustly detect concept use, a concept recognition mechanism must employ text processing techniques such as synonym expansion and word morphology. Compound expressions referring to concepts must also be handled so that, for example, *major credit card* and *charge card* can be determined to be equivalent.
(2) Words or phrases representing relationships between domain concepts must also be detected. In the above example, words like *present* and *have* represent these relationships. Recognizing these relationships requires text processing techniques similar to those required for concept recognition.
(3) The grammatical structure of sentences in the text must be analyzed to identify the way in which these relationships are used to refer to domain concepts. Recognizing the relationships between domain concepts is key to acquiring rule-like information from text. Ideally, each domain concept recognized in text should be linked to another domain concept through these relationships to determine how the concepts are related to each other. Performing this linkage requires a

grammatical analysis of the source text to identify the different parts of speech in which the concepts and relationships are used. The results of this analysis can then be used to construct chains of relationships between domain concepts, which can then be formed into rules. This process must also determine conjunctive and disjunctive use of these relationships in text.

We address these challenges with a framework for acquiring rule-like information from unstructured free text. In this paper, we focus on processing short segments of text, each typically the length of a paragraph, that contains a single regulation or requirement. The context of the text (i.e., the domain) will be assumed, as opposed to the case where knowledge about the goal or context of the text is required. The goal of the method is to generate a single rule from each text segment. Our approach uses the OWL ontology language and its associated Semantic Web Rule Language (SWRL). The approach requires the existence of an OWL-based domain ontology describing the core concepts in the source text. It uses domain concepts and concept relationships represented in this ontology. It also uses existing domain rules written in SWRL. We apply NLP techniques to identify new rules within the text. In particular, our framework uses WordNet to help identify terms in free text and then uses the Stanford Parser to find grammatical relationships between these terms [6]. In analyzing grammatical relationships, our framework uses OWL concepts and SWRL rules in the existing domain ontology to generate new SWRL rules encoding chains of relationships between concepts in the source document. We show how SWRL's tight integration with OWL supports a principled extraction process and can help ensure semantic consistency when adding new rules.

The paper is organized as follows. We first overview related work. We then describe the sub-methods within our framework. Next, we describe the development of a Java-based implemented of this system. We then present an evaluation based on automatically generating a set of SWRL rules from online text-based car rental requirements. We end with a discussion of the results and conclude that our framework can accurately generate new rules from text.

2 Related Work

Automatic acquisition of rule-like knowledge from data has a long history. The association rule mining field is perhaps the most active [7], though a variety of other methods have been used [8]. The general aim is to discover important relationships between variables in structured data that can be encoded as rules. The expansion of online information repositories has steered work towards extracting knowledge from less structured data sources. In the scientific field, the availability of large number of abstracts and full-text publications has driven the development of many new approaches. Initial work concentrated on automatically classifying the subjects of papers in a corpus; this information was used to find papers related to particular research questions. Further work employed deeper textual analysis techniques to infer relationships between the entities described in the papers themselves. For example, Madkour *et al.* [9] described a method for extracting interactions between proteins from MEDLINE papers. Efforts on non-scientific areas include extracting rules from Wikipedia [10].

Many knowledge extraction efforts have used ontologies in the key role of providing structured terminologies. Recently, researchers have begun to attempt to derive ontologies from text by automatically extracting domain terms from a corpus and finding pair-wise relationships between them [1-4, 11-15]. A variety of approaches have been adopted, and range from simple term matching to techniques that use word stemming and compound word recognition. In some cases, a domain ontology provides an initial controlled vocabulary for identifying terms. Other approaches attempt to generate a domain ontology from scratch using an analysis of the core terms in a corpus. Another focus of work attempts to construct a subsumption hierarchy from the terms. Again, a variety of techniques are used to find such relationships. Documents can be analyzed for syntactic patterns that indicate relationships between terms. Template-based approaches have been used to encode syntactic patterns. Statistical methods have also been adopted to detect term co-occurrence, which can indicate relationships. These approaches are often combined, but remain limited to inferring relationships between pairs of concepts.

In contrast, acquiring domain knowledge in form of rules is more challenging because the relationships rules can model are significantly more complex [16]. Instead of detecting relationships between pairs of concepts, these approaches must automatically link a series of these relationships together to build compound requirements. These compound requirements can be encoded as rules. Few approaches to ontology-based rule extraction are described in the literature. Duboue and McKeown described a system for capturing content selection rules from free text [17]. Content selection rules identify the parts of a corpus that are relevant to a certain topic. Their method used a Frame-based knowledge representation format to drive statistical methods to produce these types of rules from short segments of user-supplied free text. This text is assumed to contain relevant information that can be encoded using rules. Manine *et al.* [4] presented an approach for acquiring gene interaction rules from text, which were then encoded using ontologies. The approach used an existing ontology as an hypothesis language. This ontology was supplied as input to an inductive logic algorithm, which then used it to learn inference rules from pre-selected free text. Park and Lee [18] developed an ontology-based method to extract rules semi-automatically from web documents. Like other rule acquisition approaches, the method required an existing domain ontology and manual selection of relevant web pages as method input. This approach used very basic NLP techniques based on WordNet so was limited in its ability to handle complex source text. Of note in this approach was its use of the eXtensible Rule Markup Language (XRLM) [19]. This XML-based language was designed to mark up web pages that contain rule-like content. It included a sub-language called Rule Identification Markup Language (RIML). This sub-language was designed to allow users to tag implicit rules in a web page and to identify the components of such rules. It could be used to automatically acquire rules from text. However, XRML or RIML were not widely adopted and few systems have used it for automatic rule acquisition.

A general limitation of the rule acquisition methods described here is that they did not support a general-purpose rule extraction framework, and were restricted to use in particular domains.

3 Methods

Our rule extraction framework requires two inputs: existing knowledge and free text. The knowledge is in the form of an OWL ontology that describes a particular domain. In addition to basic definitions of core concepts in the domain, the ontology of existing knowledge contains SWRL rules that encode deductive relationships. The free text encodes knowledge of the domain in unstructured natural language in English. The goal is to formalize new knowledge in the text as SWRL rules. Each piece of text encoding a rule may be a few sentences long and is assumed to contain requirements or regulations. In our current framework, the text has been already identified in the source to contain rule-like information about concepts in the domain ontology.

Our framework relies upon the existing SWRL rules to serve as templates that can guide the extraction of new rules. Unlike many other rule languages, SWRL is not general purpose and is designed work directly with OWL. All entities referred to in a SWRL rule must exist in the OWL ontology in which the rules are developed. SWRL provides six main types of SWRL atoms that govern interactions between SWRL and OWL (see Table 1). The rules themselves have a simple Horn-like structure with a body and a head. Bodies and heads contain conjunctions of atoms. Of the six atom types, class and object property are the primary source of information about entities in an ontology and the relationships between them. These atoms refer to OWL classes, which capture classification information about individuals, and OWL object properties, which relate individuals to each other. Our method currently focuses on these two atom types, though we plan to extend it to support built-in and data valued property atoms, which will allow the representation of numerical criteria in rules.

Table 1. The six types of SWRL atoms defined by the SWRL Submission. Examples of each are shown. Entity names such as `Person` and `hasLicense` refer to OWL classes or properties.

SWRL Atom Type	Example Atom
Class atom	`Person(?x), Car(?y)`
Individual property atom	`hasLicense(?x, ?y)` `hasLocation(?x, ?y)`
SameAs/DifferentFrom atom	`sameAs(?x, ?y)` `differentFrom(?x, ?y)`
Data valued property atom	`hasName(?x, "Joe")` `hasAge(?x, ?g)`
Built-in atom	`swrlb:notEqual(?state, "CA")` `swrlb:lessThan(?g, 18)`
Data range atom	`xsd:double(?x)`

3.1 Expansion of Domain Ontology Terms

As noted, we start with an existing OWL ontology that encodes domain information as a set of OWL classes and object properties. We use the names of these OWL entities to produce an expanded list of equivalent or related terms. If the OWL entity names are meaningful in the domain, we use these terms; otherwise, we use the RDFS label annotation property associated with each entity. In the first step, we focus on the OWL properties from the ontology. These property names are the initial set of terms that are the basis of matching text to rules. Using WordNet, we extend the list of relevant terms for each property to the list of synonym terms and their morphological variations. For example, we extend the verb `present` to terms such as `show`, `submit`, and `give`. These terms are used in text analysis to detect equivalent relationships. We perform an equivalent process to expand the names of OWL domain classes. This expanded list is used to detect equivalent domain concepts referred to in text.

3.2 Finding Dependencies in Text

In the second step, we use the Stanford Parser (available at nlp.stanford.edu) to analyze the grammatical relationships in each sentence in the text. The Stanford Parser is a statistical parser that finds the most likely parse tree for a piece of text (limited to 71 words), based on the parse trees it has been trained on. The parser presents the relationships in the parse tree as predicates representing binary relationships between pairs of terms. The predicates are abbreviations for grammatical relationships. Predicate arguments are terms from the text. Table 2 shows a selection of these abbreviations.

Table 2. Some abbreviations used by the Stanford Parser to denote grammatical relationships

Abbreviation	Explanation
Det	determiner
nsubject	nominal subject
Aux	auxiliary
Amod	adjectival modifier
nn	noun compound modifier
dobj	direct object

For example, the parser identifies nine dependencies in the sentence *All drivers must meet the renting location's minimum age requirements*. These dependencies are:

det`(drivers-2, all-1),` *nsubj*`(meet-4, drivers-2),` *aux*`(meet-4, must-3),`
det`(requirements-10, the-5),` *amod*`(requirements-10, renting-6),`
nn`(requirements-10, location's-7),` *amod*`(requirements-10, minimum-8),`
nn`(requirements-10, age-9),` *dobj*`(meet-4, requirements-10)`

The number following each term indicates its position in the sentence. These relationships can be displayed in a typed dependency graph. Figure 1 shows a graph for

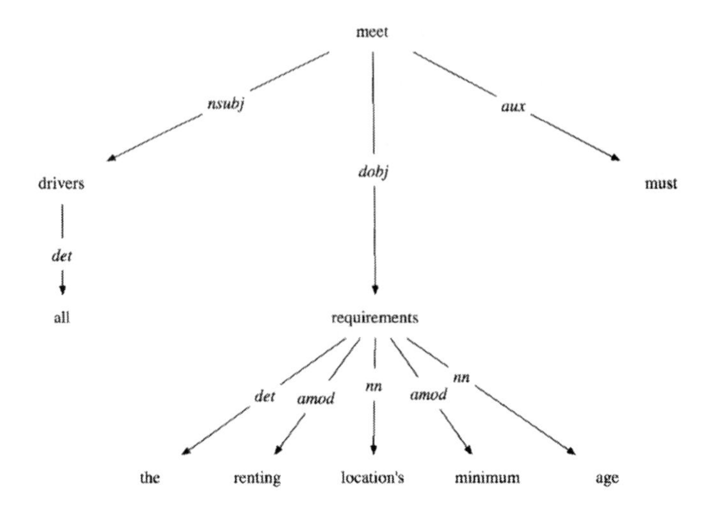

Fig. 1. Typed dependencies in the sentence *All drivers must meet the renting location's minimum age requirements* that were extracted by the Stanford Parser. Nodes are text terms and labeled edges represent relations.

this sample sentence. Text terms are shown as nodes. The dependency between two terms is depicted as a labeled edge. The direction of an edge is from the first argument of the binary relation to the second.

We take each sentence in the source text and feed them to the parser. We then use the results of this analysis to help find the relationships between terms in the text.

3.3 Finding Relationships in the Text

In the third step, we first search the text for relations corresponding to OWL properties in the domain ontology. As noted, we use the expanded synonym and morphological term list when performing this match. In the example sentence, only the word *meet* corresponds to an OWL property in the input ontology. After finding all relevant terms, we extract the dependencies involving them. Our expansion process considers only dependencies that indicate a direct object relationship. For instance, from the three dependences that involved *meet*, we only consider the direct object dependency between it and *requirements*. The noun subject relationship to *drivers* and the auxiliary relationship to *must* are secondary. Terms that are not matched are dropped so irrelevant text and dependencies are effectively ignored.

After finding first-level dependencies, we expand them by considering each dependent's dependencies. We continue these expansions iteratively until we capture all related terms from the domain ontology, effectively calculating the transitive closure of the first-level direct-object dependencies. Figure 2 shows the dependency expansion of *meet* from the sample sentence.

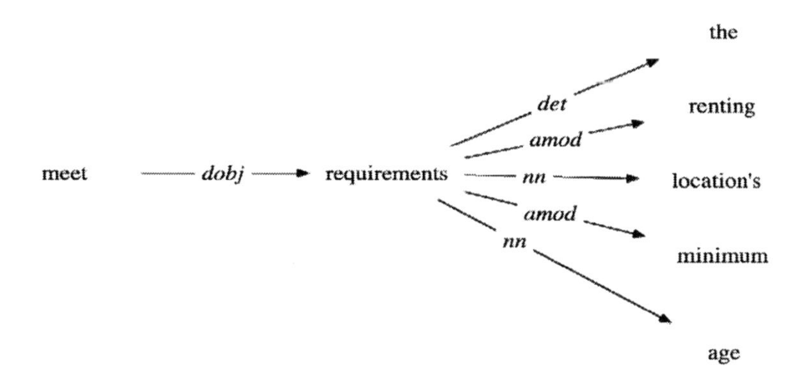

Fig. 2. Expansion of dependencies for the OWL ontology property related term *mee*t

After constructing the dependency graph for an OWL property, we extract all the node terms and consider them as related terms. Then, we sort these terms based on their original positions in the text and combine them together to build a dependent phrase. For example, for *meet* we produce the dependent phrase *the renting location's minimum age requirement*. This dependent phrase is assumed to be a domain concept.

3.4 Finding Concepts in Text

After we find dependent phrases, we try to identify OWL classes in the domain ontology corresponding to each phrase. To accomplish this alignment, we use the Needleman-Wunsch global sequence alignment algorithm [20], which is commonly used in bioinformatics to align DNA and protein sequences. It employs a dynamic-programming approach to find the best sequence alignment based on the scores of all possible alignments for two sequences. The scores depend on matches, mismatches, and gaps in each candidate alignment. We use an affine gap penalty approach, in which the gap penalty decreases linearly with the size of the gap in the alignment.

Using the Needleman-Wunsch algorithm, we compare a dependent phrase to the expanded synonym and morphological term list for all the OWL classes in the ontology to find the class that produced the best alignment score. For example, for the dependent phrase *the renting location's minimum age requirement*, we find `minimum_age_requirement` as a corresponding class.

3.5 Assembling Rule Bodies

As the next step we need to assemble each rule body using the relationships that were identified in the last step. The first stage of this process involves assembling chains of object property atoms, where each atom property contains an OWL object property corresponding to a relationship identified in the source text. If no disjunctions are identified by the parser, we generate conjunctions of relevant object property atoms. Since SWRL does not support disjunctions of atoms, rules containing disjunctions must be handled differently. Such rules can be handled by breaking such a rule into multiple separate rules. In our extraction process, we use the Stanford Parser to identify disjunctive relationships between text terms corresponding to OWL properties. We generate multiple rules for these rules containing disjunctive relationships. For example, if a requirements rule specified that a driver must present a driver's license plus cash or credit card payment in order to rent, we generate two rules. One covers the driver's license and cash requirements, and the other covers driver's license and credit card requirements. Conceptually, our method considers these multiple rules represent a single rule.

3.6 Linking Relationships to Domain Concepts

After generating rules with property atoms using the relevant OWL properties, we determine the OWL classes that type the individuals associated with the subject and object arguments of these atoms. This process ensures that we restrict generated rules to refer to specific domain concepts. Otherwise, rules could match any arbitrary entities that are associated through matched OWL properties. To extract the type of the subject individuals in an atom, we use the OWL domain restriction of the associated property, if present. The OWL class corresponding to the dependent phrase is used as the type of property atom's object individual. In addition, we use the associated properties' range classes as a sanity check in our rule extraction process. In our semantic checking, we verify that the corresponding class extracted from the text for the object argument was the same as, or is a subclass of, the class that specified as the range of the OWL property. After finding appropriate classes for all properties atoms, we generate class atoms for them. For example, for the *meet* property from the earlier example, we generate the following SWRL atoms:

```
Person(?a) ^ minimum_age_requirement(?b) ^ meet(?a, ?b)
```

Here, classes `Person` and `minimum_age_requirement` are identified through the domain and range of the `meet` object property. If no domain or range are present, no class atoms are generated.

3.7 Generating Rule Heads

As a final step, we generate rule heads. We use the structure of existing SWRL rules as templates to complete the head part of the each rule. We used these templates to extract rule heads for generated rule bodies. For example, the completed rule for the earlier sample sentence is as follows:

```
Person(?a) ^ minimum_age_requirement(?b) ^ meet(?a, ?b) ^ national(?c)
                    -> qualifiedToRentFrom(?a, ?c)
```

A limitation of our method is that we currently only handle rule heads that already exist in the rule base. The domain and range of the head property is used to align the variables in the head with the variables from the corresponding types in the body.

4 Implementation and Results

We developed a Java based implementation of our method. The implementation uses the latest 3.0 release of WordNet and version 1.6.5 of the Stanford Parser. Version 3.4.4 of the Protégé-OWL API was use to work with OWL ontologies and SWRL rules.

To evaluate our framework, we chose text on rental requirements for car rental companies. We chose all companies linked to the airport websites of the four largest cities in California [21]: Los Angeles International Airport (LAX), San Diego International Airport (SAN), San Jose International Airport (SJC), and San Francisco International Airport (SFO). We found online regulations for 17 car rental companies in these airports and used company web sites as sources of text for car rental requirement rules. We manually identified relevant text on basic car rental requirements. We used six of the 17 companies as training cases to develop an input domain ontology containing terms and relationships referred to in the training text. The six training cases were chosen because their car rental requirement information exceeded the 71-word limit for input into the Stanford Parser and thus could not be processed directly by our approach. We encoded the rental regulations of these six companies as SWRL rules. We then tested our framework on the other 11 cases, which we have provided as an Appendix. Table 3 provides a list of companies and whether they are located in LAX, SAN, SJC or SFO. The table also specifies whether or not information from the company was used as a training or test case.

Table 3. Car rental companies, their airport locations and their roles in our evaluation

No.	Company	Location(s)	Usage
1	Ace	SAN	Testing
2	Advantage	LAX, SAN, SJC	Training
3	Alamo	LAX, SAN, SFO, SJC	Testing
4	Avis	LAX, SAN, SFO, SJC	Testing
5	Budget	LAX, SAN, SFO, SJC	Training
6	Dollar	LAX, SAN, SFO, SJC	Training
7	Enterprise	LAX, SAN, SFO, SJC	Testing
8	Fox	LAX, SAN, SFO, SJC	Testing
9	Hertz	LAX, SAN, SFO, SJC	Testing
10	Midway	SAN	Testing
11	National	LAX, SAN, SFO, SJC	Testing
12	Pacific	SAN	Testing
13	Payless	LAX, SAN	Testing
14	Renty	SAN	Testing
15	Thrifty	LAX, SAN, SFO, SJC	Training
16	TravCar	SAN	Training
17	West Coast	SAN	Training

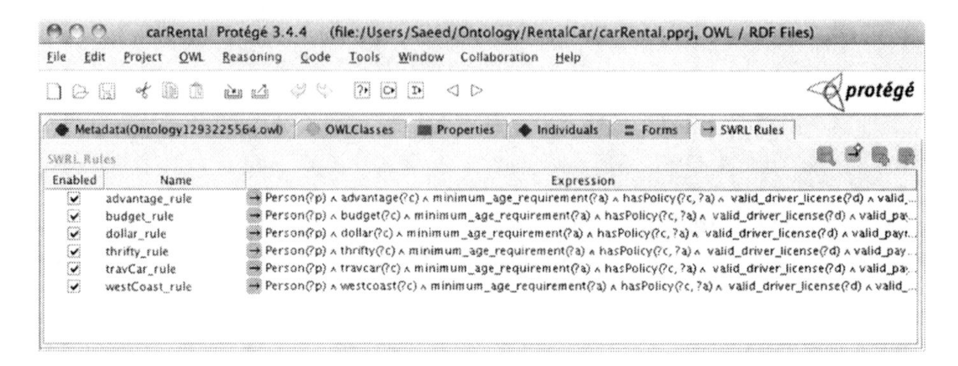

Fig. 3. Screen shot of Protégé-OWL showing set of user-developed SWRL rules describing car rental requirements for the six companies in the training set

Using the text from the six training rental companies, we first developed an OWL domain ontology describing the core entities referred to in the requirements text. The ontology contained classes representing persons, rental companies, policies, and so on, and object properties representing relationships between those entities. We also created classes representing the testing rental companies. We then developed SWRL rules that encoded the requirements for each company in the training set (shown in Figure 3). For each testing company, we applied our framework to its extracted text to generate new requirements rules.

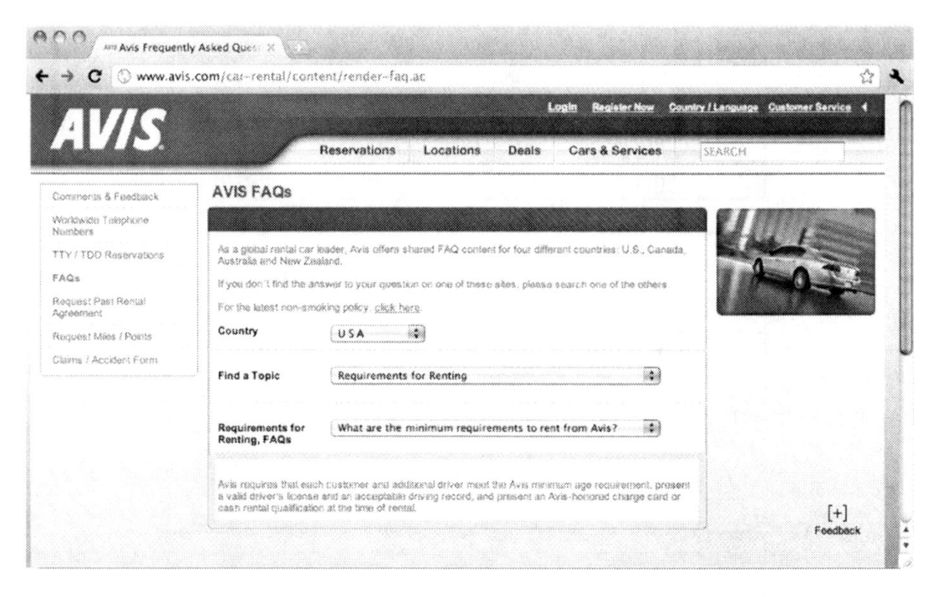

Fig. 4. The core minimum requirements for renting a car from Avis. The text in the box was used as an input in our method to automatically extract a car rental requirement.

As an example, Avis's web page (shown in Figure 4) provides information about basic requirements that must be met when renting a car [22]:

Avis requires that each customer and additional driver meet the Avis minimum age requirement, present a valid driver's license and an acceptable driving record, and present an Avis-honored charge card or cash rental qualification at the time of rental.

We applied our method on the text from the web site. The Stanford Parser correctly identified the disjunction caused by the *or* in the final clause and our method. The compound term *Avis-honored charge card* was identified as the object of the *meets* relationship and the term analysis indentified its closest match as the `credit_card` class. The following two rules were generated:

```
Person(?a) ^ credit_card(?b) ^ present(?a,?b) ^
minimum_age_requirement(?c) ^ present(?a,?c) ^ valid_driver_license(?d)
^ present(?a,?d) ^ acceptable_driving_record(?e) ^ present(?a,?e) ^
avis(?f)
-> qualifiedToRentFrom(?a ,?f)

Person(?a) ^ cash_qualification(?b) ^ present(?a,?b) ^
minimum_age_requirement(?c) ^ present(?a,?c) ^ valid_driver_license(?d)
^ present(?a,?d) ^ acceptable_driving_record(?e) ^ present(?a,?e) ^
avis(?f)
-> qualifiedToRentFrom(?a,?f)
```

The equivalent requirements from the Enterprise web site are [23]:

All Drivers Must: Meet the renting location's minimum age requirements. Have a valid driver's license. Have a major credit card in their name at the time of rental or meet the location's cash qualification requirements.

Our method extracted the following two rules from this text:

```
Person(?a) ^ credit_card(?b) ^ has(?a, ?b) ^ valid_driver_license(?c) ^
has(?a, ?c) ^ minimum_age_requirement(?d) ^ meet(?a, ?d) ^
enterprise(?e) -> qualifiedToRentFrom(?a, ?e)

Person(?a) ^ cash_qualification(?b) ^ meet(?a, ?b) ^
valid_driver_license(?c) ^ has(?a, ?c) ^ minimum_age_requirement(?d) ^
meet(?a, ?d) ^ enterprise(?e) -> qualifiedToRentFrom(?a, ?e)
```

Out of 11 test cases, we verified that in 9 cases we generated one or more rules that accurately reflected the rental company's requirements. That is, the generated rule or rules contained all relationships specified in the text. For two cases (Fox and Pacific), the generated rules were incomplete. They lacked four relationships that used terminology (such as contact phone number) not present in the training set. Our approach found 96 out of the 100 relevant relationships present in the text of the test set; we calculated that our approach provided a recall of 96%. The resulting rules did not contain any relationships that were not relevant; the precision was thus 100%.

5 Discussion

We have presented a novel framework for acquiring complex domain knowledge from text and then encoding this information as new rules. Our approach addresses a major shortcoming of prior work in which extracted knowledge is largely in the form of properties between classes or subsumption hierarchies. Considerable amounts of rule-based knowledge is available online, and our framework provides an opportunity to extend an existing rule base with new rules. Our work can thus enable the automated expansion of the rule base as new web content appears and potentially the maintenance of the rule base if the rule-based information changes.

Our approach combines OWL-based domain ontologies with NLP techniques to capture this knowledge and then represents it using the SWRL rule language. We performed an initial evaluation of this framework by applying it to a set of online regulations in the car rental domain. This approach successfully acquired rules from these sources with a high level of accuracy. The close relationship between OWL and SWRL allows us to generate rule that are not only informed by the domain ontology but work directly with that domain ontology once generated. A further advantage is that the generated rules can be validated semantically against the ontology.

We intend to analyze our approach over a variety of different sources to determine its robustness. The car rental domain that we chose is arguably simple in nature, and the accuracy of the results we achieved may be less with more complex domains. In our future work, we would thus like to identify situations in which matches are poor. The framework we have developed is generalizable, however. We thus expect that improving the robustness of certain steps in the framework can incrementally improve accuracy. In particular, we will focus on three core areas that can benefit from deeper analyses: (1) the ability to acquire information from text with complex grammatical content; (2) the sensitivity of matching to named OWL entities in the domain ontology; and (3) the ability to acquire numerical criteria from text and encode them in rules.

A shortcoming our work is that users must manually develop a detailed OWL domain ontology before applying the method. This shortcoming is shared with other similar rule extraction approaches [4, 17, 19]. A significant amount of current work is directed at automatically acquiring domain ontologies from free text. We intend to combine our method with one or more of these approaches to determine the feasibility of automatically seeding a domain ontology without user intervention. An additional shortcoming of our current approach is that users must manually select the text containing rule-like information and present that text to the method. In ongoing separate work, we are developing a method to automate this process so that the appropriate text is automatically selected for our framework. We have already developed an approach to automatically find sections of publication that correspond to SWRL rules [24]. We intend to combine this method with the framework described in the paper to produce a fully automated mechanism for finding and generating rules from text. By combining these approaches, we plan to create an overall learning system that can start with an existing set of rules, identify online text corresponding to rules, and automatically extract out new rules. By including user feedback on the accuracy within this knowledge acquisition loop, we expect that the system can iteratively improve and thus robustly transform unstructured rule-based knowledge on the web to the more formal representation needed for reasoning.

Acknowledgments. This research was supported in part by National Institutes of Health grants R01LM009607 and R01MH87756.

References

1. Yangarber, R., Grishman, R., Tapanainen, P., Huttunen, S.: Automatic Acquisition of Domain Knowledge for Information Extraction. In: Proceedings of COLING 2000: The 18th International Conference on Computational Linguistics, Saarbrücken, Germany (2000)
2. Maedche, A., Staab, S.: Ontology learning for the Semantic Web. IEEE Intell. Sys. 16(2) (2001)
3. Alani, H., Kim, S., Millard, D.E., Weal, M.J., Hall, W., Lewis, P.H., Shadbolt, N.R.: Automatic Ontology-Based Knowledge Extraction from Web Documents. IEEE Intell. Sys. 18(1), 14–21 (2003)
4. Manine, A.P., Alphonse, E., Bessières, P.: Learning ontological rules to extract multiple relations of genic interactions from text. Int. J. Med. Informat. 78(12), e31–e38 (2009)
5. Miller, G.A.: WordNet: A Lexical Database for English. Com. ACM 38(11), 39–41 (1995)
6. de Marneffe, M.C., MacCartney, B., Manning, C.D.: Generating Typed Dependency Parses from Phrase Structure Parses. In: Proceedings of 5th International Conference on Language Resources and Evaluation (LREC 2006), Genoa, Italy (2006)
7. Liu, B., Hsu, W., Ma, Y.: Integrating Classification and Association Rule Mining. In: Knowledge Discovery in Databases (1998)
8. Held, C.M., Heiss, J.E., Estevez, P.A., Perez, C.A., Garrido, M., Algarin, C., Peirano, P.: Extracting Fuzzy Rules From Polysomnographic Recordings for Infant Sleep Classification. IEEE Trans. Biomed. Eng. 53, 1954–1962 (2006)
9. Madkour, A., Darwish, K., Hassan, H., Hassan, A., Emam, O.: BioNoculars: Extracting Protein-Protein Interactions from Biomedical Text. In: BioNLP, Prague, Czech Republic (2007)
10. Shnarch, E., Barak, L., Dagan, I.: Extracting Lexical Reference Rules from Wikipedia. In: Proceedings of the 47th Annual Meeting of the ACL, Suntec, Singapore (2009)
11. Xu, F., Kurz D., Piskorski J., Schmeier S.: A Domain Adaptive Approach to Automatic Acquisition of Domain Relevant Terms and Their Relations with Bootstrapping. In: Proc. Third Int'l Conf. Language Resources and Evaluation (LREC 2002) (2002)
12. Muller, H.M., Kenny, E.E., Sternberg, P.W.: Textpresso: an ontology-based information retrieval and extraction system for biological literature. PLoS Biol. 2, e309 (2004)
13. Riloff, E., Jones, R.: Learning Dictionaries for Information Extraction by Multi-Level Bootstrapping. In: Proceedings of the Sixteenth National Conference on Artificial Intelligence (AAAI 1999), pp. 474–479 (1999)
14. Crow, L., Shadbolt, N.: Extracting Focused Knowledge from the Semantic Web. Int. J. Hum. Comput. Stud. 54, 155–184 (2001)
15. Buitelaar, P., Olejnik, D., Sintek, M.: A Protégé plug-in for ontology extraction from text based on linguistic analysis. In: Proceedings of the International Semantic Web Conference, ISWC (2003)
16. Kang, J., Lee, J.K.: Rule Identification from Web Pages by the XRML Approach. Decision Support Systems 41(1), 205–227 (2005)
17. Duboue, P.A., McKeown, K.R.: Statistical acquisition of content selection rules for natural language generation. In: Proceedings of EMNLP, pp. 121–128 (2003)
18. Park, S., Lee, J.K.: Rule identification using ontology while acquiring rules from Web pages. Int. J. Hum.-Comput. Stud. 65(7), 659–673 (2007)
19. Lee, J.K., Sohn, M.: Extensible Rule Markup Language - toward intelligent Web platform. Communications of the ACM 46, 59–64 (2003)
20. Needleman, S.B., Wunsch, C.D.: A general method applicable to the search for similarities in the amino acid sequence of two proteins. J. Mol. Biol. 48(3), 443–453 (1970)

21. California cities by population, http://en.wikipedia.org/wiki/List_of_California_cities_by_population
22. Avis information web page, http://www.avis.com/car-rental/content/render-faq.ac
23. Enterprise information web page, http://enterprise.custhelp.com/app/answers/detail/a_id/3061/session/L3NpZC9MZjFxTlNtaw%3D%3D/sno/0
24. Hassanpour, S., Das, A.K. Semantics-based Text Mining of Biomedical Concepts in Scientific Publications. Stanford Institute of Biomedical Informatics Research, Technical Report BMIR-2010-1421 (2010)

Appendix: Extracted Online Text on Basic Rental Requirements from 11 Airport-Based Rental Car Companies in California, Used as Testing Cases

1. Ace: "All drivers must possess a valid drivers license issued in their country of residence, and an acceptable means of payment as identified in the Local Policy Details page."
2. Alamo: "All Drivers: Must meet the renting location's minimum age requirements Have a valid driver's license Present a major credit card in their name at the time of rental"
3. Avis: "Avis requires that each customer and additional driver meet the Avis minimum age requirement present a valid driver's license and an acceptable driving record, and present an Avis-honored charge card or cash rental qualification at the time of rental."
4. Enterprise: "All Drivers Must Meet the renting location's minimum age requirements. Have a valid driver's license. Have a major credit card in their name at the time of rental or meet the locations' cash qualification requirements."
5. Fox: "All renters/drivers will be required at the time of rental to supply A valid drivers license, current home address, a current home and local contact number, and second contact phone number."
6. Hertz: "You must meet the renting location's minimum age requirement or qualify with the age differential. You must have a valid driver's license. You must have a valid form of payment."
7. Midway: "To rent a car from Midway car rental you must have a driver's license, and credit card present in your name at the time that you pick up the vehicle."
8. National: "All Drivers Must meet the renting location's minimum age requirements. Have a valid driver's license. Present a major credit card in their own name at the time of rental."
9. Pacific: "All drivers must be at least 21 years of age, with a valid driver license and MAJOR CREDIT CARD."
10. Payless: "All drivers must meet the renting location minimum age requirements, have a valid driver license, clean driving record, and present a major credit card in his/her own name at the time of rental."
11. Renty: "Customer needs to have a valid driver license, debit card/credit card, and valid full coverage insurance on the rental car."

Classification Rule Mining for a Stream of Perennial Objects

Zaigham Faraz Siddiqui and Myra Spiliopoulou

University of Magdeburg,
Magdeburg 39106, Germany
{siddiqui,myra}@iti.cs.uni-magdeburg.de

Abstract. We study classification over a slow stream of complex objects like customers or students. The learning task must take into account that an object's label is influenced by incoming data from adjoint, fast streams of transactions, e.g. customer purchases or student exams, and that this label may even change over time. This task involves combining the streams, and exploiting associations between the target label and attribute values in the fast streams. We propose a method for the discovery of classification rules over such a confederation of streams, and we use it to enhance a decision tree classifier. We show that the new approach has competitive predictive power while building much smaller decision trees than the original classifier.

1 Introduction

Stream mining assumes that objects arrive, update the model (e.g., a decision tree) and are then forgotten. This covers learning tasks like assessing whether a customer transaction is fraudulent, but not the task of predicting whether a customer will pay back a loan, given the customer's activities thus far. There are very few methods for supervised learning upon such objects which are *fed* by one or more transaction streams [15,12]. These methods are either limited to numerical data [12], or treat data inefficiently, i.e., over-simplify the problem by assuming attributes to be independent and thus building very deep decision trees [15]. In this study, we propose the combination of classification rules' discovery with decision tree learning over a confederation of interrelated streams for the discovery of accurate and compact decision trees.

The need to learn over objects fed by transaction streams occurs in several contexts. Consider the customer records of a company or the student records of a university. New individuals are recorded continuously, hence such data constitute a slow stream $\mathcal{T}$, which is the target of a supervised learning task – e.g. predicting the customer's affinity to a marketing campaign or a student's final rank. The purchases of the customers, or the students' presentations and exams constitute streams of transactions $\mathcal{S}^1, \ldots, \mathcal{S}^J$, whose contents affect the classification of $\mathcal{T}$.

Classification over a slow stream fed by fast transaction streams is a new problem that poses two challenges. First, the (attribute, value)-pairs of the transaction streams must be incorporated into the slow stream; this incorporation is not

N. Bassiliades et al. (Eds.): RuleML 2011 - Europe, LNCS 6826, pp. 281–296, 2011.

a stream-join: for the learning task, we cannot generate a new customer record for each transaction made by the customer. Second, appropriate classification algorithms must be designed for this new type of stream data.

In our earlier work we proposed a solution to the first problem [13]: it is called *incremental propositionalisation*, and corresponds to combining the slow stream with the fast streams in a buffer-like manner, except that the data values in the fast streams do not become records of the slow stream but rather expand the slow stream with new attributes. For the second problem, we proposed a tree classifier called TrIP [15]. However, the combination of incremental propositionalisation with decision tree learning leads to inefficient, deep classifiers with low accuracies. The reason is that the attributes from the fast stream may be correlated but incremental propositionalisation treats them as independent. In this paper, we propose classification rule mining for the discovery of attributes of high predictive power, and enhance the algorithm TrIP to exploit these attributes during learning.

The paper is organized as follows. In section 2, we formalize the new learning problem we study, and discuss literature advances that are relevant or applicable to this problem. In section 3, we present our new classification rule mining algorithm. In section 4, we compare our approach to the baseline algorithm [13] over two datasets. The last section concludes with a summary and open issues.

2 Problem Specification and Background Literature

In the previous section, we used the terms *slow stream* and *fast stream* or *transaction stream* to distinguish between two types of stream. We now explain the learning task in more detail. Then, in subsection 2.3 we elaborate on the few studies that address this problem, and on research advances from conventional stream classification, which can be extended for the task at hand.

2.1 Problem Specification

In our introductory example, we considered a slow stream of customers $\mathcal{T}$ and fast transaction streams $\mathcal{S}^1, \ldots, \mathcal{S}^J$ that feed the slow stream, e.g. the customers' purchases, the customers' complaints and reclamations, the customers' interactions with the hotline etc. The learning task concerns solely $\mathcal{T}$, e.g. predicting whether a customer will respond to a marketing campaign (Y) or not (N), or labelling customers on their Customer Lifetime Value for the company (typically in four classes A, B, C, D where A is best and D is worst). We denote the set of class labels as $\mathcal{C}$ (cf. Table 1) and allow for $o \geq 2$ labels. Obviously, the contents of the fast streams should be taken into account when building the classifier.

Learning on a Stream of Perennial Objects. The slow stream $\mathcal{T}$ exhibits three properties that are atypical for streams. Differently from conventional stream objects that are seen, processed and forgotten, objects of $\mathcal{T}$ may not be deleted: an examinations office may file away the results of a successful exam, but does not file away the students who passed the exam; a product purchase may be

Table 1. Symbols and Parameters

Notation	Description
$\mathcal{T}$	stream of perennial objects – target of the learning task
$\mathcal{S}^j$	the jth stream, $j = 1, \ldots J$, feeding $\mathcal{T}$
$\mathcal{C}$	set of class labels $\{l_1, l_2, \ldots, l_o\}$
t_i	the ith timepoint
w	size of the window, defined as number of tuples
$\mathcal{S}_i^j$	tuples from $\mathcal{S}^j$ inside the window at t_i
$\mathcal{T}_i$	objects from $\mathcal{T}$ referenced by tuples in $\cup_{j=1}^J \mathcal{S}^j$
$\mathcal{W}_i$	propositionalised objects built by combining $\mathcal{T}_i$ with $\mathcal{S}_i^j, j = 1 \ldots J$
$\mathcal{I}$	classification rule $X \rightarrow [p_1, p_2, \ldots, p_o]$: X is the antecedent (a set of (attribute,value)-pairs), and p_u is the number of tuples with antecedent X and label l_u, i.e. the "contribution" of $\mathcal{I}$ to l_u $(u = 1, \ldots, o)$
$\mathcal{L}$	lattice of classification rules
$\mathcal{F}$	set of features extracted from the lattice $\mathcal{L}$ for the classification of the stream $\mathcal{T}$, where a feature $f \in \mathcal{F}$ is the antecedent of a classification rule
τ^{max}	maximum number of features to be extracted from $\mathcal{L}$; the size of $\mathcal{L}$ is an upper boundary for this threshold
s^{min}	minimum support a rule must have, before adding a tentative rule below it to $\mathcal{L}$
$e(\mathcal{I})$	entropy of $\mathcal{I}$,: $\sum_{u=1}^{o} \rho_u log \rho_u$, where $\rho_u = \frac{p_u}{\sum_{l=1}^{o} p_l}$
$d(\mathcal{I})$	d-score of $\mathcal{I}$ as its *un*-interestingness
d^{min}	minimum permitted d-score of a rule
δ	confidence threshold for significance computations

shifted to a backup medium after completion, but the customer who did the purchase remains in the database. One can even argue that $\mathcal{T}$ is not a stream at all. However, it is obvious that new objects arrive (new customers, new students), while old objects are filed away after some time (e.g. students who completed their degree and customers who have quitted the relationship with the company). We use the term *perennial objects* or *stream of perennial objects* for the slow stream $\mathcal{T}$ (cf. notation Table 1).

Second, the objects in $\mathcal{T}$ may appear several times, e.g. whenever the properties of a customer (e.g. her address) change and whenever this customer is referenced by a fast stream (i.e. when the customer performs a transaction). Third, the label of a $\mathcal{T}$ object may change over time: a customer who earlier responded to marketing campaigns (Y) may stop doing so (label becomes N); a B-customer may become an A-customer or a C-customer. Hence, the label of a perennial object x is not a constant; at every timepoint t, at which x is observed, its label is $label(x, t)$. The learning task is to predict this label at t, given the labelled data seen thus far and given the streams that feed $\mathcal{T}$.

Observing a Stream of Perennial Objects and its Adjoint Streams. We observe the target stream of perennial objects $\mathcal{T}$ and the fast transaction streams feeding it $\mathcal{S}^1, \ldots, \mathcal{S}^J$. The term *feeding* means that the objects in $\mathcal{S}^j, j = 1 \ldots J$ reference objects in $\mathcal{T}$ and deliver new information to them.

To learn a classifier over $\mathcal{T}$ while taking the contents of $\mathcal{S}^1, \ldots, \mathcal{S}^J$ into account, we must combine $\mathcal{T}$ with the fast streams. A stream join is not an appropriate operator though: if we join a customer with her 10 purchases, we acquire 10 purchase records expanded with customer data; we rather need *one* customer object expanded with the data of 10 purchases. An appropriate operator, called *propositionalisation*, for static data has been proposed in [11]; we expanded it for stream data in [13] under the name *incremental propositionalisation*. We use this operator and describe it in subsection 2.2 below.

For simplicity, we use the term *object* for a perennial object, i.e. an element of $\mathcal{T}$, and the term *tuple* for an element of a fast stream $\mathcal{S}^j$ that feeds $\mathcal{T}$.

2.2 Incremental Propositionalisation

We use incremental propositionalisation method [13] from our earlier work to combine the stream of perennial objects with the streams feeding it. The incremental propositional algorithm uses a sliding window of w timepoints for the fast transaction streams $\mathcal{S}^1, \ldots, \mathcal{S}^J$. We denote as $\mathcal{S}_i^j$ the set of tuples from stream $\mathcal{S}^j, j = 1 \ldots J$ that are inside the sliding window at timepoint t_i.

For the stream of perennial objects $\mathcal{T}$, the incremental propositionalisation algorithm uses a *cache*: at timepoint t_i, the cache contains the perennial objects referenced by the arriving tuples in the transaction streams, i.e. the perennial objects referenced in $\mathcal{S}_i^1, \ldots, \mathcal{S}_i^J$. These perennial objects constitute $\mathcal{T}_i$.

The incremental propositionalisation algorithm [13] operates incrementally over the contents of the caches and windows at each timepoint t_i. It starts with a semi-join between $\mathcal{T}_i$ and $\mathcal{S}_i^j$ for each $j = 1 \ldots J$, so that each object $x \in \mathcal{T}_i$ is associated with the set of matching tuples $matches(x, j, i) \subset \mathcal{S}_i^j$.

Next, each set of matching tuples is summarized into a single *sub-object*: (i) each numerical attribute A in $matches(x, j, i)$ is mapped to the *min*, *max*, *count* and *average* of the A values seen in $matches(x, j, i)$; (ii) for each nominal attribute A, the algorithm generates as many columns(r_A) with counts for A as there are distinct values in $\bigcup_x matches(x, j, 0)$ at t_0. The domain of A may change after t_0, in the sense that previously unseen values emerge, while old

Original Schema

Transaction

TID	CID	PID	Time
1	1	1	1
2	1	1	1
3	2	1	1
4	2	2	1
5	1	2	2
6	1	2	2
7	2	1	2
8	1	3	3
9	3	3	3

Customer

CID	Name	Married	Income
1	David	S	20000
2	Tom	M	65000
3	Harris	M	90000

Product

PID	Price	Category
1	100	Book
2	50	DVD
3	25	CD

Natural Join

TID	CID	Name	Married	Income	PID	Price	Category	Time
1	1	David	S	20000	1	100	Book	1
2	1	David	S	20000	1	100	Book	1
3	2	Tom	M	65000	1	100	Book	1
4	2	Tom	M	65000	2	50	DVD	1
5	1	David	S	20000	2	50	DVD	2
6	1	David	S	20000	2	50	DVD	2
7	2	Tom	M	65000	1	100	Book	2
8	1	David	S	20000	3	25	CD	3
9	3	Harris	M	90000	3	25	CD	3

Propositionalised Table

CID	Name	Married	Income	Count	AVG_P	MIN_P	MAX_P	Count_Book	Count_DVD	Time
1	David	S	20000	2	100	100	100	2	0	1
2	Tom	M	65000	2	75	50	100	1	1	1
1	David	S	20000	4	75	50	100	2	2	2
2	Tom	M	65000	3	83.333	50	100	2	1	2
1	David	S	20000	3	41.667	25	50	1	2	3
3	Harris	M	90000	1	25	25	25	1	0	3

Fig. 1. (a) Interrelated streams Customer, Transaction and Product, (b) join of the three streams vs (c) propositionalization into the target stream Customer

values are no more referenced. If the domain grows larger than r_A, then values are grouped into r_A clusters on similarity: two values of A are similar, if they appear in similar tuples. The process of propositionalisation is also shown in Fig 1. Further details can be found in [13].

We denote as $\mathcal{W}_i := \mathcal{T}_i \odot \mathcal{S}_i^1 \odot \ldots \odot \mathcal{S}_i^J$ the result of combining $\mathcal{T}_i$ with $\mathcal{S}_i^j, j = 1 \ldots J$ at t_i. The objects in $\mathcal{W}_i$ are essentially the perennial objects in $\mathcal{T}_i$, expanded with data from the adjoint streams. In other words, $\mathcal{W}_i$ is $\mathcal{T}_i$ after the invocation of the operator "incremental propositionalisation".

2.3 Related Work and Background Literature

The stream learning problem described in subsection 2.1 is fairly new. It has been studied in [12] for streams of numerical signals, but the solution does not transfer to streams of conventional data records that contain categorical data. We proposed a solution for unsupervised learning on perennial objects in [14], while the problem of supervised learning on perennial objects was studied in [15].

The algorithm TrIP [15] builds upon our earlier work on incremental propositionalisation [13] to combine the slow stream of perennial objects with the fast transaction streams. It is apparent that the propositionalisation algorithm generates a large set of output columns. Moreover, it suppresses associations among the original attributes, notably associations between attribute and label in $\mathcal{T}$. This problem becomes apparent in the learning phase of TrIP [15].

TrIP is a decision tree learner for a slow stream of perennial objects that is accompanied by fast transaction streams [15]. TrIP is inspired by the CVFDT algorithm that was proposed in [10] for a conventional data stream. TrIP deals with the re-appearance of perennial objects and with the fact that these objects may change their label. However, TrIP, like all decision tree learners assumes independency of the attributes and cannot exploit cases where some attribute values acquire predictive power as the stream progresses. This issue can be dealt with classification rule miners.

Gupta et al. [8] use concept analysis for discovering classification rules incrementally: the rules are defined as concepts and are stored in one lattice per class. As new objects arrive, concepts are added/updated in the lattice. The algorithm only handles binary attributes. For discovering rules, lattice is traversed and rules are returned with the label as a consequent. It is not entirely clear how the algorithm would behave if the lattices of different classes produce the same rule.

The methods of Aydin et al., *IRIL* [1] and *ICRIL*[2] learn classification rules over streaming data but the objective is not to build a classifier, but to find interesting rules. The notion of interestingness used by the algorithm is subjective and requires user interaction.

The method of Ferrer et al. FACIL [7] is classification rule mining algorithm for numerical data streams that focuses on processing border examples. FACIL iterates over the examples *multiple times* to discover rules whose purity (i.e., the extent to which a rules contains examples from a single class) is above user-defined threshold κ. Unlike FACIL, our algorithm is a single-pass algorithm and operates both on numerical and categorical data.

Yu et al. [17] distinguish between *exact* [5,16] and *approximate* [9,4] association rule miners over streams. These studies focus on effectively mining and maintaining a growing set of rules.

Method of Veloso et al. [16] maintain only the *maximally frequent itemsets*. This results in information loss, though, hence a database scan is required to recover all the frequents itemsets and their supports. *Moment* maintains only the *closed frequent itemsets* over a sliding window [5]; for these rules there is no information loss. The authors propose a *closed enumeration tree* (CET) to store selected itemsets over a sliding window: they rank the nodes on how promising they are, and then define a boundary between closed frequent itemsets. The new rules are captured through the boundary movements.

CARMA is an approximate single-pass algorithm [9]. It stores the frequent itemsets in a lattice, which is updated incrementally. Since a newly created itemset may have missed some previously inserted tuples, CARMA maintains support intervals. If CARMA has the chance to access the tuples again, its Phase II calculates the exact support.

Our CRMPES is a single-pass algorithm inspired by CARMA and *Moment*. However, CARMA and *Moment* are designed to find *association* rules, and they build the rule lattice accordingly. In contrast, CRMPES builds a lattice of *classification* rules, and is designed to add rules in the lattice only if they have higher predictive power than the rules that are already in the lattice.

3 Incremental Classification Rule Learning

To enhance classification over a stream $\mathcal{T}$ of perennial objects, we identify attributes in the fast transaction streams $\mathcal{S}^1, \ldots, \mathcal{S}_i^J$ which have potentially high predictive power with respect to the class label in $\mathcal{T}$. To do so, our Classification Rule Miner for a stream of Perennial Objects, CRMPES, learns a lattice $\mathcal{L}$ of classification rules incrementally, derives predictive attributes from them and delivers them to a decision tree classifier.

CRMPES consists of several components that operate as follows. At each t_i, the labels from $\mathcal{T}$ are propagated to the arriving tuples of the fast streams, and the rules in the lattice are updated, as described in subsection 3.1. The lattice is grown incrementally, thereby removing uninteresting rules, as explained in subsection 3.2. Next, attributes are generated from the learned lattice, as discussed in subsection 3.3. The incremental propositionalisation producing $\mathcal{W}_i = \mathcal{T}_i \odot \mathcal{S}_i^1 \odot \ldots \odot \mathcal{S}_i^J$ at each t_i is done next to generate the input to the stream classification algorithm. This input, together with the classification rules found at t_i are used for stream classification, as explained in subsection 3.4. The notation and parameters are presented in Table 1.

Algorithm 1. CRMPES_StreamAlign

Input : $y, cnt, \mathcal{T}_i, \mathcal{L}$
Output: $\mathcal{L}$

1 $x \leftarrow$ perennial object in $\mathcal{T}_i$ that is referenced by y; $l_u \leftarrow$ label of x
2 **foreach** $\mathcal{I} \in \mathcal{L}$ **do**
3   **if** y *supports* $\mathcal{I}$ **then**
4   **if** $\mathcal{I}$ *is not "tentative"* **then** $\mathcal{I}.p_u \leftarrow \mathcal{I}.p_u + cnt$
5 return $\mathcal{L}$

3.1 Aligning the Fast Streams to the Slow Stream

Let $\mathcal{T}$ be the stream of perennial objects, and let $\mathcal{S}^1, \ldots, \mathcal{S}^J$ be the streams feeding it. As explained in subsection 2.2, we use a sliding window of length w, and denote as $\mathcal{S}_i^1, \ldots, \mathcal{S}_i^J$ the contents of these streams inside the window at timepoint t_i; the objects of $\mathcal{T}$ referenced by these tuples constitute $\mathcal{T}_i$.

The label of each $x \in \mathcal{T}_i$ is propagated to all tuples in $\cup_{j=1}^J \mathcal{S}_i^j$ that reference x, i.e. to all tuples in $\cup_{j=1}^J matches(x, j, i)$ (cf. subsection 2.2). For example, assume that we classify customers by lifetime value into classes A, B, C, D, and let customer x at timepoint t_i belong to class B: B becomes the label of all transactions performed by x that are inside the sliding window.

A classification rule $\mathcal{I}$ has the form $X \rightarrow [p_1, p_2, \ldots, p_o]$, where X is a set of (attribute, value)-pairs in accordance to the schema of one of the fast streams, and p_u is the number of tuples supporting X and having the label $l_u \in \mathcal{C} = \{l_1, \ldots, l_o\}$. We call p_u the *contribution of X to label l_u* (cf. notation in Table 1). We build a lattice $\mathcal{L}$ of classification rules incrementally as described in the next subsection.

The operation of stream alignment, i.e. label propagation and lattice updating, is depicted in Algorithm 1: CRMPES_StreamAlign takes as input the currently observed tuple y, the cache of perennial objects $\mathcal{T}_i$ and the current state of the lattice $\mathcal{L}$. Intuitively, the algorithm reads the label of the perennial object x referenced by y (Line 1), finds all classification rules supported by tuple y and, for each such rule $\mathcal{I}$, it increases the support of this label p_u (Line 7). As can be seen in Algorithm 1, though, CRMPES_StreamAlign is more elaborate. In particular, it takes the value by which the support should be increased as input *cnt*. Further, it treats "tentative" rules differently (Line 5). The nature of these rules and the particularities of CRMPES_StreamAlign are explained in subsection 3.2, when we explain how the lattice is grown and shrunk.

3.2 Building a Lattice of Classification Rules Incrementally

The core of our Classification Rule Miner, CRMPES_Core (cf. Algorithm 2), grows the lattice $\mathcal{L}$ of classification rules incrementally. At t_i, CRMPES_Core considers the tuples in $\cup_{j=1}^J \mathcal{S}_i^j$. Some of these tuples will be forgotten later, i.e. they *exit* the sliding window, while new ones, yet unseen in t_i, will *enter* the sliding window. Let OLD_i be the tuples to be forgotten at t_i, and NEW_i be the new tuples at t_i.

Algorithm 2. CRMPES_Core

```
   Input  : OLD_i, NEW_i, T_i, L, s^min, d^min, δ
   Output: L
 1 foreach y ∈ NEW_i do CRMPES_StreamAlign(y, +1, T_i, L)       /* UPDATE L */
 2 E ← ∅
 3 foreach I ∈ L do                                              /* GROW L */
 4 |   if I has no children AND is not "tentative" AND is not "locked" then
 5 |   |   if Σ_{u=1}^{o} I.p_u ≥ s^min then add I to E
 6 Expand L by creating new rules as children of the rules in E
 7 Mark the new rules as "tentative"
 8 foreach y ∈ OLD_i do CRMPES_StreamAlign(y, −1, T_i, L)       /* UPDATE L */
 9 foreach I ∈ L do                                              /* SHRINK L */
10 |   let I' be the child of I
11 |   if I is "redundant" towards I' then  mark I as "locked"
12 |   redirect accesses to I towards I'
13 |   else if Σ_{u=1}^{o} I.p_u < s^min OR e(I) − e(I') < ε then
14 |   |   mark I as "locked"
15 |   |   remove all children of I from L
16 |   |   unmark all "locked" rules that are redirecting towards I
17 |   else  umark I
18 return L
```

CRMPES_Core takes as input (1) the tuples in OLD_i and NEW_i, (2) the objects $\mathcal{T}_i$ referenced by these tuples, (3) the lattice $\mathcal{L}$ built thus far, and (4) thresholds s^{min} on the support of classification rules, d^{min} on their interestingness, and δ on the confidence in estimating rules' redundancy. CRMPES_Core traverses $\mathcal{L}$ from the root downwards, *grows* it by adding rules and *shrinks* it by removing rare, uninteresting and redundant ones, as we explain below.

UPDATE $\mathcal{L}$ with new tuples (Line 1). CRMPES_Core starts processing $\mathcal{L}$ by first updating the supports of the rules in it. It invokes CRMPES_StreamAlign for each new tuple y, whereupon the label of y is identified (cf. Algorithm 1, Line 1), and the contribution of each rule supported by y to this label is increased by $+1$ (cf. invocation of CRMPES_StreamAlign in Algorithm 2, Line 1).

GROW $\mathcal{L}$ with new rules (Lines 2-7). Arriving tuples in NEW_i may give raise to new rules that are not yet in the lattice. CRMPES_Core grows the lattice *pro-actively*. First, it identifies all classification rules that have no children and are supported by at least s^{min} tuples thus far (Lines 3-5) and then *expands* them (Line 6) by *tentative* rules (Line 7).

Lattice *expansion* is only possible for rules that have no common child yet, and whose antecedents differ by only one attribute. For each such a pair of rules, with antecedents XB and XD respectively, a common child with antecedent XBD is created and marked as "tentative". From this moment on, the contribution of XBD to the label of each arriving tuple y is increased whenever CRMPES_StreamAlign is invoked (cf. Algorithm 1, Line 5)! However, the lattice cannot grow below a tentative rule (cf. Algorithm 2, Line 4), i.e. a tentative rule cannot acquire a child until it stops being "tentative" (cf. Line 17). We explain the treatment of tentative rules in sequel.

UPDATE $\mathcal{L}$ with old tuples (Line 8). When a tuple exits the sliding window, the rules it supports must be modified: CRMPES_Core invokes CRMPES_StreamAlign for each tuple $y \in OLD_i$ with a count value of -1, so that the support of the rules is decreased (cf. Algorithm 1, Line 4). An exception is made for tentative rules whose support is not decreased.

The reason for this exception lays in the behaviour of the sliding window. Let t_i be the timepoint of creating a new tentative rule $\mathcal{I}_{XBD}$. To compute its support, all $\cup_{j=1}^{J} \mathcal{S}_i^j$ tuples should be considered. However, CRMPES_Core processes only the tuples that arrive new at t_i (cf. Line 1), while those that have already been seen are not reconsidered – although they are still inside the sliding window. Since the tuples that are getting removed have no contribution towards the support of the tentative rule, its support is not decreased. Once all such tuples have exited the window, tentative rules are unmarked, provided of course that they are worth retaining in the lattice: CRMPES_Core uses several criteria to shrink the lattice by eliminating useless rules.

SHRINK $\mathcal{L}$ by removing useless rules (Lines 9-17). CRMPES_Core uses three criteria to assess the usefulness of a rule: the rule's support, the rule's predictive power, and the rule's redundancy with respect to its children.

A rule $\mathcal{I}'$ is *redundant* if it is parent of a rule $\mathcal{I}$ and its support is not significantly higher than the support of $\mathcal{I}$. Then, the parent rule $\mathcal{I}'$ is marked as "locked" (Line 11), and all accesses to it are redirected to $\mathcal{I}$. For the significance test, we use $\chi^2 = \sum_{u=1}^{o} (p'_u - p_u)^2 / p_u$ (with critical value $\chi^2_{1-\delta}$), where p_u, p'_u are the contributions of $\mathcal{I}$, resp. $\mathcal{I}'$ to label $l_u, u = 1 \dots o$.

If the support of a rule $\mathcal{I}$ remains/drops below the threshold s^{min} (Line 13), then the rule is also marked as "locked" (Line 11). This means that the lattice cannot grow below it (Line 4). Further, all existing rules below $\mathcal{I}$ (i.e. being more specific and thus having no higher support than $\mathcal{I}$) are removed from $\mathcal{L}$ (Line 15). In contrast, rules that were earlier "locked" and redirecting to the now locked rule $\mathcal{I}$ are themselves unlocked (Line 16).

A rule $\mathcal{I}$ may have adequate support but its predictive power might not be significantly better than its parent $\mathcal{I}'$. Such rules are also marked as locked. It is based on the entropy of a rule $\mathcal{I}$: $e(\mathcal{I}) = \sum_u \rho_u log \rho_u$, where $\rho_u = p_u / \sum_l p_l$. The significance test is done using the Hoeffding bound [3,6]. It states that, if $e(\mathcal{I}) - e(\mathcal{I}') < \epsilon$ for some threshold ϵ, then the rule $\mathcal{I}$ is not better than $\mathcal{I}'$.

Classification rules that have high support and predictive power are retained in the lattice. If they were marked earlier (as "tentative" or "locked"), they are unmarked (Line 17). Retaining them in the lattice may turn other rules *redundant* though: it is possible that a small number of rules suffices for distinguishing among the classes, while the rest are redundant.

We also model the *interestingness* of a rule $\mathcal{I}$ by combining the rule's support and entropy $e(\mathcal{I})$ (cf. Table 1. We define:

$$d(\mathcal{I}) = \frac{\sum_{u=1}^{o} p_u}{w} \times (1 - e(\mathcal{I})) \tag{1}$$

where a rule is the more interesting, the higher its $d()$-score is. The weight of a rule's support ratio inside the sliding window with the 1-complement of the rule's entropy is intended to prevent rare rules with possibly low entropy from acquiring high $d()$ scores. CRMPES_Core uses the score $d()$ to rank and to eliminate the rules with scores lower than d^{min} from $\mathcal{L}$. Uninteresting rules are treated similarly to those with very low support (Lines 13-16).

3.3 Generating Features from the Classification Rules' Lattice

The lattice of classification rules built and maintained by CRMPES_Core is used to generate additional features for the learning task over the stream of perennial objects $\mathcal{T}$. A *feature* f is not a single attribute but rather the antecedent X of some classification rule $\mathcal{I}$ in the lattice $\mathcal{L}$, i.e. a set of (attribute,value)-pairs, as specified in Table 1.

Feature generation takes place at each timepoint t_i. The Feature Generation algorithm CRMPES_FGen (cf. Algorithm 3) takes as input the lattice $\mathcal{L}$ built by CRMPES_Core thus far, and it incrementally builds a set of generated features $\mathcal{F}$ of cardinality τ^{max}.

First, CRMPES_FGen ranks the classification rules in $\mathcal{L}$ on their interestingness $d()$-score, as defined in Eq. 1, thereby skipping closed and tentative rules (Line 1). Let R be an ordered list of ranked rules (Line 2), so that $R[k]$ is the rule at position k with $k = 1, \ldots, |R|$, and $R[k].antecedent$ is this rule's antecedent. At the first iteration, CRMPES_FGen selects the antecedent of the top-ranked classification rule (Line 3) and removes it from R (Line 5). At the mth iteration,

---

Algorithm 3. CRMPES_FGen

Input : $\mathcal{L}, \tau^{max}$
Output: $\mathcal{F}$

1 $\mathcal{L}' \leftarrow \{\mathcal{I} \in \mathcal{L} | \mathcal{I}$ is not "closed" and not "tentative"$\}$
2 rank $\mathcal{L}'$ on $d()$-score descending $\rightarrow R$
3 $\mathcal{F} \leftarrow \{R[1].antecedent\}$
4 $SF \leftarrow R[1].antecedent$
5 remove$(R, R[1])$
6 **for** $m = 2, \ldots, \tau^{max}$ **do**
7 $\quad \mathcal{I} \leftarrow argmin_m\{R[k]antecedent \cap SF = \emptyset\}$
8 $\quad \mathcal{F} \leftarrow \mathcal{F} \cup \{\mathcal{I}.antecedent\}$
9 $\quad SF \leftarrow SF \cup \mathcal{I}.antecedent$
10 $\quad$ remove$(R, \mathcal{I})$
11 return $\mathcal{F}$

---

the rule of highest rank is chosen among those that have an empty intersection of (attribute, value)-pairs to the set SF, i.e. to the set of (attribute,value)-pairs already in $\mathcal{F}$ (Line 7). Then, the sets and the list R are updated accordingly (Lines 8-10).

In fact, the selection of the mth rule is slightly more general than depicted in Line 7. If CRMPES_FGen finds no rule with empty intersection to SF, it considers rules in R that have minimal intersection. This implies additional scans over the list R. However, the additional cost is low, since R becomes smaller at each iteration (Lines 5, 10).

3.4 Enhancing a Decision Tree Classifier with Predictive Attributes

A learning algorithm over a stream of perennial objects receives as input a propositionalised stream [15], the schema of which is a large set of derived attributes (Section 2.2). With CRMPES, we deliver an additional set of features, derived from classification rules of high predictive power. We enhance the tree induction algorithm TrIP [15], by allowing it to choose from a list of such predictive attributes for learning.

The complete algorithm, as invoked at each timepoint t_i is outlined in Algorithm 4. At each timepoint, the contents of the fast streams are updated (Line 3), the referenced perennial objects in $\mathcal{T}$ are placed in the cache $\mathcal{T}_i$ (Line 4), the contents of the sliding window are adjusted (Line 5), and CRMPES_Core is invoked (Line 6). It returns an updated lattice, from which CRMPES_FGen derives the set of currently predictive features $\mathcal{F}$ (Line 6). Then, the data are propositionalised (Line 7) as for the conventional TrIP [15], which is invoked with an additional parameter - the set of predictive features at timepoint t_i (Line 8). ζ is the model learned and adapted by TrIP from one timepoint to the next. It can also be delivered as output (Line 9).

It must be noted that the adaptive learning of TrIP, as shown in Algorithm 4, is simplified. TrIP grows a decision tree gradually, adding subtrees as new data

Algorithm 4. CRMPES_TrIP

```
   Input  : w, s^min, d^min, δ, τ^max
   Output: ζ
 1 L ← ∅
 2 foreach timepoint t_i do
 3 |  foreach j=1,...,J do update contents of S^j into S_i^j
 4 |  update contents of T into T_i
 5 |  compute OLD_i, NEW_i using w
 6 |  L ←CRMPES_Core(OLD_i, NEW_i, T_i, L, s^min, d^min, δ)
 7 |  F ←CRMPES_FGen(L, τ^max)
 8 |  W_i ← incrementalPropositionalization(T_i, S_i^1, ..., S_i^J)
 9 |  ζ ← AdaptDecisionTree(ζ, W_i, F)
10 |_ return ζ
```

arrive, removing obsolete branches, and retaining alternative subtrees. These activities are summarized here into a function "AdaptDecisionTree()", omitting the full set of parameters. The original TrIP can be found in [15], page 646, as Algorithm 1. Our extensions are to be inserted after line 3 of the original TrIP, just before the incremental propositionalisation step (Line 7 in CRMPES_TrIP, line 4 in the original TrIP).

4 Experiments

We study the quality of the rules discovered by CRMPES and the effect of the derived attributes on the quality of the final stream classifier. We use a synthetic dataset on learning user profiles, and the dataset of the PKDD 1999 Challenge on predicting defaults in bank loans. Both datasets exhibit concept drift. Quality is measured as the area under the ROC curve (AUC) at each timepoint.

4.1 Learning User Profiles

We used a multi-relational data generator[1] to create a stream of users and adjoint streams of items and user ratings. The core idea of the data generation process is as follows. There are item descriptors and user profiles. An item descriptor is essentially a cluster centroid: items are generated as points around it. A user profile determines the affinity of a user for an item descriptor: a generated rating for an item depends on the user's affinity for the item's cluster, as set in her profile, and on the distance of that item from its cluster's centroid. A user may change from a profile to another (drift). The learning task is to predict each user's profile at each moment, given the ratings thus far.

Note that our scenario is not for predicting ratings. Item descriptors may be movie genres, user profiles may be "teenager fans of action and Gothic", "sci-fi fans", "kids liking cartoons" etc. Each profile affects the predisposition of a user towards a genre, and determines (with some variance ϱ) the ratings of the user for individual movies. Users may shift from one profile to another, since people's preferences change with time.

We specified 6 user profiles and 8 item descriptors described by 5 numerical attributes, and generated 800 items and 1000 users. Since TrIP is a binary classifier, we grouped the profiles into two classes (á three profiles).

We set the CRMPES parameters to $w = 30$ timepoints, $s^{min} = 0.05$, $d^{min} = 0.4$, $\delta = 0.95$ (for χ^2 and ϵ), and the TrIP parameters $\tau = 0.01$ and $n = 500$ objects seen before starting with learning.

For the experiments we have used three strategies: **P** uses only attributes generated by the incremental propositionalisation, while **R** uses only rule-based attributes delivered by CRMPES, and **PR** uses both. Essentially, strategy **P** corresponds to TrIP, as proposed in [15] and is our baseline. All strategies are

[1] The data generator along with further results can be downloaded from *http://omen.cs.uni-magdeburg.de/itikmd/mitarbeiter/zaigham-faraz-siddiqui.html*

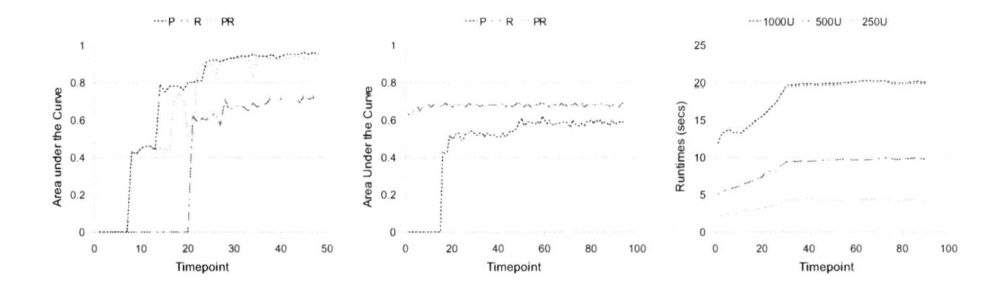

Fig. 2. (l-to-r): Results without drift for 1000 users and 800 items (a) with approximately 1500 transactions at each timepoint (b) with approximately 6500 transactions at each timepoint and (c) run times of the system for the dataset with 1000, 500 and 250 users and 6500, 3500 and 1500 transactions per timepoint

evaluated using the prequential evaluation except for the Fig 2a&b where we use hold out a part of stream data for evaluation.

The graphs in Fig 2a&b show the performance of the strategies when no drift is present. **PR** shows competitive performance for both the experiments. This is mainly due to the advantage that it draws from utilising the rich feature space. Whereas **P** and **R** experiences a drop in performance as concept becomes complex for their learning methodology. In Fig 2c the run times for our algorithm (i.e., rule mining + propositionalisation + TrIP) are shown for different dataset sizes for $w = 30$ units. They are averaged over 5 runs for each dataset size. There is overheard involve for using MySQL but run times stay linear to the size of the dataset.

In Fig 3a, we see the AUC values. At the beginning, all strategies show good performance, since the classes are rather easy to learn. After timepoint 30, the concept shift causes a performance drop. The simultaneous introduction of noise through $\varrho = 50$ prevents the strategies from recovering their earlier performance. Strategy **R** suffers most from noise and is unstable, **P** is more stable, and **PR** performs comparably or better than **P**.

In Fig 3b, we see how the size of the tree learned by TrIP varies for each of the strategies. The classification rules learned by **R** result in very large trees, so more after the concept changes at timepoint 30. The tree learned by the baseline (TrIP upon strategy **P**) is consistently much larger than the tree learned by TrIP upon **PR**. Hence, **PR** achieves comparable or better predictive performance than the baseline, while learning smaller and less volatile trees.

In a separate experiment Fig 3c&d, we show the performance with 1000 users. Here, the drift occurs around t_{50} and is the only place where **PR**'s tree grows to adjust to the drift. Strategy **R** is unable to learn the concept before the drift and shows a volatile behaviour after. Strategy **P** overtakes **PR** during $t_{50} - t_{70}$, but it is more of over-fitting than better performance as its tree is big and is forced to adjust in the subsequent time points.

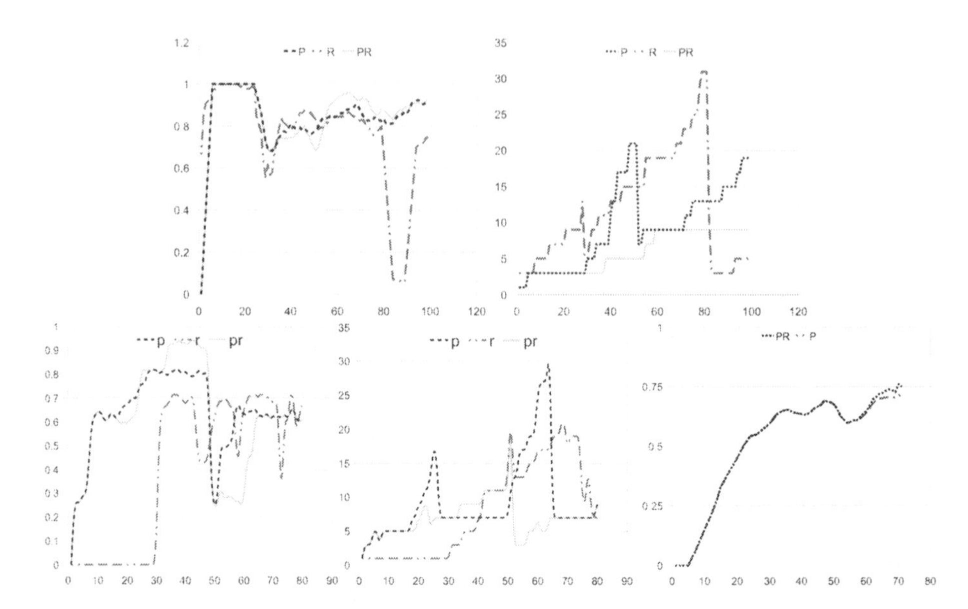

Fig. 3. TrIP with 3 strategies (l-to-r): (a & b) **AUC** and **tree size** with 150 users, (c & d) **AUC** and **tree size** with 1000 users (e) Financial Dataset with $w = 30$, size of *Account* cache=200 and size of *District* cache=40

4.2 Predicting Defaults in Bank Loans

The dataset "Financial" of the PKDD 1999 Challenge contains data on bank customers, the transactions of their bank accounts and static data on the districts they come from. The data are timestamped, so we can transform them into the dataset `District`, the stream `Transaction` and the slower stream `Account`, which contain the customer data is the target stream. The learning task is to predict whether a customer (represented by her Account) will default in paying back her loan. The originally 4 classes were already merged into two (*loan-trusted* and *loan-risk*) during the 1999 Challenge.

In [15], we stressed that the "Financial" dataset exhibits a difficult learning problem: the class distributions reflect the state of the accounts only when they have matured. Hence, labels become applicable at a much later timepoint than when the objects are introduced. So, we expect low performance at the first timepoints. We also point out that the amount of data cached per stream affects performance. We experimented with similar settings.

We set the CRMPES parameters to $\delta = 0.95$, $s^{min} = 0.01$, $d^{min} = 0.1$. For TrIP, we set $\tau = 0.01$ and $n = 200$. For the incremental propositionalisation, we allow $r = 3$ columns per nominal attribute to accommodate values and $g = 8$ columns for rule-based attributes.

We used only the baseline **P** and strategy **PR**. We see in Fig 3e that they perform similarly. Inspection of the CRMPES output showed that there are some useful rules, e.g. `balance within [-600, 600] AND penalty imposed`

→ *loan-risk*, but they were not very frequent and were not utilised by TrIP. An explanation is also the nature of the dataset: the labels are predictable only when the accounts mature, i.e. rather late. Further, the `Financial` dataset contains many nominal attributes that can be exploited directly by TrIP; numerical attributes, as in the synthetic dataset, are more difficult to exploit in a decision tree, so CRMPES brings higher advantage.

5 Conclusion

In this paper, we proposed a classification rule mining algorithm for a stream of perennial objects. Such a stream consists of objects that are of static nature, e.g., customers or university students, fed by additional streams of conventional nature, e.g. purchase transactions, product impressions, course enrolments and exams. The learning task, like predicting a customer's responsiveness to a marketing campaign or a student's final rank, refers to the static objects but is influenced by the information in the feeding streams. Learning algorithms for this kind of stream are scarce and suffer from the caveats of a very large feature space.

We have used classification rules over the perennial objects' stream to identify attributes of high predictive power. We maintain these rules in a lattice, and adjust the lattice as new data arrive in the feeding streams, allowing for drift of any of the labels. Classification rules are used to identify attributes of high predictive power for some label. These attributes are then used with priority for learning. Tree induction is performed with an existing algorithm for a perennial objects' streams: we have extended it to focus only on the prioritised attributes. Our experiments show that the enhanced algorithm has superior performance, while considering less attributes and thus consuming less space.

We have considered a binary classification problem, but our stream classification rule discovery approach is designed for an arbitrary number of labels, and can also be used for overlapping classes, i.e. for the multi-label learning problem. We intend to extend our approach towards multi-label stream learning over a stream of perennial objects.

References

1. Aydin, T., Güvenir, H.A.: Learning interestingness of streaming classification rules. In: Aykanat, C., Dayar, T., Körpeoğlu, İ. (eds.) ISCIS 2004. LNCS, vol. 3280, pp. 62–71. Springer, Heidelberg (2004)
2. Aydın, T., Güvenir, H.A.: Modeling interestingness of streaming classification rules as a classification problem. In: Savacı, F.A. (ed.) TAINN 2005. LNCS (LNAI), vol. 3949, pp. 168–176. Springer, Heidelberg (2006)
3. Catlett, J.: Megainduction: Machine Learning on Very Large Databases. Ph.D. thesis, University of Sydney (1991)
4. Charikar, M., Chen, K., Farach-Colton, M.: Finding frequent items in data streams. In: Widmayer, P., Triguero, F., Morales, R., Hennessy, M., Eidenbenz, S., Conejo, R. (eds.) ICALP 2002. LNCS, vol. 2380, pp. 693–703. Springer, Heidelberg (2002)

5. Chi, Y., Wang, H., Yu, P.S., Muntz, R.: Moment: Maintaining closed frequent itemsets over a stream sliding window. In: Proceedings of the International Conference on Data Mining, ICDM 2004 (2004)
6. Domingos, P., Hulten, G.: Mining high-speed data streams. In: Proceedings of the International Conference on Knowledge Discovery in Databases, KDD 2000, pp. 71–80. ACM, New York (2000)
7. Ferrer-Troyano, F., Aguilar-Ruiz, J.S., Riquel Jose, C.: Data streams classification by incremental rule learning with parameterized generalization. In: ACM Symposium on Applied Computing, SAC 2006, pp. 657–661. ACM, New York (2006), http://doi.acm.org/10.1145/1141277.1141428
8. Gupta, A., Kumar, N., Bhatnagar, V.: Incremental classification rules based on association rules using formal concept analysis. In: Perner, P., Imiya, A. (eds.) MLDM 2005. LNCS (LNAI), vol. 3587, pp. 11–20. Springer, Heidelberg (2005)
9. Hidber, C.: Online association rule mining. Tech. Rep. UCB/CSD-98-1004, EECS Department, University of California, Berkeley (1998), http://www.eecs.berkeley.edu/Pubs/TechRpts/1998/5677.html
10. Hulten, G., Spencer, L., Domingos, P.: Mining time-changing data streams. In: Proceedings of International Conference on Knowledge Discovery in Databases, KDD 2001. ACM, New York (2001)
11. Kroegel, M.A.: On Propositionalization for Knowledge Discovery in Relational Databases. Ph.D. thesis, University of Magdeburg, Germany (2003)
12. McGovern, A., Hiers, N., Collier, M., Gagne II, D.J., Brown, R.A.: Spatiotemporal relational probability trees. In: Proceedings of the International Conference on Data Mining, ICDM 2008 (2008)
13. Siddiqui, Z.F., Spiliopoulou, M.: Combining multiple interrelated streams for incremental clustering. In: Winslett, M. (ed.) SSDBM 2009. LNCS, vol. 5566, pp. 535–552. Springer, Heidelberg (2009)
14. Siddiqui, Z.F., Spiliopoulou, M.: Stream clustering of growing objects. In: Gama, J., Costa, V.S., Jorge, A.M., Brazdil, P.B. (eds.) DS 2009. LNCS, vol. 5808, pp. 433–440. Springer, Heidelberg (2009)
15. Siddiqui, Z.F., Spiliopoulou, M.: Tree induction over perennial objects. In: Gertz, M., Ludäscher, B. (eds.) SSDBM 2010. LNCS, vol. 6187, pp. 640–657. Springer, Heidelberg (2010)
16. Veloso, A., Meira, J.W., Carvalho, M., Possas, B., Parthasarathy, S., Zaki, J.: Mining frequent itemsets in evolving databases. In: Proceedings of the 2nd SIAM International Conference on Data Mining (2002)
17. Yu, P.S., Chi, Y.: Association rule mining on streams. In: Encyclopedia Database Systems (2009)

A Case for Learning Simpler Rule Sets with Multiobjective Evolutionary Algorithms

Adam Ghandar[1], Zbigniew Michalewicz[1,2], and Ralf Zurbruegg[3]

[1] School of Computer Science,
University of Adelaide, Adelaide, SA 5005, Australia
[2] Institute of Computer Science, Polish Academy of Sciences,
ul. Ordona 21, 01-237 Warsaw, Poland
and
Polish-Japanese Institute of Information Technology,
ul. Koszykowa 86, 02-008 Warsaw, Poland
[3] School of Commerce, University of Adelaide,
Adelaide, SA 5005, Australia

Abstract. Fuzzy rules can be understood by people because of their specification in structured natural language. In a wide range of decision support applications in business, the interpretability of rule based systems is a distinguishing feature, and advantage over, possible alternate approaches that are perceived as "black boxes", for example in facilitating accountability. The motivation of this paper is to consider the relationships between rule simplicity (the key component of interpretability) and out-of-sample performance. Forecasting has been described as both art and science to emphasize intuition and experience aspects of the process: aspects of intelligence manifestly difficult to reproduce artificially. We explore, computationally, the widely appreciated forecasting "rule-of-thumb" expressed in Ockham's principle that "simpler explanations are more likely to be correct".

1 Introduction and Background

The combination of evolutionary algorithms and fuzzy systems has led to many and varied successful applications. In this paper, we a fixed size integer representation to of fuzzy rules and multiobjective EAs to learn classification rules. We compare the performance with results reported for benchmark datasets; and examine the generalizability of learned rules. Compared with other evolutionary methods proposed to learn rules, the approach presented involves less specialization to the rule learning problem. We use a mixed integer and floating point problem representation of fixed size, a key feature is that it remains within the framework of a standard EA needing no additional parameters or routines.This allows us for instance to use different evolutionary algorithms when useful and makes implementation more straight forward.

Genetic Fuzzy Systems (GFS) are a category of techniques for learning fuzzy systems, or parts of them, using evolutionary computation. The definition could be extended to include the categories of other nature inspired population based

N. Bassiliades et al. (Eds.): RuleML 2011 - Europe, LNCS 6826, pp. 297–304, 2011.

heuristics such as particle swarm optimization, ant systems, etc. They are part of recent trends, in soft computing and computational intelligence, to combine neural networks, fuzzy systems and a range of heuristic techniques. We apply several multiobjective evolutionary algorithms, including NSGAII and a steady state version of NSGAII SSNSGAII [2], and SPEA2 [11]. In addition, we adapt the approach to MOCell (a cellular algorithm) which increases diversity on the pareto front [9], and FastPGA which reduces CPU time expensive fitness evaluations [4].

The remainder of the paper is organized as follows. section 2 describes the approach and methodology. Section 3 provides experimental results comparing the methodology to other techniques using standard datasets. Finally section 4 concludes the paper.

2 Approach and Method

This section provides details on the approach to implementing an evolving fuzzy rule system for classification. We describe the classification problem and the tradeoff between classifier accuracy and simplicity, followed by the fuzzy rule based approach.

2.1 Description of the Problem and Multiple Objectives

We consider classifiers to be rulebases which can define a mapping $D : \Re^n \rightarrow \Omega$ from a vector of observations $\mathbf{x} = x_1, \ldots, x_n \in \Re^n$ to a set of c class labels $\omega_1, \ldots, \omega_c \in \Omega$. The problem considered in this paper is to utilize the relationship between classifier characteristics simplicity and accuracy to promote generalizable classifiers. This is through defining two primary conceptual objectives in the classifier design: accuracy in classification and simplicity of the classification rules. Given a decision vector $\mathbf{g}$, a series of "genes" which on decoding specify a fuzzy rulebase classifier. there are two objectives denoted $f_{error}(\boldsymbol{x})$ (the accuracy objective) and $f_{complexity}(\mathbf{x})$, (the rulebase simplicity objective). We can express this problem as follows:

$$\text{minimize } \mathbf{z} = f_{error}(\mathbf{x}), f_{complexity}(\mathbf{x}).$$

The accuracy objective performance is a measure of the classification error in determining the class of a set of examples T. Each example is a tuple containing crisp feature observations y_i and a matching class $c_i = (y_1, y_2, \ldots, y_n, c_i) \in C$. The is measured as follows:

$$f_{error}(\mathbf{x}) = 1 - \frac{\text{No. correct classifications}}{\text{Total No. of training examples}}.$$

A set of fuzzy if-then rules always contains three main sources of complexity:

1. the number of rules,
2. the number of statements about linguistic labels within each rule (i.e. the number of inputs in the rules),
3. the complexity of the qualifiers or membership functions (e.g. if a rule uses the qualifier "high", then how is high defined).

It is not possible to reduce the output complexity except possibly by changing to a different type of fuzzy system. Therefore, $f_{simplicity}$ is decomposed into three components (which are modeled as separate objectives in the evolutionary approach). These objectives are: counting the *number of rules* used in classification, and the second is the *average number of inputs used per rule* = total number of inputs/number of rules. And so, for this multiobjective problem, given two evolved fuzzy rulebase solutions, $\mathbf{x_1}$ and $\mathbf{x_2}$, we can say that $\mathbf{x_1}$ dominates $\mathbf{x_2}$ iff

1. $f_{error}(\mathbf{x_1}) < f_{error}(\mathbf{x_2})$ and,
2. $f_{No.rules}(\mathbf{x_1}) < f_{No.rules}(\mathbf{x_2})$ and,
3. $f_{No.inputs/rule}(\mathbf{x_1}) < f_{No.inputs/rule}(\mathbf{x_2})$.

If one of these conditions is true, then we can say t $\mathbf{x_1}$ dominates $\mathbf{x_2}$ in that objective.

2.2 Fuzzy Rule Based Classifiers

In the evolutionary approach, a fundamental aspect of the method is to define of a mapping between the representation of fuzzy rules that is used in application (termed the phenotype) and the internal representation that is used in the evolutionary process (called the genotype).

A single rule r_k of M rules that make up a rulebase has the following form:

$$R_k : \text{if } x_1 \text{ is } A_1 \wedge \ldots \wedge x_n \text{ is } A_n; \text{ then } (z_{k,1}, \ldots, z_{k,c})$$

where $x_1 \ldots x_n$ are feature observations that are described by linguistic labels $A_1 \ldots A_n$, these are common in the different rules. Examples of possible descriptions are low, high, medium etc. A rulebase is a set of rules $r_1, r_2, \ldots, r_k$. The consequent is interpreted as a degree of certainty an observation is a member in each class given the pattern of features specified in the antecedent if part. The output is calculated analytically in the approach from training data:

$$z_{k,i} = \frac{\text{Sum of matching degrees of rule k with examples of class i}}{\text{Sum of total matching degrees of rule k for all examples}}$$

We implement classifiers of the Tageki-Sugeno-Kang form (TSK) including types 1 to 4, see for instance [8].

The genotype is the the internal representation for the evolutionary process. The genotype comprises of ordered slots to contain each rule (and within each rule, the input and consequent components), and these slots have a boolean switch to indicate whether the rules (or rule component) are active. Rulebases are represented internally using a sequence of integers and floating point values.

3 Experimentation

The approach is examined using five separate datasets from the UCI Machine Learning repository. Due to limited space, additional information on the datasets may be found at UCIML website [1].

[1] http://archive.ics.uci.edu/ml/

Table 1 shows results for the datasets reported in the literature. Table 2 shows the average best result from 30 runs for the MOEA and fuzzy system evaluation methods that were tested. Those results we obtained that were as good, or better than, previous best results are marked with an asterix in table 2.

Table 1. Results for classification error that have been reported in the literature and references

Dataset	Reported Error	Reference
Breast Cancer	4.1 - 6.5	[7,10]
Iris	0.5 - 4	[3]
Glass	24.4, 32.06	[1,6]
Ionosphere	13.1 (C4.5 algorithm res. = 5.9), 5-6 (Fung's res.)	[3,5]
P I Diabetes	26 - 27 (C4.5 was 24.4)	[3]

Table 2. Average best results of the methods tested (from 30 runs). NB * means better or as good as results used as a comparison found in the literature (table 1).

	NSGAII	SPEA2	SSNSGA	FPGA	Cell
BC					
FS 1	6.35*	6.44*	7.32	10.53	7.86
FS 2	37.5	39	38.9	39.72	37.87
FS 3	4.47*	4.29*	5.33*	7.11	6.17
FS 4	36.11	38.2	38.9	37.5	39.1
Iris					
FS 1	1.67*	2.29*	4.16	3.33*	5
FS 2	0.83*	2.5*	1.67*	5	3.33*
FS 3	2.08*	1.67*	1.67*	3.33*	4.16
FS 4	4.17	3.33*	1.67*	4.16	1.67*
Glass					
FS 1	36.05	35.19	32.57	33.14	34.3
FS 2	34.88	41.86	34.89	40.69	42.44
FS 3	30.81*	28.49*	30.81*	33.72	30.23*
FS 4	38.95	37.2	37.21	36.05	41.86
Ionosphere					
FS 1	14.084*	15.84	18.66	19.71	23.94
FS 2	60.3	59.32	58.09	64.789	62.67
FS 3	16.54	19.71	20.422	21.83	17.25
FS 4	64.12	63.98	63.38	60.91	63.03
Diabetes					
FS 1	23.7*	23.86*	20.13 *	21.76*	22.89*
FS 2	25.32	25.81	28.24	24.18	28.41
FS 3	22.72*	18.83 *	21.1 *	20.29*	19.96*
FS 4	29.38	26.79	27.59	23.53*	25.32

Table 3. Regression equations with form $ClassificationError = Intercept + (NoRules)X_1 + (NoInput)X_2$ together with coefficient of determination (R^2). Results where no tradeoff was found are not included (TSK FS 2 and 4 sometimes did not provide a tradeoff between complexity and interpretability in the more complex datasets).

	Intercept	No.Rules Coef.	No.Input Coef.	R^2
Breast Cancer Dataset				
TSK FS 1				
SPEA2.Error	31.8	-4.07 (p = 4.56e-66)	-2.77 (p= 9.34e-40)	0.68
NSGAII.Error	27.87	-4.81 (p = 1.07e-47)	-2.27 (p= 2.48e-31)	0.73
TSK FS 3				
SPEA2.Error	27.99	-7.3 (p = 1.01e-14)	-1.43 (p= 1.94e-46)	0.72
NSGAII.Error	29.22	-6.43 (p = 7.38e-33)	-2.58 (p= 8.24e-25)	0.65
Glass Dataset				
TSK FS 1				
SPEA2.Error	60.37	-5.12 (p = 2.53e-02)	-0.61 (p= 4.96e-22)	0.37
NSGAII.Error	55.52	-1.43 (p = 2.77e-07)	-1.35 (p= 8.9e-03)	0.16
TSK FS 2				
SPEA2.Error	64.02	-3.85 (p = 3.82e-42)	-2.67 (p= 5.3e-26)	0.62
NSGAII.Error	65.46	-1.52 (p = 8.4e-48)	-4.45 (p= 1.80e-02)	0.45
TSK FS 3				
SPEA2.Error	60.35	-0.84 (p = 9.4e-31)	-3.96 (p= 1.39e-01)	0.43
NSGAII.Error	61.89	-5.06 (p = 3.06e-25)	-2.2 (p= 7e-36)	0.5
TSK FS 4				
SPEA2.Error	59.37	0.15 (p = 9.48e-34)	-3.39 (p= 8.05e-01)	0.37
NSGAII.Error	59.55	-1.58 (p = 1.15e-31)	-3.04 (p= 3.17e-04)	0.33
Ionosphere Dataset				
TSK FS 1				
SPEA2.Error	58.08	-3.67 (p = 3.61e-02)	-0.83 (p= 4.81e-110)	0.83
NSGAII.Error	61.48	-4.62 (p = 2.05e-11)	-5.89 (p= 9.77e-59)	0.82
TSK FS 3				
SPEA2.Error	62.07	-2.04 (p = 1.35e-43)	-11.47 (p= 3.55e-34)	0.8
NSGAII.Error	58.92	-3.62 (p = 4.84e-02)	-1.78 (p= 1.42e-45)	0.64
TSK FS 4				
SPEA2.Error	62.07	-2.04 (p = 1.35e-43)	-11.47 (p= 3.55e-34)	0.8
NSGAII.Error	58.92	-3.62 (p = 4.84e-02)	-1.78 (p= 1.42e-45)	0.64
Pima Indians Diabetes				
TSK FS 1				
SPEA2.Error	33.26	-2.15 (p = 9.02e-10)	-0.53 (p= 7.74e-24)	0.4
NSGAII.Error	31.54	-0.77 (p = 6.41e-05)	-0.43 (p= 1.16e-02)	0.14
TSK FS 2				
SPEA2.Error	32.5	0.61 (p = 3.1e-16)	-1.02 (p= 7.91e-02)	0.17
NSGAII.Error	32.97	-1.92 (p = 5.89e-01)	0.08 (p= 2.58e-05)	0.08
TSK FS 3				
SPEA2.Error	28.04	-0.13 (p = 2.69e-27)	-1.07 (p= 6.58e-01)	0.38
NSGAII.Error	36.2	-4.08 (p = 1.30e-08)	-0.55 (p= 6e-44)	0.51
Iris Dataset				
TSK FS 1				
SPEA2.Error	51.34	-8.65 (p = 2.13e-109)	-5.05 (p= 2.16e-27)	0.74
NSGAII.Error	61.34	-18.81 (p = 1.79e-97)	-6.13 (p= 2.53e-68)	0.74
TSK FS 2				
SPEA2.Error	64.23	-28.75 (p = 1.25e-49)	-4.85 (p= 2.85e-69)	0.81
NSGAII.Error	61.04	-29.38 (p = 3.05e-21)	-2.96 (p= 8.57e-48)	0.71
TSK FS 3				
SPEA2.Error	56.07	-19.56 (p = 1.92e-77)	-4.85 (p= 1.68e-68)	0.75
NSGAII.Error	52.35	-18.33 (p = 2.15e-62)	-4.34 (p= 6.76e-62)	0.72
TSK FS 4				
SPEA2.Error	61.85	-35.07 (p = 3.16e-29)	-3.05 (p= 3.98e-85)	0.8
NSGAII.Error	61.28	-28.98 (p = 6.13e-36)	-3.21 (p= 4.02e-77)	0.78

Table 4. Comparison of the best performance VS simplicity for IN and OUT sample results for the No. of Rules and the No. of Input

	OUT Rules	IN Rules	OUT Input	IN Input
Breast Cancer Dataset				
TSK FS 1				
SPEA2.Error	4	6	1.2	3
NSGAII.Error	6	8	2.14	2.33
TSK FS 3				
SPEA2.Error	3	6	1.25	1.57
NSGAII.Error	5	4	1	1.4
Glass Dataset				
TSK FS 1				
SPEA2.Error	2	6	1.67	2.71
NSGAII.Error	4	7	1.4	3.25
TSK FS 2				
SPEA2.Error	3	6	1.75	2
NSGAII.Error	6	5	1.28	1
TSK FS 3				
SPEA2.Error	7	8	3.5	3.44
NSGAII.Error	4	8	3.2	2.77
TSK FS 4				
SPEA2.Error	5	7	1.67	2.25
NSGAII.Error	6	6	2.28	2.42
Ionosphere Dataset				
TSK FS 1				
SPEA2.Error	3	2	7	6.33
NSGAII.Error	3	3	6	6
TSK FS 3				
SPEA2.Error	2	2	6	6.33
NSGAII.Error	1	3	2	7.5
Pima Indian Diabetes				
TSK FS 1				
SPEA2.Error	4	5	1.6	1.83
NSGAII.Error	2	6	0.67	2.28
TSK FS 2				
SPEA2.Error	5	6	1	2
NSGAII.Error	7	8	2.5	2.56
TSK FS 3				
SPEA2.Error	4	7	1.4	2.875
NSGAII.Error	4	7	2.4	2.375
TSK FS 4				
SPEA2.Error	5	8	1.17	2.33
NSGAII.Error	6	7	1.86	1.625
Iris Dataset				
TSK FS 1				
SPEA2.Error	5	7	1.5	1.625
NSGAII.Error	4	4	1.2	1
TSK FS 2				
SPEA2.Error	4	7	1	0.875
NSGAII.Error	7	7	1.125	1.125
TSK FS 3				
SPEA2.Error	4	8	0.8	1.11
NSGAII.Error	5	6	0.83	1
TSK FS 4				
SPEA2.Error	8	8	1.11	1.11
NSGAII.Error	3	6	0.75	0.85
AVERAGE	4.4	6	2.0	2.5

Examples of good overall performance was most common when fuzzy systems of tsk type 1 and 3 were used. The more complex rule aggregation methods did not seem to translate into improved performance in the learned classifiers. However, the more complex tnorm used to aggregate the rule inputs in tsk 3 systems did produce better performance. Generally, these two approaches did achieve respectable results, except in the Ionosphere dataset.

Table 4 shows the simplicity objectives and the classification error solutions in the 5 datasets. Table 3 shows results of fitting a linear model of the relationship between simplicity and accuracy (other models could be used but a linear approach provides balance that allows some insight to be extracted in the general case. In iris the error was reduced, on average, by 3-5% for each increase in average inputs by 1 and by around 25% for additional rules. The linear model of the relationship between simplicity and error (table 3) shows that accuracy is increased by adding rules in all cases and that its impact on the error is statistically significant. The gradient of improvement as additional rules and inputs are added varies in the different cases considered and shows whether additional complexity is useful (ie a shallow gradient means more complexity is useful).

4 Conclusion

This paper has provided an overview the application of a genetic fuzzy system for learning classifiers. It was found that by looking at the best solution overall for out of sample testing, that in comparison to methods in the literature, this approach to learning classification systems was able to perform comparably or better in almost all of the datasets tested. In the introduction we suggested that randomized algorithms might provide some insight into a computer approximation of the "simpler explanations are better" heuristic. The approach showed that there is a clear nexus between simple models and out of sample performance: in over 95% of the test runs the performance the best performing out of sample solution was simpler than the best performing in sample solution. The experiments show interpretability objectives in multiobjective evolutionary algorithms for learning fuzzy rules can lead to rules with greater prediction capability as well as avoiding supercilious complexity.

References

1. Athitsos, V., Sclaroff, S.: Boosting nearest neighbor classifiers for multiclass recognition. Boston University Computer Science Tech. Report No, 2004-006 (February 2004), athitsos@cs.bu.edu
2. Deb, K., Pratap, A., Agarwal, S., Meyarivan, T.: A fast and elitist multiobjective genetic algorithm: Nsga-ii. IEEE Transactions on Evolutionary Computation 6(2), 182–197 (2002)
3. Eggermont, J., Kok, J.N., Kosters, W.A.: Genetic programming for data classification: partitioning the search space. In: SAC, p. 1001 (2004)

4. Eskandari, H., Geiger, C., Lamont, G.: FastPGA: A dynamic population sizing approach for solving expensive multiobjective optimization problems. In: Obayashi, S., Deb, K., Poloni, C., Hiroyasu, T., Murata, T. (eds.) EMO 2007. LNCS, vol. 4403, pp. 141–155. Springer, Heidelberg (2007)
5. Fung, G., Dundar, M., Bi, J., Bharat Rao, R.: A fast iterative algorithm for fisher discriminant using heterogeneous kernels. In: ICML (2004)
6. Jiang, Y., Zhou, Z.-H.: Editing training data for knn classifiers with neural network ensemble. In: Yin, F.-L., Wang, J., Guo, C. (eds.) ISNN 2004. LNCS, vol. 3173, pp. 356–361. Springer, Heidelberg (2004)
7. Zhang, J.l.: Selecting typical instances in instance-based learning. In: Proceedings of the Ninth International Machine Learning Conference, pp. 470–479 (1992)
8. Kuncheva, L.I.: How good are fuzzy if-then classifiers? IEEE Transactions on Systems, Man, and Cybernetics, Part B 30(4), 501–509 (2000)
9. Nebro, A.J., Durillo, J.J., Luna, F., Dorronsoro, B., Alba, E.: Mocell: A cellular genetic algorithm for multiobjective optimization. Int. J. Intell. Syst. 24(7), 726–746 (2009)
10. Mangasarian, O.L., Wolberg, W.H.: Selecting typical instances in instance-based learning. Proceedings of the National Academy of Sciences, 91–93 (1990)
11. Zitzler, E., Laumanns, M., Thiele, L.: Spea2: Improving the strength pareto evolutionary algorithm. Technical report (2001)

Algorithms for Rule Inference in Modularized Rule Bases*

Grzegorz J. Nalepa, Szymon Bobek, Antoni Ligęza, and Krzysztof Kaczor

AGH University of Science and Technology,
Al. Mickiewicza 30, 30-059 Kraków, Poland
{gjn,szymon.bobek,ligeza,kk}@agh.edu.pl

Abstract. In the paper an extended knowledge representation for rules is considered. It is called Extended Tabular Trees (XTT2) and it provides a network of decision units grouping rules working in the same context. The units are linked into an inference network, where a number of inference options are considered. The original contribution of the paper is the proposal and formalization of several different inference algorithms working on the same rule base. Such an approach allows for a more flexible rule design and deployment, since the same knowledge base may be used in different ways, depending on the application.

1 Introduction

Rules constitute a cardinal concept of the rule–based expert systems (RBS for short) [4]. Building such systems requires creating a knowledge base, which in case of RBS can be separated into two parts: fact base containing the set of facts and rule base containing the set of rules. To make use of these two parts, the inference engine must be provided. The inference engine is responsible for generating findings, based on the current state of the fact base using rule conditions. In the first task of the inference mechanism the conditional parts of the rules are checked against the facts from the fact base. This task is performed by *pattern matching algorithm*. The output of the algorithm is the set of rules, which conditional parts are satisfied. This set of rules is called a *conflict set*. The next task of the engine is the execution of the rules from the *conflict set*. There are many different algorithms for determining an execution order of the rules.

A rule-base can contain thousands or even millions rules. Such large rule-bases cause maintenance problems and cause inefficiency of inference (a large number of rules may be unnecessary processed). The modularization of the rule-base that introduces structure to the knowledge base can be considered as the way to avoid them. Rules can be grouped in modules, to facilitate the maintenance of a large set of rules.

The main focus of this paper is the inference in the structured rule bases. Sect. 2 presents knowledge base structuring and inference control algorithms in the well-known expert system shells. The discussion includes three main pattern matching algorithms. In Sect. 3 the issue of knowledge modularization as well as the motivation is given. In Sect. 4 the main concepts of the XTT2 knowledge representation method are introduced.

* The paper is supported by the PARNAS Project funded from NCN (National Science Centre) resources for science.

N. Bassiliades et al. (Eds.): RuleML 2011 - Europe, LNCS 6826, pp. 305–312, 2011.

Sect. 5 introduces the inference methods for XTT2 knowledge bases. A practical case study is presented in Sect. 6. The conclusions of the paper are included in Sect. 7.

2 Classic Rule Inference Algorithms

An expert system shell is a framework that facilitates creation of complete expert systems. Usually, they provide most of the important functionalities: rule language, inference algorithm, explanation mechanism, user interface, knowledge base editor.

CLIPS [4] is an expert system tool that is based on the Rete algorithm. It provides its own programming language that supports rule-based, procedural and object-oriented programming. *JESS* [3] is a rule engine and scripting environment derived form CLIPS and written entirely in Java. It uses CLIPS rule syntax. *Drools* [1] provides a unified and integrated platform for Business Rules, Workflows (Processes) and Events. All these shells share similar inference control solutions.

Every inference algorithm performs the following operations: 1) *Match* rule LHSs (Left Hand Sides) to determine which are satisfied according to the content of the working memory (WM). 2) *Conflict set resolution* selects rules(s) (*instantiation(s)*) that has satisfied LHS. 3) *Action* Perform the actions in the RHS (Right Hand Sides) of the selected rule(s). 4) Goto 1. The first step is a bottleneck of inference process. The algorithms, which are presented in this section, try to address this problem.

The *Rete algorithm* [2] is an efficient pattern matching algorithm for implementing production rule systems. The main advantage of the Rete algorithm is that it tries to avoid iterating over production and WM by storing the information between cycles. Each pattern stores the list of the elements that it matches – when WM is changed only the changes are analyzed. Rete also can avoid iterating over production set. When the WM is changed, the altered working elements are let in to the a tree-like structure (*network*) that was compiled previously from the patterns (rules). Each node of the network tries to match the given working element. If it matches, then the copy of the element is passed to all the successors of the node. The leaves of the Rete tree contain information about changes to be applied to the conflict set.

The main idea of the *TREAT algorithm* [6] is to exploit the *conflict set support* for temporarily redundant systems. The conflict set is explicitly retained across production system cycles which allows for the following advancements comparing to Rete: 1) in case of addition of WM element, conflict set remains the same, and constrained search for new instantiation of only those rules that contain newly added WM element is performed. 2) deletion from WM triggers direct conflict set examination for rules to remove. No matching is required to process deletion since any instantiation of the rule containing removed element is simply deleted.

Gator algorithm. Both Rete and TREAT offer static networks that dos not depend on the characteristic of the system. This very often leads to the creation of networks that are not optimal for some knowledge bases. To address this problem a new discrimination network algorithm called Gator was proposed. It is based on Rete, but additionally implements mechanisms for optimizing network structure according to specific knowledge base characteristic. It can be said that Rete and TREAT are special cases of Gator and as reported in [5] it outperforms TREAT and Rete in most cases.

3 Knowledge Modularization Techniques

Most of expert systems have flat knowledge base, so the inference mechanism has to check each rule against each fact. When the knowledge base contains a large number of rules and facts this process becomes inefficient. This problem is addressed by providing a structure in the knowledge base that allows for checking only a subset of rules.

CLIPS can organize rules into so called *modules* that allow for restriction of access to their elements from other modules. They can be compared to global and local scoping in other programming languages. Modularization of knowledge base helps managing rules, and improves efficiency of rule-based system execution. Each module has its own pattern-matching network for its rules and its own agenda. Only module that has *focus* set is processed by the inference engine. The current focus can be dynamically switched in RHS of the rule or can be arbitraly set at the begining of the inference process.

Jess provides *modules* mechanism that helps to manage large numbers of rules. Modules also provide a control mechanism: the rules in a module will fire only when that module has the focus, and only one module can be in focus at a time. The main difference between CLIPS module and Jess module is that the second one can be considered as nothing more than a namespace for rules. In terms of efficiency the modules mechanism does not influence on the performance of the *conflict set* creation.

Drools have a built-in functionality to define the structure of the rulebase which can determine the order of the rules evaluation and execution. This functionality is provided by the *jBPM5* component. The rules can be grouped in a ruleflow–groups which defines the subset of rules that are evaluated and executed. Ruleflow–groups have a graphical representation as the nodes on the *ruleflow* diagram. They are connected with the links what determines the order of its evaluation. However, there is no policy which determines when a rule can be added to the ruleflow-group. Due to this fact, the rules groupping can cause problems in the rule base especially in case of large rulebases.

The limitations of rule inference in existing shells give motivation for this research. A flexible and expressive rule formalization method is considered. It allows for proposing different formalized inference modes for modularized rule bases.

4 Formalization of Modularized Rule Bases with XTT2

XTT2 rule representation method is formalized with the use of the Attributive Logic with Set Values over Finite Domains ALSV(FD) [8]. This calculus was proposed to increase the expressive power of the rule language, as well as to open up possiblity of fromalized design and analysis of rules. In this logic it is assumed tha the state of a rule-based system is described using attributes. Each attribute has the set of allowed values which it can take (a domain) A domain is assumed to be a finite (discrete) set. In ALSV(FD) two types of attributes are identified: *simple* taking only one value at any time, and *generalized* taking multiple values at any time. Using a set of relational operators formulae are built. These formulae form rule conditions.

ALSV(FD) triples e_i are defined as follows: $(A_i, \propto, V_i)$ for attributes that can take sets as a value and $(A_i, \propto, d_i)$ for attributes that can take a single value, where A_i is an attribute, $\propto$ is an ALSV(FD) operator. The V_i is a set of values from the attributes domain and d_i is a single value from the attribute domain.

XTT2 *Rule* Let us consider the set of all rules defined in the knowledge base denoted as $\mathbb{R}$. A single XTT2 rule is a triple: $r = (\mathbb{COND}, \mathbb{DEC}, \mathbb{ACT})$ where $\mathbb{COND} \subset \mathbb{E}$, $\mathbb{DEC} \subset \mathbb{E}$, where $\mathbb{E}$ is the set of ALSV(FD) triples and $\mathbb{ACT}$ is a set of actions to be executed when a rule is fired. A rule can also be written using LHS and RHS: $LHS(r) \rightarrow RHS(r), DO(\mathbb{ACT})$, where $LHS(r)$ and $RHS(r)$ correspond respectively to the condition and decision parts of the rule r, and $DO(\mathbb{ACT})$ involves executing actions from a predefined set. Actions are not included in the RHS of the rule because it is assumed that they are independent from the considered system, and the execution of actions does not change the state of the system.

Rule Schema. Let us consider a concept of a *rule schema*. Each rule has a schema that is a pair of attributes sets: $h(r) = (H^{cond}, H^{dec})$, where H^{cond} and H^{dec} sets define the attributes occuring in the conditional and decision part of the rule. A schema is used to identify rules working in the same situation (operational context). Such a set of rules can form a decision component in the form of a decision table. A schema can also be considered a table header.

Decision Component (Table). Let us consider a *decision component* (or table). It is an ordered set (sequnce) of rules having the same rule schema, defined as follows: $t = (r_1, r_2, \ldots, r_n)\ \forall_{i,j}: r_i, r_j \in t \Rightarrow h(r_i) = h(r_j)$ where $h(r_i)$ is a schema of the rule r_i. In XTT2 the rule schema h can also be called the schema of the component (or table). Components are connected (linked) in order to provide inference control.

Inference Link. An *inference link* l is an ordered pair: $l = (r, t),\ l \in \mathbb{R} \times \mathbb{T} \cup \{\bot\}$ where $\mathbb{R}$ is the set of rules in the knowledge base, and $\mathbb{T}$ is the set of tables in the knowledge base. A single link connects a single rule (a row in a table) with another table. An empty link is denoted as $\bot$. A structure composed of linked decision components is called a XTT2 knowledge base.

XTT2 *Knowledge Base.* The XTT2 *knowledge base* is the set of components connected with links. It can be defined as an ordered pair: $X = (\mathbb{T}, \mathbb{L})$ where: $\mathbb{T}$ is a set of components (tables), $\mathbb{L}$ is a set of links, and all the links from $\mathbb{L}$ connect rules from $\mathbb{R}$ with tables from $\mathbb{T}$. Links are introduced during the design process according to the specification provided by the designer. The knowledge base forms an inference network.

5 XTT2 Inference Algorithms Formalization

Below, we describe three algorithms for inference control in the XTT2 network (see 1). In order to define and formalize inference approaches a general algorithm is given first.

Main Inference Algorithm
INPUT:

$\mathbb{U}$ – an ordered set of tables, $\mathbb{U} \subset \mathbb{T}$; the function z determining the number of tokens needed for a table execution: $z\colon \mathbb{T} \rightarrow \mathbb{N} \times \mathbb{N}$ and $z(t) = (k_n, k_r)$ where k_n is the number of tokens required for execution of a given table, and k_r a number of received tokens; initial state s_0. $\mathbb{U}$ and z are built using the selected algorithm: DDI, TDI, GDI.

OUTPUT: the final state of the system: s_n.

1. If $\mathbb{U} = \emptyset$ then STOP.
2. Initialize the current state $s_c \leftarrow s_0$.
3. In a loop, process all tables in $\mathbb{U}$:
   (a) Select the next table from $\mathbb{U}$ as t.
   (b) For the table t if $k_r < k_n$, where $z(t) = (k_n, k_r)$ then go to step 3a.
   (c) In a loop, process all rules in table t:
      i. Select next rule in table t as r.
      ii. Fire rule r, that changes the system state $s_c \leftarrow s'$.
      iii. If there exists a link from r in t to a table t', and $k'_r < k'_n$, where $z(t') = (k'_n, k'_r)$, then $k'_r \leftarrow k'_r + 1$.
4. $s_n \leftarrow s_c$.
5. STOP.

The *Data-Driven Inference* algorithm identifies start tables, and puts all the tables that are linked to the initial ones in the XTT2 network into a FIFO queue. When there are no more tables to be added to the queue, the algorithm fires selected tables in the order they are popped from the queue.

Data-Driven Inference Algorithm

INPUT: set of tables: $\mathbb{T}$, set of schemas: $\mathbb{H}$.
OUTPUT: ordered set of tables to be fired: $\mathbb{U}$, and corresponding values of z.

1. Find the set of start tables $N_1 \subset \mathbb{T}$ containing tables where conditional attributes are independent of other attributes (in the sense of table schemas): $N_1 \leftarrow \{t_i : h(t_i) = (H_i^{cond}, H_i^{dec}), \forall j : h(t_j) = (H_j^{cond}, H_j^{dec}), H_i^{dec} \cap H_j^{cond} = \emptyset\},\ i \neq j$
2. In a loop:
   (a) If $N_1 \leftarrow \emptyset$ then STOP.
   (b) Build set of tables $N_2 \subset \mathbb{T}$ containing these tables which have the same set of attributes in their conditional part (H^{cond}) as the set of attributes in the conclusion part of the tables (H^{dec}) from N_1:
   $N_2 \leftarrow \{t_k : \forall_i t_i \in N_1 : H_k^{cond} = H_i^{dec}\}$ and $N_2 \cap (\mathbb{U} \cup N_1) = \emptyset$
   (c) $\forall t_k \in N_2 : z(t_k) = (0, 0)$.
   (d) $\mathbb{U} \leftarrow \mathbb{U} \cup N_1$.
   (e) $N_1 \leftarrow N_2$.

The forward-chaining strategy is suitable for simple tree-like inference structures. However, it has limitations in a general case, because it cannot determine tables having multiple dependants.

The *Token-Driven Inference* is based on monitoring the partial inference order defined by the network structure with tokens assigned to tables. A table can be fired only when there is a token at each input. Let us consider $\mathbb{L}$ a set of all links, and $\mathbb{T}$ is set of all tables. Two functions $prev$ and $leaves$ are introduced: $prev$ returns a set of previous tables determined by links. $leaves$ returns a set of start tables determined by links.

Token-Driven Inference Algorithm

INPUT: set of tables: $\mathbb{T}$, set of links: $\mathbb{L}$.
USES: $leaves(t_i, N)$, $prev(t)$.

OUTPUT: ordered set of tables to be fired: $\mathbb{U}$, corresponding values of z

1. Find the set of tables $N_1 \subset \mathbb{T}$ where decision attributes constitute system response.
2. In a loop:
   (a) If $N_1 \leftarrow \emptyset$ then STOP.
   (b) Find the set $N_2 \subset \mathbb{T}$ of previous tables for each tables belonging to N_1:
   $N_2 \leftarrow \{t \in \mathbb{T} \colon t \in prev(t_i)\}\ \forall_i t_i \in N_1$, where $t \notin (\mathbb{Q} \cup N_1)$
   (c) Find the number of start tables for all tables in N_2:
   $z(t) = (|leaves(t, \emptyset)|, 0)$ for every $t \in N_2$.
   (d) $\mathbb{U} \leftarrow \mathbb{U} \cup N_1$
   (e) $N_1 \leftarrow N_2$

This model of inference execution covers the case of possible loops in the network, e.g. if there is a loop and a table should be fired several times, the token is passed from its output to its input, and it is analyzed if can be fired; if so, it is placed in the queue.

The *goal-driven approach* works backwards with respect to selecting the tables necessary for a specific task, and then fires the tables forward so as to achieve the goal. One or more output tables are identified as the ones that can generate the desired goal values and are put into a LIFO queue. As a consequence, only the tables that lead to the desired solution are fired, and no rules are fired without purpose. The algorithm of building a stack for the goal-driven inference can be defined as follows.

Goal-Driven Inference Algorithm

INPUT: set of tables: $\mathbb{T}$, set of schemas: $\mathbb{H}$, where $h(t_i) = (H_i^{cond}, H_i^{dec})$ is a schema of table $t_i \in \mathbb{T}$.
OUTPUT: ordered set of tables to be fired: $\mathbb{U}$, and corresponding values of z

1. Find the set of tables $N_1 \subset \mathbb{T}$, that have conclusion attributes constituting a required system response (the goal): $N_1 \leftarrow \{t_i \in \mathbb{T} \colon \forall_i \nexists t_j\ H_i^{dec} = H_j^{cond},\ i \neq j\}$
2. In a loop:
   (a) If $N_1 \leftarrow \emptyset$ then STOP.
   (b) Build set of tables $N_2 \subset \mathbb{T}$ containing these tables which have the same set of attributes in their conclusion part as the set of attributes in the conditional part of the tables from N_1: $N_2 \leftarrow \{t_k \in \mathbb{T} \colon \forall_i H_k^{dec} = H_i^{cond}\},\ t_i \in N_1$
   (c) $z(t) = (0, 0)$ for every $t \in N_2$
   (d) $\mathbb{U} \leftarrow \mathbb{U} \cup N_1$
   (e) $N_1 \leftarrow N_2$

The Goal-Driven Inference may be particularly suitable for situations where the context of the opeartion may clearly defined and it is possible to clearly identify the knowledge component that needs to be evaluated.

6 Simple Case Study

The implementation of the XTT2 method includes two representations: textual suitable for processing by a rule engine, and visual aimed at a design tool. The visual one is

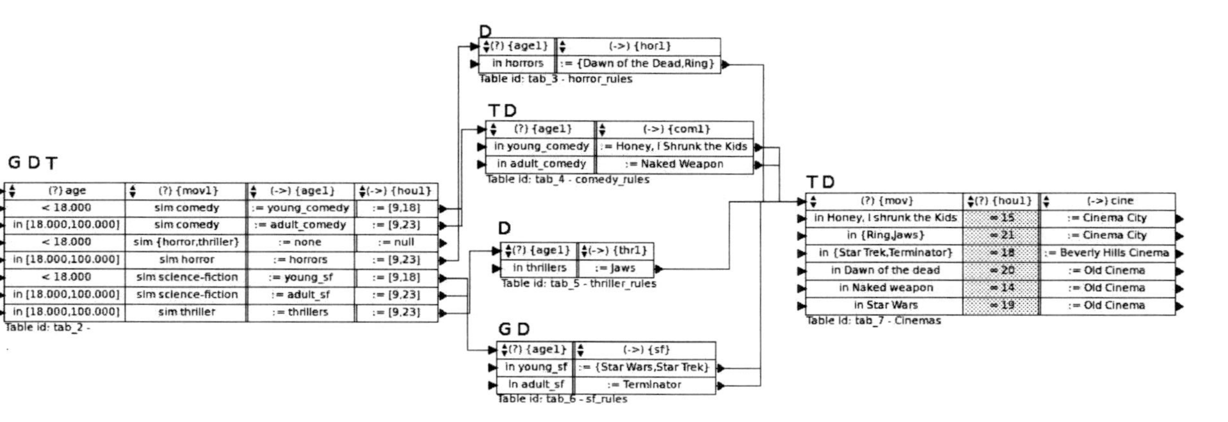

D Data Driven Inference - Tables fired by this mode are marked with D. In the example it was assummed that user age is 21 and movie preference is comedies

G Goal Driven Inference - Tables fired by this mode are marked with G. In the example it was assumed that user age is 21 and movie preference is science-fiction and as a Goal table, the "tab_7 - Cinemas" table was selected.

T Token Driven Inference - Tables fired by this mode are marked with T. In the example it was assummed that user age is 21 and movie preference is comedies.

Fig. 1. Different inference modes

supported by the HQEd graphical editor. The textual one is called HMR (*HeKatE Meta Representation*). It is directly processed by a dedicated inference engine for XTT2 rule bases – HeaRT [7]. It implements the custom inference control algorithms. Depending on the problem that has to be solved, different inference algorithm can be selected to improve efficiency of the reasoning process. Applying different inference modes to the same knowledge base can be compared to asking system different questions.

In Fig. 1 three queries to the simple XTT2 system were presented. The system, based on user profile and age is supposed to suggest a cinema to go to watch a movie. Three possible ways of reasoning are possible thanks to the three inference modes described in Sect. 5: *Data Driven* – to answer the question what time and what films a customer can see in which cinemas; *Goal Driven* – what science-fiction films are suitable for a customer; *Token Driven* – the same as Data Driven, but with highly improved efficiency, due to omitting tables that do not led to the solution.

7 Concluding Remarks

In this paper the issue of providing different inference algorithms for modularized rule bases was tackled. Modularization is useful in case of larger rule bases where number of rules working in the same context are related on the logical level. While existing systems provide certain technical means of rule set decomposition, the inference algorithms they use do not support efficient inference in the decomposed rule base.

The original contribution of the paper is the introduction of practical inference algorithms for modularized (non-flat) rule bases built with the XTT2 representation. The algorithms allow for reusing the same rule base for different inference tasks and use-case scenarios. While the approach is oriented towards a custom rule language, it can be considered a more generic one. In fact, the XTT2 language is expressive enough to cover the semantics of classic CLIPS-like production rules languages.

References

1. Browne, P.: JBoss Drools Business Rules. Packt Publishing (2009)
2. Forgy, C.: Rete: A fast algorithm for the many patterns/many objects match problem. Artif. Intell. 19(1), 17–37 (1982)
3. Friedman-Hill, E.: Jess in Action, Rule Based Systems in Java. Manning (2003)
4. Giarratano, J., Riley, G.: Expert Systems. Principles and Programming, 4th edn. Thomson Course Technology, Boston (2005) ISBN 0-534-38447-1
5. Hanson, E.N., Hasan, M.S.: Gator: An Optimized Discrimination Network for Active Database Rule Condition Testing. Tech. Rep. 93-036, CIS Department University of Florida (December 1993)
6. Miranker, D.P.: TREAT: A Better Match Algorithm for AI Production Systems; Long Version. Tech. Rep. 87-58, University of Texas (July 1987)
7. Nalepa, G.J.: Architecture of the HeaRT hybrid rule engine. In: Rutkowski, L., Scherer, R., Tadeusiewicz, R., Zadeh, L.A., Zurada, J.M. (eds.) ICAISC 2010. LNCS, vol. 6114, pp. 598–605. Springer, Heidelberg (2010)
8. Nalepa, G.J., Ligęza, A.: HeKatE methodology, hybrid engineering of intelligent systems. International Journal of Applied Mathematics and Computer Science 20(1), 35–53 (2010)

Modularity in the Rule Interchange Format

Carlos Viegas Damásio[1], Anastasia Analyti[2], and Grigoris Antoniou[3]

[1] CENTRIA, Departamento de Informática Faculdade de Ciências e Tecnologia
Universidade Nova de Lisboa, 2829-516 Caparica, Portugal
cd@di.fct.unl.pt
[2] Institute of Computer Science, FORTH-ICS, Crete, Greece
analyti@ics.forth.gr
[3] Institute of Computer Science, FORTH-ICS, and
Department of Computer Science, University of Crete, Crete, Greece
antoniou@ics.forth.gr

Abstract. The adoption of standards by the knowledge representation and logic programming communities is essential for their visibility and impact. The Rule Interchange Format is a fundamental effort in this direction that should be supported by users, developers and theoreticians. For this reason, it is essential to the community to discuss the recommendations published by the W3C RIF Working Group. In particular, this paper presents the semantics of Rule Interchange Format (RIF) of multi-documents, analyses it and some deficiencies are elicited. A more general approach is proposed as an alternative semantics for multi-documents. As a side important result, some relevant problems in the semantics of RIF-FLD are also discussed and possible ways out are proposed.

Keywords: Semantic Web, Rule Interchange Format, Modularity, Logic Programming, Language Issues, Many-valued Semantics.

1 Introduction

The development of the Semantic Web requires appropriate modular constructs for the combination of rulebases and ontologies. This is an essential problem to software engineering and its difficulty rockets with the distributed and woven character of the Semantic Web. The simplest mechanism is the basic importing of ontologies or rulebases, like the ones available in the Web Ontology Language [21,20] and Rule Interchange Format [27]. Others address the problem of extracting and reusing subsets of ontologies in order to avoid using irrelevant parts of knowledge and thus reducing complexity of reasoning (e.g. see [14,16,18] and references therein). Packaged-Based Description Logic [6] is a general approach of contextualized interpretations of ontologies with semantic mappings among names, addressing several fundamental issues in a theoretical sound way. Compositionality and modularity of reasoning for logic programming languages has been studied for a long time [8] and recently have obtained novel results for Answer Set based semantics [19,13]. Finally, the syntactic modular constructs for

N. Bassiliades et al. (Eds.): RuleML 2011 - Europe, LNCS 6826, pp. 313–328, 2011.

logic programming systems for programming-in-the-large have been extensively analysed and several approaches appear in the literature (e.g. [17,5]).

This paper results from the attempt to align the syntax and semantics of our Modular Web Framework [4,5], which allows the safe and controlled use of weak negation in the Semantic Web, with the general RIF Framework for Logic Dialects (RIF-FLD [27]). Unfortunately, this proved to be impossible due to general problems identified both in the semantics of ordinary formulas and of document formulas in RIF-FLD. Here we report the identified problems, discuss and advance proposals for their correction.

The Rule Interchange Format Framework for Logic Dialects [27] proposes two forms of structuring logical documents, via import and module mechanisms. The import mechanism allows the use of profiles in order to include in a RIF logical theory other logical theories with a specific semantics or syntax, e.g. RDF or OWL. The semantics of import with profiles is left open for the RIF dialects to define the intended behaviour. The import mechanism without profile corresponds roughly to the textual import of the contents of RIF documents, modulo local constants, and will be discussed in detail in this paper. The module mechanism allows the remote linking of external theories to the enclosing RIF document where it is used, and will also be analysed.

This paper start by illustrating the MWeb approach with a motivating example. Next, we present the basics of the RIF-FLD semantics, and in particular describing the semantics of some connectives and elicit their problems. Subsequently we describe the syntax of RIF document formulas, and overview in detail the corresponding semantics and its singular features. The deficiencies of the current proposal will be pointed out and an alternative semantics encompassing solution will be provided. The changes in the definition of some connectives require also a generalization of the notion of model, and the corresponding notion of logical entailment, which are briefly treated. Conclusions finish this work.

2 The MWeb Approach

The Modular Web framework [4,5] addresses in a principled way several aspects of knowledge sharing and integration in the Semantic Web. The MWeb framework provides mechanisms supporting safe uses of non-monotonic negation in scoped closed and open world assumptions in logic rules for Semantic Web applications, under the full control of rulebase providers and consumers. In order to make the MWeb approach widely applicable, we have started the alignment with the RIF syntax as well as an attempt to semantically extend RIF-FLD framework to encompass MWeb's semantics. Several issues have been elicited in this process, which are better explained with a concrete MWeb rulebase example.

Typical MWeb rulebases can be found in figures 1 and 2 where Geographical data is provided and used to describe information about universities[1]. Every

[1] The examples can be tried out with the implementation publicly available at `http://centria.di.fct.unl.pt/~cd/mweb`

MWeb rulebase has an interface, and a logical document part where knowledge is specified by facts and rules. The current MWeb syntax is akin to RIF's presentation syntax, where the # operator expresses class membership in RIF, while ## subclass inclusion. Moreover, we also allow F-logic like frames of the form $o.[p_1\text{-»}v_1, \ldots, p_2\text{-»}v_n, \ldots]$ (equivalent to $o.[p_1\text{-»}v_1]$, and $o.[p_2\text{-»}v_2]$, and ...) represent that object o is related via property p_1 to value v_1, etc. With this information, the meaning of the logical part of both rulebases is immediate.

```
GEO interface (geo.mw)
:- rulebase 'http://geography.int'.

:- prefix xsd = 'http://www.w3.org/2001/XMLSchema#'.
:- prefix geo='http://geography.int#'.
:- import('rdf.mw',interface).

:- defines local closed class(geo:Continent).
:- defines local open class(geo:Country) wrt context class(geo:PoliticalEntity).
:- defines local open ?X.[ rdf:type -» geo:Country ] wrt context class(geo:PoliticalEntity).
:- defines local definite class(geo:City), class(geo:PoliticalEntity).
:- defines local definite property(geo:located_in), property(geo:part_of),
                          property(geo:city_name).
```

```
GEO rulebase (geo.rb)
:- import('rif.rb', rulebase).
:- import('rdf.rb', rulebase ).

geo:Africa # geo:Continent.           geo:America # geo:Continent.
geo:Antarctica # geo:Continent.          geo:Asia # geo:Continent.
geo:Europe # geo:Continent.           geo:Oceania # geo:Continent.

geo:Country ## geo:PoliticalEntity.

geo:EU.[ geo:part_of -» geo:Europe, rdf:type -» geo:PoliticalEntity].
geo:Spain.[ geo:part_of -» geo:EU, rdf:type -» geo:Country ].
geo:Portugal.[ geo:part_of -» geo:EU, rdf:type -» geo:Country ].
geo:Cataluna.[ geo:part_of -» geo:Spain, rdf:type -» geo:PoliticalEntity ].

geo:Barcelona.[ geo:located_in -» geo:Cataluna, rdf:type -» geo:City,
                geo:city_name -» "Barcelona"^^xsd:string ].
geo:Lisboa.[ geo:located_in -» geo:Portugal, rdf:type -» geo:City,
             geo:city_name -» "Lisboa"^^xsd:string, geo:city_name -» "Lisbon"^^xsd:string ].

?X.[ geo:located_in -» ?Z ] :- ?Y.[ geo:part_of -» ?Z ], ?X.[ geo:located_in -» ?Y ].
```

Fig. 1. Geographic MWeb Rulebase

The interface document provides an Internationalized Resource Identifier (IRI) for the rulebase, an optional base IRI address as well as prefixes for shortening writing of IRIs. More important, the interface can (textually) import other interfaces. In Fig. 1 and Fig. 2, an interface defining the vocabulary of the RDF language is imported (not shown). An optional `vocabulary` declaration can be used to list the vocabulary of the rulebase. Next, follow two blocks of declarations. The first block defines the predicates being defined in the MWeb rulebase, and correspond to a generalization of the export declarations found in logic programming based languages. The second block corresponds to a generalization of import declarations, as shown in the rulebase of Fig. 2.

```
INST interface (inst.mw)
:- rulebase 'http://institution.int'.
:- prefix xsd = 'http://www.w3.org/2001/XMLSchema#'.
:- prefix geo='http://geography.int#'.
:- prefix inst = 'http://institution.int#'.
:- import('rdf.mw',interface).

:- defines local normal class(inst:Institution).
:- defines local normal inst:address(?ID,?NAME,?STREET,?NUMBER,?CITY,?COUNTRY).

:- uses definite class(geo:Country).
:- uses definite property(geo:located_in), property(geo:city_name).
:- uses definite property(rdf:type) from 'http://geography.int#'.
```

```
INST rulebase (inst.rb)
:- import('rdf.rb', rulebase ).

:- defines internal definite inst:address/5.

?ID # inst:Institution :- inst:address( ?ID, ?_, ?_, ?_, ?_ ).

inst:address(inst:UBAR,"Universitat Barcelona"^^xsd:string,
    "Calle 1"^^xsd:string,2,"Barcelona"^^xsd:string).
inst:address(inst:UNL, "Universidade Nova de Lisboa"^^xsd:string,
    "Rua 2"^^xsd:string,3,"Lisboa"^^xsd:string).

inst:address(?ID,?NAME,?STREET,?NUMBER,?CITY,?COUNTRY) :-
    inst:address(?ID,?NAME,?STREET,?NUMBER,?CITYNAME),
    ?CITY.[ geo:city_name -> ?CITYNAME ],
    ( ?CITY.[ geo:located_in -> ?COUNTRY ] ) @ 'http://geography.int',
    (?COUNTRY.[ rdf:type -> geo:Country ] ) @ 'http://geography.int'.
```

Fig. 2. Institutional MWeb Rulebase

The interesting feature of the MWeb framework is that besides scope (i.e. internal, local, or global), different reasoning modes can be associated to predicates (i.e. definite, open, closed, or normal). This allows control of monotonicity of reasoning by the producer and consumer of the knowledge. In what follows, we use the term predicates to mean an ordinary predicate, a class or a property.

Global and local predicates are visible in the Semantic Web, the difference being that local predicates can only be declared in a single rulebase; internal predicates are not visible. Normal predicates are general predicates which can use weak negation in the bodies, and therefore are non-monotonic. The remaining predicates cannot use weak negation in the bodies of rules, but strong negation is allowed. Closed predicates are used to make closed-world assumptions with respect to the rulebase vocabulary, or with respect to the provided context in the declaration. For instance, declaring the class `geo:Continent` closed means that everything which is not concluded to be a continent in the geographic MWeb rulebase of Fig. 1 is assumed to be non-continent. In practice, this corresponds to define the class by the program containing the facts in the program plus the extra logical rule: `neg ?X # geo:Continent :- naf ?X # geo:Continent.`

The rule expresses that every ?X which cannot be proved to be a continent (naf ?X # geo:Continent) then it is known not to be a continent (neg ?X # geo:Continent). In intuitive terms, the above rule states that the list of continents provided is exhaustive. This illustrates the extra power of having two forms of negations, and why we require them in our MWeb language. Open predicates implement open-world assumptions, where unknown information can be either true or false. This is captured by a rule like the one above and its dual with respect to strong negation. Definite predicates are monotonic predicates which can use the monotonic strong negation. Also note in Fig. 1 that the `geo:Country` class is made open and exported in two ways, the last one in the form of frames representing RDF triples. The relationship between RIF predicate # and `rdf:type` frames is captured by the rules in `'rdf.rb'`, which is imported by `'geo.rb'`. The import of document `'rif.rb'` provides the rules for capturing the semantics of # and ##, and is redundant since it is imported as well in `'rdf.rb'`.

Regarding the `uses` declarations, a rulebase must specify the import mode of the predicate which is combined with the defining mode. In general, the predicate is obtained (called) at runtime from all rulebases defining it, except when an explicit rulebase list is provided specifying the providing rulebases (as in the last declaration of Fig. 2). A used predicate can be complemented with extra rules in the logical part. However, one can explicitly indicate the rulebase to call with the `@` operator and thus uses the original predicate, as shown in Fig. 2.

From this short presentation of MWeb, it is concluded that we require mechanisms to represent the interface, the logical document, import documents, call predicates in other modules, as well as two forms of negation. We will see that RIF-FLD presents difficulties/problems in any of these issues.

3 Basics of Rule Interchange Format Semantics

The Rule Interchange Framework for Logic Dialects [27] provides the general syntax and semantics for the rule languages to be used in the Semantic Web. The syntax and semantics is quite flexible and general having 13 distinct kinds of terms and 9 kinds of formulas, which can be further extended. It supports the usual conjunctive, disjunctive, rule, and quantified formulas and provides also two forms of negation, namely symmetric (strong) and default negation. Additionally, it includes document and remote formulas. Document formulas are used for defining the semantics of formulas in multi-documents (e.g. for defining the notion of module) and remote formulas are used for querying other documents inside a formula in a RIF document.

Specific dialects like RIF Core [26], RIF Basic Logic Dialect [23] have been specified but none uses default negation (designated `Naf` by RIF) nor symmetric negation (designated `Neg`). The other main recommendation being developed by W3C RIF group is RIF Production Rule Dialect [28] which uses only default negation over sets of ground facts, and cannot be applied to predicates defined by rules. Additionally, there have been defined some specialized RIF Dialects to cover the syntax of semantics of disjunctive logic programs under the stable model semantics RIF-CASPD ([24]) and well-founded semantics with default and strong (symmetric) negation RIF-CLPWD ([25]). However, the approach followed in the definitions of RIF-CASPD and RIF-CLPWD is against the current trends in the literature for defining the semantics of logic programs [22,10,9] because of the way RIF-FLD semantics has been defined. Namely, RIF-CASPD and RIF-CLPWD resort to an explicit quotient syntactic definition in order to obtain the intended models, while in the approaches of [22,10,9] this is fully captured model-theoretically by appropriate definitions of the truth-value lattices and interpretation of logical connectives. A "minimization" or preferential entailment is still necessary, as in RIF-FLD semantics.

The details of the syntax and semantics of RIF-FLD are long and involved, and cannot be fully presented in this paper. Therefore, we will focus on the relevant parts of the recommendation where we found some problems. For further information, the reader is referred to the standards defined by the RIF W3C Working Group [27] and to the recent overview [7]. RIF-FLD semantics is based on a complex semantic structure with more than a dozen kinds of different mappings, for capturing the intended meaning of each of the type of terms that the language allows. However, for our purpose is enough to analyse the underlying set of truth-values as well as the semantics of negations and rule formulas.

Definition 1 (Set of truth-values [27]). *Each RIF dialect must define the set of truth values, denoted by* **TV**.

1. *This set must have a partial order, called the truth order, denoted* $\leq_t$. *In some dialects,* $\leq_t$ *can be a total order.*
2. *In addition,* **TV** *must be a complete lattice with respect to* $\leq_t$.
3. **TV** *is required to have two distinguished elements,* **f** *and* **t**, *such that* $\mathbf{f} \leq_t elt$ *and* $elt \leq_t \mathbf{t}$ *for every* $elt \in \mathbf{TV}$.
4. **TV** *has an operator of negation,* $\sim: \mathbf{TV} \to \mathbf{TV}$, *such that*
   - $\sim$ *is a self-inverse function: applying* $\sim$ *twice gives the identity mapping.*
   - $\sim \mathbf{t} = \mathbf{f}$ *(and thus* $\sim \mathbf{f} = \mathbf{t}$*).*

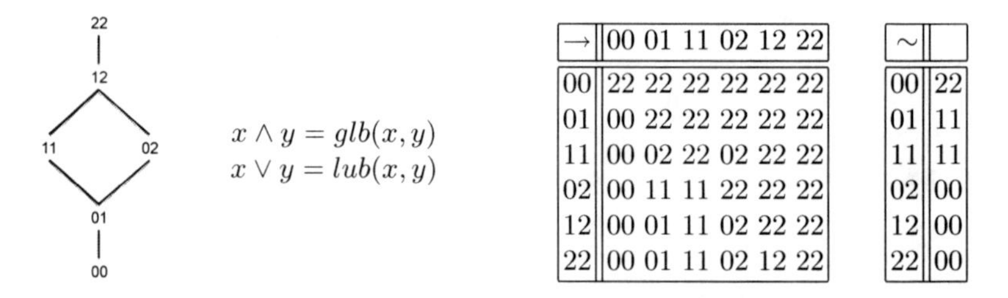

→	00	01	11	02	12	22
00	22	22	22	22	22	22
01	00	22	22	22	22	22
11	00	02	22	02	22	22
02	00	11	11	22	22	22
12	00	01	11	02	22	22
22	00	01	11	02	12	22

~	
00	22
01	11
11	11
02	00
12	00
22	00

Fig. 3. Truth values and truth-tables for Partial Equilibrium Logic (WFS) [9]

Notice that the condition forcing the existence of elements **f** and **t** is redundant since this follows immediately from **TV** being a complete lattice. Conjunction and disjunction are interpreted as greatest lower bound (glb) and least upper bound (lub) in **TV**. The first significant remark is that the only sensible and widely adopted constraint imposed to negation operators has not been stated: a negation operator must be anti-monotonic, i.e. reverse the truth ordering. Formally, for every $elt_1, elt_2 \in \mathbf{TV}$ if $elt_1 \leq_t elt_2$ then $\sim elt_2 \leq_t \sim elt_1$. The other constraints are questionable, as we explain below.

$\mathbf{TV} = \{-2 < -1 < 0 < +1 < +2\}$

$x \wedge y = \min(x, y)$
$x \vee y = \max(x, y)$

$\rightarrow$	-2	-1	0	$+1$	$+2$
-2	$+2$	$+2$	$+2$	$+2$	$+2$
-1	$+2$	$+2$	$+2$	$+2$	$+2$
0	$+2$	$+2$	$+2$	$+2$	$+2$
$+1$	-1	-1	0	$+2$	$+2$
$+2$	-2	-1	0	$+1$	$+2$

$\sim$	
-2	$+2$
-1	$+2$
0	$+2$
$+1$	-1
$+2$	-2

$-$	
-2	$+2$
-1	$+1$
0	0
$+1$	-1
$+2$	-2

Fig. 4. Truth values and truth-tables for Equilibrium Logic (*ASP*) [22]

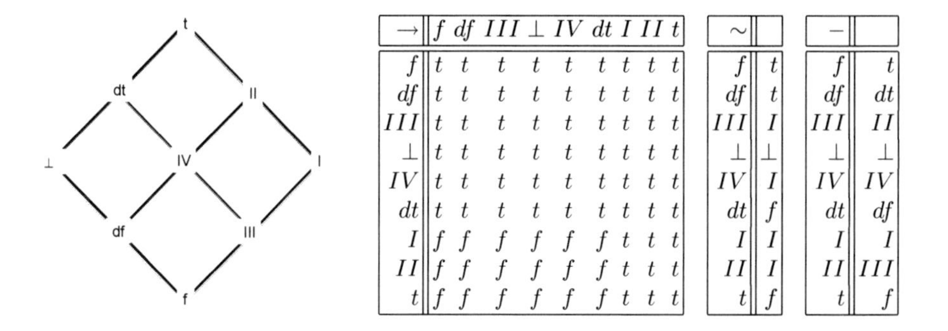

$\rightarrow$	f	df	III	$\bot$	IV	dt	I	II	t
f	t	t	t	t	t	t	t	t	t
df	t	t	t	t	t	t	t	t	t
III	t	t	t	t	t	t	t	t	t
$\bot$	t	t	t	t	t	t	t	t	t
IV	t	t	t	t	t	t	t	t	t
dt	t	t	t	t	t	t	t	t	t
I	f	f	f	f	f	f	t	t	t
II	f	f	f	f	f	f	t	t	t
t	f	f	f	f	f	f	t	t	t

$\sim$	
f	t
df	t
III	I
$\bot$	$\bot$
IV	I
dt	f
I	I
II	I
t	f

$-$	
f	t
df	dt
III	II
$\bot$	$\bot$
IV	IV
dt	df
I	I
II	III
t	f

Fig. 5. Truth values and truth-tables for Nine Logic ($WFSX_p$) [11]

The interpretation of the negations is then defined in RIF-FLD as follows, where $TVal_{\mathbf{I}}$ is the truth-valuation function from the set of formulas other than document formulas and remote formulas to the set of truth-values **TV**. Document formulas and remote terms are analysed in the next section.

Definition 2 (Truth-valuation for negations [27]). *Let Φ be a RIF well-formed formula other than a document formula or a remote formula, and* **I** *be a semantic structure.*

- $TVal_{\mathbf{I}}(\texttt{Neg Neg } \Phi) = TVal_{\mathbf{I}}(\Phi)$.
- $TVal_{\mathbf{I}}(\texttt{Naf } \phi) = \ \sim TVal_{\mathbf{I}}(\Phi)$.

While the interpretation of `Neg` is rather loose, just requiring that the double negation law is obeyed, on the contrary, the interpretation of `Naf` is too strong.

$$\mathbf{TV} = \{F_0 < F_1 < F_2 < \ldots < 0 < \ldots < T_2 < T_1 < T_0\}$$

$$x \rightarrow y = \begin{cases} T_0 \text{ if } x \leq y \\ y \text{ otherwise} \end{cases}$$

$\sim$	F_0 F_1 $\ldots$ F_n $\ldots$ 0 $\ldots$ T_n $\ldots$ T_1 T_0
	T_1 T_2 $\ldots$ T_{n+1} $\ldots$ 0 $\ldots$ F_{n+1} $\ldots$ F_2 F_1

Fig. 6. Truth values and truth-tables of the Infinite Valued Semantics (WFS) [10]

The essential problem with the previous definition is that the negations of Equilibrium Logic [22] underlying Answer Set semantics [15] and extensions are ruled out by RIF-FLD semantics. The same happens to Well-founded Semantics with Explicit Negation and its extensions [2,1,12]. The reason is the same for all these semantics since the double negation law for default negation does not hold, as can be seen in Figures 3-6 (the truth-table for symmetric negation is $-$).

Moreover, the remaining condition imposing that the negation of true is false and vice-versa is not even obeyed by the infinite-valued logic [10] presented in Fig. 6, which can be seen as the proper model-theoretical definition of well-founded semantics. Thus, both conditions imposed by Def. 1 discard all the (recent) model-theoretical approaches found in the literature for the major semantics of logic programming. In fact, a common general condition that all these semantics obey is that negation is anti-monotonic, which is not enforced. The double negation law for strong negation holds in the shown cases, corresponding to the major semantics in the literature.

The semantics of rule-implication also brings problems to some of the above-mentioned semantics since one of the imposed constraints is again not obeyed.

Definition 3 (Truth-valuation for rule implication [27]). *Let Φ be a RIF well-formed formula other than a document formula or a remote formula, and* **I** *be a semantic structure.*

1. $TVal_{\mathbf{I}}(head\ \texttt{:-}\ body) = \mathbf{t}$ *if* $TVal_{\mathbf{I}}(head) \geq_t TVal_{\mathbf{I}}(body)$;
2. $TVal_{\mathbf{I}}(head\ \texttt{:-}\ body) <_t \mathbf{t}$ *otherwise.*

All the mentioned model-theoretical semantics for logic programming with negation(s) obey to the first condition imposed. However, the second condition is not satisfied by the Equilibrium Logic and by the Well-founded Semantics with Explicit Negation (the ones having strong negation – see figures 4 and 5). For this reason, we suggest discarding completely the second condition from the semantics of rule implication. This is related to the notion of logical entailment, which we will discuss subsequently. However, we require first the notion of multi-structure to be able to introduce the notion of logical entailment.

4 Rule Interchange Format Document Formulas

The RIF document formulas provide the general encapsulation of the RIF group of Formulas. Note that group formulas are not document formulas, and a document formula is associated to at most one group formula.

Definition 4 (Document and Group Formulas [27]). *The presentation syntax of document and group formulas of RIF-FLD is captured by the following EBNF grammar.*

```
Document ::= IRIMETA? 'Document'
      '(' Dialect? Base? Prefix* Import* Module* Group? ')'
Dialect  ::= 'Dialect' '(' Name ')'
```

```
Base     ::= 'Base' '(' ANGLEBRACKIRI ')'
Prefix   ::= 'Prefix' '(' NCName ANGLEBRACKIRI ')'
Import   ::= IRIMETA? 'Import' '(' LOCATOR PROFILE? ')'
Module   ::= IRIMETA? 'Module' '(' (Const | Expr) LOCATOR ')'
Group    ::= IRIMETA? 'Group' '(' (FORMULA | Group)* ')'
```

For our purposes we are interested solely in the `Import` and `Module` directives. The import directive has a mandatory `LOCATOR` which specifies where the corresponding document can be found. Locators include for instance *URLs* but others can be defined by the dialect. The module directive has a an argument (a logical *Term*) before `LOCATOR` which will be used to refer to the module in remote terms of the form Φ @ *Term*, which can be found at `LOCATOR`.

A first issue is immediately recognized: RIF-FLD does not have the notion of interface. There are two easy solutions for this problem, always depending on using a document (formula) to express the interface information. A first solution relies on the use of meta-annotations to provide the missing information, while the other alternative requires assertion of specific formulas in a new vocabulary to express this information, as is done for instance with RDF schema or OWL2 `Declaration` axiom. We tend to prefer the latter approach, since this would allow to use RIF's `Import` to express our own `import` (in interfaces and logical parts of MWeb), and RIF's `Module` to capture our `uses` declaration.

The semantics of document formulas is captured by semantic multi-structures, i.e. a special set of RIF-FLD semantic structures. See [27,7] for full details. Semantic structures are an extension of first-order logic semantics in order to be able to assign meaning to every kind of (HiLOG) terms and formulas in the language, including for instance datatypes and remote terms. These semantic structures are built from a set of truth-values **TV** (see the previous section), datatypes, the domain **D** (or universe) and several total mappings to interpret the different RIF-FLD formulas. In particular, we need for our discussion the total mapping $\mathbf{I}_C$ mapping constants in the countable infinite set of constant symbols `Const` to elements of the domain **D**, and $\mathbf{I}_{truth}$ mapping elements of the domain **D** to truth values in **TV** for evaluating arbitrary formulas (see [27] for more details). A significant feature of the RIF-FLD semantics is that any formula is mapped first into an element of the domain, and afterwards the mapping $\mathbf{I}_{truth}$ is used to determine its truth-value.

Definition 5 (Semantic multi-structures [27]). *A semantic multi-structure,* $\hat{\mathbf{I}} = \{J, K; I^{i_1}, I^{i_2}, \ldots; M^{j_1}, M^{j_2}, \ldots\}$, *is a set of semantic structures such that*

- J *and* K *are the usual RIF-FLD semantic structures; and*
- I^{i_k} *and* M^{j_k}, *where* $k = 0, 1, 2, \ldots$, *are semantic structures adorned with locators of RIF-FLD document formulas (one can think of adorned structures as locator-structure pairs). The locators used in* $\hat{\mathbf{I}}$ *must be of the kinds allowed in the* `Import` *and* `Module` *directives.*

The semantic structures J, K, *and all the structures* I^{i_k} *in the import group are required to be identical in all respects except that the mappings* J_C, K_C, *and* $I_C^{i_k}$ *(for all* i_k*), which interpret constants in the semantic structures, may differ* *on those constants in* `Const` *that belong to the* `rif:local` *symbol space. The semantic structures* M^{j_k} *in the last group have many more degrees of freedom: they are required to agree with the other structures in* $\hat{\mathbf{I}}$ *only to the extent that the mappings* $M_C^{j_k}$ *must coincide with* J_C*,* K_C*, and* $I_C^{i_k}$ *on all constants in* `Const` *except the ones in the* `rif:local` *symbol space.*

As detailed in [27], the first semantic structure, J, is used to interpret non-document formulas (i.e. the group formula and its contents). The structure K is used for document formulas. The structures in the middle group, I^{i_k}, are optional; they are used to interpret imported documents (via the `Import` directive). All structures in that group must be adorned with the locators of distinct documents. The structures in the last group, M^{j_k}, are also optional; they are used to interpret documents that are linked as remote modules to other documents (via the `Module` directive). The structures in that group must also be adorned with locators of distinct documents. However, the same locator can adorn a structure in the import group and a structure in the module group.

Mark that `rif:local` constants are interpreted locally in each document, either in imported or module documents. The import structures must coincide except for these constants, while modules must interpret constants in the same way except for the `rif:local` constants. This simplifies a lot matters, but some approaches like Package-Description Logics refuse such a condition [6] having explicit mechanisms for mapping of vocabulary between different packages, in particular constants. We will not address this issue in this paper but can be identified as a potential problem of the RIF multi-document semantics.

Definition 6 (Imported document [27]). *Let* Δ *be a document formula and* `Import(loc)` *be one of its import directives, where* `loc` *is a locator of another document formula,* Δ'*. In this case, we say that* Δ' *is directly imported into* Δ*. A document formula* Δ' *is said to be imported into* Δ *if it is either directly imported into* Δ *or it is imported (directly or not) into another document, which itself is directly imported into* Δ*.*

Definition 7 (Remote module [27]). *Let* Δ *be a document formula and let* `Module(n loc)` *be one of its remote module directives*[2]*, where* `loc` *is a locator for another document formula,* Δ'*. In this case, we say that* Δ' *is a directly linked remote module of* Δ*. A document formula* Δ' *is said to be a linked remote module for* Δ *if it is either directly linked to* Δ *or it is linked (directly or not) to another document, which is directly linked to* Δ*.*

Notice that the import relation and the linked module relation are made independent by the previous definitions, which is in our opinion a major source of problems. However, some relation between them is imposed by the next definition, which specifies how remote formulas are handled by linking to the interpretation of remote modules:

[2] Note that n is the term used to refer to the module.

Definition 8 (Term-interpreting mapping for remote term refs [27]). *Let Δ be a document formula and $\hat{\mathbf{I}} = \{J, K; I^{i_1}, I^{i_2}, \ldots; M^{j_1}, M^{j_2}, \ldots\}$ be a semantic multi-structure that contains semantic structures for all the documents that are imported into Δ or linked to it as remote modules (directly or indirectly). Let $\Phi@r$ be a remote term that appears in Δ or one of its imported or linked documents, say Δ', and let $L \in \hat{\mathbf{I}}$ be a semantic structure. If there is a unique remote module directive* `Module(`$n\ j_k$`)` *in Δ' such that $L(r) = L(n)$ then $L(\Phi@r) = M^{j_k}(\Phi)$. If no such remote module directive exists or if such a directive is not unique, then $L(\Phi@r)$ is indeterminate, i.e., it can be any element in the domain of L. Truth valuation is extended as $TVal_L(\Phi@r) = I_{truth}(L(\Phi@r))^3$.*

In our reading, the previous definition has two problems. First, if there is a module directive inside an imported document, say i_l, then the corresponding semantic structure will not be added to $\hat{\mathbf{I}}$ since the import relation does not include them (modules are not followed by the import). But, then the module directive `Module(`$n\ j_k$`)` in Δ_{i_l} will be used to provide meaning to the remote term $\Phi@r$ via the (possibly) non-existing M^{j_k} semantic structure. An even more strange behaviour occurs for import directives inside modules, which are ignored by the previous definition. An example of these situations can be found in Fig. 7, which is based on the rulebases described in Section 2.

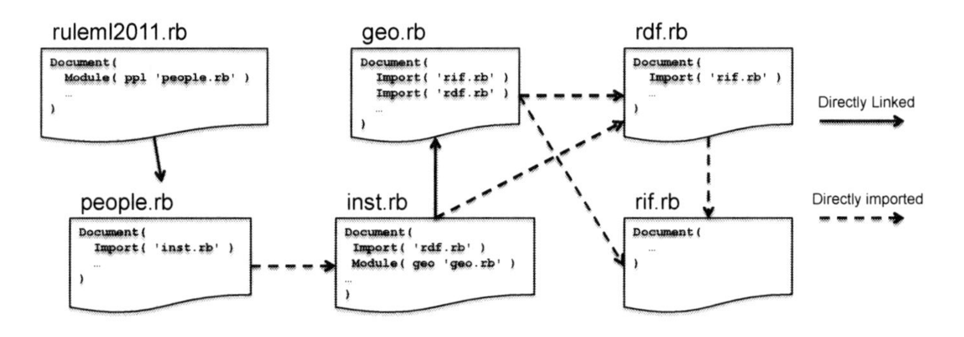

Fig. 7. Multi-document example

When trying to assign meaning to the document formula in 'ruleml2011.rb', the multi-document structure will only include semantic structures for documents in 'people.rb', while one would expect to have semantic structure for all documens in the figure, and in particular the module in 'geo.rb'. Additionally, there is a problem lurking which is that imported documents in different modules are interpreted by the same semantic structure, which does not make sense at all. In the figure, one would expect a different semantic structure for interpreting the imported document 'rdf.rb' in rulebases 'inst.rb' and 'geo.rb'. To complete the overview of the RIF-FLD semantics for document formulas we just need to introduce the truth-valuation of all formulas, document or not:

[3] I_{truth} is a total mapping $\mathbf{D} \rightarrow \mathbf{TV}$ used to define truth valuation for formulas.

Definition 9 (Truth valuation in multi-document structures [27]). *Let Δ be a document formula and let $\Delta_1 \dots \Delta_n$ be all the RIF-FLD document formulas that are imported (directly or indirectly, according to the previous definition) into Δ. Let $\Gamma, \Gamma_1, \dots, \Gamma_n$ denote the respective group formulas associated with these documents. Let $\hat{\mathbf{I}} = \{J, K; I^{i_1}, I^{i_2}, \dots; M^{j_1}, M^{j_2}, \dots\}$ be a semantic multi-structure whose import group contains semantic structures adorned with the locators $i_1 \dots i_n$ in the documents $\Delta_1 \dots \Delta_n$. Then we define:*

$$TVal_{\hat{\mathbf{I}}}(\Delta) = glb_t(TVal_K(\Gamma), TVal_{I^{i_1}}(\Gamma_1), \dots, TVal_{I^{i_n}}(\Gamma_n)).$$

For the non-document formulas Φ then $TVal_{\hat{\mathbf{I}}}(\Phi) = TVal_J(\Phi)$.

5 Alternative Semantics for Multi-documents

Our approach to the semantics of multi-documents is based on separating the interpretations of import from module directives. We take care first of import via importing multi-structures, which will be used to interpret documents as well as modules. A semantic importing multi-structure corresponds to RIF-FLD multi-structure without the optional module semantic structures.

Definition 10 (Semantic importing multi-structures). *A semantic importing multi-structure, $\tilde{\mathbf{I}} = \{J_{\mathbf{I}}, K_{\mathbf{I}}; \mathbf{I}^{i_1}, \mathbf{I}^{i_2}, \dots\}$, is a set of semantic structures of the form where*

- *$J_{\mathbf{I}}$ and $K_{\mathbf{I}}$ are the usual RIF-FLD semantic structures; and*
- *$\mathbf{I}^{i_k}$ where $k = 0, 1, 2, \dots$, are semantic structures adorned with locators of RIF-FLD document import formulas.*

The semantic structures $J_{\mathbf{I}}$, $K_{\mathbf{I}}$, and all the structures $\mathbf{I}^{i_k}$ in the import group are required to be identical in all respects except that the mappings $J_{\mathbf{I}_C}$, $K_{\mathbf{I}_C}$, and $\mathbf{I}_C^{i_k}$ (for all i_k), which interpret constants in the semantic structures, may differ on those constants in `Const` *that belong to the* `rif:local` *symbol space.*

Each module as well as the main document will have a corresponding semantic importing multi-structure in our new notion of modular semantic multi-structure.

Definition 11 (Modular semantic multi-structure). *A modular semantic multi-structure is a set $\overline{\mathbf{M}} = \{\tilde{\mathbf{M}}^{?j_0}, \tilde{\mathbf{M}}^{j_1}, \tilde{\mathbf{M}}^{j_2}, \dots\}$ of semantic importing multi-structures such that*

- *$\tilde{\mathbf{M}}^{?j_0}$ is a semantic importing multi-structure, for providing the interpretation of the main document, which might be adorned with a locator j_0; and*
- *$\tilde{\mathbf{M}}^{j_k}$ where $k = 0, 1, 2, \dots$ are semantic importing multi-structures adorned with locators of RIF-FLD document module formulas,*

Moreover, all the mappings of constants in the semantic structures composing $\tilde{\mathbf{M}}^{?j_0}, \tilde{\mathbf{M}}^{j_1}, \tilde{\mathbf{M}}^{j_2} \dots$ must coincide on all constants in `Const` *except the ones in the* `rif:local` *symbol space.*

The rationale of modular semantic multi-structures is that each module may interpret differently their imported documents but must all coincide in the non-local constants. Remote term references will be interpreted in the corresponding semantic importing multi-structure.

Definition 12 (Term-interpreting mapping for remote term references). *Let Δ be a document formula and $\overline{\mathbf{M}} = \{\tilde{\mathbf{M}}^{?j_0}, \tilde{\mathbf{M}}^{j_1}, \tilde{\mathbf{M}}^{j_2}, \ldots\}$ be the modular semantic multi-structure with optional locator j_0 such that*

- $\tilde{\mathbf{M}}^{?j_0}$ *is a semantic importing multi-structure, containing an ordinary semantic structure for all the documents that are imported into Δ (directly, or indirectly);*
- $\tilde{\mathbf{M}}^{j_k}$ *is a semantic importing multi-structure, containing an ordinary semantic structure for all the documents that are imported into Δ^{j_k} (directly, or indirectly), where Δ^{j_k} is the document formula of a module located in j_k;*
- *if a directive* `Module(`n j_m`)` *occurs in any document formula of Δ or Δ^{j_k} or in any document imported or linked by them, then the corresponding semantic importing multi-structure $\tilde{\mathbf{M}}^{j_m}$ must occur in $\overline{\mathbf{M}}$. The locator j_0 of main document is mandatory if it occurs in some* `Module` *directive.*

Let $\Phi@r$ be a remote term that appears in Δ (resp. Δ^{j_k}) or in one of its imported documents, say Δ', and let $L \in \tilde{\mathbf{M}}^{?j_0}$ (resp. $L \in \tilde{\mathbf{M}}^{j_k}$) be an ordinary semantic structure. If there is a unique remote module directive `Module(`n j_m`)` *in Δ' such that $L(r) = L(n)$ then $L(\Phi@r) = J_{\tilde{\mathbf{M}}^{j_m}}(\Phi)$. If no such remote module directive exists or if such a directive is not unique, then $L(\Phi@r)$ is indeterminate, i.e., it can be any element in the domain of L. Truth valuation is extended as $TVal_L(\Phi@r) = I_{truth}(L(\Phi@r))$.*

The conditions of Definition 12 guarantee that imported modules are treated separately in the several modules, and that each semantic importing multi-structure contains all the imported modules directly or indirectly. Furthermore, all modules occurring in a document formula or any imported or remote linked document have a corresponding semantic importing multi-structure.

Returning to the example of Fig. 7, we will have in the modular semantic multi-structure three semantic importing multi-structures. The one for the main document located in `'ruleml2011.org'` has no importing semantic structures. The importing multi-structure for document in `'geo.rb'` contains importing semantic structures for `'rdf.rb'` and `'rif.rb'`. The remaining importing semantic structure results from module in `'people.rb'`, and contains three importing structures for `'rdf.rb'`, `'rif.rb'`, and `'inst.rb'`. Note that it is not needed a semantic importing multi-structure for `'inst.rb'` since this document is never mentioned in a `Module` declaration. Finally, the semantics for multi-documents can be appropriately defined by extending the truth-valuation function for semantic importing and modular semantic multi-structures.

Definition 13 (Truth valuation in multi-document structures). *Let Δ be a document formula and let $\Delta_1 \ldots \Delta_n$ be all the RIF-FLD document formulas that are imported (directly or indirectly, according to the previous definition)* *into Δ. Let $\Gamma, \Gamma_1, \ldots, \Gamma_n$ denote the respective group formulas associated with these documents. Let $\tilde{\mathbf{I}} = \{J_{\mathbf{I}}, K_{\mathbf{I}}; \mathbf{I}^{i_1}, \mathbf{I}^{i_2}, \ldots\}$ be a semantic importing multi-structure whose import group contains semantic structures adorned with the locators $i_1 \ldots i_n$ in the documents $\Delta_1 \ldots \Delta_n$. Then we define:*

$$TVal_{\tilde{\mathbf{I}}}(\Delta) = glb_t(TVal_{K_{\mathbf{I}}}(\Gamma), TVal_{\mathbf{I}^{i_1}}(\Gamma_1), \ldots, TVal_{\mathbf{I}^{i_n}}(\Gamma_n)).$$

For the non-document formulas Φ then $TVal_{\tilde{\mathbf{I}}}(\Phi) = TVal_{J_{\mathbf{I}}}(\Phi)$.

Consider now a modular semantic multi-structure $\overline{\mathbf{M}} = \{\tilde{\mathbf{M}}^{?j_0}, \tilde{\mathbf{M}}^{j_1}, \tilde{\mathbf{M}}^{j_2}, \ldots\}$ for any formula (document or not) φ then $TVal_{\overline{\mathbf{M}}}(\varphi) = TVal_{\tilde{\mathbf{M}}^{?j_0}}(\varphi)$.

Basically, the original truth-valuation for multi-document structures is adopted by semantic importing multi-structures, and the semantics of a document is provided by the semantic importing multi-structure of its document formula captured by $\tilde{\mathbf{M}}^{?j_0}$. Notice that the other semantic importing multi-structures in $\overline{\mathbf{M}}$ only affect the semantics of the original document via remote terms, which is apparently the intention under the RIF-FLD semantics for remote modules.

6 Models and Logical Entailment

The notion of model by RIF-FLD follows a standard approach of classical logic and some fuzzy logics:

Definition 14 (Models [27]). *Let $\mathbf{I}$ be a semantic structure or multi-structure. We say that $\mathbf{I}$ is a model of a formula, Φ , written as $\mathbf{I} \models \Phi$ iff $TVal_{\mathbf{I}}(\Phi) = \mathbf{t}$. Here Φ can be a document or a non-document formula.*

The only comment that this definition deserves is that it restricts the usual notion of model in many-valued logics by limiting the distinguished truth-values to $\mathbf{t}$. However, for instance, the logic underlying paraconsistent well-founded semantics with explicit negation has three distinguished truth-values. We suggest generalizing the above definition by allowing a set of truth-values $\mathbf{DV}$ and substituting the condition $TVal_{\mathbf{I}}(\Phi) = \mathbf{t}$ by $TVal_{\mathbf{I}}(\Phi) \in \mathbf{DV}$ and additionally enforcing that $\mathbf{t} \in \mathbf{DV}$. Notice that this definition is an extension of Def. 14 and does not have any impact in already existing dialects. Finally, let us discuss logical entailment:

Definition 15 (Logical entailment [27]). *Let Φ and Ψ be (document or non-document) RIF-FLD formulas. We say that $\Phi \models \Psi$ iff for every intended semantic multi-structure $\hat{\mathbf{I}}$ it is the case that $TVal_{\hat{\mathbf{I}}}(\Phi) \leq_t TVal_{\hat{\mathbf{I}}}(\Psi)$.*

This is a natural definition of logical entailment for many-valued logics, and the relationship to the original definition of rule implication is obvious since $\Phi \models \Psi$ iff $\models \Phi \rightarrow \Psi$, i.e. it is assumed the deduction meta-theorem. However, the notion of logical entailment adopted for instance in Equilibrium Logic [22] resorts again to the notion of designated truth-values. Accordingly, an alternative more encompassing notion of logical entailment for the RIF-FLD framework would be that $\Phi \models \Psi$ iff $\models \Phi \rightarrow \Psi$ iff for every intended semantic multi-structure $\hat{\mathbf{I}}$ it is the case that $TVal_{\hat{\mathbf{I}}}(\Phi \rightarrow \Psi) \in \mathbf{DV}$, which captures the notion of logical entailment for all the logics presented in Section 3, and generalises Def. 15.

7 Conclusions and Further Work

This paper brings out some issues in the RIF-FLD semantics, for negation connectives, rule implication, models and logic entailment, as well as for multi-documents, all necessary to capture the Modular Web framework [4,5]. It has been shown that the adoption of double negation law for the semantics of negation hinders the RIF intention of providing a sufficient general semantics capable of capturing in a natural way an interesting subset of existing semantics for rule-based systems, namely for extended logic programming under Answer Set Semantics [15] or Well-founded Semantics with Explicit Negation [3,2]. It is argued that the only natural condition to impose is anti-monotonicity of the negation symbol. Problems are also found in the semantics of rule implication, and suggested the removal of one of the conditions. The notion of model is generalized and a proposal for new definition of logical entailment is also advanced. All these proposals are backwards compatible with any existing RIF-FLD dialects. Finally, the semantics of multi-documents in RIF-FLD has been detailed and problems brought out. These issues have been formally corrected according to what seems to be the spirit of [27]. In this way, we expect to succeed in the alignment of the syntax and semantics of our Modular Web framework.

References

1. Alcântara, J., Damásio, C.V., Pereira, L.M.: An encompassing framework for paraconsistent logic programs. J. Applied Logic 3(1), 67–95 (2005)
2. Alferes, J.J., Damásio, C.V., Pereira, L.M.: A Logic Programming System for Non-monotonic Reasoning. Journal of Automated Reasoning 14(1), 93–147 (1995)
3. Alferes, J.J., Pereira, L.M.: On Logic Program Semantics with Two Kinds of Negation. In: Proc. of JICSLP 1992, pp. 574–588 (1992)
4. Analyti, A., Antoniou, G., Damásio, C.V.: A Principled Framework for Modular Web Rule Bases and Its Semantics. In: KR 2008, pp. 390–400. AAAI press, Menlo Park (2008)
5. Analyti, A., Antoniou, G., Damásio, C.V.: MWeb: A principled framework for modular web rule bases and its semantics. ACM TOCL 12(2):#17, 41 (2011)
6. Bao, J., Voutsadakis, G., Slutzki, G., Honavar, V.: Package-based description logics. In: Stuckenschmidt, H., Parent, C., Spaccapietra, S. (eds.) Modular Ontologies. LNCS, vol. 5445, pp. 349–371. Springer, Heidelberg (2009)
7. Boley, H., Kifer, M.: A guide to the basic logic dialect for rule interchange on the web. IEEE Trans. Knowl. Data Eng. 22(11), 1593–1608 (2010)
8. Bugliesi, M., Lamma, E., Mello, P.: Modularity in Logic Programming. Journal of Logic Programming 19(20), 443–502 (1994)
9. Cabalar, P., Odintsov, S.P., Pearce, D., Valverde, A.: Partial equilibrium logic. Ann. Math. Artif. Intell. 50(3-4), 305–331 (2007)
10. Cabalar, P., Pearce, D., Rondogiannis, P., Wadge, W.W.: A purely model-theoretic semantics for disjunctive logic programs with negation. In: Baral, C., Brewka, G., Schlipf, J. (eds.) LPNMR 2007. LNCS (LNAI), vol. 4483, pp. 44–57. Springer, Heidelberg (2007)

11. Damásio, C.V., Pereira, L.M.: A model theory for paraconsistent logic programming. In: Pinto-Ferreira, C., Mamede, N.J. (eds.) EPIA 1995. LNCS (LNAI), vol. 990, pp. 377–386. Springer, Heidelberg (1995)
12. Damásio, C.V., Pereira, L.M.: A Survey of Paraconsistent Semantics for Logic Programs. In: Gabbay, D., Smets, P. (eds.) Handbook of Defeasible Reasoning and Uncertainty Management Systems, vol. 2, pp. 241–320. Kluwer Academic Publishers, Dordrecht (1998)
13. Dao-Tran, M., Eiter, T., Fink, M., Krennwallner, T.: Modular nonmonotonic logic programming revisited. In: Hill, P.M., Warren, D.S. (eds.) ICLP 2009. LNCS, vol. 5649, pp. 145–159. Springer, Heidelberg (2009)
14. Doran, P., Tamma, V., Iannone, L.: Ontology module extraction for ontology reuse: an ontology engineering perspective. In: Proc. of ACM-CIKM 2007, pp. 61–70. ACM, New York (2007)
15. Gelfond, M., Lifschitz, V.: Logic programs with Classical Negation. In: 7th International Conference on Logic Programming (ICLP 1990), pp. 579–597 (1990)
16. Grau, B.C., Horrocks, I., Kazakov, Y., Sattler, U.: A logical framework for modularity of ontologies. In: Proc. IJCAI 2007, pp. 298–304. AAAI, Menlo Park (2007)
17. Kifer, M.: Flora-2: An object-oriented knowledge base language (2007), `http://flora.sourceforge.net/`
18. Konev, B., Lutz, C., Walther, D., Wolter, F.: Semantic modularity and module extraction in description logics. In: Proc. of ECAI 2008, pp. 55–59. IOS Press, Amsterdam (2008)
19. Oikarinen, E., Janhunen, T.: Modular Equivalence for Normal Logic Programs. In: Proc. of ECAI 2006, pp. 412–416 (2006)
20. W3C OWL Working Group (ed.) OWL 2 Web Ontology Language Document Overview. W3C Recommendation (October 27, 2009)
21. Patel-Schneider, P.F., Hayes, P., Horrocks, I.: OWL Web Ontology Language Semantics and Abstract Syntax. W3C Recommendation (February 10, 2004)
22. Pearce, D.: Equilibrium logic. Annals of Math. and Artificial Intelligence 47(1-2), 3–41 (2006)
23. Boley, H., Kifer, M. (eds.) RIF Basic Logic Dialect. W3C Recommendation (June 22, 2010)
24. Heymans, S., Kifer, M. (eds.) RIF Core Answer Set Programming Dialect, 2009. RuleML specification (December 17, 2009)
25. Kifer, M. (ed.) RIF Core Logic Programming Dialect Based on the Well-founded Semantics, 2009. RuleML specification (August 13, 2010)
26. Boley, H., Hallmark, G., Kifer, M., Paschke, A., Polleres, A., Reynolds, D. (eds.) RIF Core Logic Dialect, W3C Recommendation (2010) (June 22, 2010)
27. Boley, H., Kifer, M. (eds.) RIF Framework for Logic Dialects, W3C Recommendation (2010) (June 22, 2010)
28. de Sainte Marie, C., Hallmark, G., Paschke, A. (eds.): RIF Production Rule Dialect. W3C Recommendation (June 22, 2010)

Overview of Knowledge Formalization with XTT2 Rules*

Grzegorz J. Nalepa, Antoni Ligęza, and Krzysztof Kaczor

AGH University of Science and Technology,
Al. Mickiewicza 30, 30-059 Kraków, Poland
{gjn,ligeza,kk}@agh.edu.pl

Abstract. The paper discusses a new formalized knowledge representation for rule-based systems called XTT2. This hybrid knowledge representation combines decision diagrams with extended decision tables. A single decision table contains a set of rules of similar structure operating within a common context. The structure of XTT2 constitutes a hierarchical knowledge representation consisting of lower level knowledge components, where specification is provided by a set of rules working in the same context, and at the higher level, where the decision diagram defines the overall structure of the knowledge base. This model has a concise formalization which opens up possibility for rigorous design and verification. The focus of the paper is on the presentation of the formal aspects of the approach starting from an initial logical specification.

1 Introduction

Formalization of knowledge within a rule-based system can be based on mathematical logic or performed on the basis of engineering intuition. Distinctive examples of rule-based languages emerging from elegant logical formalism include Prolog and Datalog. On the other hand, modern rule-based shells, such as CLIPS, Jess, or Drools, follow the classical paradigm where the rule language is just a programming solution, with no formal definition in the sense of rigorous logical formalism.

The main objectives for introducing a formalization of the rule language are: 1) providing a transparent logical framework enabling in-depth analysis of expressive power and formal properties of the rule base; 2) speeding up the design process – formalized rule language opens possibility to partially formalize the design process which can in turn lead to better design error detection at early design stages; 3) allow for a superior knowledge base quality control – formal methods can be used to identify logical errors in rule formulation [2]; 4) simplifying knowledge translation – partially formalized translation to other knowledge representation formats are possible; 5) propose custom inference modes – structured rule bases require alternative inference strategies [4].

The rule representation discussed in this paper is called XTT2 (*Extended Tabular Trees version 2*). This hybrid knowledge representation combines decision diagrams and decision tables. It forms a transparent and hierarchical visual representation of

* The paper is supported by the AGH UST Grant 11.11.120.859.

N. Bassiliades et al. (Eds.): RuleML 2011 - Europe, LNCS 6826, pp. 329–336, 2011.

the decision tables linked into a network structure. Such knowledge representation assures high density of data presentation. This is due to the fact that the XTT2 model represents rules using the ALSV(FD) (*Attributive Logic with Set of Values over Finite Domains*) logic [4] and decision tables. It is much more expressive than the classic (mostly propositional) rule languages, e.g. it allows for formal specification of non-atomic values of attributes in rule preconditions.

The approach discussed in this paper is based on certain concepts related to dynamic system modeling. The primary assumption is that the rule-based model is a dynamic system having certain *internal state*. The state is described using some *attributes*, that describe certain crucial properties of the system. The state is represented by the set of current *attribute values*. A statement that an attribute has a given value can be interpreted as a *fact* in terms of classic expert systems. The *dynamics* of the system – transitions between states – is modeled using *rules*. For this paper we assume a simple model where given an initial state, the system performs reasoning process that includes firing number of rules and reaching a final state – producing a certain decision. The conditional parts of the rules take the form of a conjunction of atomic formulae in the ALSV(FD) logic which are the *attribute-operator-value* triples. The decision part of the rule includes statements that modify the system state in case the rule is fired (the proper decision) and possibly some actions to be executed.

In the next section an introduction to ALSV(FD) logic is given. In Sect. 3 a proposal of the formalization of the approach is given. A practical example and evaluation follows. Then a short discussion of related works is presented. The paper ends with concluding remarks.

2 Attributive Logic with Set Values over Finite Domains

In [1] a thorough discussion of attributive logics has been given. It includes a formal framework of SAL (Set Attributive Logic) that provides syntax, semantics for calculus where attributes can take *set values*. Here an improved version of SAL, called ALSV(FD) is considered. The formalism is oriented towards Finite Domains (FD) and its expressive power is increased through the introduction of new relational symbols enabling definitions of atomic formulae. Moreover, ALSV(FD) introduces a formal specification of the partitioning of the attribute set needed for practical implementation, and a more coherent notation.

Simple and Generalized Attributes. Let $\mathbb{A}$ denote the set of all attributes used to describe the system. Each attribute has a set of admissible values that it takes (a domain). $\mathbb{D}$ is the *set of all possible attributes values*: $\mathbb{D} = \mathbb{D}_1 \cup \mathbb{D}_2 \cup \cdots \cup \mathbb{D}_n$ where $\mathbb{D}_i$ is the domain of attribute $A_i \in \mathbb{A}$, $i = 1 \ldots n$. Any domain $\mathbb{D}_i$ is assumed to be a *finite*, discrete set. In the general case, the domain can be ordered, partially ordered or unordered.

In ALSV(FD) two types of attributes are identified: *simple* ones taking only one value at a time, and *generalized* ones taking multiple values at a time. Therefore, we introduce the following partitioning of the set of all attributes: $\mathbb{A} = \mathbb{A}^s \cup \mathbb{A}^g$, $\mathbb{A}^s \cap \mathbb{A}^g = \emptyset$ where: $\mathbb{A}^s$ and $\mathbb{A}^g$ are respectively the sets of simple and generalized attributes.

A *simple attribute* A_i is a function (or a partial function) of the form: $A_i : \mathbb{O} \rightarrow \mathbb{D}_i$ where: $A_i \in \mathbb{A}^s$, $\mathbb{O}$ is a set of objects, $\mathbb{D}_i$ is the domain of attribute A_i.

The definition of *generalized attribute* is as follows: $A_i\colon \mathbb{O} \to 2^{\mathbb{D}_i}$ where: $\mathbb{O}$ is a set of objects and $2^{\mathbb{D}_i}$ is the set of all possible subsets of attribute A_i domain $\mathbb{D}_i$.

Attribute A_i denotes a property of an object. The formula $A_i(o)$, where $o \in \mathbb{O}$, denotes the value of property A_i of object o. However, here we assume that only one object (in this case it is the system being described) with a specific property name exists. This is why the following *notational convention* is used: the formula A_i simply denotes a *value* of the attribute A_i.

State Representation. The current values of all attributes are specified within the contents of the knowledge base. From logical point of view the *state* of the system is represented as a logical formula of the form: $s\colon (A_1 = S_1) \wedge (A_2 = S_2) \wedge \ldots \wedge (A_n = S_n)$ where A_i are the attributes and S_i are their current values. Note that $S_i \in \mathbb{D}_i$ for simple attributes and $S_i \subseteq \mathbb{D}_i$ for generalized ones.

The ALSV(FD) has been developed to describe rules. In order to do so, it provides certain expressions to represent conditions and actions of rules. These expressions are the atomic formulae of ALSV(FD). Their syntax is presented next.

Atomic Formulae Syntax. Let A_i be an attribute from $\mathbb{A}$, and $\mathbb{D}_i$ the domain related to it. Let V_i denote an arbitrary subset of $\mathbb{D}_i$ and let $d_i \in \mathbb{D}_i$ be a single element of the domain. The legal atomic formulae of ALSV(FD) along with their semantics are presented below, for simple and general attributes respectively. If V_i is an empty set (the attribute takes no value), we shall write $A_i = \emptyset$.

In the case when the value of A_i is unspecified, we shall write $A_i = null$. If the current attribute value is of no importance , we shall write $A = any$.

More complex formulae can be constructed with *conjunction* ($\wedge$) and *disjunction* ($\vee$); both of these have classical meaning and interpretation. For enabling efficient verification, there is no explicit use of negation in the formulae.

The meaning of these formulae is presented as follows. For the simple attributes: $A_i = d_i$ means that the value of A_i is precisely defined as d_i. $A_i \in V_i$ means that the current value of A_i belongs to V_i. $A_i \neq d_i$ means that shorthand for $A_i \in \mathbb{D}_i \setminus \{d_i\}$. $A_i \notin V_i$ means that shorthand for $A_i \in \mathbb{D}_i \setminus V_i$. For the generalized attributes: $A_i = V_i$ means that A_i equals to V_i (and nothing more). $A_i \neq V_i$ means that A_i is different from V_i (at least one element). $A_i \subseteq V_i$ means that A_i is a subset of V_i. $A_i \supseteq V_i$ means that A_i is a superset of V_i. $A_i \sim V_i$ means that A_i has a non-empty intersection with V_i. $A_i \not\sim V_i$ means that A_i has an empty intersection with V_i.

Formulae Semantics. The semantics of the atomic formulae is as follows:

- If $V_i = \{d_1, d_2, \ldots, d_k\}$, then $A_i = V_i$ means that the attribute takes as its value the set of all the values specified with V_i (and nothing more).
- $(A_i \subseteq V_i) \equiv (A_i = U_i)$ for some U_i such that $U_i \subseteq V_i$, i.e. A_i takes *some* of the values from V_i (and nothing out of V_i),
- $(A_i \supseteq V_i) \equiv (A_i = W)$, for some W such that $V_i \subseteq W$, i.e. A_i takes *all* of the values from V_i, and
- $(A_i \sim V_i) \equiv (A_i = X_i)$, for some X_i such that $V_i \cap X_i \neq \emptyset$, i.e. A_i takes *some* of the values from V_i.

For a complete discussion of the syntax and semantics of ALSV(FD) see [4].

The ALSV(FD) has been introduced with practical applications for rule languages in mind. In fact, the primary aim of the presented language is to formalize and extend the notational possibilities and expressive power of rule languages. The ALSV(FD) logic formulae correspond to simple statements (facts) about attribute values. These formulae are then used to express certain conditions. Using this formalism a complete solution that allows for building decision rules is discussed in the next section.

3 Formalization of Modularized Rule Bases

The goal of the definitions presented here is to formalize the structure of the knowledge base. Moreover, they are used to organize the process of the design and possible translation of the knowledge base.

Rule Conclusion and Decision. Two identifiers are used to denote attributes as well as operators in rule parts: *cond* corresponds to the *conditional* part of a rule, and *dec* corresponds to the *decision* part of a rule. Using it, two subsets of the attribute set can be identified. $\mathbb{A}^{cond}$ is a subset of attributes set $\mathbb{A}$ that contains attributes present in the conditional part of a rule. $\mathbb{A}^{dec}$ is a subset of attributes set $\mathbb{A}$ that contains attributes present in the decision part.

Relational Operators in Rules Considering the syntax of the legal ALSV(FD) formulae the legal use of the relational operators in rules is specified. The set of all operators has been divided into smaller subsets that contain all the operators, which can be used at the same time.

The set of all relational *operators* that can be used in rules is defined as follows: $\mathbb{F} = \mathbb{F}^{cond} \cup \mathbb{F}^{dec}$ where: $\mathbb{F}^{cond}$ is a set of all operators that can be used in the conditional part of a rule. $\mathbb{F}^{cond} = \mathbb{F}_a^{cond} \cup \mathbb{F}_s^{cond} \cup \mathbb{F}_g^{cond}$ where:

- $\mathbb{F}_a^{cond}$ contains operators, that can be used in the rule conditional part with all attributes. The set is defined as: $\mathbb{F}_a^{cond} = \{=, \neq\}$
- $\mathbb{F}_g^{cond}$ contains operators that can also be used in the rule conditional part with generalized attributes. The set is defined as: $\mathbb{F}_g^{cond} = \{\subseteq, \supseteq, \sim, \not\sim\}$
- $\mathbb{F}_s^{cond}$ is the set that contains the operators, which can be used in a rule conditional part with simple attributes. The set is defined as: $\mathbb{F}_s^{cond} = \{\in, \notin\}$. ALSV(FD) also allows for using the following operators $<, >, \leq, \geq$ which provide only a variation for $\in$ operator. These operators can be used only with attributes whose domains are ordered sets.

$\mathbb{F}^{dec}$ is a set of all operators that can be used in a rule decision part: $\mathbb{F}^{dec} = \{:=\}$. The operator $:=$ allows for assigning a new value to an attribute.

Moreover, to specify in the rule condition that the value of the attribute is to be $null$ (unknown) or any (unimportant) the operator $=$ is used. To specify in the same rule part the value of the attribute is not $null$ the operator $\neq$ is used.

ALSV(FD) *Triples.* The ALSV(FD) triples are the "building blocks" of rules. Let us consider the set $\mathbb{E}$ that contains all the triples that are legal atomic formulae in ALSV(FD). The triples are build using the previously defined relational operators:

$$\mathbb{E} = \{(A_i, \propto, d_i), A_i \in \mathbb{A}^s, \propto \in \mathbb{F} \setminus \mathbb{F}_g^{cond}, d_i \in \mathbb{D}_i\} \cup \\ \{(A_i, \propto, V_i), A_i \in \mathbb{A}^g, \propto \in \mathbb{F} \setminus \mathbb{F}_s^{cond}, V_i \in 2^{\mathbb{D}_i}\}$$

XTT2 *Rule.* Let us consider the set of all rules defined in the knowledge base denoted as $\mathbb{R}$. A single XTT2 rule is a triple: $r = (\mathbb{COND}, \mathbb{DEC}, \mathbb{ACT})$ where: $\mathbb{COND}, \mathbb{DEC} \subset \mathbb{E}$, and $\mathbb{ACT}$ is a set of actions to be executed.

A rule can be written using LHS (*Left Hand Side*) and RHS (*Right Hand Side*): $LHS(r) \rightarrow RHS(r), DO(\mathbb{ACT})$ where $LHS(r)$ and $RHS(r)$ correspond respectively to the condition and decision parts of the rule r, and $DO(\mathbb{ACT})$ involves executing actions from a predefined set. Actions are not included in the RHS of the rule because it is assumed that they are independent from the considered system, and the execution of actions does not change the state of the system.

Any rule can also be presented in the following form:
r: $[\phi_1 \wedge \phi_2 \wedge \cdots \wedge \phi_n] \rightarrow [\theta_1 \wedge \theta_2 \wedge \cdots \wedge \theta_m], DO(\mathbb{ACT})$ where: $\{1, \ldots, n\}$ and $\{1, \ldots, m\}$ are the sets of identifiers, $n \in \mathbb{N}$, $m \in \mathbb{N}$ $\phi_1, \ldots, \phi_n \in \mathbb{COND}$ and $\theta_1, \ldots, \theta_m \in \mathbb{DEC}$. From a logical point of view, the order of the atomic formulae in both the precondition and conclusion parts is unimportant.

Rule Firing. Considering the previous definitions, firing a single XTT2 rule r involves the following basic steps: 1) Checking if *all* the ALSV(FD) triples in the $\mathbb{COND}$ part are satisfied. 2) If so, changing the system state by evaluating triples (assigning new values to attributes) in the $\mathbb{DEC}$ part. 3) Executing actions defined by $\mathbb{ACT}$; actions do not change attribute values.

Having the structure of a single rule defined, the structure of the complete knowledge base is introduced. The knowledge base is composed of tables grouping rules having the same attributes lists (rule schemas).

Rule Schema. Let us consider a concept of a *rule schema*. Each rule has a schema that is a pair of attributes sets: $h = (H^{cond}, H^{dec})$ where H^{cond} and H^{dec} sets define the attributes occuring in the conditional and decision part of the rule.

A schema of the rule can be defined as follows: $\forall r = (\mathbb{COND}, \mathbb{DEC}, \mathbb{ACT}) : h = (\text{trunc}(\mathbb{COND}), \text{trunc}(\mathbb{DEC}))$ where the function *trunc* transforms the set of atomic formulae into a set of attributes that are used in these triples. A schema is used to identify rules working in the same situation (operational context). Such a set of rules can form a decision component in the form of a decision table. A schema can also be considered a table header.

Decision Component (Table). Let us consider a *decision component* (or table). It is an ordered set (sequence) of rules having the same rule schema, defined as follows:
$t = (r_1, r_2, \ldots, r_n)$ $\forall_{i,j}: r_i, r_j \in t \Rightarrow h_i = h_j$ where h_i is a schema of the rule r_i. In XTT2 the rule schema h can also be called the schema of the component (or table). Components are connected (linked) in order to provide inference control.

Let us observe Figure 1. On the left table t_1 is represented. It is an example of a table having three rules: r_1, r_2, r_3. These rules have the same schema
$h_1 = (\{A_1, A_2, A_3\}, \{A_4, A_5\})$. This means that respective ALSV(FD) triples contain given attribute e. g. a triple $e_{2,3}$ is a part of rule r_2 and it contains the attribute A_3.

To simplify the visual representation a convetion is introduced, where the schema of a table is depicted on the top of the table.

Inference Link. A link l is an ordered pair: $l = (r,t),\ l \in \mathbb{R} \times \mathbb{T} \cup \{\bot\}$ where: $\mathbb{R}$ is the set of rules in the knowledge base, and $\mathbb{T}$ is the set of tables in the knowledge base. A single link connects a single rule (a row in a table) with another table. An empty link is denoted as $\bot$. A structure composed of linked decision components is called a XTT2 knowledge base.

XTT2 *Knowledge Base.* It is the set of components connected with links. It can be defined as an ordered pair: $X = (\mathbb{T}, \mathbb{L})$, where: $\mathbb{T}$ is a set of components (tables), $\mathbb{L}$ is a set of links, and all the links from $\mathbb{L}$ connect rules from $\mathbb{R}$ with tables from $\mathbb{T}$. Links are introduced during the design process according to the specification provided by the designer. The knowledge base can be perceived as an inference network.

Let us observe that a number of specific structures of knowledge bases could be considered including decision trees. In such a decision tree-like structure nodes would consist of single decision components. So, the XTT2 knowledge base can be seen as a generalization of classic decision trees and tables.

4 Practical Example

An example of the XTT2 knowledge base is presented in Figure 1. The knowledge base is composed of three tables (components), and two links: $X_1 = (\{t_1, t_2, t_3\}, \{l_1, l_2\})$ On the first component (t_1) the rule schema, corresponding to the table header can be observed. There are nine rules, three in each of the tables. In the first table the conditional and decision parts are presented (action-related part is ommited for brevity). If the rule r_1 from the table t_1 is fired the inference control would be passed to the table t_2 through the link l_1. If the rule r_3 is fired the inference control would be passed to the table t_3 through the link l_2. This is the case of a simple forward chining mode, other inference modes are also possible.

For practical example of rules, imagine a system recommending books to different groups of persons depending on their age and reading preferences. The age of a

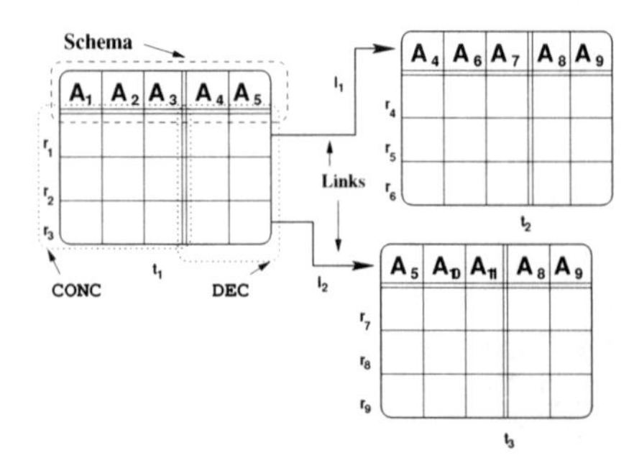

Fig. 1. Example of an XTT2 knowledge base

reader and his/her preference could be represented by the following attributes: $\mathbb{A} = \{fav\_genres, age, age\_filter, rec\_book\}$ with corresponding domains:
$\mathbb{D} = \mathbb{D}_{fav\_genres} \cup \mathbb{D}_{age} \cup \mathbb{D}_{age\_filter} \cup \mathbb{D}_{rec\_book}$, defined as:
$\mathbb{D}_{fav_genres} = \{$horror, handbook, fantasy, science, historical, poetry$\}$,
$\mathbb{D}_{age} = \{1 \ldots 99\}$,
$\mathbb{D}_{age_filter} = \{$young_horrors, young_poetry, adult_horrors, adult_poetry,
$\mathbb{D}_{rec\_book} = \{$ 'It', 'Logical Foundations for RBS', 'The Call of Cthulhu"$\}$.
In this case the second attribute is a simple one, where as the first and third are generalized ones. The third one contains book titles that can be recommended to a reader. In the example, both fav_genres, and age, attributes are input, age_filter is internal, and rec_book is an output one.

Following the example, a state can be defined as: $(age = 16) \wedge (fav\_genres = \{horror, fantasy\})$ This means, that a given person is 16 years old and she or he likes reading horror and fantasy books. In fact, it is a partial state where only the values of the input attributes are defined. It is sufficient for the inference process. To specify the full state the values of the remaining attributes should be defined as $null$.

Consider example of the following rules:
$r_1 : [age < 18 \wedge fav\_genres \supseteq \text{horror}] \longrightarrow [age\_filter := \text{young\_horrors}]$
$r_2 : [age = \_ \wedge fav\_genres \in \{\text{science}\}] \longrightarrow [age\_filter := \text{all\_science}]$
$r_3 : [age\_filter \in \{\text{young\_horrors, adult\_horrors}\}] \longrightarrow [rec\_book := \text{'It'}]$
Having the defined state, it can be observed, that rules r_1 and r_3 can be fired.

The implementation of the XTT2 method includes two representations: a) textual suitable for processing by a rule engine, and b) visual aimed at a design tool. The textual representation of XTT2 is called HMR (*HeKatE Meta Representation*). HMR allows for textual definition of all the XTT2 concepts. The visual representation of XTT2 is supported by the HQEd graphical editor. Both of this two representations can be used to design the system. However, the visual representation is more convenient. In fact, the textual form of HMR can be written directly or automatically generated by the HQEd tool according to the visual representation. The textual representation is processed by HeaRT [3] tool which is a dedicated inference engine for XTT2 rule bases implementing the custom inference algorithms.

5 Related Work

Considering the use of decision tables our approach is similar to Vanthienen's research on decision tables. In the paper [6] it is presented how the rule-based system can created with the help of PROLOGA (*Procedural Logic Analyzer*) system, which is an interactive rule-based tool for computer-supported construction and manipulation of decision tables. The problems of maintenance, efficiency and verification of a large knowledge bases are also discussed. In [5] an approach to a knowledge modularization is described in order to increase an efficiency of verification.

However, in XTT2 the perspective is on state-base representation. Moreover, practical inference issues in structured rule bases are considered. The Vanthienen's works do not describe an influence of the knowledge base modularization on the inference process. This is why, XTT2 provides dedicated inference engine (HeaRT), which allows for using the advanced inference strategies. In comparison to Vanthienen's works, XTT2 provides a stronger formalism and more expressive rule language.

The implicit rule base structure is an important feature of XTT2. Rules are grouped into decision tables, and the inference control is designed during design. Therefore the XTT2 representation is highly optimized towards rule base structuring. This is different from all Rete-based solutions, including all the three previously mentioned, that is CLIPS, Jess, and Drools. This feature makes the visual design much more transparent and scalable. It also greatly improves the inference process. The well known inference algorithms like Rete, and others (e.g. Treat or Gator) do not work well with modularized knowledge bases (for details see [4]).

6 Concluding Remarks

In this paper a rigorous formalized language called XTT2 for building rule-based systems has been proposed. The approach is based on the ideas of using a formal, attributive logic based approach for rule description. Moreover, it allows to identify a structure of the rule base, by using extended decision tables grouping rules working in the same context. This approach seems superior to wide-spread rule-based solutions thanks to the transparent and scalable visual representatio. It opens up possibility of formal verification on the logical level.

References

1. Ligęza, A.: Logical Foundations for Rule-Based Systems. Springer, Heidelberg (2006)
2. Ligęza, A., Nalepa, G.J.: Rules verification and validation. In: Giurca, A., Gasevic, D., Taveter, K. (eds.) Handbook of Research on Emerging Rule-Based Languages and Technologies: Open Solutions and Approaches, pp. 273–301. IGI Global, Hershey (2009)
3. Nalepa, G.J.: Architecture of the HeaRT hybrid rule engine. In: Rutkowski, L., Scherer, R., Tadeusiewicz, R., Zadeh, L.A., Zurada, J.M. (eds.) ICAISC 2010, Part II. LNCS, vol. 6114, pp. 598–605. Springer, Heidelberg (2010)
4. Nalepa, G.J., Ligęza, A.: HeKatE methodology, hybrid engineering of intelligent systems. International Journal of Applied Mathematics and Computer Science 20(1), 35–53 (2010)
5. Vanthienen, J., Mues, C., Aerts, A., Wets, G.: A modularization approach to the verification of knowledge based systems. In: 14th International Joint Conference on Artificial Intelligence (IJCAI 1995) - Workshop on Validation & Verification of Knowledge Based Systems, Montreal, Canada (August 20-25, 1995), http://eprints.soton.ac.uk/36413/
6. Vanthienen, J., Dries, E.: Illustration of a decision table tool for specifying and implementing knowledge based systems. In: ICTAI, pp. 198–205 (1993)

HalVA - Rule Analysis Framework for XTT2 Rules*

Grzegorz J. Nalepa, Szymon Bobek, Antoni Ligęza, and Krzysztof Kaczor

AGH University of Science and Technology,
Al. Mickiewicza 30, 30-059 Kraków, Poland
{gjn,szymon.bobek,ligeza,kk}@agh.edu.pl

Abstract. Quality and reliability issues are important in development and exploration of rule-based systems. In the paper a formalized knowledge representation for rules called XTT2 is considered. It is a rule language based on an expressive attribute logic called ALSV(FD). A custom runtime and verification framework for XTT2 called HalVA is proposed. It allows for verification of certain formal properties of rules, including determinism, subsumption or completeness.

1 Introduction

Rule-Based Systems have been in use for several decades in various branches of engineering. In fact, they constitute straightforward, intuitive, and powerful scheme for encoding operational knowledge. Among numerous rule-based languages and tools, one can mention classical solutions, such as Clips, its reincarnation in Java, JESS, Drools, ILOG Rules and many other. All of them offer relatively matured solutions with respect to knowledge encoding and inference.

One of the critical issues concerning development of practical rule-based application is the *reliability* and *safety* of the system. In order to assure correct behavior, certain intrinsic characteristics of the rulebase should be assured. Among other, the system should work correctly for any admissible input data and produce deterministic, consistent solutions. Unfortunately, none of the above systems offers an appropriate solution in this area.

This paper is focused on expressive, formalized rule language called XTT2 (*eXtended Tabular Trees* version 2) [4]. We start with describing a logic in use which is the key issue for knowledge verification. Together with the XTT2 rule encoding scheme it provides an account for formal verification of rules for XTT2.

The paper is organized as follows. In Sect. 2 a state of the art is briefly discussed with the motivation for the research given. Then the introduction to the ALSV(FD) logic providing means for rule formalization is put forward. Rule formalization with XTT2 is briefly discussed in Sect. 3. Practical approach to verification of XTT2 rules is outlined in Sect. 4, followed by conclusions.

* The paper is supported by the BIMLOQ Project funded from 2010–2012 resources for science as a research project.

N. Bassiliades et al. (Eds.): RuleML 2011 - Europe, LNCS 6826, pp. 337–344, 2011.

2 State-of-the-Art and Motivation

Expert systems are widely used in areas where computer high performance and infallibility are important. In some cases failure of the expert systems can have serious consequences, though it is crucial to ensure that the system works correctly in every possible situation. Many tools and methodologies that support rule-based systems verification have been developed over the time, but none of them covers all the needs that such systems should have. Anomalies in the set of rules can cause the serious faults in system responses. Therefore the analysis of knowledge base is a significant step during developing rule-based system.

The issue of verification and validation were discussed by many authors. According to [6] verification and validation procedures of the system can be understood as one of the following: anomaly detection, formal verification, parallel use, rule base visualization to aid review, code review, testing. That study shows, that verification of the rule based systems is dominated by testing and code review. This approach highly depend on human skills, since incorrectly written test may produce wrong results. Formal verification and anomaly detection are not so widely used despite the fact that those methods usually have strong logical foundations and in most cases exceed testing and debugging approach.

Apparently, the classic verification tools developed in the 90' are not commonly used. Based on comparison of existing verification tools in [5] one can draw a conclusion, that the main reason why formal verification is not widely used among expert system developers is that it requires *formal knowledge representation*. In fact, most of these tools are usually based on propositional or predicate logic. MELODIA uses propositional logic and flat rule base. CLINT, COVER, SACCO uses predicate logic and a flat rulebase. Moreover, IN-DEPTH introduces a hierarchical representation, COVADIS uses simple production rules language with a flat rulebase, whereas KRUST uses frames. However, common expert system shells such as CLIPS, Jess or Drools do not provide formal knowledge representation, so it is not possible to use these tools. Although there are some analysis tools that are dedicated to aforementioned shells like CRSV-CLIPS [1,5] for CLIPS, Drools Verifier for Drools, their aim is not to provide formal verification, but to offer a framework for writing tests.

Motivation for research presented here is to provide an expressive formalized rule language that allows for *formal verification*. The XTT2 language is expressive enough to cover the semantics of classic CLIPS-like languages, as well as the business rules oriented Drools. The actual study of the expressiveness and the mapping is out of scope of this paper. The focus here is to present practical verification algorithms for XTT2. They are oriented towards formal verification of selected formal rule properties, and use the notation based on the ALSV(FD) introduced in the next section.

3 Formalization of Modularized Rule Bases

Knowledge representations based on attributes are not only common, but also very intuitive. This kind of logic is omnipresent in various applications.

It constitutes the basis for construction of relational database tables, attributive decision tables and trees, attributive rule-based systems and is often applied to describe the state of dynamic systems and autonomous agents. Here we consider the Attributive Logic with Set Values over Finite Domains (ALSV(FD)) [4].

Let us now consider a set of all attributes used to describe the system $\mathbb{A}$. Each attribute $A_i \in \mathbb{A}$ has a set of allowed values (a domain) $\mathbb{D}_i$. Let $\mathbb{D}$ be the *set of all attributes values*: $\mathbb{D} = \mathbb{D}_1 \cup \mathbb{D}_2 \cup \cdots \cup \mathbb{D}_n$ where $\mathbb{D}_i$ is the domain of attribute $A_i \in \mathbb{A}$. Any domain $\mathbb{D}_i$ is assumed to be a *finite* (discrete) set. In a general case, the domain can be ordered, partially ordered, or unordered.

In ALSV(FD) two types of attributes are identified: *simple* taking only one value at any time, and *generalized* ones taking a set of values at any time. Therefore, we introduce the following partitioning of the set of all attributes: $\mathbb{A} = \mathbb{A}^s \cup \mathbb{A}^g$ where: $\mathbb{A}^s$ - the set of simple attribute names. $\mathbb{A}^g$ - the set of generalized attribute names. Let $\mathbb{O}$ denote a set of potential objects, and let $\mathcal{T}$ denote a discrete set of time instants. A *simple attribute* A_i is a function (or partial function) of the form: $A_i\colon \mathbb{O} \times \mathcal{T} \to \mathbb{D}_i$. The definition of *generalized attribute* can be written as follows: $A_i\colon \mathbb{O} \times \mathcal{T} \to 2^{\mathbb{D}_i}$ Attribute A_i denotes a property of certain objects at a certain instant of time. The formula $A_i(o)$, where $o \in \mathbb{O}$, is the value of property A_i of object o. For simplicity the explicit specification of object is not present (the whole system is considered as one object) and explicit reference is only to the current instant of time. As a consequence, simplified atomic formulae of the form $A_i = d$ where $d \in \mathbb{D}_i$ or $A_i = V$ where $V \subseteq \mathbb{D}_i$ are used further on.

The current values of all attributes are specified within the contents of the knowledge base. From the logical point of view the *state* of the system is represented as a logical formula of the form: $(A_1 = S_1) \wedge (A_2 = S_2) \wedge \ldots \wedge (A_n = S_n)$ where A_i are the attributes and S_i are their current values; note that $S_i = d_i$ $(d_i \in \mathbb{D}_i)$ for simple attributes and $S_i = V_i$, $(V_i \subseteq \mathbb{D}_i)$ for complex ones.

The rule formalism considered here is called XTT2 and provides a formalized rule specification. This section starts from presentation of operators needed to express rules, then single rule formulation using the ALSV(FD) concepts, and then provides definitions for grouping similar rules into decision units (tables) linked into an inference network.

Rule Conclusion and Decision. In XTT2 each rule can be divided into two parts: *condition* and *conclusion* (*decision*). Therefore, two identifiers will be used to denote attributes as well as operators in rule parts: *cond* corresponds to the *conditional* part of a rule, and *dec* corresponds to the *decision* part of a rule.

Relational Operators in Rules. Considering the syntax of the legal ALSV(FD) formulae the use of the relational operators in rules can be specified. The set of all *operators* can be defined as follows: $\mathbb{F} = \mathbb{F}^{cond} \cup \mathbb{F}^{dec}$ where: $\mathbb{F}^{dec} = \{:=\}$ is a set of all operators that can be used in a rule decision part. The operator $:=$ allows for assigning a new value to an attribute. $\mathbb{F}^{cond} = \{=, \neq, \subseteq, \supseteq, \sim, \not\sim, \in, \notin\}$ is a set of all operators, that can be used in a rule conditional part. ALSV(FD) also allows for using the following operators $<, >, \leq, \geq$ which provide only a variation for the $\in$ operator.

ALSV(FD) *Triples.* Considering the legal ALSV(FD) atomic formulae the $\mathbb{E}$ set can be introduced. It contains all the triples that are legal atomic formulae in ALSV(FD) using the relational operators defined previously:
$\mathbb{E} = \{(A_i, \propto, d_i), A_i \in \mathbb{A}, \propto \in \mathbb{F}, d_i \in \mathbb{D}_i\} \cup \{(A_i, \propto, V_i), A_i \in \mathbb{A}, \propto \in \mathbb{F}, V_i \in 2^{\mathbb{D}_i}\}$
XTT2 *Rule.* Let us consider the set of all rules defined in the knowledge base denoted as $\mathbb{R}$. A single XTT2 rule is a triple: $r = (\mathbb{COND}, \mathbb{DEC}, \mathbb{ACT})$ where: $\mathbb{COND}, \mathbb{DEC} \subset \mathbb{E}$, and $\mathbb{ACT}$ is a set of actions to be executed.

A rule can be written using *LHS* (*Left Hand Side*) and *RHS* (*Right Hand Side*): $LHS(r) \rightarrow RHS(r), DO(\mathbb{ACT})$ where $LHS(r)$ and $RHS(r)$ correspond respectively to the condition and decision parts of the rule r, and $DO(\mathbb{ACT})$ involves executing actions from a predefined set. Actions are not included in the *RHS* because it is assumed that they are independent from the considered system, and the execution of actions does not change the state of the system.

Any rule can also be presented in the following form:
$r\colon [\phi_1 \wedge \phi_2 \wedge \cdots \wedge \phi_n] \rightarrow [\theta_1 \wedge \theta_2 \wedge \cdots \wedge \theta_m], DO(\mathbb{ACT})$ where: $\{1, \ldots, n\}$ and $\{1, \ldots, m\}$ are the sets of identifiers, $n \in \mathbb{N}$, $m \in \mathbb{N}$ $\phi_1, \ldots, \phi_n \in \mathbb{COND}$ and $\theta_1, \ldots, \theta_m \in \mathbb{DEC}$. From a logical point of view, the order of the atomic formulae in both the precondition and conclusion parts is unimportant.

Rule Schema. Let us consider a concept of a *rule schema.* Each rule has a schema that is a pair of attributes sets: $h = (H^{cond}, H^{dec})$ where H^{cond} and H^{dec} sets define the attributes occuring in the conditional and decision part of the rule.

A schema of the rule can be defined as follows: $\forall r = (\mathbb{COND}, \mathbb{DEC}, \mathbb{ACT})$: $h = (\text{trunc}(\mathbb{COND}), \text{trunc}(\mathbb{DEC}))$ where the function *trunc* transforms the set of atomic formulae into a set of attributes that are used in these triples. A schema is used to identify rules working in the same situation (operational context). Such a set of rules can form a decision component in the form of a decision table. A schema can also be considered a table header.

Decision Component (Table). Let us consider a *decision component* (or table). It is an ordered set (sequnce) of rules having the same rule schema, defined as follows: $t = (r_1, r_2, \ldots, r_n)$ $\forall_{i,j} : r_i, r_j \in t \rightarrow h_i = h_j$ where h_i is a schema of the rule r_i. In XTT2 the rule schema h can also be called the schema of the component (or table). Components are connected (linked) in order to provide inference control.

Inference Link. A link l is an ordered pair: $l = (r, t),\ l \in \mathbb{R} \times \mathbb{T} \cup \{\bot\}$ where: $\mathbb{R}$ is the set of rules in the knowledge base, and $\mathbb{T}$ is the set of tables in the knowledge base. A single link connects a single rule (a row in a table) with another table. An empty link is denoted as $\bot$. A structure composed of linked decision components is called a XTT2 knowledge base.

XTT2 *Knowledge Base.* It is the set of components connected with links. It is an ordered pair: $X = (\mathbb{T}, \mathbb{L})$, where: $\mathbb{T}$ is a set of components (tables), $\mathbb{L}$ is a set of links, and all the links from $\mathbb{L}$ connect rules from $\mathbb{R}$ with tables from $\mathbb{T}$. Links are introduced during the design process according to the specification provided by the designer. The knowledge base forms an inference network.

Let us now proceed to the descussion of the main verification tasks for the XTT2 rules as well as corresponding algorithms.

4 Rule Verification Tasks

4.1 Formal Definition of Verification Tasks

Consider the legal atomic formulae. Any single atomic formula $e_i = A_i \propto V_i$ can be considered as a kind of a *constraint* imposed on the values of the domain $\mathbb{D}_i$ of A_i. Let us define the so-called *set of examples* of e_i as follows: $[e_i] = \{d \in \mathbb{D}_i: \quad e_i \textit{ is satisfied by } d\}$ for simple attributes, and $[e_i] = \{V \subseteq \mathbb{D}_i: \quad e_i \textit{ is satisfied by } V\}$ for generalized ones. In fact, the set of examples for an atomic formula e is a set of legal attribute values satisfying this formula. For example, consider $D_i = \{0, 1, 2, 3, 4, 5, 6, 7, 8, 9\}$ and a formula $e_i = A_i \geq 7$. Then the set of examples for e_i is given by $[e_i] = \{7, 8, 9\}$.

In the following sections we shall consider simplified rules of the form: $e_1 \wedge e_2 \wedge \ldots \wedge e_n \longrightarrow h$ where h is an atomic formula assigning specific value to some decision attribute. Let LHS denote the set of preconditions of the rule, i.e. $LHS = \{e_1, e_2, \ldots, e_n\}$.

Below, we consider definitions of some most common problems to be detected and eliminated in rule-based systems.

Inconsistency of a single rule. can be result of the two following situations: 1) in the preconditions of the rule there are two logically inconsistent atomic formulae and 2) in the preconditions of the rule there exists an atomic formula logically inconsistent with the conclusion. The first situation can happen if there exist some atomic formulae $e_i, e_j \in LHS$, such that: $[e_i] \cap [e_j] = \emptyset$. The second situation takes place when $[e^i] \cap [h] = \emptyset$. Obviously, in both cases, the formulae must define constraints referring to the same attribute.

Inconsistency of a pair of rules. means that there exists a state satisfying the preconditions of each rule, but conclusions define different values of the same attribute. Consider two rules with preconditions given by LHS_k and LHS_l. The preconditions of these rules can be simultaneously satisfied if and only if, for any pair of atomic formulae e_i, e_j, such that $e_i \in LHS_k$ and $e_j \in LHS_l$, e_i and e_j define constraints over the same attribute the following condition s satisfied: $[e_i] \cap [e_j] \neq \emptyset$. If the above holds, and simultaneously the rules define different values of the same conclusion attribute, then the rules are inconsistent.

Completeness. is defined as the ability to react for every admissible input values. This means that the Cartesian Product of domains of attributes of a group of rules is covered by the rule preconditions. Consider a group of rules with preconditions defined with use of attributes $A_1, A_2, \ldots, A_n$. The Cartesian Product of the domains of these attributes will be denoted as $\mathbb{U}$. Now, consider a single rule $e_1 \wedge e_2 \wedge \ldots \wedge e_n \longrightarrow h$. The Cartesian Product of states covered by preconditions of the rule is given by $P = [e_1] \times [e_2] \times \ldots \times [e_n]$ The completeness holds if and only if, for any $u \in \mathbb{U}$, there exists a rule with P such that $u \in P$.

Subsumption of conditions. It takes place, if and only if there are two atomic formulae referring to the same attribute, but one of them is weaker then the other. Let e_i and e_j be two atoms belonging to preconditions of some examined formula. The subsumption holds if and only if $[e_i] \subseteq [e_j]$, i.e. e_j subsumes e_i. Obviously, if e_i is satisfied, then e_j must be satisfied as well, but not vice versa. The subsumed condition e_i can be eliminated.

Subsumption of a pair of rules. takes place, if and only if one of the rules can be fired always when the second one (and perhaps also in some more states), and the rules have the same conclusion. The subsumption holds in fact among the joint precondition formulae. Let P_k, P_l denote the Cartesian Products of states covered by the respective formulae. Subsumption holds if and only iff $P_i \subseteq P_j$ In more operational terms, the subsumption can also be defined as follows. Consider two rules with preconditions constructed over the same attributes. Rule l subsumes rule k if and only if, for any $e_i \in LHS_k$ there exists $e_j \in LHS_l$, such that $[e_i] \subseteq [e_j]$, i.e. e_j subsumes e_i. Obviously, if e_i is satisfied, then e_j must be satisfied as well, but not vice versa. The more general rule l cannot have any extra atoms in preconditions, i.e. each of its preconditions must cover some atom in preconditions of rule k. The subsumed rule k can be eliminated.

Identity and equivalence of rules. takes place when two rules can also be identical or equivalent. Detection of identical rules is a trivial case. Rules are equivalent if they both can be fired for the same set of input states and they have identical conclusions. Equivalence of preconditions can be easily defined as mutual subsumption.

4.2 Verification Algorithms

Inconsistency of a single rule. Inconsistency within a single rule can be understood on in two ways: presence of inconsistent conditions , and inconsistency between one of the conditions and conclusion To discover inconsistency between conditions within a single rule following steps should be performed:

1. Create a list of all attributes from condition part of the rule.
2. Take first attribute from the list and find all other conditions containing the attribute. If there are no attributes left on the list, stop.
3. Calculate intersections of sets that are covered by selected conditions. If the intersections is an empty set, report inconsistency.
4. Delete previously selected attribute and go to step 2.

Warning about potential inconsistency between conditions and conclusion of the rule is generated when the same attributes exist in both conditional and decision part of the rule.

Inconsistency of a pair of rules. Inconsistency between a pair of rules are understood as a situation when decision parts of two rules are different, but there is a state when both rules are true. To discover inconsistency between a pair of rules, following steps should be performed:

1. Designate states that two rules from the same context cover.
2. Calculate intersection of those states.
3. In case the intersection is not an empty set and decision parts of both rules differ, report inconsistency.

Completeness. The most difficult part of logical verification is completeness test. To check if the system is complete, all possible input data has to be passed to the system, and depending on the system response, the conclusion about completeness is produced. The completeness tests described in this section are limited to a group of rules – the single XTT2 table, not entire system. Checking entire system for completeness is an issue far more complicated, and practically not possible. Two approaches to this problem were developed and tested: Cartesian product of partition of domains, Decision Tree.

The approach with Cartesian product of partitions of domains was not efficient for bigger problems, where domains were partitioned into a lot of pieces by a lot of rules within a XTT2 table. To enhance performance of the completeness test, the approach with decision tree of system states was proposed. An idea of this algorithm is to create a tree, where each branch represents a state that should be covered. Every level of the tree corresponds to attributes that shall cover states denoted by it. The completeness test is based on depth-first search algorithm. The enhancement lies in the fact that when the branch is found that is not covered by any condition of rules from analyzed XTT2 table, this branch, with all its successors are cut and are not analyzed.

Subsumption of a pair of rules. Subsumption of a pair of rules is similar to the case of inconsistency of a pair of rules described in Sec. 4.2. One rule subsumes the other if its condition part is more general and decision part is the same.

A test for the presence of this kind of subsumption is done as follows:

1. Designate states that are covered by rules from given context (XTT2 table)
2. Calculate intersections of this states
3. In case the intersections is not an empty set and decision parts of the rules are the same, report subsumption error

Identity and equivalence of rules. Problem of discovering equivalent rules is reduced to finding rules in which: order of conditions were changed, one or more conditions were duplicated, and one or more conditions are logically equivalent.

5 Summary and Future Work

The original contribution of the paper is the proposal of a formal verification framework for XTT2. It is an expressive rule language, with possible mapping to some common rule shells. In the paper verification algorithms for important anomalies were given and their implementation was presented.

The implementation of the XTT2 method includes a textual representation called HMR (*HeKatE Meta Representation*). It is directly processed by HeaRT [3] tool which is a dedicated inference engine for XTT2. HeaRT also implements a *verification framework*, called HalVA (HeKatE Verification and Analysis) [2]. The framework implements the discussed verification algorithms as plugins. Verification plugins can be run from the interpreter or from the design environment using a communication module.

To further improve the efficiency of the algorithms, a new method of investigating system properties is proposed as a future work. The new approach is based on analyzing logical dependencies between condition parts of rules, rather than on algebra of sets (as it is now in domain partitioning approach). This method requires defining special rules for every operator from ALSV(FD) logic that would be used to conclude about existence of anomalies in system. Verification would be therefore domain independent, and specific values, or sets of values would not be considered explicitly but *intensionally* instead – based on aforementioned rules.

References

1. Culbert, S.: Expert system verifications & validation. In: Proc. of First AAAI Workshop on V,V & Testing (August 1988)
2. Ligęza, A., Nalepa, G.J.: Proposal of a formal verification framework for the XTT2 rule bases. In: Tadeusiewicz, R., Ligęza, A., Mitkowski, W., Szymkat, M. (eds.) CMS 2009: Computer Methods and Systems: 7th Conference, Kraków, Poland, November 26-27, pp. 105–110. AGH University of Science and Technology, Cracow, Oprogramowanie Naukowo-Techniczne, Kraków (2009)
3. Nalepa, G.J.: Architecture of the HeaRT hybrid rule engine. In: Rutkowski, L., Scherer, R., Tadeusiewicz, R., Zadeh, L.A., Zurada, J.M. (eds.) ICAISC 2010, Part II. LNCS (LNAI), vol. 6114, pp. 598–605. Springer, Heidelberg (2010)
4. Nalepa, G.J., Ligęza, A.: HeKatE methodology, hybrid engineering of intelligent systems. International Journal of Applied Mathematics and Computer Science 20(1), 35–53 (2010)
5. Tsai, W.T., Vishnuvajjala, R., Zhang, D.: Verification and validation of knowledge-based systems. IEEE Trans. on Knowl. and Data Eng. 11, 202–212 (1999), `http://dx.doi.org/10.1109/69.755629`
6. Zacharias, V.: Development and verification of rule based systems — A survey of developers. In: Bassiliades, N., Governatori, G., Paschke, A. (eds.) RuleML 2008. LNCS, vol. 5321, pp. 6–16. Springer, Heidelberg (2008), `http://dx.doi.org/10.1007/978-3-540-88808-6_4`

Rewriting Queries for Web Searches That Use Local Expressions

Rolf Grütter[1], Iris Helming[1], Simon Speich[1], and Abraham Bernstein[2]

[1] Swiss Federal Research Institute WSL, Birmensdorf, Switzerland
{rolf.gruetter,iris.helming,simon.speich}@wsl.ch
[2] University of Zurich, Department of Informatics Zurich, Switzerland
bernstein@ifi.uzh.ch

Abstract. Users often enter a local expression to constrain a web search to a geographical place. Current search engines' capability to deal with expressions such as "close to" is, however, limited. This paper presents an approach that uses topological background knowledge to rewrite queries containing local expressions in a format better suited to standard search engines. To formalize local expressions, the Region Connection Calculus (RCC) is extended by additional relations, which are related to existing ones by means of composition rules. The approach is applied to web searches for communities in a part of Switzerland which are "close to" a reference place. Results show that query rewriting significantly improves recall of the searches. When dealing with approx. 30,000 role assertions, the time required to rewrite queries is in the range of a few seconds. Ways of dealing with a possible decrease of performance when operating on a larger knowledge base are discussed.

Keywords: Local Expression, Query Rewriting, Region Connection Calculus (RCC), Web Ontology Language (OWL), DL-safe SWRL Rules.

1 Introduction

Web searches are quite often constrained by local references (e.g., place names or expressions for spatial relations between places) [1, 2]. However, existing search engines are weak in supporting spatial queries. While local expressions, such as "close to", may be used as strings in a query, they are usually evaluated according to the frequency of their occurrence in the indexed documents and not according to their meaning in natural language. For some queries, Google[1] returns resources of real world entities which are "close to" or "in the surroundings of" a reference place. However, this feature is limited to government agencies and commercial enterprises such as hotels, surgeries and offices in urban areas, in a way similar to the yellow pages[2].

[1] http://www.google.ch/
[2] http://yellow.local.ch

N. Bassiliades et al. (Eds.): RuleML 2011 - Europe, LNCS 6826, pp. 345–359, 2011.

Localized versions of standard search engines, such as Google, Yahoo[3] and Bing[4], offer the option of displaying query results in the national language or from hosts in the respective country. In addition, there are a number of search engines whose scope is limited to a single country or a geographical region. These engines support queries and return results in the language of the country (e.g., the Chinese search engine Baidu[5]). They also provide local information, such as yellow and white pages. As a motivating example will show, the advantage of a localized search goes beyond "just" finding yellow and white pages in a national language.

This paper presents an approach to support web searches by rewriting queries using topological background knowledge which is created from the administrative structure of a country and from a tessellation of micro regions. The latter establish consistent units for the analysis of spatial mobility. Applying our approach to web searches that use local expressions significantly improves recall. When using an X86-based PC operating on a knowledge base holding about 30,000 role assertions, query rewriting takes 6,317.54 ms on the average.

The paper is organized as follows: Section 2 provides an overview of the Region Connection Calculus (RCC) and DL-safe SWRL rules. RCC is used as a foundation of the formalism which is introduced in section 4. DL-safe SWRL rules are used – together with OWL DL – to implement the formalism which is described in section 5. The same section also shows how queries are rewritten. In section 6, the approach is applied to web searches for communities which are "close to" a reference place and the results of this application are presented. Section 7 discusses related work and section 8 concludes with an outlook on future work.

This paper extends previous work [3] by (i) refining the basic formalism and separating it from background knowledge, (ii) considering spatial mobility as an additional source of knowledge, and (iii) evaluating the approach on the basis of web searches in a realistic scenario.

2 Region Connection Calculus and DL-Safe SWRL Rules

The Region Connection Calculus (RCC) is an axiomatization of certain spatial concepts and relations in first order logic [4]. The basic theory assumes just one primitive dyadic relation: C(x, y) read as "x connects with y". Individuals (x, y) can be interpreted as denoting spatial regions. The relation C(x, y) is reflexive and symmetric.

Using the primitive relation C(x, y) a number of intuitively significant relations can be defined. Of these relations, PP ("proper part of"), PPi ("inverse proper part of"), PO ("partially overlaps"), EQ ("equal to") and DR ("discrete from") form a jointly exhaustive and pairwise disjoint set, which is known as RCC-5. Similar sets of one, two, three and eight of these relations are known as RCC-1, RCC-2, RCC-3 and RCC-8, respectively. PP and PPi are subsumed by the relations P ("part of") and Pi ("inverse part of"). RCC also incorporates a constant denoting the universal region, a

[3] http://ch.search.yahoo.com
[4] http://www.bing.com
[5] http://www.baidu.com

sum function and partial functions giving the product of any two overlapping regions and the complement of every region except the universe [4].

According to Randell et al. [4], regions support either a spatial or temporal interpretation. For a spatial interpretation, a topological model is provided. According to this model, regions are interpreted as sets of points in a point-based universe and C(x, y) holds if the topological closures of regions x and y share (at least) a common point. In order to comply with the model-theoretic semantics of Description Logics (DL), the RCC relations are interpreted in this paper as binary relations between individual regions in an abstract domain.

In order to infer new from existing knowledge or to check consistency of a knowledge base holding spatial relations, so-called composition tables are used. The entries in these tables share a uniform inference pattern which can be formalized as composition axioms of the general form $\forall x \forall y \forall z\ [S(x, y) \wedge T(y, z) \rightarrow R_1(x, z) \vee \ldots \vee R_n(x, z)]$ where S, T, and R_i are variables for relation symbols.

RCC composition rules can be implemented as DL-safe SWRL rules. DL-safe SWRL rules are function-free Horn rules with the restriction that each variable in the rule occurs in a non-DL-atom in the rule body [5]. This is ensured by adding special non-DL-literals such as $\mathcal{O}(x)$ to the rule body, and by adding a fact $\mathcal{O}(a)$ for each individual a to the knowledge base.[6] While in theory DL-safe SWRL rules support complex, i.e., disjunctive, heads (or negation in the rule body) [6], there is currently no implementation that supports this feature. However, since the RCC relations are jointly exhaustive [4], it is always possible to replace a negative atom, for instance ¬disconnectedFrom(z, y), by a, possibly auxiliary (cf. section 4), positive atom, for instance connectsWith(z, y).

3 A Motivating Example

Think of a woman taking up a new job in the community of Dietlikon (which is located in the canton of Zurich). She might not be familiar with this part of Switzerland, but still wants to find a home which is close to her place of work. Before calling a housing agency she might want to inform herself about the communities close to Dietlikon by searching the web. The retrieval problem triggered by her information need can be put as follows: "For every community that is close to the community of Dietlikon, retrieve all resources from the web." Note that housing agencies on the web usually offer the opportunity of searching within a selectable Euclidean distance from a reference place. Euclidean distance, however, can be tricky when looking for close places. It does not consider conditions such as topography and local public infrastructure.

To make local expressions such as "close to" meaningful, the approach presented in this paper uses topological background knowledge in terms of spatial relations between administrative units and functional micro regions. Administrative units establish the institutional structure of a country. They are typically organized into a

[6] For the evaluation (cf. section 6) it was sufficient to add a fact $\mathcal{O}(a)$ for each individual a. The requirement that $\mathcal{O}$ must not be a concept from the DL knowledge base was not considered.

set of partially ordered partitions. Units of the same partition share the same type. Each unit is administered by a local authority. Switzerland, for instance, is organized into 26 cantons, 147 districts and 2551 communities [7]. Micro regions, on the other hand, do not contribute to a country's administration. They have been established as consistent units for the analysis of spatial mobility and "encode" things such as the behavior of commuters. In Switzerland, the tessellation of micro regions consists of 106 units [7]. Whereas these form a partition similar to those of administrative units, this does not align with the partial ordering of the latter. However, micro regions still align with the smallest units of institutional organization in that a given community is part of a single micro region only.

It is well documented that administrative boundaries influence how people perceive distance (cf. section 7). Some evidence for this comes from the fact that boundaries, for instance of districts, often take course along natural boundaries such as ridges or watercourses thereby "encoding" some prominent topographic features. Districts further divide a country into units performing decentralized administrative tasks in areas such as health (hospitals), education (schools) and judiciary (courts) [7]. Hence, districts – and administrative units in general – suggest themselves as a foundation for a formalism of proximity. Administrative units, however, do not always properly reflect functional properties such as local public infrastructure. In order to include these, the presented approach also considers a tessellation of functional micro regions. Note that the work presented here is still in progress. Further factors influencing the perception of proximity on different scales of social organization may be added in the future.

Fig. 1. Eight communities close to the community of Dietlikon. Shaded areas show different districts. The bold line borders the functional micro region of Glattal-Furttal.

The formalism introduced in the following section is defined on a topological structure.[7] This is the basic idea: A region z is close to a region x if another region y is *a priori* close to x and z connects with y. Note that the type of x implicitly encodes a scale factor: What is close to a community is not the same as what is close to a district.[8] In the next section, this basic rule is refined and linked to two different sources of background knowledge. In order to get back to the example, our approach evaluates the eight labeled communities in Figure 1 as being close to Dietlikon. They are in the intersection of communities that are part of or externally connected to the district of Bülach and those that are located in the micro region of Glattal-Furttal (bold borderline).

4 A Formalism for Proximity

4.1 The Basic Composition Rule

In order to formalize local expressions, RCC is extended by additional relations. In the context of this paper, $\mathsf{CL}(x, y)$, which is read as "x is close to y", is introduced as a *weakly asymmetrical* relation, in accordance with empirical evidence [9]. Against the background of knowledge considered in this paper, this means that the relation is usually symmetrical, if x and y are members of the same administrative partition (e.g., both are communities), but asymmetrical, if y is a member of a more fine-grained partition than x (e.g., y is a community and x a district) or else, if x is a non-administrative region. $\mathsf{CL}(x, y)$ is further irreflexive, intransitive and not antisymmetric.

The additional RCC relation is related to the existing ones by means of a composition rule in such a way that the rule is a necessary condition for the relation:

Composition rule 1. $\forall x \forall y \forall z\ [\mathsf{CL_{ap}}(y, x) \wedge z\{\mathsf{P}, \mathsf{PO}\}y \rightarrow \mathsf{CL}(z, x)]$; informally, a region z is close to a region x if another region y is *a priori* close to x and z is part of or partially overlaps y.

The subscript ap in the name of the relation $\mathsf{CL_{ap}}(y, x)$ stands for "a priori". $\mathsf{CL_{ap}}(y, x)$ is derived from background knowledge. In this paper we consider two sources of background knowledge, (1) a country's organization into different levels of administrative partitions (cf. section 4.2) and (2) tessellations of different granularity consisting of different types of functional regions (which may cross a country's borders).

Even though tessellations of different granularity may be organized as a system of partitions similar to that of administrative regions, this does not have to be the case. Our approach requires, however, that each administrative region must be related to exactly one functional region. In the current implementation (cf. section 5.1) we use

---

[7] This is consistent with Shariff, Egenhofer and Mark [8] who conclude that, for a large set of spatial-relation terms, topology is a more important parameter of the semantics than metric.

[8] Worboys [9] argues that for nearness the subject-referent dichotomy plays a dominant role in that the referent creates the scale in which the relation has context.

the weak notion of "located in" which is introduced as subsumed by "spatially related" – the most general RCC relation.

4.2 A Partially Ordered and Typed System of Partitions

Definition 1 uses the Boolean RCC function SUM and the RCC relation DR to reformulate the well-known notion of a partition in terms of RCC. The RCC function $\mathsf{SUM}_{i \in I}\, x_i$ is defined as $\forall z\, [\mathsf{C}(z, y) \leftrightarrow \bigvee_{i \in I} \mathsf{C}(z, x_i)]$ for a region y [4]. As is customary, lower case letters are used for variables denoting individuals.

Definition 1 (Partition in RCC). A family of regions $(x_i)_{i \in I}$ is a partition of a region y if the following holds:

- $y = \mathsf{SUM}_{i \in I}\, x_i$ where I is a finite index set; this implies $\forall x_i\, \mathsf{P}(x_i, y)$;
- $\forall x_i \forall x_j\, \mathsf{DR}(x_i, x_j)$ for $i \neq j$;
- regions $(x_i)_{i \in I}$ are named for all $i \in I$.

We consider only a small subset of partitions, namely those whose elements are typed by kind of administrative region. For instance, $\mathsf{Community}(x_i)$ says that x_i is of type Community. Multiple typing of regions is not considered, that is, the concepts used for typing are mutually disjoint. Similarly, a given type is used for a single partition only. This allows distinguishing the partitions by their types.

In order to account for the different scales of social organization a *partial order* on the system of partitions in RCC is defined by comparing partitions with regard to their granularity.

Definition 2 (Partial Order on Typed Partitions). Let $C(x_i)_{i \in I}$ and $D(y_k)_{k \in K}$ be partitions of the same region of types C and D, respectively. We say that $C(x_i)_{i \in I}$ is *more fine-grained* than $D(y_k)_{k \in K}$, denoted by $C(x_i)_{i \in I} \preceq D(y_k)_{k \in K}$, if each element of $C(x_i)_{i \in I}$ is a (possibly improper) subset of an element of $D(y_k)_{k \in K}$. A partial order on typed partitions is reflexive, transitive and antisymmetric.

This means that each element of $D(y_k)_{k \in K}$ is partitioned by elements of $C(x_i)_{i \in I}$. For instance, $\mathsf{Community}(x_i)_{i \in I}$ and $\mathsf{District}(y_k)_{k \in K}$ are both typed partitions of a canton and each element of $\mathsf{District}(y_k)_{k \in K}$ is partitioned by elements of $\mathsf{Community}(x_i)_{i \in I}$.

Definition 3 (Minimal Partial Order on Typed Partitions). We say that a partial order on typed partitions is *minimal* with regard to a given conceptualization, denoted by $C(x_i)_{i \in I} \preceq_{\min} D(y_k)_{k \in K}$, if the conceptualization does not provide a type for any $(w_j)_{j \in J}$ such that $C(x_i)_{i \in I} \preceq (w_j)_{j \in J} \preceq D(y_k)_{k \in K}$. A minimal partial order on typed partitions is *intransitive*.

For instance, if a given conceptualization provides the administrative types District and Community, any partial order comprising a non-typed partition of intermediate granularity is not minimal. Definition 3 excludes unwanted partitions such as those consisting of a mash of districts and communities. For further information cf. [3].

4.3 Refining the Formalism

The above introduced background knowledge can be used to formalize the notion of *a priori* closeness as shown in composition rule 2.

Composition rule 2. $\forall x_a \in (a_i)_{i \in I}\ \forall y_a \in (a_i)_{i \in I}\ \forall b \in (b_k)_{k \in K}\ \forall w\ [\mathsf{P}(x_a, b) \wedge y_a\{\mathsf{P}, \mathsf{EC}\}b \wedge \mathsf{LOC}(x_a, w) \wedge \mathsf{LOC}(y_a, w) \rightarrow \mathsf{CL_{ap}}(y_a, x_a)]$; informally, a region y_a is *a priori* close to a region x_a, if (i) x_a and y_a belong to the same administrative partition $(a_i)_{i \in I}$ (e.g., both are communities); (ii) y_a is part of or borders the same region b of the next upper level of administrative partitions $(b_k)_{k \in K}$ (e.g., a district) of which x_a is part; and (iii) x_a and y_a are located (LOC) in the same functional region w of appropriate granularity; EC stands for "externally connected to".

Note that in composition rule 2 the scope of the quantifiers for x_a, y_a and b is limited to the elements of the respective partitions. This also applies to composition rule 1', a refinement of composition rule 1 which uses the consequence of composition rule 2 in the rule body. Composition rules 1' and 2 are implemented in our rule base.

Composition rule 1. $\forall x_a \in (a_i)_{i \in I}\ \forall y_a \in (a_i)_{i \in I}\ \forall z\ [\mathsf{CL_{ap}}(y_a, x_a) \wedge z\{\mathsf{P}, \mathsf{PO}\}y_a \rightarrow \mathsf{CL}(z, x_a)]$; informally, a region z is close to a region x_a of an administrative partition $(a_i)_{i \in I}$ if another region y_a of the same administrative partition is *a priori* close to x_a and z is part of or partially overlaps y_a.

5 Rewriting Queries That Use Local Expressions

5.1 Representing Topological Background Knowledge

For the evaluation of composition rules 1' and 2 three partitions of administrative units and a tessellation of functional micro regions are asserted as background knowledge in an OWL DL Knowledge Base ($\mathcal{KB}$), consisting of a TBox $\mathcal{T}$ and an ABox $\mathcal{A}$. Rules are implemented in a DL-safe SWRL rule base ($\mathcal{RB}$) (not shown). The notation used for the $\mathcal{KB}$ is adopted from [10]. The expressivity of the description language is $\mathcal{ALCHOIF}$. Note that the complexity of the approach is determined by DL complexity.

Partitions are represented in $\mathcal{T}$ by (anonymous) concepts that are made up of individual names, also called *nominals*, $\{a_1, \ldots, a_n\}$. Nominals are linked to types by axioms of the form $C \sqsubseteq \{a_1, \ldots, a_n\}$. In order to disallow multiple typing, the concepts used for typing are defined as mutually disjoint, i.e. $C \sqsubseteq \neg D$.

The subsumption hierarchy of RCC relations [4] is implemented as a hierarchy of roles. The role partOf and the roles subsumed by partOf are described as functional roles, thereby making sure that an individual region a_i can be part of a single region b_j only. This overrides the transitivity of the RCC relation $\mathsf{P}(x, y)$ and prevents, for instance, communities from being related to cantons (or to countries or continents if these were represented).

Disjunctions of RCC relations in the bodies of composition rules, such as {P, PO}, are represented by auxiliary roles subsuming the roles partOf and partiallyOverlaps, for instance. This has some similarity with the design of RCC-12 [11]. RCC-12 relations generalize the RCC-8 relations in such a way as to allow composition rules for being expressed as (non-disjunctive) Horn rules.

Partitions are asserted in $\mathcal{A}$ as partOf(a_i, b_j), or any of the roles subsumed by partOf(a_i, b_j), for all applicable $a_i \in \{a_1, \ldots, a_n\}$ and $b_j \in \{b_1, \ldots, b_m\}$. In so doing, $\mathcal{A}$ is closed with regard to nominals denoting administrative regions.[9] A minimal partial order on typed partitions (cf. section 4.2) is implemented by asserting partOf(a_i, b_j) or any of the roles subsumed by partOf(a_i, b_j) only for those pairs of individuals (a_i, b_j) for which holds $C(a_i)_{i \in I} \preceq_{\min} D(b_j)_{j \in J}$. All individuals in the ABox are asserted as being different from each other.

5.2 Rewriting Queries

Algorithm 1. Function **CLOSETO** computes $(Q \sqcap \exists \mathsf{closeTo}.\{a\})(z)$ from $\mathcal{KB}$ and $\mathcal{RB}$ using composition rules 1' and 2 (cf. section 4.3).

FUNCTION CLOSETO
INPUT: Knowledge Base $\mathcal{KB} = \{\mathcal{T}, \mathcal{A}\}$, Rule Base $\mathcal{RB}$, Concept Q, Individual a
OUTPUT: Set<Individual>
0. $U \leftarrow \emptyset,\ V \leftarrow \emptyset,\ W \leftarrow \emptyset,\ X \leftarrow \emptyset,\ Y \leftarrow \emptyset,\ Z \leftarrow \emptyset$
1. $\{b\} \leftarrow \{b \mid \mathcal{A} \models \mathsf{partOf}(a, b)\}$
2. $U \leftarrow \{u_{i \in I} \mid \mathcal{A} \models \mathsf{partOfOrExternallyConnectedTo}(u_i, b)\}$
3. $\{c\} \leftarrow \{c \mid \mathcal{A} \models \mathsf{locatedIn}(a, c)\}$
4. $V \leftarrow \{v_{j \in I} \mid \mathcal{A} \models \mathsf{locatedIn}(v_j, c)\}$
5. $Y \leftarrow U \cap V$
   FOR $(y_k \in Y;\ Y \neq \emptyset;\ Y \setminus y_k)$ {
6. $\quad X \leftarrow X \cup \{x_{m \in M} \mid \mathcal{A} \models \mathsf{partOfOrPartiallyOverlaps}(x_m, y_k)\}$ }
7. $W \leftarrow \{w_{n \in N} \mid \mathcal{A} \models Q(w_n)\}$
8. $Z \leftarrow X \cap W$
9. **OUTPUT** Z

[9] Note that partOf(a_i, b_j) and the roles subsumed by partOf(a_i, b_j) are used for asserting partitions into administrative regions only.

The terms used in a query reveal how a user conceptualizes a domain. Query concepts can, thus, be used to determine the scale on which spatial relations are to be evaluated. For the evaluation (cf. section 6), conjunctive queries of the form $\forall z\ [Q(z) \wedge \mathsf{CL}(z, a)]$ are used, which are expected to return the set of those individuals of type Q that are close to a given individual a. In this query, the type of individual a, for instance Community, determines the scale for the evaluation of $\mathsf{CL}(z, a)$.

Algorithm 1 show the steps (0–9) to take when rewriting a query. The query $\forall z\ [Q(z) \wedge \mathsf{CL}(z, a)]$ is implemented in DL by the concept assertion $(Q \sqcap \exists \mathsf{closeTo}.\{a\})(z)$. Given an ABox $\mathcal{A}$ and a concept description $Q \sqcap \exists \mathsf{closeTo}.\{a\}$, the retrieval problem is thus to find all individuals z in $\mathcal{A}$ such that $\mathcal{A} \models (Q \sqcap \exists \mathsf{closeTo}.\{a\})(z)$.

6 Evaluation

6.1 Material and Methods

We compare the results of two series of web searches using 170 pairs of conceptually (although not syntactically) consistent queries according to two different strategies. According to the first search strategy, the queries are entered into the search engine as a set of strings. According to the second search strategy, the queries are semantically rewritten and the resulting queries are fed into the search engine. The knowledge required to rewrite the queries is held in a consistent DL knowledge base and a DL-safe SWRL rule base as described in section 5.1. The knowledge base holds 12 concepts, 21 roles, 210 individuals, 603 concept assertions and 29,003 role assertions. Pellet 2.0[10] is used in order to rewrite the queries. Using Pellet 2.0 to reason on OWL DL knowledge bases returns sound and complete results [12]. Reasoning on SWRL rule bases is sound, but not necessarily complete [13]. However, the rewritten queries that were considered for our motivating example in section 3 were also complete. The search engine used for the comparison is GoForIt.[11]

In order to compare the searches, recall and precision are calculated. GoForIt is based on the Open Directory Project (ODP).[12] Different from ODP's search engine, however, GoForIt not only searches the directory's content, but also the categorized resources. This allows extracting all figures necessary for the calculation of recall and precision. The numbers of relevant resources in the result sets are found by summing up the figures in the relevant categories. To give an example, rewriting the query `<Gemeinden "in der Nähe von" Dietlikon>` (i.e. German for communities close to Dietlikon) returns the names of eight communities (cf. Fig. 1). The relevant categories of a search using the disjunction of these names are `Nürensdorf`, `Dübendorf`, `Rümlang`, `Wallisellen`, `Kloten`, `Wangen-Brüttisellen`,

[10] http://clarkparsia.com/pellet
[11] http://www.goforit.com/
[12] http://www.dmoz.org/

Bassersdorf and Opfikon. For the calculation of recall, the returned resources in these categories are related to the sum of all resources (not only of those found by the engine) of the same categories. We thus make the common assumption that manually categorized resources are more relevant than those found by a search algorithm. For the calculation of precision, the returned resources are related to the numbers of resources (whether relevant or not) in the result sets. A two-sided, pairwise t-test has been performed on the resulting recall values to show the significance of our results.

This analysis is complemented by measuring the time required to rewrite the queries.

6.2 Results

Searches without Query Rewriting. In this part of the evaluation the retrieval problem stated in section 3 is put in terms of the strings <Gemeinden "in der Nähe von" Dietlikon>. Similar queries are framed for the remaining 169 communities in the canton of Zurich.[13] The results from web searches using such strings are summarized in Table 1. They are discussed below.

Table 1. Results from searches without query rewriting (n = 170)

	Total relevant	Total matches	Relevant matches	Recall	Precision
Mean	191.39	14.65	0.10	0.00	--
Max	381	750	1	0.01	1.00
Min	20	0	0	0.00	0.00

Searches with Query Rewriting. In this part of the evaluation the retrieval problem is put in terms of the following SPARQL query [14]:

```
SELECT ?z
WHERE {
  ?z rdf:type exp:Community .
  ?z rdf:type [a owl:Restriction;
  owl:onProperty exp:closeTo;
  owl:hasValue exp:Dietlikon] .
}
```

The result of the SPARQL query is fed into the search engine: <Nürensdorf OR Dübendorf OR Rümlang OR Wallisellen OR Kloten OR Wangen-Brüttisellen OR Bassersdorf>. Similar queries are framed for the remaining 169 communities. The numbers of community names resulting from query rewriting range between 6 and 24. The results from the searches are summarized in Table 2.

[13] Note that we excluded the community of Zurich from the analysis. The rewriting algorithm returns intuitively satisfactory results for 170 communities, but not for Zurich. It seems that for communities like Zurich a topological model also has to take into account the impact of urban agglomeration.

Table 2. Results from searches with query rewriting (n = 170)

	Total relevant	Total matches	Relevant matches	Recall	Precision
Mean	191.39	8,843.50	154.35	0.81	0.07
Max	381	30,880	305	0.91	0.31
Min	20	520	17	0.69	0.00

6.3 Discussion

Recall of all searches without query rewriting is low. Only 17 out of 170 searches return a relevant match. The reason for this is that GoForIt does not return resources of entities that are "close to" the reference places as does Google for government agencies and commercial enterprises in urban areas (cf. section 1). Precision is undefined for 102 searches which makes the calculation of a meaningful average infeasible.

Query rewriting significantly ($p < 0.01$) increases recall of the searches. Precision is defined for all searches with query rewriting, at a consistently low level, however. When appraising precision one should keep in mind that the method of calculation disregards the ranking algorithm of the search engine. Precision of the n-best results is much higher. All 170 searches are located in the quadrant of the recall × precision matrix (not shown) that is far from the precision axis (i.e. recall > 0.5) and close to the recall axis (i.e. precision < 0.5). According to Salton and McGill [15], this characterizes broad searches put in general terms.

Overall response time is determined by the time required to rewrite the queries. When using an X86-based PC with a clock rate of 2,533 MHz and a Random Access Memory of 4 GB to operate on the knowledge/rule base described in section 5.1, the time required for query rewriting ranges between 5,608 ms and 19,452 ms (6,317.54 ms on the average). This is acceptable except for six queries which take over 10,000 ms to be rewritten.

The evaluation assumes that query rewriting properly interprets the intended meaning of the expression "close to" in the given context (which remains to be seen). However, even if our approach approximated the meaning of "close to" only roughly, it would still be useful to improve the searches. This can be seen from a comparison of the average total matches in Tables 1 and 2.

7 Related Work

7.1 Administrative Boundaries Influence the Perception of Distance

Maki [16] showed that the affiliation to a category, such as a state, plays an important role in human perception of locations. Subjects should decide about the location of two cities regarding their orientation east-west. If the cities in question belong to different states, the reaction times were significantly shorter than with cities which belong to the same state. The term "categorization effect" refers to the fact that human beings are able to judge faster about entities on a continuum if they can make use of category information.

Carbon and Leder [17] showed that the membership to different political systems, structures or hierarchies influences the estimation of distance between two cities. In their experimental setting, subjects should estimate distances between cities east and west of the former border inside of Germany. Compared to pairs inside the same part of the former republic, distances were overestimated if the cities in question belonged to different parts.

Based on investigations in natural-language corpora, Hois and Kutz [18] are providing parameters which influence the human perception of space. Among these is "domain-specific knowledge of entities" which refers to things such as granularity. Granularity in our approach is modeled via different layers of administrative regions.

7.2 Using Local Expressions in Web Searches

Mark and Egenhofer [19] describe an experiment to test how people think about spatial relations between unbranched lines and simply connected regions. For the predicates "the road crosses the park" and "the road goes into the park" there was a great deal of consensus among the subjects. The authors conclude that the so-called 9-intersection model forms a sound basis for characterizing line-region relations and that many spatial relations can be well-represented by particular subsets of the primitives differentiated by the 9-intersection model.

Different from the approach described here, Mark and Egenhofer [19] use verbs to term natural language predicates and not prepositional phrases. This is reasonable, because in their cases, verbs catch the intuition of the predicates better than any other word class. Independent of the word class used, their results suggest that natural language predicates can, in principle, be aligned with spatial relations as identified by a mathematical model. This supports a similar suggestion for spatial relations between simply connected regions made by the approach described here.

The European SPIRIT project addressed the shortcomings of web search facilities when considering geographical context [20]. It developed methods supporting spatially-aware information retrieval on the Internet. The core component of the system is a geographical ontology that provides a model of the terminology and structure of geographic space. The geographical ontology supports "part-of", "contains", "overlap" and "adjacency" relations between geographic places. Together with the disambiguated place name such relations are used to derive the desired geographical search extent for the query. While "part-of", "contains", "overlap" and "adjacency" can be mapped onto the RCC relations, they are arbitrarily chosen and do not form a jointly exhaustive and pairwise disjoint set of relations. Relations that do not fall into any of the four categories (e.g., "disconnected from") and relations that extend RCC (e.g., "close to") are undefined.

Bishr [21] proposes to encode spatial inferences in the Semantic Web Rule Language (SWRL) [22]. Even though not explicitly mentioned, the examples are provided in an RCC-like style. The proposal can, in principle, be aligned with the approach presented here. Different from [21], however, we introduce additional relations and provide an implementation.

Schokaert, De Cock and Kerre [23] (in [24]) suggest augmenting the structured information available to a local search service, such as Google Maps, with information extracted from the web. They show how nearness information in natural language and information about the surrounding neighborhood of a place can be translated into fuzzy restrictions and how such fuzzy restrictions can be used to estimate the location of a place with an unknown address.

While the idea of augmenting the structured information available to a local search service with information extracted from semi- and unstructured data, i.e. documents on the web, is appealing, it requires that the latter is available in abundance. The "vast amount" [23] of data addressed by the authors, together with the kinds of examples they provide, suggest that their approach is targeted on mass searches. In our case, the resources on the web, which could possibly be used to augment the searches, are scarce (cf. section 6).

8 Conclusion and Outlook

We introduced an approach to rewrite queries for web searches that use local expressions. Query rewriting makes use of topological background knowledge that is implemented in an OWL DL knowledge base and a DL-safe SWRL rule base. Applying the approach to searches for communities which are "close to" a reference place shows that query rewriting significantly improves recall of the searches.

The spatial relations between two simply connected regions identified by the 9-intersection model mentioned in section 7 equal the RCC-8 relations. To the best of our knowledge, experiments testing natural language predicates for compliance with these relations in a way similar to that described for unbranched lines and simply connected regions [19] have not been performed so far. Likewise, no experiments have been performed with the newly introduced relation "close to". Whether the described approach is empirically well founded or not remains to be seen.

Our approach requires that topologies of administrative units are available in RCC. State-of-the-art geographic information systems (GIS) and spatial databases provide ways and means to compute such topologies from GIS layers. In Switzerland the relevant GIS layers can be downloaded from the website of the Swiss Federal Statistical Office.[14] Other European countries such as the United Kingdom and Germany offer similar services. Technically, the approach is, thus, applicable to many countries. Whether the semantics of the relation "close to", expressed as rules applied to the generated topologies, differs between countries remains to be seen.

The current prototype operates on topological knowledge that covers a part of Switzerland. Since the knowledge base grows by the square of the number of regions asserted, we expect the performance to decrease when extending the coverage area. This applies even though an off the shelf PC was used for the evaluation, which could easily be replaced by a faster one. Future work will explore ways of dealing with this expected decrease of performance. This will include distribution of knowledge bases and outsourcing of individuals in a database or a triple store which are known to scale better than in-memory storage structures. An even better way might be to move expensive knowledge processing from run-time to design-time. This requires that search engines are enabled to use topological background knowledge when crawling

[14] http://www.bfs.admin.ch/bfs/portal/de/index/dienstleistungen/geostat/datenbeschreibung/generalisierte_gemeindegrenzen.html

the web and indexing resources. Operating on index entries such as `<Nürensdorf: "close to" Dietlikon>` at run-time is expected to be much faster than rewriting queries.

The approach presented in this paper distinguishes between the basic formalism and the way how background knowledge is used in order to ground the relation $\mathsf{CL}_{ap}(y, x)$. This separation clears the way for using alternate sources of background knowledge. Put the other way round, it facilitates the use of alternate approaches to compute proximity on the basis of the background knowledge provided in this work. Accordingly, we intend to use travel time as calculated by a route planning algorithm to estimate spatial closeness and to relate the results to those obtained by the approach presented here in the near future.

Acknowledgements. This research was funded by and conducted in cooperation with the Swiss Federal Office for the Environment (FOEN) and the Swiss National Science Foundation (SNF).

References

1. Sanderson, M., Kohler, J.: Analyzing geographic queries. In: Proceedings of the Workshop on Geographic Information Retrieval (SIGIR). ACM Press, New York (2004)
2. Wang, L., Wang, C., Xie, X., Forman, J., Lu, Y., Ma, W.-Y., Li, Y.: Detecting Dominant Locations from Search Queries. In: Proceedings of the 28th Annual International ACM SIGIR Conference on Research and Development in Information Retrieval (SIGIR 2005). ACM, New York (2005)
3. Randell, D.A., Cui, Z., Cohn, A.G.: A Spatial Logic based on Regions and Connections. In: Nebel, B., Rich, C., Swartout, W. (eds.) Proceedings of the 3rd International Conference on Principles of Knowledge Representation and Reasoning (KR 1992), pp. 165–176. Morgan Kaufmann, San Mateo (1992)
4. Motik, B., Sattler, U., Studer, R.: Query Answering for OWL-DL with Rules. J. Web Semant., 549–563 (2004)
5. Motik, B., Horrocks, I., Rosati, R., Sattler, U.: Can OWL and Logic Programming Live Together Happily Ever After? In: Cruz, I.F., et al. (eds.) ISWC 2006. LNCS, vol. 4273, pp. 501–514. Springer, Heidelberg (2006)
6. Bundesamt für Statistik: Räumliche Gliederungen der Schweiz (2011), `http://www.bfs.admin.ch/bfs/portal/de/index/regionen/11/geo.html`
7. Shariff, A.R., Egenhofer, M., Mark, D.: Natural-Language Spatial Relations Between Linear and Areal Objects: The Topology and Metric of English-Language Terms. International Journal of Geographical Information Science 12(3), 215–246 (1998)
8. Worboys, M.F.: Nearness Relations in Environmental Space. International Journal of Geographical Information Science 15(7), 633–651 (2001)
9. Grütter, R., Scharrenbach, T., Waldvogel, B.: Vague Spatio-Thematic Query Processing – A Qualitative Approach to Spatial Closeness. Transactions in GIS 14(2), 97–109 (2010)
10. Baader, F., Nutt, W.: Basic Description Logics. In: Baader, F., Calvanese, D., McGuinness, D.L., Nardi, D., Patel-Schneider, P.F. (eds.) The Description Logic Handbook: Theory, Implementation and Applications, 2nd edn., pp. 47–104. Cambridge University Press, Cambridge (2007)

11. Schockaert, S.: Reasoning About Fuzzy Temporal and Spatial Information From the Web. Ph.D. thesis, Ghent University (2008)
12. Sirin, E., Parsia, B., Grau, B.C., Kalyanpur, A., Katz, Y.: Pellet: A Practical OWL-DL Reasoner. J. Web Semant., 51–53 (2007)
13. Parsia, B.: Understanding SWRL (Part 3): Some tricky bits. Weblog Clark & Parsia, LLC, Thursday (September 13, 2007), `http://weblog.clarkparsia.com/2007/09/13/understanding-swrl-part-3-some-tricky-bits/`
14. Prud'hommeaux, E., Seaborne, A.: SPARQL Query Language for RDF. W3C Recommendation (January 15, 2008), `http://www.w3.org/TR/2008/REC-rdf-sparql-query-20080115/`
15. Salton, G., McGill, M.J.: Introduction to modern information retrieval. McGraw-Hill, New York (1983)
16. Maki, R.H.: Categorization and Distance Effects With Spatial Linear Orders. Journal of Experimental Psychology: Human Learning and Memory 7(1), 15–32 (1981)
17. Carbon, C.-C., Leder, H.: The Wall Inside the Brain: Overestimation of Distances Crossing the Former Iron Curtain. Psychonomic Bulletin & Review 12(4), 746–750 (2005)
18. Hois, J., Kutz, O.: Natural Language Meets Spatial Calculi. In: Freksa, C., Newcombe, N.S., Gärdenfors, P., Wölfl, S. (eds.) Spatial Cognition VI. LNCS (LNAI), vol. 5248, pp. 266–282. Springer, Heidelberg (2008)
19. Mark, D.M., Egenhofer, M.J.: Modeling Spatial Relations Between Lines and Regions: Combining Formal Mathematical Models and Human Subjects Testing. In: Egenhofer, M.J., Mark, D.M., Herring, J. (eds.) The 9-Intersection: Formalism and its Use for Natural-Language Spatial Predicates. Technical Report 94-1, National Center for Geographic Information and Analysis, University of California, Santa Barbara, CA (1994)
20. Jones, C.B., Purves, R., Ruas, A., Sanderson, M., Sester, M., van Kreveld, M., Weibel, R.: Spatial Information Retrieval and Geographical Ontologies: An Overview of the SPIRIT Project. In: Proceedings of the 25th Annual International ACM SIGIR Conference on Research and Development in Information Retrieval, pp. 387–388. ACM Press, New York (2002)
21. Bishr, Y.: Geospatial Semantic Web. In: Rana, S., Sharma, J. (eds.) Frontiers of Geographic Information Technology, pp. 139–154. Springer, Heidelberg (2006)
22. Horrocks, I., Patel-Schneider, P.F., Boley, H., Tabet, S., Grosof, B., Dean, M.: SWRL: A Semantic Web Rule Language Combining OWL and RuleML. W3C Member Submission, World Wide Web Consortium (May 21, 2004), `http://www.w3.org/Submission/SWRL/`
23. Schockaert, S., De Cock, M., Kerre, E.E.: Location approximation for local search services using natural language hints. International Journal of Geographic Information Science 22(3), 315–336 (2008)
24. Jones, C.B., Purves, R.S.: Special Issue: Geographical Information Retrieval. International Journal of Geographic Information Science 22(3), 219–360 (2008)

Implementing General Purpose Applications with the Rule-Based Approach

Igor Wojnicki

Institute of Automatics, AGH – University of Science and Technology
wojnicki@agh.edu.pl

Abstract. Using Rule Based Systems (RBS) for implementing general purpose applications makes verification of their formal properties feasible – especially conformance of such applications to their design. To make the RBS approach suitable for general purpose applications an RBS architecture and a certain knowledge representation should be engineered. The paper proposes both the architecture (the Four Layer Architecture – FLA) and an example knowledge representation (Extended Tabular Trees – XTT^2). A prototype RBS and an example application which acknowledges the approach are also discussed.

1 Introduction

The main motivation to use a Rule Based System (RBS)[8] for implementing general purpose applications is its reliability. Entire application logic is defined formally, which allows for analysis of its properties[5]. It can be verified if the application is implemented properly and if it covers all of the requirements.

There are two main issues while applying an RBS for implementing general purpose applications. These are: the single-pass inference process (the interactivity issue), and not well defined separation between the application logic and the interface with the environment (the separation issue).

An RBS based on a single-pass inference process just reads all its inputs runs, completes and generates all outputs. Any interactivity in this case is quite limited, such a behavior is highly non interactive then. The interactivity issue can be addressed by introducing an ability to read inputs and write outputs during the inference process to the inference algorithm.

The separation issue regards poorly separated application logic and the interface with the environment. It makes alteration of the application subject to programmer's mistakes[2,3]. Also upon altering the application logic one can unintentionally disrupt its communication with the environment. To solve the separation issue the Four Layer Architecture (FLA) is proposed. It consists of: the application knowledge base, the environment knowledge base, the environment routines, and the inference engine. Such an architecture is inspired by the *Model-View-Controller* (MVC[1]) approach known from Software Engineering[1].

[1] Trygve Reenskaug made the original MVC note at Xerox PARC in 1978 `http://heim.ifi.uio.no/~trygver/themes/mvc/mvc-index.html`

N. Bassiliades et al. (Eds.): RuleML 2011 - Europe, LNCS 6826, pp. 360–367, 2011.

The application knowledge base resembles the *Model*, the environment knowledge base is the *Controller*, while the environment routines is the *View*. In such a case the application logic (the application knowledge base) does not need to be altered in order to change its communication with the environment i.e. provide a different user interface, provide data from different sources, port or embed entire RBS, etc.

2 Architecture Overview

According to the proposed approach, an application consists of the *application knowledge base*, the *environment knowledge base* and the *environment routines* (the fourth layer is the actual *inference engine*). The *environment knowledge base* bridges the *application knowledge base* and the *environment routines* in a declarative way. It defines relationship between rules and routines. It indicates what routines are called in order to deliver input data from the environment to the inference engine upon checking rule conditions. It also indicates what routines should be called after firing the rules to deliver outcomes to the environment. The purpose of the *environment routines* is to deliver data from/to the inference engine, they are clearly separated from the *application knowledge base.*

For example, having rules based on Attributive Logic[5], each attribute is assigned to a class. The attribute class indicates if the attribute interacts with the environment, if appropriate *environment routine* should be called upon referencing it or not. It is either *state* or one of the *non-state* classes: read-only (*ro*), write-only (*wo*), and read-write (*rw*). The *state* class indicates that the attribute does not interact with the environment, no *environment routine* is called upon referencing it. If the attribute's value comes (is read) from the environment the *ro* class should be assigned. If the attribute's value goes (is written) to the environment the *wo* class should be assigned. For a bi-directional interaction, writing or reading, the *rw* (read-write) class should be used.

Actual data transfer between the environment and attributes is provided through *environment routines* which are also called *triggers*[4]. If an *ro* or *rw* attribute is referenced by the inference engine while checking rule conditions appropriate trigger is executed in order to deliver the value to the engine. If an *wo* or *rw* attribute is referenced by the inference engine while firing a rule appropriate trigger is executed in order to deliver the value to the environment.

Assignments between attributes and appropriate triggers constitute the *environment knowledge base.* For an attribute of *ro* class, an *ro trigger* is assigned, for a *wo* class, a *wo trigger*, for an *rw*, both *ro* and *wo triggers.* Triggers are executed by the inference engine. An *ro trigger* sets the attribute value, it reads it from the environment, delivering to the inference engine. An *wo trigger* writes (or sends) the value to the environment.

3 Example Rule Representation and Run-Time

To implement the application knowledge base of the proposed Four Layer Architecture the XTT^2 (*EXtended Tabular Trees – Mark 2*) knowledge representation is used (any rule representation might be used, FLA is designed to be rule representation independent; XTT^2 is used as a proof of concept). At the visual level it is composed of decision tables. A single table is presented in Fig. 1. The table represents a set of rules based on common attributes. A single rule can be read as follows:

```
IF (A1  o11  a11) and...(An o1n a1n) THEN (B1=b11)...(Bp=b1p)
```

where `A1`...`An` are attributes used in the condition part, `o11`...`o1n` are logical operators, `B1`...`Bp` are attributes used in the decision part; `a11`... `a1n` and `b11`...`b1p` are expressions evaluating to single values or sets of values. Every attribute has assigned a type and an indication whether it can hold single or multiple values. XTT^2 includes two main extensions compared to the classic RBS: non-atomic attribute values (sets of values can be used both in conditions and decisions), non-monotonic reasoning support (sets of values providing assert/retract like functionality in decisions). Each table row corresponds to a decision rule. Tables can be linked in a graph-like structure. A link is followed when the corresponding rule is fired. Interconnected tables may form cycles which make the inference process loop over.

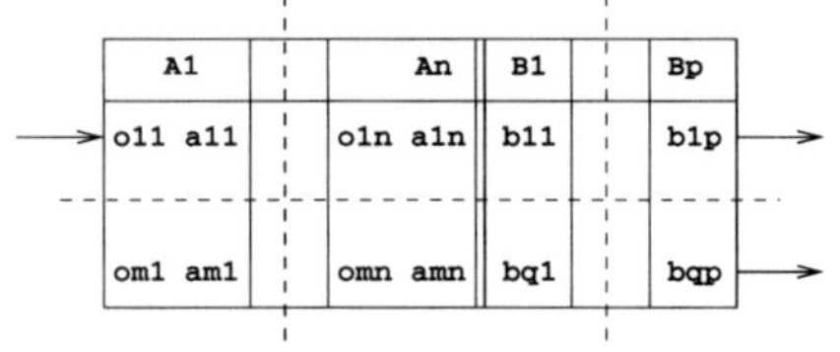

Fig. 1. A single XTT^2 table

A table corresponds to a number of rules, processed in a sequence. If a rule is fired and it has a link, the inference engine processes the rules in another table the link points to. Each rule corresponds to a *Horn* clause: $\neg p_1 \vee \neg p_2 \vee \ldots \vee \neg p_k \vee h$ where p_i is a literal in SAL (Set Attributive Logic[5]) in a form $A_i(o) \in t$ where $o \in O$ is a object referenced in the system, and $A_i \in A$ is a selected attribute of this object, $t \subseteq D_i$ is a subset of attribute domain A_i. Rules are interpreted using a unified knowledge and fact base, that can be dynamically modified during the inference process using set based assignments in the rule decision part. The approach has been extended and redesigned several times to make it more robust, flexible and easy to use[6,7,9]. Moreover, it has been successfully applied to model classic rule-based expert systems.

To verify the proposed approach a run-time environment is created. It is capable of processing rules and interacting with the environment, thus implementing the inference engine and providing appropriate means to call the environment routines. Attribute values can be read or written multiple times during the inference process. The run-time is named *Beating HeaRT* (HeaRT stands for HeKatE Run-Time). It is one of the tools provided by the HeKatE Project (see `http://hekate.ia.agh.edu.pl`).

XTT^2 becomes rule representation providing the *application knowledge base*. The attributes are assigned to *ro*, *wo*, *rw* classes. Appropriate *environment knowledge base* is defined. At each step, if a *non-state* attribute is involved, appropriate values are read from, or written to, the environment by launching corresponding triggers (the *environment routines*). The inference process is highly interactive.

Summarizing, the Beating HeaRT provides a complete run-time with input/output capabilities implementing the Four Layer Architecture, which enables multi-pass rule interpretation.

4 Example Application

In the following section an example of FLA/XTT-based application, a simple text editor, is presented. The application is highly interactive, calling different triggers multiple times during the inference process.

The application knowledge base is given in Fig. 2. This visualization is slightly enhanced comparing to the one presented in Sect. 3. The enhancements are targeted toward easier table and rule identification. Each of the tables has a unique identifier displayed in its bottom-left corner. Furthermore, each rule within a table is uniquely labeled (the last column). The tables, form a directed graph with optional cycles. A cycle indicates that under certain conditions the inference process loops over.

There are the following attributes present in the system: *key* (character type, single value, *state* class), *inkey* (character, single value, *ro* class), *ochar* (character, multiple values, *state* class), *outchar* (character, multiple values, *wo* class), *ichar* (character, multiple values, *state* class), *inchar* (character, multiple values, *ro* class), *cursor* (integer, single value, *wo* class), and *chars* (character, multiple values, *wo* class).

There are several operators used in the condition and decision parts of the rules. These are: logical operators which evaluate to true or false (*eq* – equals, *neq* – not equals, *gt* – greater than, *lt* – less than, *in* – in ($\in$), *notin* – not in ($\notin$)), evaluative operators which evaluate to a value or set of values (*add* – add, *sub* – subtract, *insert* – insert at given index (in case of multivalued attributes), *remove* – remove from given index) and modification operators which modify attribute's value (*assign* – assign a value).

The proposed editor application is capable of reading in characters into a buffer (the *chars* attribute) which contents is displayed at any change (since *chars* is *wo* class). The *cursor* attribute represents cursor position in the buffer. The *inkey* attribute holds a single key sequence typed by the user (*ro* class attribute). There are several key sequences with special meaning, these are (ˆ stands for *Ctrl* key): ˆ*o*: open a file, ˆ*s*: save the buffer to a file, *backspace*: erase a character left of the current cursor position, *left*: move the cursor left by one character, *right*: move the cursor right by one character, ˆ*q*: quit the editor. Any other incoming key sequence should insert a corresponding character at the current position of the cursor into the buffer. The *key* attribute holds the same value as *inkey* however it is a state class attribute. It allows to access this value as many times as needed without reading another value from the environment.

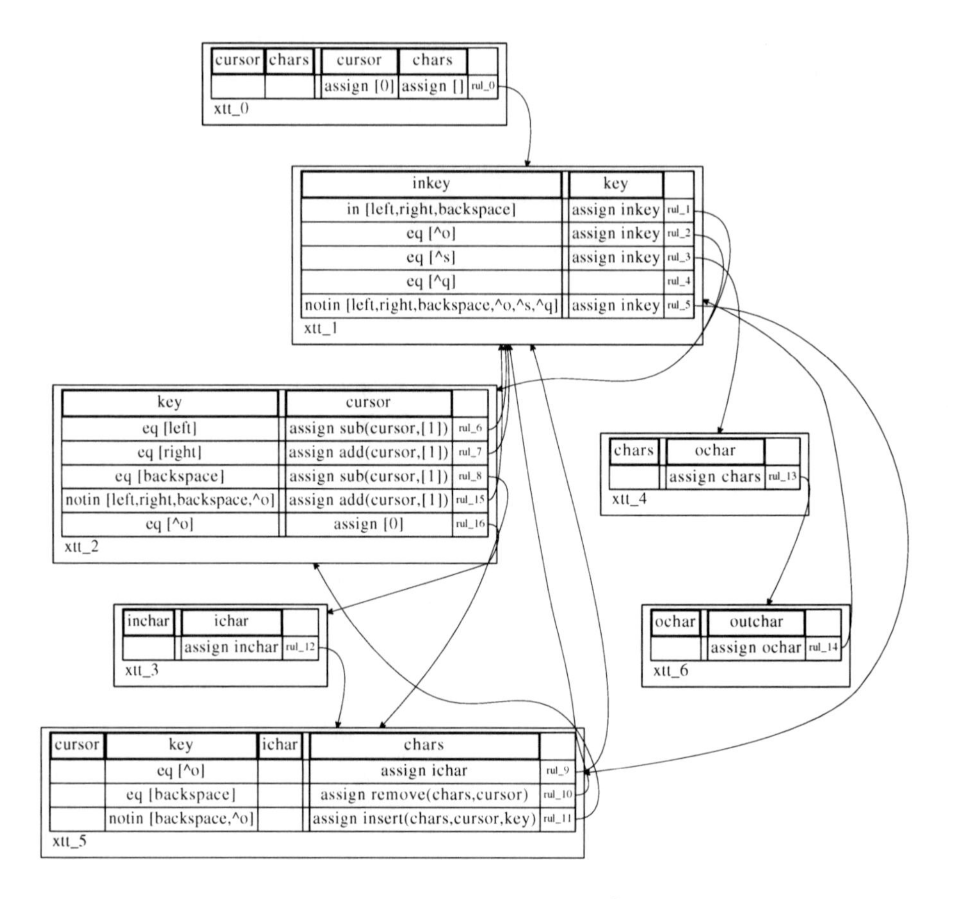

Fig. 2. Editor Case, XTT^2

The *outchar* and *inchar* attributes (*wo* and *ro* class respectively) provide means to write entire buffer contents to or read it from the environment at once (i.e. transferring it from or to a file). The *ochar* and *ichar* attributes are similar to *outchar* and *inchar* but they are of state class.

The inference process is started with a table labeled *xtt_0*. It presets values of *cursor* and *chars* to 0 (zero) and empty, respectively. The *xtt_1* is the main logic of the application. It assigns a value to *key* based on the value of *inkey* and forces the inference process to follow to the appropriate table based on this value. If such a value has influence on the cursor position (*left, right, backspace*, or *^o*) then the inference process switches to *xtt_2* (the rules: *rul_1*, *rul_2*). If it is *^s*, saving the buffer content, the inference switches to *xtt_4* (the *rul_3* rule). If it is *^q* then the rule *rul_4* without an outgoing link is fired which concludes the inference process. Otherwise *rul_5* is fired which leads to *xtt_5*. The *xtt_2* table is responsible for changing the *cursor* value (representing the cursor position). It utilizes the *sub* and *add* operators. For example the *rul_6* decision should be read as: $cursor = cursor - 1$. The *xtt_5* table modifies the buffer by changing the *chars* values. It assigns *chars* the values of *ichar*, if ^*o* sequence is pressed (the *rul_9* rule). Otherwise it inserts another value into *chars* (*rul_10*) or removes a value (*rul_11*). There are *remove* and *insert* operators used, the former removes a value from a multi-valued attribute, at a given index, the latter inserts it respectively. Other XTT[2] tables should be self-explanatory at this point.

```
% inkey attribute
io(att_12,ro_trigger,get_character).
% inchar attribute
io(att_8,ro_trigger,read_chars_from_file).
% outchar attribute
io(att_10,wo_trigger,write_chars_to_file).
% chars attribute
io(att_3,wo_trigger,display_chars).
% cursor attribute
io(att_4,wo_trigger,display_cursor).
```

Fig. 3. Editor Case, IOD interfacing Prolog

To make the application communicate with the environment, to obtain typed in characters, to display buffer contents and to react to control sequences, appropriate trigger routines have to be implemented and assigned to *non-state* attributes. The assignment provided by the IOD (Input Output Declarations, a language for defining the *environment knowledge base*) is presented in Fig. 3. It is expressed with a three argument predicate `io/3` (IOD is based on Prolog language syntax for simplicity). The first argument is the attribute unique identifier, the second indicates the trigger class (either *ro trigger* or *wo trigger*) and the routine name to spawn as a trigger. Lines starting with % are comments. The IOD in Fig. 3 states that the `get_character` trigger is called upon referencing the *inkey* attribute (*att_12* attribute identifier) to obtain its value. This action takes place if the attribute is in the condition part of a rule since *inkey* is of *ro* class. The `write_chars_to _file` and `read_chars_from_file` are called upon referencing the *outchar* attribute (unique identifier: *att_10*, *wo* class) in the decision part and the *inchar* attribute (unique identifier: *att_8*, *ro* class) in the condition part, respectively. The `display_chars` and `display_cursor` are called upon referencing the *chars* (unique identifier: *att_3*, *wo* class) and the *cursor* (unique identifier: *att_4*, *wo* class) in the decision part, respectively. The above trigger routines are written in Prolog.

An alternative IOD for the same application knowledge base is given in Fig. 4. The trigger routines are implemented in Java. Comparing with the IOD for Prolog there is a slight change due to semantics differences between Java and Prolog languages. The third argument of the `io` predicate consists of three entries: the class name, the method name and the object reference. The class and the method implement appropriate trigger routine. The reference is optional and it allows to call methods on existing objects (already instantiated). If the reference is not present every time a trigger is called an object of the given class is created and

```
% inkey attribute
io(att_12,ro_trigger,['EditorWindow',get_character,editor]).
% inchar attribute
io(att_8,ro_trigger,['EditorWindow',read_chars_from_file,editor]).
% outchar attribute
io(att_10,wo_trigger,['EditorWindow',write_chars_to_file,editor]).
% chars attribute
io(att_3,wo_trigger,['EditorWindow',display_chars,editor]).
% cursor attribute
io(att_4,wo_trigger,['EditorWindow',display_cursor,editor]).
```

Fig. 4. Editor Case, IOD interfacing Java

appropriate method is executed. If the reference is present, an object is created upon the first call of the trigger. Any subsequent calls regard that object.

To start an XTT^2 based application the application knowledge base has to be loaded in along with corresponding IOD. Based on the IOD the run-time chooses appropriate module to handle either Prolog or Java based trigger routines. Then the inference process is started by indicating the initial XTT^2 table.

The presented application is highly interactive. The user can type in characters, backspace, move the cursor, save the buffer into a file, or read it in. The inference process ends upon obtaining *^q* sequence (see the *rul_4* rule, Fig. 2), from the user.

5 Summary and Further Research

Implementing general purpose software can be achieved through applying the Four Layer Architecture (FLA) and choosing appropriate knowledge base representation to support its interactivity (XTT^2).

A test case application, a simple text editor, confirms applicability of the proposed approach to design and implement general purpose applications with RBS. The application is presented with two separate interfaces, a textual one, implemented in Prolog, and a graphical one, implemented in Java. No changes to the application logic are required to switch between these two interfaces upon run-time. To run the application the Beating HeaRT run-time environment is presented which provides the FLA. The run-time interprets the application knowledge base stored as XTT^2 rules. as well as given IOD (the environment knowledge base), and triggers appropriate routines (the environment routines) written in Prolog or Java.

An ongoing research focuses on providing a comprehensive set of reusable trigger routines performing common tasks such as: file operations, user interfaces and interactions with the underlying operating system. There are also plans to replace the proposed IOD language with Input/Output Markup Language (IOML) based on XML. Some changes in the inference algorithm are also under consideration, including backtracking or parallel rule interpretation.

References

1. Burbeck, S.: Applications programming in smalltalk-80(tm): How to use model-view-controller (mvc). Technical report, Department of Computer Science, University of Illinois, Urbana-Champaign (1992)
2. Friedman-Hill, E.: Jess in Action, Rule Based Systems in Java. Manning (2003)
3. Giarratano, J.C., Riley, G.D.: Expert Systems. Thomson (2005)
4. Leś, W., Łosiewicz, M.: The xtt inference engine and the java virtual machine coupling. Master's thesis, AGH – University of Sience and Technology (2009)
5. Ligęza, A.: Logical Foundations for Rule-Based Systems. Springer, Heidelberg (2006)
6. Nalepa, G.J., Ligęza, A.: A graphical tabular model for rule-based logic programming and verification. Systems Science 31(2), 89–95 (2005)
7. Nalepa, G.J., Wojnicki, I.: Proposal of visual generalized rule programming model for Prolog. In: Seipel, D., et al. (eds.) INAP, WLP: Proceedings, Wurzburg, pp. 195–204. Bayerische Julius-Maximilians-Universitat (September 2007)
8. Negnevitsky, M.: Artificial Intelligence. A Guide to Intelligent Systems. Addison-Wesley, Harlow (2002) ISBN 0-201-71159-1
9. Wojnicki, I., Nalepa, G.J.: Prolog hybrid operators in the generalized rule programming model. In: Seipel, D., et al. (eds.) INAP, WLP: Technical Report 434, pp. 205–214. Bayerische Julius-Maximilians-Universitat (September 2007)

OWL Web Ontology Language as a Scripting Language for Smart Space Applications

Espen Suenson, Johan Lilius, and Iván Porres

Department of Information Technologies,
Åbo Akademi University,
Turku, Finland
givenname.surname@abo.fi

Abstract. We describe a scripting language for smart space applications based on the OWL Web Ontology Language. The design goals of the scripting language are: I. A syntax that easily expresses common script applications for smart spaces. II. Based on OWL to enable synergy with semantic web technologies. III. Ease of implementation by using existing OWL reasoners.

We motivate the design of the scripting language and give some examples of how to use it. Furthermore, we will give a formal definition of the syntax and semantics of the scripting language based on the OWL 2 definition.

Keywords: OWL, smart space, ontology, scripting, semantic web.

1 Introduction

The Semantic Web is based on the architecture of the World Wide Web. However, there is also a wish to permit greater interoperability between portable devices, and in particular to permit portable devices to discover and exchange information about their immediate physical environments, that is, their context. A Smart Space is an idea of connecting such devices in a local way similar to the Semantic Web. [9] In this paper we define a smart space as a local network about the size of a room consisting of smart phones, tablet PCs and the like, that is, devices that are fairly computationally powerful.

Smart-M3 is a communication infrastructure for smart devices conceived by Nokia. In Smart-M3, computational devices (smart phones and others) communicate within a limited physical space through a central database, the System Information Broker (SIB). The communication is in the form of RDF. [3] A program that communicates with the SIB is called a Knowledge Processor (KP). An application may consist of several KPs acting together, KPs residing on other devices and programs not communicating directly with the SIB. The KPs do not communicate with each other since this is done via the SIB.

In this paper we describe a scripting language for simple smart space applications. The language targets the Smart-M3 platform. The first design goal of

N. Bassiliades et al. (Eds.): RuleML 2011 - Europe, LNCS 6826, pp. 368–375, 2011.

our scripting language is that it should make it easier to make smart space applications. To satisfy this design goal our scripting language must make it easy to express simple tasks, see the examples of section 3.

The second design goal is that the scripting language is based on OWL. [7] Hence we will refer to the scripting language as OWL Script. By building on well deliberated standards we hope to save some of the work of inventing new standards and to enable greater interoperability between standards.

The third design goal is that OWL Script should be able to be implemented without expending the effort to create a compiler or interpreter from ground. The use of OWL means that it is possible to use existing OWL reasoning engines as the computational core of OWL Script.

The main research question that we are trying to answer is how to make a practically oriented scripting layer that combines the ideas of smart spaces and the Semantic Web technologies. 'Practical' is meant to be understood both from from the point view of the scripting programmer as well as of the scripting language implementer.

2 Related Work

Luukkala and Niemelä have proposed to use an Answer Set Programming implementation as the basis for rule based computation on top of the Smart-M3 platform. [4] Their approach provides for rule based constraint programming in a way that is computationally more powerful than using OWL. However, in their approach variables can only hold single individuals. We believe that our approach where variables refer to sets provides for more intuitive scripts with regard to smart spaces.

Oliver and Honkola suggests using the WQL query language of Smart-M3 to implement scripts similar to those considered in this paper. [5] However, they do not describe the scripting language in detail.

As the individual scripts in our approach have a form similar to 'IF a THEN b', OWL Script, if viewed as a collection of rules, bears some resemblance to a production rule system (with implementations such as Drools). However, the focus of our work is not on the rules as a system, but rather on the individual 'rule' level and its expression in OWL. Each script or 'rule' will execute independently.

The Rule Interchange Format [8], RuleML [2] and REWERSE I1 Rule Markup Language are rule formats that can be executed. However, the purpose of these formats is mainly to serve as interchange formats between different rule notations, hence they do not address specifically a syntax suitable for smart space scripting or implementation via OWL reasoners.

A number of OWL reasoning engines exist which could conceivably be used as back ends in implementing the proposed scripting languages. To name some: Pellet, Hermit, the Jena framework, Bossam and Racer.

3 Programming with OWL Script

Shown in table 1 is an example KP in OWL Script. It checks whether a named user is listed as busy in the SIB, and whether there's a call to his phone. If so, the phone's voicemail is activated by inserting a command in the SIB that will presumably be read by the phone at a later time and acted upon.

Table 1. OWL Script programming example

```
with  user = /User and /Id == "peter.smith@abo.fi"
      phone = /Phone /Owner user
      busyUser = user and /Busy
      ringingPhone = phone and /IncomingCall

when busyUser, ringingPhone

then  insert /ActivateVoicemail( ringingPhone )
```

The program has three clauses. The 'with' clause defines an ontology in the KP that we can think of as a declaring local variables. Any variable that has the '/' access modifier prefixed will be fetched from the SIB. Variables without access modifiers are local to the KP. All variables are sets, so even though we assume that there's only one user with a given 'Id', the variables 'phone' and 'ringingPhone' could easily be conceived to have multiple members.

The 'when' clause decides if the KP will take any action. In this case, if both 'busyUser' and 'ringingPhone' are nonempty sets, the 'then' clause will be carried out. The 'then' clause specifies the action that will be taken if the KP fires. In our example a unary predicate will be inserted into the SIB over the set 'ringingPhone'.

Table 2. OWL Script programming example

```
when /SIB_Location and /EmployeeRestaurant,
     dev/Time > "11:00:00" ^^xsd:time,
     dev/Time < "13:30:00" ^^xsd:time

then  insert /AtLunch( user )
```

In table 2 we see an example that lists the user as busy in the SIB if he is present in a restaurant and it is around lunch time. The example demonstrates communication with the hosting device through the use of the 'dev/' access modifier. We also see that some things are outside the scope of OWL Script and must be provided by the device, such as the current time.

4 Syntax

The syntax of OWL Script is defined by extending the syntax of OWL 2 Functional Syntax and adding the syntactical categories for those things that are exclusive to OWL Script.

Table 3. Extension of the OWL 2 syntax

<table>
<tr><td>AccessModifier</td><td>:=</td><td>'/' | 'dev/'</td></tr>
<tr><td>NonlocalIdentifier</td><td>:=</td><td>AccessModifier IRI</td></tr>
<tr><td>Quantifier</td><td>:=</td><td>nonNegativeInteger |
'min' nonNegativeInteger |
'max' nonNegativeInteger |
'only'</td></tr>
<tr><td>Class</td><td>+=</td><td>NonlocalIdentifier</td></tr>
<tr><td>ObjectProperty</td><td>+=</td><td>NonlocalIdentifier</td></tr>
<tr><td>DataProperty</td><td>+=</td><td>NonlocalIdentifier</td></tr>
<tr><td>DataRange</td><td>+=</td><td>('==' | '>' | '<') Literal</td></tr>
<tr><td>ClassExpression</td><td>+=</td><td>'(' ClassExpression ')' |
ClassExpression 'and' ClassExpression |
ClassExpression 'or' ClassExpression |
ClassExpression ',' ClassExpression |
[Quantifier] PropertyExpression</td></tr>
<tr><td>PropertyExpression</td><td>:=</td><td>ClassExpression ObjectPropertyExpression ClassExpression |
'?' ObjectPropertyExpression ClassExpression |
ClassExpression ObjectPropertyExpression '?' |
DataPropertyExpression DataRange</td></tr>
<tr><td>ClassAxiom</td><td>+=</td><td>ClassExpression '=' ClassExpression</td></tr>
</table>

The extension of the OWL syntax is based on the OWL 2 Functional Syntax definition. [7] The extensions are shown in table 3 in extended BNF notation. The '+=' symbol that is used in some places instead of the normal ':=' means that the syntactic categories of OWL 2 are augmented with the productions shown, that is, those productions can be used in addition to those already defined in the standard. Syntactic categories that are not defined here are defined in the OWL 2 standard.

The access modifiers '/' and 'dev/' are the only extensions of the basic OWL 2 syntax that cannot be expressed in ordinary OWL 2. The rest of the extensions in table 3 can be regarded as syntactic sugar for OWL 2 expressions. Of course, the constructs of table 4 cannot be expressed in OWL.

Disregarding the access modifiers, the body of the 'with' and 'when' clauses is standard OWL with added syntactic shortcuts. The 'then' clause builds a set of RDF triples and directs insertion or removal of triples. The full syntax for KPs is shown in extended BNF notation in table 4.

Table 4. OWL Script syntax

RDFExpression	:=	**NonlocalIdentifier** '(' **ClassExpression** ')' |
		NonlocalIdentifier '(' **ClassExpression** ',' **ClassExpression** ')' |
		NonlocalIdentifier '(' **ClassExpression** ',' **Literal** ')'
Action	:=	'new' **IRI** |
		'insert' **RDFExpression** |
		'remove' **RDFExpression**
KnowledgeProcessor	:=	['with' { **Axiom** }] 'when' **ClassExpression** 'then' { **Action** }

It should be noted that the presented syntax is ambiguous, but that the ambiguity can be resolved by the proper use of parentheses.

5 Semantics

The semantics of an OWL ontology O is given in terms of an interpretation $\mathsf{I} = (\Delta_\mathsf{I}, \Delta_\mathsf{D}, \cdot^\mathsf{C}, \cdot^\mathsf{OP}, \cdot^\mathsf{DP}, \cdot^\mathsf{I}, \cdot^\mathsf{DT}, \cdot^\mathsf{LT}, \cdot^\mathsf{FA})$ where Δ_I is an object domain of individuals and Δ_D is a data domain of data values, $\cdot^\mathsf{C}$ is the class interpretation function, $\cdot^\mathsf{OP}$ is the object property interpretation function, $\cdot^\mathsf{DP}$ is the data property interpretation function, $\cdot^\mathsf{I}$ is the individual interpretation function, $\cdot^\mathsf{DT}$ is the datatype interpretation function, $\cdot^\mathsf{LT}$ is the literal interpretation function and $\cdot^\mathsf{FA}$ is the data facet interpretation function. [6]

To describe the contents of the SIB and hosting device triple stores we define additionally the interpretation functions $\cdot^{\mathsf{C}^\mathsf{SIB}}, \cdot^{\mathsf{OP}^\mathsf{SIB}}, \cdot^{\mathsf{DP}^\mathsf{SIB}}, \cdot^{\mathsf{C}^\mathsf{dev}}, \cdot^{\mathsf{OP}^\mathsf{dev}}$ and $\cdot^{\mathsf{DP}^\mathsf{dev}}$.

To describe the semantics of variables with access modifiers we require the following to hold given $/\mathsf{name}$ in O:

$$
\begin{aligned}
&\text{if } /\mathsf{name} \in \mathsf{V_C} \text{ then}\\
&\qquad x \in (\mathsf{name})^{\mathsf{C}^\mathsf{SIB}} \Rightarrow x \in (/\mathsf{name})^\mathsf{C}\\
&\text{if } /\mathsf{name} \in \mathsf{V_{OP}} \text{ then}\\
&\qquad (x,y) \in (\mathsf{name})^{\mathsf{OP}^\mathsf{SIB}} \Rightarrow (x,y) \in (/\mathsf{name})^\mathsf{OP}\\
&\text{if } /\mathsf{name} \in \mathsf{V_{DP}} \text{ then}\\
&\qquad (x,y) \in (\mathsf{name})^{\mathsf{DP}^\mathsf{SIB}} \Rightarrow (x,y) \in (/\mathsf{name})^\mathsf{DP}
\end{aligned}
$$

where $\mathsf{V_C}$, $\mathsf{V_{OP}}$ and $\mathsf{V_{DP}}$ are the vocabularies of classes, object properties and data properties in O.

We define exactly similar requirements to hold for the device interpretation functions $\cdot^{\mathsf{C}^\mathsf{dev}}, \cdot^{\mathsf{OP}^\mathsf{dev}}$ and $\cdot^{\mathsf{DP}^\mathsf{dev}}$. Note that the vocabulary membership conditions can be resolved syntactically.

We need to define the semantics for the rest of the syntactic additions we have made to OWL. We do this by extending the domain of the interpretation functions $\cdot^{\mathsf{DT}}$ and $\cdot^{\mathsf{C}}$ from the OWL 2 Direct Semantics definition. [6] The extension of $\cdot^{\mathsf{DT}}$ is given in table 5. The extension of $\cdot^{\mathsf{C}}$ is given in table 6. We have added only one axiom form to the syntax, the condition that it imposes is given in table 7.

Table 5. Extension of the datatype interpretation function

Data Range	Interpretation $\cdot^{\mathsf{DT}}$
`== lt`	$\{(\mathsf{lt})^{\mathsf{LT}}\}$
`> lt`	$(\mathsf{DT})^{\mathsf{DT}} \cap (\mathsf{xsd:minExclusive}, \mathsf{lt})^{\mathsf{FA}}$
`< lt`	$(\mathsf{DT})^{\mathsf{DT}} \cap (\mathsf{xsd:maxExclusive}, \mathsf{lt})^{\mathsf{FA}}$

where DT is the datatype of the literal `lt` if different from rdf:PlainLiteral; otherwise it is xsd:integer.

Table 6. Extension of the class expression interpretation function

Class Expression	Interpretation $\cdot^{\mathsf{C}}$
`( CE )`	$(\mathsf{CE})^{\mathsf{C}}$
`CE₁ and CE₂`	$(\mathsf{CE}_1)^{\mathsf{C}} \cap (\mathsf{CE}_2)^{\mathsf{C}}$
`CE₁ or CE₂`	$(\mathsf{CE}_1)^{\mathsf{C}} \cup (\mathsf{CE}_2)^{\mathsf{C}}$
`CE₁ , CE₂`	$\begin{cases} \delta \text{ if } \exists x, y : x \in (\mathsf{CE}_1)^{\mathsf{C}} \text{ and } y \in (\mathsf{CE}_2)^{\mathsf{C}} \\ \emptyset \text{ otherwise} \end{cases}$ where $\delta \subseteq \Delta_{\mathsf{I}}$ and $\delta \neq \emptyset$
`CE₁ OPE CE₂`	$\{x \mid \exists y : (x,y) \in (\mathsf{OPE})^{\mathsf{OP}} \text{ and } x \in (\mathsf{CE}_1)^{\mathsf{C}}, y \in (\mathsf{CE}_2)^{\mathsf{C}}\}$
`n CE₁ OPE CE₂`	$\{x \mid \#\{y \mid (x,y) \in (\mathsf{OPE})^{\mathsf{OP}} \text{ and } x \in (\mathsf{CE}_1)^{\mathsf{C}}, y \in (\mathsf{CE}_2)^{\mathsf{C}}\} = n\}$
`min n CE₁ OPE CE₂`	$\{x \mid \#\{y \mid (x,y) \in (\mathsf{OPE})^{\mathsf{OP}} \text{ and } x \in (\mathsf{CE}_1)^{\mathsf{C}}, y \in (\mathsf{CE}_2)^{\mathsf{C}}\} \geq n\}$
`max n CE₁ OPE CE₂`	$\{x \mid \#\{y \mid (x,y) \in (\mathsf{OPE})^{\mathsf{OP}} \text{ and } x \in (\mathsf{CE}_1)^{\mathsf{C}}, y \in (\mathsf{CE}_2)^{\mathsf{C}}\} \leq n\}$
`only CE₁ OPE CE₂`	$\{x \mid \forall y : (x,y) \in (\mathsf{OPE})^{\mathsf{OP}}, x \in (\mathsf{CE}_1)^{\mathsf{C}} \text{ implies } y \in (\mathsf{CE}_2)^{\mathsf{C}}\}$
`? OPE CE`	$\{x \mid \exists y : (x,y) \in (\mathsf{OPE})^{\mathsf{OP}} \text{ and } y \in (\mathsf{CE})^{\mathsf{C}}\}$
`CE OPE ?`	$\{y \mid \exists x : (x,y) \in (\mathsf{OPE})^{\mathsf{OP}} \text{ and } x \in (\mathsf{CE})^{\mathsf{C}}\}$
`DPE DR`	$\{x \mid \exists y : (x,y) \in (\mathsf{DPE})^{\mathsf{DP}} \text{ and } y \in (\mathsf{DR})^{\mathsf{DT}}\}$

The quantified forms of the syntactic forms '`? OPE CE`', '`CE OPE ?`' and '`DPE DR`' have been omitted since they are similar to the forms shown. `CE` is a class expression, `OPE` is an object property expression, `DPE` is a data property expression and `DR` is a data range.

Table 7. Extension of the class expression axiom satisfaction conditions

Axiom	Condition
`CE₁ = CE₂`	$(\mathsf{CE}_1)^{\mathsf{C}} = (\mathsf{CE}_2)^{\mathsf{C}}$

We emphasize that the extensions are merely syntactical, they do not extend the computational power of OWL. In other words, it is possible, though not always efficient, to implement the extensions in ordinary OWL. In particular, the syntactic form '$\mathtt{CE}_1$, $\mathtt{CE}_2$' can be implemented as $(\exists\top.(\mathsf{CE}_1)^{\mathsf{C}})\sqcap(\exists\top.(\mathsf{CE}_2)^{\mathsf{C}})$ (borrowing notation from [1]) and the form '`CE OPE ?`' can be implemented with the use of the OWL inversion operator ObjectInverseOf.

To define the semantics of the parts of OWL Script that doesn't directly extend OWL, we first define an interpretation function for RDF expressions, $\cdot^{\mathsf{RDF}}$. The definition of $\cdot^{\mathsf{RDF}}$ is given in table 8.

The semantics of the 'Action' syntactic category is as follows: An action of the form '`new IRI`' defines a new blank RDF node x such that $(\mathsf{IRI})^{\mathsf{C}} = \{x\}$. An action of the form '`insert RDFE`' indicates that the RDF triple set $(\mathsf{RDFE})^{\mathsf{RDF}}$ is to be written to the SIB or the hosting device triple store, depending on the access modifier. Similarly, '`remove RDFE`' indicates triple sets that are to be deleted.

The triple sets to be inserted or removed may be described by several actions. The complete sets are written atomically to the SIB and the hosting device, but the writing operations to the SIB and the device are not atomic with respect to each other. Conflicts between 'insert' and 'remove' actions are resolved in favor of insertion.

We can now define the semantics of a KP '`with O when CE then A`'. Let I be an interpretation that satisfies O under the additional SIB and device store requirements. If $(\mathsf{CE})^{\mathsf{C}} \neq \emptyset$ then the actions A are carried out and updates the SIB and device triple stores according to the definition above of action semantics.

Table 8. RDF expression interpretation function

RDF Expression	Interpretation $\cdot^{\mathsf{RDF}}$
`NLI ( CE )`	$\{((x)^{\bar{\mathsf{I}}}, \mathsf{rdf:type}, \mathsf{IRI}) \mid x \in (\mathsf{CE})^{\mathsf{C}}\}$
`NLI ( CE₁ , CE₂ )`	$\{((x)^{\bar{\mathsf{I}}}, \mathsf{IRI}, (y)^{\bar{\mathsf{I}}}) \mid x \in (\mathsf{CE}_1)^{\mathsf{C}}$ and $y \in (\mathsf{CE}_2)^{\mathsf{C}}\}$
`NLI ( CE , lt )`	$\{((x)^{\bar{\mathsf{I}}}, \mathsf{IRI}, \mathsf{lt}) \mid x \in (\mathsf{CE})^{\mathsf{C}}\}$

where IRI is the IRI of the non-local identifier `NLI` and $\cdot^{\bar{\mathsf{I}}}$ is the inverse of $\cdot^{\mathsf{I}}$.

6 Conclusion

The scripting language we present demonstrates that it is feasible to use OWL as a programming language in a limited domain setting. We believe that OWL Script is easy to use for examples similar to the ones we have given. As we work on incorporating further domains and examples, the language can be extended to accomodate these.

The most important task of our future research is to make an implementation of OWL Script and see how well it performs in practice, in particular to gauge how suitable the syntax is to script programmers.

References

1. Baader, F., Nutt, W.: Basic description logics (2003)
2. Grosof, B.N., Gandhe, M.D., Mahesh, D.G., Finin, T.W.: Sweetjess: Inferencing in situated courteous ruleml via translation to and from jess rules. In: Proceedings of the ISWC 2002 International Workshop on Rule Markup Languages for Business Rules on the Semantic Web, Sardinia, Italy (June 2002/2003)
3. Honkola, J., Laine, H., Brown, R., Tyrkko, O.: Smart-m3 information sharing platform. In: IEEE Symposium on Computers and Communications, pp. 1041–1046 (2010)
4. Luukkala, V., Niemelä, I.: Enhancing a smart space with answer set programming. In: Dean, M., Hall, J., Rotolo, A., Tabet, S. (eds.) RuleML 2010. LNCS, vol. 6403, pp. 89–103. Springer, Heidelberg (2010)
5. Oliver, I., Honkola, J.: Personal semantic web through a space based computing environment. In: Proceedings of the 2nd International Conference on Semantic Computing (2008)
6. W3C recommendation: Owl 2 web ontology language direct semantics (2009), `http://www.w3.org/TR/2009/REC-owl2-direct-semantics-20091027/`
7. W3C recommendation: Owl 2 web ontology language structural specification and functional-style syntax (2009), `http://www.w3.org/TR/2009/REC-owl2-syntax-20091027/`
8. W3C Working Group Note: Rif overview (2009), `http://www.w3.org/TR/2010/NOTE-rif-overview-20100622/`
9. Wang, X., Dong, J.S., Chin, C., Hettiarachchi, S., Zhang, D.: Semantic space: An infrastructure for smart spaces. IEEE Pervasive Computing 3, 32–39 (2004)

Rule-Based Complex Event Processing for Food Safety and Public Health

Monica L. Nogueira and Noel P. Greis

Center for Logistics and Digital Strategy, Kenan-Flagler Business School,
The University of North Carolina at Chapel Hill,
Kenan Center CB#3440, Chapel Hill, NC 27599 U.S.A.
{monica_nogueira,noel_greis}@unc.edu

Abstract. The challenge for public health officials is to detect an emerging foodborne disease outbreak from a large set of simple and isolated, domain-specific events. These events can be extracted from a large number of distinct information systems such as surveillance and laboratory reporting systems from health care providers, real-time complaint hotlines from consumers, and inspection reporting systems from regulatory agencies. In this paper we formalize a foodborne disease outbreak as a complex event and apply an event-driven rule-based engine to the problem of detecting emerging events. We define an evidence set as a set of simple events that are linked symptomatically, spatially and temporally. A weighted metric is used to compute the strength of the evidence set as a basis for response by public health officials.

Keywords: Rules engine; complex event processing; answer set programming.

1 Introduction

Even though the U.S. food supply is one of the safest in the world, thousands of foodborne illness cases still occur each year [7]. Surveillance and response to foodborne disease suffer from a number of systemic and other delays that hinder early detection and confirmation of emerging contamination situations. At the onset of an outbreak it is often impossible to link isolated events that may be related to events reported by other data sources. Once distinct events are suspected to be related, public health officials create a cluster and look for confirmatory evidence as part of a lengthy investigatory process. Latencies in the process could be reduced by the earlier availability and synthesis of other confirmatory information, often outside formal public health channels, including information from private companies and consumers.

In practice, local public health departments are usually the first to pick up the signals of foodborne disease. These signals may correspond to reports of illness generated by different types of events, e.g. E1: a patient with symptoms of gastro-intestinal distress seeking medical attention at a hospital emergency room or visiting a private physician's office; E2: laboratory test results for an ill patient which confirm a causative pathogen, e.g. *Salmonella*; and E3: a cluster of ill patients due to a common pathogen. Routinely, a state's syndromic surveillance system collects data from local

N. Bassiliades et al. (Eds.): RuleML 2011 - Europe, LNCS 6826, pp. 376–383, 2011.

health care providers about events of type E1, E2 and E3 on a continuous basis, reporting them to the Centers for Disease Control and Prevention (CDC).

However, other events can signal an emerging foodborne disease outbreak. Many public health authorities and food industry operators, e.g. food manufacturers and grocery stores, maintain complaint hotlines (E4) where consumers report foodborne illness or a suspected adulterated food product. Consumer complaints made directly to public agency hotlines, e.g. local health departments (LHDs), state departments of agriculture or departments of environment and natural resources, are officially recorded and may lead to an investigation, at the discretion of the receiving agency.

A public food recall notification (E5) may also signal existing illness cases. Food manufacturers may voluntarily recall of one of their food products due to positive test results for foodborne pathogens, unintentional adulteration, mislabeling, or the presence of an allergen or hazardous material in the food product. Recalls may also be advised by authorities after routine inspections conducted by the U.S. Department of Agriculture (USDA), U.S. Food and Drug Administration (FDA), and state agencies.

Food facility inspection reports (E6), which list violations to the food code applicable to such facilities, provide another signal that may help to identify the root cause of a contamination situation. Evaluation of the type, severity, recurrence, and other characteristics of past code violations for a specific facility and the product(s) it manufactures could help link such operations as a probable source of contamination.

Microblogging and social media networks, i.e. Twitter or Facebook, are non-standard data sources that hold the potential, yet to be realized, to provide real-time information about emerging food contamination situations. Bloggers posting microblog messages (E7) about illness after eating a certain food product or at a particular restaurant can provide timely warning about an emerging problem.

The paper is organized as follows. Section 2 discusses the motivation and challenges in representing the food safety domain using rules. Section 3 presents our rule-based event model and describes the inference engine developed for our application. An illustrative example of the domain is shown in Section 4. Conclusions and directions for future research are discussed in Section 5.

2 Motivation and Challenges

Data associated with event types E1–E7 described above are collected by separate information systems and maintained and managed by distinct governmental agencies. Hence, in responding to the twin challenges of early detection of and rapid response to emerging outbreak situations, a central problem is how to access, process and interpret more events more quickly, thus reducing the time, scale, and scope of an emerging event. Framing the problem of outbreak detection as a complex event addresses a major failure of current surveillance methods. Current syndromic surveillance systems utilize statistics-based cumulative sum algorithms, i.e. CUSUM, to detect increases in illness reporting numbers and to determine that a foodborne disease outbreak may be emerging or is on-going. Alerts are normally generated by the system when the number of illness cases assigned to a certain syndrome, e.g. fever, respiratory, or gastrointestinal distress, exceeds the threshold determined for that particular syndrome for the geographic area originating these events, i.e. county, and the local population baseline. These alerts are typically based solely on reported illness cases, type E1 to E3 events above. Consideration of event types E4 to E7 aids in the detection of emerging outbreaks before they are sufficiently advanced to rise above the threshold of traditional CUSUM statistical methods.

To better understand the investigatory processes for outbreak detection, consider the following situation. A couple experiences severe gastrointestinal ulceration (GIU) symptoms after eating at a local restaurant chain and seeks medical attention at the emergency room of their local hospital. Two separate illness reports are entered into the health care system to be reported to the state's public health syndromic surveillance system. If the number of reported GIU and foodborne-related cases does not exceed the corresponding threshold for GIU syndrome in the area, then no alert will be generated by the CUSUM algorithm and detection of an emerging situation will be delayed. However, consider that another person falls ill after eating at a different branch of the same food chain and calls a consumer complaint hotline to make a report. Currently, this event will be registered in the receiving agency's database but not automatically passed along to public health syndromic surveillance systems. Consider that another person, also ill after eating at that chain, reports the illness on a personal blog. Both these events occur "under the radar" of public health and are not currently picked up as evidence of a possible emerging contamination.

3 Rule-Based Event Modeling

With respect to rule-based event modeling, our work: (1) extracts relevant information from unstructured text, i.e. web-based recall notifications, to generate events that trigger a rule-based inference engine to "reason" about what it knows in light of the new information encoded by this event; (2) semantically links different types of events by employing (simple) ontologies for food, U.S. geographic regions, North Carolina counties, and foodborne diseases; (3) implements a rule-based inference engine using the Answer Set Programming (ASP) paradigm to identify evidence sets that signal an emerging foodborne disease outbreak; (4) computes an Event Evidence Indicator for newly formed evidence sets as a measure of the strength of the evidence in support of such sets; and (5) reduces latency in outbreak detection by identifying emerging outbreaks when the number of cases affecting individual counties falls below the statistical threshold.

3.1 Event Model

An *event* is defined as the acquisition of a piece of information that is significant within a specific domain of interest to the application. In this application the domain of interest is food safety. We distinguish between two different types of events: simple events and materialized complex events. Simple events include both *atomic* events and *molecular* events. Atomic events have a distinct spatio-temporal identity, i.e. they take place at a particular place and time that is relevant to the determination of the complex event. An example of an atomic event would be a single reported case of gastrointestinal illness, an FDA recall, or a consumer complaint. Molecular events can be thought of as atomic events that are "linked together" by evidence, for example that are joined through previous evidence or by public health experts outside the system. Molecular events could include a confirmed cluster of two or more *Salmonella* cases as determined by DNA fingerprinting. An *event stream* is defined as the sequence of simple events received by the complex event processing (CEP) system that are assigned a timestamp from a discrete ordered time domain and a geostamp consisting of a longitude and latitude geocode. An atomic event has a single timestamp and geostamp; molecular events may have multiple timestamps and geostamps. As defined by [4], CEP consists of techniques and tools that enable the understanding and control of event-driven information systems.

A *complex* or materialized event is an event that is inferred by the engine's rules evaluation of the occurrence of other simple events. For example, in our application the materialized event is a foodborne disease outbreak.

3.1 Semantic Model

Our representation allows for incomplete information which is indicated by a unique reserved symbol of the representation language. Sparse data is an inherent characteristic of the problem, and one of our goals is to detect outbreaks when the number of illness cases has not yet exceeded thresholds employed by traditional statistical methods. The events of interest are described by the following concepts.

A *patient illness case* record contains information about an event of type E1 and uniquely identifies a patient; his county of residence; time and date of visit to health care provider; syndrome or diagnosis assigned; and the disease-causing pathogen. This record will be updated to confirm the pathogen identified by a laboratory test when an event of type E2 corresponding to this patient enters the system. A simple ontology of foodborne diseases and related syndromes is employed to enable the semantic link of diagnosis data and pathogen data across different types of events.

By definition, an illness cluster – a molecular event – is formed by a number of patients with a common diagnosis caused by the same pathogen (as identified by laboratory test results or other causal links). The cluster patient with the earliest disease onset date is referred to as "patient#1." Events of type E3 are represented by two different types of records: (a) a *cluster* record provides information that uniquely identifies a specific cluster; and (b) a *cluster illness case* record contains information about a specific patient of the cluster defined by a *cluster* record. A *cluster* record contains a unique identification code, the disease-causing pathogen, number of counties affected by the outbreak, number of patients in the cluster, the unique identification code of patient#1, and date of patient#1 visit to a health care provider. A *cluster illness case* record contains that cluster identification code, and the patient's unique identification code and county of residence. A *cluster illness case* record acts as a pointer to the more complete *patient illness case* record for that patient.

A consumer complaint call, an event of type E4, is represented by three types of records. A *complaint caller* record provides a unique call identification code, date and time of call, and information about the caller, e.g. caller's county of residence; type of illness codified using the responding agency's medical code; and number of people that fell ill because of the product. A *complaint food operator* record informs about the manufacturer or retailer the caller has complained about. A *complaint food product* record lists the food product and its FDA food code, date of manufacturing, and other information provided by the caller. A food ontology semantically links recalled food products to those implicated by consumer complaint calls. Neighboring relations among North Carolina counties and cities are described by a separate ontology. A recall notification, an event of type E5, is represented by two types of records. A *recall* record contains the event unique identification code, the recall-issuing agency, date and time of its release, recalling company, recalled food product, reason for the recall, e.g. presence of allergen or pathogen, known number of illnesses, and number of geographic areas affected. U.S. geographic areas are defined by a simple ontology which includes all U.S. states and regions as defined by the U.S. Census Bureau. An associated *recall area* record defines a geographic area affected.

3.2 ASP Rule-Based Inference Engine

In this work, we use a form of declarative programming known as Answer Set Programming (ASP) [5], to represent the rule-based CEP of the food safety domain and to search for/detect emerging outbreaks and other information of interest to public health officials. ASP has been applied to industrial problems, but to the best of our knowledge it has not been used in food safety applications.

The ASP paradigm is based on the stable model/answer set semantics of logic programs [1, 2] and has been shown to be a powerful methodology for knowledge representation, including representation of defaults and multiple aspects of reasoning about actions and their effects, as well as being useful in solving difficult search problems. In the ASP methodology, search problems are reduced to the computation if the stable models of the problem. Several ASP solvers – programs that generate the stable models of a given problem encoded in the ASP formalism – have been implemented, e.g. Cmodels, DLV, Smodels, etc. In what follows we provide the basic syntactic constructs and the intuitive semantics of the ASP language used in this work. A complete formal specification of the syntax and semantics of the language can be found at [2, 6].

A signature Σ of the language contains constants, predicates, and function symbols. Terms and atoms are formed as is customary in first-order logic. A literal is either an atom (also called a positive literal) or an atom preceded by $\neg$ (classical or strong negation), a negative literal. Literals l and $\neg l$ are called contrary. Ground literals and terms are those not containing variables. A consistent set of literals does not contain contrary literals. The set of all ground literals is denoted by $lit(\Sigma)$. A rule is a statement of the form:

$$h_1 \vee \ldots \vee h_k \leftarrow l_1, \ldots, l_m, \mathit{not}\ l_{m+1}, \ldots, \mathit{not}\ l_n\,. \quad (1)$$

where h_i's and l_i's are ground literals, *not* is a logical connective called negation as failure or default negation, and symbol $\vee$ corresponds to the disjunction operator. The head of the rule is the part of the statement to the left of symbol $\leftarrow$, while the body of the rule is the part on its right side. Intuitively, the rule meaning is that if a reasoner believes $\{l_1, \ldots, l_m\}$ and has no reason to believe $\{l_{m+1}, \ldots, l_n\}$, then it must believe one of the h_i's. If the head of the rule is substituted by the falsity symbol $\perp$ then the rule is called a constraint. The intuitive meaning of a constraint is that its body must not be satisfied. Rules with variables are used as a short hand for the sets of their ground instantiations. Variables are denoted by capital letters. An ASP program is a pair of ⟨Σ, Π⟩, where Σ is a signature and Π is a set of rules over Σ, but usually the signature is defined implicitly and programs are only denoted by Π. A stable model (or answer set) of a program Π is one of the possible sets of literals of its logical consequences under the stable model/answer set semantics.

Our encoding – the set of rules of program Π – contains roughly 100 rules, while event records (in ASP, rules with an empty body, also called "facts") and the ontologies describing facts, utilized for experiments, are in the hundreds. We use the DLV system [3] as our ASP solver. To illustrate the ASP methodology, a few (simplified) rules used by our engine to detect emerging clusters are shown below. Rule (2) means that if neighboring counties A and B reported a small number of cases of food-related illnesses, due to pathogen P and/or syndrome S, this constitutes evidence for the engine to create a suspected cluster with associated case records generated by rules of form (3). Thus, an emerging outbreak affecting A and B, due to pathogen P, is computed by rule (4).

$$suspcluster(A,B,P,S) \leftarrow neighbors(A,B), minreached(A,P,S), minreached(B,P,S). \quad (2)$$

$$suspcluster\_illness(A,B,Id,P,A) \leftarrow suspcluster(A,B,P,S),\ P\ != S,\ patient\_illness(Id,H,M,AmPm,Day,Mon,Y,A,Sys,P). \quad (3)$$

$$susp\_outbreak(A,B,P) \leftarrow suspcluster(A,B,P,\_). \quad (4)$$

Suspected clusters are linked by (5) to existing recalls of food products affecting the state or the geographic region where it is located. Recalls of food distributed directly to a state or a more specific region, as computed by (5) and (6), are of higher interest.

$$more\_specif\_susprecall\_linked(R1,A,B,F1,M1,L1) \leftarrow susprecall(R1,A,B,F1,M1,L1),\ susprecall(R2,A,B,F2,M2,L2),\ subregion(L1,L2),\ R1\ != R2,\ not\ other\_more\_specif(A,B,L1,R2). \quad (5)$$

$$other\_more\_specif(A,B,L1,R2) \leftarrow susprecall(R2,A,B,\_,\_,L2),\ susprecall(R3,A,B,\_,\_,L3),\ subregion(L3,L1),\ R2\ != R3. \quad (6)$$

3.3 Evidence Set and Event Evidence Indicator

The set of linked events that provide evidence of the materializing of a complex event is called the *Evidence Set*. An evidence set is associated with a degree of uncertainty as to whether an emerging outbreak event will materialize based on the information in the event data. Rule (7) below exemplifies the computation of elements of the evidence set. Intuitively, the rule meaning is that the engine will conclude that there is evidence that a complaint call C, from county T implicating a food product F1 of type FC–per the FDA Code, is connected to a materialized cluster of illness P affecting neighboring counties A and B, if this call can be linked to an existing recall R of food F2 manufactured by company M at location L, if food F2 is also of type FC.

$$evidence(A,B,P,S,R,F2,M,L,F1,FC,T) \leftarrow suspcluster(A,B,P,S),\ nccounty(T),\ suspcall(C,A,B,F1,FC,T),\ susprecall(R,A,B,F2,M,L),\ type\_of(F2,FC). \quad (7)$$

The engine computes a measure of the strength of the evidence supporting the conclusion of an emerging complex event through a ranking that ranges from 0, or no evidence, to a maximum of 7, highest evidence rating. The computation of the *Event Evidence Indicator* (EVI) is based on the number and strength of the relationships that connect the events in the evidence set and corresponds to the weighted summation of EVI components calculated for the subsets formed when linking pairs of different types of events. For example, we compute the EVI component for the set of all events corresponding to a suspected cluster and incoming recall notification. The engine also uses EVI to determine what suspected outbreaks to "push" to users and, thus, possibly produce a lower number of false positives, i.e. outbreaks not confirmed later.

4 Illustrative Application

The ASP rule-based inference engine was implemented in the *North Carolina Foodborne Events Data Integration and Analysis Tool* (NCFEDA) shown in Figure 1. In this application, incoming food-related event streams are processed by the *Events Manager* components: (1) a set of databases; and (2) the Event Trigger Module. The databases store all food-related events and geocoded datasets across all contributing NCFEDA public and private sector stakeholders. The Events Manager continuously monitors the databases for new incoming events that are determined by the *Event Trigger Module* as possible triggers. As noted earlier, triggers are events that could include a case related to a foodborne illness, a cluster of illnesses, a recall notification, or a consumer complaint. Inspection reports and microblog messages will be added in the future. The *Event Trigger Module* is composed of *translation units* that convert incoming database event records to ASP *facts* to be evaluated by the ASP inference engine together with all facts describing the domain within a chosen time period.

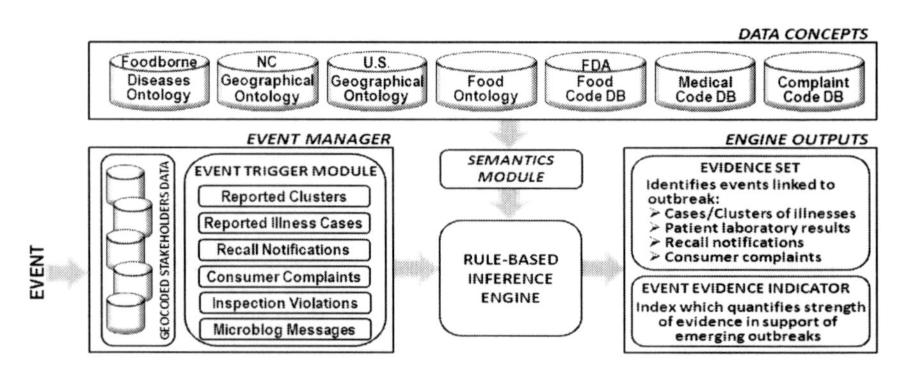

Fig. 1. NCFEDA CEP High-level Diagram

NCFEDA's web scraping tool (not shown in Figure 1) retrieves recall notifications issued by the FDA and USDA directly from their websites generating recall events which are sent to the Events Manager for storing and processing. Upon arrival of a new such event, the Events Manager sends the free-text record to the Event Trigger Module's recall translation unit which (1) parses the recall record text; (2) utilizes the

Semantics Module and ontologies for extraction of any relevant recall information from the text; and (3) generates the recall's corresponding ASP facts.

NCFEDA's *Rule-based Inference Engine* consists of the ASP program containing (a) 100 inference rules for the food safety domain; (b) new and (selected) previously stored facts describing the current situation being monitored; and (c) the DLV solver. Arrival of new events triggers computation of new stable models of the assembled program which will determine whether there is an emerging outbreak event occurring.

5 Conclusions and Future Directions

A primary contribution of this paper has been to frame the outbreak detection problem as a complex event where events include not only structured event data (e.g. case information) but also unstructured event data (e.g. recall or complaint data). We develop semantic models that are able to extract meaningful information from unstructured text data that can serve as event triggers. Using ontologies and rules we are able to discover semantic links between events that provide evidence of an emerging outbreak event. Identification of events that comprise the evidence set is accomplished using ASP. Finally, we introduce a novel concept, the Event Evidence Indicator, which quantifies the strength of evidence in support of an emerging event as a basis for response by public health officials. We successfully implemented these concepts in the NCFEDA prototype. This work is on-going and we are continuing to further develop the rule-based inference engine and the computational strategy for the Event Evidence Indicator.

Acknowledgments. This work was funded by the Department of Homeland Security and Institute of Homeland Security Solutions under Contract# HSHQDC-08-C-00100.

References

1. Gelfond, M., Lifschitz, V.: The stable model semantics for logic programming. In: Kowalski, R., Bowen, K. (eds.) Intl. Logic. Progr. Conf. Symposium, pp. 1070–1080. MIT Press, Cambridge (1988)
2. Gelfond, M., Lifschitz, V.: Classical negation in logic programs and disjunctive databases. New Generation Computing 9, 365–385 (1991)
3. Leone, N., Pfeifer, G., Faber, W., Calimeri, F., Dell'Armi, T., Eiter, T., Gottlob, G., Ianni, G., Ielpa, G., Koch, C., Perri, S., Polleres, A.: The DLV System. In: Flesca, S., Greco, S., Ianni, G., Leone, N. (eds.) JELIA 2002. LNCS (LNAI), vol. 2424, pp. 537–540. Springer, Heidelberg (2002)
4. Luckham, D.C.: The Power of Events: An Introduction to Complex Event Processing in Distributed Enterprise Systems. Addison-Wesley Longman Publishing, Boston (2001)
5. Marek, V.W., Truszczynski, M.: Stable models and an alternative logic programming paradigm. In: The Logic Programming Paradigm: a 25-Year Perspective, pp. 375–398. Springer, Berlin (1999)
6. Niemela, I., Simons, P.: Extending the Smodels System with Cardinality and Weight Constraints. In: Logic-Based Artificial Intelligence, pp. 491–521. Kluwer Academic Publishers, Dordrecht (2000)
7. Scallan, E., et al.: Foodborne illness acquired in the United States–Major pathogens. Emerg. Infect. Dis. 17(1), 7–15 (2011)

Author Index